INSIDE AND OUTSIDE CANADIAN ADMINISTRATIVE LAW

Essays in Honour of David Mullan

Inside and Outside Canadian Administrative Law

Essays in Honour of David Mullan

EDITED BY
GRANT HUSCROFT AND MICHAEL TAGGART

UNIVERSITY OF TORONTO PRESS
Toronto Buffalo London

Toronto Buffalo London
Printed in Canada

ISBN-13: 978-0-8020-9245-8
ISBN-10: 0-8020-9245-4

Printed on acid-free paper

Library and Archives Canada Cataloguing in Publication

Inside and outside Canadian administrative law : essays in honour of David Mullan / edited by Grant Huscroft and Michael Taggart.

ISBN-13: 978-0-8020-9245-8
ISBN-10: 0-8020-9245-4

1. Administrative law – Canada. I. Mullan, David J., 1946– II. Huscroft, Grant III. Taggart, Michael IV. Title.

K3400.I58 2006 342.71′06 C2006-904039-7

University of Toronto Press acknowledges the financial assistance to its publishing program of the Canada Council for the Arts and the Ontario Arts Council.

University of Toronto Press acknowledges the financial support for its publishing activities of the Government of Canada through the Book Publishing Industry Development Program (BPIDP).

Contents

Foreword

It is a situation that happens every day in law firms, administrative tribunal offices, and judicial chambers. An administrative law issue has arisen. The issue is difficult. The need for answers is urgent. The time is running out. In this situation, for as long as the administrative law bar in Canada can remember, there is only one question:

'What does Professor Mullan have to say about the issue?'

Invariably, after just a brief search, we find one of his timely conference papers, one of his incisive articles, or one of his classic texts. Sure enough, David Mullan's insights are there – very recent, practical ones, exactly on point, on the very issue that just a short time ago seemed so intractable. Soon afterward, the insights find their way into the work product: a research memorandum, an opinion letter, a legal brief, oral argument or rulings and reasons for judgment, often becoming the very essence of it.

David's contribution does not end there. Chances are that he taught the writer or the recipient of the work product, shaping his or her fundamental understanding of the area. Or perhaps the writer or recipient attended one of the innumerable conferences to which David volunteers his time. Or perhaps the writer or recipient has read work product shaped by David's work or authored by someone shaped and influenced by David.

David's contribution is unique, profound, and unparalleled in quality and extent. It is fair to say that administrative law in the modern era in Canada was born in 1968 when the Honourable James McRuer released his great five-volume report, *Inquiry into Civil Rights*. Two years later, David came to Canada and from that time has acted like a loving parent over this area of law, watching over it, nurturing it, helping it to develop. As a result, we in Canada today are the beneficiaries of a mature system of administrative justice that is practical, fair, and reflects our finest values and traditions.

I had the privilege of teaching alongside David for several years in our upper-year seminar, 'Advanced Constitutional Law,' at Queen's University. From that close vantage point, I have observed in my dear friend an exceptionally rare trifecta of qualities: intelligence but quiet humility, compassion but unceasing dedication to standards of excellence, and, above all else, uncompromising integrity in all that he does.

There is no better way to recognize David and his marvellous contribution than to publish this exceptional collection of papers in his honour. Sincerest congratulations to the editors, Grant Huscroft and Mike Taggart, and to all of the contributors.

David Stratas
Heenan Blaikie LLP
Toronto

Acknowledgments

This is a book of essays in honour of David Mullan. We explain why he is so deserving of a *Festschrift* in the first chapter and will confine ourselves here to giving thanks to those that made this volume possible.

First of all, thanks to Liz Mullan for her support and advice. Second, we want to acknowledge the contributors to this volume. Their enthusiastic participation speaks volumes for the high regard David Mullan is held in throughout the common law world. There was no shortage of people wanting to contribute, but unfortunately there was not space for everyone. Third, we thank our research assistants: at London, Ontario, Chris Cheung, Sarah Shody, Meghan Butler, and Cameron MacDonald; at Auckland, Katy Nathan and Mark Utting.

Financial support for the production of this volume was provided by David Stratas and from research funds from the University of Auckland Law School and the University of Toronto Law School.

Finally, the University of Toronto Press and Stephen Kotowych have supported this project enthusiastically from the beginning. We thank Stephen, Anne Laughlin, and Diane Mew for their support, and outstanding editorial assistance.

The primary object of a *Festschrift* is to add to the corpus of legal knowledge while paying a public tribute to a distinguished and deserving scholar. It should also be a pleasure to be involved in, and it certainly was for us.

Grant Huscroft and Michael Taggart

Acknowledgments

Contributors

Alfred C. Aman, Jr. is Roscoe C. O'Byrne Professor of Law, University of Indiana at Bloomington, and Director of the Indiana University Institute for Advanced Study.

Philip Bryden is Professor and Dean of Law, University of New Brunswick.

Geneviève Cartier is Professor of Law, Sherbrooke University.

Hugh Corder is Professor and Dean of Law, University of Cape Town.

Paul Craig is Professor of English Law, University of Oxford, and a Fellow of St. John's College.

Robin Creyke is Alumni Professor of Administrative Law, Australian National University.

David Dyzenhaus is Professor of Law and Philosophy, University of Toronto.

John M. Evans is a Judge of the Appellate Division of the Federal Court of Canada.

Grant Huscroft is Associate Professor of Law, University of Western Ontario.

K.J. Keith is a Judge of the International Court of Justice.

Denis Lemieux is Professor of Law, Laval University.

Wade MacLauchlan is President of the University of Prince Edward Island.

Beverley McLachlin is Chief Justice of the Supreme Court of Canada.

Janet McLean is Professor of Law, University of Dundee.

Lorne Sossin is Associate Professor of Law, University of Toronto.

Michael Taggart is Alexander Turner Professor of Law, University of Auckland.

Mark D. Walters is Associate Professor of Law, Queen's University, Ontario.

INSIDE AND OUTSIDE CANADIAN ADMINISTRATIVE LAW

Essays in Honour of David Mullan

David Mullan: In Appreciation

GRANT HUSCROFT AND MICHAEL TAGGART

David Mullan was born in Australia, but from a young age was raised and educated in New Zealand. Like many before and since, he left New Zealand to undertake postgraduate study overseas and subsequently made his academic career in Canada. In the more than thirty-five years David Mullan has spent here, he has become Canada's leading administrative law scholar and one of the best known and regarded administrative lawyers in the common law world. As is their wont, New Zealanders like to claim Mullan as one of their greatest legal exports.

David Mullan graduated with an LL.B. and a first class LL.M. from Victoria University of Wellington. He left New Zealand in 1970 to undertake further postgraduate work at Queen's University in Kingston. Apart from five years teaching at Dalhousie University in the mid-1970s, Queen's Law School and Kingston, Ontario, have been his home. Since the late 1960s, he has produced a prodigious amount of high-quality writing that has won the admiration and respect of scholars, students, practitioners, and judges. His pre-eminence in the field of administrative law has been recognized by his peers, his students, and his university.

In 1996 David Mullan was awarded the Canadian Association of Law Teachers' Academic Excellence Award (the equivalent of a lifetime achievement award). In turn, the Law Society of Upper Canada conferred on Mullan an Honorary LL.D. degree in 2002. Queen's University and its alumni have honoured both David Mullan's research and his teaching. He was the first holder of the Osler, Hoskin & Harcourt Chair of Constitutional and Administrative Law. David Mullan has been a distinguished visitor at the University of Sydney Law School several times and a regular visitor to New Zealand law schools, not to mention the law schools of Canada.

Like many that have made another country their home, David Mullan has made considerable efforts to understand the history of his adopted country, including that of Quebec. He has spent considerable time in Quebec and has made a real effort to reach out to the Quebec legal academic community, doing more than most English-Canadian scholars.

In 2004 David Mullan took early retirement from Queen's University, but since then he has been anything but idle. He has continued to work as a member of the Ontario Human Rights Tribunal, a vice-chair of the Ontario Workplace Safety and Insurance Appeals Tribunal, and as a panelist under the North American Free Trade Agreement. Such is the esteem in which he is held professionally that he was appointed the City of Toronto's first Integrity Commissioner in 2004. He has worked hard to establish that important office, and at the same time continued to work as a consultant and prolific writer and presenter on administrative law issues.

It probably could go without saying that the contributors do not intend by this *Festschrift* to put David Mullan 'out to pasture.' Whatever post-full-time law teaching holds for David Mullan, there is no doubt that he will continue to think, talk, and write about administrative law for a long time to come.

The editors' associations with David Mullan have different beginnings but ultimately became entwined. Grant Huscroft was a student of David Mullan's at Queen's Law School in the early 1980s and, as with so many other students, this sparked his interest in public law. When it came time to undertake postgraduate work, Grant emulated Mullan in reverse and headed to New Zealand. He pursued postgraduate study at the Faculty of Law in the University of Auckland where he met Michael Taggart, who had commenced his law-teaching career in Canada a few years earlier.

It was about that time that Taggart was considering where to spend his first research leave (or sabbatical, as it used to be called). Having admired David Mullan's work since he was a law student, and having taught administrative law in Canada out of the first edition of the celebrated Evans, Janisch, Mullan, and Risk casebook,[1] Taggart wrote to Mullan, and received a characteristically warm and enthusiastic invitation to spend the year in Kingston. So Huscroft went back to Canada in 1987, and Taggart spent a great year at Queen's University in 1989 (due in no small part to the hospitality of our honorand). In 1991 Huscroft left the Ontario public service to join the Faculty of Law at the University of Auckland. David Mullan's friendship and scholarship was one of the many things Huscroft and Taggart had in common as colleagues for a decade at Auckland. In 2002 Huscroft returned to Canada to teach at the University of Western Ontario. Shortly thereafter David Mullan signalled he was to take trial early retirement. It seemed that the writing was on the wall: David Mullan would slip quietly out of full-time teaching to pursue his writing and many other interests. The editors decided that this should not happen without the opportunity for a scholarly celebration of his enormous contribution to administrative law teaching and research. Hence the idea for this *Festschrift* was born.[2]

There are a number of things that mark David Mullan as a special person and remarkable teacher/scholar. First and foremost, like every excellent teacher, David cared deeply about the learning and welfare of his students. He invested enormous amounts of energy and time over the years in preparing for class, producing high-quality teaching materials, and supporting and mentoring students. He was always popular with students, and his courses were sought after. The real measure of the success of a law teacher is not popularity, however, but how he is remembered five, ten, fifteen or more years after law school. Invariably David Mullan is remembered as among the best – a scholar of the highest standards who inspired admiration and affection. Many of his former students became his friends.

The second thing that stands out is David Mullan's loyalty and commitment to institutions and people. For more years than he probably cares to remember David was Dean of Postgraduate Studies at Queen's and in this capacity he assisted a large number of students. In the same vein, his involvement in mooting appeared almost constant: travelling all across Canada with Queen's mooting teams to the numerous competitions. He was there with his students through their triumphs and their lows; and so it has been with Queen's Law School itself. David was never tempted by the many opportunities that came his way to go elsewhere. The same qualities of loyalty and commitment shown to the institution he cares about are exhibited to his many friends and colleagues. He has helped many to establish academic careers.

The third aspect is his service to the profession. David Mullan has always had a close and cordial relationship with the legal profession and the judiciary, and has contributed regularly to seminars, conferences, and continuing legal education programs across Canada. He is a much sought after speaker. Not for him, an 'ivory tower' disdain for those working in the trenches of the law. A vast amount of time and energy went into his long-term editorship of the *Administrative Law Reports* and his contributions to the *Canadian Encyclopedic Digest* (fortunately published as separate, stand-alone books). The care and skill in the exposition of law is evident to all who have read and benefited from this work, which complements his pioneering theoretical and doctrinal work that has been extremely influential in academic circles. He has straddled the divide between town and gown, and is equally respected on each side for the many contributions he has made to both.

The fourth aspect is David Mullan's significant contribution to Commonwealth administrative law. One of the icons of the New Zealand advertising industry is a campaign for a carbonated beverage called Lemon & Paeroa, produced only in New Zealand.[3] Making a virtue out of this uniqueness, a series of ads declared the drink to be 'world famous in New Zealand.' In law, as in many other parts of the academy, it is hard to become world famous from places like New Zealand and Canada. The concerns and legal responses can seem so local, the conditions uncongenial to generalization beyond one's borders, the publication outlets limited and parochial, cultural cringe can hang over, and the presence of a larger and dominant neighbour can deflect the limelight. One of David Mullan's many achievements is that he has become genuinely world famous from Canada.

English-speaking Canada and New Zealand have several other things in common: a colonial and common law heritage, a Westminster-style liberal democracy, and a common language. Moreover, the peoples get on well together. From the early 1950s, some talented New Zealand lawyers bucked the trend to go to Oxbridge or London, and headed for the alternately greener and whiter pastures of Canada. A pioneer in this regard was Jack Northey, who was one of Professor Bora Laskin's most memorable doctoral students at the University of Toronto in the early 1950s,[4] and whose writing on New Zealand administrative law sparked some of David Mullan's earliest publications as a legal academic.[5] David Mullan was part of a later and much larger wave of New Zealand lawyers who came to Canada in the 1960s and 1970s. Indeed at one stage just about every law school in common law Canada boasted at least one New Zealander. Like David Mullan, many of them have made major contributions to their adopted country.

These foreign-trained lawyers brought to Canada not only a high degree of technical ability and analytical skill, but also an abiding interest in what can be called common law comparativism. This can be summed up as a curiosity about how problems are dealt with elsewhere in the common law world and a facility and confidence in finding out. All colonies imported imperial laws, but as the bounds of imperialism loosened (albeit at very different rates) the bright side of an increasing mature, indigenous legal system carried with it the risk of insularity.

These law teachers (from New Zealand, as well as Australia and elsewhere) were an insurance policy against that risk materializing.

Moreover, and as importantly, these bridges built by foreign-trained lawyers not only carried other traditions, experiences, and laws to Canada, but also allowed good Canadian laws and developments to be sent back to the rest of the common law world. These foreign scholars were, in other words, translators and transmitters of Canadian law to the rest of the common law world.[6] This was an especially important role in administrative law because, for a variety of reasons, Canada has been the 'natural meeting ground'[7] of the British and American administrative law traditions. David Mullan has been an astute observer and careful translator. Moreover, as attested to earlier, he has encouraged the movement of scholars and his students around the common law world.

The fifth notable thing about David Mullan is his passion for the law, sport, and for life, a passion underpinned by an enormous capacity both for work and socializing. His love of sports – everything from horse racing to rugby – is well known. He has remained a loyal supporter of New Zealand's national rugby team, the All Blacks, as well as its less successful cricketers. His love of entertaining friends, and his generosity in doing so, is also well known. Many people have enjoyed the hospitality David and Liz have provided over the years.

In short, there are ample reasons to celebrate David Mullan's career and achievements to date. There is no better gift to a scholar than the scholarship of others written in appreciation. With this in mind, we identified the broad themes in David Mullan's work – procedural fairness; scope of review and deference; the interrelationship of administrative law, human rights, and the rule of law; the legitimacy of state regulation and tribunal adjudication; and common law comparativism – and invited contributions on these themes from scholars who had engaged with his work and had some association with him. This volume is the result.

On behalf of the contributors, we offer this book in appreciation of David Mullan: scholar, teacher, and friend.

NOTES

1 J.M. Evans, H.N. Janisch, David J. Mullan, and R.C.B. Risk, *Administrative Law: Cases, Text, and Materials* (Toronto: Emond Montgomery Publications Ltd, 1980). The book is discussed in Wade MacLauchlan and Philip Bryden's contribution to this volume.

2 The editors were aware that a special 'Administrative Law' issue of the *Queen's Law Journal* was dedicated to David Mullan in 2002: 'Focus on Administrative Law' (2002) 27 Queen's L.J. 389–916 (Spring 2002). That, however, was an exclusively Canadian affair and it was evident that Mullan's many friends and admirers wanted to express their appreciation in a stand-alone *Festschrift*.
3 Richard Wolfe and Stephen Barnett, *From Jandals to Jaffas: The Best of Kiwiana* (Auckland: Random House, 2003), 48–9.
4 See B. Brown, 'Jack Northey' in N. Tarling, ed., *Auckland Minds and Matters* (Auckland: Auckland University Press, 2003), 105.
5 See, e.g., D.J. Mullan, 'Developments in New Zealand Administrative Law (1971–72)' (1973) 35 (2) N.Z.J. Pub. Admin. 1; D.J. Mullan, 'One Plus Five Equals Six?' [1971] N.Z.L.J. 512; D.J. Mullan, 'Procedural Codes – A Second Opinion' [1973] N.Z.L.J. 41.
6 The earliest exemplar of this in administrative law in Canada is the Englishman John Willis, who studied at Oxford and then Harvard Law School and came to Canada in 1933 and stayed. See M. Taggart, 'Prolegomenon to an Intellectual History of Administrative Law in the Twentieth Century: The Case of John Willis and Canadian Administrative Law' (2005) 43 Osgoode Hall L.J. 223, and the contributions to a *Festschrift* for Willis comprising a special Administrative Law issue of the *University of Toronto Law Journal*: (2005) 55 U.T.L.J. 311–887.
7 H.N. Janisch, 'Review Essay' (1977–78) 4 Dal. L.J. 824 at 830.

Academe and the Courts: Professor Mullan's Contribution

THE RIGHT HONOURABLE BEVERLEY McLACHLIN, P.C.

This celebration of Professor David Mullan's scholarship situates his work in the course of the powerful currents that have defined Canadian legal academic and judicial cultures. My contribution will focus on the changing roles of academics and judges as, from their different perspectives, they engage in a common project of education and elaboration of the law.

I begin with a historical discussion of the relationship between judges and academics, tracing its evolution from mutual and sometimes hostile isolation to active interaction in pursuit of different, yet common and overlapping endeavours. Central to this evolution has been the development of a mature approach to the law as a critical discipline, abetted in Canada by the introduction of the *Charter* in the early 1980s, and a better understanding of the different but complementary roles of law professors and judges. The result, as Professor Mullan's scholarship in administrative law attests, has been the emergence of a new tradition of vibrant, critical scholarship and open, engaged judging.

Academe and the Courts: A Historical Perspective

To understand the relationship between the courts and legal academe, we must begin with history. We must look at both institutions to see how they have evolved and become what they are today. In the common law tradition, the history of courts and of legal academe is largely one of isolation. Each operated in its own sphere. Those spheres were not equal. Courts were regarded as the founts of the law; academics tended to confine themselves to respectful summarization of what the courts and Parliament did. That relationship, which held throughout the nineteenth and much of the twentieth century, began to change in the latter part of the past century. A new tradition of critical and vibrant legal analysis developed in the universities; law became recognized as a worthy and unique critical discipline. The courts changed, too. Facing problems of new complexity, they began to look to academic comment for help. An emerging spirit of cooperation between judges and law professors ended their mutual isolation and markedly increased the calibre of the pedagogical and jurisprudential endeavours in which each engaged. Most recently, the *Charter* signalled a broader role for legal academics in the work of the courts, which has been fulfilled by an increase in the quality and volume of legal academic scholarship.

The Anglo-European Context

In England, the Bar early on took control of legal education and access to the profession, to the exclusion of the universities.[1] The universities taught canon law and Roman law, but not the law applied in the royal courts.[2] Thus, education in the common law was a matter for practitioners. Around 1400, the Inns of Court appeared and began to undertake legal education on a somewhat organized basis.[3] However, the training provided was narrow and vocational.[4] By the reign of Elizabeth I, the Inns' monopoly over the teaching of the law was expanded to include the regulation of admission to practise.[5]

The path to the judiciary was also controlled by the profession. Its stranglehold on the judiciary arose from the unique history of the development of the common law in England. In early years, judges of the royal courts were mostly clergymen.[6] Some may have possessed a background in Roman and canon law. They may also have been trained by apprenticing with older judges.[7] However, in the fourteenth century the practice of recruiting common law judges from the ranks of the clergy came to an end.[8] Henceforth, judges were selected from the practising bar – a tradition that continues in certain common law jurisdictions.

As a consequence of this history, the legal profession monopolized education and admission to the profession and the judiciary. This eliminated any power or authority legal academics could claim over the development or interpretation of the law. As noted by Professor Langbein of Yale Law School: 'The English legal tradition was shaped ... by court practice rather than by university study. The bearers of the English common law were pleaders and judges, as opposed to professors.'[9]

Indeed, even in the late nineteenth century, the dominant view among English lawyers was that the common law simply could not be taught in the universities and could only be learned by apprenticeship in chambers or at the law courts.[10] The absence of any significant role for the universities in relation to English law meant that there was no academic criticism of the judiciary or practising bar.

It also meant that there was no significant English legal literature. Indeed, '[f]rom 1256, when Bracton stopped writing, until 1758, when Blackstone started his lectures at Oxford, there was hardly a single book on English law that could be described as literature.'[11] The legal writing that did appear in the nineteenth century was not particularly developed. In 1883 Dicey was acutely aware of the paucity of English legal literature and lamented that: 'Our best works ... are at bottom a mere accumulation of notes on detached points of curious rather than useful learning. They are deficient in all general conceptions, in all grasp of principles, in all ideas of method.'[12]

Legal academics were, as a result, viewed 'on a lower plane' than judges or practitioners.[13] Academics seemed paralysed by a fear of analysis, which could lead to criticism of judges – unthinkable given the academics' lower standing. Fortunately, this is no longer the case in the United Kingdom. Nevertheless, the historical rift between academics and judges had a major influence on the development of the common law that is felt to this day.[14]

The lack of prestige of law schools and low status of academic lawyers is a recurring motif in the social history of English law,[15] although some argue it has been overplayed.[16] Its core themes are both the lack of analytical, synthetic academic works discussed above and the failure of legal teaching to become established or accepted in the universities. The mid-to-late nineteenth century is 'generally presented as a dreary procession of disappointments and missed opportunities.'[17]

Affairs did not improve much until the Second World War, when the English law school expanded its role and became an entrenched academic faculty.[18] This general picture is supported by the available statistics. As Twining documents, in 1909 there were 109 reported law teachers in England, and by 1933–34 this had risen to only 130. The insignificance and traditional subservience of academics to the Bar led Professor L.C.B. Gower to comment as recently as 1950 that[19]

> [n]o professor as such has ever been 'elevated' to the high court bench, no judge has ever 'descended' from the bench to a professorial chair and nothing is more nauseating than the patronising air of much humility usu-

> ally affected by one of his majesty's judges when addressing an academic gathering ... it is my submission that English teachers of law suffer from an acute inferiority complex and that this is a bad thing for the profession as a whole.

The division between the practice and theory of law in the United Kingdom, however, led to the development by academics of certain unoccupied fields of law where they could make law instead of the judges. The academic development of conflict of laws by Dicey and Cheshire was an example of such an area, demonstrating the valuable role of academics in organizing disparate judicial decisions within a theoretical framework.[20] The transformative possibilities of this type of scholarship were limited by the rule that an academic author could only be cited by courts after the author's death.[21] This rule discouraged any topical analysis of recent cases by academics or real dialogue with courts.

The civil law systems of Europe evolved in a manner diametrically opposite to the development of English common law. Universities guided the development of the civil law and only relatively recently has it been admitted that judicial decisions may be a source of law. In contemporary civil law theory, academic scholarship is regarded as a secondary source of law. As Professor MacDonald has said about the civil law, '[s]cholarly opinion is not simply writing *about* law; it is, in some measure, thought to be constitutive of law.'[22]

Canada, as inheritor of both the civil and common law systems, drew from both. Early common law scholarship in Canada adopted the descriptive, deferential role. However, the tides of change could not be resisted and, like the civil law where academics played a central role in legal development, legal academics now play an increased and important role in the work of the courts throughout Canada. It is to a discussion of the Canadian legal academic and judicial context that I now turn.

The Development of Canadian Legal Academe

Although common law legal teaching began at Dalhousie University in 1883, university teaching in both civil and common law subjects was limited during the nineteenth century.[23] No parallel existed to the United States professional academic law schools that blossomed during the 1870s. Standards for becoming a lawyer varied widely across Canada, generally comprising an apprenticeship supplemented by lectures given by practitioners or the rare full-time faculty member.

The Canadian legal academic of the 1920s and 1930s typically worked in an environment characterized by high teaching loads, stultified professional interchange of ideas, and an ethos that discouraged criticism and creativity. The major sources of ideas were journals and books from the United Kingdom and the United States, as opposed to Canadian sources.[24] The work produced during this period was largely taxonomic, classifying the law and legal rules and mimicking the type of legal work prevalent in the United Kingdom. There was little critical or evaluative work.[25]

Not much changed in the following decades: law schools of the 1940s and 1950s were small, and legal education was still largely controlled by the profession as opposed to academics. 'Few practitioners' texts existed, even in subjects such as contracts or commercial law; most published scholarship addressed issues of doctrinal, black-letter law ...'[26] Academic legal research and writing had little impact on the actual practice of the law; practitioners and judges rarely referred to legal treatises or articles. In 1950 Chief Justice Rinfret notoriously remarked during the hearing of the *Rentals Reference*[27] that 'the Canadian Bar Review is not an authority in this Court,' explicitly importing the traditional English aversion to legal periodicals.[28] As the Arthurs Report notes, 'legal practice was conducted without apparent difficulty, notwithstanding the lack of libraries holding secondary materials, or (until the 1970s) a distinctively Canadian index to secondary literature.'[29] This was to be expected since even after the Second World War law professors were a rare commodity – most law teaching was done by practitioners.

However, change was on its way. In the 1960s and 1970s, the number of law schools mushroomed. So did the cohort of law professors, from a meagre forty or so in 1950 to over six hundred in the early 1980s.[30] The changes were not only numeric; a new professionalism took root in Canadian legal academe. As the credentials of legal academics improved, their numbers increased, the training of law graduates ameliorated, and the scholarly community grew. The legal academic community quickly started to be recognized as a source of legal knowledge and expertise.[31] In 1950 the appointment of Vincent C. MacDonald to the Supreme Court of Nova Scotia marked the first full-time law teacher appointed to the bench in Canada, and was followed in the 1960s and 1970s by further judicial appointments of academics. Even the Supreme Court of Canada started to welcome lawyers with firm connections to law schools, including Louis-Philippe Pigeon in 1967, Bora Laskin in 1970, and Jean Beetz in 1974.[32] Most importantly, the taboo against criticism of judicial reasoning began to lose its grip. A growing awareness that the law could and should be analysed, questioned, and reviewed for its impact began to take hold.

The new spirit that swept legal academe in the 1960s and 1970s slid toward retrenchment in the 1980s. The growth in law schools and academic staff of the 1960s and 1970s plateaued in the late 1970s: 'Excitement gave way to concern, retrenchment and introspection.'[33] And this, when, in the eyes of some at least, Canadian academe had yet to achieve excellence. Professor Harry Arthurs put it thus in his 1976 Horace E. Read Memorial Lecture to the Faculty of Law at Dalhousie University: 'Canadian legal scholarship, in all of its manifestations, is often inadequate, sometimes acceptable, but seldom – on an objective scale – first class.'[34]

The concern with the quality of Canadian legal scholarship led to the pivotal *Law and Learning* study of Canadian legal academic scholarship. The study divided the body of Canadian legal literature into at least four types of research: conventional texts and articles; legal theory, or research designed to yield a unifying theory or perspective by which legal rules may be understood; law reform research designed to accomplish change in the law; and fundamental research designed to secure a deeper understanding of law as a social phenomenon.[35] Professor Arthurs's taxonomy of Canadian legal scholarship is now recognized as the dominant means of ordering the work of legal academic scholars. Professor Mullan's contribution to Canadian legal scholarship, as will be discussed below, has contributed to all four strands.

Two decades later, many of the recommendations of the Arthurs Report remain unfulfilled.[36] Yet the scope and breadth of Canadian legal research have undeniably increased since the early 1980s. The proliferation of student and faculty-edited law reviews, the growing pools of research funding in the form of Canada Research Chairs and Social Sciences and Humanities Research Council awards, the efforts made to increase the size and quality of Canadian graduate programs, and an emerging body of inter-disciplinary and transnational scholarship all attest to the vibrancy of the Canadian legal academic community.

The Development of the Canadian Judiciary

While legal academic scholarship struggled for legitimacy, Canada's judiciary went through its own growing pains. The parallel was noted by Chief Justice Dickson (then puisne judge of the Supreme Court of Canada) in a 1981 speech to Dalhousie Law School: '[a] common feature of the judiciary and the law schools of this country is that each, in a sense, reached maturity within the last 30 years.'[37]

The 1867 *Constitution Act* did not set up a Supreme Court; it merely provided that Parliament could create a Supreme Court (unlike the situation in the United States). The implication was that the Supreme Court was not viewed as essential to our constitutional structure. Indeed, until 1949 the Judicial Committee of the Privy Council served as our final court of appeal. As Chief Justice Dickson put it, '[m]any appeals were taken directly to London from a provincial court of appeal without even a courtesy stop at Canada's highest court.'[38] Even when the Supreme Court of Canada decided cases, it was bound to apply English precedent. For some time after appeals to the Privy Council were abolished there was little discernible change in the Supreme Court's approach, which remained conservative and deferential to English authority.[39]

The status of the Supreme Court of Canada improved gradually, in parallel with that of the academic community. Just as academics in the 1960s and 1970s started to build a distinctively Canadian body of legal academic scholarship, justices appointed in the late 1960s and 1970s began to assert a uniquely Canadian vision and to develop a distinct Canadian jurisprudence. Chief Justice Dickson himself acknowledged the importance of cooperation between judges and academics as a result of the fact that 'the effective law-making power of our final court of appeal is tangibly restricted to those possibilities which appear sound in the light of prevailing views about those fundamental issues.'[40]

The Chief Justice was in the vanguard, it must be said. Many lawyers and judges remained reluctant to accept a full role for academics in the legal reasoning of the courts. On the other hand, to many academics, the growing dialogue between the Supreme Court of Canada and the academic community by the early 1980s had not resulted in sufficiently high calibre legal reasoning and judgment. Thus, Chief Justice Dickson continued to advocate for closer links, arguing that '[t]he success of the Court in fashioning legal rules depends very much, of course, on the calibre of its judges, but it depends also on the legal culture of the country and the way in which that legal culture informs and develops the materials available to the Court.'[41] Paul Weiler put it thus in his influential 1975 law review article: '[t]he deficiencies in Canadian judicial performance are, in large measure, a product of the failure of Canadian legal theory.'[42] In arguing for a growth in the role of scholarship at the

Supreme Court of Canada, Weiler concluded that 'twenty-five years after [the Supreme Court of Canada] became our final court of appeal, it is high time to get the scholarly task underway.'[43]

Chief Justice Dickson presciently predicted that the patriation of the Constitution and the newly entrenched *Charter* in 1982 would create new opportunities for 'mutual inspiration and instruction' between judges and the professoriate.[44] He issued the rallying cry that 'the door must now be open for the integration of academic law into the mainstream of Canadian law if we are ever to develop a distinctly Canadian jurisprudence.'[45] The growing interchange between academics and judges would result from the more liberal, contextual approach that characterized the interpretation of *Charter* rights.

The changing relationship between the judiciary and academics in the late 1980s and 1990s was formally recognized through the growth of judicial education initiatives. It was informally nurtured by the abundant use of academic sources in the development of the Court's *Charter* jurisprudence. These formal and informal links between the judiciary and academia will be discussed in turn.

Judicial education was institutionalized through the creation of the National Judicial Institute (NJI) in 1988 to improve the quality of judicial decision-making.[46] It was a successor to the Canadian Institute for the Administration of Justice established in 1974 to provide some measure of judicial education.[47] The NJI acts through judicial educators, many of whom are members of the law faculties of Canadian universities. In addition, federally appointed judges can take sabbaticals as part of the Study Leave Fellowship program of the Canadian Judicial Council. Judges spend time at a Canadian faculty of law teaching, studying, and researching. This allows them to be exposed to academic developments in the law, and to legal academics and law students.

The use of scholarly works by the courts increased markedly after the Arthurs Report and with encouragement from both the judiciary and academics. Chief Justice Dickson's prediction that the use of academic scholarship would increase in the era of the *Charter* was borne out, as evidenced in a 1993 study by Black and Richter which found that the frequency of citations to academic scholarship by the Supreme Court of Canada had tripled in a generation.[48] Black and Richter's study further found that *Charter* cases were more likely than non-*Charter* cases to cite academic authority.[49] The results of this study confirm those of Bale, who found that the number of references by the Supreme Court of Canada to periodical literature increased from 59 citations in 1985 to 204 in

1992.[50] The growing importance of academic commentary to *Charter* law-making was more recently confirmed in a public address by Justice Bastarache to the University of Alberta Faculty of Law.[51] He speculated that the increased use of academic works is due, in part, to the growing law-making function of the Court, the competing policy considerations underlying many *Charter* challenges, and the far-reaching effects of many decisions under the *Charter*.[52] His comments bear out most of Chief Justice Dickson's earlier predictions about the future course of academic scholarship and the Court.

For some, the Supreme Court's jurisprudence in the last two decades of the twentieth century was too radical. In England and Australia, for example, both judges and academics regarded much of the Supreme Court's work with more than a little suspicion. The Court's openness to critical and creative academic thinking was seen by some as a threat to the stability and predictability of the law. The Court's robust interpretation of *Charter* rights, including equality rights and aboriginal rights, as well as its willingness to reshape the law of fiduciary responsibility and common law tort doctrines, attracted scepticism and sometimes overt criticism from those who viewed its jurisprudence from distant, more conservative shores. At the same time, Canadian jurisprudence found new adherents abroad. The *Charter* jurisprudence of the Court has entered the mainstream of world legal thought. The Supreme Court's cases are read and considered in courts from South Africa to Europe to Asia. More and more, Canadian judges and academics are invited to share their views on democracy, federalism, and human rights at conferences around the world. Internationally, Canadian jurisprudence has assumed a unique identity – known, criticized, admired, but undeniably relevant.

Within Canada, the story is similar. The newly academic and assertive brand of judging that emerged in the 1980s attracted criticism. Academics, politicians, and members of the press expressed fears about 'judicial activism' and the power of unelected judges to shape society. Yet the new Canadian jurisprudence also found adherents. Many academics approved of the new approach to the law; indeed, for some the Court was often too conservative. Members of the public continue to bring their cases to the Court and opinion polls consistently show high levels of public confidence in the judiciary. People may like or dislike a particular decision of the Court, but they nevertheless continue to regard it as a vital institution capable of resolving with integrity and intelligence the difficult issues that arise in our complex, multi-cultural society.

The Academic and Judicial Roles: Convergence and Contrast

The last thirty years have been years of great change and growth for Canadian legal academe and for Canadian courts. It is no accident that both have grown in similar directions in the same historical period. The respective roles of judges and of academics are very different. Yet they are intersecting and complementary. Strength and growth in one promote strength and growth in the other, as the brief history set out above attests.

It is worth pausing to consider the similarities and differences between the roles of judges and legal academics, and why it is that these two roles complement each other.

First, the similarities. The first is obvious: judges and academics spend most of their working lives trying to explain the law. Legal academics teach students, write articles, and speak at conferences. Judges render decisions from the bench, and occasionally communicate their vision of the law through speeches and articles. Both academics and judges employ research assistants, clerks, and other students whom they mentor in their understanding of the law. The second similarity flows from the first: judges and academics are both teachers. Judges are not professional teachers; yet reasons for judgment play a pedagogical role for lower courts and lawyers, and are the primary pedagogical material in our law schools. These similarities give rise to a third commonality – the ability of judges to sometimes function as academics and of academics to sometimes become judges. The members of legal academe, like judges, are lawyers, writers, and teachers. Members of each profession share a common passion for the law and its development. They are engaged in a common endeavour: using the institution of the law for the betterment of society. Finally, as the phenomenon of globalization reaches into the field of law, both judges and legal scholars are increasingly called on to address transnational issues and develop an understanding of the international dimensions of their roles.[53]

But there are also differences in the roles of judges and legal academics – differences that explain why the two professions complement each other so well. Law professors are free to adopt causes and espouse agendas; judges are not. Law professors can choose their area of study; judges are obliged to consider only the cases that come before them. Law professors are permitted to be provocative and adversarial; judges must strive to remain neutral, unbiased, and objective, in fact and in the public's perception. Law professors can criticize others ferociously and defend themselves aggressively; judges must remain above the fray and cannot reply to criticism. Law professors have greater freedom to align their time with their priorities; judges are kept busy with imposed priorities. Law professors can play with broad theoretical frameworks and test interdisciplinary interlocks; judges are stuck with the facts of the case before them. Law professors can specialize in a particular area of the law and become highly knowledgeable in its minutiae; judges are condemned to the life of the generalist. Finally, law professors can float ideas without fear that they may not work out; judges know that what they say will have serious consequences for the parties before them and often for many others, not to mention the future development of the law. Judges solve problems; academics analyse them.

In sum, law professors can roam where judges cannot, and in ways that judges cannot. They can point out weaknesses in the law. They can suggest new departures and developments. They can serve as critics, and at their best, as guides. All this is invaluable to the judge.

A healthy relationship between the world of legal academe and the world of the court depends on the independence of each calling. The academic who worries about whether a judge will approve of her criticism is an academic working with one hand tied. The academic should respect the judge as a person and the institution, so long as they function with integrity. But constructive criticism of perspectives and errors of the judge's product is beneficial. Similarly, the judge cannot worry about whether the academics like what she writes. The judge's duty is to decide the case in light of the facts, law, and arguments presented in court to the best of her ability, not to worry about winning favour with the outside world. The relationship between judges and legal academics is one of tension but, at its best, healthy and productive tension.

Legal academics must remain independent. Their main task is to teach and to explicate the law by writing, not to help judges. Whether academic pieces should even strive to be useful to judges is a debate that has raged in the United States,[54] Canada,[55] and in Australia.[56] I would argue that so long as law professors retain their independence and integrity, they can and should have an eye out for how their work can advance the development of the law. Scholarship for scholarship's sake is important, but so is the rational and relevant development of legal doctrine through legislation and judicial decisions. Legal academics and practitioners should 'share the fundamental belief that scholarship that seeks to inform and guide practitioners, legislators, other policy-makers, and judges is a valuable, indeed necessary, component of any law school's [and legal academic's] mission.'[57]

If we accept that academics may properly have regard for how their work can advance the law, the next question is how this can be done most effectively. Canada's experience in two decades of *Charter* litigation provides a prime example of effective interaction between legal academe and the courts. The courts were faced with the monumental task of doctrinally defining the expansive guarantees of the *Charter.* Time after time, right after right, from free speech to liberty to equality, they found the necessary historic, social, and analytic context between the pages of Canada's law reviews. The great bulk of legal scholarship produced in this exciting era was of high quality and hence highly useful. A little of it fell prey to three faults that can reduce the usefulness of academic writing to judges: excessive analysis that loses itself and its relevance in minutiae; personal attacks on judges rather than their decisions; and lack of objectivity that transforms legitimate criticism into little more than a rant.

What, then, of judges? They too must write from a stance of independence. Helping professors fill casebooks and law journals may be an incidental by-product of their work, but cannot be their main focus. Yet judges too have learned that their work may be better if they have an eye out for how the legal scholars will interpret it. The days of judgments consisting of a few cryptic paragraphs capable of being understood only by the litigants and their lawyers are gone. Judges now strive to give full reasons that can be understood by strangers to the case, and to do so in a way that clearly and, with luck, concisely, sets out the facts and applicable legal principles. They want the parties, the judicial community, and legal academe to be able to understand their rulings and appreciate why they are making them. The result is better law.

In summary, the roles of legal academics and judges as they have evolved are both different and complementary. They work with the same subject matter and share the same goal: the clear articulation and reasoned development of legal principles and values. Yet their roles are different and independent. These differences make legal academics valuable to the judiciary and the judiciary important to legal academe.

Professor Mullan: Academic Change-maker

Against this background, I turn to the subject of this volume, the work of Professor Mullan. Many tributes have been paid him. From my perspective as a jurist, let me advance this observation: Professor Mullan's work stands as a testament to the power of a law professor to assist judges and influence the development of the law. Fiercely independent and not infrequently critical, he has pointed out problems and suggested solutions. He has done so in a way that has enhanced the respect Canadians hold for the courts and the esteem in which Canadian legal scholarship is more widely held.

I earlier contrasted the old-fashioned academic, concerned more with the taxonomy of the law than its content, with the modern academic, engaged in the creative enhancement of Canadian law and its institutions. Professor Mullan belongs to the latter category. Through the publication of texts, articles, case comments, his involvement in law reform activities, and judicial education, Professor Mullan has helped build a new critical and creative standard for legal academics – one that has enriched not only academe but the work of lawyers and the courts. Nowhere has this been more apparent than in his contribution to the area of which I have the most knowledge: the jurisprudence of the Supreme Court of Canada.

Professor Mullan's scholarship cuts a bold swathe through most aspects of this Court's administrative law jurisprudence. His work has been formally referred to by the Supreme Court of Canada in at least eighteen decisions, and in several of those cases multiple works were cited.[58] This Court has cited his academic works in the areas of standards of review, the doctrine of collateral attack, *audi alteram partem*, and legitimate expectations, to name a few. This statistical snapshot, though, does not provide an accurate sense of Professor Mullan's full contribution. His textbook, *Administrative Law*,[59] remains a point of first reference for discovering the principles of law underpinning a particular dispute before the Court. As well, Professor Mullan has made an inestimable contribution through his work educating the students who arrive as law clerks to the judges at the Supreme Court of Canada, either by teaching them directly, or through the casebook he has co-authored and that forms the basis of administrative law teaching in Canada today.[60]

Consider what current members of the Supreme Court of Canada have had to say about Professor Mullan's scholarship:

- 'Professor Mullan's mastery of the field of administrative law means his analysis provides insight into how cases fit together and how new decisions will alter the existing status quo' (Bastarache J.).

- 'The common law may be overwhelmed by information if there is no intellectual filter to provide more than a useful shopping list of judicial holdings ... Professor Mullan has played a special role in focusing the Court on what is really happening in administrative law, tying together strands of jurisprudence in the field' (LeBel J.).
- 'One of Professor Mullan's key skills is bringing coherence to the area, extracting important principles to guide the future development of the law' (Abella J.).
- 'Through synthesizing and providing frameworks Professor Mullan pushes the Court to simplify rather than over-complicate, encouraging the Court to be more understandable' (Binnie J.).
- 'In particular, Professor Mullan produces a timely comment on just about everything this Court produces, rarely stating merely what the case held, but pointing out where the decision was good and what needs to be fixed' (Binnie J.).
- 'Because Professor Mullan has so mastered his subject, he is able to quickly respond to new developments with objective and dispassionate analysis, commenting with thoroughness and objectivity. He is an exemplar of the shift in the role of academics in the common law world' (LeBel J.).
- 'Professor Mullan's work has been invaluable in providing the broader context in which a particular administrative law problem arises' (Bastarache J.).
- 'Professor Mullan is particularly interested in how the law is going to work in the real world and *if* it works in the real world' (Binnie J.).
- 'His strong sense of the history and the future of administrative law allow him to be a fair, confident and measured commentator of this Court's work' (Abella J.).

These comments highlight three ways in which Professor Mullan's scholarship has contributed to the work of the courts: first, through creating an architecture of administrative law; second, by analysing and constructively criticizing the developing of the case law; and third, by providing insight into the broader context in which administrative law problems arise.

Perhaps Professor Mullan's greatest contribution has been to provide an intellectual framework for the ordering of Canadian administrative law. He has taken full advantage of the freedom enjoyed by academe to move beyond the concerns of whether this or that case was correctly decided, to the broader task of building the architecture of our country's administrative law – the broad framework that knits together past judicial decisions and orients the problems of the future. Professor Mullan's textbooks and articles, spanning two decades, on deference to administrative tribunals,[61] the proper role of administrative tribunals,[62] and *audi alteram partem*[63] attest to his ability to pull together divergent strands of a complex, sometimes seemingly incomprehensible subject. All this is done in a way that is as dismissive of useless formalism as it is attentive to function: what academics have taught courts to call the 'purposive approach.' Through his extensive powers of synthesis, Professor Mullan has helped rationalize and modernize Canadian administrative law.

Professor Mullan's power to paint the big picture, however, has not come at the cost of detail and reflective nuance. He has not merely stitched divergent patches of administrative law together; he has done this in a way that is attentive to the different colours and threads of his primary material – the legislation and cases on administrative law. Along with other administrative law scholars of the new generation, his work bridges the distance between academic commentary and judicial decision-making. His recent case comments on *Blencoe v. British Columbia (Human Rights Commission)*[64] and *Ocean Port Hotel Ltd. v. British Columbia (General Manager, Liquor Control and Licensing Branch)*[65] provide examples of his quick and analytical response to decisions of the Supreme Court of Canada. His long-time editorship of, and innumerable annotations for, the *Administrative Law Reports* further evidence his detailed consideration of legal developments and his ability to weave them into the existing fabric of the law.

Professor Mullan's third contribution exemplifies the critical role academic lawyers can play in providing the broader social, economic, and political context within which legal problems are situated. One important element of this context is the *Charter.* Another is international law. Professor Mullan's work situates modern Canadian administrative law in these contexts and, having done so, goes on to integrate it into broader human rights and economic concerns. His recent article in the *Indiana Journal of Global Legal Studies* is an excellent example of his wide perspective on administrative law.[66]

Nowhere has Professor Mullan's broad perspective on administrative law been better demonstrated than in the paper he presented at the event marking the 125th anniversary of the Supreme Court of Canada.[67] Professor Mullan argued that historically the case law of the Supreme Court of Canada has demonstrated significant deference to the judgment and choices of administrative tribunals, refuting the notion that the Supreme Court of Canada's current deferential approach to the expertise and operational imperatives of administrative tribunals was a novel development. Creating coherence out of inarticulate randomness, Professor Mullan concluded that in fact a strong commitment to the sovereignty of Parliament informed the Supreme Court's early administrative law decisions, though he cautions that up until the Second World War, administrative law was in its infancy and judicial scrutiny of administrative action was a relatively recent phenomenon. Professor Mullan concluded with a characteristic word of advice to the judiciary. He spoke of persistent administrative law knots that need to be untangled, including the 'appropriate judicial response to deregulation, downsizing and contracting out and especially resolving how the courts should deal with the increasing blurring of the lines between the public and private domains.'[68]

Establishing analytic architecture, commenting on current developments, and situating administrative law in context are not insignificant accomplishments. They attest to Professor Mullan's understanding of his primary role as an academic lawyer and his secondary, but no less significant, role in assisting courts to develop the law in a coherent and responsive way that meets society's evolving needs. Through clear analysis, objectivity, and a deft combination of big-picture thinking and attention to detail, he has made a contribution that leaves administrative law, one of the most complex fields of modern legal study, far clearer and richer than he found it.

Conclusion

The work of scholars such as Professor Mullan shows how far the legal community has come in its common project of legal education. The ancient separation of the judiciary from academia and the contempt in which academics were held has been transformed into a powerful collaborative endeavour that has improved the work of each. By encouraging the participation of academics, the judiciary has improved the quality of its legal reasoning. By actively developing a critical, analytical, and theoretical scholarship that engages with judicial decisions, academia has developed a uniquely Canadian body of legal studies. Critical, analytical scholarship has been especially useful to the Supreme Court of Canada in the era of the *Charter*. In particular, it has provided the Court with much of the historical analysis, current context, and insight into the rigorous analysis that must inform all judicial rule-making. Building on this solid foundation of dialogue and mutual respect, both courts and scholars must not be complacent, but must ensure that their respective journeys lead them to the common port of justice.

NOTES

1 John Dawson, *The Oracles of the Law* (Ann Arbor: University of Michigan Press, 1968) at 34–48.
2 J. Langbein, 'Trinity Hall and the Relations of European and English Law from the Fourteenth to the Twenty-First Centuries' in H. Felter, ed., *Trinity Hall 650th Anniversary Milestone Lectures* (Cambridge, UK: Trinity Hall, 2001) 75 at 76; B. Dickson, 'The Relationship of Judges and Law Schools: "Allies in the Common Course"' in L. Lévesque, comp., *Speeches Delivered by the Right Honourable Brian Dickson*, vol. 1 (Ottawa: Supreme Court of Canada, 1993) 179 at 184.
3 Dawson, *supra* note 1 at 39.
4 Ibid. at 45.
5 Ibid. at 42.
6 Ibid. at 5.
7 Ibid. at 6.
8 Ibid. at 11.
9 Langbein, *supra* note 2 at 76.
10 A.V. Dicey, *Can English Law be Taught at the Universities?* (London: Macmillan and Co., 1883) at 1. Dicey, however, did not share this view and, in his 1883 inaugural lecture at Oxford, he sought to demonstrate the weakness of the existing system of English legal education and stake out a complementary role for the universities in educating lawyers.
11 Dawson, *supra* note 1 at 47.
12 Dicey, *supra* note 10 at 12; see also William Twining, *Blackstone's Tower: The English Law School* (London: Sweet & Maxwell, 1994) at chap. 6.
13 L.C.B. Gower, 'English Legal Training' (1950) 13 Mod. L. Rev. 137 at 198.
14 Dickson, *supra* note 2 at 186.
15 Twining, *supra* note 12 at 25.
16 Ibid. at fn. 13.
17 Ibid. at 24.
18 Ibid. at 26.
19 Gower, *supra* note 13 at 198.

20 See Dickson, *supra* note 2 at 185. Today, of course, academics make significant contributions to many fields of law in the United Kingdom, including, in particular, administrative law: see M. Beloff, 'The Academic Influences on Judicial Review' in R. Gordon, ed., *Judicial Review in the New Millennium* (London: Sweet & Maxwell, 2003) at 91.

21 The Right Honourable Lord Woolf, 'The Atlantic Divide' (1999) 34 Tulsa L.J. 657 at 663. For a detailed discussion of this UK rule by Canadian legal academics, see Gordon Bale, 'W.R. Lederman and the Citation of Legal Periodicals by the Supreme Court of Canada' (1993–4) 19 Queen's L.J. 36 at 51–52, and G.V.V. Nicholls, 'Legal Periodicals and the Supreme Court of Canada' (1950) 28 Can. B. Rev. 422.

22 Roderick A. MacDonald, 'Understanding Civil Law Scholarship in Quebec' (1985) 23 Osgoode Hall L. J. 573.

23 For a detailed history, see Bora Laskin, *The British Tradition in Canadian Law, Hamlyn Lectures 21st Series* (London: Steven & Sons, 1969) chap. 3 [Laskin, 'Hamlyn Lectures']; see also J. Willis, *A History of Dalhousie Law School* (Toronto: University of Toronto Press, 1979) at 19.

24 R. Risk, 'Canadian Law Teachers in the 1930s: "When the World was Turned Upside Down"' (2004) 27 Dal. L.J. 1; Laskin, 'Hamlyn Lectures,' *supra* note 23 at 89–92.

25 Laskin, 'Hamlyn Lectures,' *supra* note 23 at 92.

26 H.W. Arthurs, 'National Traditions in Labor Law Scholarship: The Canadian Case' (2002) 23 Comp. Lab. L. J. 645 at 655; Laskin, 'Hamlyn Lectures,' *supra* note 23 at 89.

27 *Reference Re the Wartime Leasehold Regulations*, [1950] S.C.R. 124.

28 Nicholls, *supra* note 21; Bale, *supra* note 21. An Australian contribution to the citation debate can be found in R. Smyth, 'Academic Writing and the Courts: A Quantitative Study of the Influence of Legal and Non-Legal Periodical Articles in the High Court' (1998) 17 U. Tasm. L. Rev. 164.

29 Consultative Group on Research and Education in Law, *Law and Learning Report to the Social Sciences and Humanities Research Council of Canada* (Ottawa: Minister of Supply and Services, 1983) at 65 [Arthurs Report].

30 Ibid. at 18.

31 Ibid.; Bora Laskin, 'A Judge and His Constituencies' (1976–7) 7 Man. L.J. 1.

32 Bale, *supra* note 21 at 58–59.

33 Ibid. at 22.

34 Quoted in Dickson, *supra* note 2 at 193. These concerns were amplified by Professors Edward Veitch and R.A. MacDonald, 'Law Teachers and Their Jurisdiction' (1978) 56 Can. Bar Rev. 710.

35 Arthurs Report, *supra* note 29 at 66.

36 Roderick A. MacDonald, 'Still "Law" and Still "Learning"?'(2003) 18 Can. J.L. & Soc. 5; Constance Backhouse, 'Revisiting the *Arthurs Report* Twenty Years Later,' ibid. at 33.
37 Dickson, *supra* note 2 at 190.
38 Ibid. at 190–1.
39 For an in-depth discussion of the continuing reliance on English law during this period, see Laskin, 'Hamlyn Lectures,' *supra* note 23 at chap. 2.
40 Dickson, *supra* note 2 at 195, quoting Paul C. Weiler, 'Of Judges and Scholars: Reflections in a Centennial Year' (1975) 53 Can. Bar Rev. 563 at 563.
41 Dickson, *supra* note 2 at 191.
42 Weiler, *supra* note 40 at 563.
43 Ibid. at 575.
44 Dickson, *supra* note 2 at 196.
45 Ibid.
46 <http://www.nji.ca/>.
47 T. David Marshall, *Judicial Conduct and Accountability* (Toronto: Carswell, 1995) at 53.
48 Vaughan Black and Nicholas Richter, 'Did She Mention My Name? Citation of Academic Authority by the Supreme Court of Canada, 1985–1990' (1993) 16 Dal. L.J. 377.
49 Ibid. at 389.
50 Bale, *supra* note 21 at 56. It should be noted, however, that this part of the study was primarily concerned with comparing the number of citations to Canadian law journals with those to foreign legal periodicals.
51 Michel Bastarache, 'The Role of Academics and Legal Theory in Judicial Decision-Making' (1999) 37 Alta. L. Rev. 739.
52 Ibid. at 739.
53 Claire L'Heureux-Dubé, 'The Importance of Dialogue: Globalization and the International Impact of the Rehnquist Court' (1998) 34 Tulsa L.J. 15; Christopher McCrudden, 'A Common Law of Human Rights? Transnational Judicial Conversations on Constitutional Rights?' (2000) 20 O.J.L.S. 499; Anne-Marie Slaughter, 'Judicial Globalization' (2000) 40 Va. J. Int'l L. 1102.
54 The contours of the debate are summarized well in a series of articles by Judge Edwards of the U.S. Court of Appeals, DC Circuit: Harry Edwards, 'The Growing Disjunction Between Legal Education and the Legal Profession' (1992) 91 Mich. L. Rev. 34; Harry Edwards, 'The Growing Disjunction Between Legal Education and the Legal Profession: A Postscript' (1993) 91 Mich. L. Rev. 2191; Harry Edwards, 'Another Postscript to the Growing Disjunction Between Legal Education and the Legal Profession' (1994) 69 Wash.

L. Rev. 561 [Edwards, Another Postcript]. For a British perspective on Edwards's arguments, see Woolf, *supra* note 21 at 663–65.

55 See Bastarache, *supra* note 51; and the response by Professor Hutchinson: Allan C. Hutchinson, 'The Role of Judges in Legal Theory and the Role of the Legal Theorists in Judging (or "Don't Let the Bastaraches Grind You Down")' (2001) 39 Alta. L. Rev. 657.

56 John Gava, 'Law Reviews: Good for Judges, Bad for Law Schools?' (2002) 26 Melbourne U.L. Rev. 560.

57 Edwards, 'Another Postscript,' *supra* note 54 at 571.

58 *Doucet-Boudreau v. Nova Scotia (Minister of Education)*, [2003] 3 S.C.R. 3; *Toronto (City) v. C.U.P.E., Local 79*, [2003] 3 S.C.R. 77; *Ellis-Don Ltd. v. Ontario (Labour Relations Board)*, [2001] 1 S.C.R. 221; *Dr. Q. v. College of Physicians and Surgeons of British Columbia*, [2003] 1 S.C.R. 226; *Mount Sinai Hospital Center v. Quebec (Minister of Health and Social Services)*, [2001] 2 S.C.R. 281; *Blencoe v. British Columbia (Human Rights Commission)*, [2000] 2 S.C.R. 307; *Baker v. Canada (Minister of Citizenship and Immigration)*, [1999] 2 S.C.R. 817; *R. v. Consolidated Maybrun Mines Ltd.*, [1998] 1 S.C.R. 706; *Dagg v. Canada (Minister of Finance)*, [1997] 2 S.C.R. 403; *Domtar Inc. v. Quebec (Commission d'appel en matière de lésions professionnelles)*, [1993] 2 S.C.R. 756; *Canada (Attorney General) v. Mossop*, [1993] 1 S.C.R. 554; *Italy (Republic) v. Boilard*, [1982] 1 S.C.R. 320; *Homex Realty and Development Co. v. Wyoming (Village)*, [1980] 2 S.C.R. 1011; *Northern Telecom Ltd. v. Communications Workers of Canada*, [1980] 1 S.C.R. 115; *Martineau v. Matsqui Institution*, [1980] 1 S.C.R. 602; *Harelkin v. University of Regina*, [1979] 2 S.C.R. 561; *Nicholson v. Haldimand Norfolk (Regional) Police Commissioners*, [1979] 1 S.C.R. 311; and *Canada (Minister of National Revenue) v. Coopers and Lybrand Ltd.*, [1979] 1 S.C.R. 495.

59 David J. Mullan, *Administrative Law* (Toronto: Irwin Law, 2001).

60 David J. Mullan, *Administrative Law: Cases, Text and Materials*, 5th ed. (Toronto: Emond Montgomery, 2003). See MacLauchlan and Bryden's contribution to this volume, 'Learning Administrative Law from David Mullan: An Appreciation of Evans, Janisch, Mullan and Risk, *Administrative Law: Cases, Text, and Materials*.'

61 For example, David J. Mullan, 'Judicial Deference to Administrative Decision-Making in the Age of the *Charter*' (1986) 50 Sask. L. Rev. 203; David Mullan, 'The Supreme Court of Canada and Tribunals – Deference to the Administrative Process: A Recent Phenomenon or a Return to Basics?' (2001) 80 Can. Bar Rev. 399 [Mullan, 'Deference to the Administrative Process'].

62 David Mullan, 'Tribunals and Courts – The Contemporary Terrain: Lessons from Human Rights Regimes' (1999) 24 Queen's L. J. 643.

63 David J. Mullan, 'Policing the *Consolidated-Bathurst* Limits - Of Whistle-blowers and Other Assorted Characters' (1993) 10 Admin. L. R. (2d) 241; David J. Mullan, 'Annotation to *Consolidated-Bathurst Packaging Ltd. v. International Woodworkers of America*' (1986) 16 Admin. L. R. 37; David J. Mullan, '*Consolidated-Bathurst* and the Dominion Stores Pension Fund Case: Different Approaches or Reconcilable Differences?' (1987) 21 Admin. L. R. 215.

64 [2000] 2 S.C.R. 307; David J. Mullan, 'Ocean Port Hotel and Statutory Compromises of Tribunal Independence' (2002) 9 C.L.E.L.J. 193.

65 [2001] 2 S.C.R. 781; David J. Mullan and Deirdre Harrington, 'The *Charter* and Administrative Decision-Making: The Dampening Effects of *Blencoe*' (2002) 27 Queen's L.J. 879.

66 David Mullan and Antonella Ceddia, 'The Impact on Public Law of Privatization, Deregulation, Outsourcing and Downsizing: A Canadian Perspective' (2003) 10 Ind. J. Global Legal Stud. 199.

67 Mullan, 'Deference to the Administrative Process,' *supra* note 61.

68 Ibid. at 431.

Learning Administrative Law from David Mullan: An Appreciation of Evans, Janisch, Mullan, and Risk, *Administrative Law: Cases, Text, and Materials*

H. WADE MacLAUCHLAN AND PHILIP BRYDEN

By all accounts Professor David Mullan was a remarkable teacher of administrative law. In presenting the Canadian Association of Law Teachers Award for Academic Excellence to David Mullan in 1996, Hudson Janisch (himself an outstanding law teacher) made special mention of Mullan's dedication to the education of his students and in particular to the teaching of administrative law. This dedication was recognized by Queen's University, where Professor Mullan spent most of his teaching career, with the presentation of the Queen's Alumni Award for Excellence in Teaching. So it is, in our view, entirely fitting that a volume recognizing David Mullan's contributions to administrative law should include reflections on the way he influenced the teaching of administrative law.

To some extent, of course, Professor Mullan's many former students are better placed than we are to write about his gifts as an educator. As teachers of administrative law ourselves, however, we believe that we can best reflect on the influence Mullan had on the teaching of the subject by writing about the casebook *Administrative Law: Cases, Text, and Materials* he co-authored with John Evans, Hudson Janisch, and Dick Risk.[1]

EJMR was Canada's first commercially published administrative law casebook. Emond Montgomery published the first edition in 1980 and there were five editions, the fifth published in 2003. *EJMR* survived attrition in the ranks of its collaborators, with Dick Risk's name disappearing from the list of authors in the fourth edition, which appeared in 1995.[2] The fifth (and in many ways the best) edition was brought out by Mullan alone.[3] It is no sign of disrespect to the contributions made by the other authors to say that the casebook represents one of Mullan's most significant contributions to the way Canadian academics and practitioners have thought about administrative law for the past twenty-five years.

Our observations on *EJMR* are in two parts. In the first, we consider how the book delineated the boundaries of administrative law for Canadian law teachers. More specifically, we discuss the ways in which *EJMR's* identification of the principal governmental institutions to be considered by students of administrative law, the relevant legal and quasi-legal norms that need to be addressed, and the nature of the audience for an administrative law text represent the dominant paradigm for administrative law teaching in Canada, and differ from the 'continentalist' tradition that is also ably represented in Canada. In the second part of this essay we look at the evolution of *EJMR* over five editions and nearly twenty-five years and explore what the changes in the book tell us about the development of Canadian administrative law.

Demarcating Administrative Law as a Discipline in Canada

EJMR dominated its field so thoroughly that it is fair to say that it had no rivals in English Canada. In 1987 Butterworths published an administrative law casebook by Daniel Baum,[4] but this book does not appear to have captured the imagination of Canadian law teachers. It did not go into a second edition and is now out of print. While some Canadian administrative law texts were written with use as teaching materials in mind (the most notable being *Principles of Administrative Law* by David Jones and Anne De Villars, now in its fourth edition),[5] for the most part Canadian law teachers prefer casebooks over texts, and *EJMR* has been the administrative law casebook of choice in English Canada from the time the first edition of the book was published to the present day.

Of course, as Mr Justice Blair of the Ontario Court of Appeal observed in his review of the first edition, *EJMR* is 'not merely a "case book": it is a textbook in which carefully edited excerpts from cases, articles and other books are appropriately arranged to illustrate the subject.'[6] Indeed, the most frequent criticism of *EJMR* was that there was too much text to allow the book to be used efficiently as a teaching tool. In their review of the first edition, Professors Bob Franson and Howard Kushner of the University of British Columbia observed:[7]

> It is hard to see how any introductory course can effectively cover the whole book. A course nominally rated at forty-five hours, like the introductory administrative law course at the University of British Columbia,

> can only sample from it. We used the book for the first time in our forty-five hour introductory course and found that we were only able to cover half the book. It was clear from the students' reactions that even that modest coverage was too much and will have to be reduced next year. The question raised, for us at least, is whether it is fair to expect the students to buy a book when you are able to cover less than half of it.

For some Canadian teachers of administrative law, the answer to Franson and Kushner's question was 'no,' and those who adopted this view tended to develop their own course materials, typically narrower in scope than *EJMR*. For example, for most of his career at the University of British Columbia, Philip Bryden taught administrative law using his own materials, although he returned to using the *EJMR* casebook on moving to the University of New Brunswick in 2004. For other law teachers, whatever disadvantages the *EJMR* materials may have had in terms of length[8] were more than made up for by the overall quality of the book. In his review of the second edition of the casebook, Wade MacLauchlan (who used the *EJMR* casebook throughout his administrative law teaching career) noted: 'From a personal perspective, as one who has mercifully not had the experience of "getting up" a whole set of materials to teach a course in administrative law, my overwhelming sense is: "How could I ever have walked into the classroom if it had not been for *EJMR*?"'[9]

Whether or not one used *EJMR*, the approach the four authors took to the subject tended to shape the way Canadian legal academics thought about teaching administrative law. Although *EJMR* was the first commercially published administrative law casebook in Canada, we would not claim that the authors originated the teaching of administrative law in Canadian law schools. The shape and content of the five editions of the book reflect mainstream administrative law thinking throughout the English-speaking world, and the influence of leading scholars such as S.A. de Smith and H.W.R. Wade in England, K.C. Davis and Richard Stewart in the United States, and John Willis, Paul Weiler, and Harry Arthurs in Canada is readily apparent. What we would say is that the approach to administrative law taken in the *EJMR* casebook established the dominant paradigm for administrative law teaching in this country.

So pervasive is the *EJMR* way of thinking about administrative law that its peculiar features only become apparent by contrasting it with an alternative vision of the scope of administrative law. Fortunately, a Canadian example of such an alternative vision can be found in the magisterial multi-volume treatise by René Dussault and Louis Borgeat, *Traité de droit administratif*.[10] It is convenient to describe this vision as the 'continentalist' approach to administrative law. In our view, the foundational difference between the *EJMR* version of administrative law and the continentalist tradition is that, in *EJMR*, administrative law is the body of law used by citizens to constrain administrative action, while in the continentalist tradition, administrative law is the body of law used by the administrative arm of government to control and mobilize its own operations. The continentalist tradition does not ignore the elements of external control reflected in the *EJMR* paradigm, but these elements represent only a subset of the continentalist picture of administrative law, and a relatively small subset at that. Four of the five volumes of the English-language edition of Dussault and Borgeat's treatise are devoted to the law governing governmental contractual and tortious liability, governmental collection and use of information, the role of government as an employer and owner of property, and governmental collection and spending of money. Only one volume is devoted to the law by which judges supervise the exercise of governmental decision-making authority, which is the focus of the English-Canadian administrative law tradition reflected so ably in *EJMR*.[11]

The implications of this basic difference in approach go beyond the volume of legal material covered. It influences the types of governmental institutions on which the authors focus their attention, the types of legal and quasi-legal norms that are emphasized, and the nature of the audience for which the books are written. We will explore each of those elements in turn.

Principal Governmental Institutions

It is only a slight exaggeration to say that, at an institutional level, the preoccupation of *EJMR* is the relationship between courts and administrative tribunals. The authors made no bones about the significance of the courts to their approach to administrative law. Thus, in the preface to the first edition, they observed: 'Although entitled *Administrative Law*, our book is very much concerned with the part of administrative law that is associated with the courts.'[12] The authors recognized that this focus requires justification, and to their credit they devoted several pages of the introduction in the first edition to their explanation.

In particular, the authors provided five reasons for the central place they gave to judicial review of administrative action.[13] The first was that the influence of judicial review on administrative practice could not be estimated by the relatively infrequent occasions on which participants in administrative proceedings have recourse to judicial review. In other words, what happens on judicial review often sets the boundaries within which administrative practice may vary from agency to agency. Secondly, the authors noted that the courts are an important forum in which persons affected by administrative determinations can challenge those decisions. A third and related point was that lawyers advising persons affected by administrative decisions have to be aware of the prospect of judicial review and its limitations. Fourth, a study of the role and limitations of the courts and their procedures in contrast with other governmental institutions helps to inform students about the legal process, something that in the view of the authors lies 'at the core of legal education.'[14] Finally, the authors believed that study of the role of courts in administrative decision-making emphasized another important element of legal education, namely the interpretation of statutes.

The other institution that assumes pride of place in *EJMR* is the administrative tribunal. The authors do not, of course, make the mistake of assuming that quasi-judicial tribunals are the only institutions to which administrative law applies. They take account of the work of government departments and municipalities, but their emphasis is on the diverse and amorphous group of institutions known variously as agencies, boards, commissions, and tribunals. The authors do a very good job of exposing students to the wide range of institutions that fall under this heading, though some instructors, including Professor MacLauchlan, supplemented the book with readings designed to provide students with a more in-depth understanding of one or more agencies.[15] The authors do not, however, explore how these institutions are staffed or financed, nor is more than sporadic consideration given to how these organizations are managed or how they operate on a day-to-day basis. In *EJMR*, administrative law operates as a constraint on the way administrative agencies make decisions, and the only times the text explores agency management are in those instances in which a party affected by a decision seeks to challenge the lawfulness of the decision on the ground that management unlawfully interfered with the decision.

For Dussault and Borgeat, in contrast, the institutional focus of administrative law is much broader. They pay considerable attention to agencies, boards, and commissions, but they devote much more space than the authors of *EJMR* to departmentalized structures and municipal institutions, and they also discuss at length central agencies and Crown corporations, institutions that receive barely a mention in *EJMR*. The distance between Dussault and Borgeat's conception of administrative law and that of the authors of *EJMR* is revealed most clearly when we consider their respective discussions of personnel management. Dussault and Borgeat devote half of the second volume of the English-language edition to the law governing the management of government personnel, and the focus of this discussion is almost exclusively on individuals who would be classified as members of the public service. There is no substantive discussion of the legal rules governing the employment of civil servants in *EJMR*. The personnel side of the structure and operation of tribunals only appears in the fourth and fifth editions of *EJMR*, as the authors begin to consider the emerging body of law governing tribunal independence.

Relevant Legal and Quasi-legal Norms

Just as the authors of *EJMR* give their work a different institutional focus than is found in Dussault and Borgeat's treatise, they tend to emphasize different types of legal rules and norms. In light of *EJMR's* emphasis on judicial review of administrative decision-making, it is hardly surprising that the elaboration of common law rules of fair procedure and the interpretation of enabling legislation by agencies and courts take pride of place in *EJMR*. In the fourth and fifth editions of the book, the *Charter* and statutory rules of administrative procedure found in legislation such as the Ontario *Statutory Powers Procedure Act*[16] and the Quebec *Administrative Justice Act*[17] began to assume greater prominence, but this did not alter the essential character of *EJMR*. It is a book about the constraints the common law places on adjudicative decision-making by agencies exercising statutory powers.

To be fair, the authors (and Hudson Janisch in particular) devote significant space to administrative rules, both in a specific chapter on rule-making and in a chapter on the techniques used to shape the exercise of discretion.[18] Useful as this material is, however, it can be severed fairly easily from the rest of the text, and therefore presents an easy target for exclusion by instructors who find it challenging to cover all the material found in the book. Moreover, even within *EJMR's* consideration of the different techniques available to agencies to structure their discretion, the discussion of what Lorne Sossin describes as 'soft law'[19] is not particularly elaborate. *EJMR* teaches students about the use of rules, adjudicative precedents, and non-binding guidelines, and about the legal boundaries between rules and guidelines, but the different shapes that administrative 'guidance' takes and the ways in which guidelines might interact with more traditional legal norms are not given significant emphasis.

The types of legal norms emphasized in Dussault and Borgeat's treatise differ from the norms highlighted in *EJMR* in two basic respects. First, Dussault and Borgeat pay considerable attention to the legal norms that civil service managers and their legal advisors employ on a day-to-day basis. Many of these rules are found in statutes, from legislation governing the civil service to freedom of information and privacy laws to financial administration legislation. As noted earlier, it is not that the common law of judicial review is unimportant for Dussault and Borgeat; rather, it occupies a much smaller part of their vision of administrative law than for the authors of *EJMR*.

The other major difference is that 'guidelines' or 'directives' play a much larger role than that ascribed to them in *EJMR*. Dussault and Borgeat do not offer particularly profound insights into the ways in which judicial review can shape the exercise of administrative discretion, but they provide their readers with a fairly sophisticated understanding of the legal status of directives and the ways in which they are employed to influence personnel and financial management in the public sector.[20]

The Audience for the Book

It may seem self-evident that the audience for which an administrative law casebook is written is the group of law teachers and students who are going to use it in their law school classes. Less obvious are the assumptions we as law teachers make about the types of professional careers our students are likely to have and how their law school education helps to prepare them for those careers. Needless to say, the authors of *EJMR* do not attempt to dictate the career paths of their students and it is evident from their work that they realized that their students would likely play a variety of roles both within and outside the legal system. That said, it is equally clear that the *EJMR* text is predominantly designed to prepare students to become lawyers who will represent participants in administrative proceedings and in litigation contesting administrative decisions.

The authors provide a relatively catholic view of the array of clients these lawyers represent. The decisions excerpted run the gamut from prison discipline and social assistance cases involving individuals, to matters involving regulated industries, the environment, or labour relations where the parties are often large institutional actors. The lawyers in these proceedings sometimes represent government agencies, whether before administrative tribunals or the courts, and it is relatively easy for an instructor to use the materials to encourage students to imagine themselves in the position of a member of an administrative tribunal or a judge. What *EJMR* does not do is encourage students to think of themselves as public service managers with operational responsibility for the institutions making the decisions set out in the book. Nor, for the most part, is *EJMR* concerned with institutional design or the match between public policy goals and legislative responses. The book encourages students to develop a sophisticated understanding of the public policy goals of the agencies and tribunals that are addressing particular problems, but it tends to take the institutional setting as a given rather than to explore larger public policy questions of whether a particular institutional response is a good fit for the problem under consideration.[21] The authors of *EJMR* undoubtedly have the public policy expertise to provide examples that would enable their students to engage in this type of discussion. Their choice not to treat this type of material as a priority for inclusion in their book reflects a reasonable judgment that this public service management and macro-level public policy lies at the periphery of the work done by most Canadian administrative lawyers rather than at its core.

Once again, the Dussault and Borgeat treatise presents a fascinating contrast with *EJMR*. Public administration and macro-level public policy analysis are treated as different disciplines from administrative law in *EJMR*. Dussault and Borgeat begin their treatise with a discussion of public administration[22] and define administrative law as 'the entire set of rules relating to the organization, operation and control of the Administration.'[23] This emphasis on the organization and operation as well as the control of the administrative apparatus of the state suggests that Dussault and Borgeat saw their audience as public service managers and public policy-makers as well as lawyers who were acting for persons affected by administrative decisions. It is not that Dussault and Borgeat saw no distinction between law and public policy, or administrative law and public administration. Rather, they sought to identify the legal dimension of the organization and operation of the administrative apparatus of the state, and to integrate that dimension within their consideration of the role the law played in controlling the behaviour of administrative actors.

Conclusion

The point of the preceding discussion is not to suggest that *EJMR* presents an impoverished version of administrative law in comparison to Dussault and Borgeat. Rather, *EJMR* defines the scope and content of administrative law in a manner that serves the needs of a particular audience, but in doing so deflects into other disciplines (notably public administration and public policy studies) matters that could just as easily fall under the heading of administrative law. The dominance of their approach to the teaching of administrative law in both English-language and French-language law schools in Canada reflects the success of the *EJMR* authors in gauging the type of educational program that Canadian law teachers wanted for their administrative law students. While the general outlines of this program remained constant, *EJMR* evolved significantly over the course of the five editions of the book. Moreover, a set of course materials extending to more than 1,400 pages reflects a remarkable commitment by the authors to determining how students learn best, and how students come to terms with a dynamic and evolving discipline. It is to this subject, the sophistication of *EJMR* as a set of teaching materials and their evolution over five editions, that we turn in the second part of this essay.

Learning and Interpreting Canadian Administrative Law through *EJMR*

Over the course of its first five editions, *EJMR* has played a crucial role as the lead interlocutor of Canadian administrative law. This has not been an easy task. The field has changed dramatically and dynamically. Judicial review has evolved to a remarkable degree in barely three decades. Because courts prefer to express their authority in the careful and sometimes awkward language of precedent, it is a sizeable challenge for the authors of administrative law study materials to keep track of 'trends' and to present the field in a balanced and up-to-date manner. These twenty-five years have included many changes in legislation and administrative institutions and practices. In the broader context of public policy, there have been fiscal and ideological shifts, with significant variations from jurisdiction to jurisdiction across Canada. In our understanding of what works – and does not work – in public administration, we are always trying to innovate and improve. On top of all this, the *Charter* has undergone two decades of interpretation and development. For students, and for teachers, of administrative law, it is a huge challenge to keep pace with and interpret this sizeable and constantly evolving body of jurisprudence and legal development.

When the authors of *EJMR* produced their first edition in 1980, they faced a climate of dynamic change, notably with the significant developments in administrative law jurisprudence of the 1970s. There were undoubtedly temptations to pronounce a new world.[24] Instead of taking what might have been the easy road of reductionism and facile clarity, the authors of *EJMR*, and eventually David Mullan alone, chose dialogue. From the first edition, a central feature of *EJMR* was the 'note.' These are not the standard 'see also...' commentaries that appear in the footnotes of law review articles or monographs, a medium that all four of the original authors had admirably practised and mastered. Rather, the notes of *EJMR* are richly pedagogical and dialogical. They repeatedly ask readers to 'consider,' to 'reflect,' and to be alert to 'context.' The following comment is illustrative:[25]

> Perhaps the most that can be asked of the law in this area is that it forces judges to address the relevant questions. The law cannot constrain judges who are so predisposed from doing 'the wrong thing'. It should, however, help others to consider thoughtfully what 'the right thing' is and not hamper them from doing it.

This comment comes as the last word, in the fifth edition, of a 125-page chapter entitled 'The Standard of Review.' This chapter takes readers through a constructive and well-organized series of steps: 'Establishing the Modern Standard,' 'Life after *CUPE*: Two Steps Back and One Forward?,' 'Deviations from the Modern Standard', 'Extending the Reach of Deference Theory,' 'Rearticulating the Modern Standard,' 'Focusing on the Nature of the Question,' and 'Some Concluding Thoughts.' Readers are encouraged to be alert to context, to the mix of law and facts, to the interrelationship of substantive issues and remedies, to the diversity of administrative decision-making contexts, and to the underlying importance of interpretation. They are continually encouraged to reflect, to be alert to subtle doctrinal shifts, and to reach a better understanding of the world of administrative law. The tone of the commentary in *EJMR* is never patronizing, neither of judges nor of the primary readership, students. *EJMR* does not rush to judgment. There are occasional hints along the lines of 'we share your pain ...,' but even these comments are rare. *EJMR* is not a complainer's text. It is *hard working*, and it *embraces* the discipline. *EJMR* offers a conscientious, optimistic, and comprehensive account of the dynamic quality of administrative law as a discipline.

This says a lot about the quality, the experience, and the commitment of the authors of *EJMR*, and of David Mullan as the remaining author of the fifth edition. It is very easy to become complainers about administrative law, as professors or as students. The sheer volume, the diversity, and the shifting standards of administrative law make it an exceptionally challenging field to embrace. It is especially challenging for law students encountering administrative law for the first time, early in their law school careers. Administrative law stands out from other courses. The standard approach to introductory or survey courses in law school, at least for the good students, is to do the work, keep up, figure out a doctrinal edifice or a flowchart, incorporate an appropriate measure of debate, offer a balanced and context-sensitive assessment, and move on. In administrative law, both the volume and the underlying diversity require more of students. It has never been easy to figure out the doctrinal edifice or flowchart of administrative law. And then, even when students begin to understand the 'edifice,' the many elements of context, of policy, of strategy, or of multi-layered decision-making necessitate a further level of sophistication and patience.

EJMR more than meets these challenges. The good student who stays on top of administrative law through *EJMR* will become a sophisticated interpreter and practitioner. As for the flowchart, it has never been easy to 'can' administrative law, but by the fifth edition of *EJMR* it has gotten easier. The field is now clearly framed in three parts: Procedures, Substantive Review, and Remedies. The introduction has become more elegant with successive editions, with the fifth edition receiving a helping hand from Justice L'Heureux-Dubé's judgment in *Baker v. Canada (Minister of Citizenship and Immigration)*.[26] Her decision is reproduced in its entirety, taking up the entire chapter on 'The Role of Judicial Review,' followed by a series of twenty-seven notes. These notes tell much about David Mullan's approach to teaching and learning administrative law. The first four deal with 'The Legislative Structure and Decision-Making Chain,' and notes 1 and 2 read as follows:[27]

> 1. What was the direct legislative source of the minister's 'humanitarian and compassionate' discretion? Was it the *Immigration Act*, section 114(2) or another instrument?
> 2. What is somewhat peculiar about the contents or terminology of section 2.1 of the *Immigration Regulations*?

This is an important administrative law lesson: go back to the authorizing text, and work rigorously with the statutory/regulatory language and relationships. Notes 3 and 4 raise questions about ministerial guidelines and delegation. Notes 5 and 6 ask students to look closely at the scope of review permitted from the minister to the Federal Court Trial Division, from the Trial Division to the Court of Appeal, and from the Court of Appeal to the Supreme Court of Canada, and ask whether students 'accept the Supreme Court's reasoning' on the issue of the scope of review. Mullan goes on to pose twelve questions on procedural issues, beginning with the factors that determine the scope of entitlement to procedural fairness. By the time students have worked their way through note 10, they have been asked to think about the relationship between statutory interpretation and common law procedural requirements, and between *Charter* and common law procedural claims. These are not just 'did you notice ...?' queries. Within the notes, students are asked the following:[28]

> 9. ... Does [reference to the expertise of the decision-maker] mean that the court is partially abdicating its role as the guardian of the common law and as the body best located to make judgments on whether statutory or prerogative authorities have provided sufficient procedural protections to affected persons or constituencies?
> 10. ... What difference would or should it make either here or more generally if the procedural claim is being advanced within a section 7 rather than simply a common law framework?

Students are then taken through a series of notes on specific procedural issues, including the right to an oral or in-person hearing, the right to reasons, and bias. They are required to return to the notes of the original immigration officer and to consider whether those notes were in fact the 'reasons for decision' of the minister. They are asked to reflect on the extent of overlap between the Court's reasoning on the bias issue and its treatment of a further claim that there had been an abuse of discretion for taking account of irrelevant factors or failing to take account of relevant matters. These are challenging questions, especially for students in their second week of studying administrative law. They are challenging questions for seasoned teachers and practitioners.

The questions on substantive review begin with why the Court went on to deal with substantive arguments, having found in Baker's favour on procedural grounds. Mullan's notes then turn to the choice of standard of review, asking 'How is it feasible to conceive of abuse of discretion within a range of various standards of review?' He asks students to go back and study the criteria for determining the standard of review and to think carefully about the Court's choice of the intermediate standard of 'unreasonableness,' then asks: 'Is the court holding that this means that the decision of the official is judged by whether it is in an overall sense "unreasonable," or is the court really speaking about unreasonableness in a different sense?'

Mullan's notes then take students through a rigorous consideration of how the Court dealt with the abuse of discretion issue, including what it means to insist that a decision-maker must be 'alert, alive and sensitive.' Finally, he turns to remedies, asking:[29]

> 25. What remedy does the court provide after holding that the appeal should be allowed? How far does this go towards Mavis Baker's ultimate goal of remaining permanently in Canada? More generally, what does this say about the capacities of judicial review?

The notes conclude with a review of scholarly commentaries on *Baker*, with questions on the relevance of international law and on the significance of *Baker* for the unity of public law. Throughout these notes, and throughout the fifth edition of *EJMR*, David Mullan offers a formidable combination of teaching skill and incisive scholarship. For the generations of students who have struggled with the doctrinal edifice or flowchart of administrative law, or who have been frustrated by partial glimpses of the underlying administrative, legislative, and factual context, Mullan's introductory chapter on the role of judicial review captures the dynamic that weaves itself throughout administrative law. Notably, he takes us through all the steps from the underlying legislation, regulations, ministerial guidelines, international obligations, and facts; through the successive steps in judicial review and appeal; through the 'choice of procedure' issues; through substantive review of reasonableness and abuse of discretion; through remedial considerations; and, finally, through what it meant to Mavis Baker, who challenged her deportation order from December of 1992 and became a permanent resident of Canada in December of 2001.

David Mullan's approach of introducing students *thoroughly* to the range of issues and debates in administrative law through the lens of a single case is reminiscent of John Willis, who was famous for teaching the entire subject through three cases: *Canadian Wheat Board v. Nolan*,[30]

Roncarelli v. Duplessis,[31] and *Smith and Rhuland Ltd. v. The Queen*.[32] Once having given students a good grounding and structure through *Baker* and its analysis, Mullan departs from Willis, and proceeds to work through a further 1,400 pages and thirteen chapters of material. Many would question whether such a volume of material and such comprehensive treatment could be manageable in the scope of a single course. As we noted earlier, there is a long-standing debate among administrative law teachers regarding how much coverage can be justified, at the risk of sacrificing understanding and subtlety. *EJMR* has chosen to favour volume and comprehensiveness, while aiming to compensate with clarity of presentation and analytical elegance. These are achieved in an admirable measure, especially by the 2003 fifth edition under the sole authorship of David Mullan.

Students who do their work early in the course (something that cannot always be taken for granted) have an ability to move at a decent pace (which is surely required) and with a respectable degree of nuance (it is impossible to study or properly understand administrative law without an astute sense of strategy, institutional relationships, legislative and policy context, remedies and facts, together with the doctrine of judicial review). Those who stay on top of it find that they almost anticipate David Mullan's questions and reflections; those who fall behind face massive frustration. For this, David Mullan would make no apology. *EJMR* is the product of a hard worker. It approaches administrative law as a hard-working subject. And it cannot be said that *EJMR* sacrifices understanding or subtlety in the name of coverage.

The fifth edition of *EJMR* is especially pleasing because it is elegantly written and hence a good read. It is not a forced march across the administrative law landscape. A knowledgeable reader can let the fifth edition fall open at any page or chapter and pick up the debate. This is a high compliment. Even for the less seasoned reader, *EJMR* is accessible. The structure is clear. The level of debate is challenging but manageable, with a serious effort. Once the reader catches on to the rhythm and perspective of David Mullan's notes, *EJMR* is a fine text. It works as a set of study materials, and students would be well advised to hang on to it as a continuing reference.[33]

By encouraging debate, favouring comprehensive treatment, offering a coherent structure, and insisting on dialogue, *EJMR* has made a mighty contribution to the field of administrative law in Canada. We now benefit from more than two decades of lawyers who have learned administrative law with *EJMR* as their source material.[34] While they may well have wished for more answers and fewer questions from *EJMR* during their days of study, it is reassuring to know that many of English Canada's leading administrative lawyers under the age of fifty used *EJMR* and hence are probably employing the dialogical, dynamic, and hard-working approach to the field that they saw modelled in the text. Not every student who used *EJMR* became an ardent practitioner of this approach, but it is safe to say that, without *EJMR*, we would be less confident that Canada has produced a new generation of administrative law interlocutors.

This brings us back to how David Mullan and his *EJMR* co-authors approached the dynamic character of administrative law. There are so many temptations to declare a new level of certainty, on the one hand, or to scream with frustration, on the other. As teachers, we are always expected to say that we are 'getting somewhere.' When *EJMR* first appeared in 1980, we *were* getting somewhere. A new majority on the Supreme Court of Canada in the 1970s had undertaken to create a modern Canadian administrative law jurisprudence. While the Canadian *Charter of Rights and Freedoms* was not adopted until 1982, there was a developing rights consciousness informed by common law, human rights statutory developments, and the idea of an unwritten bill of rights. The 1970s saw many reforms of administrative law statutory regimes and institutions, and of judicial review and courts in some jurisdictions. We had moved beyond treating the administrative state as a novelty, or an exception to the judicial norm. There could not have been a more propitious time to introduce a new set of national study materials. Wisely, the authors of *EJMR* chose not to declare too many victories or to make unwarranted assertions of doctrinal clarity or advancement. Instead, they provided us with an important new tool for an ongoing dialogue. In so doing, *EJMR* was in step with the dynamic (and many would say still uncertain) character of administrative law, as it was to continue to evolve over the subsequent two decades.

At the beginning of the 1970s, Canadian courts, led by the Supreme Court of Canada, were mainly preoccupied with the correct application and occasional clarification of precedent-determined rules. There was widespread criticism that the leading administrative law precedents were out of step with the modern administrative state and demonstrated an anti-administration bias.[35] By the end of the 1970s, the Supreme Court had enunciated a new policy of curial deference in substantive review, notably in *CUPE, Local 963 v. New Brunswick Liquor Corporation*,[36] and a more flexible 'fairness' approach to administrative procedures, with *Nicholson v. Haldimand-Norfolk Regional Board of Commissioners of Police*,[37] the leading precedent. These decisions, together with related or further interpretations from the Supreme Court,[38] prompted an active body of jurisprudence in superior, appellate, and federal courts. By the first edition of *EJMR* in 1980, there was no shortage of material – or debate.

Over the course of five editions of *EJMR*, David Mullan and his co-authors remained fundamentally optimistic. They tracked jurisprudential developments carefully, looking for doctrinal coherence. They have been assiduous about pointing out incoherence, problems of principle, or backsliding, where appropriate. Throughout, *EJMR* has been marked by patience and a willingness to probe, to question, to criticize, and to engage in dialogue.

Over and above its comprehensive treatment of procedural and substantive review, *EJMR* lays out other important lessons for students of administrative law. Remedies are addressed on a continuing basis throughout the materials, and then brought together comprehensively in four concluding chapters. Some issues, such as 'the Crown' are given a lower profile in later editions. Other issues, such as interpretation and the inclusion of underlying statutory and regulatory texts, are accorded increasing space and sophisticated treatment with each successive edition. Of necessity, the interpretation of the *Charter* is accorded greater attention with each edition. Administrative practice and institutional processes receive more attention, especially on issues that are the subject of legislative reform or that have been challenged on judicial review.

From its first to its fifth edition, *EJMR* has evolved into a very important instrument for the development of administrative law in Canada. For students and teachers, it sets an agenda, a framework, and a dialogue. For those who decide to be serious and hard-working administrative lawyers, it is both a way-finder and a companion. *EJMR* is a 'chatty' companion, one that insists on an incessant and probing dialogue about administrative law. Above all, *EJMR* is motivated by a *commitment* to administrative law as a discipline, a commitment that rises to what might be called *passion*, for those who stay at it.

That is the ultimate lesson of *EJMR*: *you have to stay at it.* To his great credit, no one exemplifies this quality better than David Mullan. He stayed at *EJMR*, from its first to its fifth edition, and ultimately became the sole remaining author. He stayed at Canadian administrative law through four decades of dynamic development. And, through *EJMR*, he has shared with two generations of students (and two generations of law professors) a thoroughgoing, dialogical, and passionate tool that embraces administrative law – and leaves us wanting to stay at it.

Conclusion

We conclude this essay by returning to our initial observation that David Mullan was a remarkable teacher of administrative law. Those of us who did not sit in his classroom over the years can only envy the many students who began their study of administrative law in his classes. This essay speaks for David Mullan's bigger classroom: for the thousands of students, scores of teachers, and two generations of administrative law scholars who can say that, through *EJMR*, David Mullan taught them administrative law.

NOTES

1 J.M. Evans, H.N. Janisch, David J. Mullan, and R.C.B. Risk, *Administrative Law: Cases, Text, and Materials* (Toronto: Emond Montgomery, 1980) ['*EJMR*'].
2 J.M. Evans, H.N. Janisch, and David J. Mullan, *Administrative Law: Cases, Text, and Materials*, 4th ed. (Toronto: Emond Montgomery, 1995). The second edition was published in 1984 and the third edition in 1988.
3 David J. Mullan, *Administrative Law: Cases, Text, and Materials*, 5th ed. (Toronto: Emond Montgomery, 2003).
4 Daniel Baum, *Cases and Materials on Administrative Law* (Toronto: Butterworths, 1987).
5 David Jones and Anne De Villars, *The Principles of Administrative Law*, 4th ed. (Scarborough, ON: Thompson Canada Ltd., 2004).
6 Hon. D.G. Blair, 'Book Review of *Administrative Law: Cases, Text, and Materials* by John M. Evans et al.' (1981) 59 Can. Bar Rev. 438 at 438. In his review essay discussing the fourth edition of *EJMR*, Michael Taggart identified the challenges associated with the tendency of the book to serve both as a set of teaching materials and as a treatise for administrative lawyers. As he put it: 'This Janus-like quality – looking to both students and practitioners – has been a considerable strength, in my opinion, but as the book has grown with each edition the risk has increased of its either falling between the markets or, more likely, becoming less attractive as a teaching book.' Michael Taggart, 'Outside Canadian Administrative Law' (1996) 46 U.T.L.J. 649 at 661.
7 Robert Franson and Howard Kushner, Book Review of *Administrative Law:*

Cases, Text, and Materials by John M. Evans et al. (1982) 16 U.B.C. L. Rev. 382 at 384.

8 The authors were sensitive to this criticism, though they did not always let it dominate their decisions. The first edition was 1,085 pages long, including the index. The second edition was reduced in size by nearly 100 pages, and including the index it was 994 pages long. The book grew again in the third edition, and despite the removal of the index had 1,194 pages. The fourth edition was the longest, and with the restoration of an index, it reached a whopping 1,519 pages. In bringing out the fifth edition, Professor Mullan managed to trim some 80 pages of text, but it is still 1,438 pages long including the index.

9 H. Wade MacLauchlan, 'Book Review of *Administrative Law: Cases, Text, and Materials* by John M. Evans et al.,' 2nd ed. (1985) 17 Ottawa L. Rev. 437 at 450.

10 René Dussault and Louis Borgeat, *Traité de droit administratif*, t. 1–3, 2nd ed. (Québec: Les Presses de l'Université Laval, 1989). The first edition of this treatise, titled *Traité de droit administratif canadien et québécois*, was authored by Dussault alone and was published in two volumes by Les Presses de l'Université Laval in 1974. Carswell published a five-volume English edition titled *Administrative Law: A Treatise*, translated by Murray Rankin and Donald Breen, from 1985 to 1990. The best single-volume representation of Canadian continentalist tradition is Patrice Garant, *Droit administratif*, 5th ed. (Cowansville, QC: Éditions Yvon Blais, 2004).

11 We do not wish to overstate our case by suggesting that *EJMR* completely ignores such issues as freedom of information and the tortious liability of government. What we would suggest, however, is that these issues are treated as aspects of the law governing administrative disclosure and as remedies rather than as central themes deserving of significant consideration in their own right.

12 *EJMR*, *supra* n. 1 at ii.

13 Ibid. at 13–15.

14 Ibid. at 14.

15 See MacLauchlan, *supra* note 9 at 442–43.

16 R.S.O. 1990, c. S-22.

17 R.S.Q., c. J-3.

18 The preface to the *EJMR* second edition, *supra* note 2 at v, identifies Professor Janisch as the author primarily responsible for the section 'Changing Attitudes towards Rulemaking' in chapters 2 and 13, which deal with confining and structuring the use of discretion, which encompasses the use of rules for this purpose. The first edition had a chapter devoted specifically to

rule-making (chapter 3) and this organizational feature re-emerged as chapter 3 in the third edition, once again being attributed primarily to Professor Janisch. (preface to third edition *supra* n. 2, at vii). The preface to the fourth edition, (*supra* n. 2 at v), identifies Professor Janisch as having contributed chapter 4 on 'Rulemaking' and chapter 14 on 'Discretion, Rules and Policy.'

19 See, for example, Lorne Sossin, 'Discretion Unbound: Reconciling the *Charter* and Soft Law' (2002), 45 Canadian Public Administration 465; Lorne Sossin and Charles W. Smith, 'Hard Choices and Soft Law: Ethical Codes, Policy Guidelines and the Role of Courts in Regulating Government' (2003), 40 Alberta L. Rev. 867.

20 See René Dussault and Louis Borgeat, *Administrative Law: A Treatise*, 2nd ed., trans. by M. Rankin (Toronto: Carswell, 1990), vol. 1 at 329–40 (legal status of directives), vol. 2 at 33–35, 49–50 and 122–37 (use of directives for personnel management), and vol. 2 at 256–69 and 322–45 (use of directives for financial management).

21 Stephen Breyer's *Regulation and its Reform* (Cambridge, MA: Harvard University Press, 1982) is an example of a book that addresses this type of problem. Additionally, Breyer and Stewart's administrative law text devotes chapter eight to the organization and management of the Federal Trade Commission, a major American administrative agency. Stephen Breyer and Richard Stewart, *Administrative Law and Regulatory Policy* (Boston: Little, Brown, 1979).

22 Dussault and Borgeat, *supra* note 20, vol. 1 at 1–11.

23 Ibid. at 12.

24 At the time of the publication of the first edition of *EJMR*, Mullan was Canada's most active commentator on the changing jurisprudence of administrative law: 'Fairness: The New Natural Justice?' (1975) 25 U.T.L.J. 281; 'Standing after *McNeil*' (1976) 8 Ottawa L. Rev. 32; 'Recent Developments in Nova Scotian Administrative Law' (1978) 4 Dal. L.J. 467; '*Martineau and Butters v. Matsqui Institution Inmate Disciplinary Board*: Its Potential Impact on the Jurisdiction of the Trial Division of the Federal Court' (1978) 24 McGill L.J. 92; 'Developments in Administrative Law: The 1978–79 Term' (1980) 1 Sup. Ct. L. Rev. 1; 'Mr. Justice Rand: Defining the Limits of Court Control of the Administrative and Executive Process' (1979–80) 18 U.W.O. L. Rev. 65. In 1980, Mullan also produced a 275–page second edition of his *Administrative Law* chapter in the *Canadian Encyclopedic Digest*, 2nd ed. (Toronto: Carswell, 1973).

25 *EJMR*, fifth edition, *supra* note 3 at 824.

26 [1999] 2 S.C.R. 817 [*Baker*].

27 *EJMR*, fifth edition, *supra* note 3 at 83.

28 Ibid. at 84.
29 Ibid. at 86–87.
30 [1952] A.C. 427, 3 D.L.R. 433 (J.C.P.C.).
31 [1959] S.C.R. 121.
32 [1953] 2 S.C.R. 95. Willis compiled a set of materials, most recently in 1971, which he used to teach administrative law at the University of Toronto and at Dalhousie Law School.
33 *EJMR* has been cited five times by the Supreme Court of Canada as a reference or source of authority between 1983 and 2004. We suspect it is used with much greater frequency by former students who find it a familiar tool for analysing administrative law situations. Citation of David Mullan's body of work by the Supreme Court of Canada is discussed in Chief Justice McLachlin's contribution to this volume.
34 One of the authors, Wade MacLauchlan, studied administrative law at the University of New Brunswick in 1979–80, with David Townsend as professor (teaching the course for the first time), using an advanced photocopied draft of the first edition of *EJMR*.
35 This has been commented on by many authors. For example, see H. Wade MacLauchlan, 'Transforming Administrative Law: The Didactic Role of the Supreme Court of Canada' (2001) 80 Can. Bar Rev. 281, particularly the commentaries on cases referred to at notes 1–9; Philip Bryden, 'Canadian Administrative Law: Past, Present, and Future – Where We've Been' (1991) Queen's L.J. 7; Harry Arthurs, 'Protection Against Judicial Review' (1983) 43 R. du B. 277.
36 [1979] 2 S.C.R. 277.
37 [1979] 1 S.C.R. 311.
38 David Mullan was the pioneering editor of the Supreme Court Law Review's annual essay on the Court's administrative law jurisprudence: 'Developments in Administrative Law: The 1978–79 Term' (1980) 1 Sup. Ct. L. Rev 1. Mullan continued in this role for six essays, through to (1985), 7 Sup. Ct. L. Rev 1. He was succeeded by his *EJMR* co-author John Evans, who produced five essays from 1984–85 to 1988–89. Wade MacLauchlan and Philip Bryden have both subsequently served in this capacity.

The Uneasy Relationship between Independence and Appointments in Canadian Administrative Law

LORNE SOSSIN

To what extent does the proper functioning of administrative justice depend on the assurance of some degree of independence for those who adjudicate? For these purposes, what does independence mean?

– David Mullan[1]

David Mullan has made a career of asking big questions. I believe there is no greater tribute to his contributions to the field of Canadian administrative law than attempting to investigate some of these questions. In this essay, I take up the challenge to explore the meaning of independence in the context of the administrative justice system.[2] Specifically, I argue that tribunal independence presupposes some merit constraints on who the government may appoint to adjudicative tribunals (and how those appointments may be made), and that it is striking that the criteria for independence developed at common law do not make clear whether such merit constraints operate, and if so, to what extent.[3]

Administrative tribunals are part of the executive branch and are appointed by the government of the day pursuant to statutory parameters. Those same tribunals, however, where they perform adjudicative functions, must be seen to be independent of executive influence. This tension is a by-product of a larger one. Tribunals are provided with a statutory mandate to adjudicate disputes, but in many cases they are also vehicles for the implementation of government policy. The logic of the tribunals suggests they are intended to be expert bodies, and many appointments reflect this fidelity to expertise. Tribunal appointments also have served, however, as a means of rewarding political loyalties and ensuring kindred individuals are in positions of authority.[4] The

Supreme Court has exhibited ambivalence in the face of challenges to the independence of tribunals. Chief Justice McLachlin captured this ambivalence in *Ocean Port Hotel Ltd. v. British Columbia (General Manager, Liquor Control and Licensing Branch*:[5]

> Administrative tribunals, by contrast, lack this constitutional distinction from the executive. They are, in fact, created precisely for the purpose of implementing government policy. Implementation of that policy may require them to make quasi-judicial decisions. They thus may be seen as spanning the constitutional divide between the executive and judicial branches of government. However, given their primary policy-making function, it is properly the role and responsibility of Parliament and the legislatures to determine the composition and structure required by a tribunal to discharge the responsibilities bestowed upon it.

This analysis is divided into three sections. First, I provide a review of the independence doctrine as it has developed to date. Second, I explore how the appointment issue has figured into this legal terrain. Finally, I suggest a better framework for integrating appointments into the law of tribunal independence. While my understanding of this area of administrative law owes much to the clarity of thought David Mullan has brought to administrative law, I am not at all certain he would agree with all of my conclusions. Hopefully, this instalment in the debate will impel him to continue to develop his own views on this question.

The Tension between Adjudicative Tribunals and Courts and the Scope of Independence

There is an inexorable (and perhaps not unintended) tension between adjudicative tribunals and courts. On the one hand, these are bodies created to perform much the same functions as courts: to hear evidence, reach findings of fact, and apply the relevant law and determine remedies. On the other hand, tribunals are executive bodies whose structure and mandate can be created, modified, or repealed at the will and whim of the legislature.[6] Thus, when looked at formally, the separation of powers suggests that the measure of independence enjoyed by tribunals will be fluid and subject to the policy preference of the legislature that creates the tribunal. This presumes, however, that the executive is a single integrated whole. In the Canadian constitutional order, it is not. The executive is more properly understood as a web of constitutionally mediated relationships.[7] For example, the political executive, represented by the cabinet, has a relationship with the civil service that is premised on the constitutional convention of bureaucratic neutrality.[8] I would argue that adjudicative tribunals similarly enjoy a distinctive and nuanced relationship with the political executive, based in part on the constitutional constraints imposed by the rule of law. In this sense, tribunals are neither an integrated part of a single executive whole, nor a headless fourth branch of government unaccountable to the executive.[9]

Leaving aside the constitutional dynamics, when looked at functionally certain protections and constraints follow wherever a body has a 'purely' adjudicative mandate (and this would distinguish such bodies from boards and agencies with regulatory mandates, where policymaking, investigation, and enforcement may accompany an adjudicative function). Is there a compelling reason why someone coming before an adjudicative tribunal should enjoy fewer protections of decision-making impartiality and independence than someone coming before a court – especially since many tribunals have jurisdiction that once belonged to the courts?[10]

It is often said that far more rights are determined by tribunals than courts.[11] As David Mullan observed:[12]

> given the highly significant role that administrative justice plays in the lives of ordinary Canadians, and the reality that many administrative tribunals perform adjudicative functions very typical of those exercised by the courts, there is a strong countervailing sense that greater degrees of independence may be part of the key to a more professional and competent corps of adjudicators.

Thus, the nature and scope of tribunal independence may vary depending on whether or not a formal, functional, or rights perspective is adopted. This tension has been exacerbated by the judicial approach to the issue of tribunal independence, which has focused almost exclusively on the relationship between tribunal independence and the constitutional doctrine of judicial independence.[13]

In *Valente v. The Queen*[14] the Supreme Court of Canada noted that, broadly speaking, the test for independence in the judicial setting is 'the one for reasonable apprehension of bias, adapted to the requirement of independence.'[15] The Court further noted that, although there is obviously a close relationship between independence and impartiality, they are nevertheless separate and distinct values or requirements:[16]

> The word 'impartial' ... connotes absence of bias, actual or perceived. The word 'independent' in s. 11(d) reflects or embodies the traditional constitutional value of judicial independence. As such, it connotes not merely a state of mind or attitude in the actual exercise of judicial functions, but a status or relationship to others, particularly to the Executive Branch of government, that rests on objective conditions or guarantees.

In terms of independence, Le Dain J. (writing for the Court) quoted with approval the following statement by Sir Guy Green, Chief Justice of Tasmania:[17]

> I thus define judicial independence as the capacity of thc courts to perform their constitutional function free from actual or apparent interference by, and to the extent that it is constitutionally possible, free from actual or apparent dependence upon, any persons or institutions, including, in particular, the executive arm of government, over which they do not exercise direct control.

In *Canadian Pacific Ltd. v. Matsqui Indian Band,*[18] with very little discussion of the separation of powers or the different pressures that might operate in judicial and executive decision-making contexts, Lamer C.J., writing for a minority, held that the test for institutional independence enunciated in *Valente* applied, with added flexibility, to administrative tribunals.[19] Lamer C.J. stated:[20]

> I begin my analysis of the institutional independence issue by observing that the ruling of this court in *Valente, supra*, provides guidance in assessing the independence of an administrative tribunal ...
>
> Where a party has a reasonable apprehension of bias, it should not be required to submit to the tribunal giving rise to this apprehension. Moreover, the principles for judicial independence outlined in *Valente* are applicable in the case of an administrative tribunal, where the tribunal is functioning as an adjudicative body settling disputes and determining the rights of parties. However, I recognize that a strict application of these principles is not always warranted.

Matsqui involved appeals from tax assessments of real estate within reserves. The particular issue was whether or not lands granted to Canadian Pacific by the Crown were, by definition, excluded from lands 'within a reserve.' Canadian Pacific lost at the tribunal level, so applied to the Federal Court, Trial Division for judicial review. Canadian Pacific argued that the provisions permitting band members to sit on the assessment appeal tribunal raised a reasonable apprehension of bias. Joyal J. struck out the application on the ground that the issues raised could be litigated within the assessment appeal structure itself.[21] Joyal J. did not deal with reasonable apprehension of bias. An appeal to the Federal Court of Appeal was allowed.[22] The band appealed to the Supreme Court of Canada, where Canadian Pacific argued that the assessment appeal procedures were not an adequate alternative to judicial review because the appeal tribunals themselves gave rise to a reasonable apprehension of bias, in part based on the tribunals' lack of independence. Lamer C.J. concluded that the *Valente* principles apply to administrative tribunals on the basis of natural justice principles, but that the test for institutional independence may be less strict than for courts:[23]

> Therefore, while administrative tribunals are subject to the *Valente* principles, the test for institutional independence must be applied in light of the functions being performed by the particular tribunal at issue. The requisite level of institutional independence (i.e., security of tenure, financial security and administrative control) will depend on the nature of the tribunal, the interests at stake, and other indices of independence such as oaths of office.
>
> In some cases, a high level of independence will be required. For example, where the decisions of a tribunal affect the security of the person of a party (such as the immigration adjudicators in *Mohammad, supra*), a more strict application of the *Valente* principles may be warranted. In this case, we are dealing with an administrative tribunal adjudicating disputes relating to the assessment of property taxes. In my view, this is a case where a more flexible approach is clearly warranted.

Although Lamer C.J. carried fewer judges on this point than Sopinka J. (who would have preferred to see how the tribunal functioned in practice before resolving the independence question),[24] his view was nonetheless adopted by the Court in subsequent cases. One of the cases that extended the analogy to the judicial independence methodology was *2747–3174 Québec Inc. v. Quebec (Régie des permis d'alcool).*[25] In *Régie*, the Court adopted with approval Lamer C.J.'s approach, but clarified and refined the suggestion in *Matsqui* that administrative tribunals are subject to the *Valente* principles of institutional independence. The Court acknowledged that the requisite level of institutional independence may be lower for liquor regulators than for a court, and concluded that the 'directors' (adjudicators) of the Régie had sufficient security of tenure because they could not be simply removed at pleasure (that is, without cause):[26]

> In my view, the directors' conditions of employment meet the minimum requirements of independence. These do not require that all administrative adjudicators, like judges of courts of law, hold office for life. Fixed-term appointments, which are common, are acceptable. *However, the removal of adjudicators must not simply be at the pleasure of the executive.* Le Dain J. summarized the requirements of security of tenure as follows in *Valente*, at p. 698:
>
>> ... that the judge be removable only for cause, and that cause be subject to independent review and determination by a process at which the judge affected is afforded a full opportunity to be heard. The essence of security of tenure for purposes of s. 11(d) is a tenure, whether until an age of retirement, for a fixed term, or for a specific adjudicative task, that is secure against interference by the Executive or other appointing authority in a discretionary or arbitrary manner.

Thus, in *Régie* the focus of the Court was on the 'objective guarantees' apparent from the statute and regulations, not the experience of the Régie adjudicators. Sopinka J.'s interest in seeing how a tribunal functioned in practice, rather than how it was structured on paper, appears to have drifted from view.[27] In other words, appointments at pleasure violated the common law standard of independence because this suggested an absence of security of tenure, not because 'at pleasure' appointments themselves lacked sufficient safeguards in practice against the government's misuse of its appointment power.

Neither the *Valente* principles nor, by extension, the common law standard of independence applicable to tribunals address the question of appointments. The logic of independence appears to be that, irrespective of who is appointed or how, once they are members of a tribunal, the real question is whether the tribunal member is subject to any ongoing influence, by reason of a lack of security of tenure, a lack of financial independence, or a lack of administrative independence. Put simply, independence does not seem to constrain the government's appointment power in any way. Why is this so? Can an adjudicative body be seen as independent if its members are appointed based on patronage rather than merit (or if this view is widely perceived because qualified people are passed over for appointment while the party faithful receive positions)?[28]

Appointments in Canadian Administrative Law

While there may be broad agreement that the appointment power and institutional independence are related concepts, how this might be supervised by the judiciary is far from clear. A given person's qualification or lack thereof for a tribunal position is difficult to ascertain. Immigration and Refugee Board members, for example, are primarily required to make credibility findings. No special training or educational program certifies expertise in this area. Why should a government not seek to put into decision-making positions adjudicators who broadly reflect its outlook on policy goals? Once again, the lack of any meaningful supervision over judicial appointments themselves casts a shadow over the judicial supervision of administrative appointments.

Perhaps not surprisingly, judicial consideration of the government's appointment power has been rare. In *Hewat v. Ontario*,[29] the Ontario Court of Appeal examined the issue of institutional independence in the context of a labour relations tribunal.[30] The appellants were vice-chairs of the Ontario Labour Relations Board who had been appointed by order-in-council for a fixed term of three years. The appointments were made by an NDP government interested in significant labour reform. For reasons widely understood to be based on political incompatibility, a subsequently elected Conservative government in Ontario revoked their appointments mid-term by way of an order-in-council, and the vice-chairs challenged the validity of these orders. The Ontario Divisional Court found the orders revoking the appointments were invalid because the statute made clear that the appointments were for a fixed term, but declined to order that the vice-chairs be reinstated, awarding damages instead. The vice-chairs appealed, arguing that if they were not reinstated to their positions 'then the government is putting tribunal officers in the same position as employees generally – they can be dismissed at will so long as the employer is prepared to pay damages.'[31] The Ontario Court of Appeal noted that a remedy of reinstatement was impractical given the length of time that had passed since the revocations had occurred. However, the court acknowledged the validity of the vice-chairs' arguments regarding the institutional independence of the board if the government were able to revoke appointments at will, on payment of compensation:[32]

> I do not see the issues before this court as bringing into play constitutional safeguards against the conduct of government. Indeed, it would be intellectually naïve not to recognize that elected governments must have room to make political decisions and to conduct themselves in a manner to assure that their political policies are implemented. We were told by counsel that, until recently, the practice over the past 25 years has been to make appointments to tribunals that have *quasi*-judicial functions for a fixed period of three years with the expectation gleaned from experience that in normal circumstances there would be repeated renewals of that term. There are many tribunals, agencies and boards in this province, each with different responsibilities, and it would be difficult to lay down any single rule or practice that would be suitable for all. That having been said, the Ontario Labour Relations Board in its quasi-judicial functions must of necessity maintain a public perception of independence from government if the public is to have any respect for its decisions. Indeed, it is difficult to imagine how any tribunal with quasi-judicial functions could maintain the appearance of integrity to those who appear before it, without some degree of independence.

The court's analysis addresses only part of the story. If the Conservative government's attempt to revoke appointments on partisan grounds was met with judicial disapproval, does this also cast doubt on the validity of the original NDP appointments, which arguably were based on equally partisan considerations? In my view, this is a plausible extension of the logic of *Hewat*, but Canadian courts have been unwilling to view appointments as a question of independence.

The link between appointments and independence was raised squarely in *CUPE v. Ontario (Ministry of Labour)*.[33] The case concerned the discretion of ministers of labour in Ontario to appoint chairs to interest arbitration panels in the hospital sector pursuant to the *Hospital Labour Disputes Arbitration Act*.[34] Chairs of interest arbitrations were previously chosen from a group composed largely of experienced and mutually acceptable individuals. The minister changed the process such that retired judges were appointed. The central issue in the appeal was whether this change breached the duty of fairness by interfering with the impartiality and independence of the arbitrators and raising a reasonable apprehension of bias, and/or interfering with the legitimate expectations of the applicant union. The Divisional Court dismissed the application.

The Court of Appeal reversed this finding and found that the change in appointment schemes violated the institutional independence of the arbitration boards and also constituted a breach of the legitimate expectations of the applicant. With respect to the breach of independence finding, Austin J.A., writing for the court, held that retired judges who were appointed effectively at pleasure and on an ad hoc basis lacked financial security and security of tenure. He also found that the minister (and the government generally) had a financial stake in the outcome of the labour arbitrations and thus it created a perception of bias for the minister alone to be responsible for appointments of chairs for the arbitration panels. The court's holding suggested that while the minister had discretion to appoint anyone who in his opinion was 'qualified,' this discretion was in fact limited to those qualified people who would be perceived as independent. This would represent a significant check on the minister's appointment power (and could effectively limit his options to the roster of mutually agreed-upon arbitrators, from which most appointments had been made prior to the minister's change).

The Supreme Court's landmark decision in *Ocean Port* suggested a different approach. In *Ocean Port*, the Court confirmed that the guarantee of institutional independence in adjudicative tribunal settings is not a constitutional right, but rather a common law protection, and as such, is vulnerable to the government overriding it through ordinary statutory language at any time for any reason.[35]

Ocean Port involved an investigation by a senior inspector with the Liquor Control and Licensing Branch, which led to allegations that Ocean Port Hotel Ltd., the operator of a hotel and pub, had committed five infractions of the *Liquor Control and Licensing Act* and accompanying regulations. Following a hearing, another senior inspector with the branch concluded that the allegations had been substantiated and imposed a penalty that included a two-day suspension of Ocean Port's liquor licence. Ocean Port appealed to the Liquor Appeal Board by way of a hearing *de novo*. The findings on four of the five allegations were upheld and the penalty was confirmed. Ocean Port appealed to the Court of Appeal arguing, among other things, that the Liquor Appeal Board lacked the requisite institutional independence. Pursuant to section 30(2)(a) of the act, the chair and members of the Liquor Appeal Board 'serve at the pleasure of the Lieutenant Governor in Council.' In practice, members are appointed for a one-year term and serve on a part-time basis. All members but the chair were paid on a per diem basis. The chair established panels of one or three members to hear matters before the board 'as the chair considers advisable.' The Court of

Appeal concluded that members of the board lacked the guarantees of independence required to impose penalties and set aside the board's decision.[36] However, the Supreme Court of Canada pointed out that, even if the tribunal did not meet the common law natural justice requirements for institutional independence, this was not fatal to its ability to function:[37]

> It is well-established that, absent constitutional constraints, the degree of independence required of a particular government decision-maker or tribunal is determined by its enabling statute. It is the legislature or Parliament that determines the degree of independence required of tribunal members. The statute must be construed as a whole to determine the degree of independence the legislature intended.

The Court went on:[38]

> Confronted with silent or ambiguous legislation, courts generally infer that Parliament or the legislature intended the tribunal's process to comport with principles of natural justice.
>
> In such circumstances, administrative tribunals may be bound by the requirement of an independent and impartial decision-maker, one of the fundamental principles of natural justice: *Matsqui, supra* (*per* Lamer C.J. and Sopinka J.); *Régie, supra,* at para. 39; *Katz v. Vancouver Stock Exchange,* [1996] 3 S.C.R. 405, 139 D.L.R. (4th) 575. Indeed, courts will not lightly assume that legislators intended to enact procedures that run contrary to this principle, although the precise standard of independence required will depend 'on all the circumstances, and in particular on the language of the statute under which the agency acts, the nature of the task it performs and the type of decision it is required to make': *Régie, supra,* at para. 39.
>
> However, like all principles of natural justice, the degree of independence required of tribunal members may be ousted by express statutory language or necessary implication ... Ultimately, it is Parliament or the legislature that determines the nature of a tribunal's relationship to the executive. It is not open to a court to apply a common law rule in the face of clear statutory direction. Courts engaged in judicial review of administrative decisions must defer to the legislature's intention in assessing the degree of independence required of the tribunal in question.

In *Ocean Port,* the Court concluded that the provincial legislature 'spoke directly to the nature of the appointments to the Liquor Appeal

Board': under its enabling legislation, the chair and members of the board 'serve at the pleasure of the Lieutenant Governor in Council.'[39] With respect to this language, the Court stated:[40]

> In my view, the legislature's intention that Board members should serve at pleasure, as expressed through s. 30(2)(a) of the Act, is unequivocal. As such, it does not permit the argument that the statute is ambiguous and hence should be read as imposing a higher degree of independence to meet the requirements of natural justice, if indeed a higher standard is required ... Where the intention of the legislature, as here, is unequivocal, there is no room to import common law doctrines of independence, 'however inviting it may be for a Court to do so': *Re W.D. Latimer Co. and Bray* (1974), 6 O.R. (2d) 129 at 137, 52 D.L.R. (3d) 161 (C.A.).

The Court clarified the scope and implication of *Ocean Port* in *Bell*,[41] particularly in the context of 'purely' adjudicative administrative settings. *Bell* involved complex pay equity litigation that had dragged on for years, often ending up in the Federal Court based on challenges to the impartiality and independence of the Canadian Human Rights Tribunal, which was conducting the hearing.[42] This appeal raised two concerns. First, the tribunal was said to lack independence because the Canadian Human Rights Commission, a party of interest in the proceedings, has the power to issue binding guidelines interpreting the Canadian *Human Rights Act* in 'classes of cases.' Second, the tribunal was said to lack independence because its chair has discretion over whether sitting members can continue to hear cases that continue past the expiry of their terms. While the act clearly authorized both powers, Bell argued that because the tribunal was purely adjudicative it should enjoy the constitutional protections of 'adjudicative independence,' and alternatively, that section 2(e) of the *Canadian Bill of Rights*, which guarantees a 'fair hearing', is a quasi-constitutional protection which rendered inoperative statutory provisions inconsistent with the standards of independence and impartiality.

The tribunal rejected Bell's position and directed that the hearings should proceed. The Federal Court, Trial Division, allowed Bell's application for judicial review, holding that even the narrowed guideline power of the commission unduly fettered the tribunal, and that the chairperson's discretionary power to extend appointments did not leave tribunal members with a sufficient guarantee of tenure.[43] The trial judge quashed the proceedings on the basis that the institutional structure of the tribunal was inconsistent with the protection afforded under section 2(e) of the *Bill of Rights*.[44] The Federal Court of Appeal reversed that judgment.[45] The Supreme Court unanimously upheld the judgment of the Court of Appeal. Writing jointly for the Court, McLachlin C.J. and Bastarache J. also rejected the attempt by Bell to delineate a category of tribunals, known as 'quasi-judicial' or 'purely adjudicative,' which would be subject to a constitutional judicial independence standard. The determination of the particular standard of independence and impartiality required in a particular setting must involve a contextual rather than a categorical analysis:[46]

> To say that tribunals span the divide between the executive and the judicial branches of government is *not* to imply that there are only two types of tribunals – those that are quasi-judicial and require the full panoply of procedural protections, and those that are quasi-executive and require much less. A tribunal may have a number of different functions, one of which is to conduct fair and impartial hearings in a manner similar to that of the courts, and yet another of which is to see that certain government policies are furthered. In ascertaining the content of the requirements of procedural fairness that bind a particular tribunal, consideration must be given to <u>all</u> of the functions of that tribunal. It is not adequate to characterize a tribunal as 'quasi-judicial' on the basis of one of its functions, while treating another aspect of the legislative scheme creating this tribunal – such as the requirement that the tribunal follow interpretive guidelines that are laid down by a specialized body with expertise in that area of law – as though this second aspect of the legislative scheme were external to the true purpose of the tribunal. All aspects of the tribunal's structure, as laid out in its enabling statute, must be examined, and an attempt must be made to determine precisely what combination of functions the legislature intended that tribunal to serve, and what procedural protections are appropriate for a body that has these particular functions.

In light of their analysis of the Human Rights Tribunal, McLachlin C.J. and Bastarache J. concluded that a high degree of independence applies to the tribunal and that neither of the powers challenged infringed that standard. In particular, they characterized the guideline-making power as akin to the power of cabinet or a ministry to make regulations. An administrative tribunal's impartiality cannot be said to be compromised because it is bound to apply the 'law' relevant to a particular setting. They concluded: 'The Act therefore evinces a legislative intent, not simply to establish a Tribunal that functions by means of a quasi-judicial process, but also to limit the interpretive powers of the

Tribunal in order to ensure that the legislation is interpreted in a non-discriminatory way.'[47] That the Commission's guidelines were subject to the *Statutory Instruments Act*[48] and the process for developing guidelines involved consultations analogous to the legislative process further distinguished them from mere administrative guidelines in the Court's eyes.[49] The Court was not persuaded that the chair's power to extend the term of members past the expiry of their term adversely affected the independence or impartiality of the tribunal, especially since a similar power relating to provincial court judges was upheld as consistent with judicial independence in *Valente*.

The Supreme Court of Canada considered the distinction between administrative and judicial independence again in *Ell v. Alberta*.[50] The issues were whether the principle of institutional independence applied to justices of the peace and if so, whether the legislated removal of certain respondent justices from office contravened the principle. The Court concluded that the principle applied to the respondents, but that their removal did not contravene the principle because it was necessary for institutional reform and was not 'a disguised attempt to remove any particular justices of the peace from office.'[51] In coming to this conclusion the Court stated:[52]

> In modern times, it has been recognized that the basis for judicial independence extends far beyond the need for impartiality in individual cases. The judiciary occupies an indispensable role in upholding the integrity of our constitutional structure: see *Provincial Court Judges Reference, supra*, at para. 108. In Canada, like other federal states, courts adjudicate on disputes between the federal and provincial governments, and serve to safeguard the constitutional distribution of powers. Courts also ensure that the power of the state is exercised in accordance with the rule of law and the provisions of our Constitution. In this capacity, courts act as a shield against unwarranted deprivations by the state of the rights and freedoms of individuals. Dickson C.J. described this role in *Beauregard, supra*, at p. 70:
>
> > [Courts act as] protector of the Constitution and the fundamental values embodied in it – rule of law, fundamental justice, equality, preservation of the democratic process, to name perhaps the most important.
>
> This constitutional mandate gives rise to the principle's institutional dimension: the need to maintain the independence of a court or tribunal as a whole from the executive and legislative branches of government.

While this reasoning appears sound, the Court clarified that it applied only to presiding justices of the peace who were responsible for judicial functions. Non-presiding justices of the peace, who are responsible for administrative functions, would not have the benefit of the independence protection. At the same time, however, there are hints in *Ell* that the boundary between judicial and administrative independence may not be well defined. For example, when referring to the fact that independence is a relative rather than absolute standard, Major J. cites both administrative and judicial case law.[53] He concludes that '[t]he level of security of tenure that is constitutionally required will depend upon the specific context of the court *or tribunal*.'[54]

As *Bell* and *Ell* were attempting to clarify the boundary between various kinds of tribunals and courts, the Court returned to the question of appointments in the *Retired Judges* case.[55] In that case, the Court upheld the Ontario Court of Appeal's conclusion that the appointment of retired judges to serve as chairs of hospital labour arbitration boards should be quashed, but for significantly different reasons.

Whereas the Ontario Court of Appeal viewed the case principally as one about independence, the Supreme Court viewed the case principally as about the scope of ministerial discretion. On the issue of independence, the majority of the Court in the *Retired Judges* case held that the legislature specifically conferred the power of appointment on the minister and that, absent a constitutional challenge, a statutory regime expressed in clear and unequivocal language on this specific point prevails over common law principles, citing *Ocean Port*. Binnie J., writing for the majority, explained the significance of *Ocean Port* in the following terms:[56]

> In that case, the members of the provincial liquor licensing appeal board, who were empowered to impose penalties on liquor licences for non-compliance with the Act, were appointed to serve 'at the pleasure' of the executive. Some licencees successfully argued before the British Columbia Court of Appeal that 'at pleasure' appointees lacked the security of tenure necessary to ensure their independence. The Board's decisions were therefore set aside. On further appeal to this Court, however, it was held, per McLachlin C.J., that 'like all principles of natural justice, the degree of independence required of tribunal members may be ousted by <u>express</u> statutory language or <u>necessary</u> implication.' (para. 22 [emphasis added])

The Supreme Court's ground for interfering with this discretion was that the *Hospital Labour Disputes Arbitration Act* (*HLDAA*) provided that, where the management and labour nominees to a board of arbitration cannot agree on the appointment of a chair, then 'the Minister shall appoint as a third member a person who is, in the opinion of the Minister, qualified to act.' Because the minister had no basis to conclude that the retired judges he wished to appoint were 'qualified to act,' the majority of the Court held that the appointments were patently unreasonable.

Binnie J. considered the cross-examination of government officials, who confirmed that the minister did not inquire into the experience or expertise of the retired judges in the field of labour relations. For the minister, their qualification arose simply from their judicial background and their expertise in neutral decision-making. Binnie J. declared, 'we look in vain for some indication in the record that the Minister was alive to these labour relations requirements.'[57] Just as the Court was required to quash a decision that frustrated the objects and purposes of the minister's statutory discretion in *Roncarelli v. Duplessis*,[58] so Binnie J. argued judicial intervention was required in this case.

For the dissenting justices, the legislative provision itself indicated that there are no obvious factors of particular relevance to the formation of the minister's opinion on who is qualified to act. Because there are no obvious factors implied by this broad grant of authority, there could be no 'obvious' or 'immediate' defect in the minister's choice of one particular factor (the generalist expertise of retired judges) over another (the specialized knowledge of labour arbitrators). In such circumstances, Bastarache J. concluded the minister's decision cannot be characterized as 'clearly irrational' or so flawed that 'no degree of curial deference could allow it to stand.'[59]

While the majority decision in the *Retired Judges* case suggests that a court will intervene in the appointment process to ensure the executive fulfill the requisite legislative mandate, the decision does not go so far as to suggest there is a generalized common law or constitutional requirement that tribunals appointments be made according to objective criteria of merit rather than subjective criteria of political desirability. Indeed, following the Court of Appeal decision in the *Retired Judges* case, a number of statutes in Ontario were amended to state clearly that appointees did not have to have any specific qualifications in order to act.[60] The question remains: has Canadian administrative law neglected the issue of whether anything other than merit-based appointments to adjudicative tribunals may satisfy the requirements of tribunal independence? It is to this question that I now turn.

The Importance of Appointments for Independence

While it is a widely shared view that public confidence in the administrative justice system would be enhanced by a merit based system of appointments, it is not clear how such a system might accommodate the legitimate policy-making role of tribunals.[61] In my view, in order to give effect to concerns for independence in appointment processes, two principles must animate the discussion.

The first principle is transparency. When the Canadian Bar Association Task Force on Administrative Appointments asked the federal government for a description of the appointment process, it was told that no such description existed and that each order-in-council appointment was a separate matter to be considered on its own merits. The task force concluded, 'This appears to be an arbitrary way to conduct public business.'[62]

If government wishes to use tribunals to make policy through the selection of politically desirable tribunal members, this should be done explicitly and should include a direct justification. There are many reasons why an appointment process might involve factors other than merit, or where merit itself might be construed more broadly. These could include the importance of having tribunals that reflects the diverse make-up of a community, or regional or linguistic balance. However, all of these concerns can be added to a transparent appointment policy, through guidelines or other instruments. The critical question is whether there exist criteria which could be legitimate but which need not be transparent. This brings us to the crux of the matter: Is patronage a legitimate criterion for appointments to adjudicative bodies? I believe it is not – which is not to say that a qualified person of the same party affiliation as the government in power should be excluded from positions for which she or he is suitable. Where the selection criteria are stated to be objective, related to core competencies and vetted according to merit based criteria, but appointees nonetheless reflect only the prevailing policy preferences of the government, or loyalty to the party in power, the integrity of the administrative justice system is imperiled.

A second principle is the rule of law. Administrative adjudication, irrespective of the statutory environment in which it takes place, arguably requires a minimum degree of competence and impartiality that a purely political appointment process cannot guarantee. Where policy goals are attained through adjudicative action, competence and impartiality also should be seen as central to the policy agenda itself. This logic could lead to constitutionalizing minimum appointment criteria, which would mean that some minimum standards would prevail over even expressly worded statutory provisions purporting to suggest that no qualifications are required for a given adjudicative provision. I note that this is a different question than that considered in *Ocean Port*, which was whether the *Valente* framework of judicial independence could prevail in the administrative tribunal context over clear statutory provisions in conflict with that framework. Once one sees independence as a broader spectrum of protection, the question becomes less clearly decided on a sharp distinction between tribunals and courts. Clearly, the rule of law must apply in both settings.

The principles of transparency and the rule of law do not suggest simply one kind of appointments process. One could imagine a plethora of possible schemes that would address both concerns. These could involve ministerial variations or a central appointments secretariat. These could involve statutory provisions, regulations, or guidelines. These could be led by an Attorney General's Office or could be driven by Management Board, the executive department responsible for managing the civil service. These could involve arm's length appointment committees or enhanced power to tribunal chairs over appointments. Certainly arm's length processes are more likely to inspire confidence that an appointment is merit-based than processes controlled by a minister or her staff, but much depends on context. I would echo the observation offered by the Canadian Bar Association Task Force in its report, *The Independence of Federal Administrative Tribunals and Agencies*:[63]

> In suggesting that the government reform the appointment process, we are not suggesting that they abdicate responsibility for it. No government will give up the discretion to make appointments, nor should it. There is nothing wrong with the government making the final decision on appointments. This is a perfectly legitimate function of the executive. Nor should a government hesitate to appoint someone simply because they have been active in politics ... What must be avoided is for political 'qualifications' to be a determining or major factor in the appointment process.

Below, I briefly review several recent reform initiatives to the appointment of adjudicative tribunals that demonstrate this diversity.

The sponsorship scandal, which has included aspersions cast on Liberal patronage appointments to head crown corporations, has contributed to heightened public interest in the appointments process at the federal level.[64] The federal government's response has been to tighten parliamentary oversight over executive appointments as part of its attempt to remedy the 'democratic deficit.' The government has also announced an overhaul to appointments for the Immigration and Refugee Board, historically seen as tainted by patronage appointments. These reforms have occurred against the backdrop of the first serious attempt to reform judicial appointments in a generation. While this reform initiative has focused on Supreme Court appointments and the extent to which a parliamentary role would be introduced into that process, wider questions have been asked about the transparency and credibility of judicial appointments.[65]

In Quebec, the adoption of the *Loi sur la justice administrative*[66] brought significant changes to the appointment process. With this statute, the Assemblée nationale provided a mandatory process for the selection, appointment, and renewal of terms of the TAQ members (and also brought similar changes to other enabling statutes of the tribunals such as the Commission des lésions professionnelles et the Régie du logement). Members of TAQ can be appointed only if they possess the professional knowledge required by law and ten years of relevant expertise.[67] For each of the tribunal's sections (there are four), the statute prescribes the type of professionals who can be appointed: lawyers or notaries, doctors, psychiatrists, social workers, and 'évaluateurs agrées.' Board members are chosen through a procedure for recruitment and selection established by regulation.[68] The duration of the initial term is five years for all board members and their term can be renewed for an additional five years.[69] The renewal of a term is also examined by a committee and follows a procedure established by regulation. Since the *Barreau de Montréal* case,[70] the renewal committee is independent from the government. The Court of Appeal held that it infringed section 23 of the Quebec *Charter of Human Rights and Freedoms*[71] to have a member of the government or the president of the TAQ sit on the committee. Quebec has addressed the appointments problem by adding another layer to the fabric of administrative justice in the province and providing that appellate layer with court-like attributes.

In British Columbia, the *Administrative Tribunals Act*[72] has focused on simplifying the existing panoply of tribunals rather than adding new complexity. This legislation includes provisions relating to appointments, which focus on the distinction between appointments to adjudicative tribunals and non-adjudicative tribunals.[73] A similar approach was recommended in the federal context by the Canadian Bar Association Task Force in the early 1990s. The task force called on the federal government to enact a Federal Tribunals and Agencies Act, which would broadly guarantee the independence of federal adjudicative tribunals and establish an independent commissioner for tribunals to provide supports to tribunal members analogous to those provided to judges by the commissioner for federal judicial affairs.[74] The recommended legislation was never enacted.

In the federal context, the impetus for appointments reform was scandal, patronage, and partisan politics. In Quebec and British Columbia, the reform to administrative appointments appeared to emerge from a policy process in search of a more coherent administrative justice system. In Nova Scotia, reform resulted in part at least from a legal challenge. The challenge involved Archie Kaiser, a law professor with Dalhousie University, who applied unsuccessfully for a position on a mental health tribunal. He filed a complaint with the Nova Scotia Human Rights Commission alleging he was not selected for the appointment because he was not a supporter of the Liberal government, then in power in Nova Scotia.[75] Kaiser claimed that the tribunal members appointed by the Nova Scotia government were not objectively viewed as more qualified than Kaiser. The government initially fought the claim but ultimately settled and, as part of that settlement, agreed to a series of reforms to the appointments process that effectively would remove discretion over appointments from the ministers and give it to non-partisan advisory committees.[76] This example reveals the conundrum of reconciling a merit system of appointments with the policy-implementing (or policy-making) role of tribunals. While Kaiser may well have had more expertise and experience in the mental health field of law than those appointed in Nova Scotia, what if the goal of the Nova Scotia government was to introduce new and different perspectives on mental health into the system? Is this an illegitimate approach to the government's mental health policy agenda? In my view, the answer is not clear cut and will depend on the circumstances. Viewing appointments as one of the indicia of independence places an onus on government to justify its appointments on legitimate grounds. If the Nova Scotia government wishes to pursue law reform through mental health board appointments, the government should justify the appointments on those terms. Transparency strengthens both political and legal forms of accountability.

I want to conclude this discussion with a more detailed look at a current reform project under way in Ontario. The reform project has been initiated by the Administrative Justice Working Group (AJWG), a diverse group of legal practitioners[77] that has been meeting since 2003 to encourage broad discussion in the legal community about the need for reform of the administrative justice system in Ontario. This group has called on the Ontario government to 'commit itself to an open, transparent, accessible, merit-based and competitive process for the recruitment and appointment of members to Ontario's quasi-judicial rights tribunals.'[78]

The AJWG has advanced the following fundamental principles to animate appointments to adjudicative tribunals:

- regular posting of appointment opportunities for members, including public advertising as appropriate in accordance with established guidelines;
- public advertising of all chair positions;
- standard qualifications standards that reflect the adjudicative responsibilities of the position;
- commitment to selection of members based on results of competitive process led by tribunal chair;
- appointments based on the recommendation of the tribunal chair, in accordance with success in competitive process and identified needs of tribunal;
- reappointments pursuant to recommendation of tribunal chair based on performance appraisals;
- appointment terms of a standard duration including standard probationary and non-probationary terms;
- publication of both standard and tribunal-specific criteria for appointments; and
- statutory entrenchment of key components of the reformed process.

The focus of the AJWG's advocacy efforts has been on tribunal advisory committees. The AJWG has proposed that the chair of each quasi-judicial tribunal be responsible for establishing a process for member recruitment that includes the participation of a tribunal advisory committee. Each tribunal would establish its own advisory committee to include representatives of the legal bar and the litigating public that appears before the tribunal, including key stakeholder groups.[79] Prior to a recruitment initiative, the advisory committee would be able to provide input or advice with respect to any identified gaps in the tribunal's adjudication panel in terms of, for example, diversity, gender balance, background skills and experience, and so on. In some cases, the chair might wish to include members of the advisory committee in the selection process for new adjudicators. The inclusion of stakeholder groups in the appointment process is not uncontroversial. It appears to introduce the possibility of capture and ulterior agendas that represent the heart of the problem with the status quo.

Under the AJWG proposal, the establishment and maintenance of a well-functioning tribunal advisory committee would form part of the key responsibilities of every chair of a quasi-judicial tribunal, as set out in their Memorandum of Understanding (MOU) with their minister. Under the MOU, the chair would be responsible for ensuring that the tribunal's advisory committee was representative of the tribunal's predominant user communities and an effective forum for informed public input.

The AJWG also contemplates the creation of an Administrative Justice Policy Committee to develop and oversee implementation of policies for quasi-judicial tribunals in a number of areas including member recruitment. For example, the composition and appropriate roles and responsibilities of tribunal advisory committees would be the subject of a policy guideline developed by the provincial oversight committee. This committee would be composed of representatives of key stakeholders in the Ontario administrative justice sector, including public members. At minimum, the provincial committee would include members nominated by the Society of Ontario Adjudicators and Regulators, the Ontario Bar Association (that is, Administrative Law Section, Labour Section, Workers' Compensation section), Legal Aid Ontario, and the attorney general. It is expected that the committee would include a senior lawyer at the Ministry of the Attorney General and at least three members of the public with some experience or background in the administrative justice system. On an on-going basis, the provincial oversight committee would be responsible for considering and approving province-wide guidelines in areas such as the role of advisory committees, member recruitment, performance appraisal and the procedure for public complaints.[80] These recommendations build on the initiative of the Society of Ontario Adjudicators and Regulators (SOAR), which published its Principles for Appointments to Adjudicative/Regulatory Tribunals in 1997.[81]

The AJWG proposal would remove the unchecked influence of partisanship over tribunal appointments but risks replacing it with the unchecked influence of stakeholder groups. It indirectly raises a fundamental question: Is partisanship of one kind or another inherent in the appointments context? Or, put differently, which constituency *should* influence tribunal appointments? This question has no easy answer, in part because Canadian administrative law has devoted so little attention to the issue of policy-making in tribunals. Perhaps the differing views of the government, of stakeholders, and of the tribunals themselves creates a constructive tension in this regard. These are questions that deserve to be contested and which, under the current practice of appointment by executive prerogative, are rarely even raised.

After successive politicization of appointments by the NDP and Conservative governments in Ontario, can this trend be reversed? While the Ontario government has yet to engage in any comprehensive appointments reform, the Liberal government elected in 2003 has implemented a policy under which all adjudicative appointments are publicly advertised. Of course, independence and appointments are merely one aspect of sector reform on the table. The government's own review of its agencies, boards, and commissions has unearthed serious concerns in the tribunal community regarding low salaries paid to full and part-time adjudicators, overlapping and inefficient tribunal mandates, outmoded statutes, and so forth.

The proposals and initiatives discussed in this section focus on the relationship between tribunals and the governments that appoint them. There is a final, further perspective on which I wish to close, which is the relationship between tribunals and those affected by their decision-making. A tribunal that has direct accountability to the public or to stakeholders obviates the need for government appointments. For example, municipal councils and school boards are examples of administrative decision-makers elected directly by the public. In other cases, legitimacy is a matter of the ongoing confidence of key stakeholder groups (for example, labour boards). Still other administrative bodies may rely on their technical or scientific expertise for legitimacy in their policy-making functions (for example, energy boards). Each of these, for different reasons, has enjoyed a measure of independence from the vicissitudes of government appointments preferences. It is worth emphasizing that insulation from the political process in these settings has largely been achieved through legislative and policy initiatives. Recourse to legal constraints should not be misused as a means of frustrating the legitimate authority of governments to pursue their policy agendas. Where those agendas are advanced improperly through partisan appointments to adjudicative tribunals, however, in my view courts cannot abnegate their responsibility to intervene.

Viewed from a broader vantage point, all tribunals are created for a purpose. That purpose will drive the logic of an appointments process. The purpose of municipal councils suggests its members should be elected. The purpose of labour boards suggests representatives of labour and employers should play a strong role in the adjudicative process. The purpose of adjudicative tribunals suggests the logic of a credible, transparent, and merit-based appointment system. When called on, courts should be capable of articulating this logic and the legal consequences that follow – consequences that may include merit-based constraints even to at-pleasure appointments.[82] This is analogous, in my view, to the opinions expressed by courts respecting tribunal expertise in standard of review cases. As in those cases, the courts should not view the appointments issue in the abstract, but rather in contextual terms, and should be alive to the practical realities of tribunals as well as the political realities of government.

Conclusion

In commenting on the renewed interest in appointments and independence, David Mullan offered the following observation:[83]

> Especially critical in recent litigation have been issues of the impact on independence of government proposals to change the composition of tribunals either by non-renewal of expiring appointments or even dismissal. The early case law in this domain rejected such challenges on the basis that those seeking renewal would realize that the government of the day would be looking at their performance in terms of their overall discharge of their duties in terms of the general philosophy and dictates of the empowering statute. It was simply inappropriate to presume that members of a tribunal might act in such a way as to favour government interests in particular cases in order to enhance their chances of reappointment. More recently, confronted by the specter of governments blatantly and unapologetically using their powers of appointment, reappointment and dismissal to achieve political ends and political rebalancing, such arguments are now making some headway.

A focus on independence must, in my view, include a focus on the broader context of appointments decision-making. It is not simply a matter of security of tenure or financial independence or control over administration – though these are clearly important guarantees – but also a question of transparency and the rule of law. Those who are affected by tribunal decision-making have a right to expect an independent hearing before an independent adjudicator. Prior to the Supreme Court's decision in *Ocean Port*, Mullan speculated that the independence principle from the *Provincial Judges Remuneration Reference*[84] could apply to tribunals as well: 'If the Preamble can be deployed to challenge compromises of independence in the case of non-section 96 judges, it is not much of a stretch to extend that to adjudication by tribunals.'[85]

While the Supreme Court has removed this possibility with its decision in *Ocean Port*, this does not preclude the notion that administrative law imposes constraints on the government's appointment power. One type of constraint is the limit on ministerial discretion developed in *Roncarelli* and applied in the appointment's context in the *Retired Judges* case. Another type of constraint, in my view, must remain tied to the notion of independence. This must be an approach to independence tailored to the diverse and distinctive sphere of administrative justice, not one grafted from the judicial context. As I have attempted to demonstrate in this paper, Canadian administrative law has neglected to develop such an approach to independence.

All adjudication must be premised on protections ensuring that the outcome of decision-making is determined on the merits. This merits premise can only truly be ensured by decision-makers appointed on the basis of a merit-based system of appointment. As Rosalie Abella observed, 'The public will only have confidence in tribunals if they have confidence that they are not seen as the dumping grounds for post-electoral rewards.'[86] Integrating appointments within a culture of adjudicative independence for tribunals represents a significant step toward ensuring public confidence in administrative justice in Canada.

NOTES

I am grateful to Grant Huscroft and Michael Taggart for asking me to participate in this collection and for their constructive comments on an earlier draft of this paper. I realize more with each research project how indebted I am to David Mullan for his thought-provoking scholarship, mentorship, and friendship. I also wish to acknowledge Amanda Gibson, Leslie Zamojc, and Zimra Yetnikoff for their superb research assistance.

1 David J. Mullan, '*Ocean Port Hotel* and Statutory Compromises of Tribunal Independence' (2002) 9 C.L.E.L.J. 184 at 193 [Mullan, 'Ocean Port'].

2 On the importance of administrative justice systems generally, see *Paul v. British Columbia (Forest Appeals Commissioner)* [2003] 2 S.C.R. 585, which affirms that a wide range of tribunals will enjoy jurisdiction to hear and decide constitutional challenges as well as resolving the disputes for which the tribunal was established. See Justice John Evans's contribution to this volume.

3 By 'adjudicative tribunal' I refer broadly to tribunals whose primary purpose is the impartial resolution of disputes. In Ontario, for example, this would capture the Human Rights Tribunal of Ontario, the Ontario Labour Relations Board, the Ontario Rental Housing Tribunal, the Social Benefits Tribunal, and the Workplace Safety and Insurance Appeals Tribunal. I do not mean to suggest there are no constraints for appointments to other kinds of agencies, boards, and commissions, but I believe the strongest case for linking appointments to independence arises in the adjudicative context. For a judicial approach to the functional similarity of adjudicative tribunals and courts, see *AG (Quebec) v. Blaikie*, [1979] 2 S.C.R. 1016. While emphasizing the distinction between tribunals and courts, the Court more recently highlighted the added independence requirements of adjudicative tribunals at common law in *Bell v. Canadian Telephone Employees Association*, [2003] 1 S.C.R. 884 at para. 22 [*Bell*]. For a discussion on classifying tribunals as adjudicative and non-adjudicative, see Ed Ratushny, *The Independence of Federal Administrative Tribunals and Agencies in Canada* (Ottawa: Canadian Bar Association, 1990) at 46–47.

4 Numerous studies have detailed the use of tribunals for partisan appointments. These studies tend to rely on impressionistic accounts of governments advancing their ideological or partisan agenda through tribunal appointments. See, for example, Ron Ellis, 'Super Provincial Tribunals: A Radical Remedy for Canada's Rights Tribunals' (2002) 15 Can. J. Admin. L. & Prac. 15; Donald Chiasson, 'Government Perspective on Administrative Tribunals' (2000–1) 14 Can. J. Admin. L. & Prac. 199; and S. Ronald Ellis, 'Appointment Policies in the Administrative Justice System: Lessons from Ontario Four Speeches' (1999) 11 Can. J. Admin. L. & Prac. 205. There is, of course, nothing new in such observations. See *Independent Administrative Agencies: A Framework for Decision Making*, report no. 26 (Ottawa: Law Reform Commission of Canada, 1985) at 77.

5 [2001] 2 S.C.R. 781 at para. 24 [*Ocean Port*].

6 See J.M. Brown and J.M. Evans, *Judicial Review of Administrative Action in Canada*, looseleaf (Toronto: Canvasback, 1998) at 11:4120, who note that

where an executive body appears before an executive tribunal, a conflict does not inherently arise. See also Philip Bryden and Ron Hatch, 'British Columbia Council of Administrative Tribunals Research and Policy Committee: Report on Independence, Accountability and Appointments Process in BC Tribunals' (1999) 12 Can. J. Admin. L. & Prac. 235.

7 For discussion, see L. Sossin, 'The Ambivalence of Executive Power in Canada' in Adam Tomkins and Paul Craig, eds., *The Executive and Public Law: Power and Accountability in Comparative Perspective* (Oxford: Oxford University Press, 2006).

8 For discussion, see L. Sossin, 'Speaking Truth to Power? The Search for Bureaucratic Independence' (2005) 55 U.T.L.J. 1.

9 As Katrina Wyman put it, 'The doctrine of tribunal independence is not concerned with establishing administrative tribunals as a fourth branch of government': Katrina Miriam Wyman, 'The Independence of Tribunals in an Era of Ever Expanding Judicial Independence' (2001) 14 Can. J. Admin. L. & Prac. 61 at 100.

10 For a review of these functional arguments, see J. Harsel, 'Tribunals in the System of Justice: The Need for Independence' (1997) 4 Austrl. J. Admin. L. 200. See also J. Teague, 'Tribunals and the Judicial Arm of Government' in R. Creyke ed., *Administrative Tribunals: Taking Stock* (Canberra: ANU, 1992).

11 See, e.g., *Cooper v. Canada (Human Rights Commission)*, [1996] 3 S.C.R. 854 at para. 70 (McLachlin J. dissenting).

12 Mullan, '*Ocean Port,*' *supra* note 1 at 212.

13 For a broader discussion and critique of the analogy to judicial independence, see Wyman, *supra* note 9. See also L. Sossin and G. Heckman, 'How Canadian Administrative Law Protections Measure up to International Human Rights Standards' (2005) 50 McGill L.J. 193. In earlier cases, such as *Consolidated-Bathurst v. I.W.A.*, [1990] 1 S.C.R. 282, the term 'judicial independence' was used by the Supreme Court to characterize the common law standards applicable to a labour tribunal, lending credence to the view that it was the adjudicative nature of a tribunal's powers that determined the level of independence protections imposed by law rather than whether the tribunal was 'judicial' or 'executive' in origin.

14 *Valente v. The Queen*, [1985] 2 S.C.R. 673 [*Valente*].

15 Ibid. at 168. The test for a reasonable apprehension of bias adopted in *Valente* and subsequently is that stated by de Grandpré J. in *Committee for Justice and Liberty v. National Energy Board*, [1978] 1 S.C.R. 369 at 394: '. . . the apprehension of bias must be a reasonable one, held by reasonable and right minded persons, applying themselves to the question and obtaining thereon the required information. In the words of the Court of Appeal that

test is "what would an informed person, viewing the matter realistically and practically – and having thought the matter through – conclude. Would he think that it is more likely than not that Mr. Crowe, whether consciously or unconsciously, would not decide fairly."'

16 Ibid. at 169–70.

17 'The Rationale and Some Aspects of Judicial Independence' (1985), 59 A.L.J. 135 at 135, quoted in ibid.

18 [1995] 1 S.C.R. 3 [*Matsqui*].

19 While Sopinka J. appeared to write for the greatest number of judges on this point, Lamer C.J.'s decision has become the predominant articulation of institutional independence in Canada. Further, while Lamer C.J.'s reasons suggest judicial independence would only be breached where *all* the *Valente* criteria are not met, it has come to be understood that if *any* of the criteria are breached, a reasonable apprehension of bias will result. For discussion, see Richard Haigh and Jim Smith, 'Independence after *Matsqui*' (1998) 11 Can. J. Admin. L. & Prac. 101.

20 *Matsqui, supra* note 18 at paras. 75, 79–80.

21 [1993] 1 F.C. 74 (T.D.).

22 [1993] 2 F.C. 641 (C.A.)

23 *Matsqui, supra* note 18 at paras. 83–85.

24 Ibid. at paras. 117–23.

25 [1996] 3 S.C.R. 919 [*Régie*].

26 Ibid. at para. 67–68 [emphasis added].

27 The central exception to this claim is *Katz v. Vancouver Stock Exchange*, [1996] 3 S.C.R. 405 at para. 1.

28 Both 'patronage' and 'merit' are notoriously difficult to define. Patronage may be seen as limited to conferring appointments on the 'party faithful' or on a broader group of those with kindred convictions on policy matters. The Oxford English Dictionary defines patronage as 'The control of appointments to offices, privileges, etc., in public service.' A series of Supreme Court cases use the term 'patronage' as though its meaning were self-evident. For example, in *Ell v. Alberta*, [2003] 1 S.C.R. 857 at para. 45, the Supreme Court observed, 'Historically, there was a widespread belief that appointment to office was solely on political grounds. The McRuer Commission (1968) described the situation in Ontario as a 'mockery of judicial office [that is] bound to depreciate respect for law and order in the community' (p. 518). *It is hoped that patronage in the appointment process has been at least lessened, if not eradicated, since the time of that report.* Unquestionably, the perception that appointment to judicial office is political in nature undermines public confidence in the administration of justice' [emphasis added].

For the purposes of this paper, I use patronage to connote appointments where partisan affiliation represents a primary justification for a tribunal appointment. I use merit to connote a system of appointments based on objective assessments of expertise and suitability for tribunal appointments. For a discussion of the merit principle, see *Lavoie v. Canada*, [2002] 1 S.C.R. 769 at para. 22 and *O.P.S.E.U. v. Ontario (Attorney General)*, [1987] 2 S.C.R. 2 at 44.

29 (1998), 37 O.R. (3d) 161 (C.A.) [*Hewat*].

30 For discussion of the significance of this case, see Katrina Wyman, 'Appointments to Adjudicative Tribunals: Politics and Courts' (1999) 52 U. T. Fac. L. Rev. 101. See also Craig Flood, '*Hewat* v. *Ontario*' (1998) 6 C.L.E.L.J. 263.

31 *Hewat*, *supra* note 29 at 166.

32 Ibid. at 169.

33 (2000) 51 O.R. (3d) 417 (C.A.), aff'd [2003] 1 S.C.R. 539 [*Retired Judges*]. Grant Huscroft analyses this decision in his contribution to this volume.

34 R.S.O. 1990, c. H.14. Section 6(5) provides: 'Where the two members appointed by or on behalf of the parties fail within ten days after the appointment of the second of them to agree upon the third member, notice of such failure shall be given forthwith to the Minister by the parties, the two members or either of them and the Minister shall appoint as a third member a person who is, in the opinion of the Minister, qualified to act.'

35 For a more detailed appraisal of *Ocean Port*, see Philip Bryden, 'Structural Independence of Administrative Tribunals in the Wake of *Ocean Port*' (2003) 16 Can. J. Admin. L. & Prac. 125; M. Rankin, 'Case Comment: *Ocean Port Hotel Limited v. B.C. (General Manager, Liquor Control)*' (1999), 57 The Advocate 709; and L. Sossin, 'Developments in Administrative Law: the 2001–2002 Term' (2002) 18 Sup. Ct. L. Rev. (2nd) 41.

36 (1999), 174 D.L.R. (4th) 648.

37 *Ocean Port*, *supra* note 5 at para. 20.

38 Ibid. at paras. 20–22.

39 Ibid. at para. 25.

40 Ibid. at para. 27.

41 *Supra* note 3.

42 See, e.g., *Bell Canada v. Canadian Telephone Employees Assn.*, [1998] 3 F.C. 244 (T.D.).

43 [2001] 2 F.C. 392 (T.D.).

44 Ibid. at paras. 129–30.

45 [2001] 3 F.C. 481 (C.A.).

46 *Bell*, *supra* note 3 at para. 22.

47 Ibid. at para. 26.

48 *Statutory Instruments Act*, R.S.C. 1985, c. S-22.

49 McLachlin C.J. and Bastarache J. elaborated: 'While it may have been more felicitous for Parliament to have called the Commission's power a power to make 'regulations' rather than a power to make 'guidelines,' the legislative intent is clear. A functional and purposive approach to the nature of these guidelines reveals that they are a form of law, akin to regulations. It is also worth noting that the word used in the French version of the Act is '*ordonnance*' which leaves no doubt that the guidelines are a form of law.' (*Bell, supra* note 3 at para. 37.

50 [2003] 1 S.C.R. 857 [*Ell*].

51 Ibid. at para. 38.

52 Ibid. at paras. 22–23.

53 Ibid. at para. 30: 'The manner in which the essential conditions of independence may be satisfied varies in accordance with the nature of the court or tribunal and the interests at stake. See *Canadian Pacific Ltd.* v. *Matsqui Indian Band*, [1995] 1 S.C.R. 3, at para. 83, *per* Lamer C.J. and *Therrien* (*Re*), [2001] 2 S.C.R. 3, 2001 SCC 35, at para. 65, where the Court advocated a contextual approach to judicial independence.'

54 Ibid. at para. 31 [emphasis added].

55 *Supra* note 33.

56 Ibid. at para. 117.

57 Ibid. at para. 181.

58 [1959] S.C.R. 121 at 140.

59 Ibid. at para. 36.

60 See T. Kuttner and L. Jacobs, 'The Expert Tribunal' (Canadian Institute for the Administration of Justice Roundtable Paper, 2003), citing, among other examples, the *Back to School Act (Toronto and Windsor)*, 2001, S.O. 2001, c.1, ss. 11(4) and (5).

61 For discussion, see P. Aucoin and E. Goodyear-Grant, 'Designing a Merit-Based Process for Appointing Boards of ABCs: Lessons from the Nova Scotia Reform Experience' (2002) 45 Canadian Public Administration 301.

62 Ratushny, *supra* note 3 at 56.

63 Ibid. at 58.

64 The 'sponsorship affair' refers to the alleged mismanagement of funds directed by the federal government to sponsor events in Quebec following the 1995 referendum as part of a national unity strategy, which has led to parliamentary committee hearings, a public inquiry headed by Justice Gomery, and a series of civil and criminal legal proceedings. The sponsorship program and alleged improprieties with its management and operations are detailed in a 2003 report of Canada's auditor general: Auditor

General of Canada, Report of the Auditor General of Canada – Sponsorship Program, Advertising and Public Opinion Research (Minister of Public Works and Government Services, 2003) online: http://pwgsc.gc.ca/sponsorship/text/sponsorship-report-e.html.

65 See conference material from Judicial Appointment in a Free and Democratic Society, April 19, 2003, at http://www.law-lib.utoronto.ca/Conferences/judiciary/. See also the report of the Canadian Association of Law Teachers Panel on Supreme Court Appointments at http://www.acpd-calt. org/english/docs/SupremeCourt_panel.doc.

66 L.R.Q., c. J-3. For more discussion, see F. Houle and L. Sossin, 'Policy-Making in Tribunals,' presented to the Canadian Institute for the Administration of Justice Administrative Law Roundtable (June 2004).

67 Ibid. at s. 41.

68 Ibid. at s. 42.

69 Ibid at ss. 46–48

70 (2001), 22 D.L.R. (4th) 470 (Que. C.A.).

71 R.S.Q., c. C-12.

72 S.B.C. 2004 c. 45.

73 The legislation purports to render mandatory the selection and appointment of presidents and board members of administrative tribunals in British Columbia on the sole basis of merit.

74 Ratushny, *supra* note 3, at 50–51.

75 This case is discussed in Aucoin and Goodyear-Grant, *supra* note 61. The terms of the settlement are available at *Kaiser v. Nova Scotia (Executive Council)*, [2002] N.S.H.R.B.I.D. No. 1.

76 The settlement and its implications are discussed in Aucoin and Goodyear-Grant, *supra* note 61 at 311–12. See also Dean Jobb, 'Fewer patronage appointments pledged in settlement of lawsuit by Halifax law professor' Lawyer's Weekly (8 February 2002).

77 I disclose that I am a member of this group. The group includes private bar lawyers, academics, members of the Ontario Bar Association Workers Compensation, Administrative Law and Labour Law sections, lawyers and legal workers in the Legal Aid Ontario clinic system, and several former members, vice-chairs and chairs of various Ontario adjudicative tribunals.

78 Administrative Justice Working Group, 'Recommendations to Improve the Appointments Process for Ontario Non-Regulatory Tribunals' (February 2005) [unpublished, on file with author].

79 At least one Ontario tribunal, the Workplace Safety and Insurance Appeals Tribunal, already has an advisory committee that includes stakeholder representatives.

80 The proposal also explores various options for the appointments of members to this policy committee.

81 See http://www/soar.on.ca/soar-appoint.htm. The guiding principles include:

1 The appointment process for tribunals should be transparent, open and fair. It should be coordinated centrally and implemented in a consistent way across the tribunal sector.
2 The tribunal chair should participate in the selection process, and his or her recommendations should be considered by the government and the all-party committee of the legislature when the ultimate selection is made and confirmed.
3 Persons chosen for appointment to tribunals must be competent to carry out the work of the tribunal.
4 Provided that a person is otherwise qualified, close affiliation with a political party should not be cause for disqualification.
5 An adequate budget for training of new and continuing members is a central requirement for excellence within the tribunal sector.
6 In order to ensure independence and impartiality, both in fact and in appearance, an appointment should be for a fixed term during good behaviour. Normally, reappointments should be available, conditional on merit. The system of reappointments must be designed to preserve the effectiveness, integrity and impartiality of the institution.
7 The duration of appointments, and the basis for compensation, should be specified in legislation.
8 Details of a member's obligations and responsibilities should be specified by contract at the beginning of the appointment.

82 Of course, the Supreme Court has already developed the idea of procedural constraints on at-pleasure appointments: *Knight v. Indian Head School Division* 19, [1990] 1 S.C.R. 653.

83 D. Mullan, *Administrative Law* (Toronto: Irwin Law, 2001) at 346.

84 *Reference regarding the Remuneration of Judges of the Provincial Court of Prince Edward Island*, [1997] 3 S.C.R. 3.

85 Ibid. at 347.

86 Rosalie Silberman Abella, 'Canadian Administrative Tribunals: Toward Judicialization or Dejudicialization?' (1988) 2 Can. J. Admin. L. & Prac. 1 at 10.

Where Do Tribunals Fit into the Australian System of Administration and Adjudication?

ROBIN CREYKE

Fourteen years ago David Mullan was the keynote speaker at the first workshop on tribunals to be held in Australia.[1] In his paper, Mullan not only set out to paint a picture of the special features of Canadian tribunals, but also explored issues surrounding their independence – independence from the courts, from the executive, and from the legislature – and the extent to which developments in Canada arising from the *Bill of Rights* and the *Charter of Rights and Freedoms* provided constitutional independence for tribunals.[2] It is a mark of his prescience as an academic, as well as the entrenchment of thinking about the architecture of government, that the topic has as much currency today as it did then. This paper addresses the issues raised by Mullan in the contemporary Australian context, and seeks to elucidate the place of tribunals in the framework of Australian government.

Tribunals and Adjudication

Both Canada and Australia have embraced the tribunal mode of adjudication, but one is hard-pressed to identify how many tribunals each country has, not least because no satisfactory definition of a tribunal has yet been devised.[3]

What Is a Tribunal?

The word 'tribunal' has defied definition. Is an adjudicator who makes an interim determination in a building payment dispute a tribunal?[4] Are bodies that mediate or arbitrate rather than decide tribunals?[5] Are bodies, that are principally policy-making, such as the Australian

Broadcasting Authority or Ministers of the Crown, tribunals?[6] Are those who investigate and settle disputes, such as ombudsmen, or health rights commissioners, tribunals? As these questions indicate, the distinction between a tribunal and other administrative decision-makers is 'somewhat arbitrary.'[7]

At the 1992 workshop on tribunals it was pointed out that 'categorisation of tribunals is unlikely to be solved by etymological means and ... a functional approach may be the only way to identify them.'[8] That task was attempted by the Australian Law Reform Commission (ALRC) in the late 1990s. In its *Managing Justice* inquiry, the commission categorized tribunals according to six dichotomies: policy and court-substitute tribunals; review tribunals and primary decision-making bodies; first- and second-tier review tribunals; tribunals that adjudicate disputes about pre-existing legal rights and entitlements, and tribunals that exercise arbitral power to create legal rights and obligations; tribunals that adjudicate and tribunals that use other dispute resolution processes such as mediation; and tribunals that determine rights between private parties, and between government and private parties.[9] While these dichotomies are useful, they are descriptive rather than definitive. The ALRC noted of tribunals that '[t]he legislation prescribing their structure, powers and practices mandates forms of adjudication which are often quite different from adjudication in a court' and simply concluded that they are bodies which 'provide decision making and dispute resolution processes which are "alternative" to traditional court proceedings.'[10] The commission made no attempt to elaborate upon those differences or to identify criteria to assess what is a tribunal.

There have been legislative attempts at identifying what is distinctive about tribunals. The *Administrative Law Act 1978* (Vic.) defined a tribunal as:[11]

> a person or body of persons (not being a court of law or a tribunal constituted or presided over by a Judge of the Supreme Court) who, in arriving at the decision in question, is or are by law required, whether by express direction or not, to act in a judicial manner to the extent of observing one or more of the rules of natural justice.

This definition fails to isolate tribunals from other decision-makers. The rules of natural justice apply to ministers, officials and various other public decision-makers as well as tribunals. The *Legislation Act 2001* of the Australian Capital Territory defines tribunal to include 'any entity that is authorised to hear, receive and examine evidence' – another overly broad definition.[12]

Nor has the Council of Australasian Tribunals (COAT),[13] set up in 2002 as the peak coordinating body for tribunals in Australasia, taken the matter further. The COAT constitution defined tribunal as 'any Commonwealth, State, Territory or New Zealand body whose primary function involves the determination of disputes, including administrative review, party/party disputes and disciplinary applications but which in carrying out this function is not acting as a court.'[14] This definition could include ombudsmen, and privacy and other specialist commissioners who have as a 'primary function' the 'determination of disputes.'

The problem with these inclusive definitions is that once the meaning of tribunal embraces ordinary decision-makers, the concept of 'tribunal' as a special and distinct adjudicative entity is lost. Hence the issue of what it is to be a tribunal remains open for exploration.

What is clear, however, is that the label covers a diverse and expanding group which is capable of affecting many aspects of people's lives, from professional disciplinary issues, to complaints about process, to objection against decisions. 'Tribunal' also embraces multiple forms of dispute resolution: orthodox adjudication by individuals, those who investigate and make recommendations, as well as those who simply assist the parties to reach a mutually agreed solution to a dispute. This paper adopts the more orthodox and narrow definition of a tribunal as an individual or body that provides a dispute resolution process as an alternative to traditional court proceedings.

Contrast between Canadian and Australian Tribunals

The most noticeable distinction between the Canadian and Australian tribunal landscapes is that Australia has embraced the generalist tribunal – that is, a tribunal with jurisdiction across public administration. Having a general jurisdiction tribunal does not mean that other specialist tribunals cease to exist. However, such a tribunal has the advantage of economies of scale – shared resources and membership, common premises, more uniform standards, and increased profile – that a specialist tribunal lacks.

Although the general jurisdiction tribunal has attracted the attention of Canadian scholars, including that of David Mullan in an early study,[15] there has been little support for its importation into Canada.[16]

Introduced at the federal level in 1976, the general jurisdiction tribunal model has spread to almost every state and territory in Australia. Only the Northern Territory and Queensland as yet have no form of merit review tribunal with authority to review decisions across the whole of government,[17] although there have been proposals to introduce such a body in both jurisdictions.[18]

In other respects, recent Australian developments have more closely aligned the Australian and Canadian tribunal scenes. In 1992 Mullan cited Canadian labour relations boards and arbitrators as an effective collective bargaining tool in Canada not found in Australia. However, that role has long been performed by a comparable body in Australia – the Australian Industrial Relations Commission (AIRC) – although it has not always been perceived as a member of the tribunal fold. The reason for this is that the original body was a court, the Court of Conciliation and Arbitration, established in 1904.[19] This federal court was set up with both arbitral and judicial powers, a mixture of functions said to breach the separation of powers principle in the Australian Constitution. This combination of functions was successfully challenged in the *Boilermakers'* case on that constitutional ground.[20] In the aftermath, the arbitral function was assigned to the Conciliation and Arbitration Commission, now the AIRC, and the judicial function was given to a court, and is now exercised by the Federal Court of Australia.

This separation of functions did not detract from the continuing effectiveness of the arbitral body. As one commentator described it, Australia has developed 'a system of bargaining based on industry-wide awards and a strong centralized tribunal ... and the tribunal still underpins Australian industrial relations ... [in a manner which] is uniquely Australian.'[21] Recognition of the AIRC as a tribunal may have been slow but it was cemented when it was included in the ALRC's comprehensive examination of Australian federal tribunals carried out between 1997 and 1999.[22]

In 1992 Mullan could say that '[i]n a way that is still not as true in Australia, tribunals in Canada also play a very significant role in economic regulation of business.'[23] Today Australia has moved much closer to the position in Canada. Bodies now exist throughout Australia to regulate the former government-owned utilities, such as energy and water distribution and supply, transport, and to monitor anti-competitive behaviour. Tribunals too have emerged in these areas. Most prominent is the Australian Competition Tribunal, a federal body.[24] Other bodies hearing disputes in the area of utility and business regulation include the Australian Capital Territory's Essential Services Consumer Council, and the Ombudsman offices which handle some of these matters in the states and the Northern Territory.

The Australian Competition Tribunal is a significant body because of the nature of the issues it deals with and the national scope of its work. The tribunal reviews determinations of the Australian Competition and Consumer Commission to approve or revoke otherwise anti-competitive arrangements such as company mergers and acquisitions and claims of exclusive dealing, as well as disputes relating to certain practices of ocean carriers. It also determines the merits of claims of denial of access to essential facilities, notably in the energy and transport fields.

The tribunal's review jurisdiction is not high volume. One source lists a dozen cases for the financial year ending 2004.[25] Another suggests that in this period the tribunal heard three matters, eleven proceedings were commenced and another nine matters were finalized.[26] Nonetheless, though its hearings may not be numerically significant, that is compensated for by their importance and far-reaching effect. For instance, cases handled in 2003–4 included an attempted takeover of Air New Zealand by the Australian national carrier Qantas,[27] access to gas pipelines,[28] the supply of pathology services in public hospitals,[29] the exclusive award of tender services,[30] and EFTPOS interchange access fees.[31] It is clear that in Australia tribunal adjudication in the area of economic regulation of business is now playing a significant role, which will only increase in the future.[32]

Constitutional Constraints on Tribunals

The Australian Constitution has shaped the jurisdiction of tribunals. Chapter III of the *Constitution* restricts the exercise of the judicial power of the Commonwealth to courts covered by Chapter III. A concomitant restriction is that such courts are not permitted to exercise non-judicial power. Although the notion of 'judicial power' has proved elusive, core features have been identified.[33] One such feature is the ability to make binding and authoritative decisions.[34] Since by definition tribunals are not Chapter III courts, they may not exercise federal judicial power. As a consequence they are denied the authority to make final decisions, a constitutional inhibition that has set the limits of their jurisdiction.[35] Federal legislation giving tribunals powers which breach this prohibition will be struck down as unconstitutional. As mentioned earlier, the most spectacular example was the dismemberment of the Court of

Conciliation and Arbitration after nearly sixty years of productive existence.[36] But there have been other, almost as cataclysmic, consequences for federal tribunals.

It was separation of powers that prevented the Australian government's attempts to expedite the enforcement power of the Human Rights and Equal Opportunity Commission (HREOC). That commission is the national anti-discrimination and human rights protection body. It makes determinations, for example, of unlawful discrimination, but was not able to enforce its findings because enforcement was considered part of the judicial power of the Commonwealth. In an attempt to avoid the cost and delays of a rehearing before the Federal Court to obtain an enforceable order, the federal government passed legislation that in effect deemed registration of HREOC 'determinations' at the Federal Court to be orders of the court.[37] As the majority of the High Court expressed it in *Attorney-General (Commonwealth) v. Breckler*: 'Registration, an administrative act, converted a non-binding administrative determination into a determination' which was 'binding, authoritative and curially enforceable.'[38] This deemed 'enforceable order' was held to be an exercise of judicial power, and the scheme was struck down.[39] The outcome limited 'the capacity of the federal Parliament to establish non-judicial tribunals with effective dispute resolution powers'[40] and has seen a diminution of HREOC's stature and workload in favour of state and territory equivalent bodies that are not caught by Chapter III.[41]

Other federal tribunals have also faced challenges to their constitutionality. The president of the Commonwealth's general jurisdiction tribunal, the Administrative Appeals Tribunal (AAT), is a judge of the Federal Court. The judicial presidency of the AAT led to the claim of a breach of Chapter III. It was argued that as a Federal Court judge the president was prohibited from exercising powers which were not judicial. Since an essential function of a merit review tribunal is to make decisions about factual questions, this function of tribunals was argued to fall outside the precincts of 'judicial power' and hence was not capable of being performed by a federally appointed judge.[42] Ultimately, the judicial president was found to be exercising power in a personal, not a judicial, capacity thus avoiding the constitutional trap.[43]

Other tribunals have also weathered calls for constitutional disqualification on the basis of their exercise of judicial power. For example, the continued operation of the Superannuation Complaints Tribunal, a body established by federal legislation, was thrown into doubt on the ground that it was determining disputes traditionally within the area of private law.[44] The tribunal undertakes review of decisions by trustees of superannuation funds in both the public and private sectors by reference to a 'fair and reasonable' standard.[45] This was held by the Full Federal Court to be an exercise of judicial power. The High Court of Australia rejected the argument. The majority held that the rights and obligations of the parties were established under the trust deed and the tribunal did no more than arbitrate a dispute in accordance with the terms of the deed. In other words, the tribunal was not establishing new rights and obligations for the parties. Furthermore, the determinations of the tribunal did not have a conclusive character.[46] Had the decision not been overturned there would have been serious implications for the federal government's retirement incomes policy.

A less high-profile but equally significant decision related to the Social Security Appeals Tribunal (SSAT). The SSAT is a high-volume, second-tier tribunal which reviews decisions concerning income support. In *Re Registrar, Social Security Appeals Tribunal; Ex parte Townsend,*[47] the jurisdiction of the tribunal was challenged on the ground that it made binding determinations. The High Court upheld the constitutional validity of the Tribunal. Toohey J. found that a federal tribunal which exercises an adjudicative function by construing legislation and applying it to factual claims does not infringe Chapter III. The outcome was unexpected given that, for all intents and purposes, SSAT decisions are accepted as authoritative by the parties. The result may be explicable more in terms of the inferior status of the tribunal than on grounds of principle. At the same time, had the exercise of functions by the SSAT been found to breach Chapter III, the finding would have sounded the death-knell for all federal merits review tribunals. Pragmatic considerations may well have swayed the court in reaching this outcome.

This chronology of major cases indicates that, while there have been spectacular shipwrecks on the shoals of Chapter III, federal tribunals have generally survived the constitutional reef. At the same time the drafters of federal legislation must always be alert to its existence since failure to do so can cause grief to even long-established bodies in the adjudicative fold.

Tribunal Processes: General

A common feature of the tribunal systems in Australia and Canada is that decision-making procedures and processes have been supplemented by common law principles. In Australia this has been most marked in relation to the two tribunals established under the *Migration*

Act 1958 (Cth): the Refugee Review Tribunal (RRT) and the Migration Review Tribunal (MRT). An attempt was made to establish an exhaustive legislative code of procedure for the two tribunals.[48] As the Explanatory Memorandum to the bill enacting the provisions stated, it 'provides a code for decision-making to replace the current common law rules of natural justice' and aims to 'replace the uncodified principles of natural justice with clear and fixed procedures which are drawn from those principles.'

Despite the explicit wording in the legislation, the High Court, by majority, held that the act did not exclude the common law rules of natural justice.[49] The result was that the failure by the RRT to give an applicant the opportunity to comment on the tribunal's finding that political changes in Bangladesh since the applicant had fled the country made it unlikely he would suffer persecution should he be returned was a breach of the common law rules of natural justice, albeit it was not a requirement under the statutory code. The federal government has since enacted further legislation to negate the impact of the High Court decision, the effect of which has yet to be judicially determined.[50]

Model Procedures for Tribunals

As Mullan has noted, fundamental administrative law issues are raised by the extent of the procedural obligations imposed on tribunals.[51] As in Canada, the procedure of Australian tribunals is generally found in the specific legislation establishing the tribunal. Unlike the position in Canada, however, no Australian jurisdiction has yet introduced template legislation[52] providing generic rules for its tribunals akin to the United States' *Administrative Procedure Act 1946*, or the United Kingdom's *Model Rules of Procedure for Tribunals*.[53]

Prior to the 1970s, Australia had a disparate collection of tribunals with widely varying functions and procedures. The *Report of the Commonwealth Administrative Review Committee* (Kerr Committee Report),[54] which established the framework for modern Australian administrative law, recommended that there should be provisions 'prescribing the minimum procedural standards for all Commonwealth administrative tribunals.'[55] This task was allocated to the Administrative Review Council (ARC), the body set up to monitor the development of a national system of administrative law.[56]

Although most Kerr Committee recommendations were adopted, no general procedure statute for tribunals was ever implemented. The consequence is that variations in tribunal procedure continue to abound and even fundamental procedural issues – the extent of a tribunal's review powers, what standard of proof to apply, who bears an onus of proof, what evidential rules should be adopted – are not prescribed. These procedural issues have been left to individual tribunals to tease out.[57] This they have done, often establishing principles applicable to all Australian tribunals. For example, the AAT established that a tribunal permitted to exercise 'all the powers and discretions of the original decision-maker' exercises contemporaneous not historical review,[58] and that when a tribunal has to meet the 'satisfaction standard' the evidence must at least be probative.[59]

Nonetheless, Australian tribunals still present a spectrum of procedural models. Their processes range from adversarial to investigative, and include mediation, arbitration, and other forms of alternative dispute resolution. Indeed, some tribunals are capable of adopting within the one matter processes from several alternative models.[60] That flexibility has its advantages. At the same time, there are costs since those appearing before a tribunal must ensure they are aware of any procedures peculiar to that particular tribunal.

In light of this situation, it is not surprising that the first project undertaken by the Council of Australasian Tribunals is the development of a practice manual for tribunals. The manual is to list generic principles as well as those governing the operations and jurisdiction of each particular tribunal.[61] It will be interesting to see whether the manual succeeds in setting out common procedural standards, an objective which has so far eluded the tribunal movement in Australia.

The Adversarial/Inquisitorial Debate

In the late 1990s there was considerable dissatisfaction with the adversarial method of tribunal proceedings in Australia.[62] This was evidenced in academic writings[63] and in the request by the Commonwealth attorney-general that, as part of the civil justice inquiry, the ALRC explore the 'civil and administrative law procedures in civil code jurisdictions.'[64] The nub of the 'civil code procedure' element was whether a more inquisitorial style of proceedings could be adopted in Australian courts and tribunals.

In the course of the inquiry the ALRC proposed that there be a legislative obligation on tribunals 'to enquire into any relevant fact in issue where the fact is relied on by an applicant, a finding in relation to that fact is necessary in order for the tribunal to reach its decision, and it is practicable for the tribunal to inquire into that fact.'[65] In the result, faced with hostility on the part of some tribunals, the ALRC watered down its support for a more investigative tribunal model. The final report recommended that '[t]ribunal processes can and should be arranged to permit enhanced inquiry by tribunals, discontinuous hearing processes, and resolution of certain issues on the papers' and '[t]he Commission's proposals in this regard should not be taken to threaten the flexible decision making processes adapted to different types of case.'[66] In other words, the inquiry stopped short of recommending a full-blown investigative model, thus preserving the status quo.

Although some Australian tribunals had been set up to be overtly inquisitorial and have been granted investigative powers,[67] a recent study has concluded that the failure to provide investigative staff and to resource tribunals to carry out investigations, coupled with the strength of the adversarial culture, has stifled the willingness of tribunal members to adopt a more investigative or inquisitorial approach. [68] Despite the legislative intention that these bodies operate in a non-adversarial manner, the opportunities for their members to take a more proactive role in tribunal hearings is availed of infrequently and the 1990s vision of a more investigative tribunal model in Australia is unlikely to materialize.

Other Methods of Dispute Resolution

At the same time, while inquisitorial methods may not have been adopted, there has been an increased focus on alternative methods of dispute resolution. Such processes include mediation, conciliation, arbitration, case appraisal, and neutral evaluation, either on their own or in conjunction with a determination.[69] Alternative dispute resolution (ADR) may be undertaken by external mediators, or carried out in-house, for example, by trained tribunal members or staff. Facilitative techniques such as requiring expert witnesses to give evidence concurrently – the so-called 'hot tub' process – is another technique for assisting parties to compromise on matters in dispute and is increasingly being relied on in cases depending on expert or technical evidence.[70]

These processes can be used to overcome deficiencies in the adversarial system. As Sourdin noted, use of experts in this non-adjudicative role can assist tribunal members who lack technical expertise in a subject area to embrace questioning and discussion techniques, and can facilitate outcomes by dealing with issues beyond the purely legal, such as communication issues or future relationships.[71] These outcomes are consistent with all five objectives for the civil justice system identified by the ALRC during the civil justice inquiry; namely, that the process should be 'just, accessible, efficient, timely and effective.'[72] It is significant in this context that over 80 per cent of cases before the peak general jurisdiction tribunal in Australia, the Commonwealth AAT, settle at the preliminary conference stage of proceedings.[73]

In some jurisdictions, these techniques have been so successful that they are perceived as a threat to the court system. For example, the Queensland Supreme Court was said to be sufficiently concerned about the decline in commercial litigation to suggest the Court 'was prepared to 'compete for more business' by offering to fast track large commercial cases.[74] Members of the bar have also noted a diminution in commercial work as the 'big law firms move strongly into mediation, now a standard requirement for commercial litigation ... preferred by many clients, who see it as a cheaper, private and more predictable way to settle disputes.'[75] So the availability of ADR as tools for tribunals can only enhance their attractiveness to litigants.

However, ADR also has its critics. Mixed responses were given to an empirical survey of Commonwealth officials on the comparative value of external review by courts and tribunals, and alternative dispute resolution. Excluding the high 'no opinion' responses, some 40 percent of respondents agreed or strongly agreed that ADR has a drawback; while only 25.8 percent disagreed or strongly disagreed. Comments included: ADR 'can hide bad compromises or good compromises about originally bad decisions'; 'it also means that unreasoned precedents aren't set'; and one officer argued that 'consent decisions need to be backed by an explanatory minute detailing the reasons for the concession.'[76]

The concerns emerging from these comments raise the fundamental problem with ADR, namely, that dispute settlements are confidential and this detracts from the precedent-setting role of the courts and tribunals. Mediated outcomes are seen also as denying the opportunity for exposure of error by government agencies, permitting officials to continue to make decisions which may be unlawful, and preventing the development of reasoned judgments to guide agency decision-makers.[77] Clearly there are advantages in using alternatives to traditional adjudicative techniques. Deciding native title disputes is one such area, avoiding lengthy commercial litigation and obtaining satisfaction of a grievance against government that does not warrant a formal hearing are others. At the same time, the number of cases in which mediation has been used by the AAT, for example, has not increased in the previous three years.[78] While not doubting the value of ADR in many situations, it is clear that it must be used selectively and that reliance on such techniques will never wholly supplant the adjudicative model.

Tribunals and Independence from the Legislature

Federal and state parliaments exercise control over tribunals in various ways. Aside from the controls exercised during the legislative process, monitoring of tribunals by the legislature occurs regularly. Tribunals must present annual reports, and tribunal executive officers appear before parliamentary committees. Parliamentary committees also inquire into particular issues arising in tribunals. In addition, since tribunals are wholly creatures of statute, the level of independence permitted a tribunal is a matter primarily for the legislature. There can be no quarrel with Mullan's comment that the legislature which creates a tribunal should as a consequence be able to 'hold them to account and, ultimately, to change or abolish them.'[79] Nonetheless, there are limitations.

Constitutional Restrictions on Tribunals

Mention has already been made of constitutional inhibitions on tasks which can be asked of federal tribunals.[80] By contrast, the absence of formal separation of powers limitations has freed state and territory legislatures to grant functions akin to judicial functions to tribunals in a manner which is not possible at the federal level in Australia.

In practice, however, small 'c' constitutional issues, such as the concept of separation of powers, do impinge on state and territory bodies. For example, judicial review powers, traditionally associated with courts, could in theory be bestowed on a state or territory tribunal. Although from time to time there have been suggestions that state and territory tribunals can exercise judicial review powers, to date no Australian legislature has given review powers to a body which is not a court.[81] This inhibition is a tacit recognition of the political value of restricting judicial power to the court system.

Limits of Parliaments' Ability to Mould Tribunals

There are other limitations on parliaments' ability to restrict the powers of tribunals. Legislation is a creature of the democratic process and that process may inhibit legislative change. A spectacular example touching tribunals occurred in Australia at the end of the 1990s. Tribunals which have a national coverage are expensive, particularly when offices are needed in each of the eight state and territory capitals and regional offices are required as well. Nor was it seen as organizationally desirable to have the proliferation of federal specialist tribunals that had occurred since the Kerr Committee reported in 1971.

Following a report of the Administrative Review Council in 1995 into the federal tribunal system,[82] the federal government proposed an ambitious amalgamation of federal tribunals. The existing high-volume, second-tier tribunals were to be merged with the Commonwealth AAT to become the Administrative Review Tribunal (ART). The specialist tribunals were to become divisions of the ART's first tier and there was to be an appellate panel. The two bills to effect this change – the *Administrative Review Tribunal Bill 2000* and the *Administrative Tribunal (Consequential and Transitional) Bill 2000* – were, in combination, the largest package of federal legislation since federation. The work involved in their drafting was prodigious.

The bills were defeated in the Senate, on party lines, on 14 February 2001 – a defeat that was seen as a major blow to the government. The defeat followed extensive criticism in the national media,[83] detailed parliamentary examination,[84] and debate at a one-day seminar, jointly sponsored by the Australian Institute of Administrative Law and the Senate Legal and Constitutional Legislation Committee, held in Parliament House, Canberra, on 25 October 2000, in which the leaders of all the major political parties participated.[85]

Broadly, the attempt foundered because the bills attempted to create an executive-style tribunal that was perceived to restrict the independence of the ART, diminish the quality of review and erode the rights of applicants. To illustrate, the presidency of the ART was to be open to a non-lawyer, in contrast to the position of its predecessor, the AAT, the president of which has always been a judicial officer. The president of the ART was to be a chief executive officer rather than an adjudicator[86]; all members' terms were for fixed and limited terms; the president was to have extensive, non-reviewable powers of direction; there was a contraction of the rights to an oral hearing, to representation, to second-tier merits review, and to decision-making by a multi-member panel; hearings on the papers were to be common; there was to be no statutory qualifications for membership of ART; and the selection of members was not to be by a 'neutral' agency of government, but by the minister of the department the decisions of which were being reviewed.

Ultimately the ART would have been less independent, and there was to be less opportunity for review since review by the appeal panel was strictly limited and the opportunities for review – for example, in the income support area – were thereby reduced. The ultimate irony was that three major federal tribunals – the Veterans' Review Board, and the two migration tribunals (RRT and MRT) – were not to be included under the umbrella of the ART, largely for political reasons. Their omission sounded the death-knell for the proposed amalgamation. If the body was not to be a comprehensive and integrated one, not even the financial benefits of the proposed amalgamation would have materialized. As it transpired, the proposal was perceived as an attack on tribunal independence and this proved unpalatable to the public that voiced its disapproval through the parliamentary process.

Parliaments and Tribunal Independence

On several occasions in recent Australian history, governments faced with under-performing tenured judicial officers or tribunal members have chosen to restructure the institution rather than directly remove those members. For example, when the Commonwealth Conciliation and Arbitration Commission was abolished in 1988 and replaced by the Industrial Relations Commission, all former members, except Justice Staples, were appointed to the new commission. The 'Staples affair' as it was known was criticized for use of the reconstitution device to avoid proper dismissal processes. The practice was seen to breach fair process requirements and to undermine rule of law values. There was a parliamentary report on the matter and not surprisingly a Joint Select Committee of the Commonwealth Parliament recommended guaranteed tenure for members of tribunals.[87] That recommendation has never been implemented and the terms of tribunal members have, on occasions, continued to be shortened, sometimes to an alarming degree.

The securing of the independence of tribunals is a complex issue. Tenure is one aspect; methods and terms of appointment of members and funding are other key issues. Nonetheless, the independence of tribunals is essential if they are creditably to perform their adjudication function and earn the respect of members of the public. As the *Better Decisions* report noted, 'it is crucial that members of the community feel confidence that tribunal members are of the highest standard of competence and integrity, and that they perform their duties free from undue government or other influence.'[88] Parliaments can contribute to that perception by ensuring that the appointments processes of members, and the methods of operation of tribunals, are consistent with these objectives and that terms of members are sufficient to guarantee independence.

Importance of Parliaments' Understanding of Tribunal Operations

The earlier discussion on the inquisitorial/adversarial debate highlighted a signal failure of understanding on the part of the federal Parliament of 'inquisitorial process.' To illustrate, the statutes setting up those Commonwealth tribunals which were intended to operate in an inquisitorial manner – the migration tribunals, the Commonwealth AAT, and the Social Security Appeals Tribunal[89] – have as their objectives that they should operate in a manner which is 'fair, just, economical, informal and quick.'[90]

The problem with this formula is that it comprises two clusters of internally inconsistent objectives.[91] These competing objectives reflect the imperatives for the introduction of tribunals in Australia, namely, the desire to further the speediness and efficiency of hearings in high-volume jurisdictions while not abandoning the traditional adjudicative virtues of fairness and justice. In failing to indicate which of the alternatives – being 'economical, informal and quick' or being 'fair or just' – should take precedence, Parliament has created a conundrum for tribunals. Nor has Parliament furthered the investigative objective for tribunals by ensuring that they are set up with the investigative staff and the funding to undertake that role. Examples of this kind indicate that parliamentary ignorance or insensitivity can hamper tribunal independence and detract from tribunals' stature in the eyes of the public.

Independence of Tribunals from Executive

Mullan's discussion under this topic in 1992 referred to statutory appeals to cabinet, and cabinet and other ministers' directives on general policy as well as issues of tenure and performance appraisal. To these issues he added the response of tribunals to oversight bodies, including the ombudsman. Several differences are apparent between the Canadian and Australian experiences in these areas.

Cabinet and Tribunal Decisions

To an Australian, the focus in Mullan's paper on statutory appeals to and directives by cabinet is alien. Doctrinally, cabinet is a silent actor in the field of administrative law in Australia. The few judicial review cases in which cabinet has played a part[92] have simply noted that since cabinet is not referred to in the relevant legislation there was no doubt that a court could not review the cabinet decision. Moreover, cabinet decisions are regarded as non-justiciable. As Bowen C.J. noted in *Minister for Arts, Heritage and Environment v. Peko-Wallsend Ltd*,[93] '[i]t is to Cabinet that the highest decisions of policy affecting Australian are brought' and it may be 'inappropriate for this court to intervene to set aside a Cabinet decision.'[94]

His Honour went on to say: 'Should the Parliament ever take the step of passing an Act expressly conferring duties or powers and discretions upon Cabinet it would be time to consider whether decisions under such an enactment were open to review by the courts.'[95] In other words, in the absence of any statutory backing for cabinet as a decision-maker in Australia, decisions by cabinet will continue to be implemented through the relevant minister alone. Certainly, the notion of appeals to or statutory directives by cabinet is foreign to an Australian administrative lawyer.

Ombudsman and Tribunal Decisions

A second alien concept relates to ombudsman review of the merits of tribunal decisions. Australian tribunals are accountable to auditors-general and to the ombudsman, both being independent statutory agencies. However, there are statutory limits on the extent to which both the ombudsman and the auditor-general can monitor the decisions of tribunals.

In Canada, tribunals are also subject to supervision by the equivalent supervisory agencies. However, the agencies' jurisdiction over tribunals appears to be more extensive than in Australia. Hence, in 1992 Mullan noted with some dismay that the Ontario Court of Appeal had held that the provincial ombudsman had jurisdiction over the province's system of tribunals.[96] This allowed the ombudsman to scrutinize the merits of tribunal decisions in particular cases. Although the Ontario ombudsman cannot overturn a decision of an administrative tribunal, he or she has wide powers to direct that a tribunal decision be remade according to the findings of the ombudsman's office.[97]

To an Australian, such a role for the ombudsman is simply not possible as the law stands. Legislation prohibits the ombudsman from so acting.[98] The jurisdiction of Australian ombudsman offices relates to 'a matter of administration'[99] and then only of a department or a 'prescribed authority.' The expression 'prescribed authority' has been defined specifically to exclude courts or tribunals. The only exception is administrative action by tribunal officials.[100] Although, from time to time there has been litigation about whether an investigation has related to a 'matter of administration' or has strayed into complaint-handling, and there have been narrow[101] and broader interpretations of what is 'administration,'[102] ombudsman offices have consistently adhered to the principle that they do not investigate tribunal or court decisions.[103]

Although the ombudsman does not review the decisions of tribunals, the obverse is not true. A quirk of the federal *Ombudsman Act 1976* (Cth) is that it authorizes the ombudsman to refer a matter to the Commonwealth AAT for an advisory opinion on a legal question.[104] The power has, however, been exercised once only in nearly thirty years,[105] suggesting that this option was unnecessary in light of other avenues of redress. The infrequency of usage may also explain why this facility has not been replicated in other Australian jurisdictions. A more narrowly focused right may have been more effective. Such a right exists in Ontario, where the Ontario ombudsman can seek a declaratory order from the Ontario Divisional Court but solely on jurisdictional issues relating to review of tribunal decisions.[106]

Government Policy and Tribunals: General

More familiar to an Australian audience is the difficulty posed for tribunals of dealing with issues of government policy. Despite the fact that tribunals exercising merits review are described as 'standing in the shoes' of the primary decision-maker, the shoes are from a different last. In particular, tribunals, being independent statutory bodies, are freed of any obligation to apply government policy. Notwithstanding this freedom, governments continue to attempt to impose policy on tribunals, with varying degrees of success.

The issue of the role of government policy in tribunal decision-making arose early in the life of the Commonwealth AAT. In the absence of any guidance in its legislation, the first president of the Commonwealth AAT, Brennan J., in *Re Drake and Minister for Immigration and Ethnic Affairs (No 2)*[107] devised what have become classical principles to guide tribunals on how to deal with policy. The question in *Drake* concerned deportation policy, a policy that had been developed by the minister for immigration and tabled in Parliament.

While noting that a distinction needed to be drawn between high-level and more routine policy, Brennan J. suggested the following practice should apply, at least when the policy, as it was in *Drake*, had been devised by a minister:[108]

> When the Tribunal is reviewing the exercise of a discretionary power reposed in a Minister, and the Minister has adopted a general policy to guide him in the exercise of the power, the Tribunal will ordinarily apply that policy in reviewing the decision, unless the policy is unlawful or unless its application tends to produce an unjust decision in the circumstances of the particular case. Where the policy would ordinarily be applied, an argument against the policy itself or against its application in the particular case will be considered, but cogent reasons will have to be shown against its application, especially if the policy is shown to have been exposed to Parliamentary scrutiny.

Although this carefully crafted pronouncement has avoided many problems, over time governments have devised other strategies to impose their views on the meaning of legislation on adjudicative bodies.[109] In Victoria, New South Wales, and Western Australia, the legislation establishing the general-jurisdiction tribunals provides that the tribunal is obliged to apply a statement of policy in reviewing a decision, but only if certain preconditions are met. This is the most overt example of government imposing policy on tribunals. The preconditions include that the policy is lawful, and that the relevant minister certifies in writing that the policy was in force at the time the decision was made.[110] This is one approach. A second relates to ministerial directions.

Directions and Tribunals

Particular difficulties have been caused by ministerial or other directions that impact on the decision-making of independent statutory bodies such as tribunals, especially when the directions are authorized by statute. This in turn raises questions about the degree to which the review is an exercise of discretionary judgment. Two issues arise: is the direction simply a policy or guide? If so, generally speaking the discussion above applies, although under a system of responsible government the level of independence permitted an independent body such as a tribunal remains something of a vexed question. Generally, however, the cases have held that the body must still exercise an independent judgment, although the terms of the direction are a relevant consideration.[111]

Second, if the statute couches the power to issue directions in an obligatory form, how should the tribunal respond without compromising its independence? The answer depends on the format of the statutory authorization. In each of the cases referred to, the courts reached a result by a process of statutory construction. If the power is to issue a 'general direction' or a 'direction,' there are conflicting decisions.[112] The specificity of the directions power, the terms of the statute, and the interests affected generally dictate the outcome.[113] Another factor influencing the outcome is whether the statutory power to give directions is required to be tabled in Parliament. Tabling is a safeguard against unnecessary use of such authority and gives an added force to the direction, making it more likely that the tribunal should comply.[114] Other safeguards against misuse of the directions power require ministerial certification or gazettal.[115]

Tenure, Performance Appraisal, and Tribunal Independence

If policy and the ability to issue directions are overt examples of the impact of the executive on tribunal independence, there are other less direct means. Through the appointments process and by appraisal of members' performance the executive possesses a subtle means of exercising authority over tribunal members. Both processes raise perennial issues affecting tribunal independence.[116]

The *Better Decisions* report noted that the terms of tribunal members at the time of the report varied from two to seven years.[117] Given the changing needs of users of tribunals, the Administrative Review Council did not favour tenure for tribunal members. It opted for fixed terms of between three and five years,[118] albeit that such terms should be renewable.[119] While the *Better Decisions* report took the view that independence should be secured by means other than tenurable positions, the report also maintained that the selection and appointment process should be 'rational, merit-based and transparent.'[120]

Claims of political bias and affiliation in tribunal appointments have periodically been made. In response, reports have recommended, for example, that tribunal positions be advertised, that there be a register for those interested in positions, and that there be publicly available selection criteria relevant to the tribunal's functions.[121] Most tribunals now advertise for members, but selection criteria are still not uniformly provided. Some agencies have opened a register for those people interested in tribunal appointment, but it is unclear what use is made of these expressions of interest. Ministers retain the right to veto suggested appointments. Control by the executive of the selection and appointments processes means there is a real possibility government can shape the membership of a tribunal.

A more contentious issue is performance appraisal of members. Tribunals, such as the migration tribunals, have introduced performance measures and targets, and members who consistently fall below these benchmarks may face non-renewal of their terms. For example, in the Migration Review Tribunal the target for a full-time member is 325 cases per year.[122] A caseload of that magnitude means a full-time member would be conducting hearings on most days. Given that the preparation for and writing up of the hearing is time-consuming such a target makes little allowance for administrative and evidential problems and more complex issues.

To its credit, however, the MRT policy does acknowledge the need to take account of the mix of cases, and of changes to work practices or legislation in assessing performance. The tribunal also accepts that it must provide members with information, training and professional development in order to assist them to achieve their targets.[123]

As the Administrative Review Council noted in its discussion paper on merits review:[124]

> too much pressure to conform to an expected norm could threaten members' willingness to fearlessly make what they believe to be the right decision in individual cases. It might also affect the degree of motivation of some members ... Performance is inevitably a consideration when it comes to re-appointment, but if criteria are not clear and public, there will always be a suspicion about the basis of re-appointment decisions.

While advocating performance appraisal schemes for members, the ARC rejected standards involving outcomes in particular cases.[125] In other words, the council was alive to the possibility that if members were required to meet targets this could impact significantly on a member's independence.[126] Similarly, the ALRC in its *Managing Justice* inquiry expressed concern that productivity standards 'may have a direct and very real effect on decisions about how cases are to be conducted.'[127] The commission warned that there could be a resultant loss of confidence in the tribunal review process and an increased number of judicial review applications if productivity standards which focused on outcomes in particular cases were to be introduced.

Setting clear timelines for handing down decisions is important. Having targets also provides certainty for members and an incentive to improve performance. On the other hand, there is a concomitant obligation on the part of management to undertake training of members to ensure that they have the requisite skills to meet these requirements. A balance must be maintained between these competing pressures to avoid a diminution of members' independence.

Independence of Tribunals from Courts

In 1992 Mullan described the relationship between courts and tribunals in Canada as one of 'considerable tension,'[128] a description that applies equally today in the antipodes. The reasons are complex, but one of them is that the courts, as Mullan appreciated, see tribunals 'as a challenge to their own adjudicative authority.'[129] A graphic illustration is the Chief Justice of the Supreme Court of Victoria's description of administrative tribunals as 'the tiger in the jungle.'[130]

Self-preservation may be one motivation for the courts' concerns; disinterested belief in their role as tribunal monitor is another. The predominant motivation is the second. History has shown that the courts jealously guard their right to supervise tribunals. Their tenacity is evident in the cases following the introduction of a comprehensive privative clause in the *Migration Act 1958* (Cth).[131] At odds with this position is the fact that courts will, on occasions, defer to the decisions of tribunal, thus illustrating another and important strand in this complex relationship.

Judicial Monitoring of Tribunals

The role of the courts in controlling the exercise of their powers by tribunals is an ancient one, tied to the prerogative writs. The authority to issue the writs was granted to the supreme courts of the Australian colonies when they were established. Sourced initially in letters patent, the jurisdiction was gradually expanded, initially by charters of justice, and later by legislation passed first by the imperial Parliament and then by local legislatures. The upshot is that the jurisdiction of the state superior courts – their inherent jurisdiction – came to parallel that of the common law courts in England.[132] Superior courts set up by statute such as the High Court of Australia,[133] the Federal Court of Australia,[134] the Federal Magistrates Court[135] and the supreme courts of the territories also have been granted the prerogative writ jurisdiction.[136]

The courts have relied on their inherent or statutory judicial review powers to police tribunal decision-making. Indeed, so rigorous was the Federal Court for a period that the judges were criticized by the High Court for being too zealous – by concerning themselves with the 'looseness in the language ... [and] with unhappy phrasing' of the reasons of the administrative decision-maker.[137] The High Court noted: 'The reasons of an administrative decision-maker are meant to inform and not to be scrutinised upon over-zealous judicial review by seeking to discern whether some inadequacy may be gleaned from the way in which the reasons are expressed.'[138]

The danger of this over-zealous analysis of reasons is that the superior court is stepping outside its judicial review role and hence intruding into the area of merits review.[139] Any blurring of the boundaries between judicial review (the purview of the courts) and merits review (the province of tribunals) has consistently been eschewed by the highest Australian courts,[140] not least because Australia has a well-developed system of merits review and the separation of powers doctrine applies strictly in the federal arena.[141]

The control exercised by the courts is also apparent in the more demanding standards imposed on tribunals than on inferior courts. The prerogative writ jurisdiction permits superior courts to review both inferior courts and tribunals for jurisdictional error. Two strands of jurisprudence about jurisdictional error are discernible. The narrower conception of jurisdictional error, requiring error in relation to a statutory precondition to the exercise of the power, was applied to lower level courts.[142] By contrast, for tribunals, the High Court applied the wider conception of jurisdictional error, accepting that jurisdictional error could be committed by a tribunal at any stage of decision-making.[143]

The justifications given by the Court for this differential treatment is the lesser training and judicial experience of tribunal members and that tribunals are not subject to any formal doctrine of precedent. As the High Court expressed it in *Craig v. South Australia*:[144]

> Putting to one side some anomalous exceptions, the inferior courts of this country are constituted by persons with either formal legal qualifications or practical legal training. They exercise jurisdiction as part of a hierarchical legal system entrusted with the administration of justice under the

> Commonwealth and State constitutions. In contrast, the tribunals other than courts which are amenable to certiorari are commonly constituted, wholly or partly, by persons without formal legal qualifications or legal training. While normally subject to administrative review procedures and prima facie bound to observe the requirements of procedural fairness, they are not part of the ordinary hierarchical judicial structure.

The High Court's attitude reflects an apparent lack of confidence in the quality of tribunal adjudication and this has been a persistent view of tribunals by the judiciary. Admittedly the views are not held universally by judges, nor applied uniformly. Otherwise, Australian courts could never have adopted a form of deference to tribunal decisions. Nonetheless, the more demanding standards imposed on tribunals reflects a distrust of them by some judges. Negative comments by the judiciary about tribunal judgments and competence has the potential to downgrade the impact of their jurisprudence. In turn this may have an adverse impact on the stature of tribunals in the eyes of the public, and is capable of undermining their effectiveness as adjudicators.

Deference

In light of these attitudes, it is not surprising that the High Court has denied that Australia has a formal doctrine of deference[145] in the sense in which that term is used in the United States[146] and in Canada.[147] Courts are unlikely to approve of a tribunal's decisions when they are anxious to preserve their supervisory role and remain sceptical of the competence of tribunal members. Despite these attitudes, there is a practical doctrine of deference in Australia in the sense that judges do defer to the opinions and decisions of tribunals in certain situations. As the court noted in *Corporation of the City of Enfield v. Development Assistance Commission*:[148]

> The weight to be given to the opinion of the tribunal in a particular case will depend upon the circumstances. These will include such matters as the field in which the tribunal operates, the criteria for appointment of its members, the materials upon which it acts in exercising its functions and the extent to which its decisions are supported by disclosed processes of reasoning.

Given that in practice judges do on occasions defer to tribunal decisions, the questions posed are: Deference to what? Or to whom? The answers to these questions could be either deference to an agency's interpretation of the legislation Parliament has directed it to administer, or deference to the special position, expertise, or skill of the decision-maker.[149]

Australian judges have generally declined to defer to tribunals' interpretation of legislation. They regard that function as a peculiarly appropriate element of their judicial role. The view is bolstered by the separation of powers doctrine, and the fact that under the Constitution Chapter III courts alone can make authoritative and conclusive decisions on issues of law. As the full court of the Federal Court said in *Tracy v. Repatriation Commission:*[150]

> This court respects the administrator's competence in the area of the ascertainment of the facts in all cases where the court exercises the jurisdiction conferred upon it to carry out the judicial review of decisions; it is the administrator's duty to respect the court's position as interpreter and guardian of the relevant law.

There is, however, a long-established practice in Australia of deferring to the practical and factual decisions, and on occasions to matters of statutory interpretation, of specialist tribunals. Such an approach necessitates a restrictive interpretation of judicial review. This is particularly noticeable in relation to decisions on industrial relations matters, as illustrated by comments made by several members of the High Court in *Attorney-General for Queensland v. Riordan:*[151]

> If the [Australian Industrial Arbitration] Commission proposes to exercise powers of conciliation and arbitration by reason of the Commission's opinion that a 'threatened, impending or probable industrial dispute' exists, a court on an application for prohibition must give great weight to that opinion. The Commission is far better equipped than a court to assess the industrial situation ...
>
> Practical consideration will demand that considerable deference be paid to the opinion of the Commission in its ascertainment of the existence or absence of a dispute, the matters in dispute and the parties to a dispute. The establishment of the Commission as an independent tribunal with specialized jurisdiction, constituted by members with appropriate expertise, provides one reason for this latitude. Another is the organization of the Commission, with industry panels within which members may acquire

general knowledge about the background to claims not easily reproduced by evidence in formal proceedings.

Similar comments have been made about the skills and experience of administrators,[152] the technical expertise of trademarks tribunals,[153] professional disciplinary tribunals,[154] and ministers of the crown.[155]

Deference is another name for judicial restraint in the scrutiny of administrative reasons, discussed earlier. If reasons statements are the principal means of discovering jurisdictional errors, it follows that courts have no option but to examine reasons to decide whether an error has been made. At the same time, as the *Wu Shan Liang* case[156] demonstrated, the courts must beware of trespassing into the field of merits review. The courts have shown that they appreciate that Australia has an extensive system of merits review and, as a consequence, often demonstrate restraint where administrative decisions are amenable to a comprehensive appeal on the merits.[157] So, in practice, the exercise of restraint is more common than might be expected in a country which ostensibly denies the existence of any formal deference doctrine.[158]

Privative Clauses

For a court to choose to refrain from exercising its review powers is one thing; for Parliament to restrict the role of courts is quite another. The effect of a privative clause is to deny or limit the courts' supervisory jurisdiction. The courts generally resist this for two reasons: the judges see any reduction of their role as inimical to their constitutional task of policing the legality of administrative action; they are also wary of permitting tribunal members to make final and authoritative decisions.[159] The consequence is that courts generally view privative clauses with suspicion and read them restrictively where possible.

In relation to the High Court of Australia, this view is supported by the constitutionally guaranteed judicial review jurisdiction of that court under section 75(v) of the Constitution. As Mason A.C.J. and Brennan J. commented in *R v. Coldham; Ex parte Australian Workers' Union*, '[t]he jurisdiction of the Court conferred by section 75(v) of the Constitution to grant mandamus and prohibition directed to an officer of the Commonwealth cannot be ousted by a privative clause.'[160]

Of course, this constitutional guarantee of the High Court's jurisdiction is in conflict with parliamentary sovereignty. Nonetheless, compromise solutions have been reached. In the *Hickman* case, the High

Court recognized the effectiveness of the privative clause to oust the court's jurisdiction provided 'the purported exercise is a *bona fide* attempt to exercise the power, it relates to the subject matter of the legislation, and it is reasonably capable of being referred to in the power (that is, does not on its face go beyond the power).'[161] Moreover, the Court acknowledged that the guarantee in section 75(v) was only to the grant of the remedies and was 'silent about the circumstances in which the [constitutional] writs may issue.'[162] That was left to the general law to determine.[163]

Defining the limits of these two approaches has been the focus of judicial attention on migration legislation.[164] The federal Parliament sought to restrict judicial review of migration decisions by enacting a comprehensive form of privative clause to oust the jurisdiction of the Federal Court and, with limited exceptions,[165] the High Court. That would have given unsupervised decision-making powers to the migration tribunals. This attempt foundered in the High Court of Australia. In *Plaintiff S157/2002 v. Commonwealth*,[166] that court retained its review role over most migration decisions by affirming that a privative clause cannot oust the jurisdiction of the High Court to review an administrative decision for jurisdictional error.[167]

A key question remained, however. What is jurisdictional error for this purpose? Was it to be the narrow or the broader version of jurisdictional error referred to earlier? Or was it to be a new species of jurisdictional error with a constitutional flavour reflecting the renaming by the High Court of the prerogative writs referred to in section 75(v) as 'constitutional writs'?[168] Jurisdictional error is undefined, and cases since *Plaintiff S157/2002* have focused on the circumstances that will attract the section 75(v) jurisdiction.[169] The outcome is to be determined in each case as a matter of statutory construction. Nonetheless, there are certain bedrock errors which are jurisdictional for the purpose of section 75(v) review: fraud, bad faith, breaches of natural justice which impact on the outcome, jurisdictional errors which are critical to the outcome, and errors of law which indicate a lack of understanding by a decision-maker of their role.[170]

The result is that, in the exercise of its section 75(v) powers, the High Court is unlikely to permit a privative clause to exclude its review of a tribunal decision in which one of these errors has had a significant effect on the decision. Whether other courts, the jurisdiction of which is not constitutionally guaranteed, will follow the High Court's lead is not yet determined. In cases in which a 'Commonwealth officer'[171] or 'the Commonwealth'[172] is involved, there would be little point in taking a different view given that the matter could always be taken to the High Court. For decisions not involving the Commonwealth, a different interpretation may be adopted. In summary, Australian courts tend to resist any diminution of their review powers, even in the face of a privative clause, thus preserving their role of policing tribunals' decision-making powers.

Independence of Tribunals as Protected by Rights Jurisprudence and Bill of Rights

Tribunals in Canada and Australia do not have any constitutionally guaranteed status.[173] Nonetheless, as Mullan pointed out in relation to the *Canadian Bill of Rights* (1960) and the *Canadian Charter of Rights and Freedoms* (1982), there may be some constitutional protection embedded in those instruments.

In Canada, both section 2(e) of the *Bill of Rights* and section 11 of the *Charter* establish the right to adjudication by an 'independent and impartial' tribunal. However, that right can only be invoked when the person claiming the right has been charged with a criminal offence.[174] At the same time, as Mullan noted,[175] some judges on the Canadian Supreme Court have interpreted 'fundamental justice' in section 7 of the *Charter*[176] as having ramifications for proceedings other than criminal proceedings.[177] The question of what amounts to fundamental justice arises when the 'life, liberty and security of the person' is affected. Mullan hypothesized that this may have ramifications for the security of tenure of tribunals since certain standards of independence apply to arbiters (whether judicial or tribunal members) under section 11 of the *Charter*.[178] Several Canadian scholars, however, have noted the limited impact of section 7 on administrative decision-making.[179]

What relevance has this for Australia since it has no bill of rights, nor an equivalent to the Canadian *Charter of Rights and Freedoms*? One Australian jurisdiction, the Australian Capital Territory (ACT), has recently enacted rights legislation. Since there are parallels between this legislation and the Canadian *Charter*, a comparison with the Canadian position is instructive, not least because there is as yet a paucity of jurisprudence on the impact of the ACT's new law.

Rights in Australia

It had long been bemoaned in some quarters that Australia is among the few developed nations not to have introduced a bill of rights.[180]

That is no longer true with the advent in the ACT of the *Human Rights Act 2004* (HRA). A central provision in that act is the requirement that '[i]n working out the meaning of a Territory law, an interpretation that is consistent with human rights is as far as possible to be preferred.'[181] As that muted obligation indicates, the effect of the HRA is intended not to be intrusive. In addition, there may be constitutional restrictions on the exercise by the ACT Supreme Court of its powers under the HRA. As Stellios points out these restrictions take three forms:[182]

> First, that the conferral of the declaration power on the ACT Supreme Court might be invalid as either contrary to the *Kable* doctrine[183] or outside the scope of authority conferred by the *Australian Capital Territory (Self-Government) Act 1988* (Cth). Secondly, that it may not be possible to appeal an exercise of power under the declaration provision to a federal court.[184] Thirdly, that following the High Court decision in *Wilson v Minister for Aboriginal and Torres Strait Islander Affairs*,[185] Federal Court judges could not sit as judges of the ACT Supreme Court when called upon to exercise the power in s 32 ...Central to all three constitutional problems is the proposition that an exercise of power under s 32 [HRA] does not involve the exercise of Commonwealth judicial power.

Features of the legislation are that breaches of the rights[186] result in no more than a declaration of incompatibility by the ACT Supreme Court, to which a response must be provided by the territory's attorney-general.[187] International law may be considered in interpreting the human rights standards.[188] However, the introduction of such material must be weighed against the desirability of relying on the ordinary meaning of the legislation, of not prolonging proceedings, and whether the international material interpreting the international norms is readily accessible.[189] A committee of the ACT Parliament scrutinizes bills and subordinate legislation against the human rights standards in the act.[190] A failure of a bill to comply with the human rights standards in the act, however, does not invalidate the operation of any territory law.[191]

An assessment of the effect of the HRA on tribunals requires an examination of section 18 of the act. That provision states:

> 18(1) Everyone has the right to liberty and security of person. In particular, no-one may be arbitrarily arrested or detained.
> (2) No-one may be deprived of liberty, except on the grounds and in accordance with the procedures established by law.

The comparable provisions in the Canadian *Charter* are sections 7–9, which state:

> 7. Everyone has the right to life, liberty and security of the person and the right not to be deprived thereof except in accordance with the principles of fundamental justice.
> 8. Everyone has the right to be secure against unreasonable search or seizure.
> 9. Everyone has the right not to be arbitrarily detained or imprisoned.

Despite the apparent breadth of scope of sections 7–9 of the *Charter*, Peter Hogg has noted that '[t]he Charter of Rights has not had much direct influence on administrative law, because ... most administrative tribunals or officials do not dispose of the "life, liberty and security of the person" guaranteed by section 7.'[192]

That view could be echoed in relation to s. 18 of the HRA. Indeed, the position is even weaker in relation to the HRA since the reference to 'the procedures established by law' (s. 18(2)) is more specific and therefore less open to interpretation than 'the principles of fundamental justice' in section 7 of the *Charter*. And in Canada even 'the principles of fundamental justice' has only been argued to raise a possibility of importing administrative standards, including those affecting the independence of tribunal decision-making.[193]

In summary, the relevance of s. 18 of the HRA for the independence of tribunals is doubtful for these reasons: tribunals for the most part do not make decisions about 'liberty and security,' there is no explicit requirement in the HRA for the independence of tribunals, the Canadian jurisprudence is ambivalent about the administrative law impact of their equivalent provisions, and the language of s. 18 suggests that the HRA is unlikely to have an impact in this area. However, it is too soon to conclude definitively whether these assessments will be borne out in practice.

Integrity Arm of Government

Mullan's 1992 paper had as an overarching theme the place of tribunals in the structure of government. That structure has traditionally been categorized into three arms: the legislative, the executive and the judicial arms of government. Institutional integrity between the three is facilitated by maintaining a degree of separation between them – the traditional Montesquieuan view. Recent discussions have indicated that this view of the shape of government may need revision.

While it has long been accepted that the separation is imperfect because incomplete, there are other problems with the 'Trinitarian' division. Many of the institutions of government fit awkwardly into the tripartite structure. As Spigelman C.J. of the New South Wales Court of Appeal noted in a recent national lecture series, there is a group of institutions which largely operate outside the orthodox triumvirate:[194]

> over the years a number of ... institutions have, by legislation and practice, developed an independence which has become institutionalized and often entrenched. Such institutions perform supervisory rules with respect to each of the other three branches, legislative, executive or judicial – although most are concerned with the Executive.

Spigelman C.J. identified such institutions as the auditor-general, anti-corruption bodies, ombudsman offices, integrity commissions, royal commissions, inquiries into corrupt or improper conduct, statutory rights to information, and rights to make public sector disclosures.[195]

His Honour did not mention tribunals, but it is arguable that they too should be covered by the integrity arm umbrella. Although tribunals are often categorized as an element of the executive arm, this too is inaccurate. Tribunals are neither part of the judicial arm, nor, since they are exempted from requirements which apply to officials such as compliance with policy, are they part of the executive. Tribunals, since they do not fit easily into the traditional three arms of government, but are, at the same time, a key accountability mechanism, deserve a place in the integrity or fourth branch of government.

That view has been endorsed by John McMillan, prominent administrative law scholar and presently federal ombudsman, who listed in addition to the institutions and rights referred to by Spigelman C.J.: 'administrative tribunals, ... privacy commissioners, ... information commissioners, human rights and anti-discrimination commissions, public service standards commissioners, and inspectors-general of taxation, security intelligence and military discipline.'[196]

Classifying these institutions outside the tripartite division of powers avoids the previous political malformation. At the same time, viewing them as a collective invites the question: What characteristics do they have in common? Some of those have been identified earlier. Spigelman C.J. nominated independence, and performance of a supervisory role, usually in relation to the executive. McMillan referred to 'legal compliance, good decision-making and improved public administration' in conjunction leading to 'institutional integrity.'[197]

Placing tribunals in the company of these integrity branch institutions will only be accepted if tribunals possess the majority of these characteristics. Certainly tribunals are involved in assessment of whether decisions are lawful and meet administrative law standards. Underlying these standards is the objective of encouraging good decision-making and improving public administration. In sum, these functions are part of tribunals' supervisory role. On these grounds tribunals certainly qualify for membership.

Conclusion

Whether tribunals are included in a fourth branch under any new allocation of government powers is one issue. At present even the notion of a fourth arm is embryonic, much less which institutions of government should be included. However, if that suggestion is accepted, it would follow that similar protection for tribunals to that provided to other bodies suggested for the integrity arm would need to be instituted. For example, methods of appointments, tenure and length of terms of members, whether terms of members are renewable, performance appraisal of members and to which bodies (Parliament, a neutral agency?), in addition to the courts, would tribunals be accountable, are all matters which trench on their independence. Funding sources, which have not hitherto been discussed, also play a role. Finally, the attitude towards, degree of understanding of, and respect accorded to, tribunals by the other arms of government also affects their independence. At present, these are areas in which tribunals are most vulnerable.

If tribunals are to take their place as one of the integrity branch institutions, it is in these areas that thought and work is needed. The juxtaposition of tribunals with the other integrity arm institutions confirms what earlier discussions in this paper have identified. Complex and subtle though these issues may be it is essential to tribunal independence that satisfactory solutions to them be assured.

NOTES

I was assisted in the preparation of this paper by Elizabeth Southwood, whose work I gratefully acknowledge.

1 The papers were published in Robin Creyke, ed., *Administrative Tribunals: Taking Stock* (Canberra: Faculty of Law, Australian National University, 1992) [Creyke, *Administrative Tribunals*].

2 David Mullan, 'Where Do Tribunals Fit into the System of Administration and Adjudication? – A Canadian Perspective' in ibid. at 1 [Mullan, 'A Canadian Perspective'].

3 Australian Law Reform Commission, *Review of the Adversarial System of Litigation: Federal Tribunal Proceedings* (Sydney: Issue Paper 24, 1998) at paras 2.1–2.9 [ALRC, *Federal Tribunal Proceedings*]. See also Robin Creyke, 'Overview' in Creyke, *Administrative Tribunals, supra* note 1 at iii [Creyke, 'Overview'].

4 *Brodyn Pty Ltd t/as Time Cost and Quality v. Davenport & Anor,* [2004] N.S.W.C.A. 394 (3 November 2004), a payment claim made under the *Building and Construction Industry Security of Payment Act 1999* (NSW).

5 E.g., the Human Rights and Equal Opportunity Commission and the National Native Title Tribunal.

6 ALRC, *Federal Tribunal Proceedings, supra* note 3 at para. 2.4.

7 Justice Robert Fisher, 'Improving Tribunals' Decisions and Reasons' [2003] N.Z. Law Rev. 517 at 534.

8 Creyke, 'Overview,' *supra* note 3 at iii.

9 ALRC, *Federal Tribunal Proceedings, supra* note 3 at para. 2.6.

10 Ibid. at para. 12.2.

11 *Administrative Law Act 1978* (Vic.), s. 2. Surprisingly, this definition excludes the major Victorian tribunal, the Victorian Civil and Administrative Tribunal, which is headed by a Supreme Court judge.

12 *Legislation Act 2001* (A.C.T.), Sch. 1 – Dictionary.

13 A body that is to replicate the Council of Canadian Administrative Tribunals.

14 *Constitution of the Council of Australasian Tribunals,* cl. 2(1).

15 David J. Mullan, 'Alternatives to Judicial Review of Administrative Action – The Commonwealth of Australia's Administrative Appeals Tribunal' (1983) 43 R. du B. 569.

16 T. Ison, *The Administrative Appeals Tribunal of Australia: A Study Paper Prepared for the Law Reform Commission of Canada* (Ottawa: Law Reform Commission of Canada, 1989) indicated tepid support for the notion, but the suggestion was never adopted.

17 ALRC, *Federal tribunal proceedings, supra* note 3 at paras 2.1–2.9.

18 Northern Territory Law Reform Committee, *Report on the Review of Administrative Decisions and an Administrative Tribunal* (Darwin: September 2004); Queensland Parliament Legal, Constitutional and Administrative Review

Committee, *The Accessibility of Administrative Justice* Discussion Paper (December 2005) at [3.2]. See also Robin Creyke, 'Tribunals and Access to Justice' (2002) 2 Queensland University of Technology L.J. 67.

19 *Conciliation and Arbitration Act 1904* (Cth).

20 *R v. Kirby; Ex parte Boilermakers' Society of Australia* (1956), 94 C.L.R. 254 [*Boilermakers'* case]. See generally Fiona Wheeler, 'The *Boilermaker*'s Case' in H.P. Lee and George Winterton, eds, *Australian Constitutional Landmarks* (Cambridge: Cambridge University Press, 2003) at 160.

21 Tina Crisafulli, 'Conciliation and arbitration' in T. Blackshield, M. Coper and G. Williams, eds, *The Oxford Companion to the High Court of Australia* (Melbourne: Oxford University Press, 2001) at 129.

22 ALRC, *Federal Tribunal Proceedings, supra* note 3; Australian Law Reform Commission, *Review of the Federal Civil Justice System* (Sydney: Discussion Paper No. 62, 1999) [ALRC, *Civil Justice System*]; Australian Law Reform Commission, *Managing Justice: A review of the federal civil justice system* (Sydney: Report No. 89, 1999) [ALRC, *Managing Justice*]. Note, however, that the current federal government has proposed to give the wage setting role of the AIRC to a new Australian Fair Pay Commission. Other existing functions are to be retained by the AIRC. The shape of the proposed legislation is currently being determined.

23 Mullan, 'A Canadian Perspective,' *supra* note 2 at 2.

24 Established under the *Trade Practices Act 1965* (Cth), continued under the *Trade Practices Act 1974* (Cth). Prior to 1995, the Australian Competition Tribunal was known as the Trade Practices Tribunal.

25 http://www.austlii.edu.au/au/cases/cth/ACompT/recent.cases.html.

26 *Federal Court of Australia, Annual Report 2003–04* (Canberra: 2004), App. 5, at 129.

27 *Qantas Airways Ltd*, [2004] A.Comp.T. 9.

28 *Application by East Australia Pipeline Ltd*, [2004] A.Comp.T. 8; *Application by Orica Ic Assets Ltd Re Moomba to Sydney Gas Pipeline System*, [2004] A.Comp.T. 2; *Application by GasNet Australia (Operations) Pty Ltd*, [2003] A.Comp.T. 6.

29 *Australian Association of Pathology Practices Inc*, [2004] A.Comp.T. 4.

30 *Nursing Agreement Association of Australia*, [2003] A.Comp.T. 2.

31 *Re EFTPOS Interchange Fees Agreement*, [2004] A.Comp.T. 7.

32 Justin Gleeson, 'Administrative Law Meets the Regulatory Agencies: Tournament of the Incompatible?' (2005) 44 AIAL Forum 28; John Tamblyn, 'Administrative Law Meets the Regulatory Agencies: Tournament of the Incompatible?' (2005) 44 AIAL Forum 39; Robin Creyke, 'Current and Future Challenges in Judicial Review Jurisdiction: A Comment' (2003) 37 AIAL Forum 42.

33 *Precision Data Holdings v. Wills* (1991), 173 C.L.R. 167 at 188–90 [*Precision Data*]; *Wilkinson v. Clerical Administrative and Related Employees Superannuation Pty Ltd* (1998), 152 C.L.R. 332 [*Wilkinson*].

34 *Huddart Parker & Co Pty Ltd v. Moorehead* (1909), 8 C.L.R. 330 at 357 [*Huddart Packer*]; *R v. Coldham; Ex parte Australian Workers Union* (1983), 153 C.L.R. 415 at 419 and 427–28; *Brandy v. Human Rights and Equal Opportunity Commission* (1995), 183 C.L.R. 245 at 258 [*Brandy*].

35 *Huddart Parker, supra* note 34 at 357.

36 *Boilermakers'* case, *supra* note 20.

37 *Sex Discrimination and Other Legislation Amendment Act 1992* (Cth) and *Law and Justice Legislation Amendment Act 1993* (Cth).

38 *Attorney-General (Commonwealth) v. Breckler* (1999) 197 C.L.R. 83 at 110, per Gleeson C.J., Gaudron, McHugh, Gummow, Hayne and Callinan JJ [*Breckler*].

39 *Brandy, supra* note 34.

40 A. Blackshield and G. Williams, *Australian Constitutional Law and Theory: Commentary and Materials*, 3rd ed. (Sydney: Federation Press, 2002) at 627.

41 *Clyne v. East* (1967), 68 S.R.(N.S.W.) 385; *Building Construction Employees and Builders' Labourers Federation of New South Wales v. Minister for Industrial Relations* (1986), 7 N.S.W.L.R. 372.

42 *Precision Data, supra* note 33 at 188; *Rola Co (Aust) Pty Ltd v. Commonwealth* (1945), 69 C.L.R. 185 at 203.

43 *Drake v. Minister for Immigration and Ethnic Affairs* (1979), 46 F.L.R. 409; *Hilton v. Wells* (1985), 157 C.L.R. 57; *Grollo v. Palmer* (1995), 184 C.L.R. 348.

44 *Wilkinson, supra* note 33.

45 *Superannuation (Resolution of Complaints) Act 1993* (Cth).

46 *Breckler, supra* note 38.

47 (1995) 130 A.L.R. 163.

48 *Migration Act 1958* (Cth), Division 3, Subdivision AB.

49 *Re Minister for Immigration and Multicultural Affairs; Ex parte Miah* (2001), 206 C.L.R. 57.

50 *Migration Legislation Amendment (Procedural Fairness) Act 2002* (Cth).

51 Mullan, 'A Canadian Perspective,' *supra* note 2 at 3.

52 See Margaret Allars, 'A General Tribunal Procedure Statute for New South Wales?' (1993) 4 P.L.R. 19 (comparing the situation in New South Wales with that in Ontario).

53 Council on Tribunals, *Model Rules of Procedure for Tribunals* (London: Report Cm 1434, 1991).

54 *Commonwealth Administrative Review Committee Report 1971* (Canberra: Parliamentary Paper No. 144 of 1971) [Kerr Committee report].

55 Ibid. at 101.

56 Ibid. at 117.

57 John McMillan, 'Merit Review and the AAT: A Concept Develops' in John McMillan, ed., *The AAT – Twenty Years Forward: Passing a Milestone in Commonwealth Administrative Review* (Canberra: Administrative Appeals Tribunal/Australian Institute of Administrative Law/Law Faculty, Australian National University, 1998) at 32.

58 Subject only to specific legislation to the contrary. For cases establishing this principle; see *Re Greenham and Minister for Capital Territory* (1979), 2 A.L.D. 137.

59 *Re Pochi and Minister for Immigration and Ethnic Affairs* (1979), 2 A.L.D. 33.

60 E.g., although Commonwealth AAT hearings tend to be adversarial, hearings are preceded by one or two preliminary conferences which are towards the inquisitorial end of the spectrum, and use of mediation is increasing at the tribunal: *Administrative Appeals Tribunal Annual Report 2003–04* (Canberra: Commonwealth of Australia, 2003–4), App. 3 at Table 3.9 [*AAT Annual Report*].

61 Ibid. at 42 and 47.

62 Australian Law Reform Commission, *Review of the Adversarial System of Litigation: Rethinking the Federal Civil Litigation System Issues* (Canberra: Australian Law Reform Commission, Paper No. 20, 1997) at paras 1.5–1.13 [ALRC, *Rethinking the System*].

63 Two texts of conference papers were produced at Griffith University: H. Stacy and M. Lavarch, eds, *Beyond the Adversarial System* (Sydney: The Federation Press, 1999); and C. Sampford, S. Blencowe, and S. Condlin, eds, *Educating Lawyers for a Less Adversarial System* (Sydney: Federation Press, 1999). See also A. Creighton, 'An Adversarial System: A constitutional requirement' (1999) 74 Reform 65; Sir Anthony Mason, 'Future of Adversarial Justice' (2000) 27 Brief 20.

64 ALRC, *Managing Justice*, *supra* note 22 at 3 (Terms of Reference).

65 ALRC, *Civil Justice System*, *supra* note 22 at para. 9.54.

66 Ibid. at para. 9.14.

67 E.g., to require the production of documents and to summon witnesses.

68 N. Bedford and R. Creyke, *Inquisitorial Processes in Australian Tribunals* (Melbourne: Australian Institute of Judicial Administration, 2006) at 49–51.

69 All these ADR methods, together with conferencing under the auspices of a trained conference registrar, are now forms of dispute resolution available to the Commonwealth AAT: *Administrative Appeals Tribunal Amendment Act 2005* (Cth), s. 3, Sch. 1 (amending s. 3(1) of the principal act).

70 Sofia Frew and Michael Sassella, 'Concurrent Expert Evidence in the AAT:

The NSW Experience' in S. Argument, ed., *Administrative Law: Problem Areas – Reflections on Practice* (proceedings of the Australian Institute of Administrative Law National Forum for 2003, forthcoming).

71 T. Sourdin, 'Facilitating the resolution of disputes before tribunal' (paper presented at the 8th annual Australian Institute of Judicial Administration Tribunals Conference, Sydney, 9–10 June 2005) at 14–15 [Sourdin, 'Facilitating'].

72 ALRC, *Rethinking the System, supra* note 62 at paras 3.9–3.18.

73 *AAT Annual Report, supra* note 60 at App. 3, Table 3.4.

74 Sourdin, 'Facilitating,' *supra* note 71 at 5, citing (2002) 5 A.D.R. Bulletin 16, referring in turn to the *Brisbane Courier Mail* (16 April 2002).

75 Lucinda Schmidt, 'Too quiet, so bar takes advice,' *Australian Financial Review,* 4 November 2005 at 52.

76 Robin Creyke and John McMillan, 'Executive Perceptions of Administrative Law – An Empirical Study' (2002) 9 Aust. J. of Admin. L. 174.

77 Ibid. at 174.

78 *AAT Annual Report, supra* note 60 at App. 3, Table 3.9.

79 Mullan, 'A Canadian Perspective,' *supra* note 2 at 5.

80 See *supra* text accompanying notes 33 to 47.

81 The Hon. Mr Paul Whelan, Minister for Police, Second Reading Speech for the *Administrative Decisions Tribunal Bill 1997,* N.S.W. Legislative Assembly, *Hansard Debates* (29 May 1997) at 9605.

82 Administrative Review Council, *Better Decisions: Review of Commonwealth Merits Review Tribunals* (Canberra: Report No. 39, 1995) [ARC, *Better Decisions*].

83 E.g., *Sydney Morning Herald,* 20 March 1997 at 3; *Canberra Times,* 28 April 1997 at 1; *Sydney Morning Herald,* 30 June 1997 at 16; *Australian Financial Review,* 30 June 1997 at 3; *Brisbane Courier Mail,* 1 July 1997 at 3; *Australian,* 1 July 1997 at 5; *Australian Financial Review,* 1 July 1997 at 4; *West Australian,* 1 July 1997 at 30; *Australian,* 2 July 1997 at 1 and 4; *Sydney Morning Herald,* 5 July 1997 at 39; *ABC Radio National,* 'The Law Report,' 22 July 1997, transcript, 1–10.

84 Department of the Parliamentary Library, Bills Digest No. 40, 2000–01 *Administrative Review Tribunal Bill 2000,* 7 September 2000; Bills Digest No. 80, 2000–01 *Administrative Review Tribunal (Consequential and Transitional Provisions) Bill 2000,* 7 February 2001; Senate Legal and Constitutional Legislation Committee, *Inquiry into the Provisions of the Administrative Review Tribunal Bill 2000 and the Provisions of the Administrative Review Tribunal (Consequential and Transitional Provisions) Bill 2000,* February 2001 (a majority report).

85 The proceedings are published in (2000) 27 AIAL Forum, and comprise that entire volume.

86 This issue has now been resolved. All general jurisdiction administrative tribunals in Australia, with the exception of the AAT in the Australian Capital Territory, are headed by a statutorily appointed judicial officer.

87 *Report of the Joint Select Committee on Tenure of Appointees to Commonwealth Tribunals* (Canberra: Parliamentary Paper 289, 1989).

88 Ibid. at para. 4.4.

89 The only tribunal that lacks this statutory objective is the Veterans' Review Board. It is safe to say, however, that the Veterans' Review Board would regard these objectives as applying to it also.

90 This statutory formula applies to the Social Security Appeals Tribunal and both migration tribunals: *Social Security (Administration) Act 1999* (Cth), s. 141; *Migration Act 1958* (Cth), s. 353 (Migration Review Tribunal), s. 420 (Repatriation Review Tribunal). This rubric is found in the legislation of the Commonwealth AAT: *Administrative Appeals Tribunal Act 1975* (Cth), s. 2A.

91 *Sun Zhan Qui v. Minister for Immigration and Ethnic Affairs* (unreported, Federal Court of Australia, 6 May 1997, [1997] 324 F.C.A. per Lindgren J. (rev'd (1997) 81 F.C.R. 71, but not on this point); his views were cited with approval by the High Court of Australia in *Minister for Immigration and Multicultural Affairs v. Eshetu* (1999), 197 C.L.R. 611 at 643 (Gummow J.); see also 628 (Gleeson C.J. and McHugh J.) and 668 (Callinan J.).

92 *South Australia v. O'Shea* (1987), 163 C.L.R. 378 [*O'Shea*]; *Minister for Arts, Heritage and Environment v. Peko-Wallsend Ltd* (1987), 15 F.C.R. 274 [*Peko-Wallsend*]. The confidentiality of cabinet documents is statutorily protected under the freedom of information and privacy legislation, but this is a specialist area.

93 *Peko-Wallsend*, *supra* note 92.

94 Ibid. at 279.

95 Ibid. at 280.

96 Mullan, 'A Canadian Perspective,' *supra* note 2 at 6.

97 The function may not be exercised until after the exercise of any rights of appeal or merit review: *Ombudsman Act 1990* (Ont.), s. 14(4).

98 E.g., *Ombudsman Act 1976* (Cth), s. 5(2).

99 Ibid. s. 5(1).

100 Ibid. s. 3(1). There is an exception but it only applies to administrative action of the chief executive officer of a tribunal.

101 *Booth v. Dillon (No. 1)*, [1976] V.R. 291; *Booth v. Dillon (No. 2)*, [1976] V.R. 434; *Booth v. Dillon (No. 3)*, [1977] V.R. 143; *Glenister v. Dillon*, [1976] V.R. 550;

Glenister v. Dillon (No. 2), [1977] V.R. 151; *City of Salisbury v. Biganovsky* (1990), 54 S.A.S.R. 117.

102 *Botany Council v. The Ombudsman* (1995), 37 N.S.W.L.R. 357; *Anti-Discrimination Commissioner v. Acting Ombudsman*, [2002] Tas. S.C. 24.

103 Dennis Pearce, 'The Jurisdiction of Australian Government Ombudsmen' in Matthew Groves, ed., *Law and Government in Australia* (Sydney: Federation Press, 2005) at 114–18 and 133–35.

104 *Ombudsman Act 1976* (Cth), ss. 10A and 11.

105 *Re Reference under the Ombudsman Act 1976 s 11 for An Advisory Opinion; Ex parte Director-General of Social Services* (1979), 2 A.L.D. 86.

106 *Ombudsman Act 1990* (Ont.), s. 14(5).

107 *Re Drake and Minister for Immigration and Ethnic Affairs (No. 2)* (1979), 2 A.L.D. 634 [*Drake (No. 2)*], a decision upheld on appeal by the full court of the Federal Court: *Drake v. Minister for Immigration and Ethnic Affairs* (1979), 46 F.L.R. 409.

108 *Drake (No. 2)*, ibid. at 645.

109 John McMillan, 'Review of Government Policy by Administrative Tribunals' (1998) 9 Law and Policy Papers 27. See also Robin Creyke and John McMillan, *Control of Government Action* (Sydney: LexisNexis, 2005), chap. 11 [Creyke and McMillan, *Government Action*].

110 *Administrative Decisions Tribunal Act 1997* (N.S.W.), s. 64(1); *Victorian Civil and Administrative Tribunal Act 1998* (Vic.), s. 25(3); *State Administrative Tribunal Act 2004* (W.A.), s. 28. Although a similar provision was to have been introduced for the Commonwealth ART had the bills been passed, no such provision was made in the subsequent amendments to the AAT's legislation: *Administrative Appeals Tribunal Amendment Act 2005* (Cth).

111 *Bread Manufacturers of New South Wales v Evans* (1981), 180 C.L.R. 404; *R v Anderson; Ex parte Ipec-Air Pty Ltd* (1965), 113 C.L.R. 177; *Ansett Transport Industries (Operations) Pty Ltd v. Commonwealth* (1977), 139 C.L.R. 54. See also Sir Anthony Mason, 'Administrative Review: The Experience of the First Twelve Years' (1989) 18 Federal Law Review 122 at 131.

112 *Aboriginal Legal Service Ltd v. Minister for Aboriginal and Torres Strait Islander Affairs* (1996), 69 F.C.R. 565, where a general direction did not support a direction about a specific funding decision; cf. *Aboriginal Development Commission v. Hand* (1988), 15 A.L.D. 410, in which the general directions power permitted a direction for a statutory body to cooperate with the minister.

113 *Hughes Aircraft Systems International v. Airservices Australia* (1997), 76 F.C.R. 151; *Sanders v. Snell* (1998), 196 C.L.R. 329; *Project Blue Sky Inc v. Australian Broadcasting Authority* (1998), 194 C.L.R. 355, where a provision that the Authority 'is to perform its functions in a manner consistent with' a bilateral treaty, had to be complied with; *N.S.W. Farmers' Association v. Minister*

for Primary Industries and Energy (1990), 21 F.C.R. 332, where a statutory power to give directions 'in exceptional circumstances' and to avoid 'conflict with major government policies' bound the independent statutory body; *Smoker v. Pharmacy Restructuring Authority* (1994), 53 F.C.R. 287, where a statutory requirement that the authority 'must comply with ... guidelines' meant the guidelines were binding on the authority; cf. *Riddell v. Secretary, Department of Social Security* (1993), 42 F.C.R. 443, where a statutory requirement that 'the Secretary must act in accordance with directions from time to time in force' did not result in invalidity, since the Federal Court found the direction impermissibly fettered the discretion of the decision-maker.

114 For example, *Migration Act 1958* (Cth), s. 499(1); *Social Security (Administration) Act 1991* (Cth), s. 9.

115 *Administrative Decisions Tribunal Act 1997* (NSW) s 64; *Victorian Civil and Administrative Appeals Tribunal Act 1998* (Vic) s 57.

116 Lorne Sossin discusses the relationship between the appointment process and tribunal independence in the Canadian context in his contribution to this volume.

117 Administrative Review Council, *Review of Commonwealth Merits Review Tribunals* (Canberra: Discussion Paper, 1994) at para. 4.75 [ARC, *Merits Review Tribunals*].

118 ARC, *Better Decisions, supra* note 82 at 172 (recommendation 41).

119 Ibid. (recommendation 42).

120 Ibid. at para. 4.35.

121 Commonwealth Parliament Joint Standing Committee on Migration, *The Immigration Review Tribunal Appointments Process* (Canberra, December 1994). See also ARC, *Better Decisions, supra* note 82 at para. 4.47.

122 *Migration Review Tribunal Annual Report 2003–04* (Canberra: Commonwealth of Australia, 2004) at 27.

123 Ibid.

124 ARC, *Merits Review Tribunals, supra* note 117 at para. 4.94.

125 A view repeated by the ALRC, *Managing Justice, supra* note 22 at para. 9.20.

126 ARC, *Better Decisions, supra* note 82 at p 173 (recommendation 46); ALRC, *Managing Justice, supra* note 22 at para. 9.17.

127 ALRC, *Civil Justice System, supra* note 22 at paras 12.154 and 12.156.

128 Mullan, 'A Canadian Perspective,' *supra* note 2 at 10.

129 Ibid.

130 Chief Justice Warren, 'The Growth in Tribunal Power' (speech delivered to the Council of Australasian Tribunals, 15 April 2004, Melbourne, Victoria) at 5–6.

131 *Migration Act 1958* (Cth), s. 474. The cases were spearheaded by the High

Court's decision in *Plaintiff S157/2002 v. Commonwealth* (2003), 211 CLR 476. See also *Minister for Immigration and Multicultural Affairs v. Al Masri* (2003), 126 CLR 54; *NAAV v. Minister for Immigration and Multicultural Affairs* (2002), 123 CLR 298; *Lobo v. Minister for Immigration and Multicultural Affairs* (2003), 132 CLR 93; *NAGV v. Minister for Immigration and Multicultural Affairs* (2003), 130 CLR 46.

132 C. Cook, R. Creyke, R. Geddes, and D. Hamer, *Laying Down the Law*, 6th ed. (Sydney: LexisNexis, 2005) at paras 3.6–3.10.

133 *Australian Constitution*, ss. 71, 73, 75, 76 and 77.

134 *Federal Court Act 1976* (Cth).

135 *Judiciary Act 1903* (Cth), s. 44. See also Australian Law Reform Commission, *The Judicial Power of the Commonwealth* (Canberra: Report No. 92, 2001) at paras 2.48, 3.18, and 12.27–12.35.

136 High Court of Australia: *Australian Constitution*, s. 75(v); Federal Court of Australia: *Judiciary Act 1903* (Cth), s. 39B; Supreme Court of the ACT: *Australian Capital Territory (Self-Government) Act 1989* (Cth), s. 48A; Supreme Court of the Northern Territory: *Supreme Court Act* (N.T.), s. 14.

137 *Minister for Immigration and Ethnic Affairs v. Wu Shan Liang* (1996), 185 C.L.R. 259 [*Liang*]; citing the full court of the Federal Court in *Collector of Customs v. Pozzolanic* (1993), 43 F.C.R. 280. See *Liang*, ibid. at 272, per Brennan C.J., Toohey, McHugh and Gummow JJ.

138 Ibid. at 272.

139 John McMillan, 'Federal Court v. Minister for Immigration' (1999) 22 AIAL Forum 1.

140 *Attorney-General (NSW) v. Quin* (1990), 170 C.L.R. 1 at 36, per Brennan J.

141 Creyke and McMillan, *Government Action*, *supra* note 109 at chap. 3.

142 S.D. Hotop, *Principles of Australian Administrative Law*, 6th ed. (Sydney: Law Book Co, 1985) at 248; E.I. Sykes, D.J. Lanham, and R.R.S. Tracey, *General Principles of Administrative Law*, 2nd ed. (Sydney: Butterworths, 1984) at 48; H. Woolf, J. Jowell, and A. Le Sueur, *de Smith, Woolf & Jowell's Principles of Judicial Review* (London: Sweet & Maxwell, 1999) at 94; John Basten, 'Constitutional Elements of Judicial Review' (2004) 15 P.L.R. 187 at 189 [Basten, 'Constitutional Elements'].

143 *Minister for Immigration and Multicultural Affairs v. Yusuf* (2001), 206 C.L.R. 323 at 351 (McHugh, Gummow, and Hayne JJ.) at 339–40 (Gaudron J.); Caron Beaton-Wells, 'Judicial Review of Migration Decisions; Life after *S157*' (2005) 33 Federal Law Review 170 [Beaton-Wells, 'Life after *S157*'].

144 *Craig v. South Australia* (1995) 184 C.L.R. 163 at 176–7.

145 *Corporation of the City of Enfield v. Development Assessment Commission* (2000) 199 C.L.R. 135 [*City of Enfield*]. See Margaret Allars, 'Chevron in Australia:

A Duplicitous Rejection?' (2002) 54 Admin. L.R. 569 [Allars, 'Chevron in Australia'].

146 *Chevron, USA, Inc v. Natural Resources Defense Council, Inc*, 467 U.S. 837 (1984); *INS v. Cardoz-Fonseca*, 480 U.S. 421 (1987). See also Justice Ronald Sackville, 'The Limits of Judicial Review of Executive Action – Some Comparisons Between Australia and the United States' (2000) 28 Fed. L.R. 315, and see Alfred C. Aman Jr's paper in this volume.

147 *Canadian Union of Public Employees, Local 963 v. New Brunswick Liquor Corp*, [1979] 2 S.C.R. 227; *Canada (Attorney General) v. Public Service Alliance of Canada*, [1993] 1 S.C.R. 941; *McTague v. Canada (Attorney-General)*, [2000] 1 F.C. 455; cf. *Canada (Attorney General) v. Mossop*, [1993] 1 S.C.R. 554. See also David Dyzenhaus, 'The Politics of Deference: Judicial Review and Democracy' and Madame Justice Claire L'Heureux-Dubé, 'The "Ebb" and "Flow" of Administrative Law on the "General Question of Law"' both in Michael Taggart, ed., *The Province of Administrative Law* (Oxford: Hart Publishing, 1997) at 279 and 331, respectively, and the paper by Grant Huscroft in this volume.

148 *City of Enfield*, *supra* note 145 at 154, per Gleeson C.J., Gummow, Kirby, and Hayne JJ. This view is always subject to the courts' retaining their role of ensuring that a tribunal keeps within its jurisdictional limits.

149 Allars, 'Chevron in Australia,' *supra* note 145; Mark Aronson, 'The Resurgence of Jurisdictional Facts' (2001) 12 P.L.R. 17; Administrative Review Council, *The Scope of Judicial Review* (Canberra: Discussion Paper, 2003) at 38–40; T.R.S. Allan, 'Doctrine and Theory in Administrative Law: An Elusive Quest for the Limits of Jurisdiction' [2003] P.L. 429.

150 *Tracy v. Repatriation Commission* (2000), 61 A.L.D. 361 at 366, per Burchett, Sundberg and Hely JJ.

151 *Attorney-General for Queensland v. Riordan* (1997), 146 A.L.R. 445 at 451, per Brennan C.J. and McHugh J. See also *R v. Ludeke; Ex parte Queensland Electricity Commission* (1985), 159 C.L.R. 178 at 184 (Brennan C.J. and McHugh J.) and 469 (Kirby J.).

152 *Australian Broadcasting Commission Staff Association v. Bonner* (1984), 2 F.C.R. 561 at 576.

153 *City of Enfield*, *supra* note 143 at 154.

154 *Kalil v. Bray* (1977), 1 N.S.W.L.R. 256 at 262; *Filo v. Pharmacy Board of N.S.W.* (1975), 3 N.S.W.D.C.R. 269 at 276.

155 *O'Shea*, *supra* note 92; *Murpheyores Inc Pty Ltd v. Commonwealth* (1976), 136 C.L.R. 1.

156 *Liang*, *supra* note 137.

157 *Tuite v. Administrative Appeals Tribunal* (1993), 40 F.C.R. 483.

158 Mary Crock, 'The Scope and Purpose of Privative Clauses: Politics, Practicalities and the Deference Question' in S. Kneebone, ed., *Administrative Law and the Rule of Law: Still Part of the Same Package?* (Canberra: AIAL, 1998) at 63 [Kneebone, *Rule of Law*].

159 Stephen Gageler, 'The Underpinnings of Judicial Review of Administrative Action: Common Law or Constitution' (2000) 28 Federal Law Review 303; Bradley Selway, 'The Principle behind the Common Law Judicial Review of Administrative Action – The Search Continues' (2002) 30 Federal Law Review 218.

160 (1983), 153 C.L.R. 415 at 418 and at 427 (Deane and Dawson JJ.).

161 *R v. Hickman; Ex parte Fox and Clinton* (1945), 70 C.L.R. 598 at 614–15 [*Hickman*].

162 *Re Refugee Review Tribunal; Ex parte Aala* (2000), 204 C.L.R. 82 at 142, per Hayne J. [*Aala*].

163 Ibid. at 97 and 101, per Gaudron and Gummow JJ.

164 Mary Crock, 'Privative Clauses and the Rule of Law: The place of judicial review within the construct of Australian democracy' in Kneebone, *Rule of Law, supra* note 158; David Bennett, 'Privative Clauses – An Update on the Latest Development' (2003) 37 AIAL Forum 32; Duncan Kerr, 'Deflating the Hickman Myth: Judicial Review after *Plaintiff S157/2002 v. The Commonwealth*' (2003) 37 AIAL Forum 1; John Basten, 'Judicial Review: Recent Trends' (2001) 17 Federal Law Review 365; G Coffey, 'Privative Clauses and the Theoretical Underpinnings of Administrative Law in Australia' (2003) AIAL Forum 39; Margaret Allars, 'Of Cocoons and Small "c" Constitutionalism: The Principle of Legality and an Australian Perspective on *Baker*' in David Dyzenhaus, ed., *The Unity of Public Law* (Oxford: Hart Publishing, 2004) at 306.

165 Those exceptions were found in the provisos crafted by Dixon J. in *Hickman, supra* note 161 at 614–17, a narrow reading of which had limited their reach to protection of 'manifest jurisdictional errors or ultra vires acts' (*Church of Scientology v. Woodward* (1982), 154 C.L.R. 25 at 55–6).

166 *Plaintiff S157/2002 v. Commonwealth* (2003), 211 C.L.R. 476.

167 See Caron Beaton-Wells, 'Restoring the Rule of Law – *Plaintiff S157/2002 v. Commonwealth of Australia*' (2003) 10 Aust. J. Admin. L. 125; Simon Evans, 'Protection Visas and the Privative Clause Decision: *Hickman* and the *Migration Act 1958* (Cth)' (2002) 9 Aust. J. of Admin. L. 49; and Sarah Ford, 'Judicial Review of Migration Decisions: Ousting the *Hickman* Privative Clause?' (2002) 26 Melb. U.L.R. 28.

168 E.g. for 'constitutional writ' jurisdiction, see *Aala, supra* note 162 at 93, per Gaudron and Gummow JJ. See also Basten, 'Constitutional Elements,'

supra note 140; Jeremy Kirk, 'The Entrenched Minimum Provision of Judicial Review' (2004) 12 Aust. J. of Admin. L. 64.

169 Beaton-Wells, 'Life after *S157*,' *supra* note 143.

170 C. Sibley, 'Jurisdictional Error: Towards a Resolution of the Uncertainty' (LL.B. honours thesis, Faculty of Law, Australian National University, 2005) at 48–9.

171 Claims under s. 75(v) of the Constitution must be against 'an officer of the Commonwealth.'

172 S. 75(iii) of the Constitution must relate to a matter in which 'the Commonwealth' is a party.

173 Mullan, 'A Canadian Perspective,' *supra* note 2 at 18.

174 Canadian *Bill of Rights*, s. 2(f); Canadian *Charter of Rights and Freedoms*, s. 11(d).

175 *Migration Legislation Amendment (Procedural Fairness) Act 2002* (Cth).

176 Section 7 is set out *infra* in the text above note 192.

177 Section 11 of the *Charter* provides: 'Any person charged with an offence has the right ... (d) to be presumed innocent until proven guilty according to law in a fair and public hearing by an independent and impartial tribunal.'

178 Mullan, 'A Canadian Perspective,' *supra* note 2 at 19–20.

179 P.W. Hogg, 'The Law Making Role of the Supreme Court of Canada' (2001) 80 Can. Bar Rev. 171 at 176 [Hogg, 'Law Making Role'].

180 E.g. Justice Michael Kirby, *Through the World's Eye* (Sydney: Federation Press, 2000); Christine Debono and Tania Colwell, eds., *Comparative Perspectives on Bills of Rights* (Canberra: ANU National Institute of Social Science and Law, and Centre for International and Public Law, 2004); G. Williams, *The Case for an Australian Bill of Rights* (Sydney: University of New South Wales Press, 2004); and G. Williams, *Human Rights under the Australian Constitution* (Melbourne: Oxford University Press, 1999).

181 *Human Rights Act 2004* (A.C.T.), s. 30(1). A similar provision is found in the Canadian *Bill of Rights*.

182 J. Stellios, 'Federal Dimensions to the ACT *Human Rights Act*' (2005) 47 AIAL Forum 1 at 2.

183 *Kable v. Director of Public Prosecutions (NSW)* (1996), 189 C.L.R. 51. The *Kable* doctrine forbids the exercise by state or territory supreme courts of federal judicial power.

184 The nub of this argument is that federal jurisdiction can only be exercised in relation to a 'matter,' a term used in ss. 75–77 of the Constitution. 'Matter' has been interpreted to require that there be at least a justiciable issue between the parties, an issue that arguably may not arise when the ACT Supreme Court is only asked to pronounce upon the incompatibility of a

law with the HRA which does not quell the controversy between the parties: *Re McBain; Ex parte Australian Catholic Bishops Conference* (2002), 209 C.L.R. 372.

185 (1996), 189 C.L.R. 1. The court held that a judge of a Chapter III court may not exercise functions on behalf of the government which could impede their judicial independence.

186 Largely based on standards drawn from the *International Covenant on Civil and Political Rights*, 999 U.N.T.S. 171, 6 I.L.M. 368 (in force Mar. 23, 1976): *Human Rights Act 2004* (A.C.T.), Pt 3.

187 *Human Rights Act 2004* (A.C.T.), s. 32. The limitations on its role replicate in part those applying under the United Kingdom *Human Rights Act 1998*.

188 *Human Rights Act 2004* (A.C.T.), s. 31.

189 Ibid. at s. 38.

190 Ibid. at Pt 5. See also Peter Bayne, 'The *Human Rights Act 2004* (ACT) and Administrative Law: A First Report' (paper delivered at the Australian Institute of Administrative Law National Forum, Canberra, 30 June–1 July 2005).

191 *Human Rights Act 2004* (A.C.T.), s. 39.

192 Hogg, 'Law Making Role,' *supra* note 179 at 176–7.

193 Mullan, 'A Canadian Perspective,' *supra* note 2 at 19.

194 The Hon. James J. Spigelman, 'The Integrity Branch of Government' (2004) 2 AIAL National Lecture Series on Administrative Law 5. See also Bruce Ackerman, 'The New Separation of Powers' (2000) 113 Harv. L. R. 633 at 694.

195 Spigelman, 'The Integrity Branch of Government,' ibid. at 5–6.

196 John McMillan, 'The Ombudsman and the Rule of Law' (2005) 44 AIAL Forum at 11–12.

197 Ibid. at 12.

Administrative Law Developments in New Zealand as Seen through Immigration Law

K.J. KEITH

States have populations. How does a state determine who is to be a member of its population? That question may be divided into two: who may enter and live in the state? And who are its citizens? The citizens are part of the first group since they have rights of entry and residence.[1]

In this tribute to Professor David Mullan, I consider aspects of the ways in which the law of New Zealand over the past forty or so years has answered the first of the two questions. I focus on immigration for two reasons among others: David Mullan's specific professional interests in immigration, as demonstrated in his valuable commentary on *Baker*[2]; and his wider interests in the structuring of public power, the evolving review powers of courts and other control bodies, and the growing significance of international law and institutions for its exercise. While the particular focus does bring with it dangers of a narrowing specialization, it does, I think, allow me to give a sense of the broader developments in administrative law in New Zealand since he began his legal studies there.[3]

The common law, consistently with international law, has long recognized that states have broad powers to admit (or not) non-citizens into their territory and to expel them,[4] and to grant (or not) citizenship. Three examples show that the powers are not unlimited or uncontested. Maritime law and practice have long required coastal states to allow seafarers in distress to enter their ports.[5] For at least two centuries the laws of many states have provided for the grant of asylum, more recently by excepting political offenders from the obligation to extradite, an exception included in many extradition treaties.[6] And during and after the Great War claims that immigration and related policy should not discriminate on racial grounds were pressed by Japan and resisted, among others, by Australia, New Zealand and, to a lesser extent, Canada.[7]

Over more recent decades national prerogatives in respect of immigration and also citizenship have become increasingly subject to international limit, for instance, by the conventions on refugees, the nationality of married women, against racial discrimination and discrimination against women, against statelessness and on the rights of families and children. Customary international law has also continued to develop, for instance, by limiting (on one view) the grant of citizenship, if it is to be invoked internationally, to those who have a real and substantial connection to the country in question.[8] I return to the international law issues later, but first some facts.

New Zealand was truly terra incognita until about a millennium ago when the Maori began to inhabit an empty land. Estimates of the population at the time of European contact in 1769 range from 150,000 to 200,000. One hundred years ago the population was reaching one million and the Maori share had fallen to under 50,000. The total population reached two million in 1952 (the Maori figure was then at 120,000), and between 1950 and 1967 it gained 270,000 from permanent and long-term migrants, particularly from the United Kingdom, Ireland, and the Netherlands, some attracted by assisted passage schemes. Immigration from the Pacific Islands increased substantially from the 1960s, and, from the mid 1980s, changes in immigration policy widened the source countries, particularly from Asia. In the 2001 census Pacific Island people totalled 232,000 (about one half of them Samoan) or about 45 per cent of the Maori population, and the Asian figure had surpassed the Pacific one and stood at 238,000. Individuals may of course identify with ethnicities generations after their families migrated.

Those increases measure the net changes of those arriving in and leaving New Zealand. They are also primarily the measure of those making permanent changes in their residence. Between 1956 and 1960 permanent and long-term arrivals and departures numbered 115,000 and 64,000 respectively for a net increase of 51,000. The figures for the five years between 1990 and 1995 are 280,000 and 220,000 for a net increase of 60,000. The short-term arrivals and departures have increased much more, reflecting the great growth in air travel, from under 90,000 passengers in 1960 to four million forty years later. It is from the groups of short-term visitors that the problems that trouble the legal system principally arise. For instance, from 1975 to 1990 the net excess of short-term arrivals over departures was over 100,000, many of them from the

Pacific coming into low-skilled employment. It was in that period that the ombudsmen and the courts became increasingly involved in claims by individuals to be allowed to stay.

Immigration Legislation in Force in the 1960s

That involvement did not extend to the larger issues of immigration policy. The executive has essentially kept the broader policy in its own hands, occasionally developing it through the exercise of the treaty-making prerogative. Parliament, too, has not had a real role in broader policy matters. Its involvement in its legislative capacity has been primarily with structure and administration and to some extent with identifying and regulating distinct categories such as refugee claimants, but not with broader policy issues, including the numbers of migrants, their skills, and other qualities or their countries of origin. There is something of a paradox that in the final years of the nineteenth century and the early years of the twentieth, when the New Zealand Parliament's powers were limited by its colonial status, it had a greater involvement with substantive immigration policy.[9]

In 1961, at the outset of the period under review, Parliament did have a real opportunity to address wider policy issues when it had before it an amendment to the *Immigration Restriction Amendment Act 1920*. The 1920 act had added to the existing restrictions a bar on persons 'other than person[s] of British birth and parentage' entering without a permit. The 1961 amendment replaced 'a person of British birth and parentage' by 'a New Zealand citizen.' The consequence was that British subjects who were not New Zealand citizens no longer had the right to enter New Zealand without a permit. A perceptive senior student, later to become a distinguished High Court Judge, briefly commented on the deeper implications of the change:[10]

> The amendment was passed through the Legislature largely under a Statutes Amendment bill of many clauses and with virtually no comment apart from the remarkable statement by the Attorney-General, the Hon J R Hanan:
>
>> 'This will remove all racial discrimination from the rules governing immigration into New Zealand.' (28 November 1961, vol 329, New Zealand Parliamentary Debates, p. 3822).
>
> On its surface this short Act seems innocuous enough. Its similarity in

> effect, however, to the recent and highly controversial Commonwealth Immigrants Act 1962 (UK) – both restrict the entry of all Commonwealth peoples other than New Zealand and United Kingdom citizens respectively and leave the issue of permits to the complete discretion of the Government – is to say the least, interesting.

Parliament did not however take the opportunity to address the wider issues, the matter being seen by both parliamentary parties as one involving no controversy and accordingly appropriate for inclusion in a Statutes Amendment Bill. Nor did it in 1964 when the 1908 act and its amendments were consolidated into what became the *Immigration Act 1964*, although the minister of immigration did take the opportunity to describe the government's immigration policy.[11] The act did not itself set out the major policy, nor does its 1987 successor.[12] Rather, it conferred broad powers on the minister of immigration or, with exceptions, a delegate, to grant permits, including temporary permits, and to extend or revoke them. As discussed later, Parliament in 1991 did require the minister to publish the government's policy and officials to comply with it. While Parliament indicated the kinds of policy that may be included, it did not itself state any elements of the policy.

Under the 1964 act, the minister had power to deport persons convicted of offences committed within five years of arrival, if the offence was punishable by more than a year's imprisonment and the court recommended deportation, or if the person was sentenced to more than a year in prison. The act expressly preserved 'the prerogative of mercy.' This led to a practice under which persons who were subject to orders for deportation petitioned the governor-general for a pardon removing the conviction.[13] The executive had other arrows in its quiver. Under the *Undesirable Immigrants Exclusion Act 1919* the attorney-general could prohibit any person from landing in New Zealand if satisfied that the person was not permanently resident there and was disaffected or disloyal or of such a character that his presence in New Zealand would be injurious to the peace, order and good government of the Dominion. The attorney, on the direction of the governor-general-in-council, had power to order persons to leave New Zealand on the same grounds. Under the *Aliens Act 1948* the minister could deport aliens who had been convicted of an offence punishable by a term exceeding one year if the court recommended deportation (without any time limits as in the *Immigration Act*), or if the minister was satisfied that it was not conducive to the public good that an alien should remain and the Governor-General in Council approved the order.

I take that legislation – of 1919, 1948, and 1964 – as in force forty years ago as my starting point. David Mullan, as a good watcher, is passionate about administrative powers and controls over them and cares about the play and the players – to borrow from Spiro Zavos's outstanding *How to Watch a Game of Rugby*,[14] another Mullan passion. To borrow further from Zavos, we should aim to 'see an object in the paint with which a surface is marked, rather than simply seeing the marks'; for '[t]he more knowledge the good watcher brings to the seeing-in process, the sharper and truer it becomes.'[15]

David Mullan, from his scholarly position, has for long watched across common law countries

- the players – those who exercise the power and participate in the play;
- the processes the players are to follow;
- the powers available to the official players; and
- the remedies available to those affected by the exercise of the power.[16]

Those matters appear throughout the following account which is largely chronological and which may be seen as physiological rather than pathological, to use one of David Mullan's metaphors.

The Decision-makers in the 1960s

The primary decision-makers forty years ago were relevant ministers (immigration, justice, and the attorney). The *Immigration Act* did allow delegation to officials but with exceptions. By making those exceptions and by not providing for delegation in the 1919 and 1948 acts, Parliament recognized the greater importance of certain decisions.[17] The excepted powers were those to deport individuals following conviction on serious offences, to deport or exclude for public interest reasons, and to exempt persons or categories from statutory prohibitions or restrictions on entry. The deportation and exclusion powers were important in terms both of their impact on the individuals who had been lawfully resident in New Zealand, possibly for some time, and of the substance of the matters to be weighed. The importance of some of the deportation powers is marked as well by the need for a judicial recommendation or the approval of the Governor-General in Council. These exemptions permitted departure from bars created by Parliament, in effect a legislative power, and accordingly were reserved to a minister.[18]

The power to revoke a temporary permit – and accordingly to require the individual to leave New Zealand – could by contrast be delegated. Parliament made a judgment that that decision was not as serious as one to deport a permanent resident on statutorily prescribed grounds, although for the individual that difference might not have been apparent.[19] Officials could also be empowered to grant or extend temporary permits. The exercise of the powers could be and was informed by advisory committees, for instance on overseas students, set up purely administratively.[20]

The requirement that powers be exercised by those on whom Parliament has conferred them was brought home sharply to the department in 1978 when a number of overstayers challenged their convictions and deportation orders on the basis that the form of entry permit which they had overstayed had not been 'prescribed' by regulations made by the Governor-General in Council as the act required. Instead, the form had been approved, in terms of a provision in the regulations, by the minister. The challenge succeeded and the orders were quashed.[21]

The 1919, 1920 and 1964 legislation was silent on the process the decision-makers were to follow, with the exception that any judicial recommendation for deportation would follow a court process and was subject to appeal. Was this a case where the common law should 'supply the omission of the legislature' and require the decision-makers to follow natural justice or give a fair hearing?[22] Was there a single answer to this question or should distinctions be drawn between the refusal to grant a temporary or permanent permit, to extend a temporary permit, to revoke a temporary permit, or to remove a person following conviction or on a public interest ground? The questions increasingly came before the courts in New Zealand and elsewhere from the 1970s. They also engaged the attention of the New Zealand ombudsman, the first such body established in the Commonwealth and the subject of an early article in the *Canadian Bar Review* by Colin Aikman, David Mullan's earliest mentor in administrative law.[23]

New Institutions in the 1960s: The Ombudsman and the Administrative Division

The establishment of the Office of Ombudsman is to be seen in a broader context of major reforms of public law that began in the period following the Second World War. In the 1950s in New Zealand, as elsewhere in the common law world, attitudes to the scope of public power and in favour of greater controls over its exercise were evolving. The National Party in the 1960 election campaign proposed not only the office that became the Ombudsman, but also a Bill of Rights based on the model of the then recently enacted Canadian one and greater controls over regulation making.[24] The second proposal failed at that time, but was revived by the Labour party twenty-five years later, again on a (new) Canadian model, and enacted in 1990. The third led to modest changes, which were taken much further by Labour in 1989.[25] From the 1950s the courts had also begun to take a more active role in reviewing administrative action although not, as we shall see, in immigration cases until the late 1970s.[26]

A more systematic approach to the role of tribunals and the courts in administrative law areas also began to appear in this period, following the setting up by J.R. Hanan, the minister of justice, of the Public and Administrative Law Reform Committee in 1966 as one of a number of law reform committees.[27] The first product of its work was the establishment in 1968 of the Administrative Division of the Supreme Court, consisting of Supreme Court judges assigned by the chief justice and, as appropriate, lay (or really expert) members, with jurisdiction over appeals as provided by particular statutes.[28] As we shall see, in the 1970s the division acquired jurisdiction over some immigration appeals. The committee's main recommendation (with one dissent) was 'that an Administrative Division of the Supreme Court be established to hear appeals from certain administrative tribunals. We are satisfied that this step would offer the best assurance that the very important issues arising in such appeals are decided justly. It would be the best means of satisfying the public that each case receives a fair and thorough hearing and a carefully-considered decision.'[29]

Mr Hanan, in introducing the bill to set up the division, had put the matter at a higher level:[30]

> The creation of the division will ... return the Supreme Court to its rightful place in our constitutional system by ensuring its direct involvement in some of the most important judicial questions to be decided. In the past the Supreme Court has been bypassed. Now it will once again become the centre of our judicial system. The Bill embodies perhaps the most important change to be proposed in the history of New Zealand's judicial system.

Right at the outset, in 1968, David Mullan and Graham Taylor, while recording that the development was regarded as a milestone in New

Zealand administrative law, had expressed caution about the prospects of the division. They commented critically on two aspects in particular of the implementing legislation which differed from the model proposed by the committee: the judges were to be appointed to the division from time to time by the chief justice rather than permanently by the governor-general, and the jurisdiction of the division was limited.[31]

Twenty years later Sir Robin Cooke, a founding member of the committee, provided this background:[32]

> In the 1960s there was a sense that the kinds of questions dealt with by administrative tribunals were often more important for ordinary citizens than the issues litigated in ordinary courts. At the same time the procedures of the ordinary courts, and I am afraid some judges of the ordinary courts, were thought by some critics not to be attuned to administrative law issues between citizen and state and citizen and citizen. Other judges of the ordinary courts would be well capable of undertaking major administrative adjudication but did not have much opportunity of doing so under the existing system: so there was an important area of adjudication or 'justiciable issues' not assigned to those who in theory should be the best judges. Moreover the judicial remedies for challenging administrative action were chiefly the prerogative writs of certiorari, mandamus and prohibition. They and the case law surrounding them had an arcane air. To find substantive law secreted in the interstices of procedure was of course thoroughly commonplace and respectable, but rather old-fashioned and inconvenient.

After recalling changes made to the original proposal, Sir Robin Cooke said that the creation of the division was essentially a public affirmation of the role of the Supreme Court in administrative adjudication. That was then its true significance. He went on to wonder whether the division was still needed.

Shortly afterwards the Law Commission, building in effect on the Mullan and Taylor critique, as now supplemented by the experience of the following twenty years, recommended that the division be abolished and its jurisdiction absorbed by the High Court. The high number of judges and the low number of cases, with each judge deciding on average under five cases a year, meant that there had not been a build-up in the volume of administrative law work or in related expertise and specialization. The subject matter was no longer as special as some had seen it twenty years earlier. 'Administrative law business is part of the constitutional role of the Queen's Judges ... of determining the scope of executive power and protecting the citizen from the abuse of that power.'[33] Parliament adopted that recommendation.[34]

The Processes for Decisions under the 1960s Legislation

I return to the question whether the courts in the 1970s would 'supply the omission of the legislature' and require natural justice when, for instance, deportation orders were being made. The early judicial signs were not positive.

An Italian citizen, Mr Pagliara, had come to New Zealand with his family when he was about thirteen. After two years he went back to Italy for two years but then returned to New Zealand. When he was about twenty-four he was convicted of a drug offence and sentenced to nine months imprisonment. The sentencing court refused to recommend deportation, a matter the Crown did not pursue when it succeeded in its appeal against sentence, with the imprisonment being increased to two years. The minister of immigration was nevertheless persuaded, following a procedure that lasted about a year but of which the offender was completely unaware (he read about the decision in the newspaper!), to recommend to cabinet that he be deported under the *Aliens Act* on the public good ground; that ground did not require a recommendation from a court. The Governor-General in Council made the appropriate order. Mr Pagliara failed in his contention in a judicial review application that he was entitled to be heard before the decision was made.[35]

The court on review depended on immigration decisions of the English Court of Appeal given in 1920, 1962, and 1969[36] which it saw as treating aliens as in a special category: they had no right and no legitimate expectation of being allowed to stay in the country. The judge was also inclined to see no difference between the refusal to extend a permit – the subject matter of the most recent English decision denying a hearing, given after the ground breaking decision of the House of Lords in *Ridge v. Baldwin*[37] – and a deportation order being made against a long-term resident. Quillam J. gained further support for his decision from the use by the legislature of the word 'satisfied': 'The use of that word is not I think calculated to indicate that the Minister was being placed under an obligation to hold any inquiry or to investigate the accuracy of statements of fact presented to him, although it is no doubt the case that if he were to act on wrong information he would be subject to the criticism of Parliament to whom he is answerable.'[38]

Two years later the same judge also rejected the challenge that a member of the Ananda Marga sect had not been heard prior to a ministerial revocation of his temporary permit.[39] The judge referred to his earlier decision and the 1969 English case and said this:[40]

> The right of the minister to issue temporary permits and to revoke them is clear. The question is, whether the power to revoke is limited by the corollary that it is only to be exercised after an opportunity has been given to be heard. It does not seem to me that this can be so. The audi alteram partem principle is now well recognised and established in its application to the decisions of administrative authorities as well as to judicial and quasi-judicial tribunals. It is, nevertheless, clear that the case of aliens is firmly retained under a different category. Just as it was held in *Schmidt*'s case that a refusal to grant an extension of permit was analogous to deportation so also must it be said is the revocation of an alien's permit. More particularly, however, the whole scheme of s.14 of the Immigration Act is against any distinction being drawn. It is necessary to remember that the basis upon which s.14 proceeds is first and foremost that no alien may have any right of entry into New Zealand. The Minister may, upon certain defined grounds, permit an alien to enter. That permit may only be granted for a limited period and from the moment it is granted it is subject to revocation at any time. It is issued with that reservation. To hold that the observations of Lord Denning in *Schmidt*'s case should be made to apply to the present situation would mean that the right of revocation given to the Minister by statute could be exercised only in those areas in which the alien was first given the right to be heard. Whether or not in any particular instance it might be thought reasonable for that to be done is one thing; to hold, in effect, that it must be done in every case, is altogether another. That would be to take out of the Minister's hands the freedom of action with regard to aliens which the legislature has been at pains to confer upon him.

The role played by the ombudsmen at that time in two revocation cases provides a sharp contrast.[41] In the first, a young Samoan challenged the revocation by the minister of his temporary permit. As in the Ananda Marga case, he was given no reason. The ombudsman undertook his own inquiries into matters set out in the department's report to the Minister – to which, unlike the judge, he had automatic and full access – and concluded that some of the statements were open to question and that the young man's conduct had changed for the better. He persuaded the department to recommend to the minister a temporary trial extension of the permit. As a result, the minister cancelled the revocation order, restoring the currency of the temporary permit.[42]

In the second revocation case, the ombudsman undertook an own-motion inquiry – again something a court cannot do. The permit had been revoked, again without notice to the permit holder, in this case because the organization sponsoring the person, a sponsored student, had withdrawn its sponsorship. The department considered it was not obliged to inquire into the circumstances under which sponsorship was withdrawn. While the ombudsman accepted that view and that the department had acted within its authority in recommending revocation, he considered that before making the recommendation it should have interviewed the student to establish whether there was any special circumstance justifying a departure from, or modification of, the usual practice because it might in some circumstances be unjust:[43]

> I formed the further opinion that in this case the department could not state with confidence that it had necessarily placed before the Parliamentary Under-Secretary all relevant information to enable him to reach an informed decision in the absence of the student having been interviewed and having been given an opportunity to be heard.
>
> I recommended therefore that the existing practice be re-examined by the department. I recommended also that in the case of the student concerned she be given an opportunity to be heard so that the department might decide whether there were any material circumstances which would justify further consideration of her case. Immediate effect was given to the second of my recommendations and I have been advised by the department that it is now considering ways in which its practices and procedures can be improved.

Two other aspects of the ombudsman's role in the 1970s and early 1980s again suggest the greater effectiveness of the office compared with the courts. Two immigrants had entered on temporary permits. While they were discussing with the department the extension of their permits, the permits expired; because of mistakes in departmental processes, prosecutions for overstaying were launched. In the case in which the ombudsman was approached, he identified the errors in the departmental process. When the department:[44]

> discovered the true position [it] considered that the proper course was to continue with the proceedings on the basis that if convicted he ask the Minister of Immigration to review his case.

This did not seem to me to take adequate account of the serious consequences for the complainant of a conviction as an overstayer. While the Minister might well decide to exercise his discretion in the complainant's favour this would not alter the fact that the complainant would have a conviction recorded against him. It is my understanding that a Magistrate did not have authority to consider the circumstances leading up to the laying of the information against the complainant but only to decide whether or not the prosecution should succeed.

I therefore formed the opinion that the department had acted unreasonably in laying an information against the complainant and I recommended that the department seek the leave of the court to withdraw the information. This recommendation was accepted by the department and the Magistrate dismissed the [prosecution]. I subsequently learned that the department had received the outstanding information it required in connection with the complainant's application and that he would be granted permanent residence.

By contrast, in the case in which the matter was tested in court, the Court of Appeal rejected the overstayer's appeal based on abuse of process.[45]

A second advantage is the ability of the ombudsman to address a general issue on the basis of the accumulation of experience, something a court can do only rarely. In the late 1970s the government instituted a crackdown on illegal immigrants – referred to by the press as 'dawn raids.' Part of this crackdown involved an offer of amnesty to overstayers. A register was established on which overstayers could place their names so that their cases for remaining in New Zealand could be considered by a departmental committee against criteria laid down by the government. While their cases were under consideration, removal proceedings against the immigrants were suspended. The number of complaints about this process led the ombudsman to make a number of general procedural suggestions to the department. These improvements included publishing the criteria for the decisions; ensuring that all relevant information reached the committee; and improving the quality of the material going to the minister when the matter was one for decision at that level.[46]

In the following year the chief ombudsman made the point more generally:[47]

It is evident ... that some departments ... have progressively modified and improved their own procedures for the handling of grievances, in some cases instituting formal review and appeal machinery for this purpose. An encouraging example of this kind of development is to be found in the Immigration Division of the Department of Labour. A considerable number of complaints about immigration matters continue to come to my office but the concern expressed in my previous report about the possibility of a continuous upsurge has not been realised, largely, in my judgment, because of the measures taken by the department itself.

International Obligations Requiring Institutional Protection in the 1970s

The legislature, prompted by a proposed exercise of the treaty-making power by the executive, took significant steps in 1977 and 1978 to provide some institutional and procedural protection to those facing deportation or removal. New Zealand's ratification of the *International Covenant on Civil and Political Rights* (*ICCPR*) was then in prospect. The process of reviewing New Zealand law against that text raised a question about compliance with article 13, which provides:

> An alien lawfully in the territory of a State Party to the present Covenant may be expelled therefrom only in pursuance of a decision reached in accordance with law and shall, except where compelling reasons of national security otherwise require, be allowed to submit the reasons against his expulsion and to have his case reviewed by, and be represented for the purpose before, the competent authority or a person or persons especially designated by the competent authority.

The 1977 amendment – the addition of section 20A to the 1964 act – is not directly in point since it concerned overstayers who had been convicted of remaining without a permit, rather than lawfully resident aliens. The former group, however, were given important procedural rights which the Court of Appeal was to read in a generous way three years later. The act conferred a right of appeal, although to the minister and not, as some urged in Parliament and as finally happened fourteen years later, an independent body. Within fourteen days of the conviction, the person could, by setting out the full circumstances, request the minister to make an order that the offender not be deported from New Zealand. The minister had the power to make such an order if satisfied that, because of exceptional circumstances of a humanitarian nature, it would be unduly harsh or unjust to deport the offender from New Zealand. In that event the person was to receive a permit.

The Court of Appeal, in a ruling which parallels that made by the ombudsman in the Samoan case (but before section 20A was enacted), held that a Fijian overstayer, Mrs Daganayasi, should have had disclosed to her, before the minister made a decision under section 20A, the medical report and memoranda of the medical referee or at least their substance to allow her a reasonable opportunity to answer them.[48]

In reaching that conclusion, the court did not refer to the two earlier English Court of Appeal decisions denying natural justice rights which were relied on in the first two New Zealand cases mentioned. Rather, it emphasized the leading decisions of the House of Lords and Privy Council in *Ridge v. Baldwin* in 1963 and *Durayappah v. Fernando*[49] in 1967 and recent English decisions which had 'tended for more than a decade to use the term "fairness" instead of or as an alternative to natural justice.' David Mullan, early in his academic career in 1975, had already valuably described and assessed that development.[50] His conclusion, pointing away from the Procrustean bed within which conceptualism had until then constrained Canadian judges, was that 'fairness, if developed properly by the courts, will lead to a highly desirable simplifying of the theoretical underpinnings of the law in this area. It will also lead to a situation where the right question is at long last being asked: what procedural protections, if any, are necessary for this particular decision-making process?'[51]

That necessity was to be assessed, New Zealand courts began to say, by reference to three matters set out by Lord Upjohn in 1967 in *Durayappah v. Fernando*:[52]

> first, what is the nature of the property, the office held, status enjoyed or services to be performed by the complainant of injustice. Secondly, in what circumstances or upon what occasions is the person claiming to be entitled to exercise the measure of control entitled to intervene. Thirdly, when a right to intervene is approved, what sanctions in fact is the latter entitled to impose upon the other. It is only upon a consideration of all these matters that the question of the application of the principle [of natural justice] can properly be determined.

Even with that advance in court-made law, the ombudsman process had advantages that were illustrated by the handling of the complaint by the young Samoan: first, it led to the correcting of errors in, and the updating of, the department's report; and, second, he got to stay while Mrs Daganayasi had already returned to Fiji. On the first point, one of the three judges would have made a ruling on the adequacy of the department's findings of fact, but the other two expressly refrained from considering that matter.

The legislature addressed article 13 of the *ICCPR* more directly in 1978 when it dealt with the deportation of non-citizens lawfully resident in New Zealand. It distinguished between three groups within that class: persons convicted of certain serious offences within prescribed times; suspected terrorists; and those certified as a threat to national security. The *Aliens Act* was repealed and accordingly the discrimination from which Mr Pagliara may have suffered was removed, but the *Undesirable Immigrants Act 1919* remained, not being repealed until 1987.

In relation to the first and second groups, the minister was to make the decision, whereas in relation to the third group it fell to the Governor-General in Council. Those subject to deportation in the first group, apart from any relevant rights of appeal within the court system, were given a right of appeal to a newly established tribunal, the Deportation Review Tribunal, consisting of a legal chair and two other members. The act contained a regular set of procedural provisions designed to give the appellant a fair opportunity to be heard. Its decisions were subject to appeal on questions of law to the Administrative Division of the Supreme Court. Appeals by those in the second category of suspected terrorists were directly to the Administrative Division, which was to hear and determine the appeal as if the deportation order had been made in the exercise of a discretion, and whose decisions were final. No appeal was provided for the third group, where the Governor-General-in-Council had made the decision.

The limited scope of appeal in relation to the second group[53] and the absence of an appeal for the third may be related to the 'compelling reasons of national security' mentioned in the Covenant and to the comment in *Daganayasi* that, where national security is involved, the requirements of fairness or natural justice may well be qualified.[54] On the other side, as the court also said, in an interesting use of later legislation in the interpretation of earlier, the 1978 provisions were 'further evidence of a climate of legislative opinion in which store is set on reasonably effective appeal rights.'[55]

New Zealand proceeded to ratify the *ICCPR* later in 1978. That opened relevant New Zealand law up to periodic scrutiny by the Human Rights Committee and, with accession in 1989 to the first optional protocol to the *ICCPR*, to the prospect of individuals complaining to the committee about immigration decisions affecting them.[56]

The procedural protections to be afforded in consolidating the 1964 act and its amendments would have added a little to the 1977 amendment. The minister would not have been obliged to consider any information not supplied within the fourteen-day appeal period and would have been authorized, perhaps unnecessarily, to seek and consider all such information from any source as considered fit. The bill also stated that the minister's decision was final. Submissions on that bill proposed that the *Daganayasi* duty of disclosure should be made explicit in the legislation, a view accepted by the minister at the select committee.[57] After the change of government in 1984 a new consolidating bill recognizing the force of the earlier submissions was introduced in 1986. The appeal period was extended to twenty-one days and, consistently with *Daganayasi* (indeed beyond it), it was made explicit that if the minister proposed to take into account information that was or might be prejudicial to the appellant's case, he or she was to disclose that information to the appellant, who was to have a reasonable opportunity to rebut or comment on it. The minister was also to appoint advisory panels for the purpose of advising on an appeal, where the minister requested. The provision, with some detailed amendment, again resulting from submissions to the select committee, were carried into the 1987 act.[58]

Judicial Review Facilitated in the 1970s, but Limits on Reviewing Policy Continue

The greater willingness of the courts to intervene in immigration cases to require fair procedure was facilitated by a procedural reform creating a new application for judicial review; it was imported from Ontario in 1972 on the urging of the Public and Administrative Law Reform Committee.[59] For the most part the old arguments about whether the correct remedy had been chosen fell away, the more so when the courts recognized that the New Zealand provisions were more broadly drawn than the Ontario ones, with a further broadening occurring in 1977.[60] As Sir Robin Cooke indicated in looking back over the work of the Law Reform Committee, the difficulties in judicial review should relate to the issues and not be exacerbated by procedural problems.[61] The courts have adopted that straightforward approach.[62]

Rather, attention was now to be given to the substance of the grounds for review. Could the claimant establish that the executive action was in the circumstances reviewable? The Catholic Bishop of Christchurch and his colleagues failed to show that in 1981 when they challenged the proposed issue by the minister of immigration of temporary permits to the members of the South African rugby team planning to tour New Zealand during the apartheid era.[63] For the judges, the language of the provision empowering the minister to grant (or not) permits was clear and unequivocal and not expressly fettered in any way. Further, it was far from clear that the *International Convention on the Elimination of All Forms of Racial Discrimination* of 1965 – the claimed source of the limit on the powers – did extend to sporting contacts of the kind in question. Next, the judges stressed the special character of immigration. For Cooke J.:[64]

> Immigration is a subject linked with foreign policy. In that sense it falls within a sphere where the Courts are very slow to intervene. Nevertheless, even in statutes concerned with immigration and policy in that regard, I would not exclude the possibility that a certain factor might be of such overwhelming or manifest importance that the Courts might hold that Parliament could not possibly have meant to allow it to be ignored. Such a situation would shade into the area where no reasonable Minister could overlook a certain consideration or reach a certain result.

Richardson J. wrote to the same effect:[65]

> There are many reported cases in which Courts have decided for historical or policy reasons to decline to review the exercise of discretionary power ... Many such non-justiciable questions have a strongly political flavour. An obvious example is the conduct of foreign relations
>
> ...
>
> Immigration policy is a sensitive and often controversial political issue. The national interest does not readily lend itself to compartmentalisation of the amalgam of considerations involved, and the isolation of particular aspects of foreign and/or domestic policies as obligatory considerations which must be weighed in the balance as distinct from permissible considerations which may properly but need not be taken into account. It may be due to considerations of this kind that Parliament elected to confer the discretion under s 14 in the widest terms. The section does not specify the criteria to be weighed by the Minister in considering the grant or refusal of visas. The absence of any particularisation is some indication that the legislature regarded the determination of the national interest in the exercise of the discretion a matter for decision in the round by the Executive. On

> this approach New Zealand's international obligations within the Commonwealth, within the United Nations, and to other States Parties to the Racial Discrimination Convention and other international treaties, are subsumed along with all other foreign and domestic policy concerns within the national interest, and our obligations under the Convention do not in the present case require separate identification and discrete consideration by the Minister.

This hands-off approach might be seen as consistent with Parliament's leaving the broad prerogative of the executive unaffected or largely so.[66]

Towards Open Government from the 1980s

One striking feature of judicial review cases into the 1970s was the paucity of the information relevant to the decision provided by the executive to those affected and to the courts. Often, no or no significant reasons would be given and there would be no or no significant discovery by the crown. The general immigration policy would sometimes not be known either. As we have already seen, the ombudsmen were in a different position. From the outset the legislation gave the ombudsmen virtually full rights of access to departmental files, a right of access seen by Colin Aikman as the most important characteristic of the office.[67] But that right was an exception that was heavily contested when the legislation was being prepared. The general position thirty or forty years ago was to the contrary.

Government papers were the Queen's papers. It was for her ministers to decide whether to release them. Otherwise they remained secret as the title to the *Official Secrets Act 1951* indicated. But on 1 July 1983 all that changed with the coming into force of the *Official Information Act 1982*. (That was also the day on which the comparable Canadian and Australian statutes came into force.) Government papers were now the people's papers. They now had the right of access to official information unless there was good reason to withhold it. They also had the right to have reasons for decisions affecting them, obviously a matter of prime importance in immigration cases.

That major change was to be put in the context of other changes in the law and government practice in the direction of more open government. In particular, from the 1970s crown claims to public interest immunity in court proceedings became increasingly rare and courts increasingly have had extensive documentation, including cabinet and ministerial papers, before them, far beyond that available in earlier times and, it would appear, in comparable jurisdictions.[68] In 1962, the same year the Court of Appeal decided that the courts rather than ministers had the final say over the release of official information for court proceedings[69] and the ombudsman legislation gave that officer virtually unfettered access to government files, the Royal Commission on the State Services declared that 'Government administration is the public's business, and the people are entitled to know more than they do of what is being done and why.' That declaration led to the newly established State Services Commission directing in 1964 that the rule should now be that information should be withheld only if there is good reason for doing so. But that administrative direction was not in the end seen as effective. Legislation was needed, again Canadian research and proposals were valuable,[70] and the *Official Information Act* was the result.

That important constitutional reform has already been the subject of extensive commentary.[71] I limit my discussion to the application of the principles of open government in the 1987 *Immigration Act* as amended, especially in 1991. The 1986 bill, like the 1964 act, would have given the minister powers to give general directions excepting classes of persons from the requirement to hold a permit. The bill did not require any process or publicity before or after the giving of the directions. The submission from the Legislation Advisory Committee and a comment from the Regulations Review Committee helped the select committee, according to the acting minister, to realize that delegating legislation to the ministerial level was not only unusual but in the circumstances was also unwise. Exemptions were rather to be effected by regulations made by the Governor-General in Council.[72]

Section 36 of the 1987 act, repeating section 23 of the *Official Information Act*, requires an immigration officer or, where the minister made the decision, the minister to give, on the applicant's request, the reasons in writing for refusal to grant a permit. It is however subject to provisions to the contrary elsewhere in the act, an exception made explicit in 1991. That qualification reflects a number of provisions introduced in that year which made it clear that certain powers to grant permits or give special directions are not accompanied by correlative rights to apply (for instance, if the individual was in New Zealand unlawfully), or to have an application considered, or to have reasons.[73] In those provisions, Parliament is distinguishing in a way not contemplated in the 1964 act between specific categories of applicants.[74] Similar exceptions were also made in the 1999 security amendments.[75] With those exceptions, applicants do of course have the right to have refusals of permits explained. That giving of reasons will: show (or not) that their cases have been properly considered; provide a basis for assessing whether a further application should be made; allow an appeal to be filed where an appeal is available; or allow review by the ombudsmen or court to be sought. The giving of reasons should also have the value of requiring the decision-maker to make the decision carefully and conscientiously and of assuring the wider public of the legitimacy of the exercise of power. It may also contribute to the build up of precedent.[76] The legislation moreover requires that the appeal bodies give reasons for their decisions. Such an obligation is routinely included in legislation regulating the procedure of tribunals.[77]

Publication of Policy and Further Institutions in the 1990s

One of the ways the 1991 amendment strengthens and more clearly defines the legal framework for the operation of government immigration policy is by providing for an independent review of certain immigration decisions by reference to the government's policy. It requires the minister to publish that policy and requires immigration officers making decisions on residence permits to comply with it.[78] The minister retains the right to make exceptions to the policy. It is still however the government's policy. The 1991 amendment gives no real direction on its content.[79] That appears, for instance, from the opposition of the New Zealand First Party to a 2003 amendment act because the 'legislation allows the continuation of the Government's current policy [allowing] about 45,000 immigrants per annum'; rather the number, it considered, should be about 10,000.[80]

A second, related change was to set up the Residence Appeal Authority (now the Residence Review Board) to hear challenges to departmental residence decisions by reference to the published policy. Thirdly, as had been urged in 1977, the act established an independent body, the Removal Review Authority, in place of the minister, to decide humanitarian appeals made by overstayers. Parties may appeal on questions of law from those tribunals to the High Court and, with leave, to the Court of Appeal.[81]

The proposed creation of those two bodies raised the question whether the Refugee Status Appeal Authority – which had been established by a cabinet decision as an independent body earlier in 1991, in response in part to the rapid increase in the number of refugee claimants – should not also have a statutory base. The interests or rights of refugee claimants were to be seen as more worthy of legal protection through a properly legislated process than those who had failed in an attempt to settle in New Zealand. Refugee claimants, after all, say they have a well-founded fear of persecution on the prescribed grounds and make their claims under rules of international law by which New Zealand is bound.[82] That argument did not succeed at that time but, following the comments made by the Court of Appeal in *Butler v. Attorney-General*[83] about the unsatisfactory legal position, Parliament in 1999 did enact legislation giving effect in New Zealand law to key provisions of the 1951 Convention and 1967 Protocol and setting up the Appeal Authority. By contrast to the legislation regulating the other tribunals, no appeal is provided for, with the consequence that its decisions have come before the courts only by way of judicial review.[84]

Under one common feature in the legislation governing their activities, the tribunals (but not the Deportation Review Tribunal) are required to prepare a report on their activities each year. The reports provide welcome transparency, as do their websites. I mention three matters. The first is the number of cases each tribunal handles each year: both the Residence Review Board and the Removal Review Authority decide about 300–400 and the Refugee Status Appeal Authority 600 (although great fluctuations occur); the proportion of successful appeals is about 40 percent for the board but the relief is in almost all cases a reference back to the Immigration Service or to the minister, 10 to 18 percent for the Removal Review Authority and, since 1991, 17 percent for the Refugee Status Appeal Authority. The overall numbers are to be compared with the ombudsman's immigration workload in the late 1970s of 60 to 130 per year. Notwithstanding the existence of those tribunals, the ombudsmen still receive a significant number of immigration complaints each year, totalling 224 in the year to 31 March 2004.

Secondly, the tribunal reports indicate that only a handful of tribunal decisions are appealed to or reviewed by the courts.

Thirdly, the reports raise important questions about the status and procedure of the tribunals. The Removal Review Authority hears appeals only on the papers. It has commented more than once, but without apparent effect, that issues of credibility or possible concealment of relevant information are sometimes difficult fully to assess from the papers. 'The Authority considers that in appropriate cases the ability to have a formal hearing would greatly assist due process.'[85] Both the Residence Review Board and Refugee Status Appeal Authority participated in the recent Law Commission review of the court and tribunal system and have stressed the need for their independence, actual and apparent, to be recognized, among other things by their administration being removed from the Department of Labour to the Ministry of Justice (as with the Deportation Review Tribunal).[86]

The Growing Role of International Law

As the Refugee Convention and the legislative and adjudicative action based on it indicate, international law is increasingly significant in various areas of administration law, including immigration. New Zealand's international obligations may:

1 require it to allow the entry of, or not to expel, certain individuals;
2 require it to follow certain procedures in making entry and expulsion decisions;
3 require it to consider certain matters in making those decisions; if the matter is established, (a) the decision-making power may be limited, or (b) the matter may be something to be considered by those exercising the power.

Straightforward examples of (1) are the rights of New Zealanders as citizens,[87] the rights of Australians under the trans-Tasman travel arrangement,[88] and the rights of diplomats, consular officers, crewmembers of ships and aircraft under various international arrangements.[89] Straightforward as well is the position of those refugees whose status has already been determined by the UN High Commissioner for Refugees and who enter under the New Zealand annual resettlement quota.[90] By contrast, difficulties often arise when a refugee claim is contested under the Refugee Convention.

Among the international agreements requiring certain procedures to be followed, within (2) above, are visa waiver and visa fee waiver agreements with a range of countries[91] and, as we have seen, article 13 of the *ICCPR* which requires a fair procedure to be followed if a non-citizen who is lawfully resident is to be deported.

The Refugee Convention also comes within (3) above since it prohibits the expulsion or return of refugees and refugee claimants to the frontiers of territories where their life or freedom would be threatened on account of their race, religion, nationality, membership of a particular social group or political opinion (article 33). The Convention against Torture similarly but more absolutely prohibits the expulsion, return or extradition of persons to a state where there are substantial grounds for believing they would be in danger of being subjected to torture.[92]

Those provisions place limits on state powers to control their borders. Treaty provisions may also place limits on those limits and effectively restore the power to expel, as appears from a recent decision of the Supreme Court of Canada discussed later.[93] By contrast, other international instruments, notably the UN *Convention on the Rights of the Child,* state matters to be considered by state authorities in the exercise of their powers.[94] Those provisions have been at the centre of extensive immigration litigation in Canada, New Zealand, and Australia and accordingly the subject of much academic commentary which understandably focuses less on the other categories of international obligations which place limits of substance or of process on the exercise of state power.[95] States are not to breach those limits (for example, expulsion to the prospect of torture) or fail to give a fair hearing. The establishing of the matter in the remaining subcategory (3)(b) – a matter to be weighed – does not have that decisive consequence.

The above discussion concerns the different categories of international obligations. Also significant, of course, for national legal systems in general and the courts in particular are the ways in which the international obligations are incorporated (or not) into national law.[96] The legislative practice varies:

1 the legislation expressly requires compliance with the international obligation;[97]
2 it expressly requires that the obligation be taken into account or had regard to;[98]
3 it provides for a fair hearing, sometimes with an independent tribunal or court having a role;[99]
4 it uses general language (e.g., about humanitarian principles);[100]
5 it is silent.[101]

In the fourth and fifth cases the question for the court or other decider is whether the international obligations may or must be considered. The second formula is capable of being read, as a literal matter, requiring the decision-makers to consider but then allowing them to breach the international obligation. But against that is the standard judicial approach that legislation and statutory powers should, if possible, be read and exercised consistently with international obligations.[102] In New Zealand the directions given and published by the minister in the statement of the government's immigration policy require officials to take those obligations into account – a formula which presents the same issue as the second statutory wording listed above.[103] Even with that possible problem, the practical consequence of the published policy appears to be a reduction in litigation. The international remedies remain available to those who consider that New Zealand institutions, including the courts, have not accorded them their rights.

The Watcher's Conclusions

What would a good academic watcher make of all of this? First, in the past forty years the executive's broad power to decide who to admit and who to expel has been considerably confined. The determination of the policy in the first place, however, is in general still an unconfined prerogative. 'In general' because obligations under international law increasingly place limits on that prerogative. Further, as Parliament required in 1991, the policy must now be published, a process which makes it more subject to political and public contest even if Parliament still essentially has no legislative role in respect of the substance of the policy. Next, also under the 1991 act, the published policy is in general binding on decision-makers.

The freedom that ministers and officials once had to make decisions without publishing the policy, without complying with it, without any kind of a hearing or disclosure of information and without giving reasons and effectively being free from independent review in a court or tribunal, is long gone. The office of the ombudsman, the legislature and the courts have increasingly opened up the process, required fair procedures, and provided for independent decision-makers in particular categories of cases. The law relating to the removal of overstayers provides a good example, with the actions of the ombudsman in 1975–76, Parliament in 1977, the courts in 1980, Parliament and those making submissions in 1983–87, and Parliament again in 1991.

Those changes, secondly, increasingly recognize differences between the rights and interests of those involved. The claimants are no longer to be seen in a single category of aliens with no right, privilege, or expectation – a position taken by judges as recently as the 1970s. They are now to be seen as arranged along a continuum beginning with those who in Hohfeldian terms hold no rights, through those with privileges to those with rights.[104] The entitlements may be to procedural protections (including appeal and review), to substantive rights or both: compare for instance a disappointed non-resident applicant for a temporary permit and a long-term resident whose deportation is being sought on the basis of conviction for a serious offences. Citizens come into a further category at the end of the continuum. One increasingly prominent issue is the rights and interests of family members of the person subject to removal, with the consequence that the immigration matter may no longer simply be one involving the individual subject to deportation.[105] State interests and responsibilities, notably in respect of national security, will often also have to be weighed, as Parliament has regularly directed, for instance, in 1978 and 1999, and the Court of Appeal has recognized.[106] The changes recognize as well the great increases since the 1960s in the number of cases that have to be handled – increases that match the great growth in travel into New Zealand.

Our careful watcher, thirdly, would observe particular statutory departures in immigration from general propositions of administrative law, including requiring officials to comply with published policy,[107] providing for electronic decision-making[108] and placing a time limit on seeking judicial review.[109] Those departures help alert us to the possibly distorting effect of a particular focus, but also raise the possibility of the departure becoming the norm or at least being adopted in other particular areas of administration. They also highlight, along with the second point, the relatively unusual character of this area of administration – most of those seeking the exercise of state power have no basis of right, interest or even legitimate expectation of a favourable outcome – although in practice that does happen, as appears from rapidly increasing visitor numbers.

Fourthly, deliberate and in many cases principled choices are now made between different decision-makers, procedures and review mechanisms (including the ombudsman and the official information legislation). Through the work of law reform agencies, especially the Legislation Advisory Committee, principles for the allocation of functions, for their definition, for their processes, and for appeal and review, have been developed, tested, and increasingly applied.[110] Those processes for the preparation of legislation help reflect and protect constitutional principle and the rule of law. One particular issue in the reform of immigration legislation will be the role of the minister. This area of administration is unusual in that ministers continue to have a hands-on role in particular cases even if the role has to some extent been reduced by the publication of binding policy and the independent role of the Review Board.[111] Is there a good reason for that continued role?[112]

Fifthly, foreign borrowings continue: from Canada we have benefited from reforms of judicial review procedures, official information, the *Canadian Bill of Rights* and *Charter of Rights and Freedoms*,[113] as well as from the work of scholars and judges.

A possible judicial borrowing relates to two concluding points: first, the growing role of international law in national legal systems, in general, and in immigration law, in particular; and second, the methods of introducing change in the law and its application. The particular case, a decision of the Supreme Court of Canada, turns on the evolving meaning and application of a treaty that has been in force for over fifty years – the Convention relating to the Status of Refugees. Persons who are 'guilty of acts contrary to the purposes and principles of the United Nations' are excluded from refugee status. The appellant had been convicted of serious drug offences involving organized trafficking in heroin and sentenced to eight years imprisonment. Did those offences come within the broadly worded exclusion and deprive him of refugee status as the Federal Court of Appeal had held? No, said the majority and his appeal accordingly succeeded.[114]

The majority, stating that the wording of the Refugees Convention and the rules of treaty interpretation were to be applied, held that the Federal Court of Appeal erred in dismissing the objects and purposes of the treaty and in according virtually no weight to the indications provided in the *travaux préparatoires*. After reviewing the legislative history and aspects of subsequent practice, it made this assessment of drug trafficking against the exclusion:[115]

> There is no indication in international law that drug trafficking on any scale is to be considered contrary to the purposes and principles of the United Nations.
>
> ...
>
> The second category of acts which fall within the scope of [the exclusion] are those which a court is able, for itself, to characterize as serious, sustained and systemic violations of fundamental human rights constituting persecution.

But the majority wrote that '[i]n this case there is simply no indication that the drug trafficking comes close to the core, or even forms a part of the corpus of fundamental human rights.'[116]

The dissenters gave much greater weight to the facts about drug trafficking, beginning with the extent of the problem, its economic and social costs, its links to criminal activity and corruption and resulting threats to international political and economic stability. They continued with the United Nations activity in the area of drug control, which indicated an approach to the determination of what constituted an act contrary to the purposes and principles of the United Nations. It was only after setting out all that material that they stated their approach to interpretation:[117]

> it cannot be the case that the interpretation of an exclusion must be forever restricted. As international law develops, the content of a phrase such as 'acts contrary to the purposes and principles of the United Nations' must be capable of development ...
>
> International law is developing continuously. Courts should recognize that the guidance provided by interpretive aids such as the *travaux préparatoires* and subsequent practice must be considered in the light of the current state of the law and international understandings. The *travaux préparatoires* should be taken into account, yet this does not mean that courts are restricted to a precise interpretation of that material. Rather, consideration should be given to the underlying principles and concerns that they express with the aim of giving them a contemporary meaning... The interpretation of international legal instruments is a dynamic process which must take into account the contemporary conditions ... [and] respond to the contemporary context.

That is to say, the minority, by contrast to the majority, gave greater weight to the developing rules of international law than to the drafting history and the original understanding.[118] That weighting raises basic questions about the source of legal obligation, especially international legal obligation, and about judicial method. Is it for the courts to introduce such changes in the law or in its application? Should that be left for those with political and democratic responsibility through treaty-making and legislating? But was it not, by reference to the actions of those with that responsibility, that the judges in the minority made its assessment?

Four centuries ago Francis Bacon, writing of followers and friends, affirmed that to take the advice of some few friends is ever honourable, 'for lookers-on many times see more than gamesters.'[119] David Mullan, an expert looker-on, is an eminent and influential adviser to those of us immersed in the middle of the game.

NOTES

Thanks to Graeme Buchanan, Robert Buchanan, Ben Keith, Janet McLean, Geoffrey Palmer, and Mike Taggart for comments on drafts of this paper, to George Mason for a helpful account of the current legislation, to Tim Smith, my clerk (2003–4), for his excellent research and other assistance with this paper and many others, and to Chelsea Payne, my new clerk, for helping with the final phases.

1 This sentence is perhaps subject to qualification considering the limits that have at times been placed on the rights of citizens to return to their place of citizenship; see, e.g., the recognition of state powers in *International Covenant on Civil and Political Rights*, 19 December 1966, 999 U.N.T.S. 171, art. 12(4) (entered into force 23 March 1976, ratified by New Zealand 28 December 1978) [*ICCPR*] that 'no one shall be *arbitrarily* deprived of the right to enter his own country' [emphasis added]. See also Lord Lester of Herne Hill Q.C., 'Thirty Years On: the East African-Asian Cases Revisited' [2002] P.L. 52. But see *Immigration Act 1987* (N.Z.), 1987/74, 33 RS 163, s. 3 for an absolute statement. The right to leave may be another matter, given the powers to refuse and recall passports.

2 *Baker v. Canada (Minister of Citizenship and Immigration)*, [1999] 2 S.C.R. 817. See, e.g., David Mullan, 'Deference from Baker to Suresh and Beyond: Interpreting the Conflicting Signals' in David Dyzenhaus, ed., *The Unity of Public Law* (Oxford: Hart Publishing, 2004) at 21, with which criticism the New Zealand Supreme Court agreed in *Attorney-General v. Zaoui*, [2006] 1 N.Z.L.R. 289 at paras 16 and 40 [*Zaoui*].

3 This paper also gives me the opportunity to reflect on connections of scholarship as well as of friendship which for David and me run back in the law faculty at the Victoria University of Wellington to the deanship of Professor Colin Aikman to whose memory David pays a splendid tribute in the latest edition of David J. Mullan, *Administrative Law: Cases, Text and Materials*, 5th ed. (Toronto: Emond Montgomery, 2003). See also the notes on developments in administrative law published in the New Zealand Journal of Public Administration to which the three of us, Professor R.O. McGechan, Roger Clark, and Graham Taylor contributed from the 1940s to the 1970s, and K.J. Keith, 'Public Law in New Zealand' (2003) 1 N.Z.J.P.I.L. 3.

4 See *Attorney-General v. E*, [2000] 3 N.Z.L.R. 257 at para. 1; *R v. Immigration Officer at Prague Airport*, [2004] U.K.H.L. 55 at paras. 11–14.

5 See, e.g., International Law Commission, *Draft Articles on Responsibilty of States for Internationally Wrongful Acts*, UN GOAR, 56th Sess., Supp. No. 10, UN Doc. A/56/10 c. IV.E.1 (2001) 43 art. 24; *New Zealand Nuclear Free Zone, Disarmament, and Arms Control Act 1987* (N.Z.), 1984/86 2–940 s.12; K.J. Keith, 'Policy and Law: politicians and judges (and poets)' in B.D. Gray and R.B. McClintock, eds., *Courts and Policy: Checking the Balance* (Wellington, NZ: Brookers, 1995) 117 at 129–34.

6 See, e.g., *In re Castioni*, [1891] 1 Q.B. 149; K.J. Keith, 'Piracy and Other Perils' (2002) 16 Journal of Maritime Law Association of Australia and New Zealand 7; *Immigration Restriction Act 1899* (N.Z.), 1899/33, s. 3 (not being a political offence).

7 Margaret MacMillan, *The Peacemakers* (London: John Murray, 2001) p. 23; Lorna Lloyd, *Peace through Law: Britain and the International Court in the 1920s* (Sussex: Boydell Press, 1997) at 43–4, 162, 166. The prime minister, Rt Hon. Helen Clark, has made a formal apology on behalf of the New Zealand government in respect of Chinese New Zealanders who paid a poll tax and suffered other discrimination in the late 1800s: Helen Clark, 'Speech to Chinese New Year Celebrations' online: New Zealand Labour http://labour.org.nz/labour_team/mps/mps/helen_clark/speeches_and_releases/speech158/index.html. As early as 1925, when still chief justice and concerned to promote a broad understanding of the legislative powers of the General Assembly, Sir Robert Stout raised the question whether there should be a distinct New Zealand citizenship, see *Butterworth's Fortnightly Notes*, 3 March 1925, 7.

8 *Nottebohm Case*, [1955] I.C.J. Rep. 4; compare para. 5 of the commentary to draft article 4 on Diplomatic Protection, prepared by the International Law Commission in 2004: *International Law Commission Report on the Work of the Fifty-sixth Session* (A/59/10).

9 See, e.g., André Siegfried, *Democracy in New Zealand*, 2nd ed. (Wellington, NZ: Victoria University Press, 1982) chaps. 16 and 17. See generally 'Immigration' in *An Encyclopedia of New Zealand* (Wellington, NZ: Government Printer, 1966); 'Te Ara: The Encyclopedia of New Zealand' online: Te Ara Encyclopedia of New Zealand http;//www.teara.govt.nz; Norman MacKenzie, ed., *The Legal Status of Aliens: Pacific Countries* (London: Oxford University Press, 1937) (for earlier accounts, see the chapters on New Zealand as well as Australia and Canada).

10 R.A. McG[echan], 'Immigration Restriction Amendment Act 1961' (1964) 4 V.U.W.L.R. 34 at 39, in which he considered *Annandale v. Collector of Customs*,

[1955] N.Z.L.R. 168 and the effect of this statutory elaboration of 'British birth and parentage':

> (2) A person shall not be deemed to be of British birth and parentage by reason that he or his parents or either of them is a naturalized British subject, or by reason that he is an aboriginal Native or the descendant of an aboriginal Native of any dominion other than the Dominion of New Zealand or of any colony or other possession or of any protectorate of His Majesty.

11 N.Z., (1964) 940 New Zealand Parliamentary Debates at 2712–19. See also N.Z., *1973 and 1974 Review of Immigration Policy* [1974] A.J.H.R. E 21 [*1974 Report*].

12 The legislation has over a long period provided for the exclusion or deportation of certain categories of people, such as those who have been convicted of certain offences, deported or allegedly involved in terrorism; *Immigration Act 1987*, ss. 7, 72, 73, 91, 92.

13 Rodger Haines Q.C., 'Immigration' in Hellen Papadopoulos et al., eds, *Laws of New Zealand* (Wellington, NZ: LexisNexis NZ, 2002) at para. 10. The governor general, of course, acts on the minister's advice. The prerogative to grant a pardon and thereby remove a conviction with consequences for deportation powers based on the conviction presumably remains, even though it is no longer expressly reserved.

14 Spiro Zavos, *How to Watch a Game of Rugby* (Wellington, NZ: Awa Press, 2004) at 9.

15 Ibid. at 18, 20. Zavos was borrowing from Richard Wollheim, *Art and Its Objects* (New York: Harper and Row, 1968).

16 The structure used by David Mullan in his textbook *Administrative Law* (Toronto: Carswell, 1979).

17 The pattern of the legislation would appear to have excluded an argument based on *Carltona v. Commissioner of Works*, [1943] 2 All E.R. 560 – if it is authoritative in New Zealand.

18 In 1991, as we shall see, Parliament decided that those powers should be exercised by regulation, in effect by cabinet.

19 It is interesting that in the revocation cases discussed below the power was in fact exercised by the minister and not by a delegate.

20 See *1974 Report*, *supra* note 11 at 12–13.

21 *Ngata v. Department of Labour (Note)*, [1980] 1 N.Z.L.R. 130. The consequential issues were dealt with by amendments to the 1964 act and addressed in further litigation; see *supra* note 3 at para. 10, n. 4.

22 *Cooper v. Wandsworth Board of Works* (1863), 14 C.B.N.S. 180, 194.

23 C.C. Aikman, 'The New Zealand Ombudsman' (1964) 42 Can. B. Rev. 399 [Aikman, 'Ombudsman'].

24 For an account by a very influential insider see J.L. Robson, *Sacred Cows and Rogue Elephants: Policy Development in the New Zealand Justice Department* (Wellington, NZ: Government Printing Office 1987) chap. 25.

25 For an account of the position in the mid-1960s see C.C. Aikman, 'Administrative Law – I' and 'Administrative Law – II' in John L. Robson, ed., *New Zealand: The Development of its Laws and Constitution*, 2nd ed. (London: Stevens, 1967) chaps. 4 and 5.

26 The 1961 change in the drafting of the standard empowering section was recently recalled by the Supreme Court in one of its earliest judgments, *Zaoui v. Attorney-General*, [2005] 1 N.Z.L.R. 577 at para. 84. The later process, based on the *Regulations (Disallowance) Act 1989* (N.Z.), 1989/143, 4–2283 and amendments to Standing Orders made in 1985 may be seen at work in an immigration matter in the *Report of the Regulations Review Committee on the Complaint relating to the Immigration Regulations 1991 Regulation 32B* [1998] A.J.H.R. I 16E (N.Z.). The regulation was revoked and replaced later in 1998. See Ryan Malone, *Regulations Review Committee Digest* (Wellington, NZ: New Zealand Centre for Public Law Faculty of Law, Victoria University of Wellington, 2003) at 75 online: http://www.law.vuw.ac.nz/vuw/fca/law/files/RRC_Printer_Friendly_Digest.pdf.

27 For the work of the committees, see B.J. Cameron, 'The Law Reform Committees 1966–86' (1988) 13 N.Z.U.L.R. 123; Sir Robin Cooke, 'The Public and Administrative Law Reform Committee: The Early Years' (1988) 13 N.Z.U.L.R. 150 [Cooke, 'Public Law']; and J. Farmer, 'The Work of the Public and Administrative Law Committee' (1988) 13 N.Z.L.U.R. 155.

28 See, e.g., Richard Wild, 'The Administrative Division of the Supreme Court of New Zealand' (1972) 22 U.T.L.J. 258, and J.F. Northey, 'An Administrative Division of the New Zealand Supreme Court: A Proposal for Law Reform' (1969) 7 Alb. L.R. 62.

29 Cooke, 'Public Law,' *supra* note 27 at 152–53.

30 N.Z., (1968) 356 New Zealand Parliamentary Debates at 1067.

31 G.D.S. Taylor and D.J. Mullan, 'Recent Developments in Administrative Law' (1969) 32(1) N.Z.J.P.A. 60.

32 Cooke, 'Public Law,' *supra* note 27 at 151–52.

33 New Zealand Law Commission, *The Structure of the Courts* (Wellington, NZ: Law Commission, 1989) at paras. 465–74. The commission drew on the work of Stephen Legomsky, later published as Stephen Legomsky, *Specialized Justice: courts, administrative tribunals, and a cross national theory of specialization* (Oxford: Oxford University Press, 1990).

34 *Judicature Amendment Act 1991* (N.Z.), 1991/60, 1–538, s. 3, Sch.

35 *Pagliara v. Attorney-General*, [1974] 1 N.Z.L.R. 86.

36 *Ex p Venicott*, [1920] 3 K.B. 72; *R. v. Governor of Brixton Prison, Ex p Soblen*, [1963] 2 Q.B.243; *Schmidt v. Secretary of State*, [1969] 2 Ch. 149.
37 [1964] A.C. 40; see K.J. Keith 'Ridge v. Baldwin: 20 Years On' (1983) 13 V.U.W.L.R. 239.
38 [1974] 1 N.Z.L.R. 86 at 95.
39 *Tobias v. May*, [1976] 1 N.Z.L.R. 509.
40 Ibid. at 511–12.
41 For a useful survey, see Helen Bowie, 'The Ombudsmen and Immigration' (1982) 12 V.U.W.L.R. 277.
42 *Report of the Ombudsmen* [1975] A.J.H.R. A3 at 34–6.
43 *Report of the Ombudsmen* [1979] A.J.H.R. A3 at 42 [*1979 Annual Report*].
44 Ibid. at 40.
45 *Moevao v. Minister of Immigration*, [1980] 1 N.Z.L.R. 464.
46 *Report of the Ombudsmen* [1978] A.J.H.R. A3 at 9–10.
47 *1979 Annual Report*, *supra* note 43 at 6.
48 *Daganayasi v. Minister of Immigration*, [1980] 2 N.Z.L.R. 130 [*Daganayasi*].
49 [1967] 2 A.C. 337 [*Durayappah*].
50 David Mullan, 'Fairness: the New Natural Justice?' (1975) 25 U.T.L.J. 281 (acknowledging New Zealand influences in the paper's preparation), cited, for instance, in *Manhaas v. Bolger* (17 August 1979), Wellington, New Zealand A 219/79, Jeffries J.
51 Ibid. at 315.
52 *Durayappah*, *supra* note 49 at 349. See, e.g., the valuable judgment of Barker J. in *Chandra v. Minister of Immigration*, [1978] 2 N.Z.L.R. 559 at 569–74 [*Chandra*]; and *Daganayasi*, *supra* note 48 at 143–4. See also G.D.S. Taylor 'Fairness and Natural Justice – Distinct Concepts or Mere Semantics?' (1977) 3 Monash U.L. Rev. 191.
53 See *Robson v. Hicks Smith Ltd*, [1965] N.Z.L.R. 1113 at 1115, 1120.
54 *Daganayasi*, *supra* note 48 at 145, referring to *R v. Secretary of State for Home Department ex parte Hosenball*, [1977] 1 W.L.R. 766 at 778, where Lord Denning M.R. had referred with approval to *Liversidge v. Anderson*, [1942] A.C. 206 at 219.
55 *Daganayasi*, *supra* note 48 at 142.
56 See, e.g., *Mohammed Sahid v. New Zealand*, Communication No. 893/1999, UN Doc. CCPR/C/77/D/893/1999 (views adopted 11 April 2003).
57 Submissions were also critical of privative clauses included in the 1983 bill. Again the force of that position was accepted, although see now *Immigration Act 1987*, ss. 10(3) (enacted in 1991), 10A(4) (enacted in 2003), 13BB(3) (enacted in 2003), 125 AB(6) (enacted in 2004, the subject of an opinion by

the solicitor-general holding the provision to be a justified limit). Those provisions mainly relate to persons applying from outside New Zealand and do not prevent an application for *habeas corpus*.

58 See *Immigration Act 1987*, ss. 63–64. See *Report No.2 of the Legislation Advisory Committee* at para 56.

59 See *Fourth Report of the Public and Administrative Law Reform Committee*, January 1971, and J.F. Northey, 'An Additional Remedy in Administrative Law' [1970] N.Z.L.J. 2002.

60 *Chandra*, supra note 52 at 562–64, Barker J.; on this foreign borrowing, see David Mullan, 'One plus five equals six' [1971] N.Z.L.J. 512.

61 Cooke, 'Public Law,' *supra* note 27 at 154.

62 See, e.g., *Royal Australasian College of Surgeons v. Phipps*, [1999] 3 N.Z.L.R. 1 at 11–12; *Jones v. Sky City Auckland Ltd*, [2004] 1 N.Z.L.R. 192 at para. 29.

63 *Ashby v. Minister of Immigration*, [1981] 1 N.Z.L.R. 222.

64 Ibid. at 226, Cooke J.

65 Ibid. at 230–31, Richardson J. That judge, unlike the other two members of the court, accepted that the Convention, especially as interpreted by the committee set up under it, did extend to sporting contacts with regimes practising apartheid. But that left remaining the questions of the obligations of states parties and the relationship of those obligations to the extensive discretion of the minister.

66 See also *Patel v. Minister of Immigration*, [1997] 1 N.Z.L.R. 252 [*Patel*].

67 Aikman, 'Ombudsman' *supra* note 23 at 407; for later commentary, relevant to the role, proposed and actual, of the ombudsman under the *Official Information Act 1982* (N.Z.), 1982/156, 35 RS 403, see D.J. Shelton, 'The Ombudsmen and Information' (1982) 12 V.U.W.L.R. 233, and K.J. Keith, 'Open Government in New Zealand' (1987) 17 V.U.W.L.R. 333.

68 See, e.g., *Lange v. Atkinson*, [2000] 3 N.Z.L.R. 385 at 395–396.

69 *Corbett v. Social Security Commission*, [1962] N.Z.L.R. 878.

70 See Committee on Official Information, *Towards Open Government: General Report* (Wellington, NZ: Government Printer, 1980), Committee on Official Information, *Towards Open Government: Supplementary Report* (Wellington, NZ: Government Printer, 1981).

71 See, e.g., Ian Eagles, Michael Taggart and Grant Liddell, *Freedom of Information in New Zealand* (Auckland, NZ: Oxford University Press, 1992); G.D.S. Taylor, *Judicial Review: A New Zealand Perspective* (Wellington, NZ: Butterworths, 1991) Part III; Legal Research Foundation and New Zealand Institute of Public Law, *The Official Information Act: papers presented at a seminar held by the Legal Research Foundation and the New Zealand Institute of Public*

Law at the Old Government Building, Wellington on 25 February 1997 and at the University of Auckland on 26 February 1997 (Auckland, NZ: Legal Research Foundation, 1997).

72 N.Z., (1987) 478 New Zealand Parliamentary Debates at 7,748. See *Legislation Advisory Committee Report of June 1988* at para. 50, and also *Immigration Act 1987*, s. 150(e).

73 See, e.g., *Immigration Act 1987*, ss. 7(4), 12(4), 17(2), 18E, 25(3), 34B(3) (enacted in 2003), 35A(2), 58, 130(6): considered in *Patel, supra* note 66; *Singh v. Chief Executive of the Department of Labour*, [1999] N.Z.A.R. 258 [*Singh*]; and *Wang v. Chief Executive Department of Labour* (20 October 2004), Auckland, New Zealand CIV20044045715 (H.C.), Harrison J.

74 The title to the 1991 act indicates it was designed to strengthen and more clearly define the legal framework for the operation of government incorporating policy in particular (c) by ensuring that persons who do not comply with immigration procedures and rules are not advantaged in comparison with persons who do comply.

75 See *Immigration Act 1987*, ss. 114F(2)(a), 114K(7). These sections were inserted by *Immigration Amendment Act 1999* (N.Z.), 1999/16, 120, s. 35.

76 See, e.g., *Singh, supra* note 73.

77 See, e.g., Michael Taggart, 'The Rationalisation of Administrative Tribunal Procedure: the New Zealand Experience' in Robin Creyke, ed., *Administrative Tribunals: Taking Stock* (Canberra: Centre for International and Public Law, 1992) 91.

78 That statutory obligation means that the general proposition that policies are not to be treated as absolutes does not apply. Cf. *Chiu v. Minister of Immigration*, [1994] 2 N.Z.L.R. 541 at 550.

79 But see *Immigration Act 1987*, ss. 13B(3), 13B(3A), 13B(4). One aspect of the policy was challenged unsuccessfully in *Patel v. Chief Executive of the Department of Labour*, [1997] 1 N.Z.L.R. 102, [1997] N.Z.A.R. 264 (C.A.) with the High Court making the point that the power to make immigration policy was still the prerogative power and was not conferred by the statute.

80 *Immigration Amendment Bill 2003* (N.Z.), 2003/62–2, Commentary.

81 *Immigration Act 1987*, ss. 115, 115A, 117. For an example of a successful appeal from the Deportation Review Tribunal (also limited to questions of law) see *Wolf v. Minister of Immigration*, [2004] N.Z.A.R. 414 where Wild J. applied what he referred to as a higher level of judicial scrutiny than appropriate in challenges, say, to rating decisions.

82 The Legislation Advisory Committee made a submission to that effect. See also W.M. Wilson Q.C., *Report to the Rt Hon. W.F. Birch, Minister of Immigration on the Process of Refugee Status Determination* (29 April 1992).

83 [1999] N.Z.A.R. 205 at 218–20. This case also provides a brief history of the processes used since the early 1960s.

84 See, e.g., *Attorney-General v. E*, [2000] 3 N.Z.L.R. 257 and *Jiao v. Refugee Status Appeals Authority*, [2003] N.Z.A.R. 647. There is a further contrast within the provisions. Decisions of the High Court on appeal from the Deportation Review Tribunal and the minister in the suspected terrorist cases are final, while those relating to the residence and removal bodies can be further appealed. Such limits encourage the filing of judicial review as well as or instead of the appeal.

85 Removal Review Authority, *Annual Report* (September 2004) at 5.

86 See New Zealand Law Commission, *Delivering Justice For All: A Vision for New Zealand Courts and Tribunals*, (Wellington, NZ: Law Commission, 2004) chap. 7 at paras. 63–8 (see recommendation 142).

87 *Immigration Act 1987*, s. 3. See also *New Zealand Bill of Rights Act 1990* 1990/109, 3–1687 s. 18(2) and *ICCPR*, *supra* note 1, art. 12(4).

88 N.Z., *New Zealand Gazette* vol. 1 (1973) at 413; ministerial exemption given under *Immigration Act 1964* (N.Z.), 1964/43, 224, s. 19.

89 See, e.g., *Vienna Convention on Diplomatic Relations 1961*, adopted 18 April 1961, 500 U.N.T.S. 95 (entered into force 24 April 1964), *Convention 108 Seafarers' Identity Documents Convention 1958*, adopted 13 May 1958 by the International Labour Organization (entered into force 19 February 1961), *Immigration Act 1987* (N.Z.), s. 11.

90 New Zealand is one of only sixteen countries in the world to operate an annual refugee quota. There are 750 resettlement places.

91 See, e.g., *Immigration Regulations 1999* (N.Z.), 1999/284, 1453, Sch. 1, part 1.

92 *Convention Against Torture and Other Cruel, Inhuman or Degrading Treatment or Punishment*, 10 December 1984, 1465 U.N.T.S. 85, art. 3(1) (entered into force 26 June 1987, ratified by New Zealand 10 December 1989).

93 *Pushpanathan v. Canada (Minister of Citizenship and Immigration)*, [1998] 1 S.C.R. 982 [*Pushpanathan*].

94 *Convention on the Rights of the Child*, 20 November 1989, 1577 U.N.T.S. 3, art. 3 (entered into force 2 September 1990).

95 For recent discussions which valuably address the wider picture, see Claudia Geiringer, 'Tavita and all that: Confronting the Confusion Surrounding Unincorporated Treaties and Administrative Law' (2004) 21 N.Z.U.L.R. 66, and Treasa Dunworth, 'Public International Law' [2004] N.Z.L.Rev. 411 at 415–18. See the earlier challenging essay by David Dyzenhaus, Murray Hunt, and Michael Taggart, 'The Principle of Legality in Administrative Law: Internationalism as Constitutionalism' (2001) 1 O.U.C.L.J. 5.

96 See New Zealand Law Commission, *A New Zealand Guide to International*

Law and its Sources (Wellington, N.Z.: Law Commission, 1996) at paras. 43–64. See also Legislation Advisory Committee, *Guidelines on Process and Content of Legislation* (Wellington, NZ: Legislation Advisory Committee, 2001) chap. 6.

97 See *Immigration Act 1987*, s. 129X.

98 See ibid., s. 129X(2).

99 See ibid., s. 103.

100 See ibid., s. 22.

101 See in respect of the rights of children and families.

102 See *Zaoui*, *supra* note 2 and the cases referred to there.

103 The 1991 act does, by contrast, require officials to comply with residence policy.

104 W.N. Hohfeld, 'Some fundamental legal conceptions as applied in judicial reasoning' (1913) 23 Yale L.J. 16.

105 See articles cited at *supra* note 95 and the cases discussed there. See also *Madafferi v. Australia*, Communication No. 1011/2001, UN Doc. CCPR/C/81/D/1011/2001 (views adopted 26 August 2004) (a recent relevant Australian case before the Human Rights Committee).

106 See, e.g., *Daganayasi*, *supra* note 48.

107 See *supra* note 78.

108 *Immigration Act 1987*, ss. 10A(6), 13E(5), 125AB(5); cf. *Ankers v. Attorney-General*, [1995] 2 N.Z.L.R. 595 at 607.

109 *Immigration Act 1987*, s. 146A.

110 See especially Legislation Advisory Committee, *Legislative Change: Guidelines on Process and Content* (from 1987) which is endorsed by the *Cabinet Manual* (Wellington, NZ: Cabinet Office, 2001) at paras 5.35–5.39: Ministers putting legislation forward are required to certify compliance or justify departure. For comment, see Walter Iles, 'The Responsibility of the New Zealand Legislation Advisory Committee' (1994) 13 Stat. L.Rev. 11; G.W.R. Palmer, 'The New Zealand Legislation Machine' (1987) 17 V.U.W.L.R. 285; K.J. Keith, 'The New Zealand Legislation Advisory Committee: Choreographer or Critic' (1990) 4 P.L.R. 290.

111 But notice that the board often refers matters to the minister to consider whether to make an exception.

112 Compare the absence of ministerial powers to release certain prisoners under the *Criminal Justice Act 1985* (N.Z.), 1985/120, 41 RS 367 with their presence in the *Criminal Justice Act 1954* (N.Z.), 1954/50, 1–237.

113 As Mullan discussed in a paper first delivered in Wellington, the Bill of Rights has had only a limited impact beyond criminal procedure and freedom of expression: David Mullan, 'A Comparison of the Impact of the

New Zealand Bill of Rights and the Canadian Charter of Rights and Freedoms on Administrative Law' (2003) 1 N.Z.J.P.I.L. 115. However, s. 27, the natural justice provision of the *New Zealand Bill of Rights Act 1990*, had a role in *Zaoui*, *supra* note 2. See also *Drew v. Attorney-General*, [2002] 1 N.Z.L.R. 58 at para. 77.

114 *Pushpanathan*, *supra* note 93.

115 Ibid. at paras. 69–70.

116 Ibid. at para. 72.

117 Ibid. at paras 128–29.

118 For a New Zealand case which also contemplates an ambulatory reading of a statute by reference to international law developments, see *Sellers v. Maritime Safety Inspector*, [1999] 2 N.Z.L.R. 44 at 62. Our honorand has referred to that judgment as 'fascinating': David Mullan, 'The Role for Underlying Constitutional Principles in a Bill of Rights World' [2004] N.Z. Law Review 9 at 32. See also *Vienna Convention on the Law of Treaties 1969*, 23 May 1969, 1155 U.N.T.S. 331 art. 31(3)(c) (entered into force 27 January 1980) valuably discussed by Campbell McLachlan, 'The Principle of Systematic Integration and Article 31(3)(c) of the Vienna Convention' (2005) 54 I.C.L.Q. 279.

119 Francis Bacon, 'Of Followers and Friends' in *Essays* (1625).

Process and Substance in Judicial Review

PAUL CRAIG

This chapter examines the inter-relationship between process and substance within judicial review. The focus of the analysis is the jurisprudence of the European Community courts, the European Court of Justice (ECJ) and the Court of First Instance (CFI). European Union (EU) law is especially interesting in this respect, because many of the member states that comprise the EU have civil law legal systems, while others are grounded in the common law. EU law provides therefore a ready-made test case for legal comparativism, in the sense that the doctrine developed by the Community courts will draw on civil law and common law influences, while fashioning legal rules that are felt to be best suited to the needs of the EU.

EU law is also of particular relevance for this study because the Community courts have developed important process rules that are of real significance for the inter-relationship of process and substance. This chapter will not seek to traverse the entirety of process within EU law. The object is rather to consider the aspects of process that are of special significance for the interaction with substantive review.

The discussion begins with the duty to give reasons, a process right readily recognized in common law regimes. The analysis then turns to access to the file and the duty of care, which are either not recognized in common law regimes, or if so only to a much lesser extent. The link between these process rights and substantive review will be examined throughout the chapter, which will conclude by reflecting on the nature of this connection in more general terms.

Reasons

Process rights in the EU owe their origin to treaty articles, Community legislation, and the jurisprudence of the Community courts. The precise blend varies with the process right in question. A prime example of an important process right that was encapsulated in the original treaty is the duty to provide reasons in article 253 European Communities Treaty (EC) (formerly article 190):

> Regulations, directives and decisions adopted jointly by the European Parliament and the Council, and such acts adopted by the Council or the Commission, shall state the reasons on which they are based and shall refer to any proposals or opinions which were required to be obtained pursuant to the Treaty.

There are a number of policy rationales for the duty to provide reasons. From the perspective of affected parties, it makes the decision-making process more transparent, so that they can know why a measure has been adopted. From the perspective of the decision-maker itself, an obligation to give reasons will help to ensure that the rationale for the action has been thought through; having to explain oneself, and defend the rationality of one's choice, is always a salutary exercise. From the perspective of the ECJ, the existence of reasons facilitates judicial review, by, for example, enabling the court to determine whether a decision was disproportionate.

These policy arguments are reflected in the oft-repeated judicial statements that reasons inform the addressee of the decision of the factual and legal grounds on which it is based, thereby enabling the person to decide whether to seek judicial review and facilitate the exercise of that review by the Community courts. Thus as the ECJ stated early in its jurisprudence:[1]

> In imposing upon the Commission the obligation to state reasons for its decisions, Article 190 is not taking mere formal considerations into account but seeks to give an opportunity to the parties defending their rights, to the court of exercising its supervisory functions and to Member States and to all interested nationals of ascertaining the circumstances in which the Commission has applied the Treaty.

The scope of article 253 EC is broad: it applies to regulations, decisions, and directives adopted either by the Council, Commission, and Parliament, or by the Council and Commission alone. This is noteworthy. The duty to give reasons varies in the domestic law of the member states, but in most countries it is narrower than that in EC law. Thus article 253 imposes a duty to give reasons not only for administrative decisions, but also for legislative norms, such as regulations or directives. Many national legal systems do not impose an obligation to furnish reasons for legislative norms, or do so only in limited circumstances. The most common general formulation of the scope of the duty to give reasons can be taken from the *Sytraval* case:[2]

> [I]t is settled case law that the statement of reasons required by Article 190 [now Article 253] of the Treaty must be appropriate to the act at issue and must disclose in a clear and unequivocal fashion the reasoning followed by the institution which adopted the measure in question in such a way as to enable the persons concerned to ascertain the reasons for the measure and to enable the competent Community court to exercise its powers of review. The requirements to be satisfied by the statement of reasons depend on the circumstances of each case, in particular the content of the measure in question, the nature of the reasons given and the interest which the addressees of the measure, or other parties to whom it is of direct and individual concern, may have in obtaining explanations. It is not necessary for the reasoning to go into all the relevant facts and points of law, since the question whether the statement of reasons meets the requirements of Article 190 of the Treaty must be assessed with regard not only to its wording but also to its context and to all the legal rules governing the matter in question.

In terms of content, the obligation to give reasons will normally require: specification of the treaty article on which the measure was based; the factual background to the measure; and the purposes behind it. This is exemplified by the *Tariff Preferences* case.[3] The ECJ annulled a Council measure in part because the legal basis of the measure had not been specified. In *Germany v. Commission*[4] the Court held that it was sufficient to set out in a concise, clear, and relevant manner the principal issues of law and fact upon which the action was based, such that the reasoning which led the Commission to its decision could be understood. Where a decision is establishing a new principle, or applying it in a novel fashion, there will have to be sufficient reasons in the decision itself,[5] but on some occasions the Court will sanction the incorporation of reasons from another instrument.[6]

The content of the duty will also be affected by the very scope of article 253, applying as it does both to general legislative norms, and to individualized decisions. The degree of specificity will, therefore, depend upon the nature of the contested measure. The ECJ explicitly recognized in *Beus*[7] that the extent of the requirement to state the reasons on which a measure was based would depend on the nature of the measure in question. In the case of a regulation it might well therefore suffice for the preamble to indicate the general situation that led to its adoption, and the general objectives that it intended to achieve. It was not necessary for the regulation to set out the factual basis of the measure, which was often complex, nor was it necessary for the relevant measure to provide a complete evaluation of those facts. Where a measure is of a general legislative nature, it will be necessary for the Community authority to show the reasoning that led to its adoption, but it will not be necessary for it to go into every point of fact and law. Where the essential objective of the measure has been clearly disclosed, there is no need for a specific statement of the reasons for each of the technical choices that have been made.[8]

The ECJ may well demand greater particularity where the measure being challenged is of an individual, rather than legislative nature. Thus in *Germany v. Commission*[9] Germany produced an alcoholic drink called Brenwein, which was made from wine much of which was imported from outside the Community. The establishment of the common external tariff resulted in significant cost increases, and therefore the German government asked the Commission for permission to import 450,000 hectolitres of this wine at the old, lower rate of duty. The Commission acceded to this request in principle, but only for 100,000 hectolitres. The Commission justified this decision on the grounds that there was ample production of wine in the EC, and that the grant of the requested quota would lead to serious disturbances on the relevant product market. The ECJ found the Commission's reasoning to be insufficiently specific concerning the size of any Community surplus, and that it was unclear why there would be serious disturbances in the market.

The context in which individual decisions are taken will, however, be of importance in determining the extent of the duty to give reasons. Thus, in relation to competition, the Community courts have held that in stating the reasons for the decisions it takes in this area the Commission is not obliged to adopt a position on all the arguments relied on by the parties. It is sufficient if it sets out the facts and legal considerations having decisive importance in the context of the decision.[10]

Access to the File

An important component of the right to be heard is access to the file. The nature and significance of this right should be made clear at the outset. Access to the file may be of relevance before the decision is made by the administration, or after it has been made when an applicant seeks to challenge the decision by way of judicial review. Access facilitates understanding of the evidentiary basis on which the decision is to be made or has been made, and comprehension of the reasoning underlying it, thereby placing the individual in a better position from which to be able to proffer counter-arguments when exercising the right to be heard or challenging the decision.

It will be seen that EU law, after some initial hesitation and subject to some reservations, accords access to the file as part of the rights of the defence. This is by way of contrast to, for example, the situation in the United Kingdom, where there is no such right of access to the file prior to the initial decision being taken. Nor is there any such right when seeking judicial review: the individual must apply for discovery/disclosure of documentation from the public body, and the UK courts have placed strict limitations as to when this will be ordered.[11]

A right of access to the file is however accorded in a number of member states.[12] The fact that EU law has sanctioned access when the initial decision is being made is therefore to be welcomed as a valuable process right, as is the inclusion of this right as one component of the right to good administration in the *Charter of Fundamental Rights*.[13] The initial jurisprudence was developed in relation to competition law, but has been extended to other areas. The application of the principle of access is not especially difficult where the decision affects only one party or a small number of parties. It can, however, be problematic when the administrative decision affects a multiplicity of parties, the more so where the litigation is complex and generates a large amount of documentation, as exemplified by cases on complex horizontal cartels. The Community courts have placed certain limitations on access in such instances, and these should be critically appraised. This appraisal should, however, be fair; it has only been necessary to construct limits because of the breadth of the initial principle of access.

As noted above, the early jurisprudence on access arose in competition proceedings.[14] The ECJ initially held in *VBVB*[15] that there was no legal obligation to disclose the complete file, only those documents on which the Commission had based its decision. The Commission chose not to stick to the legal letter of this judgment, and permitted access, except where, for example, information covered by professional secrecy was involved. The CFI in *Hercules*[16] gave legal force to this administrative practice. The Commission is obliged to make available all documents obtained in the course of the investigation, save where they involve business secrets of other undertakings, confidential information, or internal Commission documents.[17] This was regarded as part of a wider principle of equality of arms, allowing addressees of a decision to examine the file so that they could effectively proffer their views on the evidentiary basis of the Commission decision.[18] It was made clear that it was not for the Commission alone to decide which documents were useful to the undertakings and that defendants should have the opportunity to examine them in order to determine their probative value for their defence. The Community courts might however not choose to annul for failure to grant access unless this adversely affects the right to a hearing. In any event, a right of access to the file is now included in the regulations governing competition.[19]

It was originally thought that the right of access to the file was confined to competition proceedings. It is clear that this is no longer the case. The Community courts have applied the reasoning from the competition cases in other contexts. Thus, in *Eyckeler* the CFI reasoned by analogy from the competition cases and held that access to the file was equally important in challenging customs' decisions. It stated that if the right to be heard was to be exercised effectively there must be access to the non-confidential documentation relied on by the Commission when it made the contested decision.[20] It was not open to the Commission to exclude documents that it did not consider relevant, since these might well be of interest to the applicant. It would moreover be a serious breach of the rights of the defence if the Commission could unilaterally exclude from the administrative procedure documents that might be detrimental to it.[21] The ease with which the CFI reasoned by analogy from competition to customs signifies the generalization of access to the file as an aspect of the right to be heard, irrespective of the subject-matter area in question, and this is in accord with the formulation in the *Charter of Fundamental Rights*.[22] At the very least it renders it all the easier for applicants contesting decisions in other areas to argue that the right should be equally applicable, and places the onus on the Commission, if it is so minded, to show why this should not be so.

The precise boundaries of the principle were tested in complex litigation in *Aalborg Portland*.[23] The case concerned a long-running Commission investigation into agreements and concerted practices engaged in by a number of European cement producers. The documentation supporting the alleged practices was very large. The Commission therefore did not append to the statement of objections the documents supporting its conclusions. It prepared a box of documents that was made available for each addressee relating to the statement of objections addressed to that firm. The Commission refused access to the chapters of the statement of objections that they had not received and refused to grant access to all documents in the investigation file. The ECJ reiterated the right of access to the file, which meant that 'the Commission must give the undertaking concerned the opportunity to examine all the documents in the investigation which may be relevant for its defence,'[24] including incriminating and exculpatory evidence.

This general principle was subject to a number of limitations. There was no access to business secrets and confidential information. There was no general principle that the parties must receive copies of all documents taken into account in the case of other persons.[25] There was no right for access to documentation that was irrelevant and bore no relation to the allegations of fact or law in the statement of objections.[26] It was for the applicant to show that the result would have been different if incriminating evidence not communicated to the applicant had been relied on by the Commission in reaching its decision,[27] although where the document not communicated was exculpatory it was only necessary to show that its non-disclosure was able to influence disadvantageously the Commission decision.[28]

It was for the CFI to make these determinations in the light of a provisional examination of certain evidence to see whether the documents 'could have had a significance which ought not to have been disregarded.'[29] The CFI in performing this task had used an 'objective link' criterion: there had to be some objective link between the document not disclosed and the finding against the relevant undertaking. The ECJ upheld this test.[30]

The application of the access principle to complex litigation of this kind is undoubtedly problematic. There are, as the applicants claimed in argument,[31] difficulties in the CFI applying the objective link criterion, since it will not have the same knowledge and understanding of the situation as the Commission. There is also a sense in which the ECJ's approach limits the force of the right of access to the file, given that the Commission's failure to respect the right will only lead to annulment if the undertakings can discharge the burden of proof of showing that the documentation to which they were denied access would have made a difference. The ECJ's approach is nonetheless understandable. It is reluctant to allow what may well be years of Commission investigation into a complex cartel to be overturned through annulment whenever the undertaking can point to something in the mass of documents that it did not have access to.

The Duty of Care/Diligent and Impartial Examination

Recognition of the Principle

The ECJ developed early in the history of the European Coal and Steel Community (ECSC) and European Economic Community (EEC) an obligation that care should be exercised in particular when discretionary determinations were made in relation to individual cases,[32] and this jurisprudence was applied especially in the context of competition[33] and state aids.[34] The principle of care 'establishes a duty on the administration carefully to examine the relevant factual and legal aspects of the individual case.'[35] While there are antecedents for this duty going back to the ECJ's early jurisprudence, it has been developed more fully in the case law of the CFI and the ECJ. The case law will be examined here and its broader implications will be considered below.[36]

In *Nolle*[37] the applicant was an independent importer of goods on which an anti-dumping duty had been imposed who had actively taken part in the investigation leading to the imposition of the duty. The applicant contended that the normal value of the product should have been based on the Taiwanese value rather than the Sri Lankan. Advocate General van Gerven stated that the Community institutions should be subject to a principle of care when applying broad discretionary powers to individual cases, and that this required the Commission to give serious consideration to the suggestion made by the applicant.[38] The ECJ followed the advocate general's line of reasoning. It considered whether the 'information contained in the documents in the case were considered with all the due care required,'[39] and concluded that the applicant had produced sufficient facts to raise doubts as to whether the choice of Sri Lanka as a reference country was really appropriate.[40]

The development of the principle of due care was given further impetus by the decision in *Technische Universitat München*.[41] The Technical University of Munich sought to import an electron microscope from Japan. Its application for exemption from customs duties was rejected on the ground that apparatus of equivalent scientific value was manufactured in the EU, this decision having been reached after having consulted experts in the area. The Bundesfinanzhof sought a preliminary ruling and made it clear that the ECJ's deferential approach to the review of discretion involving the exercise of complex technical matters did not sit easily with the approach of the German courts.[42] The ECJ held that where the Community institutions have a power of appraisal, respect for the rights guaranteed by the Community legal order was especially important. The rights guaranteed included the right of the person to make his views known, the right to have an adequately reasoned decision, and the duty of the competent institution to examine carefully and impartially all the relevant aspects of the individual case. It was only in this way that the courts could 'verify whether the factual and legal elements upon which the exercise of the power of appraisal depends were present.'[43] The ECJ annulled the contested decision on the ground, *inter alia*, that there was a breach of the duty of care by the Commission through its reliance on experts who did not possess the requisite technical knowledge in the relevant area.[44]

Subsequent decisions, such as the *British Airways* case,[45] further stressed the proximate connection between the duty to examine carefully and impartially all aspects of the case, and the obligation to give reasons, since the latter is a prerequisite to ensure that the former has been properly complied with.

Application of the Principle to Competition

The application of the principle of care has been taken up and developed by the CFI, especially in relation to competition and state aids. In the context of competition, the principle of care operates both with respect to whether to pursue an investigation and as to the conduct of the investigation if it is pursued.

The Commission is under a duty to consider a complaint submitted to it.[46] The Commission has limited resources with which to pursue competition violations, the corollary being that it will pick and choose which possible infringements are worthy of its attention. It was made clear in *Automec*[47] that the Commission cannot be compelled to conduct an investigation, and that the power to set priorities was an inherent part of the work of administration. The Commission was however obliged 'to examine carefully the factual and legal aspects of which it is notified by the complainant'[48] in order to decide whether they indicated behaviour likely to distort competition, and the ECJ would verify whether this had been done. Where the Commission decided not to pursue a complaint, it should then inform the complainant of its reasons.[49] These must be sufficient to enable the Court to review the lawfulness of the decision and make clear to the parties concerned the circumstances in which the Commission has applied the treaty.

Where the Commission decides to conduct an investigation, the principle of care applies once again, as made clear in *Asia Motor France II*[50]: the Commission must investigate with the degree of care that will enable it to assess the factual and legal considerations submitted by the complainant. To similar effect was the statement in *Metropole* that while the Commission was not obliged to investigate each of the complaints lodged with it, it must in the absence of a duly substantiated statement of reasons conduct the investigation with 'the requisite care, seriousness and diligence so as to be able to assess with full knowledge of the case the factual and legal particulars submitted for its appraisal by the complainants.'[51] It is clear moreover from cases such as *Volkswagen*[52] that the relevant duty is one of care and impartiality in the conduct of the investigation.

The Community courts have however emphasized limits on the requirement to give reasons in this context. It has held that, in stating the reasons for the decisions it has to take to ensure that the competition rules are applied, the Commission is not obliged to adopt a position on all the arguments relied on by the parties. It is sufficient if it sets out the facts and legal considerations having decisive importance for the decision.[53]

Application of the Principle to State Aids

An analogous two-stage investigative procedure operates in state aids and the Community courts have used the principle of care to foster procedural justice in this area as they have done in that of competition.

For monitoring of state aids to be effective, it is essential for the Commission to be notified of the existence of any aid proposal. It is for this reason that article 88 EC establishes a two-stage procedure for state aids. Stage one concerns prior notification of any plan to grant aid and preliminary investigation by the Commission.[54] The Commission must come to some preliminary view within two months.[55] If there are serious difficulties in reaching a decision within this time, the Commission should proceed to the more complete review.[56] This is important since other parties are entitled to be consulted under the formal investigation, but have no such rights in relation to the preliminary assessment.[57]

This can be problematic if the Commission finds that an aid is compatible with the Common Market under the preliminary assessment, but an interested party disagrees and believes that the more thorough investigation should have been initiated. In *William Cook*[58] the court held that the procedural guarantees applicable to the more detailed investigation under article 88(2) could, in such a situation, only be properly safeguarded if such parties were able to challenge a Commission decision concerning the preliminary investigation before the court.[59] Advocate General Tesauro framed his opinion against the more general procedural precepts laid down in the *Technische Universitat Munchen* case,[60] including the principle of care laid down therein, although this aspect of the case was less fully developed by the ECJ.

The judgment of the CFI in *Sytraval*[61] represents a high point in the application of the principle of care. The applicant sought the annulment of a decision rejecting a complaint about a state aid. The CFI considered in detail the arguments advanced by the applicant in the light of the available evidence and compared this to the findings made by the Commission. It held that the Commission was under a duty to give a reasoned answer to each of the objections raised in the complaint.[62] The CFI held further that when the Commission had obtained the information from its inquiries that it would use to decide whether to proceed to the second, more detailed investigation, it came under an 'automatic obligation to examine the objections which the complainant would certainly have raised if it had been given the opportunity of taking cognizance of that information.'[63] Moreover, the Commission's duty to give reasons for its decision might in certain circumstances require an exchange of views and arguments with the complainant, since the Commission needed to ascertain the view taken by the complainant of the information gathered by the Commission in the course of its inquiry, this being regarded as a corollary of its obligation to deal diligently and impartially with the inquiry by eliciting all necessary views.[64]

The ECJ was far more circumspect when the *Sytraval* case was appealed.[65] It held that the Commission was not under an obligation to conduct an exchange of views with the complainant: such an obligation could not be based on the duty to give reasons; the Commission was not obliged to give the complainant an opportunity to state its view during the preliminary inquiry; and the Commission's duty in relation to the more formal investigation was limited to giving notice to such persons in order that they could submit their comments,[66] there being no right to engage in an adversarial debate with the Commission.[67] The ECJ also rejected the CFI's decision insofar as the latter imposed an obligation on the Commission to examine of its own motion objections which the complainant would have raised had it been given the opportunity to take cognisance of the information obtained by the Commission in the course of its preliminary inquiry.[68] Notwithstanding this finding, the ECJ concluded that the Commission might be obliged where necessary to extend its investigation of a complaint beyond mere examination of the facts and law brought to its attention by the complainant. The Commission could be required in the interests of sound administration of the rules on state aid to 'conduct a diligent and impartial examination of the complaint, which may make it necessary for it to examine matters not expressly raised by the complainant.'[69]

Development of the Principle

The CFI has not sought to expand the principle of care or diligent and impartial administration in the way that it had in the *Sytraval* case. It has taken heed of the more restrictive reading given to the principle by the ECJ in that case. The CFI has accepted that in the context of state aid interested parties other than the member state responsible cannot claim a right to debate the issues with the Commission, and that this limitation applies even to the recipient of the aid.[70]

The CFI has nonetheless developed the principle in a rather different fashion in the important *max.mobil* case.[71] The essence of the applicant's complaint was that it was adversely affected by an Austrian state measure that enabled Mobilkom, a company to which Austria had granted a monopoly, to abuse its dominant position on the relevant mobile telephone market, in breach of article 86 EC. The Commission accepted part of the applicant's complaint, but rejected it in part and the applicant sought the annulment of the Commission's decision in this latter respect.

The case is of significance both for the way in which the CFI conceptualized the principle of diligent and impartial administration, and for the way in which it applied it to the instant case. These will be considered in turn.

The CFI conceptualized the principle as but part of the broader right to sound administration recognized by the *Charter of Rights*:[72]

> Since the present action is directed against a measure rejecting a complaint, it must be emphasised at the outset that the diligent and impartial treatment of a complaint is associated with the right to sound administration which is one of the general principles that are observed in a State gov-

> erned by the rule of law and are common to the constitutional traditions of the Member States. Article 41(1) of the Charter of Fundamental Rights of the European Union proclaimed at Nice on 7 December 2000 confirms that '[e]very person has the right to have his or her affairs handled impartially, fairly and within a reasonable time by the institutions and bodies of the Union.' It is appropriate to consider, first of all, the nature and scope both of that right and of the administration's concomitant obligations in the specific context of the application of Community competition law to an individual case, as called for in this instance by the applicant.

The CFI's reasoning is equally important for the way in which it applied the principle to the instant case. It acknowledged that the duty imposed on the Commission to undertake a diligent and impartial examination had been recognized in earlier case law relating to competition. The Commission accepted this, but argued that the duty recognized by the earlier jurisprudence was dependent on provisions of the treaty or secondary legislation, and that no such rights were formally granted to complainants in the context of article 86 EC. The CFI rejected this argument. It held that the duty of diligent examination was applicable for a number of reasons. It reached this conclusion in part because it stated that article 86 EC should be read in conjunction with other treaty articles on competition that did grant procedural rights to complainants.[73] This was reinforced by reliance on the general duty of supervision to which the Commission was subject,[74] from which the CFI concluded that the 'Commission's general duty of supervision and its corollary, the obligation to undertake a diligent and impartial examination of complaints submitted to it, must apply as a matter of principle, without distinction'[75] in the context of all the treaty articles concerned with competition.

A final strand of the CFI's reasoning was based on the wording of article 86(3) EC, which provides that the Commission shall ensure the application of article 86 and shall where necessary address appropriate directives or decisions to member states. The CFI held that the fact that the Commission must decide whether intervention was 'necessary' implied a duty to conduct a diligent and impartial examination of complaints.[76] The second and third strands of this reasoning are especially revealing. They demonstrate the CFI's willingness to view the application of the duty of diligent and impartial examination as a corollary of a more general duty of supervision, and to imply the duty from the wording of the relevant treaty article.

Having said this, the CFI in *max.mobil* made it clear that the precise manner in which the obligation was discharged could vary depending on the specific area to which the duty was applied and that the procedural rights accorded by the treaties or secondary legislation were an important factor in this respect.[77] This is equally clear from the CFI's more recent approach in *Technische Glaswerke* to the application of the duty in the context of state aids, where it was accepted that the limits to the duty were set by the relevant treaty articles.[78]

The CFI's willingness to draw on the duty of care is equally apparent in the *Pfizer* case,[79] which involved a challenge to the withdrawal of authorization for an additive used in feed stuffs for animals. The authorization had been withdrawn because of fears concerning the additive's effect on resistance to bacteria by humans. The CFI held that the contested regulation could be justified on the basis of the precautionary principle. It emphasized however that procedural guarantees were especially important in this context, including the duty of the competent institution to examine carefully and impartially all aspects of the individual case. It followed, said the CFI, that 'a scientific risk assessment carried out as thoroughly as possible on the basis of scientific advice founded on the principles of excellence, transparency and independence is an important procedural guarantee whose purpose is to ensure the scientific objectivity of the measures adopted and preclude arbitrary measures.'[80]

Care, Reasons, and Dialogue

Process rights can clearly interrelate in important ways, as exemplified by the connection between the duty of diligent and impartial examination, and the provision of reasons. Shapiro has explained the nature of the relationship and the tensions that can be engendered in this regard:[81]

> The basic reason that the parties push and the ECJ resists dialogue lies in the difference between transparency and participation. Courts are likely to be initially hostile to demands for dialogue. Such requests are the last resort of regulated parties who have no substantive arguments left. Moreover, if dialogue claims are judicially accepted, they lead to a more and more cumbersome administrative process because the regulated parties will be encouraged to raise more and more arguments to which the agency will have to respond. If the only instrumental value for giving reasons is transparency, the courts will resist dialogue demands. One can discover an

> agency's actions and purposes without the agency rebutting every opposing argument.
>
> ...
>
> If the ECJ sticks closely to transparency as the sole goal of Article 190, the ECJ is unlikely to move towards a dialogue requirement. Yet participation in government by interests affected by government decisions presents an increasingly compelling value in contemporary society, particularly where environmental matters are involved. The ECJ has already, however unintentionally, opened one avenue for linking participation to Article 190 by stating that the Council need not give full reasons to the Member States where they have participated in the decisions. To be sure, these ECJ opinions are transparency-based. They require that those Member States already know what was going on because they were there. Nevertheless they create an opening for counter-arguments from complainants who were not present and claim that, therefore, they need the Commission to be responsive. In short, full transparency can only be achieved through participation or through dialogue as a form of participation.

The key issue is therefore the extent to which the jurisprudence on the process rights considered above might be moving, directly or indirectly, towards a dialogue between the individual and the decision-maker, requiring the latter to respond to arguments advanced by the former. This is a theme developed interestingly by Nehl in his study of administrative procedure in EU law, who, at the time of his writing, perceived movement in this direction.[82] There is, however, rather less evidence for this proposition now.

This is in part because the case law has taken a step back from the tentative moves in this direction. The ECJ's initial approach was cautious. In the *Sigarettenindustrie* case[83] the Court held that, although article 253 required the Commission to state its reasons, it was not required to discuss all the issues of fact and law raised by every party during the administrative proceedings. It therefore dismissed the claim that the Commission had ignored the applicants' arguments, none of which had featured in the decision. We have seen that 'dents' appeared in this orthodoxy, especially in the CFI's case law and it was the CFI that was literally at the front line in hearing direct actions brought by individuals seeking judicial review. The high point of this case law was the CFI's decision in *Sytraval*,[84] which if it had been upheld by the ECJ and if it had been extended to other areas of EU law, would have laid the foundations for a dialogue requirement. The reality is that neither happened. The ECJ reined in the CFI, and rejected the more far-reaching aspects of dialogue that the latter had advanced, even within the context of state aids.

This has been confirmed by later judgments that have gone out of their way to emphasize that the process in that context is not one of adversarial debate,[85] and the courts will not allow it to be turned into one through an expansive reading of the duty of diligent administration. Nor will they allow this to occur through expansive interpretation of the duty to give reasons. Thus, as we have seen in relation to competition, the Community courts have held that in stating the reasons for the decisions it takes, the Commission is not obliged to adopt a position on all the arguments relied on by the parties. It is sufficient if it sets out the facts and legal considerations having decisive importance in the context of the decision.[86] If there is a countervailing tendency, it is an indirect by-product of the jurisprudence on access to the file, which places the individual in a better position to know the arguments that should be advanced at the hearing, thereby leading to some obligation on the Commission to respond.

There is, however, another reason for being cautious about the extent to which the Community courts might be willing to foster a dialogue requirement. This concerns the distinction between rule-making and individualized determinations. The idea of dialogue in the United States is a feature of rule-making. It emerged in part at least as a by-product or corollary of the notice and comment provisions of the *Administrative Procedure Act 1946*, with the courts requiring the agency to respond to important comments made by the parties before finalizing the draft rule.[87] It is important not to lose sight of the fact that insofar as the Community courts have moved towards dialogue, the case law has, by way of contrast, been exclusively concerned with individualized discretionary determinations. It is moreover not fortuitous that the cases in which the Community courts have been tempted to move furthest in this direction have been concerned with especially problematic decisions of this nature. Thus it is questionable whether the CFI in *Sytraval*[88] ever intended its reasoning to apply outside of the specific circumstances of state aids, with its two-stage procedure and the disadvantages that could ensue to the individual if a complaint was dismissed at the preliminary stage at which the complainant could not participate. There is a strong vein running through the judgment of the CFI seeking to develop the duty of diligent administration as a way of meeting this particular problem, and the ECJ curbed the more far-reaching aspects of this reasoning. The apposite point for present purposes is that neither the ECJ nor the CFI has shown any inclination to develop a dialogue requirement in relation to rule-making. To the contrary they have drawn a sharp distinction between rule-making and individualized determinations, and have been very reluctant to develop process rights in relation to rule-making, even in the form of bare consultation or participation, let alone in an extended form so as to foster dialogue.

Process and Substantive Review

It is clear not only that process rights can interrelate, but also that there is an interrelationship between procedural and substantive review. This is readily apparent from discussion of the specific process rights considered above. It is fitting to reflect on this more generally at the conclusion of this chapter. The inter-connection between procedural and substantive review can operate in a number of ways.

It is exemplified by the application of the duty of careful examination in *Pfizer,* where the procedural duty served to justify the requirement of scientific advice with the aim of ensuring that the resultant regulation was not substantively arbitrary.[89] The connection between process and substance is apparent once again in relation to reasons. Thus the rationale for the obligation to give reasons is in part that it will thereby enable the courts to determine whether the administration has acted for improper purposes, or has taken irrelevant considerations into account when reaching its decision. The CFI has emphasized that the reasons given must be sufficient to enable it to exercise its judicial review function, and it has scrutinized the Commission's reasoning, annulling the decision if it did not withstand examination.[90] There is in this sense a proximate connection between expansion of the duty to give reasons and closer judicial scrutiny of the administration's reasoning process in order to discover a substantive error.

The expansion of procedural review may also encourage courts to set aside the contested decision on procedural grounds, in circumstances where the process rights have enabled the court to look at the substance of the case. Nehl brings this out clearly in relation to the court's use of access to the file.[91] Thus, if the administration has not accorded full rights of access to the file the CFI or ECJ may, as we have seen, consider whether the document was relevant for the individual's case and whether its disclosure might have made a difference to the decision reached. This will require the court to consider the Commission's reasoning process in relation to the merits of the case.[92] If the court has doubts about the substantive reasoning it may then choose to uphold the applicant's procedural claim that it was denied proper access to the file.

It is moreover not fortuitous that expansion of process rights has been matched by more rigorous substantive review. It is of course perfectly possible in principle for courts to demand more by way of, for example, reasons, but still to engage in low-intensity review before finding a substantive error. The reality is, however, that expansion of process rights will at the least encourage the courts to engage in more intensive substantive review, because they have more to work with and therefore feel more confident about asserting judicial control. It is common for courts to retain their original criterion of substantive review, such as manifest error, but to apply this more exactingly. This is what has occurred in the EU, where the courts continue to use the test of manifest error, but have developed it into a far more exacting scrutiny of fact and discretion than hitherto. That is a fascinating story in its own right.[93]

NOTES

1 *Germany v. Commission*, 24/62, [1963] E.C.R. 63 at 69 [*Germany v. Commission*]; *Asia Motor France SA v. Commission*, T-7/92, [1993] E.C.R. II-669 at para. 30 [*Asia Motor France SA*]; *Asia Motor France SA v. Commission*, T-387/94, [1996] E.C.R. II-961 at para. 103 [*Asia Motor France SA II*]; *Agrana Zucker und Stark AG v. Commission*, T-187/99, [2001] E.C.R. II-1587 at para. 83 [*Agrana Zucker*]; *Azienda Agricola 'Le Canne' Srl v. Commission*, T-241/00, [2002] E.C.R. II-1251 at para. 54 [*Azienda Agricola 'Le Canne' Srl*]; *Metropole Television SA v. Commission*, T-206/99, [2001] E.C.R. II-1057 at para. 44 [*Metropole Television SA*].

2 *Commission v. Sytraval and Brink's France SARL*, C-367/95P, [1998] E.C.R. I-1719 at para. 63 [*Sytraval*]; *Netherlands and Leeuwarder Papierwarenfabriek v. Commission*, 296, 318/82, [1985] E.C.R. 809 at para. 19; *European Parliament v. Gaspari*, C-316/97P, [1998] E.C.R. I-7597 at para. 26; *Germany v. Commission*, C-301/96, [2003] E.C.R. I-9919 at para. 87; *Petrotub SA and Republica SA v. Council*, C-76/00P, [2003] E.C.R. I-79 at para. 81; *Technische Glaswerke Ilmenau GmbH v. Commission*, T-198/01, [2004] E.C.R. II-2717 at para. 59 [*Technische Glaswerke*].

3 *Commission v. Council*, 45/86, [1987] E.C.R. 1493.

4 *Germany v. Commission, supra* note 1.
5 See, e.g., *Papiers Peints de Belgique v. Commission*, 73/74, [1975] E.C.R. 1491.
6 This will occur not infrequently in areas such as the CAP, where the Commission may have to make numerous decisions or pass many regulations within a short space of time. Where this is so the Court has accepted that the Commission can refer back to a previous decision or regulation setting out the considerations which shaped the Commission's action: see, e.g., *Schwarze*, 16/65, [1965] E.C.R. 877.
7 5/67, [1968] E.C.R. 83 at 95; *Binder GmbH v. Hauptzollamt Stuttgart-West*, C-205/94, [1996] E.C.R. I-2871.
8 *Commission v. Council*, C-122/94, [1996] E.C.R. I-881 at para. 29; *United Kingdom v. Council*, C-84/94, [1996] E.C.R. I-5755 at paras. 74, 79.
9 *Germany v. Commission, supra* note 1; *Tremblay v. Commission*, T-5/93, [1995] E.C.R. II-185.
10 See cases cited at *infra* note 53.
11 P. Craig, *Administrative Law*, 5th ed. (London: Sweet & Maxwell, 2003) chap. 23.
12 *BPB Industries and British Gypsum v. Commission*, C-310/93P, [1995] E.C.R. I-865 at I-890–893, AG Leger.
13 EC, *Charter of Fundamental Rights*, [2000] O.J.C. 364/1, art. 41(2) [*Charter*].
14 J. Schwarze, *European Administrative Law* (London: Sweet & Maxwell, 1992) at 1341–57 [Schwarze, *European*]; M. Levitt, 'Access to the File: the Commission's Administrative Procedures in Cases under Articles 85 and 86' (1997) 34 C.M.L.Rev. 1413; C-D. Ehlermann and B. Drijber, 'Legal Protection of Enterprises: Administrative Procedure, in particular Access to Files and Confidentiality' [1996] Eur. Comp. L. Rev. 375; H. Nehl, *Principles of Administrative Procedure in EC Law* (Oxford: Hart Publishing, 1999) chap. 5 [Nehl].
15 *VBVB and VBBB v. Commission*, 43, 63/82, [1985] E.C.R. 19 at para. 25.
16 *SA Hercules Chemicals NV v. Commission*, T-7/89, [1991] E.C.R. II-1711 at paras. 53–54; *BPB Industries plc and British Gypsum Ltd. V. Commission*, T-65/89, [1993] E.C.R. II-389.
17 EC, Commission, *Commission Notice on Internal Rules of Procedure for Access to the File* [1997] O.J.C. 23/3, [1997] 4 C.M.L.R. 490.
18 *Solvay SA v. Commission*, T-30–32/91, [1995] E.C.R. II-1775; *ICI v. Commission*, T-36–37/91, [1995] E.C.R. II-1847 at para. 93; *Hercules Chemicals NV v. Commission*, C-51/92P, [1999] E.C.R. I-4235; *BASF Lacke & Farben AG v. Commission*, T-175/95, [1999] E.C.R. II-1581; *Limburgse Vinyl Maatschappij v. Commission*, C-238, 244–245, 247, 250, 252, 254/99P, [2002] E.C.R. I-8375.
19 See below, at 170–71.

20 *Eyckeler & Malt AG v. Commission*, T-42/96, [1998] E.C.R. II-401 at paras. 79–80.

21 Ibid. at para. 81. See also *Primex Produkte Import-Export GmbH & Co. KG v. Commission*, T-50/96, [1998] E.C.R. II-3773 at paras. 57–70; *Kaufring AG v. Commission*, T-186, 187, 190, 192, 210, 211, 216–218, 279–280, 293/97, 147/99, [2001] E.C.R. II-1337 at para. 185; *Hyper Srl v. Commission*, T-205/99, [2002] E.C.R. II-3141.

22 Article 41(2), which provides that the right to good administration includes 'the right of every person to have access to his or her file, while respecting the legitimate interests of confidentiality and of professional and business secrecy': *Charter*, *supra* note 13.

23 *Aalborg Portland A/S v. Commission*, C-204–205, 211, 213, 217, 219/00P, [2004] E.C.R. I-123 [*Aalborg Portland A/S*].

24 Ibid. at para. 68.

25 Ibid. at para. 70.

26 Ibid. at para. 126.

27 Ibid. at para. 73.

28 Ibid. at paras. 74–75.

29 Ibid. at paras. 76, 77, 101.

30 Ibid. at para. 129.

31 Ibid. at para. 115.

32 *Geitling, Mausegatt and Prasident v. High Authority*, 16–18/59, [1960] E.C.R. 17 at 20; *Koninklijke Nederlandsche Hoogovens en Staalfabrieken NV v. High Authority*, 14/61, [1962] E.C.R. 253; Schwarze, *European*, *supra* note 14; Nehl, *supra* note 14, chaps. 8–9.

33 *Societe La Technique Miniere (LTM) v. Maschinenbau Ulm GmbH*, 56/65, [1966] E.C.R. 235 at 248; *Consten & Grundig v. Commissioni*, 56, 58/64, [1966] E.C.R. 299 at 374.

34 *Gebruder Lorenz GmbH v. Germany*, 120/73, [1973] E.C.R. 1471 at 1481.

35 Nehl, *supra* note 14 at 107.

36 See below at 175–78.

37 *Nolle v. Hauptzollamt Bremen-Freihafen*, C-16/90, [1991] E.C.R. I-5163.

38 Ibid. at I-5175.

39 Ibid. at para. 29.

40 Ibid. at para. 30. See also *Nolle v. Council*, T-167/94, [1995] E.C.R. II-2589.

41 *Hauptzollamt München-Mitte v. Technische Universitat Munchen*, C-269/90, [1991] E.C.R. I-5469 [*Hauptzollamt*].

42 J. Schwarze, 'Developing Principles of European Administrative Law' [1993] P.L. 229; G. Nolte, 'General Principles of German and European Administrative Law – A Comparison in Historical Perspective' (1994) 57 M.L.R. 191.

43 *Hauptzollamt, supra* note 41 at para. 14.
44 Ibid. at para. 135. See also *Azienda Agricola 'Le Canne' Srl, supra* note 1 at paras. 53–54.
45 *British Airways plc and British Midland Airways Ltd v. Commission*, T-371, 394/94, [1998] E.C.R. II-2405 at para. 95.
46 *Demo-Studio Schmidt v. Commission*, 210/81, [1983] E.C.R. 3045.
47 *Automec Srl v. Commission*, T-24/90, [1992] E.C.R. II-2223 [*Automec Srl*]; *Bureau Européen des Médias de l'Industrie Musicale (BEMIM) v. Commission*, T-144/92, [1995] E.C.R. II-147; *Bureau Européen des Unions Consommateurs and National Consumer Council v. Commission*, T-37/92, [1994] E.C.R. II-285; *Commission and France v. Ladbroke Racing Ltd.*, C-359, 379/95P, [1999] E.C.R. I-6265; *Riviera Auto Service Etablissements Dalmasso SA v. Commission*, T-185, 189, 190/96, [1999] E.C.R. II-93; *International Express Carriers Conference (IECC) v. Commission, La Poste, UK and the Post Office*, C-449/98 P, [2001] E.C.R. I-3875.
48 *Automec Srl, supra* note 47 at para. 79.
49 *Union Francaise de l'Express (Ufex), DHL International, Service CRIE and May Courier v. Commission*, T-77/95 RV, [2000] E.C.R. II-2167 at para. 42.
50 *Asia Motor France SA, supra* note 1 at para. 36; *Asia Motor France SA v. Commission*, T-154/98, [2000] E.C.R. II-3453 at paras. 53–56; *ABB Asea Brown Boveri Ltd v. Commission* T-31/99, [2002] E.C.R. II-1881 at para. 99; *Atlantic Container Line AB v. Commission*, T-191, 212, 214/98, [2003] E.C.R. II-3273 at para. 404.
51 *Metropole Television SA, supra* note 1 at para. 59.
52 *Volkswagen AG v. Commission* T-62/98, [2000] E.C.R. II-2707 at para. 269.
53 *Asia Motor France SA, supra* note 1 at para. 31; *Siemens v. Commission*, T-459/93, [1995] E.C.R. II-1675 at para. 31; *Asia Motor France SA II, supra* note 1 at para. 104; *Industrie des Poudres Sphériques SA v. Commission*, T-5/97, [2000] E.C.R. II-3755 at para. 199; *Agrana Zucker, supra* note 1 at para. 84; *Metropole Television SA, supra* note 1 at para. 44; *Westdeutsche Landesbank Girozentrale and Land Nordrhein-Westfalen v. Commission*, T-228, 233/99, [2003] E.C.R. II-435 at para. 280 [*Westdeutsche Landesbank Girozentrale*].
54 EC, art. 88(3).
55 *Germany v. Commission*, 84/82, [1984] E.C.R. 1451 [*Germany v. Commission II*].
56 EC, art. 88(2).
57 *Gebrüder Lorenz GmbH v. Germany*, 120/73, [1973] E.C.R. 1471; *Germany v. Commission II, supra* note 55. The Commission must also be notified of any amendment to the aid proposal: *Heineken Brouwerijen BV v. Inspecteur der Vennootschapsbelasting*, 91, 127/83, [1984] E.C.R. 3435.
58 *William Cook plc v. Commission*, C-198/91, [1993] E.C.R. I-2486; *Sytraval, supra* note 2.

59 L. Hancher, 'State Aids and Judicial Control in the European Communities' [1994] Euro. Comp. L. Rev. 134.

60 *Hauptzollamt*, *supra* note 41.

61 *Sytraval and Brink's France v. Commission*, T-95/94, [1995] E.C.R. II-2651 [*Sytraval II*].

62 Ibid. at para. 62.

63 Ibid. at para. 66.

64 Ibid. at para. 78.

65 *Sytraval*, *supra* note 2.

66 Ibid. at paras. 58–59.

67 *Falck SpA and Accialierie di Bolzano SpA v. Commission*, C-74, 75/00, [2002] E.C.R. I-7869 at para. 82 [*Falck SpA*].

68 *Sytraval*, *supra* note 2 at para. 60.

69 Ibid. at para. 62.

70 *Technische Glaswerke*, *supra* note 2 at paras 192–199, relying on *Sytraval*, *supra* note 2, and *Falck SpA*, *supra* note 67.

71 *max.mobil Telekommunikation Service GmbH v. Commission*, T-54/99, [2002] E.C.R. II-313; see also *Tideland Signal Ltd v. Commission*, T-211/02, [2002] E.C.R. II-3781 at para. 37. The CFI's decision was overturned by the ECJ, and the latter decided the case on narrower grounds. The ECJ's decision is too recent for consideration in this chapter: *Commission v. T. Mobile Austria GmbH*, C-141/02P, [2005] E.C.R. I-1283.

72 *Tideland Signal* at para. 48. See also *Westdeutsche Landesbank Girozentrale*, *supra* note 53 at para. 167.

73 Max Mobil, *supra* note 71 at para. 51.

74 Ibid. at para. 52.

75 Ibid. at para. 53.

76 Ibid. at para. 54.

77 Ibid. at para. 53.

78 *Technische Glaswerke*, *supra* note 2 at paras. 191–199.

79 *Pfizer Animal Health SA v. Council*, T-13/99, [2002] E.C.R. II-3305 at paras. 170–172 [*Pfizer Animal Health SA*].

80 Ibid. at para. 172.

81 M. Shapiro, 'The Giving Reasons Requirement' [1992] U. Chicago Legal F. 179 at 203–204; reprinted in A. Stone Sweet and M. Shapiro, *On Laws, Politics and Judicialization* (Oxford: Oxford University Press, 2002) chap. 4. (references to EC, art. 190 should now be read as referring to EC, art. 253).

82 Nehl, *supra* note 14 at 155–65.

83 *Stichting Sigarettenindustrie v. Commission*, 240–242, 261–262, 268–269/82, [1985] E.C.R. 3831 at para. 88; *Remia BV and Nutricia BV v. Commission*, 42/84, [1985] E.C.R. 2545.

84 *Sytraval II*, *supra* note 61.
85 *Falck SpA*, *supra* note 67; *Technische Glaswerke*, *supra* note 2.
86 See cases cited at *supra* note 53.
87 A. Aman and W. Mayton, *Administrative Law*, 2nd ed. (St. Paul, Minn.: West Group, 2001) chap. 2; M. Shapiro, 'APA: Past, Present and Future' (1986) 72 Va. L. Rev. 447.
88 *Sytraval II*, *supra* note 61.
89 *Pfizer Animal Health SA*, *supra* note 79 at paras. 171–72.
90 See *La Cinq SA v. Commission*, T-44/90, [1992] E.C.R. II-1; *Asia Motor France SA*, *supra* note 1; Nehl, *supra* note 14 at 142–46.
91 Nehl, *supra*note 14 at 53–54.
92 See *Aalborg Portland A/S*, *supra* note 23.
93 P. Craig, *EU Administrative Law* (Oxford: Oxford University Press, 2006), chap. 13.

A 'Mullanian' Approach to the Doctrine of Legitimate Expectations: Real Questions and Promising Answers

GENEVIÈVE CARTIER

Among David Mullan's most influential contributions to administrative law is a prescient article published in 1975, 'Fairness: The New Natural Justice?'[1] In this famous piece, he criticized the Canadian judiciary for conditioning the recognition of procedural obligations on classifying public functions as quasi-judicial as opposed to administrative. The thrust of Mullan's argument was that to so condition the application of procedural obligations on the presence of inflexible and indefinable function classification was likely to cause injustice to individuals. He argued for the introduction of British procedural fairness doctrine into Canadian law, which would dispense with the 'horrors of the classification process.'[2] This would allow lawyers and judges to ask not whether a function was quasi-judicial or administrative, but rather, 'what kind of procedural protections are necessary for a particular decision making process?'[3] Mullan's 'Fairness' article marked a turning point in the law of procedural fairness in Canada. Four years later, the Supreme Court of Canada endorsed Mullan's thesis in *Nicholson v. Haldimand-Norfolk Regional Board of Commissioners of Police*,[4] and thereby contributed to the emerging understanding in the common law world that all administrative decision-making is governed by a doctrine of fairness.

In Canadian administrative law, Mullan's 'Fairness' article is rightly associated with the 'liberating effects'[5] that it produced on administrative procedure. But for the purpose of my contribution to this *Festschrift*, that article is remarkable for expressing one of Mullan's dearest themes: that administrative law must be stripped of artificial and formal concepts in order to pose and answer 'the real questions.'[6] In this paper, I will argue that this 'Mullanian' approach allowed the Supreme Court of Canada eventually to give substance to the doctrine of legitimate expectations. This may sound surprising, not least because David Mullan has on many occasions expressed profound dissatisfaction with the formal treatment of that doctrine by the Canadian judiciary. Nevertheless, in my view, the latest pronouncements of the Supreme Court on the subject are compatible with, and in fact endorse and give meaning to, Mullan's plea to eschew formalism and to concentrate on the real issues.

I present this argument in two parts. In the first part I analyse Mullan's writings on the doctrine of legitimate expectations and suggest that his critique echoes the fundamental points he made in the 'Fairness' article: the necessity to enlarge the domain of procedural protection and free administrative law from sterile classificatory exercises and formal definitions, and the need to articulate better the issues that are often masked by technicalities and formal concepts. To appreciate Mullan's standpoint fully, I review the British origins of legitimate expectations and its evolution in the United Kingdom from a procedural to a substantive doctrine, and summarize the state of Canadian law on the matter. In the second part of this article, I argue that the traditional justification put forward to support the Canadian version of the doctrine is fundamentally flawed, and that this explains Mullan's profound dissatisfaction with the Canadian approach. But I will suggest that the latest decision of the Canadian Supreme Court on the doctrine of legitimate expectations – *Mount Sinai Hospital Center v. Quebec (Minister of Health and Social Services)*[7] – exemplifies the Mullanian approach of articulating and focusing on real issues, and has resulted in a 'surreptitious insinuation'[8] in Canadian law of a substantive version of legitimate expectations. In my view, this is a very welcome development.

At the outset, I acknowledge that the doctrine of legitimate expectations can play a role in regard to various types of decision-making. My discussion, however, will be limited to cases where legitimate expectations arise in the context of the exercise of discretionary powers, and the original promise or undertaking that gives rise to that expectation is legal – that is, is not in conflict with positive law requirements, whether flowing from primary or subordinate legislation.

Asking Real Questions

David Mullan was one of the first Canadian legal academics to write about the doctrine of legitimate expectations.[9] On several occasions he expressed dismay at the Canadian judiciary's handling of the doctrine, going so far as to write that 'the likelihood that the doctrine will ever come to play a major role in Canadian Administrative Law appears slim.'[10] To understand Mullan's pessimism, an overview of U.K. law[11] and the cold shoulder it received in Canada is necessary.

In short, the administrative law doctrine of legitimate expectations requires an administrative authority that by word, deed, or practice has induced expectations in an individual that something will be done in a certain way, to take that expectation into account in the decision-making process. A typical case is the following. An administrative authority is delegated by statute the power to issue licences at its discretion. In the course of its communications with a citizen, the authority promises that a permit will be issued to him. The promise is likely to produce a legitimate expectation that the permit will be issued. Some time later, the authority refuses to issue the permit. To what extent do the promise and the expectation it generated affect the freedom of action of the decision-maker? Do they merely affect the *procedural rights* of the individual, allowing him a right to be heard before the promise is violated, with the hope that the decision-maker will change its mind and honour the promise? Or will the decision-maker be compelled to actually deliver *the substantive benefit* that was expected – that is, the permit?

In the United Kingdom the doctrine has both a procedural and a substantive aspect.[12] On the procedural side, the doctrine states that legitimate expectations may augment the *content* of procedural rights that are already available under the common law of procedural fairness in a case where a decision-maker attempts to ignore the expectation.[13] Moreover, it recognizes that legitimate expectations may generate procedural rights in cases where fairness would not otherwise apply under the common law, thus relaxing the *threshold* for access to procedural fairness.[14] On the substantive side, the doctrine now also provides that a legitimate expectation may, in some circumstances, generate a right to the substantive outcome that was expected.[15]

A detailed analysis of the U.K. case law that led to this result is beyond the scope of this paper, but two elements of the English conception of the doctrine are germane to my present purpose. The first is that the use of the doctrine of legitimate expectations has extended procedural fairness to contexts in which such procedural protection was not required under the pre-existing common law. For example, wide policy-making functions and so-called legislative functions exercised by the executive were traditionally excluded from the sphere of application of procedural fairness in administrative law.[16] The U.K. courts recognized that promises, undertakings, or practices can induce legitimate expectations and generate procedural rights even if they were made or developed in the context of functions of a legislative nature.[17] As we shall see, on several occasions Mullan criticized the Canadian approach to procedural fairness generally for excluding legislative functions from the ambit of procedural fairness. He was particularly critical of the refusal of the Supreme Court to use the doctrine of legitimate expectations to circumvent the requirements of the common law and impose procedural obligations on decision-makers exercising functions of a legislative nature. I shall return to that point in due course.

The second element of the U.K. experience to highlight is that, while the first English cases seemed to limit the consequences that could follow from the recognition of legitimate expectations to procedural rights, indications that substantive effects might also be recognized became increasingly common in the 1990s. In fact, implicit recognition of this possibility appeared in two early cases on the doctrine,[18] from which it could be understood that two conditions were considered necessary to allow an authority to go back on a promise or depart from an established practice. First, the authority had to allow the individual to make representations before breaking the promise or interrupting the practice. Secondly, it had to demonstrate that an overriding public interest required the promise to be broken or the practice to be abandoned. A legitimate expectation therefore did not confer an automatic right to the outcome or benefit expected, but it did trigger a requirement of justification on the part of the public authority. Still, it was not clear to what extent the requirement of justification expressed in those cases could lead to a substantive constraint on decision-makers and therefore constitute an express recognition of a substantive doctrine of legitimate expectations. More specifically, the question became whether courts were allowed to evaluate the justification put forward by the decision-maker departing from a promise or practice and, if so, under what standard of review.

Two positions emerged. One suggested that it was up to the authority to see whether the change was justified by the public interest, and the final outcome would be assessed under *Wednesbury* principles,[19] as in the case of every other discretionary decision. For the court, then, no condition could be imposed on decision-makers before they could change their policies, other than the conditions that apply to any exercise of discretion.[20] The other, radically different, position insisted that '[w]hile policy is for the policy maker alone, the fairness of his or her decision not to accommodate reasonable expectations which the policy will thwart remains the court's concern.'[21] Moreover, while policy decisions were to be assessed under a standard of irrationality, courts were not necessarily limited to assessing questions of fairness under such a standard: a more intrusive standard could be used.[22]

In a very important decision, *R. v. North and East Devon Health Authority, ex p. Coughlan*,[23] the Court of Appeal settled the debate in favour of the latter position. Both parties agreed that the decision-maker could not violate a promise to the individual concerned unless an overriding public interest required it,[24] thus recognizing that the existence of a promise limited the freedom of action of the authority. The court also agreed that the authority had to provide the initial judgment on whether overriding considerations existed in the circumstances, while a court could review that judgment 'if improperly reached.'[25] But Lord Woolf M.R., delivering the decision of the court, believed that the court's role was not so limited: it could go beyond considerations of 'propriety' and determine whether the authority had appropriately balanced the public and private interests in the circumstances.[26] Lord Woolf stated that judging the adequacy of the justification offered by a decision-maker to frustrate a substantive legitimate expectation was a matter for the courts, and that courts could use a more intrusive standard of review than the *Wednesbury* standard. The court was not very specific about the nature of the standard of review, but made it clear that courts were not restricted to applying a rationality standard. If a court found that a decision-maker had not complied with the requirement of the appropriate standard, the decision-maker would be bound by its word, deed, or practice.[27]

The above two features of the English version of the doctrine of legitimate expectations inform David Mullan's critique of the Canadian state of the law on that topic. Before analysing Mullan's position, however, a sketch of the Canadian approach is necessary.

Canada proved reluctant to adopt the English version of the legitimate expectation doctrine. The Canadian courts limited the doctrine to the narrowest application in its procedural aspect: they did not use it to lower the threshold for the application of procedural protection, but rather only as an element enhancing the content of those already applicable protections. The courts steadfastly refused to recognize substantive consequences in the creation and enforcement of legitimate expectations. In the first Supreme Court decision to analyse the doctrine of legitimate expectations, the Court synthesized the doctrine as follows:[28]

> The principle developed in these cases *is simply an extension of the rules of natural justice and procedural fairness.* It affords a party affected by the deci-

> sion of a public official an opportunity to make representations *in circumstances in which there otherwise would be no such opportunity.* The court *supplies the omission* where, based on the conduct of the public official, a party has been led to believe that his or her rights would not be affected without consultation.

This clearly located the doctrine in the procedural domain, and indicated that it *extended* the rules of natural justice and fairness. The Court did not clearly specify how this extension would occur, but a convincing interpretation of the case, by David Mullan,[29] suggested that the doctrine could be understood as acting as a trigger for procedural fairness by generating opportunities to participate in a decision-making process where the existing common law did not allow such an opportunity. Since the most obvious context where the common law refused to allow participation was functions considered legislative in nature, this area was the most likely to benefit from extension of the doctrine of legitimate expectations. Unfortunately, however, this interpretation did not prevail. In a subsequent decision[30] the Supreme Court established that because the doctrine of legitimate expectations was 'an extension of the rules of natural justice and procedural fairness,'[31] these rules 'do not apply to a body exercising purely legislative functions.'[32] The Supreme Court thus shut the door on the idea that legitimate expectations could lower the threshold for procedural fairness and thereby encompass legislative functions. Moreover, the Court reaffirmed that legitimate expectations could not be the source of substantive rights. The doctrine was strictly limited to the procedural domain.[33]

A few years later, the Court reiterated the Canadian version of the doctrine of legitimate expectations in *Baker v. Canada (Minister of Citizenship and Immigration).*[34] Writing for the Court, L'Heureux-Dubé J. distinguished the object of the expectation from its legal effects. The object of the expectation can be procedural or substantive. If it is procedural, it confers the right to the expected procedure. If the expectation is of a substantive benefit, there is a presumption of unfairness if the decision-maker reneges on the representation, promise, or practice that generated the expectation without according 'significant procedural rights'[35] to the holder of the expectation. In sum, under the Canadian version of the doctrine, procedural and substantive expectations can generate procedural effects (the 'procedural aspect of the doctrine'), but substantive expectations cannot generate any substantive effect ('the substantive aspect of the doctrine').[36]

In my view, Mullan's critique of the state of the law of legitimate expectations in Canada echoes two fundamental concerns he had expressed years before in his 'Fairness' article: criticizing the exclusion from the ambit of procedural fairness of a range of functions on the basis of a classification process based on questionable, formal definitions; and the failure of courts to identify and focus on real issues.

Classification, Again

While I imagine David Mullan was pleased with the Supreme Court's endorsement of his 'Fairness' article in *Nicholson*, he was extremely dissatisfied with the state of the common law of procedural fairness in Canada as it evolved in the following years. Despite the 'liberating effect'[37] of *Nicholson*, the Canadian courts proved unwilling to reconsider the immunity from procedural protection enjoyed by policy-makers and those exercising functions of a legislative nature.[38] In Mullan's words, '[b]y denying the doctrine the capacity to do work where that work was needed most ... the Court may well have in effect gutted the doctrine's potential in Canadian law.'[39]

Mullan's basic argument was that there is a logical flaw in the judicial reasoning. He understood the 'whole thrust'[40] of the doctrine to be the creation of fairness obligations in cases where such obligations did not otherwise exist. This is what the Supreme Court of Canada said in the first case involving legitimate expectations: the doctrine 'affords a party affected by the decision of a public official an opportunity to make representations *in circumstances in which there otherwise would be no such opportunity.*'[41] Yet the courts refused to apply the doctrine in precisely the domain where such obligations did not exist – that of policy or legislative functions – because judges viewed legitimate expectations as part of the rules of procedural fairness, which did not apply to functions of a legislative nature. Moreover, Mullan pointed out that the consequence of this logical flaw was aggravated by the fact that courts defined 'legislative functions' in excessively wide terms, without providing any justification for doing so.[42]

Masking Real Issues

The second recurring theme in Mullan's scholarship on legitimate expectations relates to the tendency of Canadian courts to burden the application of the doctrine with unnecessary or unjustified conditions.

In Mullan's view, this simply masked the real issues at stake and weakened the ability of the doctrine to have any meaningful effect on administrative behaviour.

Hence, he questioned the tendency of courts to require knowledge of practices and reliance on those practices for the doctrine to apply.[43] On another occasion, he criticized a judicial approach that required an applicant 'not only ... to have reason to hold ... an expectation but also a belief ... that the decision maker will in fact follow past practices.'[44] In Mullan's view, this could only encourage administrative authorities to make it clear to anyone potentially covered by the practice that the latter will not be followed. These examples illustrate Mullan's distrust of formal concepts and definitions, and his constant quest for their justification. In his view, those kinds of questions simply diverted attention from real issues: the substantive objectives that should inform the doctrine as a whole, and the fundamental values and principles of administrative law that must be kept in mind when reflecting on the specific doctrine.

In Mullan's first comment on the subject, he had already warned that courts did not ask the question from the right point of view: 'the expectation of procedures ... is created not by the nature of the power in issue *but by the conduct of the authority exercising that power.*'[45] Elsewhere, he said that the doctrine 'is concerned with an assumption of procedural entitlements arising out of the conduct of public officials.'[46] For Mullan, this is a matter of administrative probity: public authorities should keep their public promises.[47]

Mullan hoped that courts would eventually conceive the doctrine in more sympathetic terms because he was convinced that the values and principles that informed it deserved to be more clearly articulated and more firmly applied:[48]

> In these days of increasing disenchantment with the conduct of government, the doctrine of legitimate expectation at least has the potential for injecting elements of consistency and even-handed dealing into the way in which the business of government is carried on and of thereby contributing, albeit in a small way, to the re-emergence of a basis for belief in the probity and trustworthiness of such decision makers.

A Mullanian Approach to Legitimate Expectations

In my view, Mullan was right to express dissatisfaction with the Canadian version of the doctrine of legitimate expectations. Indeed, as we will see in this part, identification of the real issues at stake and analysis of the answers provided by the courts demonstrate that the traditional justification for the Canadian version of the doctrine is deeply problematic. This suggests that as long as the Canadian courts continue on this course, the values and principles that should inform legitimate expectations analysis will have to be factored into other administrative law doctrines if injustice is to be avoided. In fact, as I will argue, this is precisely what has happened. Furthermore, Mullan's abhorrence of pointless formalism and insistence on asking the right questions helped create the environment in which the Court was able to reach a principled and just result.

The Quest for Justification

As is clear from the preceding analysis, the Canadian version of the doctrine establishes a separation between substance and procedure. Hence, in a typical situation a citizen could not legally claim the substantive outcome that she was promised, but she would have the right to be heard by the decision-maker before the latter reneges.

In my view, the 'real issues' raised by this situation are the following. First, what is the justification for refusing to give substantive effects to substantive legitimate expectations? Secondly, if the citizen cannot get the substantive outcome she legitimately expected, what would be the point of giving her procedural rights?

Traditionally, Canadian courts have articulated their understanding of the doctrine of legitimate expectations under the *ultra vires* doctrine. This doctrine 'holds that the rule of law is maintained by judges seeing to it that the administration does not act arbitrarily or "beyond its powers," where powers means the authority delegated by Parliament.'[49] A decision-maker would be acting beyond its powers either when it does something that it is not legally authorized to do, or 'if in the course of doing or deciding to do something that is *intra vires* in the strict or narrow sense it acts improperly or "unreasonably" in various ways: ... [including] disregard of the rules of natural justice, unfairness, taking into account irrelevant considerations ...'[50] *Ultra vires* in the latter sense implies interpreting the delegating statute as requiring the authority to act in conformity with the principles of good administration.[51] Under the *ultra vires* doctrine the role of the courts is, therefore, to ensure that the limits of parliamentary authorization are respected by administrative authorities.

How does the *ultra vires* doctrine justify refusing to confer substantive effects on substantive legitimate expectations? The answer to this question is based on the no-fettering rule, itself an application of the *ultra vires* doctrine. When a statute purports to delegate discretionary power to a public authority, the statutory authorization is traditionally construed as conferring a 'margin of manoeuvre' on the authority, allowing it to choose the appropriate course of action in the circumstances of each of the cases that are brought to its attention. Consequently, for administrative authorities to act legally they must conform to the statutory authorization and thus preserve their freedom of action. Likewise, courts give effect to the statute in leaving unaffected this freedom to act. Concretely, this means refraining from limiting in any way the flexibility inherent in discretion. To do otherwise would violate the parliamentary authorization conferred on the decision-making authority. It would turn the intended discretion into a self-imposed rule. Hence, any attempt to fetter discretion, absent clear statutory indication to the contrary, betrays the intention of Parliament because it forces an authority to abandon the free exercise of its powers, contradicting the wishes of the people expressed through the democratic parliamentary process.[52] Put differently, if courts conferred substantive effects on those expectations, by holding decision-makers to the promises or representations made in relation to their discretion, they would affect the freedom of action of the public authority inherent in their discretion, and they would consequently violate the no-fettering rule.

As we saw however, even though Canadian courts do not accept that substantive effects flow from substantive legitimate expectations, they recognize that procedural rights can. This leads to the second question, which looks to the justification for the procedural aspect of the doctrine of legitimate expectations. It is important here to describe very briefly the two main conceptions of the nature of procedural rights.

Academic writing generally suggests that procedure is justified on the basis that it serves individual dignity, ensures accurate decisions, or a combination of these considerations.[53] Hence, some view procedure as having an essentially dignitarian, or non-instrumental, nature.[54] Procedure does not seek any specific end, but rather has an intrinsic value, linked to the dignity and autonomy of the individual, a value that is 'independent of the accuracy or soundness of the substantive decision or verdict'[55] that will eventually be made. Others insist on the instrumental nature of procedure: it ensures the accuracy or appropriateness of the decisions taken.[56] Still others contend that procedure is justified by a mixture of both instrumental and non-instrumental considerations. D.J. Galligan insists that instrumental considerations are prominent in any sound vision of procedure, notably because the best way to preserve the dignity of an individual is to ensure that the decisions which affect him are accurate: 'accurate decisions themselves constitute an important element of fair treatment, which in turn constitutes an important element of respect for persons.'[57] In other words, while it is generally recognized that procedure has, at least in part, a non-instrumental aspect linked to the dignity of the individual, it is also suggested that the best way to be true to individual dignity is to ensure the accuracy of outcome.

These general considerations inform the search for an answer to the second question: Is the procedural aspect of the Canadian version of the doctrine of legitimate expectations compatible with, or explicable under, the *ultra vires* rule?

For such a requirement to be compatible with the *ultra vires* rule, one would need to demonstrate that the donor of the power intended the decision-maker to hear the individual before it frustrates an expectation. However, discretion was traditionally interpreted as *a priori* conferring freedom of action on the decision-maker and as rebutting the presumption that good administration requires a hearing.[58] Two different kinds of reasons seemed to justify this interpretation. One is that discretion is viewed as conferring freedom of action on the decision-maker. This seems incompatible with imposing procedural 'limits' or 'constraints' on the exercise of that kind of power. The second reason is based on the difficulty of reconciling the nature of procedure with the nature of discretion. As T.R.S. Allan has pointed out, the *ultra vires* doctrine assumes an instrumental view of procedure.[59] In other words, it is aimed at enhancing the accuracy of the outcome. However, discretion was traditionally conceived as an exercise of power that allowed the decision-maker to make the choice it considers appropriate in the circumstances of each case, whether correct or not. Indeed, the essential notion of jurisdiction (simply *ultra vires* in a different guise) was that within it the decision-maker had power to be right or wrong. So the notion of accuracy involved in the idea that procedure has an instrumental virtue is problematic in the context of discretion.

In summary, requiring fair procedure in relation to discretionary decision-making does not derive from the *ultra vires* doctrine, but rather is something imposed by the courts in the interest of good administration. It follows that the subset of legitimate expectations cannot be justified in *ultra vires* terms.

It is important to stress that the Canadian version of the doctrine clearly resists the claim that the courts should enforce substantive legitimate expectations. Therefore, any conception of procedure that blurs the distinction between process and substance is likely to be problematic under the traditional view, since the suggestion that procedure might limit the decision-maker in the range of outcomes it is legally entitled to reach would violate the no-fettering rule. Procedure would then permit indirectly what is forbidden directly under the rule. Stated differently, since the Canadian version of the doctrine explicitly denies any substantive effect to legitimate expectations, it must also deny the possibility that conferring procedural rights on an individual whose substantive legitimate expectation is about to be frustrated will affect the substance of the decision. Now, since under the *ultra vires* doctrine procedure is viewed as having only an instrumental nature, it is aimed at enhancing the accuracy of the outcome. It thus affects the substance of the decision. Therefore, to impose procedural obligations on decision-makers attempting to frustrate substantive expectations would necessarily affect the substance of the decision made, and this would contradict the no-fettering rule.[60]

So the requirement of procedural fairness under the procedural aspect of the doctrine of legitimate expectations is incompatible with, or cannot be explained under, the *ultra vires* doctrine.[61] Put differently, the Canadian version of the doctrine assumes at least a significant, dignitarian aspect of procedure that cannot be accommodated within the *ultra vires* doctrine.

The traditional justification for the Canadian version of the doctrine of legitimate expectations is therefore unsatisfactory. The *ultra vires* doctrine explains the substantive aspect of that doctrine but not its procedural aspect. Even more problematic, however, the Canadian version of the doctrine, with its strong reliance on the dichotomy between procedure and substance, is itself becoming difficult to sustain. Indeed, recent attempts to move away from a view of procedure as tightly separated from substance creates a fundamental ambiguity within the judicial discourse and brings into question the structure of the Canadian version of fairness in general and legitimate expectations in particular.

In *Baker*, L'Heureux-Dubé J. indicates clearly that she does not view process and substance as existing separately. This is evidenced by her general discussion of the aims of procedural fairness,[62] and more specifically her treatment of the duty to give reasons in discretionary decisions.[63] If this is so, logically she (and her colleagues who unanimously agreed with her on this aspect) cannot endorse the traditional no-fettering rule as a justification for the Canadian version of the legitimate expectation doctrine, because the idea that government must be free to choose the appropriate course of action when endowed with discretionary powers clashes with the idea that procedure can affect substance and limit the freedom of the decision-maker. So the traditional justification for the Canadian version of the legitimate expectation doctrine is inconsistent with the approach adopted by L'Heureux-Dubé J. and the Supreme Court in *Baker.*

In sum, the traditional justification for the Canadian version of the doctrine of legitimate expectations, the *ultra vires* rule, either leads to emptying the doctrine of any meaning, or proves unable to justify its procedural aspect. Unfortunately, the Supreme Court has not addressed this serious contradiction, despite Mullan's persistent urging that it do so. As we will see, however, the Court has taken on board the values that animate the substantive version of the doctrine and as a result has been willing to achieve justice, albeit outside the framework of the doctrine of legitimate expectations.

Mount Sinai: Substantive Recognition through a Mullanian Approach

The Mount Sinai Hospital Center was originally dedicated to offering long-term care facilities for the treatment of patients suffering from tuberculosis. Over time, the incidence of tuberculosis decreased and the Center developed a general expertise in the treatment of respiratory disease. This change was not reflected in the Center's permit, but the provincial government was well aware of it and nonetheless continued to provide full funding for many years.

At some point, serious negotiations began between the Center and the government, in order to physically relocate the Center closer to its clientele. Throughout the negotiations, successive health ministers (from different governments) had promised the Center that its permit would be regularized once it was relocated, and this was addressed as one of the Center's main concerns. But once the move was completed, the minister informed the Center that he would not issue the modified permit. He considered that the requested permit would necessitate 'strengthen[ing] the establishment's capacity to deal with more acute and more complex clinical problems than at present,'[64] which would have required increased funding that the government was unwilling to grant.

The Center applied for *mandamus*, requesting that the minister be ordered to issue the permit. The Superior Court, applying the doctrine of legitimate expectations in its procedural version, ordered the minister to consult with the Center over the decision-making concerning the modified permit.[65] In the Quebec Court of Appeal, Robert J.A., speaking for a unanimous Court, relied on the notion of promissory estoppel and ordered the minister to issue the permit as he had promised.[66] In his opinion, promissory estoppel was the only route that allowed a court to constrain the minister to keep his word, since Canadian law does not enforce substantive legitimate expectations.[67]

Seven judges of the Supreme Court unanimously dismissed the appeal of the minister. Two sets of reasons were given, but neither applied either legitimate expectations or promissory estoppel. Bastarache J., speaking for a majority of the Court, approached the matter from the point of view of the exercise of discretionary power: the refusal of the minister to deliver the permit was an attempt to reverse a discretionary decision that had already been taken. Indeed, a statutory provision stated that the minister 'shall issue a ... permit if he considers that it is in the public interest.'[68] The government's behaviour indicated that the minister had indeed 'exercised' or 'exhausted' his discretion.[69] Therefore, the issue was whether 'under some general discretionary power, the Minister was entitled to reverse that original exercise of discretion at that time, in that way.'[70]

On the facts of the case, the majority concluded that the refusal of the minister did not constitute a valid reversal of the original exercise of discretion. The financial argument invoked by the minister to support his refusal was a 'vague and ungrounded funding concern' that could not justify reversing the decision already made.[71] Moreover, even after informing the Center that he refused to issue the requested permit, the minister continued to consider the Center as operating under such a permit. According to the majority, '[t]he only logical inference to be drawn [from that behaviour] is that this situation is the one that the Minister believes to be in the public interest.'[72] Bastarache J. suggested that even if the statute or some general discretionary power were interpreted as giving the minister some room to change his mind,[73] the decision not to issue the permit would not have been valid because 'the refusal was not a fair and appropriate one';[74] it was based on a policy concern that was not legitimate in the circumstances.[75] The decision had to be 'based on valid and legitimate policy concerns that are fairly invoked and based on the reality of the situation.'[76]

Binnie J., with whom McLachlin C.J. concurred, pointed out that the majority's decision focused on the minister, while it should have focused on the relationship between the minister and the Center. He viewed the crux of the matter as follows:[77]

> [S]uccessive Ministers *not only communicated their view* that the Center's change of operations ... was in the public interest (in terms which amounted to a promise that the modified permit would be issued) but *the respondents relied* on those representations and communications. *Inexplicably,* once the respondents applied for the modified permit as promised, *the ministerial wind shifted without notice* ... It is evident on the face of the letter [in which the Minister announced his intention not to modify the permit] that *no weight whatsoever was placed by the Minister on the implications for the respondents of the broken promises.*

In line with the prior cases cleaving procedural from substantive legitimate expectations, Binnie J. refused to apply the doctrine of legitimate expectations[78] to give the respondents the substantive benefit they claimed. He thought that 'treating procedural fairness as a subset of legitimate expectations may unnecessarily complicate and indeed inhibit rather than encourage the development of the highly flexible rules of procedural fairness.'[79] Moreover, he said 'there is a countervailing concern that using a Minister's prior conduct against him as a launching pad for substantive relief may strike the wrong balance between private and public interests, and blur the role of the court with the role of the Minister.'[80] Binnie J. affirmed the limitations placed on the application of the doctrine in *CAP*:[81] no substantive effects should derive from its operation and no procedural effects could be produced either in the field of 'purely ministerial decision, on broad grounds of public policy'[82] or of legislative functions.[83]

Binnie J. approached the case from the point of view of the rules concerning the abuse of discretion. Following *Baker,* he proceeded to the determination of the appropriate standard of review of the minister's decision. On the facts of the case, the nature of the function exercised ('public policy in its fullest sense'),[84] the expertise of the minister and his position in the hierarchy of the executive mandated the highest level of deference – that is, the application of the standard of patent unreasonableness.

In the circumstances, was the decision of the minister patently unreasonable? Binnie J.'s understanding of 'patent unreasonableness' is clearly narrow, approximating the extremely deferential approach famously articulated in the *Wednesbury* case. He viewed the *Baker* decision as approving the *Wednesbury* standard of unreasonableness and its application of the notion of 'abuse of discretion to substantive decision making';[85] and he defined 'patent unreasonableness' as meaning 'irrational or perverse.'[86] Thus, he rejected what he viewed as the English approach expressed in *Coughlan*, where unreasonableness had been 'subsumed ... into the global English concept of administrative fairness.'[87] Binnie J. clearly indicated that *Coughlan* did not reflect the state of Canadian law on the role of the judiciary in the regulation of government policy. While *Coughlan* expressly stated that courts were to determine whether an overriding public interest justified frustrating a substantive legitimate expectation, Binnie J. said that the Canadian attitude towards government policy was much more restrictive:[88]

> In Canada ... the courts have taken the view that it is generally the Minister who determines whether the public interest overrides or not. The courts will intervene only if it is established that the Minister's decision *is patently unreasonable in the sense of irrational or perverse* ...

On the facts of the case, however, Binnie J. found that the decision of the minister was patently unreasonable in this sense, because of the 'singular lack of recognition of the serious consequences the Minister's sudden reversal of position inflicted on the respondents.'[89] He added:[90]

> While the Court ought to be and would be sensitive to any serious policy reason offered by the Minister for a redefinition of the public interest in this case, particularly in light of the broad scope of the discretionary power to act 'in the public interest' in s. 138, no such policy reason was articulated by the Minister ...

A finding of patent unreasonableness does not automatically lead to the granting of a substantive outcome. But given the facts of this case, the only decision that would be reasonable would be to issue the modified permit. In the end, all seven judges in *Mount Sinai* concluded that in the circumstances the minister could not validly decide as he did, and that he had to give the Center the substantive benefit it claimed (that is, the permit). Although neither the majority nor the minority judges formally appealed to the doctrine of substantive legitimate expectations in reaching their conclusions, I contend that their respective approaches adhere to the same underlying values.[91]

For Bastarache J., writing for the majority, the circumstances of the case showed that the minister had indeed exercised his discretion to deliver the permit: he had promised to do so, had repeated that promise, and continued to fund the Center. The question was whether the decision of the minister not to deliver the permit was a valid revocation of the decision to issue the permit that had *already been made*. Bastarache J. did not make use of the substantive doctrine of legitimate expectations. However, his approach explicitly recognized that the behaviour of the minister and of the governmental authorities, and the relationship they had developed with the Center, were crucial elements in the determination of the making of the first decision and the validity of the purported revocation of that decision. Moreover, the purported revocation did not have any legitimate basis: it was based on a 'vague and ungrounded funding concern.'[92] The majority concluded that the behaviour of the decision-maker prevented him from contending that he had validly revoked his decision. Therefore, the first decision had to be implemented.[93]

For Binnie J., concurring in the result, the 'web of understandings'[94] that had developed between the minister and the representatives of the Center was an essential element to consider in assessing the reasonableness of the decision not to deliver the permit. He argued that in the circumstances of the case the only reasonable decision was to issue the permit. While Binnie J. expressly rejected the idea that a legitimate expectation of a substantive outcome, created by promises or representations, might constrain the decision-maker, he took into account the history of the relationships between the minister and the Center to reach his conclusion. Moreover, while reaffirming what he views as the official position of Canadian courts – that the judiciary does not intervene in the determination of the public interest – he said that the minister's sudden change of attitude was not supported by 'any serious policy reasons.'[95]

A reading of *Mount Sinai* shows that the majority used the logic of discretionary power, not the doctrine of legitimate expectations, in effect to estop the decision-maker. However, the motivation and policy justification for that stance is the same as the justifications and motivations for the U.K.-style doctrine of substantive legitimate expectations. Recall that the U.K. version of the doctrine expresses the idea that the relationships, understandings, and communications that develop or take place between a public authority and an individual are likely to affect the substance of the decision made. More generally, it establishes the need for public authorities to be responsive to the effect that their actions produce on the individuals and to frame the justification for their actions in the light of the content of the communications that took place between themselves and the individuals. A decision will be illegal if made in violation of the preceding history of the relationships, promises, engagements, and understandings that had occurred between the parties, in a context where no overriding considerations of public interest justified that departure.

Likewise, the invocation of patent unreasonableness by the minority also resonates with the part of the U.K.-style doctrine that dates back to Lord Denning's views that there must be a good reason (in other words, justification) for departing from the officially-induced expected outcome. In the absence of good reason, the decision is arbitrary and perverse in the *Wednesbury* sense.

In sum, both Bastarache and Binnie JJ.'s positions are compatible with the values and principles that inform the U.K. version of the substantive doctrine of legitimate expectations. Their reasoning focuses on the history of the relationship between the minister and the Center (especially the representations made by successive ministers and the Center's reliance on those representations), on the consequences that the relationship produced on the outcome, and on an evaluation of the legitimacy of the reasons put forward by the minister to change course.

Conclusion

In *Mount Sinai* the Supreme Court was confronted by a case that, on its facts, seemed tailor-made for application of the U.K. version of the doctrine of substantive legitimate expectations, but the Court refused to follow that approach. Nonetheless, it considerably limited the freedom of a public decision-maker to backtrack on a particular, substantive promise to exercise discretion in a specific way, for the same reasons that U.K. courts invoked in support of substantive legitimate expectations: in their decision-making processes, public authorities must take into account the expectations they induced in individuals, through their representations, declarations, and practices. Stated differently, public authorities must justify their actions, or their decision not to act or to change course, in the light of those expectations, so that although they are not prevented from changing course, they must put forward a good reason for doing so. Thus, a Mullanian approach allowed the courts to reach for the values and principles that inform the doctrine of legitimate expectations without formally appealing to that doctrine, and to apply them accordingly. From this perspective, I contend that both majority and minority judges in *Mount Sinai* endorsed Mullan's plea for concentrating on real issues, as opposed to crafting formal doctrines and articulating disputable definitions. And while there is still much to be done in terms of clarification, I think this should be seen as a promising development in the field of public accountability.

NOTES

I thank Mike Taggart and Grant Huscroft for asking me to participate in this project. As usual, Mike provided (numerous) lucid and challenging comments on a draft of this text, and I doubt the final result is an entirely satisfying answer to his queries. Grant Huscroft's rigour, patience, and sense of humour allowed me to work in a supportive environment.

David Mullan's profound significance for Canadian administrative law has been a constant inspiration for me as a Quebec administrative lawyer trying to build bridges among colleagues of the 'two solitudes.' David's interest in Quebec administrative law attests to his quest for inclusiveness. I agree with Mike and Grant that he richly deserves the honour of being the focus of the present *Mélanges*.

1 David J. Mullan, 'Fairness: The New Natural Justice?' (1975) 25 U.T.L.J. 281 [Mullan, 'Fairness'].
2 Ibid. at 299.
3 Ibid. at 300.
4 [1979] 1 S.C.R. 311 [*Nicholson*].
5 The expression is from David Mullan: see 'Confining the Reach of Legitimate Expectations – *Sunshine Coast Parents for French v. School District No. 46*' (1990) 44 Admin. L. R. 245 at 250 [Mullan, 'Confining'].
6 'Fairness,' *supra* note 1 at 300. See also 305, 313, and 325.
7 [2001] 2 S.C.R. 281 [*Mount Sinai*].
8 David J. Mullan, '*Canada Assistance Plan*: Denying Legitimate Expectation a Fair Start' (1993) 7 Admin. L.R. 269 at 290 [Mullan, 'Fair Start'].
9 Mullan, 'Confining,' *supra* note 5 is, to my knowledge, the first Canadian contribution to that topic. A selective list of contributions by other Canadian authors includes D. Shapiro, 'Legitimate Expectations and its Application to Canadian Immigration Law' (1992) 8 J.L. & Soc. Pol'y 282; G. Cartier, 'La théorie des attentes légitimes en droit administratif' (1992) 23 R.D.U.S. 75; C. Roy, *La théorie de l'expectative légitime en droit administratif* (Cowansville:

Yvon Blais, 1993); J.G. Small, 'Legitimate Expectations, Fairness and Delegated Legislation' (1994–5) 8 Can. J. Admin. L. & Prac. 129; P.A. MacPherson, 'The Legitimate Expectation Doctrine and its Application to Administrative Policy' (1995–6) 9 Can. J. Admin. L. & Prac. 141; and D. Wright, 'Rethinking the Doctrine of Legitimate Expectations in Canadian Administrative Law' (1997) 35 Osgoode Hall L. J. 139 [Wright, 'Rethinking'].

10 David J. Mullan, 'Legitimate Expectation in Canadian Public Law' in Institute for Comparative Law / Institut de droit comparé, *Contemporary Law 1998 / Droit contemporain 1998* (Cowansville, QC: Yvon Blais, 1999) 519 at 539 [Mullan, 'Expectation in Canadian Law'].

11 A detailed analysis of the emergence of the doctrine in the U.K. can be found in S. Schønberg, *Legitimate Expectations in Administrative Law* (Oxford: Oxford University Press, 2000) [Schønberg, *Legitimate Expectations*] and R. Thomas, *Legitimate Expectations and Proportionality in Administrative Law* (Oxford: Hart Publishing, 2000).

12 The doctrine has attracted considerable academic and judicial attention in the last twenty years. A selective list of academic contributions includes R. Baldwin and D. Hawthorne, 'Expectations in a Joyless Landscape' (1986) 49 Mod. L. R. 685; R. Baldwin and J. Houghton, 'Circular Arguments: The Status and Legitimacy of Administrative Rules' [1986] P.L. 239; C.F. Forsyth, 'The Provenance and Protection of Legitimate Expectations' (1988) 47 Cambridge L.J. 238; P.P. Craig, 'Legitimate Expectations: A Conceptual Analysis' (1992) 108 L.Q.R. 79 [Craig, 'Conceptual Analysis']; P.P. Craig, 'Substantive Legitimate Expectations in Domestic and Community Law' (1996) 55 Cambridge L.J. 289; Y. Dotan, 'Why Administrators Should be Bound by Their Policies' (1997) 17 O.J.L.S. 23 [Dotan]; C.F. Forsyth, '*Wednesbury* Protection of Substantive Legitimate Expectations' [1997] L. 375; C.M.G. Himsworth, 'Legitimately Expecting Proportionality?' [1996] P.L. 46; M. Elliott, 'Legitimate Expectation: The Substantive Dimension' (2000) 59 Cambridge L.J. 421; P.P. Craig and S. Schønberg, 'Substantive Legitimate Expectations after *Coughlan*' [2000] P.L. 684; Richard Clayton, 'Legitimate Expectations, Policy, and the Principle of Consistency' (2003) 62 Cambridge L.J. 93; Philip Sales and Karen Steyn, 'Legitimate Expectations in English Public Law: An Analysis' [2004] L. 564; and Ian Steele, 'Substantive Legitimate Expectations: Striking the Right Balance?' (2005) 121 L.Q.R. 301.

13 See Schønberg, *Legitimate Expectations*, *supra* note 11, chap. 2.

14 See, among others, *R. v. Secretary of State for the Home Department, ex p. Ruddock*, [1987] 2 All E.R. 518 [*Ruddock*] and *R. v. Secretary of State for Health, ex p. U.S. Tobacco International Inc.*, [1992] Q.B. 353 [*U.S. Tobacco*].

15 *R. v. North and East Devon Health Authority, ex p. Coughlan*, [2000] 3 All E.R. 850 (C.A.) [*Coughlan*].

16 That exclusion was explicitly established in *Bates v. Lord Hailsham,* [1972] 1 W.L.R. 1373.

17 See e.g. *Ruddock* and *U.S. Tobacco, supra* note 14.

18 *R. v. Liverpool Corporation, ex p. Liverpool Taxi Fleet Operators' Association,* [1972] 2 All E.R. 589, and *R. v. Secretary of State for the Home Department, ex p. Khan,* [1985] 1 All E.R. 40.

19 The *Wednesbury* principles are named after the famous dictum from Lord Greene in *Associated Provincial Picture Houses Ltd. v. Wednesbury Corporation,* [1948] 1 K.B. 223 [*Wednesbury*].

20 This position was articulated in *R. v. Secretary of State for Transport, ex p. Richmond Upon Thames London B.C.,* [1994] 1 All E.R. 577, and *R. v. Secretary of State for the Home Department, ex parte Hargreaves,* [1997] 1 All E.R. 397 [*Hargreaves*].

21 *R. v. Ministry of Agriculture, Fisheries and Food, ex p. Hamble (Offshore) Fisheries Ltd.,* [1995] 2 All E.R. 714 at 731 (Sedley J.) [*Hamble Fisheries*]. Sedley J. reasserted his position in *R. v. Secretary of State for the Home Department, ex p. Urmaza, The Times,* 23 July 1996. In *Hargreaves, supra* note 20 at 412, Hirst L.J. characterized Sedley's position in *Hamble Fisheries* as amounting to 'heresy.'

22 *Hamble Fisheries, supra* note 21,

23 *Coughlan, supra* note 15.

24 Lord Woolf recalled that '[i]n the past it would have been argued that the promise was to be ignored since it could not have any effect on how the public body exercised its judgment in what it thought was the public interest. Today such an argument would have no prospect of success.' Ibid. at para. 55.

25 Ibid. at para. 52.

26 Ibid.

27 Ibid. at para. 82.

28 *Old St. Boniface Residents Assn. Inc. v. Winnipeg (City),* [1990] 3 S.C.R. 1170 at 1204 [emphasis added] [*Old St. Boniface*].

29 He first made this suggestion in Mullan, 'Confining,' *supra* note 5 at 246.

30 *Reference Re Canada Assistance Plan (B.C.),* [1991] 2 S.C.R. 525 [*CAP*].

31 Ibid. at 557 (Sopinka J., quoting his opinion in *Old St. Boniface, supra* note 28 at 1204).

32 Ibid. at 558.

33 Ibid. at 557.

34 [1999] 2 S.C.R. 817 [*Baker*].

35 Ibid. at para. 26.

36 Ibid.

37 Mullan, 'Confining,' *supra* note 5 at 250.

38 See, e.g., ibid.; Mullan, 'Fair Start,' *supra* note 8 at 281; 'Expectation in Cana-

dian Law,' *supra* note 10 at 526; and David J. Mullan, 'The Role of the Judiciary in the Review of Administrative Policy Decisions: Issues of Legality' in M.J. Mossman and G. Otis, eds., *The Judiciary as Third Branch of Government: Manifestations and Challenges to Legitimacy* (Montreal: Thémis, 2000) 313, at 350–1 [Mullan, 'Role of the Judiciary'].

39 Mullan, 'Role of the Judiciary,' *supra* note 38 at 350, referring more specifically to *CAP, supra* note 30.

40 Mullan, 'Confining,' *supra* note 5 at 246.

41 *Old St. Boniface, supra* note 28 at 1204 [emphasis added].

42 Mullan, 'Fair Start,' *supra* note 8. Eventually, David Mullan agreed with David Wright's view that legitimate expectations would probably not be the best way to introduce more fairness in legislative functions (Wright, 'Rethinking,' *supra* note 9). This is because legitimate expectations would usually inure to the benefit of those already involved in consultation and influence, so that the best solution remains a rewriting of the common law rules and principles of procedural fairness to include legislative functions within their domain of application. See Mullan, 'Expectation in Canadian Law,' *supra* note 10 at 539 and David J. Mullan, *Administrative Law* (Toronto: Irwin Law, 2001) at 178.

43 Mullan, 'Confining,' *supra* note 5.

44 David J. Mullan, 'Annotation to *Furey v. Conception Bay Centre Roman Catholic School Board*' (1993) 17 Admin. L.R. (2d) 46 [Mullan, 'Furey'].

45 Mullan, 'Confining,' *supra* note 5 at 248 [emphasis added].

46 Mullan, 'Fair Start,' *supra* note 8 at 272.

47 Ibid. at 280–1.

48 Mullan, 'Furey,' *supra* note 44 at 49. See also David J. Mullan, 'Natural Justice and Fairness – Substantive as well as Procedural Standards for the Review of Administrative Decision-Making?' (1982) 27 McGill L.J. 250.

49 David Dyzenhaus, 'Formalism's Hollow Victory' [2002] N.Z. Law Rev. 525 at 526.

50 Dawn Oliver, 'Is the *Ultra Vires* Rule the Basis of Judicial Review?' [1987] P.L. 543 at 544.

51 As Oliver puts it, 'Parliament, or the "donor" of the *vires* or the authority, is presumed not to have intended that the authority should act in breach of ... principles of good administration. This presumption is ... rebuttable, in the sense that if ... the instrument granting the power clearly intends that these principles are not to apply, the courts will give precedence to the terms of the Act or other instrument.' Ibid. at 544–45.

More generally, Oliver argues that, although still very relevant to judicial review, the *ultra vires* rule is not the basis for it, since it cannot explain an increasing number of cases that have been judicially reviewed by superior courts. In an illuminating essay, T.R.S. Allan argues that the doctrine of *ultra vires* 'has lost its dominance' in modern public law. See Trevor Allan, 'Fairness, Equality, Rationality: Constitutional Theory and Judicial Review' in Christopher Forsyth and Ivan Hare, eds., *The Golden Metwand and the Crooked Cord – Essays on Public Law in Honour of Sir William Wade QC* (Oxford: Clarendon Press, 1998) 15 at 18 ['Fairness, Equality'].

52 See notably Craig, 'Conceptual Analysis,' *supra* note 12 at 92. For the purpose of this paper I limit my analysis to the question of discretion. Craig describes the traditional justification for refusing substantive legitimate expectations in the case of non-discretionary decisions and suggests how the traditional justification for this stance can be questioned.

53 See, e.g., Gerry Maher, 'Natural Justice as Fairness' in Neil MacCormick and Peter Birks, eds., *The Legal Mind: Essays for Tony Honoré* (Oxford: Clarendon Press, 1986) 103; Denis J. Galligan, *Due Process and Fair Procedures: A Study of Administrative Procedures* (Oxford: Clarendon Press, 1996); T.R.S. Allan, 'Procedural Fairness and the Duty of Respect' (1998) 18 O.J.L.S. 497 [Allan, 'Duty of Respect']; and Craig, 'Conceptual Analysis.' In the specific context of legitimate expectations, see Schønberg, *Legitimate Expectations, supra* note 11 at 31: 'The connection between procedure and expectations may be explained as follows. First, procedures may reduce the risk that expectations will *actually* be disappointed in a way which causes unfairness or mistrust in government, because they affect the outcomes of administrative decision-making processes ... Second, procedures may reduce the *feeling* of unfairness and mistrust ... [because procedure demonstrates that] the administration acknowledges that its action affects his autonomy and personal dignity.' [emphasis in original]. For judicial endorsement, see *R. v. Secretary of State for the Home Department Ex p. Doody,* [1994] A.C. 531 at 551.

54 The literature on this question is huge. See for example, Laurence Tribe, *American Constitutional Law,* 2nd ed. (Mineola, NY: Foundation Press, 1988); Laurence Tribe, 'Trial by Mathematics' (1971) 84 Harv. L. Rev. 1329; Allan, 'Duty of Respect,' *supra* note 53; Jerry L. Mashaw, 'Administrative Due Process: The Quest for a Dignitary Theory' (1981) 61 B.U.L. Rev. 885; Frank I. Michelman, 'Formal and Associational Aims in Procedural Due Process' in J. Roland Pennock and John W. Chapman, eds., *Due Process,* Nomos 18 (New York: New York University Press, 1977) 126. For Michelman, '[p]rocedure as the handmaiden of substantive rights ... seems a minimalist interpretation of due process.' Ibid. at 133.

55 Allan, 'Duty of Respect,' *supra* note 53 at 498. See also Allan, 'Fairness, Equality,' *supra* note 51 at 30: '[T]he precepts of natural justice reflect the

concepts of human dignity and autonomy which underlie the richer, more substantive understanding of the rule of law. The value of procedural fairness is intrinsic, not merely instrumental: a person's participation in a decision affecting his interests affirms his dignity as a citizen - one whose cooperation is sought *with the public purposes in view,* rather than someone treated essentially as an object of administration' [emphasis added].

56 See Allan, 'Duty of Respect,' *supra* note 53 at 497.

57 Galligan, *supra* note 53 at 78. In fact, Galligan expresses scepticism towards purely dignitarian conceptions of procedure. Allan captures his point as follows: '[W]e should not readily accept the idea that the value of respect for persons generates certain standards and procedures directly, without reference to outcomes.' Allan, ibid. at 498. For Allan, depending on how one conceives the goals that are to be reached through procedure, the distinction between instrumental and non-instrumental considerations is difficult to maintain: 'It remains true that participation is a largely instrumental virtue, as Galligan argues, only if we understand "authoritative standards" to include the whole range of moral values to which the citizen might intelligibly appeal in his dealings with the state. At this point, the distinction between instrumental and intrinsic virtue has itself begun to break down.' Ibid. at 502. I contend that this is particularly the case in relation to discretionary decisions.

58 A good example can be found in *Knight v. Indian Head School Division No. 19,* [1990] 1 S.C.R. 653, where Sopinka J. affirmed that for procedure to apply, the legislature must indicate that this should be so.

59 Essentially, the *ultra vires* doctrine does not accord with a justification for procedural rights that is purely based on values, like dignity. Rather, under that doctrine, '[t]he primary function of natural justice is to enable decisions affecting individuals to be tailored to their particular circumstances, in order that the legislative intention or public policy in question is fulfilled rather than frustrated.' Allan, 'Fairness, Equality,' *supra* note 51 at 30. See also Joel Handler, *The Conditions of Discretion: Autonomy, Community, Democracy* (New York: Russell Sage Foundation, 1986) at 123–5; and Lorne Sossin, 'An Intimate Approach to Fairness, Impartiality and Reasonableness in Administrative Law' (2001) 27 Queen's L.J. 809 at 847.

60 Proponents of the *ultra vires* doctrine might suggest that 'accuracy' simply means making the best possible solution given the available information, and that information will be available only if procedures, like a hearing, are in place. From this perspective, the issue of accuracy would not relate to the conformity of the decision with pre-existing law, but rather to the relationship between the decision and the facts. The latter is a substantive matter

but escapes judicial review. But in my view it is not enough that the decision-maker has all the facts: he or she has also to take them into account and give them appropriate weight.

61 Although I concentrate on the question of legitimate expectations, this incompatibility extends to procedure generally. See Oliver, *supra* note 50.

62 '[T]he purpose of the participatory rights contained within the duty of procedural fairness is to ensure that administrative decisions are made using a fair and open procedure, appropriate to the decision being made and its statutory, institutional, and social context, with an opportunity for those affected by the decision to put forward their views and evidence fully and have them considered by the decision maker.' *Baker, supra* note 34 at para. 22.

63 Ibid. at para. 25.

64 *Mount Sinai, supra* note 7 at para. 5.

65 J.E. 92–1815 (Marcelin J.).

66 [1998] R.J.Q. 2707 (C.A.).

67 Ibid. at 2723.

68 *Act Respecting Health Services and Social Services,* R.S.Q., c. S-5, s. 138.

69 *Mount Sinai, supra* note 7 at para. 100: 'This discretion was exercised when the Minister promised the Center that it would receive the modified permit, encouraged the move to Montreal, endorsed the financing campaign focussed on the role of the Center as a long-term and short-term case hospital, and continued to fund the short-term care services despite the mismatch between those services and the Center's permit.' See also para. 106.

70 Ibid. at para. 107.

71 Ibid. at para. 109. In fact, the whole rationale for the regularization of the permit was to ensure that everything would be secured as it was: long-term and short-term services, nothing more or less, under the same funding as the government had accorded for many years. Indeed, all the negotiations were based on the assumption that nothing would change as a result of the move to Montreal.

72 Ibid. at para. 110.

73 As was found in *Comeau's Sear Foods Ltd. v. Canada (Minister of Fisheries and Oceans),* [1997] 1 S.C.R. 12.

74 *Mount-Sinai, supra* note 7 at para. 114.

75 Ibid.

76 Ibid. at para. 114.

77 Ibid. at paras. 5–6 [emphasis added]. See also para. 8, where Binnie J. writes of a 'web of understandings and incremental agreements.'

78 Binnie J. also refused to apply promissory estoppel, although he admitted

that public law estoppel could apply in situations where the legislative intent does not express an overriding public interest to which the circumstances may have to yield. He thus suggests that remedies similar to substantive legitimate expectations might flow from promises and engagements.

79 *Mount Sinai*, *supra* note 7 at para. 28.

80 Ibid.

81 *CAP*, *supra* note 31.

82 *Mount Sinai*, *supra* note 7 at para. 33.

83 Legislative functions here refer to general and policy-based decisions, typically excluded from the sphere of application of the duty to act fairly.

84 *Mount Sinai*, *supra* note 7 at para. 58.

85 Ibid. at para. 53. In Binnie J.'s view, the notion of abuse of discretion was an exception to the attitude of deference that courts usually endorsed towards ministerial decision-making. This exception had long been limited to procedure in Canada, but in England, *Wednesbury* had extended it to substantive matters and *Baker* integrated this rule in Canada.

86 Ibid. at para. 63.

87 Ibid. at para. 61.

88 Ibid. at para. 63 [emphasis added].

89 Ibid. See also para. 64, where Binnie J. points to the minister's 'total lack of regard for the implications for the respondents of the Minister's broken promises.'

90 Ibid. at para. 65.

91 The approach of the Court would accord with the position of Dotan, *supra* note 12, who rejects the use of the doctrine of substantive legitimate expectations while arguing that the principles that it seeks to protect must indeed be protected. Dotan contends that courts could constrain an authority to stick to its promise or undertaking outside the structure of legitimate expectations. I agree.

92 *Mount Sinai*, *supra* note 7 at para. 109.

93 Arguably, this aspect of the decision convinced a majority of judges to join Bastarache J., because his approach seemed to avoid the appearance of judicial intrusion into executive matters: he concluded that the decision had indeed already been taken by the minister, so that it was not the Court that forced the minister to deliver the permit. The Court only concluded that the decision not to deliver the permit was not a valid revocation of the preceding decision.

94 *Mount Sinai*, *supra* note 7 at para. 8.

95 Ibid. at para. 65.

Roadblocks, Restraint, and Remedies: The Idea of Progress in Administrative Law

JANET McLEAN

In 1985 Professor David Mullan gave a talk to the Law Faculty at Victoria University of Wellington called 'Heed the Amber Light.'[1] As an undergraduate student at the time I was not entitled to attend. On that occasion, the formalities were observed – introductions were made and my presence explained by my interest in the subject matter. Those were more formal and constrained times. That was not only true of the academy but also of the nature of judicial review itself.

Professor Mullan's writings have tracked the large movements and concerns of judicial review over more than thirty-five years. During that time, what Mullan once called the formal roadblock tests,[2] whose purpose was to inhibit judges from even considering whether something had gone wrong of a public law nature, have for the most part been eliminated in favour of greater access and increased assessment of the merits. Prerogative powers are no longer immune from review, locus standi rules have been relaxed or abandoned, the administrative/judicial dichotomy has withered, fairness has been accepted as a general principle, and 'justiciability' is being steadily unpacked.

This tribute to David Mullan's work will assess the impact on remedial discretion of the elimination of these roadblocks and the easing of other formal barriers to, and consequential expansion of, judicial review. The following questions arise. How do these developments affect the existence and operation of remedial discretion? Is remedial discretion the proper place for judicial restraint to be exercised and the collective interest to be taken into account? Are the consequences of a finding of illegality better decided by public law or by private law? Has the increased accessibility of judicial review been altogether positive –

for either plaintiffs or for the internal coherence of administrative law itself?

This paper will address these questions by reference to three concerns that Mullan has consistently explored in his writings: the need to focus on the substantive rationales (rather than non-transparent mechanical tests) for maintaining judicial restraint; the desirability of understanding administrative law as a 'whole system'; and the need to be conscientious and particular in our use of language.

Three Concerns

'Proper' Judicial Restraint

Mullan's scholarship has made a significant contribution to simplifying the procedural availability of review in both Canada and New Zealand and to encouraging greater access to judicial review remedies.[3] Throughout his work, however, one detects a fair degree of caution. The concerns that motivated the historical barriers to scrutiny – such as the need to balance the interests of the collective against those of individuals, to maintain the ability of governments to govern, to respect relative expertise, and to recognize the limitations of judicial in relation to more polycentric modes of decision-making – may still be compelling. Merely removing the once defining threshold tests such as the 'duty to act judicially' or 'jurisdictional error' cannot and should not be the end of the matter. New techniques have to be devised as a means of effecting proper judicial restraint and as a proper limit on remedies.

Conscious that once judges are prepared to look, wrongs will almost inevitably be found to have occurred, Mullan has argued that these threshold tests should be replaced with more finely grained, contextual alternatives that take account of public law's distinct concerns as a substantive matter. His work on deference is one important aspect of this theme. Indeed, Mullan is careful not to reintroduce new roadblocks to judicial review through the concept of deference, while, at the same time, he reaffirms the need for proper judicial restraint, even where the *Charter* is concerned.[4] This paper will address the question of *when* the rationales for judicial restraint ought to be considered: as a threshold question; in determining whether a particular ground of judicial review has been made out; in determining whether to exercise the discretion to grant a remedy; or even later when considering the consequences that might follow a finding of invalidity?

Administrative Law as System

Such questions in themselves lead to a consideration of administrative law understood as a systemic whole. They should also cause us to pause to consider how we measure 'progress' in the law of judicial review. [5] As Mullan has warned, judicial review ought not to become another arbitrary element in the government enterprise.[6] When the highest courts in the land pronounce judicial review doctrines, they should remain mindful that either less administratively experienced lower courts or more expert administrators and tribunals (or both) may have to apply them.[7] Doctrinal pronouncements also create incentives and disincentives for aggrieved persons to take on the burden of proving public law wrongs.[8]

Linguistic Precision

The third of Mullan's preoccupations, through which this paper will explore remedial discretion, is the use of language and its potential to mislead. Throughout Mullan's work there is an acuity for, and concern about, the use of language. There is much to be found there about the role of language in judicial discourse. The language of 'fairness,' for example, has the potential to connote a particular, narrow conception or an open-textured one. [9] In the area of remedial discretion, words like 'invalidity' and 'rights' create the same possibilities for misunderstanding as the word 'fairness.' What do we mean by 'invalid,' 'unlawful,' '*ultra vires*' or, indeed, 'unreasonable'?[10] When we use the word 'rights,' are we invoking a distinctive Hohfeldian conception or making a much more radical claim to positive entitlements against the state?[11]

With these three concerns identified, let us turn now to two recent New Zealand examples that are emblematic of modern regulatory practices. Both examples involve legislative provisions that on the face of it appear to set standards that attract judicial supervision. In both cases, too, the response of the New Zealand Court of Appeal suggests that, despite the great developments in judicial review, a new formalism may have replaced the old roadblocks; judicial restraint is being exercised in new but equally opaque ways. In both cases, too, remedial discretion is used for distinctively public law purposes.[12] This discretion goes beyond the usual equitable criteria (where the focus is on the claimants' interests and conduct such as waiver, delay, and abuse of process) and takes account of 'public' matters such as the disruption to collective interests and the compromising of the ability of governments to govern.

The examples suggest that at the same time as the extent of judicial supervision has increased, the very existence of the remedial discretion, which once signaled the distinctiveness of public law as opposed to private law, is becoming increasingly difficult to sustain. The impulse toward judicial restraint tends to manifest itself at two earlier stages in the proceeding. In order to preserve a role for remedial discretion, attempts may be made to restrict review to its most narrow grounds in the first place: it is easier to exercise a discretion to refuse a remedy where the errors can be characterized as technical irregularities. Alternatively, having decided that the discretion to grant a remedy should be exercised, judicial restraint may be manifested at the point at which judges determine what should be the consequences of a finding of invalidity. When such consequentialist concerns drive the reasoning, transparency and coherence are often sacrificed. Moreover, increasingly, the existence or not of a substantive remedy will depend on private law and not public law developments.

Rights and Public Wrongs

The New Zealand Court of Appeal decision in *Daniels v. Attorney-General*[13] serves to illustrate a number of Mullan's themes, both in its stated terms and in light of the alternative ways in which it may have been decided. Where is the proper place to consider reasons for judicial constraint? What is the effect on administrative law as a whole of considering these reasons at the later remedial stage? What are the potential effects on administrative law of the various meanings of the language of rights?

The plaintiffs were the parents of fourteen special-needs children challenging the closure of separate special-needs facilities and the replacement scheme to 'mainstream' children with disabilities of varying degrees of severity in ordinary state schools. It was not alleged that any particular child had been unable to enroll in a state school after the special schools had been disestablished. Rather, the objection was to the policy of mainstreaming itself.

Two legislative provisions were of critical importance. The first was section 3 of the *Education Act 1989* that guaranteed free education in state schools for children between the ages of five and nineteen. Section 8 of that act provides:

> People who have special educational needs (whether because of disability

or otherwise) have the same rights to enrol and receive education at state schools as people who do not.

In the High Court, Baragwanath J. found that this provision entitled every student to a 'right' to education that was 'not clearly unsuitable' and that was 'regular and systematic.'[14] He took the statutory use of rights language seriously and literally. In doing so, he chose to give enforceable substance to the legislative provision.

The Court of Appeal rejected this view that the statute gave rise to a general free-standing right of the broad kind stated, held and enforceable by each individual student.[15] This, it said, was too abstract a formulation on which to base enforceable rights and correlative obligations. It treated the statutory use of rights language as subject to, and restricted by, an independent test of justiciability. While it never expressly invoked Hohfeld's scheme, its careful use of the Hohfeldian language of 'rights and correlative obligations'[16] indicates that it was purporting to assess justiciability through a Hohfeldian frame. It found the legislation, read as a whole scheme, could give rise to judicially enforceable rights of both a general and individual kind, but that these particular plaintiffs had not established such rights.[17]

Did Section 8 Give Rise to Justiciable Rights?

The Court of Appeal opined that the legislative scheme taken as a whole could, under certain circumstances, give rise to *some* legally enforceable rights and obligations. These included: rights relating to the central government's powers to intervene in the operations of local school boards; rights arising as a result of breaches of obligations owed to students at large such as failures to open schools or to make education available at requisite times; or rights arising from actions affecting individual students, such as the right of a child who needs to avail herself of special programs offered by the school to priority over other children applying from outside the school zone.[18] The court also suggested that the decision-making processes involved in assessing a particular child's needs could give rise to justiciable obligations, though it also recognized that the statute itself set out a procedure for reconsideration by an expert arbitrator. It suggested that a complete failure by the relevant official to consider whether a particular child should receive a 'special education'[19] was an instance that would attract judicial supervision. There may have been justiciable questions here but the plaintiffs did not raise them. For some reason, none of the applicants claimed or sought to prove that he or she was worse off under the new scheme.[20]

A Hohfeldian schema of rights and collateral duties was implicitly invoked by the Court of Appeal to gloss the statutory language of rights in section 3 and 8 and to confine their scope. The Court of Appeal summed it up:[21]

> while there are rights under the 1989 Act that can be enforced by Court process, those rights do not include generally and abstractly formulated rights of the kind stated by the Judge. Rather, the rights are essentially those specifically established by and under the legislation which, to recall the Judge's formulation, do in themselves provide for regularity and system and are designed to ensure appropriate quality.

The purported use of the Hohfeldian frame in this public law case tends, however, to raise as many questions as it answers. As Bamforth has suggested, 'Hohfeldian analysis seems no more likely than any other style of analysis to generate widespread agreement about the meaning of a provision.'[22] Moreover, many of the judicial review grounds no longer depend on any *direct* correlative between the rights held by an individual and a duty owed to that particular person (as we shall go on to discuss).[23] Rather, the focus of the law of judicial review is on the rectification of wrongs. If it were not for this central difference between public and private law cases, it would not be possible to separate standing questions from the cause of action itself.[24] The Court of Appeal's Hohfeldian approach was an attempt to define and restrict the applicants' 'rights' in relation to the meaning of the statute – potentially creating a new kind of roadblock of a particularly opaque kind. In my view, the focus on the statutory rights language, and the Hohfeldian turn that the Court of Appeal gave it, tended to obscure the central question. What was really missing here were not rights but rather evidence of an actionable wrong.

The Court of Appeal itself makes this point in the part of the judgment at which it considers whether its conclusions about the meaning of the statute are changed by a consideration of the case law.[25] In each case cited for the applicants' claim there is an argument that 'rights owed to that particular person were breached.'[26] Again, the rights language tends to obscure the basic question: did the actions of the officials constitute a 'wrong.' Of the cases to which the Court of Appeal was referred, the *Tandy* decision[27] promised the greatest support for the applicants' case. There, too, the statute stated that 'suitable education' 'shall' be provided. 'Suitable education' was defined as 'efficient education suitable to his age, ability, and aptitude and to any special educational needs he may have.' In *Tandy,* the House of Lords found that the local authority's decision to reduce the home tuition of an ill child from five to three hours a week on the basis of purely financial rather than educational considerations amounted to a public law wrong. In *Daniels,* any successful challenge of this kind was precluded by the fact that the government had actually increased the total funding of children with special needs. In assessing whether the case law affected its conclusions on the justiciability of section 8, the court took account of the lack of specificity about the interests at stake, the too general nature of the relief sought, and the absence of specific proven evidence of wrongs in relation to the individuals concerned.

The Successful Ground of Challenge

The Court of Appeal did uphold the High Court's finding that the minister's initial decision to disestablish the special schools in the first place was unlawful because he did not properly direct himself in terms of the statutory tests. In particular, he failed to consider whether there was alternative 'sufficient provision' in each locality before the disestablishment of the old facilities was undertaken.

In relation to this second ground, by contrast to the first, the rights or interests of the plaintiffs were completely (and in terms of the established doctrine properly) submerged in the reasoning. A Hohfeldian framework did not, indeed could not, provide a filter here. Before reform and simplification of the writs, standing to seek a declaration or injunction had been restricted to those who had a specific legal right or had suffered special damage over and above that suffered by the public in general.[28] Contemporary doctrine attenuates the separation of the plaintiffs' interests from the question of whether a public wrong has been committed. Rights and correlative duties, in a Hohfeldian or near-Hohfeldian sense, are no longer required to be established. Only the relatively low-threshold standing test of 'sufficient degree of interest' is required to be satisfied – a matter that was never at issue here, and, indeed, a threshold that has virtually been eliminated in New Zealand law. Once satisfied, however, the plaintiffs' interests in the matter are not required to be considered further as part of the grounds of challenge. These matters, which were once a precondition for bringing the cause of action itself, were, however, considered in this case as part of the decision whether to grant, and the consequences of granting, a declaration of invalidity, as we shall go on to discuss.

Human Rights: An Alternative Ground of Challenge

There was a third possible approach to the issue that, in contrast to the successful ground of challenge, places rights firmly at the centre of the arguments. The Court of Appeal was invited to treat the matter as a case involving the right to be free from discrimination. Despite receiving extensive written submissions from the respondents and the Human Rights Commission as intervenor,[29] the Court of Appeal declined to consider whether the *Human Rights Act 1993* or the *New Zealand Bill of Rights Act 1990* prohibitions on discrimination were relevant to the case. In particular, it declined to consider whether a right to freedom from discrimination proscribed certain 'failures to treat people differently' as well as 'failures to treat people the same.'[30] Declining even to engage with the human rights challenge here, or to acknowledge the human rights dimension to the case, is surely a measure of judicial deference. Whether and how such human rights claims to positive entitlements from government fit within the Hohfeldian framework is a very difficult question. What is clear, however, is that a Hohfeldian analysis could not have been an answer to a human rights-based challenge.[31] The very purpose of human rights regimes is to create justiciable claims against governments. Indeed, as Martin Loughlin argues '[t]his positivization of the basic rights of citizens has the potential to reconfigure the architecture of public law.'[32]

As we have just seen, the individual rights of plaintiffs are not *necessarily* central to defining the public wrong that is alleged to have been committed in judicial review. The presence of human rights claims, understood as positive entitlements, shifts the onus of providing lawful justification explicitly to the government (something that administrative lawyers may have long wished for). The new focus on the individual's interest as the basis of the cause of action has other important consequential effects that are not so obviously part of an administrative law reform agenda. It transforms the individual's relation to the cause of action (making it obviously central and defining) and also intensifies the expectation of what remedy should (automatically) follow a breach. This is a structural shift.

The existence of a discretion to grant a remedy is much more difficult to justify when the focus is on positive individual rights against government rather than on public wrongs. Moreover, so long as the primary emphasis is on maintaining the integrity of the administrative system rather than vindicating rights, the 'transparency increasing' and 'shaming' type methods and mechanisms of judicial review, including the declaration and its alternatives (such as ombudsmen and commissions of inquiry) are congruent with administrative law's aims. Once the emphasis shifts to vindicating rights, however, then expectations of individualized remedies tend to intensify. But because the difficulties of giving an individualized remedy in many of these human rights-based cases are the same as they ever were in traditional judicial review cases, the temptation is to vindicate rights with a damages award (with all the attendant questions of quantum and basis that that raises).[33]

Of course, some of the traditional rationales for judicial restraint in judicial review (for example, concerns about the collective good and the ability of governments to govern) may still be articulated within a discussion of human rights issues. Indeed, questions such as what is the nature and content of the right; what duty is owed to the citizen in respect of the right; and whether such a right has been breached are, in my view, the proper place in which these matters ought to be considered. In that way, a primary focus on public wrongs rather than private rights may, to some extent, be maintained. The nature of the challenge will, however, necessarily change. It is hard to imagine how the Court of Appeal could have avoided altogether the substantive issues about the 'suitability of education' as it did in the *Daniels* case, once it had embarked on the process of considering what was owed to each individual under a human rights claim, even if it eventually found a way to avoid finding a breach in this particular case.[34] The idea of positive rights against government brings much more by way of structural and fundamental changes to judicial review than may sometimes be imagined. Which 'rights' framework one chooses to apply will affect not only the degree and justificatory burden of scrutiny but also the potential consequences of public wrong-doing.

It seems likely that the Court of Appeal had the possible remedial consequences squarely in view when it chose to develop a narrowing Hohfeldian gloss on the rights language of section 8 and to avoid even considering a substantive human rights-based challenge where such a gloss would not have been available. It found instead that an administrative law breach of a much more formal and technical kind had occurred. The only unlawfulness was the minister's failure to consider whether there was alternative 'sufficient provision' in each locality before the disestablishment of the old special needs facilities was undertaken. It added that '[s]ince the Court is not at this stage concerned with remedies, we draw no consequence from that conclusion.'[35] The nature and degree of the plaintiffs' interests would receive attention once more, in the separate hearing in the High Court on remedies that was to follow.

Remedies

The remedial hearing lasted five days. The reason the matter took so long was that in considering the consequences that ought to flow from the finding that there had been an unlawful act, the plaintiffs (understandably) tried to reopen the very matters raised under the 'suitability of education' ground of challenge that had been rejected by the Court of Appeal.[36] The plaintiffs were seeking to restore the status quo that existed at the time of the minister's decision eight years before, and seemed to suggest that a declaration of invalidity would be able to achieve this result by operation of law.

The Crown's submissions went first to the question of whether the discretion to grant a remedy ought to be exercised at all. Crown counsel effectively reintroduced the absence of findings on the record that the plaintiffs' rights had been adversely affected, emphasized the technical or 'near-technical' character of the unlawful action, and argued that there would be prejudice to third parties if further remedies were awarded. The nature of the illegality, it argued, should affect whether declaratory relief ought to be granted. Failing that, the crown argued that if a declaration were granted, such a declaration would not be capable of providing the practical relief sought without other coercive remedies reestablishing the system that had existed before the unlawful decision was made. Clearly the eight years that had elapsed since the decision had been made and the position of third parties were relevant here too. [37] While the argument does not appear in the crown's submissions in precisely these terms, it may have been relevant that the decision to disestablish the schools was not a necessary *legal* precondition to the sale of buildings, establishment of teaching contracts, and so on. Those were legally independent acts. Indeed, the legislation contemplated that special education could be provided by facilities that were not established but merely funded by the minister.[38]

The judge had a number of options: to leave the Court of Appeal's finding of unlawfulness alone to convey a hortatory effect, and to otherwise withhold the judicial review remedy in the court's remedial discretion; to grant the remedy of a declaration leaving doubt about its legal consequences; or to grant the declaration and to specify its consequences (if any). The court chose the third course. At the end of the hearing, it released a short minute stating in relevant part:[39]

> 5 [a] The High Court declares that the then Minister of Education, the Hon Wyatt Creech, acted unlawfully in purporting to disestablish special classes, clinics and services pursuant to s 98(2) of the Education Act 1964 by his decision of 21 October 1998 ...
> [6] I record that no other action, in particular decisions in relation to school staffing entitlements, are thereby invalidated.

The grant of a declaration of invalidity without any consequences is the functional equivalent of denying a discretionary remedy altogether, albeit that its hortatory effect is fractionally greater. Defining the consequences (or lack thereof) of invalidity in this way achieves much the same result as denying a judicial review remedy altogether.

Unfortunately for the coherence of the law in this respect, none of the reasoning about why this course was taken was articulated in the judicial finding, though unusually, and at the insistence of crown counsel, the minute was published in the law reports. (Presumably this was intended by the Crown to serve as a disincentive for bringing future litigation of this kind.) It may be fair to assume, however, that the grant of a declaration, albeit with no consequences, may in part have served to vindicate the judge's earlier attraction to the substantive merits of the plaintiffs' case.

It is difficult to evaluate, against this example, whether the law of judicial review has progressed very far. The absence of fully articulated reasoning at the remedial stage of the hearing can be subjected to similar objections as have traditionally been directed at the threshold tests. Roadblock tests at the outset may have at least precluded wasteful, expensive, and protracted litigation.

In fact, these plaintiffs may have been so-called non-Hohfeldian or ideological plaintiffs all along.[40] At the end of the remedies hearing, counsel were invited to take instructions on the possibility of reaching an agreed settlement. A deed of memorandum was entered between the parties that guaranteed some of the very things that the Court of Appeal had assumed were already achieved by the general scheme: systematic and regular internal control and audit by the Crown of the local and nationwide provision of special education resources; regular gathering and analysis of information, improved coordination and cooperation among providers of special education, and so on. It also provided for greater local parent representation and participation in policy-making.[41]

One wonders, if this was indeed the kind of outcome that the plaintiffs had been seeking, whether other more direct means of political action would not have been at least as effective.[42] The disabilities sector is highly organized in New Zealand and a new ministerial portfolio has recently been created for better representation at cabinet of the interests of those with disabilities. Is this an efficient use of judicial time and parents' resources? Or is it an example of the use of public law litigation as just one of many possible avenues for political participation? Is that what we hoped – or rather what we originally feared – that judicial review would become?

In this case, the quality of the plaintiffs' interests, and how successfully they made a claim to rights, was determinative of the result on both of the issues discussed. Absence of rights (conceived in a narrow Hohfeldian sense) appears to have been the main rationale for judicial restraint. It has always been the case in administrative law that many public wrongs, even 'large ones' are either not, or not able, to be challenged, let alone remedied. When the plaintiffs' interests can be separated from the cause of action, as they could in relation to the issue of whether the minister had had proper regard to the legislation when deciding to disestablish special schools, it will be much easier to accept the existence of a remedial discretion.[43] Even then, the substantive rationales for judicial restraint in restricting the consequences of granting a remedy in judicial review may be largely concealed. Once the ground on which the challenge is made becomes human rights-based, the very existence of a discretion to grant a remedy will become much harder to justify and may provoke rule-of-law-type objections. We can at least hope that the increased frequency of human rights-based challenges will have the effect of focusing judicial and scholarly attention on remedial questions in public law cases – a development much to be desired. In *Daniel's* case, the real measure of judicial deference was that these claims were not even considered by the Court of Appeal. Unless we give more judicial and scholarly attention to the links between the grounds of judicial review challenge and their consequences for remedial decisions, we risk reintroducing to judicial review the arbitrary elements that we have been striving to eliminate.

Unlawful Government Charges

The second recent New Zealand example also raises questions about the expansion of judicial review, the potential for a new formalism to develop in New Zealand, and the respective effects of either approach on remedies. As with the first example, the proper uses of the remedial discretion were again at issue. Moreover, this case serves to raise additional questions about where the distinctly public law concerns about the collective good ought to be taken into account.

Waikato Regional Airport v. Attorney-General[44] involved a challenge by way of judicial review of the lawfulness of the levy of fees for border control services at regional airports operating international flights for the first time. At the same time, the government continued to fully fund border control services at the three established metropolitan airports out of ordinary appropriations. The plaintiffs objected to the initial decision to charge a levy based on the statutory scheme and alleged that there had been an unlawful delegation. They also claimed that a later decision that continued the charging regime, though made by the correct decision-maker this time, did not conform to the requirements of the statutory scheme. Their purpose was to establish a restitutionary claim for the fees already paid. The matter was heard in the High Court, Court of Appeal, and Judicial Committee of the Privy Council.

Section 135 of the *Biosecurity Act 1993* stated in relevant part:

> The Director-General ... shall take all reasonable steps to ensure that so much of the costs of administering this Act ... as are not provided for by money appropriated by Parliament for the purpose are recovered in accordance with the principles of equity and efficiency ...

On the face of it, the statute invited judicial supervision of whether targeting cost recovery from the new entrants to the market and not their older-established competitors was in accordance with the statutory requirement to ensure recovery 'in accordance with the principles of equity and efficiency.' It was subsequently established in the proceeding that, contrary to the widespread understanding within the ministry, the terms of the appropriation for border control services did not distinguish between the funding of border services at the regional and the established metropolitan airports.[45]

The three courts who approached the question each took a different view of the possible grounds of challenge. The first decision to levy the new airports took place around June 1995. The High Court found that this decision was not made by the correct person and was not arrived at by reference to the principles of equity and efficiency as required by section 135. The Court of Appeal agreed on the delegation issue, but would have upheld the decision had it been made under a proper delegation. The Judicial Committee of the Privy Council was not prepared to decide on the delegation issue[46] but agreed with the High Court that the decision had been improperly made.

The second decision of May 1998 (again about which options should be pursued in relation to cost recovery) did not give rise to any issues of delegation. This time the director-general made the decision and explicitly referred to the principles of equity and efficiency in section 135 in the process. Both the High Court and Privy Council agreed that irrelevant considerations had been taken into account, that like cases had not been treated alike, and that the director-general had not approached the question with an open mind. The Court of Appeal, by contrast and consistently with its view on the first decision, found that the second decision was valid.

The Importance of Remedial Issues

The differences between the various courts on the question of which grounds of challenge were available can be explained, and indeed may have been driven by, their different attitudes to the remedial issues – though this is not always wholly transparent. In fact, they differed on all three important questions: the substance of the public law wrongdoing, the status of the resulting decisions, and the consequences that should flow from them.

The Court of Appeal appears to have gone to the greatest lengths to find that the government had acted properly as a public law matter. Unlike the High Court and the Privy Council, the Court of Appeal allowed the government latitude to determine what equity and efficiency could reasonably be taken to mean in relation to section 135, and emphasized the breadth and the subjective language of the discretion in terms reminiscent of Lord Morris's 1968 dissent in *Padfield v. Ministry of Agriculture Fisheries and Food*.[47] It was prepared, however, to find an error: namely, that the wrong person had made the first decision. Despite this illegality,[48] the Court of Appeal declined, in the exercise of its remedial discretion, to declare the charges made under the first decision to be 'unlawful,' saying '[a]n essential requirement for restitutionary relief is thereby removed.'[49] (Whether either a successful judicial review action or an *ultra vires* act is indeed a necessary precondition for restitutionary recovery is a matter to which we shall return later.)

The characterization of the public law wrong by the Court of Appeal as a technical, procedural kind was deliberate and calculated to make it easier to withhold a remedy. The court was explicit that its reason for exercising its discretion in this way was that 'the decision in issue is not vulnerable on its merits but on the basis that although generally acquiesced in by the Director-General the charges were not imposed pursuant to an exercise by him of the statutory power to charge.'[50] The court considered it still to be within the power of the director-general to make a valid decision about charging for past services and suggested that the 'omission can be remedied without delay.'[51] It suggested that the case was one of 'procedural carelessness'[52] rather than, as the policy papers may have suggested, one in which it was thought to be too politically embarrassing and administratively difficult to pursue government policy of cost recovery in relation to the established metropolitan airports as required by the statutory scheme.[53] Such procedural carelessness as it found to have occurred could be remedied by an explicitly 'admonitory' award of costs against the attorney-general.[54] The Court of Appeal clearly did not want to open the door to a restitutionary claim and reasoned that a declaration of invalidity and consequent order for restitution would merely prompt an unnecessary accounting exercise with no consequent change in the position of the parties.

It would undoubtedly have been much more difficult for the Court of Appeal to have upheld the decision despite this invalidity, had it discovered errors of a more substantial kind. Indeed the often trivial and technical nature of errors has been commonly cited as justification for the very existence of the discretion to grant a remedy under the old prerogative writs.[55] It is hard to imagine how the High Court and Privy Council could have exercised the discretion to withhold a declaration even if they had so desired, having first found that *both* decisions were unlawful on grounds going to the substance of the decision (including failing to approach the matter with an open mind, consciously preserving an inequitable system because of the perceived trouble, difficulty, and unpopularity of changing it,[56] and, by implication, conferring an unfair advantage on the plaintiffs' competitors). The greater the error or number of errors – especially those which clothe a decision in substantive unreasonableness – the more difficult it will be completely to withhold a remedy as the Court of Appeal did. Once a court has looked inside the decision-making process and found it wanting, it is then much harder to exercise judicial restraint by way of remedial discretion. Any necessary restraint, as a matter of public law, must then be exhibited at the point at which invalidity and its consequences are determined or explained.

The Privy Council, like the court of first instance, was prepared to find errors that went to the substance of the decisions. [57] The Court of Appeal's views that the discretionary remedy was inapt and that its decision was tailored to the circumstances of the case, could no longer stand once the Privy Council overturned the Court of Appeal's decisions about validity on appeal.[58] Indeed, the Privy Council tended to avoid the language of invalidity altogether. Instead, it assessed whether a restitutionary remedy ought to be available squarely from within restitution doctrine itself. It focused, for example, on whether a defence of 'passing on' was available;[59] whether restitutionary relief ought to be available where the payment was not in the nature of a tax but where the plaintiff had received some consideration by way of border control services for the payment (even if those services would not be consideration in the ordinary sense of conferring a commercial benefit); and whether the director-general was now capable of putting in place retrospectively a lawful system of charges in respect of the whole period (it thought not).[60] It was these restitutionary matters that the Judicial Committee considered ought to inform its decision about whether relief should be available. It found that partial recovery ought to be available, 'that is, of the excess over what would have been a fair and proportionate charge.'[61] As a consequence of this approach it did not have to address whether there could be degrees of invalidity in the way that the High Court had suggested, preferring instead to use the restitutionary formulation: 'money unlawfully exacted.'[62]

In the discussion of the reasoning of the different courts thus far, we have identified three possible sites for judicial restraint: when determining whether procedural or more merits-based grounds of review have been made out; when deciding whether to withhold a finding of invalidity (more easily justified the less merits based the ground of the review); and when considering possible substantive defences to a restitutionary claim against a public authority – that is, in the substantive grounds of restitution itself. Each choice has an impact on how the public and private causes of action relate to each other – a matter to which we shall now turn.

The Relationship between the Public and Private Causes of Action: Where the Public Interest is to be Assessed

WITHHOLDING A FORMAL DECLARATION

The Court of Appeal assumed that by denying formally to declare the first decision to be invalid, a precondition for restitutionary recovery would not be satisfied.[63] That is, it assumed that public law would be the mechanism for controlling access to the private law remedy and denied the discretionary nature of the remedy in order to do so. The issues surrounding the relationship between judicial review and the restitutionary remedy are, however, much more uncertain than the Court of Appeal here suggested.

Prior to the *Woolwich* case,[64] mistake of fact or compulsion had to be shown in order to establish that there had been an unjust demand. Such actions did not depend at all on a successful separate judicial review action or on a showing that the decision was *ultra vires*. They could be brought directly against public authorities and, indeed, private bodies or persons.[65]

The House of Lords, by a three to two decision in *Woolwich Equitable Building Society v. Inland Revenue Commissioners*,[66] expanded the grounds for restitution, establishing that the very unlawfulness of the demand is prima facie enough to require its repayment without the need for mistake or compulsion to be shown.[67] In other words, 'money paid by a citizen to a public authority in the form of taxes or levies pursuant to an ultra vires demand by the authority is prima facie recoverable by the citizen as of right.'[68] Lord Goff suggested that he was not using *ultra vires* in its 'narrow and original sense' here, saying: 'I incline to the opinion that this principle should extend to embrace cases in which the tax or other levy was wrongfully exacted by the public authority not because the demand was ultra vires but for other reasons, for example, because the authority misconstrued a relevant statute or regulation.'[69]

Although *Woolwich* itself had already been the subject of a successful action for judicial review, there was no agreement among the Law Lords on whether a successful judicial review action had first to be brought.[70] In the Court of Appeal below, Glidewell and Ralph Gibson JJ. had suggested that at least one payer would first need to bring successful judicial review proceedings in order to establish that the demand was *ultra vires*.[71] In the subsequent case of *British Steel plc v. Customs & Excise Commissioners*,[72] the Court of Appeal took the clear view that the matter could be initiated by private law proceedings for restitution. The court refused to impose onerous procedural burdens – such as requiring judicial review – on plaintiffs.

The main point for present purposes is that it is by no means settled either in the United Kingdom or New Zealand whether a successful judicial review action is a precondition for recovery of unlawful demands of an expanded post-*Woolwich* kind.[73] The discussion of the point by the Court of Appeal in *Waikato* is scant and confusing. It did not apply the *Woolwich* principle, but rather found that the older doctrine of *colore officii* would apply.

The High Court in *Waikato Airport* had earlier declined to apply *Woolwich* for the reason that it did not consider that case to apply where the payer received consideration.[74] The Court of Appeal appears to have accepted this reasoning, stating that *Woolwich* was neither 'appropriate' nor 'necessary' for the plaintiffs to have a successful claim.[75] Both courts considered that there would be sufficient authority in the doctrine of *colore officii*, as established in the earlier New Zealand case of *Julian v. Mayor of Auckland*,[76] to allow recovery where: [77]

> the plaintiff is entitled to have some service performed or act done upon payment of a fee, and that service has been performed or the act done, accompanied by the demand of an illegal or illegally excessive fee. In such circumstances the payment is held not to be voluntary, and to be recoverable as having been in substance exacted ... *colore officii*.

The doctrine of *colore officii* predates modern administrative law. It effectively makes it easier to establish duress against a public authority by creating a more easily satisfied test of involuntariness where the payment is exacted by an official. Not surprisingly, given that it predates modern judicial review, *colore officii* could always be brought as a collateral claim. In fact, in the *Julian* case cited by the Court of Appeal,[78] the action was brought as a direct claim against the official. How then, could withholding a declaration of invalidity in judicial review effectively deprive the plaintiffs of a direct claim for money had and received, as the Court of Appeal reasoned? This is an attempt by the Court of Appeal to erect an altogether new roadblock against a remedy.

The Court of Appeal's approach in *Waikato Airport* appears to be unprogressive in many ways. It limits the available grounds of judicial review to the least substantive and it withholds a finding of invalidity and recovery of monies paid. One thing the approach does achieve, however bluntly and opaquely, is that it uses public law, and especially the discretionary nature of the remedy, as a means of gate-keeping access to the private law remedy. However unclear the reasoning, the Court of Appeal considers that public law rather than private law doctrines should provide the means to protect the collective public interest. Whether this approach is ultimately effective or sustainable is another matter.

RESTITUTION AS A SITE FOR JUDICIAL RESTRAINT?

Having taken a much more substantive, and many would say more progressive, approach to the identification of legal error, and found an 'unfair and unlawful system of charging,' the Privy Council in *Waikato Airport* adopted the reasoning of *Woolwich Equitable Building v. Inland Revenue Commissioners*,[79] and suggested that the absence of consideration in *Woolwich* itself was not a reason not to apply it here.[80] In contrast to the Court of Appeal, the Privy Council appears to suggest that the ordinary law of restitution should police the boundaries of the public-private law divide and in at least two possible ways: first, by allowing the determination of what amounts to an *ultra vires* payment to be decided as a matter of restitution law; second, by offering a special common law defence to public authorities who are subject to claims for restitution. I shall discuss each of these in turn.

In many of the restitution cases, the judges are struggling with the same issues that are routinely encountered, but rarely adequately discussed, in public law cases: whether nullity is a relative or absolute concept; whether there can be degrees of invalidity; and what should be the consequences that follow an error of a public law kind? Peter Birks once argued (later changing his mind[81]) in relation to fees paid for licences under an invalid scheme that 'withholding of the license itself is not duress, for the citizen can have no entitlement to a nullity. If however, the power to issue licences is itself valid and only the demand for fees is ultra vires, the fees can be recovered. For here ... he is entitled to have the licence without charge and its withholding is itself duress.'[82]

This suggests that, in certain cases, the greater the invalidity, the lower the chances of restitution. This was one of the problems that Lord Goff may implicitly have sought to address in *Woolwich* itself by his suggestion that demands, whether the result of an invalid regulation, or of misconstruing a relevant statute or regulation, could constitute unlawful demands recoverable by way of the law of restitution.[83] It is also the very difficulty acknowledged by La Forest J. in *Air Canada v. British Columbia*,[84] but, nevertheless, perpetuated as a result of that decision: restitution would not be available if the instrument of demand was constitutionally invalid, but would if there had been the misapplication of a valid law. La Forest J. sought to justify that distinction by suggesting that the constitutional error in that case was 'close to raising a mere technical issue.'[85] Viewed in its best light, this suggests that he wanted to signal a need for some more qualitative assessment of the kind and degree of unlawfulness, and that 'invalidity' was too broad a term. Ironically, it may be that through these kind of developments in restitution law, some of the old categorizations between errors going to and within jurisdiction may once again revive and flourish.[86] Of course, these different approaches mask the real issue: how much should the judges protect the public purse?[87]

There is a sense in which we may be returning 'back to the future' here. As Mark Aronson, Bruce Dyer, and Matthew Groves remind us, it was the private law action and not the prerogative writs through which administrative law initially developed:[88]

> the very origins of judicial review go back not to the prerogative writ of certiorari (which originally corrected patent error of law, rather than invalidities) but to the damages action. Assuming invalid bureaucratic action to be a nullity, the law allowed damages actions in tort. Tort, then, was the original vehicle for obtaining judicial review of administrative action as we know it.

As they recall also, tort law has not always required nullity to be shown as a precondition for recovery against a public official – negligence law is a good example. The private law of restitution, and how it defines money unlawfully exacted, may once again become the *primary* site for consideration of the collective interest.

SPECIAL DEFENCES FOR PUBLIC AUTHORITIES?

Perhaps because of the very difficulties involved in formulating a satisfactory approach to the logic and meaning of 'invalidity,' and in recognition of the fact that a court in a private law action is not able to exercise discretion to refuse to recognize the consequences of an illegality on the broad basis that it can in a judicial review decision, the Privy Council in *Waikato Airport* suggested a further strategy by which to mitigate the consequences of a finding of unlawful conduct by public authorities. If judicial restraint was needed in order to take the collective public interest into account, a defense might be developed to accommodate the needs of government.

The Privy Council would have reintroduced the 'public law element,' if it were needed, by way of a special defence against recovery for public authorities. It approved the suggestions of Lord Goff in *Woolwich*[89] and La Forest J. in *Air Canada v. British Columbia*[90] that a special defence to a restitutionary claim might be called for in '[c]ircumstances in which some very substantial sum of money may be held to have been exacted ultra vires from a very large number of tax payers.'[91] Clearly, this was not a case where the sums were so large, or the consequences of a finding of unlawful demand were so great, as to provide the basis for such a defence. It is the implications of this suggestion for the structure of both public and private law that are important for our present purpose.

A special defence for public authorities that operates from within the law of restitution has the potential to telescope consideration of the 'collective public element' into a last-minute dispensing formula. Such an approach raises the possibility of a government action being judged twice to be unlawful, initially in a judicial review proceeding and again in terms of the elements necessary to fulfill the prima facie components of an action for recovery, and yet the plaintiff may still be denied a remedy because of the consequences to the person acting unlawfully. Could the opposite ever be true that when the consequences of a finding of invalidity are not great for the person acting unlawfully that only then should recovery issue?

In practice it is difficult to imagine such a defence being successfully raised. Using the law of restitution as a site for the development of a 'public law' type defence is at odds with the traditional Diceyan account of the ordinary law. The commitment to Diceyan rule of law principles suggests that judges will be hesitant to invoke or to define the contours of such a defence. Certainly the greater the consequences of the finding of *ultra vires* for the plaintiff, the harder it will be to raise the defence as a roadblock to recovery. In any event, the possibility that such a defence might be invoked may distort the development of both public law and private law – promoting less judicial caution in finding public law errors and creating the possibility of a separate public and private law of restitution.

The difficulties for a court in judging what is likely to be the effect on the broader public interest of allowing recovery is not to be underestimated. The corollary to the *Woolwich* case is, itself, instructive on this point. Following the successful action in *Woolwich*, the British government passed legislation restricting recovery to those who had brought a successful judicial review action, that is, restricting recovery to the

Woolwich Building Society.[92] That legislation was subsequently challenged in the European Court of Human Rights in *National & Provincial Building Society v. United Kingdom*,[93] on the basis of arguments that this was retrospective legislation that interfered with the applicants' rights of access to the court and the peaceful enjoyment of their possessions, and discriminated against them and in favour of Woolwich. The applicants failed on each of these arguments. The minority in the House of Lords in *Woolwich* was proved correct in suggesting that a great burden would be imposed on the government as a result of the majority's ruling.

The happier alternative, of course, would be for the legislation to anticipate such claims in advance, though this is likely to be more difficult to formulate and justify in the fee-levying, user-pays context of *Waikato Airport* than in the more traditional tax scenario. One solution is for the legislation itself to determine in advance what the consequences of a finding of invalidity should be.[94] Another alternative is to prescribe time limits by which to claim for recovery.

What *Waikato Airport* graphically demonstrates is that consequentialist concerns about remedies may explain the differences in the ways in which the different courts approached the substance of the public wrongdoing (describing it as technical or clothing it in substantive unreasonableness); the status of the resulting decisions (illegal but not invalid, or partially invalid); and the consequences that ought to flow from such findings (the full consequences of a standard restitutionary claim, or a special public law version of restitution). It demonstrates also that the site at which the collective interest is considered makes a difference to the nature and force of the available arguments for judicial restraint. It will be much harder to make arguments about the collective public interest in the heart of the restitutionary claim itself because of our Diceyan pre-commitment to one ordinary law that applies to all bodies, public or private. The interesting unintended consequence of the expanded nature of judicial review is that a greater willingness to examine the substance of a public decision may have the effect of making the restitutionary defence the *primary* site for consideration of the collective public interest. Would we have predicted that a liberal substantive approach to judicial review would have had that effect?

Conclusion

The easing of the formal barriers to judicial review has made remedial discretion and its uses more important as a locus for taking into account the collective public interest. At the same time, the more judges are willing to find that decisions are substantively unreasonable, the more difficult it is likely to be for them to withhold a remedy through the use of the discretion. Equally, the more individual rights-focused the nature of the claim, the more difficult it will be even to justify the existence of the discretion. As a consequence, we can detect a new formalism emerging in the New Zealand Court of Appeal. In restricting the successful grounds of review to the most technical and least substantive, the court is able to preserve the remedial discretion.

When the discretion is able to be invoked in order to withhold a remedy, the reasoning tends to be opaque in ways reminiscent of the old threshold tests to review. Courts, and even at times the same court, may adopt varying views of the meaning and consequences of invalidity. At times, as we saw in the *Waikato Airport* case, this may have the effect of shifting consideration of the consequences of a finding of invalidity into the grounds of a private law action.

These developments threaten the coherence of judicial review. The consequences to the public interest ought, where possible, to be taken into account when determining whether the grounds of judicial review have been made out. This may not always be possible. At the very least, the manner and seriousness with which issues of invalidity and its consequences are discussed should be transparent and consistent. A progressive approach to judicial review must surely aspire to the values of transparency and non-arbitrariness that are core to judicial review itself and at the heart of Mullan's contribution to the subject.

NOTES

Thanks, with the usual disclaimers, to Grant Liddell, Peter Watts, Colleen Flood, Jo Manning, for helpful discussions and to Hanna Wilberg, Paul Rishworth, Sir Kenneth Keith, and the editors for their comments on an earlier draft. Thanks to Katerina Nathan, Chapman Tripp scholar, for research assistance.

1 Subsequently published as 'Substantive Fairness Review: Heed the Amber Light!' (1988) 18 V.U.W.L.R. 293 [Mullan, 'Substantive Fairness'].
2 D. Mullan, 'Judicial Deference to Executive Decision-Making: Evolving Concepts of Responsibility' (1993) 19 Queen's L.J. 137 at 147 [Mullan, 'Judicial Deference'].
3 D. Mullan, 'Some Developments in Administrative Law (1970)' (1971) 33(2)

New Zealand Journal of Public Administration 77 at 89–96; 'Developments in New Zealand Administrative Law (1971–72)' (1973) 35(2) New Zealand Journal of Public Administration 1; 'Procedural Codes: A Second Opinion' [1973] N.Z.L.J. 41; 'Reform of Judicial Review of Administrative Action: The Ontario Way' (1974) 12 Osgoode Hall L.J. 125.

4 D. Mullan, 'Judicial Deference to Administrative Decision-Making in the Age of the Charter' (1986) 50 Sask. L.Rev. 203 at 204 [Mullan, 'Age of the Charter'].

5 See also D.H. Clark, 'Natural Justice: Substance and Shadow' [1975] P.L. 27.

6 D. Mullan, 'Establishing and Applying the Standard of Review: The Struggle for Complexity?' (2004) 11 Can.J.Admin.L. & Prac. 59 at 66–68, 74–75, 90, 94, 96.

7 Mullan, 'Substantive Fairness,' *supra* note 1, 307–8, 310.

8 Exactly how and under what conditions judicial pronouncements of doctrine impact on the work of administration is only now achieving systematic evaluation. See the interesting work of S. Halliday, *Judicial Review and Compliance with Administrative Law* (Oxford: Hart Publishing, 2004).

9 Mullan, 'Substantive Fairness,' *supra* note 1 at 294.

10 In the Privy Council, e.g., counsel for the attorney-general argued that the director-general's decision may have been 'unreasonable but not ultra vires': *Waikato Regional Airport Ltd v. Attorney-General*, [2004] 3 N.Z.L.R. 1 at 4 (P.C., New Zealand).

11 Mullan's own acuity of expression is noteworthy: he uses the expression 'Charter wrongs' rather than Charter 'rights': Mullan, 'Age of the Charter,' *supra* note 4 at 223.

12 David J. Mullan, *Administrative Law Essentials of Canadian Law* (Toronto: Irwin Law, 2001) at 481 suggests that:

> the instances in which courts have proceeded through the merits of an application for judicial review, decided that the basis of review has been made out but then declined to remedy the wrong are in fact relatively rare. Far more common, particularly in recent years, are cases in which the courts determine at the outset of a hearing or on an interlocutory motion that discretionary reasons dictate that the case not be allowed to proceed.

I have not undertaken a general survey of the instances of the use of the discretion or the differences between Australian, New Zealand, and United Kingdom courts in their approaches. It should be noted, however, that in New Zealand there are no leave requirements or times limits for bringing an action.

13 [2003] 2 N.Z.L.R. 743 [*Daniels* (CA)].

14 *Daniels v. Attorney-General*, M 1615–SW99 3 April 2002 High Court Auckland, Baragwanath J. at para. 137 [*Daniels* (HC)], discussed in *Daniels* (CA), *supra* note 13 at para. 62.
15 *Daniels* (CA), *supra* note 13 at para. 83.
16 Ibid. at paras 64 ('correlative obligations'), 70 ('correlative rights'), 79 ('duties correlative'), 80 ('rights and duties enforceable through Court processes'), 81 ('judicially enforceable rights').
17 Ibid. at para. 82.
18 *Education Act 1989* (N.Z.), s 11F, discussed in *Daniels* (CA), *supra* note 13 at para. 84.
19 *Education Act 1989* (N.Z.), s 9; *Daniels* (CA), *supra* note 13 at para. 82
20 High and very high needs students were allocated individual portable entitlements under the challenged scheme. Approximately 2 percent were assessed in this category. The remainder (moderate needs students) did not receive individual entitlements. Instead, schools were directly funded according to a formula. It is not hard to imagine exactly the kind of case that might have tested the scheme: a child assessed on the margin between moderate and high special educational needs having difficulty finding proper care in a mainstream school. The Court of Appeal hints that even on the question of where the high needs and moderate needs dividing line should be drawn it may not have intervened but rather let the internal mechanisms of review and control of the programs as a whole do their work.
21 *Daniels* (CA), *supra* note 13 at para. 83.
22 N. Bamforth, 'Hohfeldian Rights and Public Law' in M.H. Kramer, ed., *Rights, Wrongs and Responsibilities* (London: Palgrave, 2001) 17.
23 I use 'direct' advisably here. Bamforth argues that, for example, once a public authority has decided to exercise its power in relation to a particular individual, then a Hohfeldian right-duty relationship may be triggered; see *ibid.* at 16 where he discusses *Cocks v. Thanet*, [1983] 2 A.C. 286 (HL).
24 The interests or 'rights' of the parents in *Daniels* case readily met any standing requirements.
25 *Daniels* (CA), *supra* note 13 at para. 84.
26 Ibid.
27 *R. v. East Sussex County Council ex p. Tandy,* [1998] A.C. 714 (C.A. & H.L.).
28 *Boyce v. Paddington Borough Council*, [1903] 1 Ch. 109.
29 *Attorney-General v. Daniels*, unreported C.A. 84/02, 31 July 2002.
30 The plaintiffs had argued the human rights grounds unsuccessfully in the High Court. Baragwanath J. viewed the protections from discrimination in the *New Zealand Bill of Rights Act 1990* (N.Z.) and the *Human Rights Act 1993* (N.Z.) as prohibiting 'failures to treat people the same' but not 'failures to

treat people differently' in order to achieve equality of outcomes (*Daniels* (HC), *supra* note 14 at paras. 95 and 97). Failure to provide special-needs education did not, therefore, in his view, constitute a breach of those Acts. It was the *Education Act 1989* itself, and particularly s. 8 that the judge considered to be the source of rights and obligations.

31 A tort law challenge would have raised different questions again. Carol Harlow suggests in 'Damages and Human Rights' [2004] N.Z.L. Rev. 426 at 431 that '[i]t is embarrassing for judges to have to say of a right with constitutional or near constitutional status that it merits a lesser remedy than those available in the traditional tort action and, to the extent that the right invoked overlaps with a right already embedded in the common law, the embarrassment is all the greater.'

32 M. Loughlin, *The Idea of Public Law* (Oxford: Oxford University Press, 2003) at 114.

33 See P. Cane, 'Damages in Public Law' (1999) 9 Otago L.R. 489; cf. Lord Woolf's discussion of this issue in *Anufrijeva v. Southwark London Borough Council,* [2004] 1 All E.R. 833 at paras 41–74; Law Commission, 'Damages under the Human Rights Act 1998': Law Comm. 266, Cm. 4853 (2000); Law Commission, *Monetary Remedies in Public Law: A Discussion Paper* (11 October 2004).

34 Cf. *Auton (Guardian ad Litem of) v. British Columbia (Attorney General)* (2005), 245 D.L.R. (4th) 1 (S.C.C.).

35 *Daniels* (CA), *supra* note 13 at para.113.

36 The Crown resisted such attempts, arguing that in determining relief the court had to avoid determining questions that went to the heart of the new scheme; such as whether mainstreaming should be preferred to the segregated provision of special education, whether there were gaps in special education policy, and what resourcing should be available.

37 Defendants' submissions for remedies hearing on 11 July 2003.

38 *Daniels* (CA), *supra* note 13 at para. 40.

39 *Attorney-General v. Daniels,* [2004] 2 N.Z.L.R. 632.

40 L.L. Jaffe, 'The Citizen as Litigant in Public Actions: The Non-Hohfeldian or Ideological Plaintiff' (1968) 116 U.Pa.L.Rev. 1033.

41 Deed of Settlement between L.S.A. Daniels and Others and the Attorney-General, August 2003.

42 At the time of writing there has been a 5 percent increase of funding for special education. The parents are claiming that it is a result of the consultation processes required by the memorandum of settlement.

43 It is arguable that the discretion to grant a remedy is not always available in judicial review cases in any event. The possible exceptions to the existence

of this remedial discretion are discussed in Sir Thomas Bingham, 'Should Public Law Remedies be Discretionary?' [1991] P.L. 64.

44 [2001] 2 N.Z.L.R. 670 (H.C.) [*Waikato Airport* (HC)]; [2002] 3 N.Z.L.R. 433 (C.A.) [*Waikato Airport* (CA)]; [2004] 3 N.Z.L.R. 1 (P.C.) [*Waikato Airport* (PC)].

45 For the clearest statement see *Waikato Airport* (PC), *supra* note 44 at para. 11, citing D. McGee, 'Interpreting Appropriations' [2001] N.Z.L.J. 197 (a note by the clerk of the House of Representatives in response to the first instance decision). See also *Waikato Airport* (CA), *supra* note 44 at para. 46.

46 Their Lordships were not prepared to determine what effect, if any, the generous delegation provisions in s. 41 *State Sector Act 1988* (N.Z.) may have had on the principle in *Carltona v. Commissioner of Works*, [1943] 2 All E.R. 560: *Waikato Airport* (PC), *supra* note 44 at para. 64.

47 [1968] A.C. 997 at 1040.

48 *Waikato Airport* (CA), *supra* note 44 at para.134 ('illegally demanded').

49 Ibid. at para. 139.

50 Ibid. at para. 138.

51 Ibid.

52 Ibid. at para. 141.

53 *Waikato Airport* (PC), *supra* note 44 at para. 56.

54 *Waikato Airport* (CA), *supra* note 44 at para. 141.

55 Equally, this is also reflected in New Zealand in s. 5, *Judicature Amendment Act 1972*, which empowers a court in a judicial review proceeding to validate a decision 'where the sole ground of relief established is a defect in form or technical irregularity' as long as no substantial wrong or miscarriage of justice has occurred.

56 *Waikato Airport* (PC), *supra* note 44 at para. 56.

57 *Waikato Airport* (HC), *supra* note 44 at paras. 179–80, 192.

58 *Waikato Airport* (PC), *supra* note 44 at para. 76.

59 Ibid. at paras. 77–78.

60 Ibid. at para. 81.

61 Ibid. at para. 84.

62 Ibid. at para. 81. See further *infra* note 84.

63 *Waikato Airport* (CA), *supra* note 44 at para. 139. There the Court of Appeal said: 'Accordingly, as a matter of discretion, we determine that declaratory relief should be withheld. We decline formally to declare that the charges made under the first decision are unlawful. An essential requirement for restitutionary relief is thereby removed.' See also *ibid.* at paras. 135–38. The Court of Appeal also denied costs to the successful appellant, making it clear that the denial was 'admonitory' in nature and in recognition of the

indulgent use of their discretion in the appellant government's favour: *ibid.* at para. 141.

64 *Woolwich Equitable Building Society v. Inland Revenue Commissioners,* [1993] A.C. 70 [*Woolwich*].

65 See *Bannatyne v. Carter* [1901] 19 N.Z.L.R. 482; *Julian v. Mayor of Auckland,* [1927] N.Z.L.R. 453.

66 *Woolwich, supra* note 64.

67 Ibid. at 173, Lord Goff.

68 Ibid. at 177, Lord Goff.

69 Ibid. Lord Jauncey dissented, suggesting that this was too broad a proposition without limitation: *ibid.* at 196. He implicitly rejects the distinction that La Forest J. had attempted to make in the *Air Canada* case, see *infra* at text accompanying note 84.

70 Lord Keith appeared to wish to resolve the matter within judicial review. He suggested that the refusal to exercise a statutory discretion to refund rates could have been subjected to successful review: *Woolwich, supra* note 64 at 153. Cf. *ibid.* at 757, Lord Goff.

71 *Woolwich, supra* note 64 at 101.

72 [1997] 2 All E.R. 366 at 379 (Saville J.) and 381 (Millett L.J.) [*British Steel*].

73 For the Canadian position, see *Garland v. Consumers' Gas Co.* [2004] 1 S.C.R. 629 (S.C.C.), where the Supreme Court held that Garland was not required to exhaust judicial review proceedings before seeking restitutionary relief.

74 Discussed in *Waikato Airport* (CA), *supra* note 44 at para. 60.

75 Ibid. at para. 134.

76 [1927] N.Z.L.R. 453.

77 Ibid. at 458; quoted by Wild J. in the *Waikato Airport* (HC), *supra* note 44 at para. 165 and by the Court of Appeal in *Waikato Airport* (CA), *supra* note 44 at para. 134.

78 *Supra* notes 75–76.

79 *Woolwich, supra* note 64.

80 *Waikato Airport* (PC), *supra* note 44 at paras 79–82.

81 P. Birks, 'Restitution from the Executive: A Tercentenary Footnote to the Bill of Rights' in P.D. Finn, ed., *Essays on Restitution* (Sydney: Law Book Company, 1990) esp. at n. 29.

82 P. Birks, 'Restitution from Public Authorities' (1980) 33 C.L.P. 191 at 196–97.

83 This was the approach subsequently taken in *British Steel, supra* note 72 at 377, Sir Richard Scott V-C.: an unlawful demand must always be an *ultra vires* demand.

84 [1989] 1 S.C.R. 1161 at 1207 [*Air Canada*].

85 Ibid.

86 See, e.g., the High Court's attempt in *Waikato Airport* (HC), *supra* note 44 at para. 179 to distinguish between *ultra vires* charges (where there is no authority at all for the demand) and 'invalid' charges (where authority did exist but it was not used or was used incorrectly); discussed on appeal: *Waikato Airport* (CA), *supra* note 44 at para. 66.

87 Wilson J. famously took a vigorously different view from La Forest J. in *Air Canada, supra* note 84, and in doing so met the underlying public policy concerns head-on: government mistakes should not be at the expense of individual taxpayers: *ibid.* at 1215.

88 M. Aronson, B. Dyer, and M. Groves, *Judicial Review of Administrative Action*, 3rd ed. (Sydney: Thomson Law Book, 2004) at 626.

89 *Woolwich, supra* note 64 at 174.

90 *Air Canada, supra* note 84 at 1204–5.

91 *Waikato Airport* (PC), *supra* note 44 at para. 82. The Privy Council cited approvingly *U.S. v. Butler*, 297 U.S. 1 (1936). See also La Forest J. in *Air Canada, supra* note 84 at 1,205.

92 *Finance Act 1991* (U.K.), ss 53, 64. For a similar government response, see *Re Eurig* [1998] 2 S.C.R. 565 (S.C.C.), where the successful litigant was able to collect immediately but the Supreme Court's order that the fees were an indirect tax and *ultra vires* was suspended for six months giving the province time to respond by introducing legislation that retrospectively imposed the same charge, but exempted Mrs Eurig.

93 Case 117/1996/736/933–935; [1997] STC 1466; 69 Tax Cas. 540.

94 See *Crown Entities Act 2004* (N.Z.), ss. 19–23.

The Codification of Administrative Law in Quebec

DENIS LEMIEUX

Administrative Law for a 'Distinct Society'

To better understand the distinctive character of administrative law in Quebec, it is relevant to consider the way in which the state is perceived in Quebec. For most Quebecers, the state is not 'them,' it is 'us,' as the state is seen as the protector and promoter of the interests of a small francophone minority in North America.

Quebecers have shown resilience to survive and, more recently, to develop political, economic, social, and cultural values that are a cross between European and North American values. In the eighteenth and nineteenth century, Quebec created unique institutions such as parishes and credit savings unions, as well as diverse associations typical of a close-knit society. Solidarity, redistribution of wealth, promotion of the French language, and equilibrium between unequal business and social interests constitute a core of values that are enshrined in fundamental laws such as the *Civil Code,*[1] the *Charter of Human Rights and Freedoms,*[2] and the *Charter of the French Language.*[3]

While some of these values are shared by all Canadians, they are more important in a relatively small community that wishes to preserve and promote its cohesion. Therefore, they are expressed in general fundamental laws that complement the constitution of Canada.

The values of solidarity and sharing led to an interventionist role of the state in economic and social fields. Hydro-Québec, the Caisse de dépôt et de placement, the Société générale de financement, and the Régie de l'assurance-maladie, along with the development of the network of local health centres, colleges, and universities, made Quebecers of the 1970s proud of the public sector they had created.

Even today, Quebec swims against the tide of privatization in maintaining most of its Crown corporations intact. The present Liberal government, led by Premier Jean Charest, has not taken steps to privatize any major Crown corporation. Instead, it proposes to make better use of private investment to promote public goals through public-private partnerships. One justification for doing so is that it would allow Quebec 'de jouer dans la cour des grands' (to play in the big leagues) – to have a voice in the business circles of Canada and, to some extent, of North America and beyond, where Hydro-Québec and the Caisse de dépôt et de placement are active players with a dual mandate: profitability and the promotion of Quebec's economic interests.

At the same time, even though the state is seen as the trustee of the collective interests of Quebecers, safeguards have been established to prevent or remedy arbitrary conduct by government officials. For instance, the Protecteur du citoyen (the Quebec ombudsman) benefits from strong public support and his recommendations are usually followed by the Quebec government. As will be shown later, administrative appeal tribunals have been empowered to adjudicate upon grievances of citizens against the state.

Members of the Quebec judiciary have shown great deference to the public interest represented by the state by upholding the legality of government policies and measures.[4] Several present and former members of the Quebec Court of Appeal were deputy ministers of justice prior to their judicial appointments, giving them substantial expertise in the working of government. As a result, the Court of Appeal is not reticent to intervene in cases of abuse of power,[5] unreasonableness or unfairness, even at the highest level of government. The codification of general principles of administrative law and fundamental values in laws of general application gives the courts a wider discretion, since those principles are formulated in general terms that allow for flexibility and evolution. Codification also confers greater legal security on the courts in exercising their supervisory role over governmental action.

These laws include not only the *Civil Code*, the *Code of Civil Procedure*,[6] the *Charter of Human Rights*, and the *Administrative Justice Act*,[7] but also some additional statutes binding the state, such as the *Access to Information Act*[8] and the *Regulations Act*,[9] both having precedence over other laws.

Therefore, statute law, rather than case law, is the first source of legal rules applying to the state. In the law schools, the teaching of administrative law emphasizes the role of statutes in defining grounds of judicial review. The common law precedents are used, whenever they are relevant, to clarify or complete statutory provisions.

It is worth mentioning that academics in Quebec have played a key role in codifying administrative law. The reports leading to the adoption of the *Civil Code*, the *Charter of Human Rights*, the *Administrative Justice Act*, and other laws of general application, were mostly the work of law professors. Some of these academics were involved in the actual drafting of these texts, and several became judges and contributed to the further development of these fundamental laws. In the rest of Canada, a special mention must be made of Professor David Mullan, an influential scholar who has regularly engaged with Quebec academics and taken Quebec developments into account in his numerous publications.[10]

Finally, the Quebec judiciary shows a strong tendency to refer to the official 'Commentaries' that accompanied the adoption of the *Civil Code*, as well as academic treatises and law review articles. The fact that the commentators were influential in the codification is reflected in the influence of academic 'doctrine' before justices trained in civil law. As one Quebec judge told me, 'You are our windows on the outside world.' Influential academics include René Dussault, Gil Rémillard, Patrice Garant, Yves Ouellette, and Jean-Louis Baudouin, not to mention their predecessors, Louis-Philippe Pigeon, Jean Beetz, Louis Marceau, and Louis Pratte.[11] Supreme Court Justice Louis LeBel also deserves special mention, since he has always been very close to academia.

In this paper, I intend to demonstrate that the provisions found in the *Civil Code* and other laws of general application embody general principles of law, and are treated accordingly by the courts. Since the *Civil Code* is 'the foundation of other laws,' which are to be interpreted in harmony with the *Charter of Human Rights*,[12] other statutes and regulations are not interpreted restrictively but are 'enriched' by the laws of general application. All laws are part of the wider 'droit commun' unless there is an express provision to the contrary, and as we will see, such a provision would be interpreted restrictively.

Administrative Law Codified

Apart from the *Civil Code*, which will be discussed later, the major legal texts embodying general principles of administrative law are the *Charter of Human Rights*, the *Administrative Justice Act*, and the *Code of Civil Procedure*.

The Impact of the Quebec Charter of Human Rights and Freedoms *in Administrative Law*

The *Charter of Human Rights* was enacted in 1975. Its main influence was the *European Convention on Human Rights*. Fundamental rights enshrined in sections 1 to 38 of the *Charter of Human Rights* have precedence over all other Quebec legislation.[13] The *Charter* itself has been described by the Supreme Court of Canada as having a quasi-constitutional character,[14] and like the *Canadian Charter of Rights and Freedoms*, it includes a rarely-used 'notwithstanding' provision.[15]

Recognized rights and freedoms under the *Charter of Human Rights* go well beyond those included in the *Canadian Charter*. For instance, grounds of discrimination include 'social condition,' which does not appear to have any counterpart under section 15 of the *Canadian Charter*.[16] Likewise, the rights to privacy and reputation,[17] while regarded as fundamental values in Canadian society, are not included in the terms 'life, liberty, and security of the person' of section 7 of the *Canadian Charter*.

The *Charter of Human Rights* contains a provision similar to section 1 of the *Canadian Charter*, which allows such reasonable limitations prescribed by law as may be demonstrably justified in a free and democratic society. Interestingly enough, that provision (section 9.1) refers to societal values found in the *Charter of Human Rights*.[18] Therefore, tribunals and courts are given wide latitude to review governmental action in the light of values in the *Charter of Human Rights*.

The *Charter of Human Rights* has also widened some general principles of administrative law. Section 23 of the *Charter of Human Rights* ensures the independence and impartiality of administrative entities exercising quasi-judicial functions,[19] as well as a full hearing before unbiased adjudicators when a person's rights are affected by an administrative decision.[20] Thus, the independence of administrative tribunals has a quasi-constitutional foundation under Quebec law, contrary to the present state of the law in other Canadian provinces.[21] It is akin to the situation under section 2(e) of the *Canadian Bill of Rights*, which grants limited protection to federal tribunals.[22]

For instance, in the *La petite maison* case,[23] the Supreme Court held that lawyers working for the Régie des permis d'alcool could not take part in the preparation of a case concerning the revocation of a liquor licence, argue the case before the board, and then advise board members as to their decision. A 'Chinese wall' had to be erected within the

Régie, isolating board members and their advisors from other Régie employees. Several Quebec administrative regulatory agencies, such as the Quebec Transport Commission, followed suit.

When the Quebec government decided to 'dejudicialize' the administrative decision-making process in favour of a quicker and more informal procedure under the *Administrative Justice Act*, it had to provide for independent review of the initial decision in order to meet section 23 requirements.[24] Initially, the government wanted to restrict the scope of section 23 to judicial tribunals, rendering it toothless, but had to retreat since there was almost total opposition.[25]

Less attention has so far been given to section 24 of the *Charter of Human Rights*, although this may soon change. Section 24 establishes a duty to a public body to follow the prescribed procedure, and to use only relevant reasons to support a decision depriving a person of his or her rights. In such circumstances, section 24 gets rid of the old distinction between 'imperative' and 'directive' procedural rules, and by implication requires the adjudicating body to justify its decision. While this last requirement is akin to the common law duty to give reasons, a quasi-constitutional status is conferred on it by its inclusion in the *Charter of Human Rights*.

Remedies under sections 49 and 52 of the *Charter of Human Rights* are for the most part 'clones' of similar remedies under sections 24(1) and 52 of the *Constitution Act 1982*, with one substantial difference. Section 49 remedies include injunction, declaration, damages – even punitive damages if the contravention of the *Charter of Human Rights* is intentional – and other *ad hoc* orders. However, the Supreme Court of Canada has held that the right to damages may be set aside by an exclusive statutory compensation scheme, for instance, a no-fault regime, even if these regimes do not allow for punitive damages.[26]

The Supreme Court position relies on the assumption that section 49 is not included in the quasi-constitutional part of the *Charter of Human Rights*, which refers only (in section 52) to sections 1 to 38. However, this fails to take into account the fact that, without section 49, fundamental rights and freedoms become mere declaratory provisions, since that section is the foundation of the power to grant injunctions and damages to an aggrieved party.

The Supreme Court further restricted the scope of section 49 by holding that the immunity of public bodies from liability incurred in their 'legislative' responsibilities (meaning rule-making) has precedence over the *Charter of Human Rights*, since that immunity possesses a constitutional character. While it is understandable that the immunity of members of a legislative body is recognized as an unwritten principle of the constitution, it is harder to justify the extension of the immunity to a municipal corporation's bylaw-making function.[27]

Despite these restrictions, the *Charter of Human Rights* has been widely used in judicial review. Contrary to section 32 of the *Canadian Charter*, which limits application of the *Charter* to legislative and government action, the *Charter of Human Rights* applies to all private and public entities. It binds the Crown,[28] and privatization or externalization of public programs presents no problem to its applicability.

The Administrative Justice Act, 1996

In 1971 a Quebec government report from a group of administrative law scholars recommended the establishment of a network of administrative appeal tribunals, mostly immune from judicial review, for the purpose of settling disputes between government departments and citizens.[29] These tribunals, which were to be supervised by an administrative court, would allow for the development of distinctive administrative law principles reconciling individual rights and the public interest. The French administrative model was a point of reference for the report's authors.

The recommendation to establish a final administrative appeal court was scrapped for constitutional reasons, but a network of appeal tribunals was created in the following years. Two such tribunals, the Professions Tribunal and the Transport Tribunal, were ruled unconstitutional by the Supreme Court since enabling legislation had presumably purported to exclude judicial review, even on jurisdictional grounds.[30] Quebec statutes were modified accordingly to allow for limited judicial review. Nevertheless, Quebec legislation includes strongly worded 'privative clauses' as a matter of course, while providing for a right of appeal to an administrative tribunal or to the Quebec (provincial) Court.

In 1987 a second government report, again from well-respected specialists in the field, recommended the unification of several appeal tribunals. The Administrative Tribunal of Quebec (ATQ) was established by the *Administrative Justice Act* as well as a Council on Administrative Justice, loosely based on the English Council on Tribunals.[31]

But the government added a second objective to this reform – uniform procedural guarantees for all governmental entities. In the exercise of administrative functions, public authorities would have to act fairly but with celerity and efficiency, taking into account the requirements of administrative justice.[32] The non-adversarial character of the procedure would be tempered by the right of a *de novo* appeal to the ATQ[33] or, in disciplinary matters, to the Court of Quebec.

Adopted in 1996, the *Administrative Justice Act* extends the duty to act fairly to all unfavourable individual decisions rendered by a government entity.[34] It also contains a set of principles of 'good governance.'[35] For instance, policy documents and directives susceptible of being used as decisional factors must be made accessible to the public.[36] In all decisions involving a form of administrative authorization, or a cease and desist order, notice of an intention to render an unfavourable decision must be sent beforehand to the interested person. It must contain the reasons sustaining the decision, particular as to the relevant facts, and provide a reasonable period (at least ten days) for the presentation of 'observations' by the affected person.[37]

The format for such a presentation will vary from written comments to a formal hearing, depending on the type of decision and whether or not section 23 of the *Charter of Human Rights* applies. In theory, section 23 is not supposed to apply at the initial stage whenever there is a *de novo* appeal to an independent and impartial tribunal or court. However, statutory restrictions on the right of appeal exist in some cases. For instance, the ATQ cannot review a decision made by some agencies when it is based on an appreciation of the public interest, rather than the application of an objective norm.[38] For decisions concerning social benefits, the agency must allow a person access to his or her file and the possibility of completing it by adding information before the decision is rendered.[39] Administrative review is encouraged and all unfavourable decisions must be made in writing, contain reasons, and specify further recourses open to the aggrieved person, other than judicial review.[40]

All these requirements go well beyond *Baker v. Canada*.[41] They give a more precise content to the duty of fairness, while preserving the use of common law precedents to interpret and complete these requirements.[42]

The subsequent provisions of the *Administrative Justice Act* (sections 9 to 13) establish the legal framework for all administrative tribunals that have jurisdiction to adjudicate disputes between a citizen and an administrative or decentralized authority. This excludes tribunals with a wider jurisdiction, such as the Rent Board, and labour tribunals, which do not adjudicate such disputes, save exceptionally in the exercise of their general jurisdiction.

The ATQ has exclusive jurisdiction to the extent provided by express statutory provisions. It is presently composed of four sections: social affairs, economic affairs, land use planning and environment, and municipal taxation.[43] The ATQ has jurisdiction on questions of law, including constitutional questions, as well as questions of fact. It may affirm or annul an initial decision, or render a fresh decision replacing the initial one. It may also refer the case back to the decision-maker.[44]

The procedure followed by the ATQ is similar to judicial procedure, so much so that in *Barreau de Montréal v. Québec (AG)*,[45] the Court of Quebec concluded that the ATQ was an administrative rather than a judicial body for the purpose of constitutional guarantees of independence, but was so close to a court that it deserved full protection under section 23 of the *Charter of Human Rights*. The recent legislative initiative granting tenure to ATQ members (instead of a five-year renewable mandate) will accentuate this judicial character, making the ATQ almost undistinguishable from a specialized judicial court.[46]

The Code of Civil Procedure *and Judicial Review*

Quebec law is less distinct when it comes to administrative law judicial remedies. The first *Code of Civil Procedure* was enacted in 1897 and the present *Code* was adopted in 1965. It is a comprehensive law of general application, like the *Civil Code*, and it was accompanied by commentaries made by its drafters. Section 33 of the *Code* recognizes that the Superior Court is the heir to the English Court of King's Bench and, as such, exercises supervisory control over all public and private entities in Quebec.

Any ambiguity is resolved by having recourse to section 20 of the *Code*, which allows the Superior Court to create new remedies if none provided in the *Code* apply in a particular situation. Inherent powers of the Superior Court are also recognized in section 46 and its inherent jurisdiction in section 31. However, section 33 establishes restrictions on judicial review.[47]

Remedies under the *Code* are a mixed bag. Prerogative writs have been codified, which has the effect of freezing them in time. For instance, section 846 provides for 'évocation' and 'révision judiciaire,' but the conditions set up by section 846 are those developed in English law centuries ago for the writs of prohibition and *certiorari*. That section uses words like 'tribunal' and 'judgment' so its scope is, in practice, limited to quasi-judicial entities.[48]

This difficulty with the use of section 846 has favoured the development of the declaratory judgment, a remedy that appeared for the first time in 1965. From the 'Commentaries' it appears that the declaratory judgment was to be a strictly private law remedy, mostly used for the interpretation of contracts and wills. But in *Duquet v. Ste-Agathe-des-Monts*,[49] the Supreme Court gave section 453 a more liberal reading, extending it to a declaration of non-applicability of a municipal bylaw to a person. Since then, it has been used to control the constitutionality or legality of statutes, regulations, guidelines, and other administrative acts.[50]

Before that, Quebec courts had created a remedy, the 'action directe en nullité,' based on the general supervisory power of section 33. This remedy allows the court to control the validity of any norm, whether statutory or administrative. Even though it was a slower remedy, it soon became widely used due to its lack of formality.[51]

Mandamus, injunction, *quo warranto*, and *habeas corpus* have also been codified without making any changes to their centuries-old conditions. Thus, the old writs, which disappeared in England and in many other common law jurisdictions, continue to rule Quebec law from their graves.[52]

Recently, the *Code* was amended to provide that all judicial proceedings must be initiated as 'requêtes' (motions to institute proceedings). Formerly, remedies were divided into actions and 'requêtes.' This has standardized remedies to a large extent, since they are now subject to a similar procedure. This has led to a more liberal interpretation of the *Code's* provisions and has allowed for the concurrent use of different remedies.

In the next few years, a new *Code of Civil Procedure* is likely to be enacted. It has been suggested that the *Code* include a single application for judicial review, like that in the *Federal Courts Act*.[53] Such a change would be welcome but would create further difficulties, such as setting up a distinction between 'public' and 'private' entities, a distinction that is now more tenuous and runs contrary to recent statutory initiatives aimed at re-engineering the state.

Administrative Law 'Civilized'

An interesting feature of administrative law in Quebec lies in its interaction with the *Civil Code*. As we will see, the principle that public bodies are, save exceptions, bound by the *Civil Code* carries with it the 'civilization' of traditional public law rules. This goes beyond the mere statutory codification of administrative law rules, since it entails a common denominator of legal principles applying both to the public and the private sector, taking into account the special situation of the state and other public bodies.

The Status of the Civil Code *in Administrative Law*

In 1866 Quebec adopted it first codification of the civil law, the *Civil Code of Lower Canada*.[54] About one hundred years later began the task of drafting a new *Code*, more attuned to a changing social and economic situation. The new *Code*, in force since 1994, has introduced a new relationship between public and private law and has 'civilized,' to some extent, the legal rules applying to public entities.

The *Code* has become the *droit commun* for public administration. In 1989, in *Laurentides Motel*,[55] the Supreme Court stated that the *Quebec Act, 1774* had introduced a dual legal regime in Quebec: civil law for all matters dealing with property and civil rights, and common law for all public law matters. However, a statutory enactment could make the civil law apply to a certain extent to public authorities,[56] and these authorities could voluntarily avail themselves of the civil law, for instance when concluding a contract.[57]

Three important provisions of the *Code* have put an end to the old civil law–common law dichotomy. Article 1376 of the *Code* stipulates that the Book on Obligations applies to the state and all incorporated public entities, save for other applicable legal rules. According to the Supreme Court in *Prud'homme v. Prud'homme*,[58] this provision constitutes a general, explicit, and new reference to the civil law. There is no longer a need to refer to a particular statutory provision to render the *Code* applicable to public entities. This is a reversal of the former presumption favouring the common law. A public body will have the burden of justifying, in a given situation, the existence of a derogatory rule. This has led the courts to reappraise the meaning and scope of public law privileges and immunities. For instance, in *Prud'homme*, Justice LeBel pondered the necessity of an immunity for local councillors when speaking at a public meeting of a local authority.[59] In *Finney*,[60] the court reviewed the purpose of an immunity provision benefiting inspectors and other agents of the Quebec bar.

Article 300 has a wider scope. It states that the legal framework of all public bodies is, first, its enabling legislation, and then the *Civil Code*.

Again, this general provision is wider than the one it replaced (article 356).[61] The *Code* will, therefore, be used whenever possible to complement particular statutory provisions applying to a public entity.[62]

Finally, the preliminary provision of the *Code*, which has normative value,[63] proclaims that the *Code* and the general civil law principles are the foundation of all other statutes, which may add to the *Code* or derogate from it. In *Finney*, the Supreme Court mentioned that the preliminary provision impliedly confers a new role on the *Civil Code* in the hierarchy of legal sources.[64]

The *Civil Code* is more than a law of general application; it is the *droit commun* in Quebec. As a corollary, all regulations, guidelines, and other administrative measures must conform to the *Code*,[65] except when derogation from it is expressly provided in the enabling act.[66]

The *Civil Code* is part of Quebec public law. In enacting the *Code*, the legislature has, to some extent, replaced common law rules with *Civil Code* provisions. Some examples are the regime of limitations of actions against the crown,[67] and the liability of a public entity for acts of agents whose actions are *ultra vires* (unless a total or partial immunity is conferred by law to that public entity).[68] The *Code* has also integrated some public law rules, particularly to confirm the special status of Crown property and claims.[69] Finally, the *Code* may be used to interpret and complete all statutory and administrative texts, including federal laws and regulations applying in Quebec.[70]

Civil Code provisions have been used for the purpose of interpreting the *Code of Civil Procedure*,[71] the *Charter of Human Rights*,[72] the *Labour Code*,[73] and many other acts and regulations.[74] However, the *Civil Code* will not be used for such purpose if there is a clear legislative intent to the contrary.[75] For instance, in labour law, a 'cession d'entreprise' (transfer of the operation of the undertaking) has a wider meaning than the sale of a company or part of it, where the transfer of union bargaining rights is concerned.[76] Although the *Civil Code* has been granted a privileged status in Quebec law, in order to ensure the fundamental character of the *Code* it is vital that the courts play their role.

A large number of government agencies and administrative tribunals have to interpret or apply civil law rules in the exercise of their functions. This is the case for labour arbitration boards, the Rent Tribunal, the ATQ, professional disciplinary boards, and many others. Unlike judgments rendered by courts, which are normally subject to appeal, decisions rendered by these tribunals and boards are often final and protected by a privative clause excluding judicial review, except on jurisdictional grounds.

According to the pragmatic and functional approach developed in *U.E.S., loc. 298 v. Bibeault*[77] and *Pushpanathan v. Canada (Minister of Citizenship and Immigration)*,[78] these tribunals and boards are treated with great deference by courts in the exercise of their supervisory functions. Should that deference extend to civil law questions? So far, court decisions on this point have been a mixed bag. Some judges have ruled that any error of law concerning a civil law rule is reviewable. Others have required that the error be manifest or patently unreasonable to justify judicial intervention.[79]

Since a large number of tribunal decisions deal with civil law issues, it is quite understandable for the courts to draw the line somewhere. On the other hand, an overly permissive approach may lead to a balkanization of the civil law, with civil law rules being given different meaning in different contexts. Substantial deference should be shown towards decisions merely applying civil law rules, while no such deference should be shown when a board or tribunal is interpreting a *Civil Code* provision or a civil law principle so as to define its meaning and scope.

The Integration of Civil Law Rules in Administrative Law

Since the adoption of the present *Civil Code*, civil law rules have been used in administrative law situations. It is noteworthy that the courts have tried to harmonize civil law and common law rules, making Quebec a laboratory for comparative law. Civil law rules have been used both to give a legal foundation to administrative measures and to prevent abuses of powers by administrative agencies.

As 'legal persons,' public entities are entitled to benefit from all ancillary powers and rights conferred by the *Code* to all such persons. This includes a wider *locus standi*, a confirmation of the *de facto* principle and, more generally, the power to adopt measures necessary for the accomplishment of statutory responsibilities.[80]

On the other hand, articles 6, 7, and 1375 of the *Code* require all public entities to act in good faith and not to abuse their dominant position in the exercise of their powers. Section 4 of the *Administrative Justice Act* refers to these civil law values among the principles of good governance applying to government agencies. These general principles apply to all phases of the decision-making process.

Among other general principles used by the courts to provide a legal framework for administrative action are the interdiction of a 'condition potestative' in an administrative decision (an obligation that depends on a condition that is at the sole discretion of the debtor),[81] the 'fin de non recevoir,'[82] and the 'préclusion promissoire' (akin to estoppel)[83], the burden of proof in civil law cases,[84] and the exclusion of evidence capable of discrediting the administration of justice.[85] The concept of 'ordre public' (public order) has also been adapted to the administrative law context so as to submit public entities to fundamental values in Quebec society.[86]

These civil law rules, which are sometimes analogous to common law rules, are even more useful in situations where self-regulation and privatization have replaced public agencies by private actors. To the extent that administrative law is no longer applicable, the civil law becomes the only bulwark against unfair or arbitrary conduct by these agencies.[87]

The last development worth mentioning is the use of the concept of bad faith in civil law suits against public authorities. In *Finney*,[88] the Supreme Court expressed the view that the requirement of good faith has different meanings, depending on the type of function exercised by the defendant. If the alleged delict arises from the exercise of a wide discretionary power of a 'political' nature, the plaintiff must prove intentional fault or abuse of power on the part of the defendant. At the other extreme, if the act is of a purely administrative nature, bad faith requires proof of a failure to act with prudence or diligence.[89]

Between these two levels of proof are actions taken in the course of an inquiry or in the supervision of a sector in virtue of a statutory duty. Since civil servants and other agents exercising such functions usually benefit from a statutory immunity for acts done (or omitted) in good faith, the Supreme Court has devised a middle approach. It requires 'faute lourde,' or gross negligence, to make a public authority liable towards an aggrieved citizen in such a situation.[90] Therefore, a civil law principle has been adapted to a public law context.

Conclusion

In the last decade, administrative law in Quebec has been profoundly changed by laws of general application that enshrine fundamental societal values. General principles of administrative law are now more likely to be found in written provisions than in case law precedents. However, the public law principles that are part of our English public law heritage are still present, even though their status and scope have been modified through their integration in fundamental laws (the *Char-*

ter of Human Rights, the *Civil Code)*, or laws of general application (*Code of Civil Procedure, Administrative Justice Act*). This has led to their harmonization with the interpretive rules and values particular to these laws.

NOTES

1 Art. 1260 C.C.Q.
2 R.S.Q., c. C-12 [*Charter of Human Rights*].
3 R.S.Q., c. C-11.
4 See, for instance, *Ass. des radiologistes v. Rochon*, [1999] J.Q. no. 894 (C.A.); *Lachine General Hosp. v. Quebec (A.G.)*, [1996] R.J.Q. 2804 (C.A); *U.L. Canada inc. v. Quebec (A.G.)*, [2003] R.J.Q. 2729 (C.A.), aff'd 2005 S.C.C. 10.
5 See *Alliance des professeurs catholiques de Montréal v. L.R.B.*, [1953] 2 S.C.R. 140 at 155; *Dlugosz v. Quebec (A.G.)*, [1987] R.J.Q. 2312 (C.A) ; *Vallières v. Courtiers J.D.*, [1998] R.J.Q. 2623 (C.A.) ; *Gestion Serge Lafrenière inc. v. Calvé*, [1999] R.J.Q. 1313 (C.A.). One exception is *Roncarelli v. Duplessis*, where the Quebec Court of Appeal sided with the premier of Quebec, who had illegally pressured the chairperson of a regulatory agency to revoke the plaintiff restauranteur's liquor licence. The Supreme Court of Canada overturned the Court of Appeal's decision: [1959] S.C.R. 121.
6 Art. 477 C.C.P.
7 R.S.Q., c. J-3.
8 R.S.Q., c. A-2.1.
9 R.S.Q., c. R-18.1.
10 I also wish to mention Murray Rankin, a senior lawyer with Arvay, Finlay, and formerly a law professor at the University of Victoria, who translated René Dussault and Louis Borgeat, *Traité de droit administratif* t. 1–3, 2nd ed. (Quebec: Presses de l'Université Laval, 1989) (English edition translated by Murray Rankin and Donald Breen, *Administrative Law: A Treatise* (Toronto: Carswell, 1985–90) and also referred regularly to Quebec administrative law developments in his writings.
11 René Dussault has been a law professor at Laval University, deputy minister of justice, president of the Office des professions, and presently a member of the Quebec Court of Appeal. Gil Rémillard was also a member of the faculty at Laval, and later became minister of justice. Patrice Garant, also from Laval, wrote influential government reports. Yves Ouellette, a law professor at the University of Montreal, was the chairman of a commission that initiated the reform of administrative justice. Louis-Philippe Pigeon, a private practitioner who taught constitutional law at Laval, wrote a book on

legal drafting and became a Supreme Court judge. Jean Beetz, also appointed to the Supreme Court of Canada, was a dean at the University of Montreal and a respected constitutional lawyer. Louis Marceau, a Laval dean, was the first protecteur du citoyen before being appointed to the Federal Court of Canada, along with Louis Pratte, another civil law specialist from Laval. This list is not exhaustive.

12 Section 52 of the *Charter of Human Rights, supra* note 2, provides: 'No provision of any Act, even subsequent to the Charter, may derogate from sections 1 to 38, except so far as provided by those sections, unless such Act expressly states that it applies despite the Charter.' Section 53 adds: 'If any doubt arises in the interpretation of a provision of the Act, it should be resolved in keeping with the intent of the Charter.'

13 Section 52, ibid.

14 *Québec (Comm. des droits de la personne) v. C.U.M.*, [2004] 1 S.C.R. 789 at para. 15 [C.U.M.].

15 Section 52, *supra* note 2.

16 On the other hand, the long list of enumerated grounds of discrimination in section 10 of the *Charter of Human Rights* is exclusive, while the enumeration found in section 15 of the *Canadian Charter* is open to the addition of analogous grounds by the court. See *Andrews v. Law Society of British Columbia*, [1989] 1 S.C.R. 143.

17 Sections 4 and 5 of the *Charter of Human Rights, supra* note 2. See *Blencoe v. B.C. (Human Rights Comm.)*, [2000] 2 S.C.R. 307.

18 Section 9.1 provides as follows:

> In exercising his fundamental freedoms and rights, a person shall maintain a proper regard for democratic values, public order and the general well-being of the citizens of Quebec. In this respect, the scope of the freedoms and rights, and limits to their exercise, may be fixed by law.

See *Syndicat Northcrest v. Amselem*, [2004] 2 S.C.R. 551 at para. 146 [*Amselem*].

19 The distinction between administrative and quasi-judicial functions, abandoned in most common law jurisdictions, is alive and well in Quebec. As a result, the courts have relied on old Supreme Court precedents like *Coopers and Lybrand v. M.N.R.*, [1979] 1 S.C.R. 495 in order to determine the relevant factors as to the applicability of section 23, since it applies only to quasi-judicial tribunals. Section 56 provides as follows:

> In section ... 23 ..., the word 'tribunal' includes a coroner, a fire investigation commissioner, an inquiry commission, and any person or agency exercising quasi judicial functions.

20 Section 23 provides as follows:

> Every person has a right to a full and equal, public and fair hearing by an

independent and impartial tribunal, for the determination of his rights and obligations or of the merits of any charge brought against him.

21 *Ocean Port Hotel v. B.C.*, [2001] 2 S.C.R. 781.

22 R.S.C. 1985, app. III; *Bell Canada v. Canadian Telephone Employees Assn.*, [2003] 1 S.C.R. 884.

23 *Québec inc. v. Québec (Régie des permis d'alcool)*, [1996] 3 S.C.R. 919.

24 Sections 1–15 of *Administrative Justice Act*, *supra* note 8. See *2437–0223 Québec inc. v. Québec (Régie des alcools)*, [2000] R.J.Q. 104 (S.C.).

25 D. Lemieux, *Justice administrative: Loi annotée*, 2nd ed. (Montreal: C.C.H., 2001) at 49.

26 *Béliveau St-Jacques v. Féd. des employées et employés de services publics inc.*, [1996] 2 S.C.R. 345. There was a strongly worded dissenting opinion by Justice L'Heureux-Dubé.

27 *C.U.M.*, *supra* note 15 at para. 17.

28 *Supra* note 2, s. 54.

29 Les tribunaux administratifs au Québec (Quebec Department of Justice, 1971) [Dussault Report]. See Lemieux, *supra* note 25 at 5–7.

30 *Québec (A.G.) v. Farrah*, [1978] 2 S.C.R. 638; *Crevier v. Québec (A.G.)*, [1981] 2 S.C.R. 220.

31 *Rapport de groupe de travail sur les tribunaux administratifs* (Quebec Department of Justice, 1987) [Ouellette Report]. See Lemieux, *supra* note 25 at 9–20.

32 *Administrative Justice Act*, s. 1. See *Une justice administrative pour le citoyen* (Quebec: Department of Justice, 1994) [Garant Report]. See also Lemieux, *supra* note 25 at 25–39.

33 *Administrative Justice Act*, ss. 14–15.

34 Sections 2 and 3 define a governmental entity as including 'government departments and bodies whose members are in the majority appointed by the Government or by a minister and whose personnel is appointed in accordance with the Public Service Act (chapter F-3.1.1). Additional government entities have been added by express reference in subsequent legislation.

35 Section 4.

36 Section 4(4).

37 Section 5.

38 For illustrations, see Lemieux, *supra* note 25 at 118–21.

39 *Administrative Justice Act*, section 6.

40 Sections 7 and 8.

41 [1999] 2 S.C.R. 817 [*Baker*]. In this case, the Supreme Court of Canada held that the common law duty to give written reasons applies only in certain circumstances, when the decision has important significance for the individual, or when there is a statutory right of appeal. Furthermore, the

requirement may not be of a formal nature. For instance, in *Baker* a junior immigration officer's notes, which were not initially sent to the petitioner, were considered to be adequate written reasons (paras. 43–44).

42 *Administrative Justice Act*, section 2.

43 Section 16.

44 Sections 15 and 112.

45 [2001] R.J.Q. 2058 (C.A.).

46 Bill 103, An Act to amend the Act respecting administrative justice and other legislative provisions, 1st sess., 37th Leg., Quebec, 2005 (assented to 17 June 2005).

47 *Administrative Justice Act*, section 33, states that all courts, excepting the Court of Appeal, and all public entities within the jurisdiction of the Quebec legislation are subject to the superintending and reforming power of the Superior Court in such manner and form as by law provided, save in matters declared by law to be of the exclusive competency of such courts or of any of the latter, and save in cases where the jurisdiction resulting from this article is excluded by some provision of a general or special law.

48 See Lemieux, *Le contrôle judiciaire de l'action gouvernementale*, looseleaf (Montréal: C.C.H.) section 20–100.

49 [1977] 2 S.C.R. 1132.

50 See Lemieux, *supra* note 48 at ch. 20–280.

51 Ibid. at ch. 20–350.

52 Ibid. at ch. 20–050, 20–150, 20-200, 20–310, and 20–400.

53 R.S.C. 1985, c. F-7.

54 Art. 1131 C.C.L.C.

55 *Laurentides Motel v. Beauport (City)*, [1989] 1 S.C.R. 705 at para. 64 [*Laurentides Motel*]. See also *Senez v. Montreal Real Estate Board*, [1980] 2 S.C.R. 555 at 562.

56 See, for instance, article 356 of the *Civil Code of Lower Canada*, and section 94 of the *Code of Civil Procedure*.

57 *Banque de Montréal v. Quebec (A.G.)*, [1979] 1 S.C.R. 565.

58 [2002] 4 S.C.R. 663, para. 26 and 31 [*Prud'homme*].

59 Ibid.

60 *Finney v. Barreau du Québec*, [2004] 2 S.C.R. 17 at para. 26 [*Finney*].

61 Article 356 of the *Civil Code* stated that political corporations 'are governed by the public law, and only fall within the control of the civil law in their relations, in certain respects, to individual members of society,' while article 300 now provides that legal persons are governed by the *Code* where the provisions of special or general acts applicable to them 'require to be complemented, particularly with regard to their status as legal persons, their property or their relations with other persons.'

62 *Doré v. Verdun (City)*, [1997] 2 S.C.R. 862 at para. 18.

63 *Prud'homme, supra* note 58 at para. 28–30.

64 *Finney, supra* note 60.

65 *Godbout v. Longueuil (Ville)*, [1995] R.J.Q. 2561 (C.A.), aff'd on other grounds [1997] 3 S.C.R. 844 [*Godbout*]; *Allendale Mutual Insur. Co. v. Hydro Québec*, [2002] R.J.Q. 84 (C.A.) at paras. 23, 33–34.

66 *Glykis v. Hydro Québec*, [2004] 3 S.C.R. 205.

67 *Civil Code*, articles 2877 and 2930; see also *Greenberg v. Gruber* (2004), J.E. 2004–1180 (C.A.).

68 *Civil Code*, article 1464. See notes 25, 57, and 59 for the recognition of a residual immunity from civil liability.

69 Articles 916, 2724 and following.

70 *Interpretation Act*, R.S.C. 1985, c. I-21, ss. 8.1 and 8.2. See also *St-Hilaire v. Canada (A.G.)*, [2001] 4 F.C. 289 (C.A.) at para. 66; *Lloyd's of London v. Pêcheries Nicol Desbois inc.* (2004), J.E. 2004–428 (C.A).

71 *Lac d'amiante du Québec ltée v. 2858–0702 Québec inc.*, [2001] 2 S.C.R. 743.

72 *Synd. des trav. et trav. de Bridgestone/Firestone de Joliette (C.S.N.) v. Trudeau*, [1999] R.J.Q. 2229 (C.A.); *Amselem, supra* note 18 at para. 146.

73 *Synd. des salariés de distributeurs de produits pharmaceutiques (FISA) v. Médis* (2000), J.E. 2000–1308 (C.A.).

74 *Goulet v. Cie d'assur. Transamérica*, [2002] 1 S.C.R. 719 at paras. 42 and 46.

75 *Souscripteurs de Montréal inc. v. Québec (Insp. gén. des instit. financ.)*, [2000] R.R.A. 42 (C.A) at paras. 8–12 ; *Laval (Ville) v. Coimac inc.*, [2001] R.J.Q. 342 (C.A).

76 Compare *U.E.S., loc. 298 v. Bibeault*, [1988] 2 S.C.R. 1048 [*Bibeault*] and *Ivanhoe Inc. v. TUAC, sect. loc. 500*, [2001] 2 S.C.R. 566.

77 *Bibeault, supra* note 76.

78 [1998] 1 S.C.R. 982.

79 Compare *Isidore Garon ltée v. Tremblay*, [2004] R.J.Q. 58 (C.A.), at paras. 30–1 (leave to appeal to S.C.C. granted 06/05/04) and *Longpré v. Gouin*, [2003] R.J.Q. 1459 (C.A.).

80 *Civil Code*, articles 300 and following. See *Québec (RAM) v. Pharmascience inc.* (2004), J.E. 2004–1699 (S.C.).

81 Article 1500. See *Club optimiste Ancienne-Lorette v. Régie des alcools, des courses et des jeux*, [1999] J.Q. no. 1606 (S.C.) (Q.L.).

82 *Sous-min. du Revenu v. Québec (P.G.)*, [2002] R.J.Q. 54 (C.A.).

83 *Centre hospitalier Mont-Sinaï v. Québec (Min. de la Santé et des serv. sociaux)*, [1998] R.J.Q. 2707 (C.A.), aff'd on different grounds [2001] 2 S.C.R. 281 [*Mount-Sinai*]. The Supreme Court of Canada is not keen on using estoppel in administrative law. See particularly the opinion of Binnie J. in *Mount*

Sinai. See also the contribution of Geneviève Cartier to this volume. Quebec courts, on the other hand, have been more receptive to the use of the 'préclusion promissoire,' since it is founded on articles 6 and 7 of the *Civil Code*, essential provisions that apply to all entities. See *Gestion Serge Lafrenière inc. c. Calvé*, [1999] R.J.Q. 1313 at 1325 (C.A.); *Sous-min. du Revenu v. Québec (P.G.)*, [2002] R.J.Q. 54 at para. 25 (C.A.); and *P.S.B.G.M. v. Williams*, [2002] R.R.A. 1060 (C.A).

84 *SAAQ v. Viger*, [2000] R.J.Q. 2209 (C.A.).

85 *Mascouche (Ville) v. Houle*, [1999] R.J.Q. 1894 (C.A.).

86 *Godbout*, *supra* note 65.

87 For illustrations, see *Royal Aviation v. Aéroports de Montréal*, [1998] R.J.Q. 2409; *Aéroports de Montréal v. Meilleur*, [1997] R.J.Q. 1516 (C.A.); and *Bourse de Montréal v. Letellier*, [1999] R.J.Q. 2839 (C.A).

88 *Finney*, *supra* note 60.

89 Article 1457 of the *Civil Code*.

90 Article 1471 of the *Civil Code* distinguishes between 'faute simple,' 'faute lourde,' and 'faute intentionnelle,' while article 1457 specifies that the degree of prudence and diligence required from a person may vary according to the circumstances. These may include the consideration of the type of functions exercised by a public authority.

Globalization, 'Local' Foreign Policy, and Administrative Law

MICHAEL TAGGART

In many ways local government law is the Cinderella of public law. The age of the city state predated the modern rise of administrative law, and as a consequence the subservience of cities to the states containing them has long since been taken for granted. Paradoxically, perhaps, the age of globalization has generated new interest in the 'local.'[1] The problems of the world are both too big and too small for states to handle, and the latter are being dispatched increasingly to sub-national levels of government. So it may turn out that the glass slipper of globalization will allow local government law entrance to the public law ball.[2]

The purpose of this essay is to pursue this broad theme through a consideration of whether local authorities can adopt and enforce 'local' foreign policy. It was David Mullan's discussion of the Canadian Supreme Court case of *Shell Canada Products Ltd v. Vancouver (City)*[3] that put this topic in my mind.[4] Indeed, almost everything I know about Canadian administrative law I have learnt from David Mullan. More than any other scholar of his generation, he has put Canadian administrative law on the international map.[5] He has never lost the instinct for common law comparativism that legal education in a small place at the bottom of the world instills.[6] It is an honour to pay tribute to a great administrative lawyer who combines the best of New Zealand and Canadian legal cultures.

Territoriality, Power, and Local Government

In the creation story of administrative law the original sin of an inferior decision-maker was to purport to act outside the conferred area of operation or its territory.[7] Such territorial errors were jurisdictional in the narrowest sense and rendered the decision void *ab initio*.[8] The paradigmatic case was local government. Indeed, the etymology of the word 'territory' is from local government. It is derived from the Latin word *territorium*, which means the area of land surrounding a town (*municipium*) that was under that town's jurisdiction.[9]

Historically, local government was pretty much the only government that mattered in Britain for all but the nobility until the nineteenth century.[10] While the boundaries of the numerous local units were of considerable significance for a variety of reasons,[11] much that went on within those boundaries was justified by crown grant, custom, and tradition until the 1830s. But by the eighteenth century there was considerable growth in centrally generated local legislation.[12] According to Joanna Innes, this reflected '[a] developing tradition of constitutional thought ... that inferior parts of government needed specific sanction from either crown or parliament for any form of authority they wished to exercise.'[13] Faced with residents more willing to challenge local authorities' actions, those local bodies increasingly sought the safe haven of statutory authorization. This was a costly business,[14] and ratepayers were attentive to what their rates were to be spent on[15] and, when disagreeable, sought to saddle the promoters with the costs of raising local legislation.[16]

It is no coincidence that this slow process of local subservience to Parliament coincided broadly with the rise of centralization. The history of English law is the gradual transference of power to the centre from the localities. Slowly, but surely, local government in the United Kingdom lost its constitutional role; that is, it lost the essential attributes of self-government that in the previous centuries defined it.[17] So in *Roberts v. Hopwood* (1925) Lord Sumner was able to say that '[t]here is nothing about a borough council that corresponds to autonomy.'[18] By the end of the nineteenth century the local authorities' relationship with the centre shifted from one with Parliament to one shaped by central government departments.[19] This had profound consequences as the degree of central control tightened over the twentieth century, squeezing whatever autonomy was left out of local authorities. The subordination of local government became manifest,[20] and the use of the language of *ultra vires*, unheard of in the local government context before the mid-nineteenth century, became ubiquitous.[21]

Compared with local government elsewhere in the common law world, local government in the United Kingdom still discharges an immense range of functions; including responsibility for[22]

> the police, for the fire service, for almost all education other than university, for the health and welfare of mothers and infants, the old and the sick, for children in need of care, for public health, for housing, for sport and recreation, for museums, art galleries and libraries, for the physical environment and the use of land, for highways, traffic and transport, and for many other matters too numerous to mention.

The reliance of local government on central government financing for the discharge of these and other functions has meant that 'local administrations are now fig-leaves for centrally determined policies.'[23] The interest of the central government was rather selective, however. As Martin Loughlin has observed, during the Thatcher years '[t]he centre was much more concerned to limit the incursions of the localities into matters of high politics ... than to give strategic direction to local authorities.'[24]

The 'powerlessness' of local government is expressed in its subordinate legal status.[25] This is what American lawyers know as 'Dillon's Rule,' named after John F. Dillon who inscribed it in his extremely influential treatise on the law of municipalities.[26] Municipal corporations in U.S. law have no residual, inherent or natural powers. They only have such powers as are expressly delegated by statute or are necessarily or fairly implied in or incident to the powers expressly granted. What is more, traditionally the courts have interpreted these powers very narrowly in order to confine local authorities. Remarkably, given the different legal paths taken in so many other respects,[27] Dillon's Rule is replicated almost word for word in the rest of the common law world.[28] In the Anglo-Commonwealth world also, local authorities – unlike private individuals, companies, and even the crown – do not enjoy any common law or so-called residual powers, and only have the powers expressly or implicitly granted by statute.[29]

Over the last hundred years there have been calls, heeded early in the United States, to rescue local government from this straitjacket of *ultra vires*. In America this movement was called 'Home Rule,'[30] and the many states that legislated for municipal home rule expressly repudiated Dillon's Rule.[31] In the Anglo-Commonwealth the phrase 'power of general competence' was preferred to municipal home rule, and although the debate dates back to at least the 1920s in the United Kingdom,[32] it has only recently been acted on.[33] In this long-running discussion the *ultra vires* doctrine has often been painted as the villain. Nearly forty years ago, the Maud Committee (1967) was of the view that[34]

> *ultra vires* as it operates at present has a deleterious effect on local government because of the narrowness of the legislation governing local authorities' activities. The specific nature of legislation discourages enterprise, handicaps development, robs the community of services which the local authority should render, and encourages too rigorous oversight by the central government. It contributes to the excessive concern about legalities and fosters the idea that the [Town] Clerk should be a lawyer.

This tether of *ultra vires* is the principal restraint on local authorities that wish to take a stand on matters of foreign policy.

'Local' Foreign Policy

In recent times there has been no shortage of controversial matters of ethical or moral concern that have engaged the attention of local government politicians and their communities. British examples include local bans on circuses with live animals, tobacco advertising on council hoardings, or hunting on council land. These and similar issues 'travel beyond'[35] the bailiwick of a particular local territory, and are often national and indeed sometimes international issues. I want to concentrate on the international dimension here for the following reasons: it is a neglected topic in Anglo-Commonwealth administrative law; the leading case is Canadian and has been analysed by our honorand; the contrast between that case and a leading House of Lords decision is stark but generally unacknowledged; and the topic permits a comparison of judicial attitudes to local government with the globalization rhetoric of an enhanced role for large cities in a shrinking world.

It has to be admitted that there are no bright lines between local, regional, national, and international issues. Indeed the word 'foreign' looks a little old-fashioned these days. In this age of technological advances and mobility it has been said there is no 'overseas' any more. Be that as it may, my focus here is on the adoption by local authorities of a 'local' foreign policy.[36] Such a policy can take many forms, as we will see, but the essential characteristic is that the local authority identifies an issue of concern in another country or region and takes a public stand in relation to that issue. Sometimes the stand may be simply symbolic, at other times it might purport to have real consequences.[37]

Some of the most common forms of expression of such local foreign policy include the naming of streets or public facilities after dissidents from particular nations or exiled or assassinated revolutionary leaders of oppressed peoples; sister city arrangements with an overt political purpose; declaration of the local authority's area as a zone free of unwanted activity (be it apartheid or nuclear weapons or waste or whatever); disinvestment of council funds or council pension funds in companies associated with offensive regimes; 'selective procurement' policies that prevent or discourage the authority from buying goods or services from companies that trade with offensive regimes or that condone practices or policies anathema to the local authority; various forms of aid or technical assistance to other localities; preferences for locally produced goods or services, or a national preference; or targeting certain foreign countries through boycotts of their goods.

Of necessity, the treatment here must be selective, and I will concentrate on three well-known administrative law cases involving anti-apartheid activity by local authorities in the United Kingdom and Canada.[38] The apartheid regime in South Africa was dismantled in 1994, but the contemporary relevance of this case law is that the strategies pioneered and honed in relation to apartheid South Africa have been deployed against other objectionable regimes. Local governments around the world increasingly want to lend support in making the world a better place both for those within and without their territorial boundaries.[39]

The Gleneagles Agreement in Leicester

The essential background to the first case to be considered – *Wheeler v. Leicester City Council*[40] – is the agreement reached by the Commonwealth heads of government at Gleneagles, Scotland, in June 1977.[41] The final communiqué of that gathering contained a statement about apartheid in sport (which instantly became known as the Gleneagles Agreement).[42] The essence of the agreement was that heads of government of the Commonwealth reaffirmed their abhorrence of apartheid in sport and accepted the obligation to combat apartheid vigorously 'by withholding any form of support for, and by taking every practical step to discourage contact or competition by their nationals' with sportspersons or organizations from South Africa. There was an acknowledgment that 'it was for each Government to determine in accordance with its laws the methods by which to best discharge these commitments,' but it was understood that 'effective fulfillment' of these commitments was essential 'to the harmonious development of Commonwealth sport hereafter.' The agreement was a case study in political compromise, which could be read every which way (and subsequently was).[43]

The Leicester City Council, which had taken a leading role in vociferously opposing apartheid, adopted the Gleneagles Agreement as its own policy in 1982. In doing so, the council committed itself to take 'every practical step to discourage' sporting contact with South Africa. This commitment was put to the test two years later when several members of the Leicester Rugby Club were selected for the English rugby tour of South Africa in 1984. The council pressured the club to press the English Rugby Union and the three players to back out of the tour, as well as demanding that the club answer a series of questions concerning its position regarding the tour and sporting links with South Africa. The questionnaire left little doubt that only answers in line with the council's anti-apartheid policies would be acceptable. The club replied reasonably and responsibly but refused to capitulate to the council's point of view.

The litigation arose from the council's decision to ban the club for twelve months from using a playing field for rugby practices and second XV matches. The club had used the field for many years and had an expectation of an annual renewal of the licence to use the ground.[44] The council was explicit in stating that this action was taken solely because it felt the club had not been vigorous enough in attempting to dissuade the Rugby Union and the players from taking part in the tour. The club brought judicial review.

At first instance, Forbes J. refused to intervene.[45] This decision was upheld on appeal. The majority of the Court of Appeal (Ackner L.J. and Sir George Waller) held: that the council had statutory power to permit the use of sports fields; that in exercising that discretion the council could take into account its other statutory functions; that one of those functions was the duty in section 71 of the *Race Relations Act 1976* (U.K.) 'to make appropriate arrangements with a view to securing that their various functions are carried out with due regard to the need ... to promote ... good relations between persons of different racial groups,' which should be interpreted to be relevant in the exercise of all the council's powers; that the council was 'fully entitled' in exercising its power over playing fields to take account of the promotion of good race relations; and finally, that it was not *Wednesbury*-unreasonable of the council to give an outward manifestation of their disapproval of the club's failure, indeed refusal, 'to take every practical step to discourage' the tour. In sum, the majority of the Court of Appeal applied orthodox relevant consideration analysis coupled with a residual application of the *Wednesbury* sieve to catch the absurd and the outrageous, and found the promotion of good race relations to be an expressly relevant consideration and the result not unreasonable in the special administrative law sense.[46]

Ackner L.J. emphasized the council's prior commitment to the Gleneagles Agreement. It was this more than anything else that insulated the council's decision from a finding of unreasonableness. The view of the council was 'no more than clearly recorded in the Gleneagles Agreement.'[47] According to the majority of the Court of Appeal the council was entitled – nay, duty-bound – by section 71 to promote good race relations and had done so by following the precepts of the Gleneagles Agreement.

The legal status of the Gleneagles Agreement is unclear. The better reading is that it did not require (as a matter of international law) the withholding of passports from nationals intent on touring South Africa, and that is the way the U.K. government interpreted it. The government never legislated the agreement into domestic law,[48] and never actually prevented individuals or groups from touring South Africa.

Whether the Leicester City Council could lawfully adopt as policy the Gleneagles Agreement was not addressed by any of the judges in *Wheeler*.[49] It was simply assumed that the council could. It is not self-evident, however, that a local authority can lawfully adopt a foreign policy, as its jurisdiction is (to use the colonial phrasing) the 'peace, order and good government' within a defined territory. As to the power to *enforce* any such local foreign policy – which was really what *Wheeler* was about – the Court of Appeal only obliquely touched on this. Sir George Waller said '[i]f this country can freely enter into an agreement to "combat the evil of apartheid by taking every practical step to discourage contact ... with sporting organizations ... from South Africa ..." [the wording in the Gleneagles Agreement], it is difficult to see how it could be unreasonable for a council in the position of Leicester City Council to take the steps they did.'[50] But this begs the question. National governments do have the power to prevent sporting tours abroad by nationals. They can exhume the writ of *ne exeat regno,* withhold/revoke passports of citizens planning to depart for South Africa, or even legislate to that effect.[51] As noted above, the U.K. government refused to take any of those steps.[52] Can then a sub-national organ of government step into the breach and mark its disapproval?[53] These issues are taken up later.

So, rather than speaking softly and carrying a big stick,[54] the Leicester City Council spoke loudly and used the only stick at its disposal to beat the disobedient club. In doing so, the council adopted wholeheartedly a political view; it favoured the pursuit of equality over the freedom of individuals to further their sporting careers, it believed sport was political and hence approved of political interference in sport, and it thought that only severing sporting (and other) relations with South Africa would help end apartheid. Many people felt that way, but could the council 'privilege' its politics at the expense of those who did not agree? The majority of the Court of Appeal said yes because it did not want to choose between equality and liberty – both being reasonable views – and so upheld the council's preference.[55] But in doing so the court chose,[56] and chose wrongly according to the dissenting judge, Lord Justice Browne-Wilkinson.

According to Browne-Wilkinson L.J. (as he then was), the law and the constitution require judges to prefer freedom of speech and conscience to equality, and so individual freedom of speech is favoured over the freedom of expression of the elected representatives of the local community. It was better that individuals be free to express lawful views over controversial matters without fear of official backlash than to be punished for standing up for what they believe. The council could not lawfully enforce the letter or the spirit of the Gleneagles Agreement against the club. It did not have to like what the club did; it had to lump it.

It is clear that Browne-Wilkinson L.J.'s starting point was completely different to that of the majority. He recognized there was a clash of fundamental principles, namely between 'the right of a democratically elected body to conduct their affairs in accordance with their own views and ... the right of freedom of speech and conscience enjoyed by each individual in a democratic society.'[57] As noted above, he resolved that clash by holding that the common law privileged the individual's freedom of expression. Such a basic constitutional right cannot be overridden by the conferral of general discretionary powers, because Parliament does not intend by so legislating to authorize the decision-maker to take into account the lawful views of those affected by the power or their willingness to express certain views. These are irrelevant considerations. Against this constitutional backdrop, section 71 could not be read as expressly or implicitly authorizing the powers to be used to 'discriminate against those who hold lawful views on racial matters.'[58]

Browne-Wilkinson L.J. stressed that he was not suggesting that the council was in any way unreasonable in wanting to distance itself from those that appeared to support sporting links with South Africa. He clearly did not want to stigmatize the council's views as unreasonable, with or without the *Wednesbury* epithet. The unlawfulness was in the council's attempt to punish those who refused to endorse its views.

On further appeal, their Lordships unanimously overturned the decision of the Court of Appeal, but for reasons different from those given by Browne-Wilkinson L.J. Lord Roskill's judgment, in particular, is characterized by assertions of unreasonableness and unfairness, and little else.[59] In line with all the judges below, Lord Roskill took an expansive view of section 71 and held the council was 'fully entitled' to pay regard to promoting race relations in exercising the power over playing fields.[60] Lord Roskill then focused on the conduct of the council in putting questions to the club that sought to force it to agree with the council's view about sporting contacts with South Africa. He thought here the Council had crossed the line between permissible persuasion and 'illegitimate pressure coupled with threats.'[61] Rather unsatisfactorily, Lord Roskill asserted without more that this was both *Wednesbury*-unreasonable and procedurally unfair due to 'the unfair manner the Council set about to achieve its objective.'[62] He expressly disavowed reliance on 'the wider ground' that had appealed to Browne-Wilkinson L.J.[63]

The only other Law Lord to give a reasoned judgment was Lord Templeman,[64] who held that the council could not use its power to punish the club for it had done nothing wrong. This was a misuse of power. Memorably, he said the laws of England are not like those of Nazi Germany, and so private citizens do not have to display zeal in pursuing an object sought by a public authority.[65]

Wheeler was influential in the determination of the two other cases I want to consider. Both of these cases involved a boycott of Shell products. Once again, it is necessary at the outset to put this anti-apartheid strategy in context.

Shell-Shocked in Two Cities

Despite extensive oil exploration in an otherwise resource-rich country, oil is the one vital raw material not found in South Africa.[66] South Africa therefore was (and is still) almost completely dependent on imported oil. The anti-apartheid movement recognized this vulnerability early on and attempted to exploit it by supporting an oil embargo. Despite international, regional, national and sub-national action in support of the oil embargo over many years, it was not successful for two reasons. The embargo was not supported or enforced by the countries that most mattered in the oil trade[67] and it was circumvented by the multinational oil and shipping companies that profited from the trade.[68]

The British Anti-Apartheid Movement focused on the activities of Shell and British Petroleum (BP), two of the biggest companies in the South African oil trade that were owned in significant proportion by British interests. Shell increasingly became the target of anti-apartheid campaigners in the 1980s because of its important oil refining and marketing role in South Africa and accusations that it was supplying the military.[69]

This tactic of targeting one leading company in an industry had been pioneered in relation to Barclay's Bank in protest at the heavy involvement of British banks in South Africa. That campaign was successful.[70] A number of local authorities supported the campaign, and they closed trading accounts with, and disinvested in, Barclay's Bank.[71] The success of the campaign against Barclay's Bank spawned another against the Royal Dutch/Shell group of companies. This campaign was not as successful, possibly because Shell swiftly and successfully challenged the legality of the boycott of its products in two cases – one in England and the other in Canada.

The first case involved the inner city London borough of Lewisham, whose opposition to apartheid through boycotting South African products dated back to the early 1960s.[72] During the 'Bank campaign,' Lewisham L.B.C. closed its account with Barclay's Bank in 1982.[73] It resolved also to disinvest, as far as legally possible, from companies with direct or indirect links with South Africa. Furthermore, Lewisham L.B.C. founded a body known as Joint Action Against Apartheid (JAAA), and some of its councillors played key roles in that organization.

In 1987, following in the footsteps of other British local authorities,[74] Lewisham L.B.C. adopted 'a policy of boycotting all Shell products subject to alternative products being available on reasonable terms.'[75] This policy was said to 'be in line with the council's commitment to promote harmonious race relations within the Borough of Lewisham.'[76] As other councils had such policies and were not challenged, it is reasonable to infer that Lewisham was singled out for its leadership role in JAAA in actively enlisting other councils' support for the Shell boycott.

Shell relied largely on *Wheeler* and the Queen's Bench Division thought this case was indistinguishable. The council was a creature of statute and did not have the powers of a natural person or any residual powers.[77] As such, it could not use its statutory powers to punish a body or person who had done nothing contrary to English law.[78] Shell U.K. was acting lawfully. The boycott was directed as much at putting pressure on Shell to get out of South Africa as it was to promote good race relations within the borough, and so the former illegitimate purpose tainted the decision and it was set aside.

Furthermore, the court held it was beyond Lewisham's statutory powers to take part in a campaign to persuade other local authorities to boycott Shell products. But Neil L.J., with whom Taylor J. agreed, was not prepared to declare the decision *Wednesbury*-unreasonable, even though he thought it was very near that line.[79] Counsel had argued that Shell had been singled out and that such discrimination was *ultra vires*, but the court did not address this point.[80]

A number of issues are raised by this decision. *Wheeler* was about the freedom of speech and conscience of the rugby club. They could not lawfully be browbeaten into conforming to the council's wishes or punished for not conforming. *Lewisham* was about the freedom of Shell to trade with whomever it liked, but the council was denied exactly that freedom by its public status. As Laws J. said at first instance in *R. v. Somerset County Council, ex parte Fewings*,[81] the principle of liberty, that everyone can do anything that is not prohibited, is for the benefit of citizens only. The rule for local authorities is the opposite: established by Parliament to further the public good, local authorities can only do what they are empowered to do. The council was forced to treat Shell the same as all other oil companies. It could not mark its disapproval of companies within the Shell group propping up the apartheid regime in South Africa.

The case concerned a total boycott, but the logic of its holding would also invalidate a more nuanced policy that expressed a preference to buy from companies not involved in South African trade. However, unlike in the United States where there was considerable experimentation with so-called 'selective procurement' strategies,[82] this was cut short in the United Kingdom by statute. The *Local Government Act 1988* (U.K.) prohibited councils from taking account of 'non-commercial considerations' in the granting of public contracts.[83] Among the considerations deemed irrelevant are 'the country of origin of supplies or the location in any country of the business activities' of the contractor or any 'political ... affiliations or interests of' of the contractors or staff.

As noted earlier in relation to *Wheeler*, there is another, unacknowledged side to these English cases. A local authority's jurisdiction is bounded by its territory. It is given statutory powers to ensure the 'peace, order and good government' within that territory. Concern with matters elsewhere, particularly in other countries, is suspect. Local authorities cannot have a foreign policy, at least not one that affects the economic interests of law-abiding businesses, clubs and individuals. Local authorities can act symbolically – witness the number of parks and gardens throughout the United Kingdom named after Nelson Mandela, and the number of sister city arrangements with South Africa in the 1980s – but it seems from the English cases they cannot go beyond that. The next case from Canada tackled this issue head on.

Vancouver[84] arose from a resolution by the City of Vancouver stating that it would not do business with Shell and declaring Vancouver to be 'Shell-Free' until the Royal Dutch/Shell group divested itself of its South African holdings.[85] The consequence was that Shell, who had up to this point supplied oil and other products to the municipality, could no longer bid to do so in the future. Instead, the council contracted with Chevron Canada Ltd. to supply the city's petroleum needs.

This was done in the full knowledge that Chevron also did business in South Africa through a subsidiary. The city targeted Shell as part of the international campaign[86] discussed earlier. The city took the position at trial that, although the resolution admittedly discriminated against Shell, it was acting in a private corporate capacity and as such 'there is no legal or statutory prohibition against such discrimination.'[87] The trial judge rejected that submission. The city was not the same as a private corporation. It was a statutory body acting under statutory powers, which it had transcended in this case because they were used to deal with matters that were beyond the city's territorial limits. The 'wrong' was occurring 'somewhere else in the world' and hence was beyond both the territorial and legal 'jurisdiction' and was irrelevant 'to the business of Vancouver.'[88] A distinction was drawn between unreasonableness and *ultra vires*. Reminiscent of the approach of Browne-Wilkinson L.J. in *Wheeler*, the trial judge did not say the city was acting unreasonably, but simply that it did not have the power to do what it wanted to do.[89]

The trial judge thought this case was indistinguishable from *Lewisham*, which he followed. He quoted also from the famous Canadian administrative law case, *Roncarelli v. Duplessis*.[90] In that case, Roncarelli's restaurant liquor licence was revoked by the provincial licensing authority on the order of the Quebec premier, who was outraged that Roncarelli stood bail for dozens of Jehovah's Witnesses. As Martland J. made clear,[91] one reason why this was unlawful was that the statutory powers were used to punish Roncarelli for doing something that was 'entirely lawful' (that is, furnishing of bail) and unrelated to the statutory purposes. That was essentially the situation in *Wheeler* and *Lewisham* as well.

Maczko J. stressed that in this case the city was refusing to contract with a company for dealing with South Africa, but in the future it might refuse to do business with the United States or with a communist country, or, indeed, because its employees have been organized by a particular trade union.[92] The court could not, and should not, be the judge of how laudable the goal is: the Court should stick to whether or not the power exists.[93] The resolution was quashed for jurisdictional error. That decision was overruled by a weakly reasoned decision of the British Columbia Court of Appeal.[94] On further appeal, the Supreme Court of Canada overturned the Court of Appeal by the narrowest possible margin and invalidated the resolutions. The Supreme Court split five to four, with Sopinka J. writing for the majority and McLachlin J. (as she then was) writing for the minority.[95] This is one of those cases where counting the heads of the judges in all the courts favoured the municipality seven to six, but the majority in the Supreme Court favoured Shell. So the case was close, and the split in the Supreme Court is intriguing.

First, the common ground should be noted. The Supreme Court of Canada was unanimous in holding that the decision-making by council was subject to judicial review. In other words, the reviewability of procurement decisions by local authorities was accepted. There had been much doubt on this point, and it may have influenced the judgment of the British Columbia Court of Appeal.[96] Second, the Supreme Court justices agreed that the council could only rely on statutory powers and that it had to exercise them for a proper purpose. There were no common law or residual powers to contract that gave the council more room to than the statute.[97]

The judgment of Sopinka J., for the majority, essentially tracks that of the trial judge. The municipality can only exercise its powers for a municipal purpose, and that means it must be 'for the good rule and government of the City.'[98] This placed a 'territorial limit on Council's jurisdiction.'[99] Sopinka J. allowed that '[n]o doubt Council can have regard for matters beyond its boundaries in exercising powers but in so doing any action taken must have as its purpose benefit to the citizens of Vancouver.'[100] Sopinka J. likewise found *Lewisham* 'highly persuasive' and saw no reason not to follow it.[101] The majority struck down the resolution as it did not benefit the citizens of Vancouver. Sopinka J. said that if he had found that the purpose was a 'municipal' one, he would have seriously considered quashing the resolution as it discriminated against Shell.[102] Such discrimination did not appear to be authorized by the council's constituent statute; indeed, some of the provisions seemed to negate discriminatory practices.

In dissent, McLachlin J. appeared to agree that the case boiled down to a question of statutory interpretation, but the answer to that question turned on the starting point adopted. Sopinka J. adopted a narrow, strict approach to construing the council's powers: unless the powers exercised fell squarely within the powers conferred, the court should not extend them by generous interpretation. In other words, it was for the court to say what the words meant and any ambiguity had to be resolved against the local authority. Although no one said so, this is the mirror image of Dillon's Rule, and similarly it had been engraved in the leading Canadian treatise on municipal corporations.[103] McLachlin J. called this approach 'pro-interventionist.'[104]

McLachlin J. preferred to interpret the statute so that the local authority had considerable room to decide what should be done in the public interest. This 'generous and flexible approach' she saw reflected in the *Wednesbury* case, where the local authority was said to have to act absurdly or irrationally before the court would intervene.[105] In any event, the court should only intervene in 'clear cases.'[106] McLachlin J. objected to the use of 'vague doctrinal terms' like irrelevant considerations, improper purpose and reasonableness as a way of substituting the judges' view of what is best for the community for that of the democratically elected municipality.[107] As we saw earlier in discussing Browne-Wilkinson L.J.'s dissent in *Wheeler*, the language of irrelevant considerations is the language of *ultra vires*. This is traditionally more hard-edged than unreasonableness review, and imposes a correctness test, which the trial judge and the majority of the Supreme Court in *Vancouver* applied.

The problem with this way of approaching review of municipal decision-making, according to McLachlin J., is that it affords no deference to the policy choices of elected local representatives. After considerable discussion, McLachlin J. concluded that 'the courts should adopt a generous, deferential standard of review towards the decisions of municipalities.'[108] Accordingly, she read the words 'provide for the good rule and government of the city' as embracing not only the immediate needs and welfare of the local inhabitants but also 'the psychological welfare of the citizens of a community who have an interest in expressing their identity as a community,' and this included 'the community expression of disapproval ... of different types of behaviour, wherever it is found.'[109] This was part of the community's right of free expression through its representatives.[110] The courts should not stand in the way of a municipality expressing its 'moral outrage' at apartheid.[111]

In *Wheeler* and *Lewisham,* for the most part the judges looked at the situation from the point of view of the rugby club and Shell, respectively. Browne-Wilkinson L.J. in *Wheeler* focused on the infringement of the rugby club's freedom of speech and conscience. The majority in the Court of Appeal in *Wheeler* thought the council should be free to take a stand against apartheid, but its judgment seems limp next to Browne-Wilkinson L.J.'s dissent. McLachlin J. gives the majority's position in *Wheeler* legal backbone by broadly interpreting the proper purposes and creating a shadowy collective 'right' of municipal free expression. But just as the judges in *Lewisham* and the House of Lords in *Wheeler* gave short shrift to the councils' position, likewise McLachlin J. gave short shrift to Shell's rights. She did not think the company had been deprived of any '"right" or entrenched privilege.'[112]

Tellingly, nowhere does McLachlin J. mention that Shell was doing nothing illegal. Clearly the absence of a breach of the positive law was not relevant to, nor did it impede, the freedom of the community through its representatives to express its views about Shell group doing business with South Africa. Nor did McLachlin J. interpret the municipality's resolution as punishing Shell, and thus she sidestepped *Lewisham* and *Wheeler.*[113] But the effect of the resolution was to pressure Shell, and, even if the municipality did not say that it intended to punish (as those in *Wheeler* and *Lewisham* did), Shell was clearly financially worse off as a result. It would have felt like a punishment.

Most strikingly, especially as she had emphasized the municipality's freedom of expression, McLachlin J. dismissed out of hand Shell's argument that the boycott of its products unreasonably limited its freedom of opinion on the issue of doing business with South Africa in breach of section 2(b) of the *Charter of Rights and Freedoms*. Assuming that a corporation can invoke that right, McLachlin J. dismissed the infringement as 'so trivial as not to merit serious scrutiny.'[114]

By fighting fire with fire, and invoking a municipality's freedom of expression, McLachlin J. was on contested ground. The position in English law is that local authorities enjoy 'no rights properly so called.'[115] The orthodox understanding is that public authorities (as part of the state) cannot invoke constitutional rights – which are included in bills of rights for the benefit of the citizen (and corporation) – against the citizen or corporation or other parts of the state.[116]

The majority and minority in *Vancouver* agreed that the municipality is a creature of statute. The municipality is like a dog on a leash with a choker chain attached to its neck. The majority would keep the dog on a short leash with the choker tight so that it could not stray from core municipal business. In contrast, the minority would have given the dog much more leash so it could wander far and wide leaving its mark on local, regional, national and even international issues. Eventually, if the dog wandered too far, the leash will go taut and the choker would grab, but only at the point that the municipality acted patently or *Wednesbury*-unreasonably.

One of the unavoidable hazards of comparative common law discussions of administrative law is that the public laws of each common law country can differ markedly because of different conditions, traditions, and doctrinal development. This is especially true of the roles and functions of local government across common law jurisdictions. In *Vancouver,* for example, the majority and minority disagreed over the relevance of the English decision of *Lewisham* because of their different views of the legal and social histories of local government in England and Canada.[117] Sopinka J.'s judgment in *Vancouver* is firmly in the 'rats, rubbish and roads' conception of municipal purpose. Many have greater aspirations for modern local government, especially for a major Pacific Rim city like Vancouver. '[T]he growing sophistication and stature of a contemporary city such as Vancouver,' McLachlin J. contended, 'requires that the scope of "municipal purposes" be determined with reference to the current reality,' and that non-traditional purposes, such as 'expression of collective values,' be included.[118]

In passing, something must be said about McLachlin J.'s doctrinal *modus operandi,* both because of its enduring importance in Canadian administrative law and its link to a point made later.[119] In her dissent, McLachlin J. brought together the 'patent unreasonableness' test (that Canadian administrative law has applied to most questions of statutory interpretation since the late 1970s) and the *Wednesbury*-unreasonableness test (that applied to statutory discretions).[120] It seems to me she did this for several reasons. The majority had unselfconsciously proceeded to apply a correctness standard without explanation. McLachlin J. wanted to remind the majority that mainstream Canadian administrative law requires a careful weighing of factors in order to determine whether 'correctness' or 'patent unreasonableness' applies. She also wanted to draw some succour from the highly deferential standard applied to review of discretionary decision-making by local authorities. The leading authority, known to all as simply *Wednesbury*,[121] involved a local authority exercising broad discretionary power. By throwing *Wednesbury* in the face of the majority, McLachlin J. said in effect that the reasons why courts show restraint in reviewing discretionary powers apply equally when interpreting a municipality's statutory powers.

'Selective Procurement': From Apartheid to Myanmar and Beyond

As regards the ability of a municipality to adopt a selective procurement policy that is directed at companies doing business in countries with poor human rights records, the majority stance in *Vancouver* severely curtails, if not rules out entirely, this sort of activity in Canada.[122] In this respect it is in line with *Lewisham*, which the majority in *Vancouver* followed. To be valid, Sopinka J.'s judgment requires the municipality adopting a selective procurement policy 'to identify a causal link between human rights abuses in a distant country and the tangible health, safety, and welfare interests that typically fall within the purview of municipalities.'[123] Moreover, a selective procurement policy would have to apply equally to all such companies, as targeting only the largest one (as in *Vancouver*) would likely be seen as impermissible discrimination.

As McLachlin J. noted, the practice of selective procurement is quite common in the United States. As we will see, there the focus of inquiry is on whether or not the constitution permits sub-national governments, state or local, to adopt foreign policy. The Canadian constitution is quite different, and, by comparison, 'silent on the issue of the rights and powers' of non-central government in international affairs.[124]

An argument was addressed to the appellate courts in *Vancouver* that such a procurement policy encroached on the federal government's exclusive power to regulate international trade and investment under section 91(2) of the *Constitution Act 1867* (U.K.), and so was *ultra vires*. Both the British Columbia Court of Appeal and McLachlin J. held that the resolutions were not unconstitutional as they were 'in pith and substance' within the provincial head of power relating to 'Municipal Institutions.'[125] Sopinka J. did not think it necessary to address this issue.[126]

American law, practice, and literature are much richer. It is frequently noted that as many as a dozen U.S. states and seventy American cities adopted some form of anti-apartheid sanctions in the 1980s.[127] As regards anti-apartheid 'selective procurement' policies, however, a careful study identified only one piece of state legislation and thirty-five municipal ordinances in the United States up to 1987.[128] Moreover, only about one-quarter of these ordinances contained hard-edged enforcement mechanisms, although those correlated with the largest municipalities with the largest purchasing power.

Although there was much debate about the constitutional validity of this state and municipal anti-apartheid legislation,[129] none was actually challenged in federal court, either before or after Congress enacted the comprehensive federal *Anti-Apartheid Act* of 1986 (U.S.).[130] The reason commonly given for the dearth of litigation in the United States is that no person or group wanted to be seen to support apartheid.[131] This is understandable given the history of racial segregation in that country.[132] However, later campaigns against human rights abuses in Myanmar (formerly Burma), modelled very much on the anti-apartheid pattern[133] and even more extensive, have been the subject of judicial consideration all the way to the U.S. Supreme Court.[134]

In most respects the American constitutional position is *sui generis*, involving intricacies of three federal heads of power (foreign relations, commerce power, and the supremacy clause). Many of these issues are unsettled, and they are canvassed exhaustively in the literature. I have neither the time nor the competence to evaluate their applicability, and moreover that is beside the present point. What is of relevance and broader applicability are the policy arguments as to whether municipalities can and should express views, take action, and legislate in relation to matters outside their territorial boundaries. A further factor that transcends the idiosyncrasy of American constitutionalism is the impact of globalization.[135]

The starting point in the American literature is that Congress has unquestioned authority to legislate on foreign affairs and can thereby preempt any state or local law dealing with such matters. The debate arises where Congress has not legislated: are municipalities then free as a matter of constitutional law to adopt a 'local' foreign policy unless and until Congress intervenes?[136] The large constitutional law literature on this question overlooks whether the municipalities have the power to adopt and enforce 'local' foreign policies as a matter of statutory interpretation and state administrative law. This state law question[137] – which is the same as that asked in Anglo-Commonwealth jurisdictions – has been ignored in the rush to the Constitution and federal courts. So it is to those sources that we must look for discussion of the policy arguments for and against 'local' foreign policy.

These arguments have been helpfully drawn together by Richard B. Bilder, and I rely heavily on his treatment in the following summary.[138] The arguments for keeping local government out of foreign policy matters include: (1) the vital national interest in the effective and efficient achievement of a national foreign policy requires that a nation 'speak with one voice' in order to ensure a unified and coherent approach; (2) local activities may directly impede, frustrate or embarrass dealings with foreign nations with adverse consequences; (3) local involvement is inconsistent with a democratic tradition that assumes a nation's foreign policy is determined by those elected by the nation as a whole, rather than by local politicians elected by far fewer people for other, more limited purposes; and (4) local government politicians and officials lack the expertise, information and resources to make sensible judgments about often complex issues of international relations.

The arguments in favour of local government involvement in matters of foreign affairs include: (1) reflecting changes in the world whereby the line between international, national, and local concern is less clear than in the past, and consequently local government has a greater role in promoting legitimate local concerns and giving voice to the views of their citizens on international and foreign policy issues of relevance and importance to them; (2) most of the local activities in question (selective procurement, nuclear free zones, sister city arrangements) do not have any direct or significant adverse impact on foreign governments or their citizens, and are unlikely to rebound on the national government (and if they do then the legislature can act); (3) local involvement in foreign policy strengthens democracy as local government is more accessible, responsive, and accountable to local citizens; and (4) the kinds of international matters that local governments involve themselves in do not require special expertise, and may serve as a healthy check on the national government or allow experimentation with innovative ideas.

How these countervailing arguments are weighed and with what result obviously will vary depending on the social, cultural, and legal histories of the society. As indicated above, the role local government has played in the United Kingdom varies greatly from that elsewhere in the Commonwealth. One can generalize from the Anglo-Commonwealth case law that the equivalents to Dillon's Rule tend to hide or at least obscure the policy arguments for and against an expanded role for local government. The formalism of this rule implies that it is apolitical when it is obviously not: it is directed at keeping local government in its place, and that is a very small place, bounded by territorial limits and focused on the physical needs of its inhabitants.

This can be seen clearly by contrasting dicta in two New Zealand cases, both uttered by Sir Ivor Richardson. In *Creednz Inc v. Governor-General*, Richardson J. said:[139]

> It is important to remember ... there is no universal rule as to the principles on which the exercise of a discretion may be reviewed: each statute or type of statute must be individually looked at. The willingness of the Courts to interfere with the exercise of discretionary decisions must be affected by the nature and subject-matter of the decision in question and by consideration of the constitutional role of the body entrusted by statute with the exercise of the power. Thus the larger the policy content and the more the decision-making is within the customary sphere of elected representatives the less well-equipped the Courts are to weigh the considerations involved and the less inclined they must be to intervene.

That case involved a challenge to an order-in-council, being the delegated legislative action of the governor-general-in-council (in effect, acting on the advice of cabinet). This is obviously at the top of the pyramid of government.

Almost without exception, over his long judicial career Sir Ivor Richardson favoured judicial restraint in administrative law.[140] The exceptional case was one involving local government. In *Mackenzie District Council v. Electricity Corporation of New Zealand*, Richardson J. delivered the judgment of the five-judge bench and set out the legal test that applied to local authorities:[141]

> As observed by Lord Templeman in *Hazell v. Hammersmith and Fulham London Borough Council* [1991] 1 All E.R. 545, 548:
>
> > 'A local authority, although democratically elected and representative of the area, is not a sovereign body and can only do such things as are expressly or impliedly authorized by Parliament.'
>
> In other words a local authority ... has only a subordinate role in our system of government. It is a statutory creation exercising the local and special purpose functions reposed in territorial authorities by Parliament. It is not to be viewed in high policy terms as the alter ego of central Government.
>
> Judicial review of the exercise of local authority powers is a standard and straightforward question of statutory interpretation. When exercising

> a statutory power a local authority must act within the powers conferred on it by Parliament and its rate-fixing decisions are amenable to review on the familiar *Wednesbury* grounds ...
>
> Rating authorities must observe the criteria laid down in the legislation. So they must call their attention to matters they are bound by the statute to consider and they must exclude considerations which on the same test are extraneous. And discretion is not absolute or unfettered. It is to be exercised to promote the policy and objectives of the statute. Even though the decision-maker has seemingly considered all relevant factors and closed its mind to the irrelevant, if the outcome of the exercise of the discretion is irrational or such that no reasonable body of persons could have arrived at the decision, the only proper inference is that the power itself has been misused.

Not surprisingly, given the tone of this passage, the local authority was held to have acted illegally, in breach of its fiduciary duty to all ratepayers, and unreasonably. Important, for my present purpose, is the absence of any deference to the elected representatives of the 'area.' They are not treated the same as elected members of the (national) Parliament, but are inferior in status, and so it seems the court can go in 'boots and all' on judicial review. Paradoxically, the (in)famous *Wednesbury* case is invoked by Richardson J.; as noted earlier, this local authority case is emblematic of judicial deference to elected local authorities.[142]

Mackenzie declared open season on local authority rate-making and, after a quick succession of successful challenges at first instance, the New Zealand Court of Appeal rapidly retreated to a highly deferential standard of review, and reinterpreted *Mackenzie* as an 'exceptional,' if not unique, case.[143]

My point here is that in the quotation from *Mackenzie's* case the court's formalistic mask slipped to reveal a condescending judicial attitude to local government. This attitude animates Dillon's Rule and its Anglo-Commonwealth equivalents.[144] While it holds sway, to contemplate the adoption and enforcement of 'local' foreign policy is unrealistic, to say the very least. And it does hold sway rather unthinkingly in the U.K. and New Zealand courts, and by a narrow margin only in Canada.

Globalization: Two-edged Sword

The very globalization that is said to be bringing cities to the fore is also constricting whatever ability they may have to fashion 'local' foreign policy that goes beyond the merely symbolic. Here, as elsewhere, globalization is a two-edged sword. Any room for local expression of political preferences on moral or ethical grounds that 'travel beyond the boundaries of any local authority area'[145] will increasingly run up against the neo-liberal economic international commitments made by their states. The outlawing of local authority anti-apartheid 'selective procurement' by U.K. statute noted earlier[146] was driven in part by the European Union directives on procurement, which require non-discrimination based on nationality and transparency in the award process. Since then, the advent of the World Trade Organization (WTO) and more ambitious international and regional trade treaties directed at government procurement have made the adoption of human rights-respecting procurement policies more difficult at best and impossible at worst.[147]

The most important treaty is the *Agreement on Government Procurement 1994* (*GPA*) administered by the WTO. There are also a number of procurement arrangements concerned with trade liberalization at the regional level. The EU directives have been noted already, and others include the *North American Free Trade Agreement* and Asia-Pacific Economic Co-operation Forum.[148]

The *GPA* came into effect on 1 January 1996. It is a plurilateral trade agreement and currently has about thirty signatories, including the United States, Canada, the EU, and Japan. Unlike its predecessor,[149] the *GPA* covers sub-national organs, including local government, if the contracting state has put them forward and the stipulated financial minima are met.[150] Many other countries, which are not signatories, oppose the *GPA* becoming a multilateral treaty (that would bind all 140 or so members of the WTO) on the ground that it would restrain their ability to use procurement to address non-trade issues, such as the environment, indigenous peoples, and human rights.

The concerns of those countries seem well founded. The *GPA* does not appear to leave much room for states (and its sub-national organs, including local government) to adopt human rights-respecting procurement policies.[151] Article 23 of the *GPA* permits discriminatory measures necessary to protect 'public morals, order or safety' and 'human ... life or health.' Respect for human rights does not fit easily here.[152]

The reaction to the 'selective procurement' policy directed against Myanmar shows the neo-liberal trade shoe pinching on the domestic U.S. legal system. By statute, the state of Massachusetts prohibited itself from contracting with corporations doing business with Myanmar. Ultimately the U.S. Supreme Court held that the Massachusetts statute was preempted or displaced by a federal law subsequently enacted on the same subject.[153] But this was not before two of America's closest trading partners, the EU and Japan, protested against the Massachusetts statute as a violation of the *GPA's* guarantee of non-discrimination on political grounds in the awarding of public contracts. Mediation failed to resolve the dispute, and the matter was set down for a hearing by a WTO dispute settlement panel in 1997. In the light of the *Crosby* litigation the hearing was first suspended and then ultimately abandoned.[154]

Conclusion

Local government law today is multi-layered and administrative law is only one layer. Local government politicians, officials, and practitioners often resent the restraints of administrative law, desiring to throw off the shackles of *vires* in order to enjoy the freedom of the fictitious legal person. So far, no legislature or court in the common law world has been willing to put local government on the private side of the hazy line between public and private law. Nevertheless, some legislatures have been willing to cut local government more slack in what it does and how it goes about its business, as demonstrated by the push for a power of general competence. The courts seem generally less willing to do so. When the real issues are addressed – and the U.K. cases discussed here show that it is easy to miss them altogether – the courts in Canada and New Zealand adopt local equivalents of Dillon's Rule. In other words, local government is to be kept very firmly in its place and within its geographic space. Local government is not conceived as constitutional in any sense.

Local government has long been recognized as providing an important buffer or intermediary role between the state and the individual. This was evident a century ago,[155] and was a key component of pluralistic thought in the first few decades of the twentieth century.[156] In the U.S. context, Jerry Frug has argued that proponents of city autonomy failed to make headway because of 'the continued liberal unwillingness to tolerate any intermediate entity that appears to threaten the interests of both the state and the individual.'[157] But the globalization literature insists that the state is besieged on all fronts, and that local authorities are simply one of many hoping to appropriate some of the state's supposedly disintegrating sovereignty in a globalizing world. It may be that cities have more involvement in international trade and the like nowadays, but it does not necessarily follow that they will be allowed to have more power to shape the course of international events. This turns ultimately on questions of administrative law.

NOTES

Thanks, with the usual caveat, for helpful comments from John Barratt, David Dyzenhaus, John Hopkins, Grant Huscroft, Benedict Kingsbury, Martin Loughlin and Janet McLean. Thanks also to Katy Nathan for research assistance.

1 Susan E. Clarke, 'The New Localism: Local Politics in a Global Era' in Edward G. Goetz and Susan E. Clarke, eds., *The New Localism: Comparative Urban Politics in a Global Era* (Newberry Park, CA: Sage Publications, 1993) at 1.
2 Something similar has been said about international law. See Peter J. Spiro, 'Globalization, International Law, and the Academy' (2000) 32 N.Y.U.J. Int'l L. & Pol. 567.
3 [1994] S.C.R. 231 [*Vancouver*].
4 See D.J. Mullan, 'The Role of the Judiciary in the Review of Administrative Law Policy Decisions: Issues of Legality' in Mary Jane Mossman and Ghislain Otis, eds., *The Judiciary as Third Branch of Government: Manifestations and Challenges to Legitimacy* (Montreal: Les Éditions Thémis, 2000) 313 at 314 [Mullan, 'Issues of Legality'].
5 David Mullan is to the last third of the twentieth century, in my view, what the pioneer Canadian administrative lawyer John Willis was to the middle third. See M. Taggart, 'Prolegomenon to an Intellectual History of Administrative Law in the Twentieth Century: The Case of John Willis and Canadian Administrative Law' (2005) 43 Osgoode Hall L.J. 223.
6 See R. Bigwood, ed., *Legal Method in New Zealand* (Wellington: Butterworths, 2001) and M. Taggart, 'The New Zealandness of New Zealand public law' (2004) 15 P.L.R. 81.
7 See Amnon Rubinstein, *Jurisdiction and Illegality* (Oxford: Oxford University Press, 1964) at 208.
8 See, e.g., *Vevers v. Mains* (1888), 4 T.L.R. 724 (Q.B.); *Baglan Bay Tin Plate Co. Ltd v. John* (1895), 72 L.J. 805; *R. v. The Assessment Committee of the Metropolitan Borough of Shoreditch, ex parte Morgan,* [1910] 2 K.B. 859 at 880 (per Farwell J.). Cf. D.M. Gordon, 'The Relation of Facts to Jurisdiction' (1929) 45 Law Q. Rev. 459 at 484–88.
9 T. Baldwin, 'The Territorial State' in Hyman Gross and Ross Harrison, eds., *Jurisprudence: Cambridge Essays* (Oxford: Clarendon Press, 1992) 207 at 209.

10 J.D.B. Mitchell, 'Constitutional Law' in *Then and Now, 1799–1974: Commemorating 175 Years of Law Bookselling and Publishing* (London: Sweet & Maxwell, 1974) 73 at 79.

11 See D. Fletcher, 'The Parish Boundary: A Social Phenomenon in Hanoverian England' (2003) 14 Rural History 177. See generally E. Halévy, 'Before 1835' in H.J. Laski, W.I. Jennings, and W.A. Robson, eds., *A Century of Municipal Progress: The Last Hundred Years* (London: Allen & Unwin Ltd, 1935) 15 [Laski et al., *Municipal Progress*].

12 See J. Hoppit, J. Innes, and J. Styles, 'Towards a History of Parliamentary Legislation, 1660–1800' (1994) 13 Parliamentary History 312.

13 J. Innes, 'The Local Acts of a National Parliament: Parliament's Role in Sanctioning Local Action in Eighteenth-Century Britain' (1998) 17 Parliamentary History 23 at 30.

14 John Prest, *Liberty and Locality: Parliament, Permissive Legislation, and Ratepayers' Democracies in the Nineteenth Century* (Oxford: Clarendon Press, 1990) at 5.

15 See e.g. N. McCord, 'Ratepayers and Social Policy' in Pat Thane, ed., *The Origins of British Social Policy* (London: Croom Helm, 1978) at 21.

16 See generally C.E. Allan, *The Rights of Local Authorities as regards Private Bills* (London: Shaw, 1900).

17 See generally M. Loughlin, 'The Demise of Local Government' in Vernon Bogdanor, ed., *The British Constitution in the Twentieth Century* (Oxford: published for the British Academy by Oxford University Press, 2004) 521 [Loughlin, 'Demise'].

18 *Roberts v. Hopwood,* [1925] A.C. 578 at 605 (H.L.). See John Willis, *The Parliamentary Powers of English Government Departments* (Cambridge, MA: Harvard University Press, 1933) at 55.

19 On the rise of the department, see B.B. Schaffer, 'The Idea of the Ministerial Department: Bentham, Mill and Bagehot' (1959) 5 Australian Journal of Politics and History 60, and Gillian Sutherland, ed., *Studies in the Growth of Nineteenth Century Government* (London: Routledge and Kegan Paul, 1972).

20 D.G.T. Williams, 'The Control of Local Authorities' in J.A. Andrews, ed., *Welsh Studies in Public Law* (Cardiff: University of Wales Press, 1970) 117 at 124.

21 See W. Ivor Jennings, 'Central Control' in Laski et al., *Municipal Progress, supra* note 11 at 417.

22 *Report of the Royal Commission on Local Government in England* (London: Her Majesty's Printing Office, Cmnd. 4040, 1969) at para. 27.

23 Andrew Saint, 'Swiping at Suburbs,' *London Review of Books* (31 March 2005) 30 at 32.

24 Loughlin, 'Demise,' *supra* note 17 at 530.

25 Gerald E. Frug, 'The City as a Legal Concept' (1980) 93 Harv. L. Rev. 1057 at 1062 [Frug, 'The City']. See also Hendrick Hartog, *Public Property and Private Power: The Corporation of the City of New York in American Law, 1730–1870* (Durham: University of North Carolina Press, 1983). For a challenge to the 'powerlessness' thesis, see Richard Briffault, 'Our Localism: Part I – The Structure of Local Government Law' (1990) 90 Colum. L. Rev. 1 [Briffault, 'Localism'].

26 See J.F. Dillon, *Treatise on the Law of Municipal Corporations*, 1st ed. (Chicago: Cockcroft, 1872) at 101–5. This book was extremely popular and went through new editions in 1873, 1881, 1890, and 1911, by which time it had grown to five volumes. See Clyde E. Jacobs, *Law Writers and the Court: The Influence of Thomas M. Cooley, Christopher G. Tiedeman and John F. Dillon upon American Constitutional Law* (Berkeley: University of California Press, 1954) at 111–12 and 190 n. 34; E.A. Gere, 'Dillon's Rule and the Cooley Doctrine: Reflections of the Political Culture' (1982) 8 Journal of Urban History 271; G.L. Clark, *Judges and the Cities: Interpreting Local Autonomy* (Chicago: University of Chicago Press, 1985).

27 See C.W. Took, 'Progress of Local Government 1836–1936' in *Law: A Century of Progress 1835–1935* (New York: New York University Press, 1937) vol. 2 at 105, and M.D. Gelfand, 'Comparative Reflections and Projections' in Martin Loughlin, M. David Gelfand, and Ken Young, eds., *Half a Century of Municipal Decline 1935–1985* (London: George Allen & Unwin, 1985) 232 [Loughlin *et al.*, *Municipal Decline*].

28 This is not to deny the heat in the discussion over whether or not 'Dillon's Rule' is still accepted as dominant in the United States. That is a larger topic than can be resolved here. I take the majority position in *Vancouver* (*supra* note 3) as affirming the equivalent doctrine in Canada, but our honorand has suggested that the law has moved on there too: Mullan, 'Issues of Legality,' *supra* note 4 at 336–38; David Mullan, 'Revisiting the Standard of Review for Municipal Decisions: When Is a Pile of Soil an "Erection"?' (1999–2000) 13 Can. J. Admin. L. & Prac. 319; David Mullan, 'Deference from *Baker* to *Suresh* and Beyond: Interpreting the Conflicting Signals' in David Dyzenhaus, ed., *The Unity of Public Law* (Oxford: Hart Publishing Ltd, 2004) 21 at 53–54.

29 See *Attorney-General v. Fulham Corporation*, [1921] 1 Ch. 440 (Ch.); *R. v. Somerset County Council, ex parte Fewings*, [1995] 3 All E.R. 20 at 25 (C.A.); *Takapuna City Council v. Auckland Regional Council*, [1972] N.Z.L.R. 705 at 711 (C.A.); *Hazell v. Hammersmith & Fulham London Borough Council*, [1991] 1 All E.R. 545 (H.L.); I.M. Rogers, *The Law of Canadian Municipal Corporations* (Tor-

onto: Carswell, 1997) at para. 63.31 [Rogers, *Municipal Corporations*]; K.A. Palmer, *Local Government Law in New Zealand*, 2nd ed. (Sydney: Law Book Company Ltd, 1993) at 47.

30 The classic early studies are F.J. Goodnow, *Municipal Home Rule: A Study in Administration* (New York: Columbia University Press, 1916) and Howard Lee McBain, 'The Doctrine of an Inherent Right of Local Self-Government' (1916) 16 Colum. L. Rev. 190 and 299 (2 Pts).

31 For a consideration of both the rhetoric and results in the cases, see Terrence Sandalow, 'The Limits of Municipal Power Under Home Rule: A Role for the Courts' (1963–64) 48 Minn. L. Rev. 643 at 661–8 [Sandalow, 'Home Rule'].

32 See William A. Robson, *The Development of Local Government* (London: Allen & Unwin, 1931) at 206–11, and I. Leigh, *Law, Politics, and Local Democracy* (Oxford: Oxford University Press, 2000) at 52–6 [Leigh, *Local Democracy*].

33 See e.g. *Local Government Act 2000* (U.K.), s. 2(1) (empowering local authorities to consider the economic, social or environmental well-being of their areas) and *Local Government Act 2002* (N.Z.), ss. 10–16 (promotion of social, economic, cultural, environmental and cultural well-being of communities in the present and the future). See also G. Hewison, 'A Power of General Competence – Should it be Granted to Local Government in New Zealand?' (2001) 9 Auckland U.L. Rev. 498, and Leigh, *Local Democracy, supra* note 32 at 56–66.

34 *Report of the Committee on the Management of Local Government* (London: H.M.S.O. 1967) at para. 283. See K. Young, 'Maud Committee (1964–67)' in John Ramsden, ed., *The Oxford Companion to Twentieth-Century British Politics* (Oxford: Oxford University Press, 2002) at 426. For a critique of each of the Maud Committee's complaints, see M. Loughlin, 'Administrative Law, Local Government and the Courts' in Loughlin et al., *Municipal Decline, supra* note 27, 121 at 137–40. See also R. Carnwarth, 'The Reasonable Limits of Local Authority Powers' [1996] P.L. 244 [Carnwarth, 'Reasonable Limits']. For similar complaints in the United States, see *Advisory Commission on Intergovernmental Relations, State Constitutional and Statutory Restrictions upon the Structural, Functional, and Personnel Powers of Local Authorities* (1962) 24, quoted by Briffault in *Localism, supra* note 25 at 8 n.11.

35 *R. v. Somerset County Council, ex parte Fewings,* [1995] 1 All E.R. 513 at 530 Q.B.) (Laws J.); aff'd by majority on a narrower point, [1995] 3 All E.R. 20 (C.A.) [*Fewings*].

36 An alternative, suggested by Thom Holterman, is 'municipal internationalization': 'Municipal Anti-Apartheid Policy and Dutch Constitutional Law' (1989) 1 R.E.D. Public 59 at 60.

37 I grew up in a landlocked borough of Auckland City that was declared by council resolution to be a 'nuclear-free zone.' No one challenged the validity of that resolution; indeed subsequently it became central government policy and is embedded in legislation (*New Zealand Nuclear Free Zone, Disarmament and Arms Control Act 1987* (N.Z.), No. 87). Such a measure was purely symbolic, however, as there were no nuclear weapons or nuclear-powered activities of any kind in the borough. Not so in Oakland, California, one of the hubs of the nuclear weapons industry in the 1980s, where the local residents voted in favour of a nuclear-free zone in 1988. The United States Department of Defense successfully challenged the constitutionality of this ordinance as it conflicted with federal legislation on the production and transportation of atomic energy and waste, and the federal power to conduct national defence. See *United States v. City of Oakland*, No. C89–3305 JPV (N.D. Cal. filed 23 August 1990)(memorandum of opinion and order granting Defense Department's motions for partial summary judgment), as discussed in C.W. Nevins, 'Note: The Constitutionality of Oakland's Nuclear Free Zone Ordinance' (1990) 18 Hastings Const. L.Q. 189. See also Luis Li, 'State Sovereignty and Nuclear Free Zones' (1991) 79 Cal. L. Rev. 1169 and G.C. Bennett, *The New Abolitionists: The Story of Nuclear Free Zones* (Elgin, IL: Brethren Press, 1987) chap. 7.

38 I have discussed these cases as part of a much broader treatment in 'The Impact of Apartheid on Commonwealth Administrative Law' (forthcoming in [2006] Acta Juridica), and here I draw freely and at times heavily on that paper. This paper was all but complete when Leighton McDonald of the Australian National University drew my attention to *Ex parte S.F. Bowser & Co; Re Municipal Council of Randwick* (1927), 27 S.R. (N.S.W.) 209 (F.C.). There the court invalidated a condition on a licence granted by a local authority to install petrol pumps that stipulated the pumps be made in Australia. The court said that a local preference for Australian-made goods 'was a matter of general concern and general interest to be dealt with by the legislature of the country, and not a body exercising limited powers of local government within a limited area' and held that 'it is no part of the functions of a local governing body to take upon itself deliberately to boycott, as far as it can within the area under its control, foreign traders who are lawfully here and who are carrying on a lawful business in a lawful way' (at 216). For the experience with 'Buy American' preference at the federal and state levels in the United States, see C.F. Corr and K. Zissis, 'Convergence and Opportunity: The WTO Government Procurement Agreement and U.S. Procurement Reform' (1999) 18 N.Y.L. Sch. J. Int'l & Comp. L. 303 at 319 [Corr and Zissis, 'Convergence'].

39 It has been said that this is a distinctive feature of the growth of economic

sanctions since the early 1990s: Gary Clyde Hufbauer and Barbara Oegg, 'Economic Sanctions: Public Goals and Private Compensation' (2003) 4 Chicago J. Int'l L. 305 at 317.

40 [1985] 1 A.C. 1054 (H.L.) [*Wheeler*].

41 For an excellent discussion of the agreement in context, see A. Payne, 'The International Politics of the Gleneagles Agreement' (1991) The Round Table (No. 320) 417 [Payne, 'Gleneagles'].

42 The communiqué is rather inaccessible. A copy is appended to Trevor Richards, *Dancing on Our Bones: New Zealand, South Africa, Rugby and Racism* (Wellington, NZ: Bridget Williams Books, 1999) 255–6 [Richards, *Dancing*]. It is quoted also in J.B. Elkind and A. Shaw, 'The Municipal Enforcement of the Prohibition against Racial Discrimination: A Case Study on New Zealand and the 1981 Springbok Tour' (1984) 55 Brit. Y.B. Int'l L. 189 at 191–92 [Elkind and Shaw, 'Case Study'].

43 See Payne, 'Gleneagles,' *supra* note 41. Trevor Richards, head of Halt All Racist Tours (HART), was concerned that 'Gleneagles had enough loopholes to drive a bus through': Richards, *Dancing*, *supra* note 42 at 184. Cf. Elkind and Shaw, 'Case Study,' *supra* note 42.

44 The case is not satisfying in one respect. It is never clear whether there was an annual contractual arrangement, which had simply not been renewed, or whether an existing long-term contractual arrangement was terminated or suspended for at least a year. It could be important in public law terms because the failure to renew an annual licence attracts procedural fairness through the doctrine of legitimate expectation, although there was no complaint on that ground here.

45 *R. v. Leicester City Council, ex parte Wheeler and others*, Queen's Bench Division, CO/1114/84, 27 September 1984, Forbes J.

46 This is the same methodology as employed in *Wednesbury*, except in *Wheeler* the promotion of race relations was an explicit mandatory relevant consideration, whereas the physical and moral well-being of the children was assumed to be implicitly mandatorily relevant in *Wednesbury*. See Michael Taggart, 'Reinventing Administrative Law' in Nicholas Bamforth and Peter Leyland, eds., *Public Law in a Multi-Layered Constitution* (Oxford: Hart Publishing Ltd, 2003) 311 at 317 [Taggart, 'Reinventing'].

47 *Wheeler*, *supra* note 40 at 1061.

48 Both Lords Roskill and Templeman made the point that Gleneagles had not been incorporated by statute into domestic law: ibid. at 1076 (Lord Roskill) and 1080 (Lord Templeman).

49 This point was made by McLachlin J. in her dissent in *Vancouver*, *supra* note 3 at 257.

50 *Wheeler*, *supra* note 40 at 1068 (Sir George Waller).

51 I say this knowing that at that time such action might well have been in breach of international law and the (then) unincorporated *European Convention on Human Rights*, but the U.K. Parliament could have done so. Moreover, it is only later that the prerogative power to issue and withdraw passports was held to be subject to judicial review, albeit on quite narrow grounds: *R. v. Secretary of State for Foreign and Commonwealth Affairs, ex parte Everett*, [1989] Q.B. 811. *Contra*, *Re Application by Mwau*, [1985] L.R.C. (Cons.) 444 (H.C., Kenya). The writ of *ne exeat regno* was sought unsuccessfully by a private citizen in *Parsons v. Burk*, [1971] N.Z.L.R. 244 (H.C.), where it was held that only the Crown had standing to seek the writ to stop nationals travelling abroad.

52 *Supra* note 48 and accompanying text.

53 *Wheeler*, *supra* note 40 at 1067 (Sir George Waller). Cf. at the central government department level: *Bradley v. Commonwealth of Australia*, (1972) 128 C.L.R. 557 at 58 (H.C.A.).

54 Teddy Roosevelt used this phrase at the start of the twentieth century to describe American foreign policy in relation to European expansion. See Nigel Rees, comp., *Cassell Companion to Quotations* (London: Cassell, 1997) at 460.

55 What is more, the majority expressly rejected the argument that the council was punishing the club for failing to endorse its views: *Wheeler*, *supra* note 40 at 1061 (Ackner L.J.) and 1067 (Sir George Waller).

56 See A. Hutchinson and M. Jones, '*Wheeler*-Dealing: An Essay on Law, Politics and Speech' (1988) 15 J.L. & Soc'y 263 at 271 [Hutchinson and Jones, '*Wheeler*-Dealing'].

57 *Wheeler*, *supra* note 40 at 1061.

58 Ibid. at 1065.

59 Accord, T.R.S. Allan, 'Racial Harmony, Public Policy and Freedom of Speech' (1986) 49 Mod. L.Rev. 121 at 122; Hutchinson and Jones, '*Wheeler*-Dealing,' *supra* note 56 at 264; Carnwarth, 'Reasonable Limits,' *supra* note 34 at 255; Martin Loughlin, *Legality and Locality: The Role of Law in Central-Local Government Relations* (Oxford: Clarendon Press, 1996) at 174.

60 *Wheeler*, *supra* note 40 at 1077.

61 Ibid. at 1078.

62 Ibid. at 1079.

63 Ibid.

64 He and Lord Roskill agreed with each other, and the other three Law Lords (Lords Bridge of Harwich, Brightman, and Griffiths) expressed agreement with both of them.

65 *Wheeler*, *supra* note 40 at 1080. The equation of freedom of speech for local

authorities with totalitarianism is simplistic. For a sophisticated and balanced approach to freedom of speech for government (national, state, and local) see Mark G. Yudof, *When Government Speaks: Politics, Law, and Government Expression in America* (Berkeley: University of California Press, 1983) chaps. 1–4 [Yudof, *Government Speaks*].

66 M. Bailey, *Shell and BP in South Africa*, 2nd ed. (London: Anti-Apartheid Movement/Haslemere Group Publication, 1978) at 6.

67 Even in 1989, when the General Assembly of the United Nations adopted a resolution on the oil embargo of South Africa by the largest majority ever: 139 votes for, 14 abstentions, and 2 against. The naysayers were the U.K. and the U.S., countries (headed respectively by Margaret Thatcher and Ronald Reagan) that were committed to a strategy of 'constructive engagement' with South Africa. See Shipping Research Bureau, 'Fuel for Apartheid: Oil Supplies to South Africa' (Amsterdam: Shipping Research Bureau, September 1990).

68 The classic study is A.J. Klinghoffer, *Oiling the Wheels of Apartheid: Exposing South Africa's Secret Oil Trade* (London: Lynne Reinner Publishing Inc, 1989).

69 Ibid. at 2, citing *Shell Out of Namibia and South Africa* (London: Anti-Apartheid Movement, August 1980) at 10. For more detailed justification, see J. Sindad, *Shell Shock: The churches and the oil embargo* (Geneva: World Council of Churches, 1989) at 13 and the Anti-Apartheid Movement, 'Shell Shadow Report,' 2nd rev. ed. (London: Anti-Apartheid Movement, 1987).

70 Klinghoffer, *Oiling the Wheels* at 9. For the American counterpart of the banks campaign, see D.R. Culverson, *Contesting Apartheid: U.S. Activism, 1960–1987* (Boulder, CO: Westview Press, 1999) chap. 6.

71 Apparently this caused some legal complications arising from a local authority's duty to act in the best financial interests of the ratepayers and to pursue investments with the highest possible return. See N. John, 'The Campaign against British Bank Involvement in Apartheid South Africa' (2000) 99 African Affairs 415 at 424 (by March 1985, fifteen British local authorities had closed accounts with Barclays Bank or adopted new policies on banking relations with South Africa). I know of only one case arising from this form of local authority protest and that concerned councillors' duties as trustees: *Martin v. City of Edinburgh District Council*, [1988] S.L.T. 329 (Outer House). For the position in the U.S., see generally Robert H. Jerry II and O. Maurice Joy, 'Social Investing and the Lessons of South Africa Disinvestment: Rethinking the Limitations on Fiduciary Discretion' (1987) 66 Or. L. Rev. 685.

72 *Local authority action against apartheid: A survey commissioned by the United Nations Centre against Apartheid* (Sheffield: Sheffield Metropolitan District

Council, on behalf of the National Steering Committee on Local Authority Action Against Apartheid, March 1985) at 9 [*Local authority action*].

73 Ibid. 9 and 27; *R. v. Lewisham London Borough Council, ex parte Shell UK Ltd*, [1988] 1 All E.R. 938 at 941 [*Lewisham*].

74 *Local authority action*, *supra* note 72 at 37.

75 Quoted in *Lewisham*, *supra* note 73 at 940.

76 Ibid.

77 Ibid. at 949.

78 Ibid. at 951.

79 Ibid. at 952.

80 Ibid. at 947.

81 *Fewings*, *supra* note 35 at 524.

82 See D.D. Caron, 'The Structure and Pathologies of Local Selective Procurement Ordinances: A Study of the Apartheid-Era South Africa Ordinances' (2003) 21 Berkeley J. Int'l L. 159 [Caron, 'Ordinances']; and Craig Forcese, 'Municipal Buying Power and Human Rights in Burma: The Case for Canadian Municipal "Selective Purchasing' Policies" (1998) 56 U.T. Fac. L. Rev. 251 [Forcese, 'Buying Power'].

83 *Local Government Act 1988* (U.K.), s. 17(e) and (f). See generally P.E. Morris, 'Legal Regulation of Contract Compliance: An Anglo-American Comparison' (1990) 18 Anglo-Am. L. Rev. 87 at 103.

84 [1994] 1 S.C.R. 231; (1991), 84 D.L.R. (4th) 157 (B.C.C.A., supplementary reasons); (1991), 81 D.L.R. (4th) 353 (B.C.C.A.); (1990), 70 D.L.R. (4th) 374 (B.C.S.C.) [*Vancouver*].

85 The resolution was not quoted in full at first instance, but it appears in the Court of Appeal judgment. The resolution went on to say 'that this motion be communicated to the federal government, local members of parliament and civic organizations, and they be encouraged to support and take similar action:' ibid. at 354 (B.C.C.A.).

86 This was stated in the preamble to the resolution: ibid. at 264.

87 Ibid. at 375, per Maczko J. (B.C.S.C.)

88 Ibid. at 378.

89 Ibid. at 377.

90 [1959] S.C.R. 121. See the contribution in this volume by David Dyzenhaus.

91 Ibid. at 142; quoted in *Vancouver*, *supra* note 84 at 379.

92 *Vancouver*, *supra* note 84 at 381.

93 Ibid. See Emily Chiang, 'Think Locally, Act Globally? Dormant Federal Common Law Preemption of State and Local Activities Affecting Foreign Affairs' (2003) 53 Syracuse L. Rev. 923 at 939 [Chiang, 'Think Locally'] (giving hypothetical scenarios less likely to be universally applauded than

anti-apartheid measures: e.g. 'selective procurement' policies against all Arab countries because they frequently perpetuate gender discrimination or against India for permitting arranged marriages or Ireland for limiting the availability of abortions).

94 The reasoning was as follows: (1) nothing in the city's constituent (provincial) legislation required it to buy goods by tender or explicitly limited the 'right' of the city to choose its suppliers; (2) a territorial 'limitation' on 'the city's commercial power' cannot be read out of the city's constituent legislation; (3) unless and until the provincial legislature places such a limitation in the legislation, and subject to the *Charter of Rights and Freedoms*, the city 'may decline, for any purpose whatsoever, to purchase goods and services from anyone whom it pleases to put, for political reasons, on its own collective blacklist.' Counsel for Shell obviously felt that the decision did not do justice to their submissions, as the Court of Appeal was requested to address and answer three submissions that had not been traversed in the first judgment. The British Columbia Court of Appeal issued 'supplementary reasons' responding to these three submissions: *Shell Canada Products Ltd v. City of Vancouver* (1981), 84 D.L.R. (4th) 157.

95 The majority consisted of Sopinka, La Forest, Cory, Iacobucci, and Major JJ. The minority consisted of McLachlin, L'Heureux-Dubé, Gonthier JJ., and Lamer C.J.

96 See generally Sue Arrowsmith, *Government Procurement and Judicial Review* (Toronto: Carswell, 1988) chap. 1 [Arrowsmith, *Government Procurement*].

97 Some uncertainty is caused by McLachlin J.'s statement that '[t]he City's refusal to do business with Shell, standing alone, is not attacked nor could it be. The City undoubtedly possesses a general power to buy its fuel from whomever it chooses. It is the reasons or motives for choosing not to deal with Shell that are attacked': *Vancouver supra* note 84 at 238. But as all council powers are statutory (as McLachlin J. recognizes: ibid. at 241), the power is necessarily limited from the outset by its delegated nature. It clouds the issue to cleave power to contract from motive in the way McLachlin J. does. The action/motive distinction also crops up later in her judgment in an unhelpful way: ibid. at 251–52.

98 Ibid. at 278.

99 Ibid. at 279.

100 Ibid.

101 Ibid. at 279–80.

102 Ibid. at 280–83. McLachlin J. disagreed: ibid. at 259–62.

103 Rogers, *Municipal Corporations*, *supra* note 29.

104 *Vancouver, supra* note 84 at 244.

105 Ibid. at 242–43.
106 Ibid. at 248.
107 Ibid. at 244.
108 Ibid.
109 Ibid. at 252.
110 Ibid.
111 The quoted phrase is from the resolution: ibid. at 264. In her judgment McLachlin J. relied heavily upon an article by Ann McDonald entitled 'In the Public Interest: Judicial Review of Local Government' (1983) 9 Queen's L.J. 62, at the start of which the Queen's law alumna 'gratefully acknowledges the patience and guidance of Professor David Mullan.'
112 Ibid. at 258.
113 Ibid. at 257–8.
114 Ibid. at 263.
115 *Fewings, supra* note 35 at 525, per Laws J. See also *Derbyshire County Council v. Times Newspaper Ltd.*, [1993] A.C. 534 (H.L.) (local authority has no right to maintain an action for defamation).
116 Yudof, *Government Speaks, supra* note 65 at 42–50.
117 *Vancouver, supra* note 84 at 256–8 (McLachlin J.) and 279 (Sopinka J.). See generally McDonald, 'In the Public Interest,' *supra* note 111 at 86–90 and Frug, 'The City,' *supra* note 25.
118 *Vancouver, supra* note 84 at 254 (McLachlin J.); (1991), 84 D.L.R. (4th) 157 at 159, per Southin J.A.
119 See *infra* notes 139–44 and accompanying text.
120 *Vancouver, supra* note 84 at 247–48.
121 *Associated Provincial Picture Houses Ltd v. Wednesbury Corporation*, [1948] 1 K.B. 223 (C.A.) [*Wednesbury*].
122 Cf. Forcese, 'Buying Power,' *supra* note 82. It is worth noting here that the City of Vancouver's resolution on Shell and apartheid South Africa was in line with that taken by the Mulroney government at the federal level and the Peterson government in Ontario. See D.R. Black, 'How Exceptional? Reassessing the Mulroney Government's Anti-Apartheid "Crusade"' in N. Michaud and K.R. Nossal, eds., *Diplomatic Departures: The Conservative Era in Canadian Foreign Policy, 1984–93* (Vancouver: UBC Press, 2001) at 173, and K.R. Nossal, ed., *Rain Dancing: Sanctions in Canadian and Australian Foreign Policy* (Toronto: University of Toronto Press, 1994) chap. 6 ('Federalism and International Sanctions: Ontario and South Africa'). See also Arrowsmith, *Government Procurement, supra* note 96 at 89.
123 *Vancouver, supra* note 84 at 272.
124 Nossal, *Rain Dancing, supra* note 122 at 113.

125 *Vancouver, supra* note 84 at 262 (McLachlin J.); (1991) 84 D.L.R. (4th) 157 at 159–60, per Southin J.A. (B.C.C.A.).

126 Ibid. at 272.

127 See e.g. Peter J. Spiro, 'Note: State and Local Anti-South Africa Action as an Intrusion upon the Federal Power in Foreign Affairs' (1986) 72 Va. L. Rev. 813 at 818.

128 Caron, 'Ordinances,' *supra* note 82 at 176. Caron points out that those involved had 'an interest in overstating both the number of ordinances and their impact.'

129 There are literally dozens of articles. Rather than give a long list here, the reader is referred to the smaller number of articles in my footnotes that contain exhaustive references.

130 See Lynn Berat, 'Undoing and Redoing Business in South Africa: The Lifting of the Comprehensive Anti-Apartheid Act of 1986 and the Continuing Validity of State and Local Anti-Apartheid Legislation' (1990–1) 6 Conn. J. Int'l L. 7, for the history and an analysis of the 1986 Act and the likely impact of its repeal on sub-federal anti-apartheid legislation.

131 See e.g. Erika Moritsugu, 'The Winding Course of the Massachusetts Burma Law: Subfederal Sanctions in Historical Context' (2002) 34 Geo. Wash. Int'l L. Rev. 435 [Moritsugu, 'Winding Course'], and Jennifer Loeb-Cederwall, 'Note: Restrictions on Trade with Burma: Bold Moves or Foolish Acts?' (1998) 32 New Eng. L. Rev. 929.

132 See F.N. Nesbitt, *Race for Sanctions: African Americans against Apartheid, 1946–1994* (Bloomington: Indiana University Press, 2004).

133 See Moritsugu, 'Winding Course,' *supra* note 131 at 449–53.

134 See *N.F.T.C. v. Crosby,* 530 U.S. 363 (2000) [*Crosby*].

135 Of the American writers, Peter Spiro has made much of the impact of globalization. See Peter Spiro, '*Crosby* as Way-Station' (2003) 21 Berkeley J. Int'l L. 146, and 'Globalization and the (Foreign Affairs) Constitution' (2002) 63 Ohio St. L.J. 649.

136 This point is well made in Chiang, 'Think Locally,' *supra* note 93 at 957–59.

137 See Sandalow, 'Home Rule,' *supra* note 31 at 646–48, and J. Weber, 'Local Government in the United States: Its Legal Status and Structure' (1984) 50 A.L.J. 723 at 723–24.

138 Richard B. Bilder, 'The Role of States and Cities in Foreign Relations' (1989) 83 Am. J. Int'l Law 821 at 827. Bilder is speaking to the U.S. situation but I have adapted his phraseology to the Anglo-Commonwealth context.

139 [1981] 1 N.Z.L.R. 172 at 197.

140 It will take more than a solitary footnote to substantiate this view, but see *Ashby v. Minister of Immigration*, [1981] 1 N.Z.L.R. 222; *Petrocorp Exploration*

Ltd v. Minister of Energy, [1991] 1 N.Z.L.R. 27 (Richardson J.'s dissent upheld by Privy Council); *Auckland Electric Power Board v. Electricity Corporation of New Zealand,* [1994] 1 N.Z.L.R. 551. Richardson J.'s approach was not followed by Privy Council: *Mercury Energy Ltd v. Electricity Corporation of New Zealand,* [1994] 2 N.Z.L.R. 385 (P.C).

141 [1992] 3 N.Z.L.R. 41 at 43 [*Mackenzie*].

142 *Wednesbury, supra* note 121. On a close and contextual reading of the case, however, the council in *Wednesbury* was actually acting in a counter-majoritarian fashion by imposing restrictive conditions on a cinema licence in order to frustrate the wishes of the majority of local body electors who had voted by poll for the opening of cinemas on Sunday. See Taggart, 'Reinventing,' *supra* note 46 at 315.

143 The retreat was sounded in *Wellington City Council v. Woolworths New Zealand Ltd,* [1996] 2 N.Z.L.R. 537 (C.A.), and *Waitakere City Council v. Lovelock,* [1997] 2 N.Z.L.R. 385 (C.A.). Richardson P. wrote the lead judgment in both cases.

144 See C.P. Gillette, 'In Partial Praise of Dillon's Rule, or, Can Public Choice Theory Justify Local Government Law' (1991) 67 Chicago-Kent L. Rev. 959 at 966.

145 *Fewings, supra* note 35 at 530.

146 *Supra* note 83 and accompanying text.

147 Just how tricky or proscriptive depends on the ideological stance of the commentator. See e.g. Christopher McCrudden, 'International Economic Law and the Pursuit of Human Rights: A Framework for Discussion of the Legality of 'Selective Purchasing' Laws under the WTO Government Procurement Agreement' (1999) 2 J. Int'l Econ. L. 3 [McCrudden, 'Economic Law'], and C. Forcese, 'Globalizing Decency: Responsible Engagement in an Era of Economic Integration' (2002) 5 Yale Human Rts. & Dev. L.J. 1 [Forcese, 'Globalizing Decency'].

148 See generally S. Arrowsmith, J. Linarelli, and D. Wallace, Jr., *Regulating Public Procurement: National and International Perspectives* (The Hague: Kluwer Law International, 2000).

149 There is an earlier agreement of more limited scope, in force since 1981, which was negotiated under the auspices of the General Agreement on Tariffs and Trade.

150 Corr and Zissisi, 'Convergence,' *supra* note 38 at 346.

151 See S. Arrowsmith, 'Public Procurement as an Instrument of Policy and the Impact of Market Liberalization' (1995) 111 L.Q.R. 235 at 270, 280 and 282–84.

152 See Forcese, 'Globalizing Decency,' *supra* note 147.

153 *Crosby, supra* note 134.

154 See Moritsugu, 'Winding Course,' *supra* note 131 at 467–9, and McCrudden, 'Economic Law,' *supra* note 147 at 23–8 for details. For the complicated background to the statutory implementation of the *GPA* by the United States, and the consequences that no state or local law can be challenged in the U.S. courts for incompatibility with the *GPA* (except by the U.S. attorney-general) and the president and Congress are not bound to compel a state or local authority to repeal any law even if a WTO dispute settlement panel finds such law to be inconsistent, see Robert J. Delahunty, 'Federalism beyond the Water's Edge: State Procurement Sanctions and Foreign Affairs' (2001) 37 Stan. J. Int'l L. 1 at 42 (discussing provisions of the *Uruguay Round Agreements Approval Act*, Pub. L. No. 103–464, 108 Stat. 4809 (1994)).

155 See G.C. Broderick, 'Local Government in England' in J.W. Probyn, ed., *Local Government and Taxation in the United Kingdom*, 2nd ed. (London: Cassell Petter Galpin & Co., 1882) at 87 (local government as an intermediate between the state and the individual citizen), discussed in J. Palmowski, 'Liberalism and Local Government in Late Nineteenth-Century Germany and England' (2002) 45 Historical Journal 381 at 389.

156 See D. Kavanagh, 'British political science in the inter-war years: the emergence of the founding fathers' (2003) 5 British Journal of Politics and International Relations 595, and more generally, A. Sanction, 'British Socialist Theories of the Division of Power by Area' (1976) 24 Political Studies 158.

157 Frug, 'The City,' *supra* note 25 at 1116.

Judicial Review from *CUPE* to *CUPE*: Less Is Not Always More

GRANT HUSCROFT

Respect for the decisions of administrative tribunals is a recurring theme of David Mullan's work. From the outset he championed the decision of the Supreme Court of Canada in *CUPE Local 963 v. New Brunswick Liquor Corporation*,[1] which heralded the adoption of a deferential approach to judicial review. The message from *CUPE* was clear: when it came to judicial review of the decisions of expert administrative tribunals, less was more.

Curial deference made sense in the context of *CUPE v. New Brunswick* – ambiguous legislation, a specialized labour relations tribunal designed to administer it, and a privative clause purporting to immunize that tribunal's decisions from judicial review – but the way forward was not clear. There were bound to be harder cases in which the apparently all-or-nothing choice between reviewing jurisdictional questions for correctness and letting decisions made within jurisdiction stand unless they were 'patently unreasonable' would not be attractive.[2] As a result, *CUPE v. New Brunswick* was subject to a process of continued development and refinement over the years as a succession of Supreme Court justices put their stamp on it, culminating in the 'pragmatic and functional approach.'[3] Through all of the change, one of the few constants was David Mullan. He understood and respected the administrative state, and tried to keep the Court true to the message of restraint Justice Dickson articulated in *CUPE v. New Brunswick*. And more than anyone else, he has been relied on by the Court as it has developed a uniquely Canadian body of law governing judicial review of substantive decisions.[4]

The basic components of that body of law are now well established:[5] there are three standards of review – correctness, reasonableness *sim-*

pliciter, and patent unreasonableness – and the choice of the standard to apply to a particular decision depends upon several factors enumerated in *Pushpanathan v. Canada (Minister of Citizenship and Immigration)*:[6]

1. Whether or not there is a privative clause, and whether it is a 'full' or a 'partial' or equivocal clause – that is, whether it purports to preclude judicial review or allow it in a limited form;
2. The relative expertise of the decision maker and the court;
3. The purpose of the legislation, and of the relevant provision in particular; and
4. The nature of the problem, and in particular whether it is one of law, fact, or a mixed question.

The problematic concept of jurisdiction that informed the Court's approach in *CUPE v. New Brunswick* was relegated to mere descriptive status in *Pushpanathan*. 'Jurisdictional' is now simply a label for a legislative provision that, following the application of the pragmatic and functional approach, a court determines must be answered correctly.[7]

The pragmatic and functional approach does not apply with precision, even assuming that courts apply it dutifully.[8] It is simply a means of structuring the discourse on deference. None of the *Pushpanathan* factors is determinative of the appropriate standard of review, nor does any particular combination of those factors require that one standard be employed rather than another. Nor does the pragmatic and functional approach mandate a single standard of review for particular statutes: different provisions of the same statute may be subject to different standards of review. In other words, the pragmatic and functional approach contemplates that decision-makers may receive greater deference in interpreting some provisions in a statute than others. Plainly, there is room for reasonable disagreement about the application of the approach, so it is not surprising that the decisions of trial courts are often overturned by provincial appellate courts. For its part, the Supreme Court of Canada continues to hear a significant number of standard of review cases annually, but no matter how many times the lower courts are 'corrected' – no matter how many times the Supreme Court purports to clarify deference doctrine – problems remain. The path of least resistance for trial court judges (and administrative law students at exam time) is to select reasonableness *simpliciter* as the default position. Better to be slightly wrong than *very* wrong, which is possible when patent unreasonableness or correctness is chosen as the test.

Twenty-seven years after *CUPE*, then, judicial review remains difficult. The Supreme Court's decision to collapse a number of historical distinctions and render all administrative decisions subject to the pragmatic and functional approach – whether subject to appeal or ostensibly final, and whether involving the interpretation of legislation or the exercise of a discretionary power – further complicates an already complicated picture. Justice Iacobucci, whose decision established the intermediate 'reasonableness *simpliciter*' review standard, asserted that ' [a] pragmatic and functional approach should not be unworkable or highly technical,'[9] but this is wishful thinking. As David Mullan has observed, 'while the theory is relatively simple, its implementation or realization has been anything but easy.'[10]

Consider some recent cases. In *Moreau-Berube v. New Brunswick (Judicial Council),*[11] the Supreme Court upheld the decision of a judicial council recommending the removal of a provincial court judge on the basis that the decision was not patently unreasonable, whereas the New Brunswick Court of Appeal had quashed the decision for jurisdictional error. In *Ryan,*[12] the Supreme Court upheld the decision of a provincial law society disbarring a solicitor on the basis that it was not unreasonable, whereas the New Brunswick Court of Appeal had overturned the decision because it was not reasonable. In *Dr. Q. v. College of Physicians and Surgeons of British Columbia*[13] a trial judge employed a correctness standard without first applying the pragmatic and functional approach, and overturned the decision of a medical disciplinary committee suspending a doctor. The trial judge's decision was upheld by the British Columbia Court of Appeal, which also failed to apply the pragmatic and functional approach. The Supreme Court applied that approach, held that the disciplinary committee's decision was subject to review for reasonableness *simpliciter* rather than correctness, and concluded that the committee's decision was not unreasonable. These cases, among many others, suggest that the temptation for lower courts to interfere with the decisions of specialist administrative tribunals remains strong, no matter how the standard of review analysis is structured.[14]

The Supreme Court has been praised for the message of restraint it has reiterated in these cases. But the Court has also been praised for its decision in *Baker v. Canada,* in which it weighed in on the exercise of ministerial discretionary power.[15] Justice L'Heureux-Dubé's decision extended the pragmatic and functional approach to include the exercise of discretionary powers in *Baker* on the basis that traditional doctrine – which limited review of discretionary decisions to specific abuse of discretion tests such as bad faith, improper purposes, and relevant/irrelevant considerations – was based on an inaccurate assumption of a dichotomy between discretionary and non-discretionary decisions. That dichotomy was inaccurate, L'Heureux-Dubé J. said, because '[m]ost administrative decisions involve the exercise of implicit discretion in relation to many aspects of decision making.'[16]

Extension of the pragmatic and functional approach in *Baker* was not supposed to result in more invasive judicial review of discretionary powers. On the contrary, L'Heureux-Dubé J. emphasized that deference was to remain the watchword:[17]

> Incorporating judicial review of decisions that involve considerable discretion into the pragmatic and functional analysis for errors of law should not be seen as reducing the level of deference given to decisions of a highly discretionary nature. In fact, deferential standards of review may give substantial leeway to the discretionary decision-maker in determining the 'proper purposes' or 'relevant considerations' involved in making a given determination. The pragmatic and functional approach can take into account the fact that the more discretion that is left to a decision-maker, the more reluctant courts should be to interfere with the manner in which decision-makers have made choices among various options. However, though discretionary decisions will generally be given considerable respect, that discretion must be exercised in accordance with the boundaries imposed in the statute, the principles of the rule of law, the principles of administrative law, the fundamental values of Canadian society, and the principles of the *Charter*.

Nevertheless, subsequent to *Baker* many argued for an expansion of the ambit of judicial review, often in attempts to impede or even preclude the implementation of political decisions. The Conservative government of Ontario Premier Mike Harris (1995–2003) was often subject to judicial review applications brought by unions and political organizations opposed to its Common Sense Revolution.[18]

That recourse to judicial review should prove to be popular when the courts are perceived as more progressive than governments should come as no surprise: any port in a storm. But the courts must be careful not to interfere with the exercise of discretionary power on the basis of hostility to the policies being pursued, or to particular policy outcomes. The perception that courts were interfering on these bases was, after all, the problem that gave rise to deference theory in the first place, albeit in the context of quasi-judicial tribunals rather than the political executive. The case for deference is different when it comes to the exercise of executive power, but it is no less strong. Indeed, courts must be aware of an additional concern that does not arise in the context of quasi-judicial tribunals: the importance of recognizing and respecting not only institutional roles but also political roles. Judicial review is no substitute for political accountability – no *legitimate* substitute, that is – however imperfect political accountability may appear.

A recent case involving CUPE, *CUPE v. Ontario (Minister of Labour)*,[19] provides a useful backdrop for a discussion of these concerns. The Supreme Court's decision has, for the most part, been approved if not praised by distinguished commentators, including our honorand.[20] In my view, however, the case reveals real difficulties with the pragmatic and functional approach, and in particular with the application of that approach to the exercise of discretionary powers.

CUPE v. Ontario (Minister of Labour)

CUPE v. Ontario arose in the context of Ontario's *Hospital Labour Disputes Arbitration Act*,[21] a statute governing collective bargaining in the health care sector. Like private sector employees, hospital employees are free to unionize under the *Labour Relations Act 1995*.[22] Unlike other employees covered by that act, however, hospital employees do not have the right to strike, nor can they be locked out by their employers. In the event that hospitals and their employees are unable to negotiate a collective agreement, the *HLDAA* requires that a collective agreement be imposed by binding arbitration.

This sort of arbitration, called interest arbitration, must be distinguished from rights or grievance arbitration, which resolves disputes concerning the interpretation or application of extant collective agreements. Interest arbitration determines the *contents* of a collective agreement – typically, but not exclusively, the wage rate – and its substitution for the right to strike and lock-out is standard Canadian practice in labour relations legislation governing essential services. Interest arbitration boards are usually tripartite: union and management each nominate one representative to the arbitration board, and those representatives nominate a third person to chair the board. In the event that the parties' representatives cannot agree on the appointment of a neutral chairperson, the minister of labour is required to make the appointment pursuant to section 6(5) of the *HLDAA*:

> Where the two members appointed by or on behalf of the parties fail within ten days after the appointment of the second of them to agree upon the third member, notice of such failure shall be given forthwith to the Minister by the parties, the two members or either of them and the Minister shall appoint a third person who is, *in the opinion of the Minister*, qualified to act. [emphasis added]

Section 7 of the *HLDAA* purports to shield the appointment of arbitration boards from judicial review by establishing a conclusive presumption of validity, protected by a privative clause:

> Where a person has been appointed as a single arbitrator or the three members have been appointed to a board of arbitration, it shall be presumed conclusively that the board has been established in accordance with this Act and no application shall be made, taken or heard for judicial review or to question the establishment of the board or the appointment of the member or members, or to review, prohibit or restrain any of its proceedings.

For some years, arbitrators considered broadly acceptable to both union and management had been appointed by the minister. In the main, they were appointed from a list of established grievance arbitrators maintained by the Ministry of Labour, and appointments were usually made by a public servant rather than the minister personally. The Harris government proposed to reform the public sector arbitration process, but its proposals were opposed by the various unions and the minister of labour indicated that the old systems would remain in place. CUPE sought assurances that arbitrators appointed under the *HLDAA* would be acceptable to them, but received no such assurance from the minister. Subsequently, the minister appointed several retired judges to act as arbitrators under the *HLDAA*, and CUPE sought judicial review.[23]

CUPE v. Ontario is in some ways a simple case, but like so many judicial review cases it quickly becomes complicated. It began as a claim that the union had been denied procedural fairness, and the union was victorious in the Ontario Court of Appeal on this basis. The union held on to its victory in the Supreme Court of Canada, but only because that court was willing to recharacterize its argument in terms of an abuse of discretion by the minister, a claim the union had not made. The complicated nature of the decision is the giveaway that all is not well here. The outcome of the case – a finding that the minister's decision to appoint retired judges as arbitrators was patently unreasonable – is anything but obvious, and requires a lengthy explanation.

CUPE's Application for Judicial Review

CUPE's application for judicial review raised several procedural objections to what it perceived as a new appointment system. Among other things, the union claimed that the appointment of judges undermined the impartiality and independence of the appointment and decision-making process under *HLDAA*; that the appointment of judges breached representations that appointments would be made in accordance with the prior practice; that failure to make appointments in accordance with that practice breached CUPE's legitimate expectation; and that the minister's personal involvement in the appointment process gave rise to a reasonable apprehension of bias and interfered with the independence and impartiality of arbitration boards appointed under the *HLDAA*.[24]

All of these complaints flowed from the fact that the minister of labour was not a disinterested party in the arbitration system. The minister of labour's colleague, the minister of health, funds the relevant institutions, and health is a significant component of government spending.[25] Thus, changes to the arbitration system that inure to the benefit of employers inure to the benefit of the government. The union believed that retired judges were likely to render decisions favourable to employers.

The Divisional Court gave the union's application short shrift, concluding that the *HLDAA* authorized the minister to appoint arbitrators and, in the absence of a constitutional violation, that was that.[26] CUPE succeeded in the Court of Appeal,[27] however, and Austin J.A. was scathing in his criticism of the minister's conduct. In his view, the minister had abandoned an established practice of appointing mutually acceptable arbitrators and unilaterally adopted a new practice of appointing retired judges. This, he held, gave rise to a reasonable apprehension of bias, as well as an appearance of interference with the institutional independence and impartiality of boards of arbitration appointed under the act. The minister's actions, he said, 'must reasonably be seen as an attempt to seize control of the bargaining process.'[28] In addition, Austin J.A. concluded that the union had a legitimate expectation that the existing appointing system would continue. It was entitled to notice of the minister's intention to change the system, as well as an opportunity to make submissions and possibly an opportunity to be heard in person.[29] The court issued declarations to this effect and made an order in the nature of prohibition, barring the minister from appointing anyone other than arbitrators who were considered mutually acceptable.[30]

CUPE *in the Supreme Court*

The Supreme Court unanimously rejected all the procedural fairness arguments that were accepted by the Ontario Court of Appeal. Writing for the Court on this aspect of the case, Binnie J. reiterated the traditional distinction between matters of process and substance. On the procedural aspect of the case, he held that the minister's interest in the outcome of the arbitration process could not bar him from exercising his statutory power. This did not mean that there was no room for procedural fairness to operate, but Binnie J. held that if there were a duty to consult prior to changing the appointment process it had been satisfied, and that there was no duty to consult in regard to appointment of arbitrators to particular cases in any event. Furthermore, he held that the union had no legitimate expectation. There was no firm practice of appointing arbitrators exclusively from the list of grievance arbitrators, or appointing only pursuant to mutual agreement, and the minister's promise 'to continue under the existing system' – a system that was ambiguous and, as the minister had said, was subject to reform – could not bind the minister's exercise of discretion. In short, CUPE's case was routed.[31]

Ordinarily that would have been the end of the matter, for the union had argued the case solely as a procedural fairness violation.[32] However, a majority of the Court (Bastarache J., McLachlin C.J., and Major J. dissenting) concluded that although the minister's decision had been made fairly it was, nevertheless, a patently unreasonable exercise of the minister's appointment power. Writing for the majority, Binnie J. began by noting that while the challenge was to the minister's exercise of the appointment power conferred under section 6(5) of the *HLDAA*, that power was only one feature of the act, which had to be read as a whole. Quoting Rand J.'s much-admired decision in *Roncarelli v. Duplessis*,[33] Binnie J. observed that although the minister's power to appoint is discretionary in nature, 'there is always a perspective within which a statute is intended to operate.'[34] It is worth returning to *Roncarelli* before considering Binnie J.'s application of the principle it establishes.

Roncarelli's *Legacy*

The facts of *Roncarelli* are notorious. Mr Roncarelli acted as surety for Jehovah's Witnesses arrested for distributing literature critical of the Quebec government, in contravention of a municipal bylaw. Acting on 'advice' from Premier Duplessis (who was also the attorney general),[35] the Quebec Liquor Commission purported to exercise its discretionary power not only to cancel Roncarelli's restaurant licence but also to preclude him from ever obtaining another licence. Rand J.'s statement that 'there is always a perspective within which a statute is intended to operate' rebutted the argument that the exercise of discretion in the licensing process was beyond judicial review. The key passage in Rand J.'s judgment is as follows:[36]

> In public regulation of this sort there is no such thing as an absolute and untrammeled 'discretion,' that is that action can be taken on any ground or for any reason that can be suggested to the mind of the administrator; no legislative Act can, without express language, be taken to contemplate an unlimited arbitrary power exercisable for any purpose, however capricious or irrelevant, regardless of the nature or purpose of the stature. Fraud and corruption in the Commission may not be mentioned in such statutes but they are always implied as exceptions. 'Discretion' necessarily implies good faith in discharging public duty; there is always a perspective within which a statute is intended to operate; and any clear departure from its lines or objects is just as objectionable as fraud or corruption. Could an applicant be refused a permit because he had been born in another province, or because of the colour of his hair? The ordinary language of the legislature cannot be so distorted.

Rand J. was careful to acknowledge that there were limits to the Court's powers on judicial review; unlimited arbitrary power exercisable for any purpose could not be inferred *without express language*. The suggestion is that, in the absence of a constitutional violation, the Court would give effect even to arbitrary power, provided only that it were conferred in explicit terms.

Here Rand J. acknowledged what was clear in 1959: parliamentary sovereignty. Parliament could make or unmake any law, however objectionable its decision may be.[37] The examples he used to illustrate the limits courts would impose upon the exercise of discretionary power are telling. No one could be denied a liquor licence, Rand J. wrote, because he was born in another province, or because of the colour of his hair. These are, of course, examples with which no reasonable person could disagree.[38] But what about examples that are not so extreme? This is, in short, the problem posed by *CUPE v. Ontario*.

CUPE *versus* Roncarelli

CUPE v. Ontario is miles away from the sort of examples Rand J. mentioned in *Roncarelli*, let alone the facts of that case. Consider the relevant differences.

The minister's appointment power in *CUPE v. Ontario* was not simply discretionary in nature. The *HLDAA* empowers the minister to appoint as an arbitrator anyone who, *in the opinion of the Minister*, was qualified to act. Here, then, is a discretionary power conferred in broad subjective terms. Recognizing that there is room for differences of opinion as to the qualifications of an arbitrator, the legislature made clear that the minister's opinion was the only one that mattered. In contrast, the discretionary power relied on by the Liquor Commission in *Roncarelli* did not contemplate the relevance of opinion, and the premier had no decision-making authority in any event. *Roncarelli* is a classic example of bad faith and abuse of power; no proper purpose was asserted in revoking Roncarelli's licence and none could have been. Moreover, it was an easy case – indeed, a rare case – because the defendant made no attempt to hide the wrongful motivation for his actions. Premier Duplessis acted as a law unto himself, confident that he need not answer to the courts. In essence, he answered Roncarelli's complaint by asking: 'So what?'[39]

In contrast, the minister of labour's decision to appoint retired judges in *CUPE v. Ontario* addressed what Binnie J. acknowledged was a relevant labour relations consideration: problems of delay and cost associated with *HLDAA* arbitration. The minister had sought to appoint '[p]eople who had spent their entire professional lives as neutrals.'[40] That was certainly a policy the minister was entitled to pursue. It may not have been *wise* from a labour relations standpoint to appoint retired judges as arbitrators; certainly, their appointment was deprecated by the expert witness.[41] But it cannot be said that the minister's decision to appoint retired judges was an act of bad faith or an abuse of power. It is not as though the minister appointed only red-haired arbitrators.[42]

Roncarelli establishes that 'there is always a perspective within which a statute is intended to operate,' but the extent to which the courts can constrain the exercise of discretionary power is, of course, contestable. The rule of law premises that justify judicial intervention to constrain the exercise of discretionary power go only so far: at some point, the legislative decision to empower the executive to make discretionary decisions must be respected. Disagreement over where this point lies is the nub of the problem in *CUPE v. Ontario*.

Inferring Fetters on Broad Discretionary Powers: Legislative History and Purpose[43]

Binnie J. grounds his decision in orthodox statutory interpretation principle: '[T]he words of an Act are to be read in their entire context and in their grammatical and ordinary sense harmoniously with the scheme of the Act, the object of the Act, and the intention of Parliament.'[44] He pays little attention to the terms of the appointment power or the privative clause, and the plain meaning of these provisions is downplayed in favour of an extensive review of the history of the *HLDAA*. Binnie J. noted that 'history, including excerpts from the legislative record, is admissible as relevant to the background and purpose of the legislation.'[45]

Until recently, however, legislative history has played a limited role in Canadian courts. In *R. v. Morgentaler*,[46] Sopinka J. held that '[p]rovided the court remains mindful of the limited reliability and weight of Hansard evidence it should be admitted as relevant to both the background and the purpose of the legislation.'[47] There, it will be recalled, history was invoked in support of arguments that the provincial legislation regulating abortion under the guise of health care was really a colourable attempt to pass criminal law, a matter of federal jurisdiction. Subsequently, in *Re Rizzo & Rizzo Shoes Ltd*[48] the Court 'recognized that [legislative history] can play a limited role in the interpretation of legislation.'[49] Although Binnie J. refers to the more limited use contemplated in *Morgentaler* – as an aid to discovering the background and purpose of legislation – he uses the legislative history for the more significant purpose of reading-in considerations into the act in order to limit the minister's discretionary appointment power:[50]

> I conclude, therefore, that, although the s. 6(5) power is expressed in broad terms, the legislature intended the Minister, in making his selection, to have regard to relevant labour relations expertise as well as independence, impartiality and general acceptability within the labour relations community ... I do not mean that a particular candidate must be acceptable to all

parties all the time, or to the parties to a particular HLDAA dispute. I mean only that the candidate has a track record in labour relations and is generally seen in the labour relations community as widely acceptable to both unions and management by reason of his or her independence, neutrality and proven expertise.

The problem here is not that Binnie J.'s interpretation is nonsensical, or even unwise. Indeed it seems sensible, but that is beside the point.[51] The Court's job is to ensure that the minister has exercised his power in conformity with the requirements of the *HLDAA*. Given that the act provides that the qualifications of arbitrators are for the *minister* to determine *in his opinion* and that the minister's appointment decision is protected by a privative clause, Binnie J.'s sensible interpretation of the act takes on a different complexion. In inferring fetters on the minister's discretion prior to establishing and applying the appropriate standard of review – fetters that are jurisdictional in nature – Binnie J. renders the concept of deference practically irrelevant. As we will see, even the most deferential standard of review will not protect the minister's decision.

Binnie J.'s interpretation seems to follow David Dyzenhaus's suggestion (echoing Dworkin) that deference as respect (rather than submission)[52] 'requires of judges that they determine the intention of the statute, not in accordance with the idea that there is some prior (positivistic) fact of the matter, but in terms of the reasons that best justify having that statute.'[53] Dyzenhaus says that judges must eschew policy considerations in deciding questions of law; such questions must be answered 'on the basis of which decision as to the law is best justified by the principles immanent within the law.'[54] But how are these principles to be determined and, more important, why is it the task of judges to determine them? Dyzenhaus assumes that it is for the court to determine, on such bases as judges consider appropriate, but it is not obvious why this is so. What allows courts to read language into a statute, and how far can they go in doing so?

This is an old problem, not unique to administrative law. Lon Fuller addressed the issue, speaking through Judges Foster and Keen in their debate about purposive interpretation in 'The Case of the Speluncean Explorers.'[55] What Judge Foster regarded as 'intelligent fidelity' in that case – giving the words of a statute a meaning 'not at once apparent to the casual reader who has not studied the statute closely or examined the objectives it seeks to obtain'[56] – Judge Keen considered illegitimate judicial reform.[57]

Randal Graham describes cases like *CUPE v. Ontario* as a problem of 'subtext,' which suggests the need for a cautious approach. Courts must give effect to what is 'necessarily implied' in legislation as well as what is set out expressly, but only so far as is required in order to avoid absurd interpretations or internal contradictions.[58] On Graham's approach, it is easy to see how *Roncarelli* is justified, but much harder to see how the same can be said of *CUPE v. Ontario*. The *HLDAA* is not absurd in the absence of the criteria Binnie J. infers, nor is it internally inconsistent. Binnie J.'s interpretation may well make the *HLDAA* a better act, but the act is not the Court's to remake. This is what Bastarache J. has in mind, I think, when he describes the case for inferring the criteria as 'affirmations and aspirations,' coming 'nowhere near the evidentiary threshold for imposing a specific restriction on the wide discretion set out in s. 6(5).'[59] Bastarache J. was unimpressed that prior ministers of labour have operated under the criteria Binnie J. inferred. However sensible they may be, past practice could not elevate them to the level of regulatory prescription.[60]

It is easy to accept that ostensibly wide discretionary powers should in some way be fettered in order to preclude the arbitrary exercise of power. It is more difficult to discern how far it is legitimate for courts to go in inferring those fetters. At the end of the day, there is a considerable difference between declaring what *cannot* be taken into account, as in *Roncarelli*, and declaring what *must* be taken into account, as in *CUPE v. Ontario*. Considerations that cannot be taken into account may be so obvious as to go without saying – especially in a case of obvious bad faith, like *Roncarelli*[61] – but considerations that must be taken into account will usually be contestable.[62] One would expect that mandatory relevant considerations – considerations that not only must be taken into account but be acted upon – would have to meet the highest threshold, but *CUPE v. Ontario* demonstrates that this is not necessarily so.

Choosing and Applying the Appropriate Standard of Review

The hard part on an application for judicial review is usually deciding on the appropriate standard of review and, hence, how invasive judicial scrutiny will be. In this case, however, there was no difficulty. All the factors in *Pushpanathan* pointed to one standard, thus the Court was unanimous in concluding that the minister's decision was entitled to the utmost deference. The Court could interfere only if it could be shown that the minister's decision to appoint retired judges was patently unreasonable.

That should have been an insurmountable hurdle for CUPE. After all, how could it be said that the appointment of retired judges was 'evidently not in accordance with reason,'[63] or that it was 'so flawed that no amount of curial deference can justify letting it stand'?[64] Or, as Binnie J. put it in applying the patently unreasonable standard in another context, how could it be said that the minister's decision to appoint retired judges as arbitrators was 'irrational or perverse ... "so gratuitous and oppressive that no reasonable person could think [it] justified"'?[65]

These and other articulations of the patent unreasonableness standard emphasize the obvious wrongness of a decision in a *Wednesbury* sense.[66] In *CUPE v. Ontario*, however, Binnie J. describes a patently unreasonable decision as one whose defect is 'immedia[te] and obvious[s], *and so flawed in terms of implementing the legislative intent* that no amount of curial deference can properly justify letting it stand.'[67] The decision to appoint retired judges could not possibly be considered *Wednesbury*-unreasonable. Indeed, it can only be considered an abuse of the minister's discretionary appointment power after a great deal of prior interpretation has occurred, and jurisdictional fetters have been inferred.[68]

Given the nature of those fetters, Binnie J.'s remarks eschewing the reweighing of considerations are irrelevant. The problem is not a failure to take them into account, or to afford them the correct weight. The considerations are in the nature of mandatory relevant considerations, and any appointment decisions not taken in accordance with them must be patently unreasonable on Binnie J.'s account.[69]

In my view, the notion that the minister of labour was not alive to the labour relations considerations at stake is simply implausible. The minister knew exactly what was at stake, having gone through lengthy and difficult consultations with unions over the *HLDAA* arbitration process. In choosing to exercise his discretionary power as he did, he knew he was buying a fight with the union, and would have expected political consequence. He would not have expected legal consequences, however, and no doubt was so advised.[70]

It is worth recalling Rand J.'s words from *Roncarelli*: '"Discretion" necessarily implies good faith in discharging public duty; there is always a perspective within which a statute is intended to operate; and any clear departure from its lines or objects is just as objectionable as fraud or corruption.'[71] For Rand J., the failure to operate within the parameters of a conferral of discretion was tantamount to fraud or corruption. This is not the sort of conclusion that should be reached lightly, and so Rand J. emphasized that departure from the statutory purpose had to be *clear*.

The problem in *CUPE v. Ontario* is that the departure from statutory purpose is not clear. The departure from practice of prior ministers *is* clear, but this should be irrelevant, especially given that the union knew the minister was unhappy with that practice and was contemplating change.[72] In any event, no amount of practice by prior ministers can crystallize jurisdictional constraints that the *HLDAA* does not establish. The conclusion that the minister's appointment of retired judges frustrates 'the very legislative scheme under which the power is conferred' is, to say the least, highly contentious as the disagreement of a substantial minority of the Court demonstrates. As Bastarache J. puts it: 'It is difficult to characterize the Minister's appointments as immediately or obviously defective, particularly when the factors are not themselves immediately or obviously ascertainable.'[73]

Taking the Standards of Review Seriously

It is easy to lose sight of the forest for the trees in so lengthy a decision, but the essential points are these: clear statutory language conferred discretionary power on the minister of labour; the minister is an expert decision-maker; and the minister's appointment decisions were protected by a strong privative clause. The minister exercised his power to appoint retired judges as arbitrators. It is difficult to see what is wrong here, let alone that anything is so wrong as to constitute an abuse of discretion that demands judicial intervention.

It would be easier to accept the decisions of a divided Court in judicial review cases if disagreement came at the level of identifying the correct standard of review. There should be more than a little embarrassment, however, in concluding that a decision is entitled to the most deferential standard of review— judicial review for *patent* unreasonableness – only to split in applying that standard, as the Court did in *CUPE v. Ontario*.

The Court has often emphasized that the lynchpin of the standard of review analysis is the intention of the legislature. In *Pushpanathan* Bastarache J. put it this way:[74]

> The central inquiry in determining the standard of review exercisable by a court of law is the legislative intent of the statute creating the tribunal whose decision is being reviewed. More specifically, the reviewing court

> must ask: '[W]as the question which the provision raises one that was intended by the legislators to be left to the exclusive decision of the Board?'

Substitute 'minister' for 'board,' and the answer to this question in *CUPE v. Ontario* is clear: the legislature intended that the minister have exclusive authority to appoint arbitrators. The problem is that the Court subordinates the explicit intention of the legislature – to establish a discretionary power and protect it with a privative clause – to the implicit intention of the legislature, which the Court infers from prior ministerial statements and the practice of prior ministers, among other things.

Prior to *CUPE v. Ontario* being argued in the Supreme Court, the Ontario legislature passed labour relations legislation in a different context stating in blunt terms that the minister can appoint an arbitrator who lacks experience, is not mutually acceptable, and does not belong to a mutually acceptable class of persons. What is more, the minister is empowered to appoint such a person regardless of any past practice, and without consultation.[75] This may seem like a ham-fisted response to the Court of Appeal's decision in *CUPE v. Ontario*, but the frustration that it demonstrates is important. If the conferral of a subjective discretion and protection of a privative clause are not respected by the Court, such a legislative response may be the only alternative to acquiescence.[76]

The Court's Labour Relations Legacy

In my view, the key to understanding the Court's decision in *CUPE v. Ontario* lies in appreciating the labour relations context in which the case arises. It has long been assumed that judicial review is illegitimate in the context of labour relations because it is likely to frustrate the development and implementation of progressive social policies favoured by the legislature[77] – an administrative law version of the *Lochner* problem.[78] Notorious cases like *Metropolitan Life Insurance Co v. International Union of Operating Engineers, Local 796*,[79] and *Port Arthur Shipbuilding Co v. Arthurs*[80] cast a long shadow.

Since *CUPE v. New Brunswick*, however, labour relations tribunals have had an easier time staking their claim to deference, and not only on the basis that the legislature sought to empower them to make the relevant decisions. The cases are replete with acknowledgments of both the expertise of labour relations tribunals and the shortcomings of the judiciary.

It is increasingly difficult to accept these sorts of justifications for deference nowadays. David Mullan is right to say that the Supreme Court's deferential approach to judicial review was developed at a time when 'competence, nay excellence had become the characteristic of many of those who were members of labour boards or who acted as arbitrators of disputes arising out of collective agreements.'[81] But labour relations tribunals are not what they used to be; it is a long time since the likes of Bora Laskin, Harry Arthurs, and Paul Weiler have been seen. Nor are the courts what they once were; the negative stereotype that supported the argument for deference is no longer relevant. The Canadian judiciary is younger and more diversified than ever before, and cannot reasonably be described as 'conservative.' Judges are drawn from a more diverse pool of lawyers than in the past, many of whom have had careers in government or experience practising before administrative tribunals, and hence considerable understanding of and experience in the administrative state.

Binnie J.'s decision in *CUPE v. Ontario* all but precludes the appointment of retired judges as arbitrators, and so vindicates the old stereotype that judges are unsuited to labour relations.[82] At the same time, however, Binnie J.'s decision demonstrates how irrelevant that stereotype has become. Although he does not acknowledge as much, CUPE was successful at least in part because a majority of the Court was sympathetic to unions' historic antipathy to judges. The majority was, in my view, making amends for the perceived misdeeds of its predecessors.[83]

Binnie J.'s decision might also be read as reflecting the Court's concern about equality, something that David Dyzenhaus has argued is often implicated in judicial review decisions. According to Dyzenhaus, *CUPE v. New Brunswick* is an example of the immanence of equality in the law of collective bargaining: '[i]t is clear that [Dickson J.'s] support for the Board's determination is driven by his sense that it preserved equality of bargaining power as between employer and employee.'[84] *CUPE v. Ontario* can be viewed in a similar fashion. There is no question that the Court of Appeal's decision was motivated by concern about equality.[85] The Court of Appeal assumed that labour unions were in a disadvantaged position because they were denied the right to strike, and the minister's decision to appoint judges as arbitrators was seen as further tilting the playing field against them. Although Binnie J. was more careful with his language than the Court of Appeal, the same concern about equality is evident in his decision.

There are two problems here. The first is that the Court simply gets it wrong: even assuming the immanence of equality, the Court's fundamental premise – the unfairness of arbitration – is arguably mistaken. The second, more fundamental, objection is that regardless of the merits of one's conception of equality, the Court should be more concerned with the limits of judicial review than it is, since these limits go to the very legitimacy of its enterprise.

As to the first problem, it is wrong to assume that interest arbitration works to the disadvantage of unions. On the contrary, it works to their benefit in important ways. For one thing, it facilitates organization efforts. Access to arbitration is a helpful tool of organization for unions seeking bargaining rights in the health care sector, especially in nursing homes and similar institutions. Health care workers who are unwilling to strike are more easily persuaded to join unions if they think that their collective agreements will be settled by arbitration. Secondly, arbitration is likely to result in a better collective agreement than could be obtained by collective bargaining, given the constraints on employers' funding. Arbitrators are far more likely to order salary increases that employers cannot afford than employers are likely to agree to them in the bargaining process. This explains why, far from seeking to *avoid* being covered by the *HLDAA*, unions almost invariably argue that they should be covered by its terms in the event that there is any doubt.[86]

From the government's perspective, this is a real problem. Wages and benefits are a significant component of the health care budget, yet routinely they are determined by arbitrators – labour relations practitioners – who have little reason to be concerned about the government's ability to pay, even though it is now a required consideration under the act.[87] The public interest is not obviously well served by all this, and one would expect the government to respond. There are problems, too, from a labour relations perspective. The availability of arbitration diminishes the likelihood of a negotiated settlement by creating incentives for the parties, both union and management, not to make hard decisions that are likely to be criticized by their constituents. Moreover, the arbitration system is marked by extensive delay and, as a result, retrospective arbitration awards, neither of which is good for labour relations.

Given this context, it is reasonable to suppose that the minister's decision was motivated by dissatisfaction with the status quo. The appointment of judges as arbitrators may have 'revealed a discontent with arbitral "expertise," and perhaps a disposition to find other chairpersons who might be more inclined to follow the [statutory] criteria faithfully.'[88] Greater attention to the ability to pay criteria could reasonably be expected to benefit the government, but that could be justified in accordance with the requirements of the *HLDAA*. It is easy to see a political complaint in all of this. It is far more difficult to see an abuse of discretion.

Conclusion

The perennial problem in judicial review in Canada lies in the need to constrain the courts – however well meaning they may be. The Supreme Court has long emphasized the need to defer to the decisions of administrative tribunals, but cases like *CUPE v. Ontario* suggest that incentive to defer to the discretionary decisions of the executive is not nearly as strong.

Once it is accepted that there are limits on the exercise of discretionary powers, how is the reach of judicial review to be limited? Everyone accepts that there is room to remedy a *Roncarelli*-type situation, but beyond this little is clear. The problem is apparent in Bastarache J.'s dissenting opinion. He accepted as 'self-evident' the proposition that discretion is never untrammelled, and that the minister could not appoint 'only members of his own political caucus, hospital CEOs, or union business agents.' He described these as extreme examples, however, and not before the Court.[89]

Lorne Sossin has suggested that it is difficult to limit the reach of judicial review given Bastarache J.'s concession,[90] but I do not think that this undermines the thrust of his opinion. I take Bastarache J. to be saying no more than that appointments made in bad faith need not be countenanced despite the deferential approach he advocates. There may well be difficulty in determining when the line is crossed – when an ill-advised appointment constitutes an abuse of discretion, and hence a patently unreasonable exercise of the appointment power – but this sort of difficulty is inherent in any case involving judicial review of the exercise of discretionary powers. Extension of the pragmatic and functional approach to include discretionary decisions was intended to move the law from the classification game the courts had long been forced to play, thereby bringing unity to the Canadian approach to judicial review of substantive decisions. It was not intended to reduce the deference accorded discretionary decisions, and especially not discretionary decisions made directly by ministers.

Ultimately, however, it may have this effect, especially if courts are unwilling to acknowledge the possibility that political accountability is an appropriate remedy, and to insist that it be used as an alternative to judicial review. It is remarkable that despite all of the context suggesting that a political decision had been made, Binnie J.'s decision does not discuss political accountability at all.

Binnie J.'s decision for the majority in *CUPE v. Ontario* is troubling because it suggests that the Supreme Court of Canada is not prepared to treat Ministers with the same respect that it has shown to administrative tribunals. If this is right, then we should expect to see more judicial review where executive action is concerned. This may not trouble those who equate deference with respect, but it should: judicial review is bound to become more political as a result. To the extent it does, its legitimacy is bound to be undermined.

NOTES

Thanks to David Dyzenhaus, Randal Graham, Brad Miller, Lorne Sossin, and Mike Taggart for their helpful comments on an earlier draft, and to my research assistants Chris Cheung and Sarah Shody. Most of all, thanks to David Mullan for his friendship and support over many years. David introduced me to public law, encouraged me to study in New Zealand, and helped me to become an academic. I am enormously grateful.

1 [1979] 2 S.C.R. 227 [*CUPE v. New Brunswick*].
2 David Mullan recognized as much before the Supreme Court created the middle-ground standard of reasonableness *simpliciter*: See David J. Mullan, 'Judicial Deference to Executive Decision Making: Evolving Concepts of Responsibility' (1993) 18 Queen's L.J. 137 at 178: 'The polarities of patent unreasonableness and correctness can no longer suffice as the only alternatives.'
3 See generally David J. Mullan, 'Establishing the Standard of Review: The Struggle for Complexity?' (2003) 17 Can. J. Admin. L. & Prac. 59 [Mullan, 'Establishing the Standard']; Lorne Sossin, 'Empty Ritual, Mechanical Exercise or the Discipline of Difference? Revisiting the Standard of Review in Administrative Law' (2003) 27 Advocates Q. 478; P. Bryden, 'Understanding the Standard of Review in Administrative Law' (2005) 54 U.N.B.L.J. 74 [Bryden, 'Understanding the Standard']; and David Jones, 'Standards of Review in Administrative Law,' paper prepared for the Canadian Institute for the Administration of Justice, 17 June 2005. I have benefited considerably from these papers in preparing this essay.
4 See Chief Justice McLachlin's contribution to this volume.

5 Procedural fairness claims are not subject to the pragmatic and functional approach, at least, not yet. David Mullan has questioned the continued viability of the process-substance distinction on a number of occasions, and has suggested that the pragmatic and functional approach be applied to procedural fairness claims. See e.g. Mullan, 'Establishing the Standard,' *supra* note 3 at 87. The Court continues to resist this development, but determinations of the relevant decision maker as to appropriate procedures may receive considerable deference. See, e.g., *Baker v. Canada (Minister of Citizenship and Immigration)*, [1999] 2 S.C.R. 817 at para. 27 [*Baker*].

6 [1998] 1 S.C.R. 982 [*Pushpanathan*].

7 Ibid., at para. 28.

8 It is remarkable that it is still necessary for the Supreme Court to insist that the pragmatic and functional approach be used. See, e.g., *Dr. Q. v. College of Physicians and Surgeons of British Columbia*, [2003] 1 S.C.R. 226. In some contexts, such as the answering of constitutional questions, it is settled that the standard of review is correctness, and as a result there may be no need to go through the analysis. See, e.g., *Barrie Public Utilities v. Canadian Cable Television Association*, [2003] 1 S.C.R. 476 at para. 66 per Bastarache J. (dissenting). But even where the standard is thought to be well established, as patent unreasonableness was understood to be established in the context of judicial review of labour relations arbitration decisions, the Court insists that the pragmatic and functional approach be applied – and it may in some cases lead to a less deferential standard. See, e.g., *Voice Construction Ltd v. Construction & General Workers Union*, [2004] 1 S.C.R. 609 [*Voice Construction*], discussed in David J. Mullan, '*Voice Construction* – One Swallow Does Not a Summer Make?' (2004) 11 Can. Lab. & Emp. L.J. 113 (arguing that patent unreasonableness is likely to remain the relevant standard for judicial review of labour relations arbitration decisions).

9 *Law Society of New Brunswick v. Ryan*, [2003] 1 S.C.R. 247 at para. 26 [*Ryan*].

10 David Mullan, *Administrative Law: Cases, Text, and Materials*, 5th ed. (Toronto: Emond-Montgomery, 2003) at 699 [Mullan, *Cases, Text, and Materials*]. Justice Scalia of the U.S. Supreme Court made a similar point more bluntly, noting that '[a]dministrative law is not for sissies.' See A. Scalia, 'Judicial Deference to Administrative Interpretations of Law' [1989] Duke L.J. 511 at 511.

11 [2002] 1 S.C.R. 249.

12 *Supra* note 9.

13 *Supra* note 8.

14 Of course, there will sometimes be good reason to overturn the decisions of administrative tribunals. In yet another case involving CUPE, *CUPE Local*

79 v. City of Toronto, [2003] 3 S.C.R. 77 [*CUPE Local 79*], a labour relations arbitrator held that a sexual assault conviction was inadequate justification for dismissal of a playground employee, and that criminal conduct had to be established to the arbitrator's satisfaction. The Supreme Court's decision to overturn the arbitrator's decision on a correctness standard is hardly surprising; the arbitrator's decision to impugn the decision of a superior court on a matter of criminal law was remarkable, and speaks volumes about the confidence of administrative tribunals in the *CUPE v. New Brunswick* era. The case is noteworthy, too, because of Justice LeBel's lengthy concurring opinion in which he questions the theoretical coherence of the three standards of review, especially the distinction between the two standards based on reasonableness.

15 See the various essays in David Dyzenhaus, ed., *The Unity of Public Law* (Oxford: Hart, 2004). David Mullan praised the Court's decision in *Baker* in his contribution to that volume, 'Deference from *Baker* to *Suresh* and Beyond – Interpreting the Conflicting Signals,' and condemned the Court's subsequent decision in *Suresh v. Canada*, [2002] 1 S.C.R. 3 for backsliding.

16 *Baker, supra* note 5 at para. 54.

17 Ibid. at para. 56. James Sprague was one of the few commentators who expressed concern about *Baker*'s potential in this regard. See James L.H. Sprague, 'Another View of *Baker*' (1999) 7 R.A.L. 163.

18 However, administrative law was largely ineffectual in restraining the Harris reforms; see David J. Mullan, 'Judging the Judgment of Judges: *CUPE v. Ontario (Minister of Labour)*' (2003) 10 Can. Lab. & Emp. L.J. 431 at 434, citing *Pembroke Civic Hospital v. Ontario (Health Services Restructuring Commission)* (1997), 36 O.R. (3d) 41 (Div. Ct.) [Mullan, 'Judging the Judgment']. *Charter* and other constitutional law challenges were more successful, however, most prominently in *Falkiner v. Ontario (Director, Income Maintenance Branch, Ministry of Community and Social Services)* (2002), 59 O.R. (3d) 481 (Ont. C.A.) (appeal to S.C.C. discontinued [2002] S.C.C.A. No. 297) and *Lalonde v. Ontario (Commission de restructuration des services de sante)* (2001) 56 O.R. (3d) 505 (Ont. C.A.). See generally, David Mullan and Antonella Ceddia, 'The Impact on Public Law of Privatization, Deregulation, Outsourcing, and Downsizing: A Canadian Perspective' (2003) 10 Indiana Journal of Global Legal Studies 199.

19 [2003] 1 S.C.R. 539 [*CUPE v. Ontario*].

20 Mullan, 'Judging the Judgment,' *supra* note 18; David Dyzenhaus, 'The Unwritten Constitution and the Rule of Law' in Grant Huscroft and Ian Brodie, eds., *Constitutionalism in the Charter Era* (Toronto: LexisNexis Butterworths, 2004) 383 [Dyzenhaus, 'Unwritten Constitution']; Lorne Sossin,

'Developments in Administrative Law: The 2002–2003 Term' (2003) 22 Sup. Ct. L.R. (2d) 21 at 38–53 [Sossin, 'Developments']; Tom Archibald, '*CUPE v. Ontario (Minister of Labour)*: Preserving the Institutional Integrity of Labour Law' (2003) 10 Can. Lab. & Emp. L.J. 457 [Archibald, 'Institutional Integrity']. Bryden, 'Understanding the Standard,' *supra* note 3 at 98, describes the decision as 'misguided' as a matter of substantive labour relations law, but does not elaborate.

21 R.S.O. 1990, c. H.14 [*HLDAA*].

22 S.O. 1995, c. 1, Sched. A.

23 Following the receipt of complaints from the president of the Ontario Federation of Labour, several judges appointed as arbitrators decided not to act. Other retired judges were willing to hear arbitration cases, however, and several were appointed to do so.

24 CUPE's claim is set out in *CUPE v. Ontario* (2000), 51 O.R. (3d) 417 at para. 47 (C.A.).

25 Austin J.A. notes that '[t]he vast bulk of total hospital revenue comes from the government': ibid. at para. 21.

26 [1999] O.J. No. 358. Southey J. relied on *Re W.D. Latimer Co. Ltd and Bray* (1974), 6 O.R. (2d) 129, approved in *Brosseau v. Alberta Securities Commission*, [1989] 1 S.C.R. 301: '[T]he actions of the Minister in appointing retired judges as chairmen of interest arbitration boards fell squarely within the authority given him in s. 6(3) of the HLDAA. It is not open to the Court in those circumstances to apply the common law doctrines on which the applicants rely to negate the statutory authority of the Minister' (at para. 18).

27 *Supra* note 24.

28 Ibid. at para. 101.

29 Ibid. at para. 102.

30 Mutual acceptability was to be determined on the basis that they were on the grievance arbitration list or were otherwise mutually acceptable to the parties. As David Mullan notes, CUPE obtained the sort of substantive outcome not normally available in regard to a procedural fairness claim, although it might have been intended as a remedy available only in the short term. See Mullan, 'Judging the Judgment,' *supra* note 18 at 443–44.

31 Justice Binnie understates things considerably when he says at the outset of his decision: 'I would dismiss the appeal, albeit for reasons that differ somewhat from those of the Court of Appeal.' *CUPE v. Ontario*, *supra* note 19 at para. 49.

32 Two interveners, the National Academy of Arbitrators (whose counsel was advised by David Mullan) and the Canadian Bar Association, made abuse of discretion-style arguments. In dissent, Bastarache J. chides Binnie J. for

assisting the union in making its argument:

> I note in passing that, in framing the allegations concerning the boards' independence and impartiality as a claim that the Minister exercised his power patently unreasonably, Binnie J. is generous. He presents this line of argument in by far its most favourable light. A reading of the respondents' factum easily suggests that they were making the argument that if the Minister appointed boards that would themselves, in operation, fall short of the demands of natural justice, he thereby breached his own duty of procedural fairness. This is certainly the implication from the respondents' arguments, in this context, that the duty of fairness required the Minister to exercise his appointment power in conformity with the principles of natural justice. As Binnie J. discusses, however, there is no sound argument in this case that the Minister acted unfairly in the sense of violating his duty of procedural fairness (ibid. at para. 45).

33 [1959] S.C.R. 121 at 140 [*Roncarelli*]. David Mullan paid tribute to Justice Rand in his Rand Lecture at the University of New Brunswick in 1995, entitled 'Underlying Constitutional Principles: The Legacy of Justice Rand,' and in 'Mr. Justice Rand: Defining the Limits of Court Control of the Administrative and Executive Process' (1979–80) 18 U.W.O.L.R. 65. See also David Dyzenhaus's Rand Lecture, 'The Deep Structure of *Roncarelli v. Duplessis*' (2004) 53 U.N.B.L.J. 111 [Dyzenhaus, 'Deep Structure'].

34 *CUPE v. Ontario, supra* note 19 at para. 91.

35 David Dyzenhaus discusses the significance of disagreement as to whether the head of the licensing commission, Archambault, acted on orders from the premier or followed his advice. See Dyzenhaus, 'Deep Structure,' *supra* note 33 at 124–28.

36 *Roncarelli, supra* note 33 at 140.

37 David Dyzenhaus has flirted with the notion that not only judges but tribunals might refuse to obey legislative commands they consider inequitable: 'I leave dangling the question whether judges and tribunals should obey the legislature's commands when these are inequitable. My own view is that when such commands reach a certain pitch of inequity, they offend against the ideals of the rule of law even when these ideals are largely implicit because there is no written constitution.' See David Dyzenhaus, 'The Politics of Deference: Judicial Review and Democracy' in Michael Taggart, ed., *The Province of Administrative Law* (Oxford: Hart Publishing, 1997) 279 at 307 n. 67 [Dyzenhaus, 'Politics of Deference']. But he does not advance this notion in his Rand Lecture: 'My claim is not then that judges can always maintain the rule of law in the face of an assault by a powerful and determined government. Rather, it is that they can at least force government into

an explicit declaration of its determination to govern outside the rule of law.' Dyzenhaus, 'Deep Structure,' *supra* note 33 at 140. The Supreme Court of Canada appears to put paid to the idea that the rule of law can be invoked to deny effect to validly enacted legislation in *British Columbia v. Imperial Tobacco Canada Ltd*. 2005 S.C.C. 49.

38 The use of extreme examples to make controversial points is a common ploy of judges seeking to expand judicial powers. Lord Cooke, then president of the New Zealand Court of Appeal, used this technique in asserting that some common law rights run so deep that even the legislature could not be presumed to be able to overcome them, citing torture as his example. The Cooke thesis is criticized by Justice Michael Kirby of the High Court of Australia in 'Lord Cooke and Fundamental Rights' in Paul Rishworth, ed., *The Struggle for Simplicity in the Law: Essays for Lord Cooke of Thorndon* (Wellington, NZ: Butterworths, 1997) 331.

39 Premier Duplessis is quoted in the appellant's factum: 'Roncarelli is identifying himself with the odious propaganda of the Witnesses of Jehovah and as a result, I have ordered the Liquor Commission to cancel his permit ...The Communists, the Nazis as well as those who are the propagandists for the Witnesses of Jehovah, have been treated and will continue to be treated by the Union National government as they deserve for trying to infiltrate themselves and their seditious ideas in the province of Quebec' (quoted from Dyzenhaus, 'Deep Structure,' *supra* note 33 at 120).

40 *Supra* note 19 at para. 92.

41 Professor Joseph Weiler testified that retired judges 'do not have tenure as arbitrators and therefore do not have the kind of independence from government that they previously enjoyed when they served on the bench. They also have no expertise in industrial relations. Certainly they lack the deep and wide experience possessed by arbitrators familiar with the industrial relations community of Ontario' (*CUPE v. Ontario*, *supra* note 19 at para. 75).

42 There is some irony in invoking *Roncarelli* in support of an argument against appointing retired judges as arbitrators, in light of Justice Rand's appointment as arbitrator in the famous dispute at Ford. Judy Fudge and Eric Tucker describe the circumstances of his appointment:

> Paul Martin, who had recently been elected to Parliament to represent Windsor, tried to get the parties to accept binding arbitration and therefore recommended Ivan Rand, a Supreme Court of Canada justice with known pro-union sympathies. On 20 December, Labour Minister Humphrey Mitchell appointed Rand as the arbitrator and the workers returned to work (Judy Fudge and Eric Tucker, *Labour Before the Law* (Toronto: Oxford University Press, 2001) 285.)

43 I am grateful to my colleague Randal Graham for helpful discussions of this section.

44 *CUPE v. Ontario, supra* note 19 at para. 106, quoting E.A. Driedger, *Construction of Statutes*, 2nd ed. (Toronto: Butterworths, 1983) at 87.

45 *CUPE v. Ontario, supra* note 19 at para. 54. The language here is based on *R. v. Morgentaler*, [1993] 3 S.C.R. 463.

46 Ibid.

47 Ibid. at 484.

48 [1998] 1 S.C.R. 27 [*Rizzo*].

49 Ibid. at para. 35.

50 *CUPE v. Ontario, supra* note 19 at para. 111. Randal Graham describes the expanded use of legislative debate in *Rizzo* as a 'radical leap' from the original decisions in which the traditional rule against the admission of such evidence was relaxed. See Randal N. Graham, *Statutory Interpretation: Cases, Text and Materials* (Toronto: Emond Montgomery, 2002) 177 [Graham, *Statutory Interpretation*].

51 In fact, it may be more controversial than it appears. The minister is called on to make appointments precisely because the parties have been unable to agree, and they are unable to agree because they have different views about the acceptability of particular arbitrators, regardless of their acceptability in the broader labour relations community, as grievance arbitrators or otherwise. In truth, some unions will never agree to some arbitrators, whether for grievance or interest arbitration, because they perceive them as pro-employer; while some employers will never agree to other arbitrators for the opposite reason. In appointing an arbitrator, even one from the list of grievance arbitrators, the minister is bound to disappoint one of parties at least some of the time.

52 Dyzenhaus proffered this conception of deference in an attempt to avoid the *ad hoc* accommodation between formal and substantive reasons for deference that characterized the Court's various decisions since *CUPE v. New Brunswick*. See Dyzenhaus, 'Politics of Deference,' *supra* note 37. Deference as respect is adopted by the Supreme Court of Canada in *Baker, supra* note 5 at para. 65; *Ryan, supra* note 9 at para. 49; and *CUPE Local 79, supra* note 14 at para. 122.

53 Dyzenhaus, 'Politics of Deference,' *supra* note 37 at 303.

54 Ibid. at 66.

55 Lon Fuller, 'The Case of the Speluncean Explorers' (1949) 62 Harv. L. Rev. 616 [Fuller, 'Speluncean Explorers'].

56 Ibid. at 625.

57 Ibid. at 634.

58 Graham, *Statutory Interpretation*, *supra* note 50 at 143–7 and 161–71.
59 Ibid. at para. 32.
60 Ibid. at para. 31. This seems correct, since when the *HLDAA* was passed there was neither a list of arbitrators nor for that matter an established arbitration profession. These developments came much later.
61 Justice Bastarache makes this point when he says that the considerations Justice Binnie infers are not 'obvious, like the fact, in *Roncarelli*, *supra*, that discretion to renew a liquor license must not be wielded to punish a person who posts bail for fellow members of a religious minority': *CUPE v. Ontario*, *supra* note 19 at para. 31.
62 Cooke J. of the New Zealand Court of Appeal once put the point this way: 'the more general and the more obviously important the consideration, the readier the Court must be to hold that Parliament must have meant it to be taken into account': *Creednz Inc. v. Governor-General*, [1981] 1 N.Z.L.R. 172 at 182 (N.Z.C.A). This seems sensible enough, but it begs the question by assuming that considerations can in fact be 'obviously important.' Whether or not they are depends largely on the purpose the court infers and, as Judge Keen demonstrated in Fuller's 'Speluncean Explorers,' *supra* note 57, this is capable of manipulation.
63 *Canada (Attorney General) v. Public Service Alliance of Canada*, [1993] 1 S.C.R. 941 at 964 (per Cory J., who described patent unreasonableness as 'clearly a very strict test').
64 *Ryan*, *supra* note 9 at para. 52. Subsequently, in *Giguère v. Chambre des notaires du Québec*, [2004] 1 S.C.R. 3 at para. 28, the Court described a patently unreasonable error as 'so gross an error, predicated on such a basic misunderstanding' of the law that it could not be permitted to stand. In *Voice Construction*, *supra* note 8 at para. 18, Major J. said that definition was difficult, 'but it may be said that the result must almost border on the absurd.'
65 *Mount Sinai Hospital Center v. Quebec (Minister of Health and Social Services)*, [2001] 2 S.C.R. 281 at para. 63, quoting *R. v. North and East Devon Health Authority, ex parte Coughlan*, [2000] 3 All E.R. 850 at para. 72.
66 Philip Bryden discusses techniques for distinguishing the categories of patent unreasonableness from reasonableness *simpliciter* in Bryden, 'Understanding the Standard,' *supra* note 3.
67 *CUPE v. Ontario*, *supra* note 19 at para. 165 [emphasis added].
68 David Mullan describes the fetters as 'jurisdictional boundaries' in 'Judging the Judgment,' *supra* note 19 at 452. See also Sossin, 'Developments,' *supra* note 20 at 43–4, arguing that the Court's definition of a patently unreasonable exercise of discretion is identical to the definition of an *ultra vires* decision in prior cases.

69 Mullan, ibid., makes this same point, albeit he endorses the correctness of the decision. He describes the qualifications as 'conditions-precedent to any valid exercise of the discretion. Whether viewed from a correctness or latent unreasonableness perspective, they were limits on the minister's powers of appointment. They were not simply considerations which had to be weighted or assessed against other factors.' Cf. Dyzenhaus, 'Unwritten Constitution,' *supra* note 20 at 400.

70 The Divisional Court made a similar point in dismissing the union's application for judicial review at first instance: 'The role of the court in deciding this application for judicial review is not to consider whether the actions of the Minister represent good policy in the labour relations field. The only concern of this court is whether the Minister has acted unlawfully by exceeding his jurisdiction.' *CUPE v. Ontario* (Div. Ct.), *supra* note 26 at para. 14.

71 *Roncarelli*, *supra* note 33 at 140.

72 In the context of this case, it is remarkable that any of the very careful correspondence from the minister – correspondence that deliberately did not satisfy the union's demands – could subsequently be considered relevant to establishing a denial of procedural fairness, as the Court of Appeal held.

73 *CUPE v. Ontario*, *supra* note 19 at para. 36.

74 *Pushpanathan*, *supra* note 6 at para. 26, citing *Pasiechnyk v. Saskatchewan (Workers' Compensation Board)*, [1997] 2 S.C.R. 890 at para. 18, per Sopinka J.

75 *Back to School Act (Toronto and Windsor) 2001*, S.O. 2001, c. 1., ss. 11(4) and (5). I would be more concerned about these provisions if they were intended to authorize the appointment of unqualified persons – red-haired arbitrators, as it were. But context is important: this was emergency legislation, the purpose of which was to end a labour dispute and get children back to school. There was no room for doubt as to the minister's ability to appoint an arbitrator to end the dispute, and it is not surprising in light of the Court of Appeal's decision that the legislature would consider it necessary to use such blunt language to protect the minister's appointment. Indeed, the legislation can be seen as an example of what in *Charter* circles is called 'dialogue theory': a legislative response to the court's interpretation of prior legislation. The difference, of course, is that in administrative law the legislature is entitled to have the last word, and need not resort to the notwithstanding mechanism in order to insist that its view prevail. The *Back to School Act* has to be seen as a repudiation of the Court of Appeal's decision, and an insistence that the minister's appointment decision be respected.

Justice Bastarache notes that this legislation demonstrates that the legislature knows how to specify relevant appointment criteria if it so chooses, making the point that the omission of any such criteria from the *HLDAA* shows that it deliberately chose not to include appointment criteria.

76 David Mullan suggests that this legislation could be added to the list of facts that were favourable to CUPE's position: 'The government's actions in securing the passage of this kind of provision is quite readily seen as a slap in the face of the Ontario Court of Appeal, and probably not calculated to win it too many friends in the Supreme Court of Canada. At the very least, a more acute political sensitivity would have led to this kind of provision being held over until the Supreme Court had rendered its judgment in CUPE' (Mullan, 'Judging the Judgment,' *supra* note 18 at note 70). I agree that this legislation might have been perceived in this way, and that it may not have been politically astute for the government to have passed it – at least, not prior to the Supreme Court's judgment. But I wonder why governments should worry about respecting the courts when the courts appear to be unconcerned about according governments the same respect. The Ontario Court of Appeal was prepared to impugn the government's motives and hold that it had acted unfairly on the basis of arguments that were rejected in their entirety in the Supreme Court. Why should governments be deferential to courts in redressing what they regard as erroneous legal decisions?

77 As David Mullan has put it:

> With greater government intervention in the private sector, increased social programs, and legislative derogation from the traditional jurisdiction of the courts came a rather different attitude on the part of the Canadian courts. While they still paid obeisance to the prerogatives of Cabinet and ministerial decision making, they were far less hospitable to the advent of many administrative tribunals and, more generally, the new social order. This was particularly so in the stance they took on those charged with administering a new regime of labour relations based on collective bargaining instead of traditional employment law as well as tribunal substitutes for the restrictive tort law applied to the lot of employees injured at work. Indeed, in a number of judgments of this era, the attitude of the courts was one of downright hostility to legislative objectives and the removal of the courts' traditional jurisdiction (Mullan, *Cases, Text, and Materials*, *supra* note 10 at 697.)

Elsewhere, Mullan has suggested that the Court's record is mixed. See David Mullan, 'The Supreme Court of Canada and Tribunals – Deference to the Administrative Process: A Recent Phenomenon or a Return to Basics' (2001) 80 Can. Bar Rev. 399.

78 *Lochner v. New York*, 198 U.S. 45 (1905). The *Lochner* era refers to a notorious

series of decisions in which the United States Supreme Court invoked economic liberty rights inferred from the due process clause of the *U.S. Bill of Rights*, frustrating the implementation of New Deal legislation including such basics of social and economic policy as health and safety laws. See generally, Laurence Tribe, *American Constitutional Law*, 3rd ed. (New York: Foundation Press, 2000) chap. 8.

79 [1970] S.C.R. 425.

80 [1969] S.C.R. 85.

81 Mullan, *Cases, Text, and Materials*, *supra* note 10 at 698.

82 Binnie J.'s decision also has the effect of elevating the stature of labour relations arbitrators and protecting their turf – which was surely the motivation for the intervention of the National Academy of Arbitrators in the Supreme Court in support of the union's position.

83 I say this despite Binnie J.'s rejection of the reasonable apprehension of bias argument against judges as a class. 'Undoubtedly,' he writes, 'there have been some judges predisposed toward management in the past, as well as some judges predisposed toward labour, but I do not think the fully informed, reasonable person would tar the entire class of presently retired judges with the stigma of an anti-labour bias' (*CUPE v. Ontario*, *supra* note 19 at para. 202). He has to say this, I think, in order to defend the judiciary. The thrust of his decision, however, all but excludes retired judges from future involvement in labour relations, which is of course what the union would prefer.

84 Dyzenhaus, 'Politics of Deference,' *supra* note 37 at 301.

85 *CUPE v. Ontario*, *supra* note 19 at para. 76: 'It is also material that these disputes are being arbitrated not by choice but rather because the right to strike to resolve them has been taken away by legislation.' The Court later expresses the view that '[t]he prohibition of strikes works powerfully against labour ...' (ibid. at para. 85), and goes over the top when it says the appointment of judges to arbitrate disputes under the *HLDAA* 'must reasonably be seen as an attempt to seize control of the bargaining process' (ibid. at para. 101).

86 Section 1(1) of the *HLDAA* makes clear that in addition to applying to hospitals and other listed institutions such as sanitariums, sanatoriums, and nursing homes, it also applies to any 'other institution operated for the observation, care or treatment of persons afflicted with or suffering from any physical or mental illness, disease or injury or for the observation, care or treatment of convalescent or chronically ill persons, whether or not it is granted aid out of moneys appropriated by the Legislature and whether or not it is operated for private gain, and includes a home for the aged.' Where

questions arise as to the scope of this residual provision (and hence whether or not the act applies), employers have usually argued that they are *not* covered by the *HLDAA*, and that the union is free to strike, while unions have usually taken the opposite position. This reflects pure self-interest on both sides, employers knowing that hospital employees have little stomach for strike action, and often little bargaining power; unions knowing that they are likely to fare better through arbitration than negotiation. See Jeffrey Sack, C. Michael Mitchell, and Sandy Price, *Ontario Labour Relations Board Law and Practice*, 3rd ed. (Toronto: Butterworths, 1998, updated in looseleaf) at paras. 9.189–9.194.

87 *HLDAA*, *supra* note 23 s. 9(1.1). See Archibald, 'Institutional Integrity,' *supra* note 20 at 470: '[E]xpertise has come to include a nagging refusal by arbitrators to apply statutory "ability to pay" criteria. By rejecting them, arbitrators continue to assert their independence from the government-as-employer.'

88 This is how Tom Archibald, who endorses the Court's decision, characterizes the minister's motivation (ibid.).

89 *CUPE v. Ontario*, *supra* note 19 at para. 40.

90 Sossin, *supra* note 20 at 50.

From Despair to Deference: Same Difference?

HUGH CORDER

From bitter searching of the heart,
Quickened with passion and with pain
We rise to play a greater part.

This is the faith from which we start:
Men shall know commonwealth again
From bitter searching of the heart.

We loved the easy and the smart,
But now, with keener hand and brain
We rise to play a greater part.

The lesser loyalties depart,
And neither creed nor race remain,
From bitter searching of the heart.

Not steering by the venal chart
That tricked the mass for private gain,
We rise to play a greater part.

Reshaping narrow law and art
Whose symbols are the millions slain,
From bitter searching of the heart,
We rise to play a greater part.

– Frank R. Scott

I was introduced to this poem[1] in the months between agreeing to write this piece and the actual writing of it. The words used struck me as particularly evocative of the fears and hopes which have surrounded the fate of South African administrative law over the past twenty years. To learn that they had been written by a leading Canadian law professor and dean,[2] and to hear them so strikingly and unmistakably rendered by one of Canada's foremost musicians of the second half of the twentieth century[3] set the seal on their use to introduce what I have to say in tribute to David Mullan.

I have not known David as long as many of my fellow contributors to this volume, yet in the past seven years we have been in close contact, and I have read much of what he has written in this period. Indeed, when putting together a required reading list for LLM students in Melbourne[4] in late 2004, three of his articles were included,[5] reflecting his leading status in Canadian administrative law and the accessibility and relevance of his work to other jurisdictions in the Commonwealth. David Mullan was also one of a small group of experts who gathered at Leeds Castle in Kent, England, in July 1999,[6] in order to assist a working group of the South African Law Reform Commission which was responsible for drafting an Administrative Justice Act for that country. David's criticism was clear, constructive, and delivered with characteristic gentle wit, such that not even the most sensitive drafter could resist its force.

I have learned much from David Mullan since then, and am very pleased to have the opportunity to write in appreciation of his scholarship, which crosses many boundaries. I have chosen to do so by comparing the state of South African administrative law amidst the despair which marked the darkness of emergency rule two decades ago with its current, much happier, condition. Despite the manifest progress, however, the sudden enthusiasm with which the notion of 'deference' has begun to feature in recent judgments gives cause for concern, in the light of the very different socio-political context within which it is applied in Canada and South Africa. This point was starkly brought home to me in early 2004, in a brief conversation with Professor Harry Arthurs,[7] who was about to lecture to the LLB class at the University of Cape Town: 'deference' was, for him, a relatively appropriate, uncontroversial, and democratic stance for a judiciary to assume in certain circumstances in the modern era, whereas for me it bore all the dreadful baggage of South Africa's apartheid past. I hope, in what follows, to explain why I reacted in this way, and to argue for a narrow and cautious embrace of the notion in South African administrative law for the foreseeable future.

The Desperate Past

Like most of its counterparts in the legal systems of the British Commonwealth, administrative law in South Africa was a late starter, and suffered under the misguided prejudices towards the subject of Albert Venn Dicey.[8] In university legal education, it only began to be taught independently of constitutional law in the mid-1970s and scholarly publications were few and far between until about the same period.[9] In the oft-quoted words of Barry Dean, administrative law in South Africa was a 'dismal science.'[10]

Being a judge-made, common law phenomenon,[11] the true test of vigour and efficacy of the subject lay in the judgments of the courts in response to challenges to the exercise of public power. Here we find early signs of a judicial approach which was anything but uncritical of the grant of executive discretion in the regulation of Asian immigration to South Africa.[12] In *Ismail v. Union Government and Registrar of Asiatics*,[13] the appeal court said that it shared the view[14]

> as to the dangerous latitude to which the practice of passing skeleton statutes, leaving all the operative machinery to be supplied by regulations and giving the widest discretion to administrative officials, has of late years extended; it is a practice of which ... the tendency ... is to supplant the proper functions of both the legislature and the judiciary by the action of the executive.[15]

Also in 1912, Sir James Rose Innes drew critical attention to 'a growing tendency in modern legislation to clothe with finality the decisions of public officials in matters which seriously affect the rights of the public.'[16] The tenor of such healthily sceptical remarks about the conditions for the exercise of governmental power began to shift substantially over the next twenty-five years,[17] as the new alliance between the broad centre of Afrikaans- and English-speaking whites consolidated its power at the expense of blacks and the working class. Cases which turned on the twin axes of South African social and racial history, and the maintenance of public order (or latterly state security), provide landmarks of a hardening of judicial attitudes in sympathy with the needs of the executive.[18] So we find judges sanctioning: the validity of a ministerial regulation that declared 'every Asiatic person to be unsuited on economic grounds' to immigrate to the Union[19]; the segregation on racial lines of public amenities, such as post offices, which caused substantial inequality[20]; and the 'unfettered discretion' of a minister to curtail the freedoms of a (white) trade union organizer, for 'Parliament may make any encroachment it chooses upon the life, liberty or property of any individual subject to its sway, and ... it is the function of the courts of law to enforce its will.'[21]

The 'executive-mindedness' evident in such judgments of the highest court in the country continued to hold sway in the ensuing decades around the middle of the twentieth century, except for a brief respite in the early 1950s. In a number of significant cases in that brief period, the appeal court preferred the interests of the individual black victim of executive high-handedness, in a manner quite out of step with the by-then accustomed approach.[22] So the judges insisted on 'substantial equality' of facilities if railway station waiting rooms were to be racially segregated,[23] and on the observance of the rules of natural justice (particularly the right to be heard) before the government banished[24] or detained[25] its political opponents. Lest it be thought that South Africa's top court had somehow become imbued with the new-found respect for human rights, internationally exemplified by the Universal Declaration of Human Rights of 1948 and the early work of the United Nations in the aftermath of World War Two, it should be noted that these judgments were delivered at a time when Parliament and the courts were locked in dispute over the apartheid government's legislative attempts to remove 'coloured' men from the common voters' roll.[26] In a sense, therefore, I would argue that these cases represent the administrative-law equivalent of those celebrated constitutional challenges.

Just as the Appellate Division eventually succumbed before the will of a determined, manipulative, and disingenuous legislature,[27] its judges returned to their former ways in the face of an executive ever frequently helping itself to greater tranches of discretionary power. The government did this chiefly to achieve two objectives; the classification and enforced separation of 'racial groups' in as complete a manner as was possible, and the ruthless suppression of all forms of popular dissent from and resistance to such policies. A series of appellate judgments of the early 1960s[28] set the pattern for the next thirty years – an approach characterized by an unquestioning deference,[29] which at times bordered on the abdication of even the limited authority to review accorded to the courts by the principle of the separation of powers and the *ultra vires* doctrine. There can be little doubt that the executive used its very broad power to appoint judges to the superior courts to ensure that very few members of the bench would upset its policies and plans.[30]

This rather bleak picture of the state of administrative law in South Africa continued until the early 1980s, when a strange bifurcation occurred in the judicial record in this area. It seems that the courts were prepared, on the one hand, to find against some of the harsher civil strictures placed on black South Africans, both as individuals and collectively. Thus the subordinate legislation by which the movement into urban areas of such people was controlled, was invalidated on review,[31] as were executive attempts to force the pace in establishing separate 'states' for black South Africans[32] and to coerce university authorities to police the politics of their students.[33] Again, in stark contrast to the rather ossified approach to the task of review normally taken by the judges,[34] the doctrine of legitimate expectation made landfall in the Appellate Division[35] not too long after it had been adopted in comparable jurisdictions.[36]

This relatively progressive image of judicial review in instances where race was the central feature is, however, eclipsed by any number of judgments where review of action taken using emergency powers was unsuccessfully sought. In apartheid's dying decade, and consequent on the introduction of a constitution[37] which attempted to co-opt the participation in government of coloured and Indian South Africans but which also firmly shut the door on black South Africans, the government increasingly resorted to emergency rule in order to retain a semblance of order over large parts of urban South Africa. While the extensive powers to curtail political activity and detain political opponents without trial afforded by the *Internal Security Act*, 1982[38] initially proved sufficient for this purpose, from mid-1985 resort was had to the almost unlimited authority contemplated in the *Public Safety Act*, 1953[39] and successive sets of regulations issued in accordance with its provisions. Time after time, those individuals and organizations targeted by government forces for repressive measures resorted to the only defence available to them under law,[40] and sought judicial review of the administrative action taken against them.

There were some successful applications initially at provincial division level[41] but these were soon overwhelmed by failures at the same level,[42] and then an almost-complete dismissal by the highest court.[43]

Much has been written about the means employed by the executive to ensure ultimate success in the courts, as well as about judicial reactions to such challenges.[44] Suffice it to say that the Appellate Division bench which heard most of the emergency-power appeals gave full effect to the ouster clause included in the act by adopting the narrowest possible reading of the *ultra vires* doctrine,[45] thus effectively denying itself and all lower courts the competence to rule on the validity of the exercise of even thoroughly vague administrative actions.[46] This had a generally chilling effect on the whole field of administrative law, for the common law authority of the superior court judges to review executive power had always been the life-blood of that part of the law. A radical renewal of the system was clearly needed, but the prospect of such an overhaul was bleak indeed, as the 1980s came to a close in a mood of despair.

Reviving Review

The effects on administrative law of the revolution which the South African legal system underwent as a consequence of the implementation of a constitutional democracy after 1994 are many.[47] Most apparent are the changes at the constitutional and statutory levels; less obvious but more significant for present purposes is the reaction of the judges to these changes in the cases that have come before the courts.

The legal superstructure has undergone the kind of revolution called for after the darkness of the previous decades. Both the transitional[48] and final constitutions[49] have provided for a right to administrative justice as part of a set of 'fair process' rights within the Bill of Rights.[50] The formulation of this right in the transitional constitution was the complex product of political compromise[51] and need not detain us further except to note that the protections it afforded have largely[52] been perpetuated in the final constitution. The 'right to just administrative action' currently in place[53] provides that:

1 Everyone has the right to administrative action that is lawful, reasonable and procedurally fair.
2 Everyone whose rights have been adversely affected by administrative action has the right to be given written reasons.
3 [Sets out the constitutional imperative for Parliament to enact legislation in this field, which it has done].

At the statutory level, the *Promotion of Administrative Justice Act*, 2000 (*PAJA*)[54] has been in force for more than five years.[55] It provides more detailed content for the rules applicable to ensure procedural fairness both to individuals[56] and groups[57] and sets out procedural guidelines for applications for review[58] and for the giving of reasons[59] for administrative action. In addition, it sets out a range of remedies for invalid administrative action.[60]

Perhaps the most important features, however, are the extraordinarily lengthy and complex attempt to define the key portal to judicial review, 'administrative action,'[61] and the codification of the grounds of review.[62] As to the meaning to be given to 'administrative action,' the essential elements are the taking of a decision of an administrative nature in the exercise of public power or performance of a public function which adversely affects someone's rights and which has a 'direct, external legal effect.' Worthy of note in the listed grounds of review are the inclusion of a 'rational connection' test[63] and '*Wednesbury*-unreasonableness,'[64] and the omission of vagueness[65] and proportionality[66] from the act. The latter grounds, however, may well be relied on by a reviewing court under the omnibus provision in *PAJA*, which stipulates that administrative action which is 'otherwise unconstitutional or unlawful' may be reviewed for that reason.[67]

These legislative provisions, read in the context of further aspects of the constitution,[68] serve to provide a strong platform for the establishment of judicial authority to insist on the adherence to high standards of good governance in the executive and public administration. In doing so, the courts must naturally strike a balance between the constitutional ideals and the limits of human and financial resources in reality, especially against the background of the preceding decades.[69] How have the judges responded?

This is not the place for a detailed and extensive account of the interpretation of section 33 and the provisions of *PAJA*.[70] For present purposes, of more interest is the general approach adopted by the courts, and particularly by the two senior courts in the hierarchy, the Supreme Court of Appeal and the Constitutional Court. What tone has been set, what atmosphere created by the appellate judiciary when confronted with the exercise of public power by government, in apparent contradiction of the constitutional expectation of lawfulness, fairness and reasonableness?

In one of the earliest cases to be decided by the Constitutional Court, a strong signal was given that the judges took the supremacy of the law of the constitution seriously, and would insist that all exercises of executive power were reviewable. In *President of the Republic of South Africa v. Hugo*[71] the court concluded unanimously that the formerly unreviewable prerogative power to pardon sentenced prisoners was now amenable to review according to the standards laid down in the constitution,[72] although the judges differed on the particular outcome in this case. Most of the disputes in this area of the law were, however, resolved at provincial division level,[73] and it took a jurisdictional dispute between the two highest courts to provoke the next significant and authoritative pronouncement on administrative justice.

Whether judicial review of administrative action after 1994 was predominantly a common law phenomenon or owed its authority to the constitution was not a matter of mere academic interest. When the drafters of the transitional constitution opted for the creation of a new, highest court to be the ultimate interpreter of matters constitutional, they did so for a number of reasons, chief amongst which was the desire to avoid granting such authority to the Appellate Division.

However, they took the matter further, for the latter court was removed entirely from the constitutional chain of interpretation, being the highest court in the land for non-constitutional matters, but without constitutional jurisdiction.[74] The atmosphere had eased somewhat by the time Parliament drafted the final constitution, and the renamed Supreme Court of Appeal was granted the authority to entertain constitutional matters as the penultimate judicial body.[75] The fact that there had been a period of almost three years in which the Supreme Court of Appeal had not enjoyed constitutional jurisdiction set the scene for a brusque exchange of views between it and the Constitutional Court which helped to define the status of administrative review.

The continued existence of administrative law in its common law guise confronted the Supreme Court of Appeal before it was granted constitutional jurisdiction in *Fedsure Life Assurance Ltd v. Greater Johannesburg Metropolitan Council*.[76] In refusing to be seized of the matter, the Supreme Court of Appeal asked whether the elevation of the basic principles of administrative law to constitutional status in the right to administrative justice had left it 'any residual or concurrent jurisdiction to adjudicate ... on administrative action ... on the grounds that [it] fell to be set aside, reviewed or corrected at common law?'[77] The Constitutional Court ducked the issue, holding that the relationship between the common law and constitutional manifestations of administrative review was not necessary to be spelt out in the context of that case.[78]

The matter arose again in *President of the Republic of South Africa v. S.A. Rugby Football Union*,[79] in which the Constitutional Court held that it was not correct to see the right to administrative justice as a mere codification of the principles of the common law. The latter would, nevertheless, be 'important though not necessarily decisive in determining not only the scope of [the right] but also its content.'[80] The Supreme Court of Appeal responded rather mischievously, choosing in the *Container Logistics* case[81] to exercise its constitutional jurisdiction 'in the interests of justice' and deciding that the entrenchment of the right to administrative justice could not have been intended to do away with the common law approach to review.[82] Furthermore, the Supreme Court of Appeal held that administrative review in its common law guise continued to exist, almost as a parallel system to that set out in the constitution, so allowing the court to set aside the administrative decision under review without reliance on the constitution.

The Constitutional Court was not amused by this stance, and the *Pharmaceutical Manufacturers* case[83] gave it the opportunity emphatically to lay down the basis for the future development of administrative review. The Constitutional Court held that it could not accept that the common law and the constitution were separate bodies of law, for 'there is only one system of law. It is shaped by the Constitution which is the supreme law, and all law, including the common law, derives its force from the Constitution and is subject to constitutional control.'[84] After pointing out that the 'parallelism' suggested by the Supreme Court of Appeal in *Container Logistics* had been regarded as highly doubtful in several prior judgments of both courts, the Constitutional Court restated its position authoritatively:[85]

> The control of public power by the courts through judicial review is and has always been a constitutional matter. Prior to the interim Constitution, this control was exercised by the courts through the application of common law principles. Since then, such control has been regulated by the Constitution. The common law principles ... have been subsumed under the Constitution, and in so far as they might continue to be relevant to judicial review, they gain their force from the Constitution. In the judicial review of public power, the two are intertwined and do not constitute separate concepts.

The common law principles would 'continue to inform the content of administrative law ... and ... contribute to their future development ... but [w]hat would have been *ultra vires* under the common law by reason of a functionary exceeding a statutory power is invalid under the Constitution according to the doctrine of legality.'[86]

These and other similar statements mark the foundations of post-apartheid judicial review of administrative action, whose importance goes far beyond the confines of the dispute with the Supreme Court of Appeal. In the context in which the rights in the Bill of Rights are at least to some extent horizontally applicable,[87] the clear position that all 'public power' falls to be measured against constitutional standards is significant. In *Pharmaceuticals*, a further aspect of this judicial power was demonstrated, in that the court decided that the authority of the president to sign a bill into law was reviewable according to the constitutionally-sanctioned principle of legality, despite not satisfying the definition of 'administrative action.'[88] It might hitherto have been argued that such a high-policy act of the executive was not subject to review, even if all agreed that President Mandela had erred. Not so, said the Constitutional Court: 'It is a requirement of the rule of law that the exercise of public power by the executive and other functionaries should not be arbitrary. Decisions must be rationally related to the purpose for which the power is given ... Rationality is a minimum threshold requirement applicable to the exercise of all public power.'[89]

Situating administrative law on such a broad and fundamental constitutional foundation cements its integral role in establishing a constitutional democracy, while acknowledging that the pursuit of executive accountability need not occur solely through its rules – administrative law need not 'do all the work,' as had tended to be the temptation before 1994.[90] All in all, the judgment in *Pharmaceutical Manufacturers* represents a refreshing and clear demarcation and description of the judicial role as regulator of executive authority and guardian of the founding values of the constitution, a far cry from the submissive timidity of the appellate judiciary under apartheid.

The references in the *Pharmaceutical Manufacturers* judgment to 'rationality' as a minimum requirement for all public power set the scene for the next major development in administrative review in the courts. It will be recalled that the South African courts had taken a very cautious view of 'reasonableness' as a ground of review. In fact, the courts denied that unreasonableness alone could ground review, preferring an approach that regarded 'gross unreasonableness' as an indication that the administrative decision-maker had failed to apply its mind to the matter.[91] This was viewed as being consistent with the distinction between review and appeal. The transitional constitution broke the mould by requiring administrative action to be 'justifiable in terms of the reasons given for it,'[92] and the final constitution took the logic further, as has been seen, in listing 'reasonable' administrative action as an entitlement.[93] Juxtaposed with the requirement that administrative action be lawful and procedurally fair, it seems clear that reasonableness demands an enquiry that goes beyond mere procedural regularity to the substance of the matter *to some extent*, thus penetrating the rather indistinct line which apparently sets appeal apart from review.[94] If this argument holds, then the courts must scrutinize the merits underlying the administrative action, raising the spectre of the separation of powers. Is it the proper judicial role to become involved to a limited degree in second-guessing the executive? If entitled to do so by constitutional authority, as seems to be the case in South Africa, how far should the judges go, to what extent should they intervene?

These are well-known dilemmas for the judiciaries in many countries, and discussion of this issue has been clothed in the language of 'deference' (in the administrative law sphere)[95] over the past decade.[96] Each jurisdiction is likely to develop its own response to the basic question, fashioned by its laws and history. In South Africa, the courts have to balance the exercise of their constitutional authority with an acknowledgment that the government of the day has an extremely strong electoral mandate to refashion the distribution of power and resources in the country, in order to try to ameliorate and begin to reverse the dreadful inequities and injustices which past regimes have perpetrated. The courts, however, must exercise care not too readily to acquiesce in the policies and plans of the executive, lest the 'executive-mindedness' of their past comes back to haunt them. The judges thus have a difficult path to tread, especially in the socio-economic sphere, in which almost by definition the polycentric quality of decisions makes the judicial process alien.[97] How have the courts responded?

At provincial level, the leading judgment[98] is that of Froneman J. in *Carephone v. Marcus*,[99] where he had to interpret the concept of 'justifiability.' He did so as follows:[100]

> [It] ... introduces a requirement of rationality in the *merit or outcome* of the administrative decision. This goes beyond mere procedural impropriety ... But it would be wrong to read into this section an attempt to abolish the distinction between review and appeal ... [In requiring justifiable administrative action], the Constitution does not purport to give courts the power to perform the administrative functions themselves, which would be the effect if justifiability ... is equated to justness or correctness. In determining [justifiability] value judgments will have to be made which will, almost inevitably, involve the consideration of the 'merits' of the matter ... Is there a rational objective basis justifying the connection made by the adminis-

> trative decision-maker between the material properly available to him and the conclusion ... eventually arrived at?

This approach clearly indicates the abandonment of the pre-1994 symptomatic unreasonableness test and goes further than the model of 'dialectical reasonableness' advanced by Lawrence Baxter some years before, relying on developments in England.[101] It took some time, however, for this interpretation to be tested in the appellate courts, and by that stage the constitutional language had been changed to that of 'reasonableness.' In addition, Parliament had seen fit to attempt to give content to the concept by including the nonsensical and outdated circularity of the *Wednesbury* test in the *PAJA*.[102]

A relatively unlikely set of circumstances caused the Constitutional Court to confront its approach to reasonableness as a ground of review. The government, in pursuit of its general policy of black economic empowerment and the redistribution of wealth, had announced that a significant proportion of the total allowable catch of different types of fish would be allocated through a permit and quota system to 'previously disadvantaged individuals.' In the event, instead of the 25 percent thus available for preferential allocation according to this criterion, only about 2 percent of the total catch was allocated in this way. Two black economic empowerment fishing consortia challenged the exercise of ministerial discretion as being unreasonable in its outcome, among other grounds, and succeeded in the Cape High Court in having the decision set aside.

The matter was taken to the Supreme Court of Appeal in *Minister of Environmental Affairs and Tourism v. Phambili Fisheries*,[103] in which the arguments about unreasonableness received short shrift. Schutz J.A., for the court, invoked 'deference' as the justification for holding that it would be entirely inappropriate for a court to intervene in as technical and policy-laden a field as the allocation of fishing permits and quotas, especially when preferential treatment for certain groups was both sanctioned and implemented.[104] One of the respondents was not deterred by this rather peremptory judgment, and took the dispute to the Constitutional Court in the *Bato Star Fishing* case.[105] The Constitutional Court dismissed the appeal unanimously, but in a remarkable manner, there being two separate judgments, each of which is concurred in by all the judges.

The judgment which appears second in the law reports, that of Ngcobo J., is unusual for a number of reasons. While it signals assent at the outset and at the end with the conclusions reached in the other judgment,[106] much of the rest of the language used tends to foreshadow a contrary outcome. Central to the discussion is a consideration of the meaning to be given to transformation of the economy and the empowerment of that part of the population which was unjustly excluded from participation in the economy under apartheid.[107] The judgment seems to be on the verge of declaring the percentage allocation of the catch dedicated to empowerment to be unreasonably small, especially in the light of public pronouncements prior to the tendering and allocation process.[108] In the end, the judgment shows restraint, perhaps conscious of the court's proper role under the separation of powers, but the reader has a real sense of the judge engaging with what it means in practical terms for economic power to be redistributed. One passage in particular gives a flavour of this approach, which is likely to recur in the future:[109]

> But transformation is a process. There are profound difficulties that will be confronted in giving effect to the constitutional commitments of achieving equality. We must not underestimate them. The measures that bring about the transformation will inevitably affect some members of the society adversely, particularly those coming from the previously advantaged communities.

From every point of view, this is a significant judgment.

So is the other judgment in *Bato Star* given by O'Regan J. This is the most influential judgment since 1994 as regards the meaning to be given to review for reasonableness. The court was confronted directly with the need to make sense of the circular definition of reasonableness in the *PAJA*,[110] and responded that it found the *Wednesbury*-style formulation adopted by Parliament to be 'unfortunate and confusing.'[111] Viewed consistently with relevant elements of the Constitution, the court held that reasonableness should be understood as requiring 'a simple test, namely, that an administrative decision will be reviewable if ... it is one that a reasonable decision-maker could not reach.'[112] This would depend on all the circumstances of the case, including 'the nature of the decision, the nature of the competing interests involved and the impact of the decision on the lives and well-being of those affected.'[113] O'Regan J. then considered whether review for reasonableness meant that the distinction between review and appeal had fallen away? Not so, O'Regan J said: 'Although the review functions of the court now have a substantive as well as a procedural ingredient, the distinction between appeals and reviews continues to be significant. [The Court's] task is to ensure that the decisions taken by administrative agencies fall within the bounds of reasonableness as required by the Constitution.'[114]

This is a refreshingly frank and, with respect, correct reading of the ambit of the administrative review power now entrusted to the judiciary by the Constitution. It acknowledges the practical reality that review includes a judicial perusal of the factual basis for administrative action to the extent necessary to determine its reasonableness. The 'rationality' of the *Pharmaceutical Manufacturers* judgment[115] is thus not enough, in that the court is now concerned not only with the process followed to reach an administrative decision, but also the effects of that decision on the parties. In advancing to this position, the court made little reference[116] to the notion of deference which had proved so attractive to the Supreme Court of Appeal in prior cases,[117] but was no doubt acutely aware of the underlying concern about the proper role of the judiciary in South Africa's democracy. It is to an assessment of the current state of play in this regard that I turn in the concluding part of this piece.

Deference with a Difference

Deference as a term of art has not been part of the lexicon of administrative law in South Africa for very long, although a particularly submissive and supine form of deference to the executive naturally characterized judicial policy in general from the late 1950s till 1990.[118] In fact, it appears that the notion of deference as applied to administrative law is best known to Canada, where its use has for some years been characterized as a convenient means of justification for the courts' curbing the ambit of their review in sectors of the administration where a high degree of discretion dependent on specialist expertise has been entrusted by the legislature to the administrator concerned.[119]

There can be no doubt, however, that administrative lawyers in the Commonwealth today 'speak of little else,'[120] and South Africa is no exception. Cora Hoexter was responsible for introducing the concept to the mainstream of South African law,[121] stimulated by the distinction drawn by Dyzenhaus between deference-as-respect and deference-as-submission.[122] In a wide-ranging, articulate and critical piece in which she lamented the continued predominance of judicial review in South

African administrative law and the opportunities lost in the recent bout of reforming the system,[123] Hoexter advocated the adoption of 'principles of restraint or deference to guide the courts' intervention in administrative law.'[124] She expressly rejected a 'return to the bad old days ... of judicial prostration to the dictates of the executive,'[125] and proposed instead the adoption of a theory of deference of the following sort:[126]

> a judicial willingness to appreciate the legitimate and constitutionally-ordained province of administrative agencies; to admit the expertise of those agencies in policy-laden or polycentric issues; to accord their interpretations of fact and law due respect; and to be sensitive in general to the interests legitimately pursued by administrative bodies and the practical and financial constraints under which they operate. This type of deference ... ought to be shaped by a conscious determination not to usurp the functions of administrative agencies; not to cross over from review to appeal.

Hoexter then proceeded to explore three themes which could appropriately inform the development of deference in South Africa: that of variability, of administrative action, and of reasonableness review,[127] and warned expressly against a misconceived notion of deference.[128] In concluding that judges would continue to exercise their review powers as they always had, she predicted rather gloomily that 'the debate about deference ... will be cancelled owing to lack of interest ... [a]dministrative lawyers will instead be debating the meaning of "rights" and other concepts.'[129]

I have set out Hoexter's views at some length, as they reflect many of the current and most important issues in South African, if not comparative, administrative law, and as they make a valuable contribution to the understanding of such issues. I do so also because, contrary to her prediction, judges have referred to her discussion of deference with a degree of enthusiasm which is both encouraging and alarming.[130]

On the one hand, it has been heartening to see the highest courts grappling openly with the development of a proper role for themselves in relation to the other branches of government, particularly in the socio-economic sphere, where the greatest potential for destructive conflict exists in a country like South Africa. Both judgments in *Bato Star* have moved the debate further in an authoritative manner, the court acknowledging that there will be complex circumstances when it will need to show 'due respect to the route selected by the decision-maker ... [while it] should not rubber-stamp an unreasonable decision simply because of the complexity of the decision or the identity of the decision-maker.'[131] In addition, the fact that the Constitutional Court holds that 'the need for Courts to treat decision-makers with appropriate deference or respect flows not from judicial courtesy or etiquette but from the fundamental constitutional principle of the separation of powers itself'[132] provides the basis for a healthy relationship between the executive and the judiciary in the future.

On the other hand, the judicial submissiveness of the past in the face of such clear violations of the rule of law combines with a degree of executive impatience with obstacles to socio-economic reform plans thrown up in the courts to create a sense of unease at the ready embrace of the notion of deference. The deliberate destruction of judicial independence by the executive in Zimbabwe provides an all-too-unsettling demonstration of the ease and speed with which courts can be cowed and manipulated.[133] There is little to suggest that South Africa is a comparable case, and it must be stressed that the official stance of the government, led by the example of former President Mandela, has been at least strictly correct in terms of the Constitution, and on occasion glowingly supportive of the courts. The executive has generally implemented judgments of the courts, although in some high-profile socio-economic awards it has struggled to deliver fully on its obligations. The only glaring instance of executive failure to comply with the judgments of the courts is to be found in the Eastern Cape Province, where the provincial government has been notoriously slow in giving effect to many judgments granting rights to social pensions to some of the poorest in South Africa.[134] This ironic situation probably has more to do with incompetence and corruption than wilful disobedience, but it has led to several expressions of judicial castigation.[135]

In sum, when one looks back at our bitter and divided past and the role of the judiciary in submitting itself to the executive and legislature, there is no reason to despair. We should rather celebrate the differences now prevalent, chief among them the Constitution and the promising first decade of judicial review. Along with the judges, all lawyers 'must rise to play the greater part,' with due respect but abundant vigilance.

NOTES

1 Frank R. Scott, 'Villanelle for Our Time' (1943).

2 Frank Scott (1899–1985) was a Canadian poet, lawyer, and intellectual. He

studied history at Oxford as a Rhodes scholar, was politically active in the Canadian socialist movement, and served as dean of law at McGill from 1961 to 1964. He won the 1977 Governor General's award for non-fiction for his *Essays on the Constitution* (Toronto: University of Toronto Press, 1977) and the 1981 Governor General's award for poetry for his *Collected Poems* (Toronto: McClelland and Stewart, 1981). See generally S. Djwa, *The Politics of Imagination: A Life of F.R. Scott* (Toronto: McClelland and Stewart, 1987) and S. Djwa and R.St.J. MacDonald, eds, *On F.R. Scott: Essays on His Contributions to Law, Literature and Politics* (Kingston, ON: McGill-Queen's University Press, 1983).

3 By Leonard Cohen, in *Dear Heather* (New York: Columbia Records, 2004).

4 In a course entitled 'Administrative law in Commonwealth Countries,' which focused mainly on the law of Australia, Canada, New Zealand, South Africa, and the United Kingdom.

5 They were: D. Mullan, 'A Comparison of the Impact of the New Zealand Bill of Rights Act and the Canadian Charter of Rights and Freedoms on Judicial Review of Administrative Action' (2003) 1 New Zealand Journal of Public and International Law 115; D. Mullan, 'Deference from *Baker* to *Suresh* and Beyond: Interpreting the Conflicting Signals' in David Dyzenhaus, ed., *The Unity of Public Law* (Oxford: Hart, 2004) 21; and D. Mullan, '*Ocean Port Hotel* and Statutory Compromises of Tribunal Independence' (2002) 9 Canadian Labour and Employment Law Journal 189.

6 This event, arranged by Professor Jeffrey Jowell of University College, London, provided an ideal opportunity for the initial drafters of South Africa's administrative law statute to hear the comments and criticisms of leading administrative lawyers from a number of countries.

7 Professor Arthurs, professor of law and political science, and president emeritus, York University, Toronto, was a guest of the Institute of Development and Labour Law, University of Cape Town, in a seminar on 'Constitutionalism and Labour Law' (paper presented to the Institute of Development and Labour Law, University of Cape Town, 23 February 2004).

8 As is well known, Dicey's influential *The Law of the Constitution* (London: Macmillan, 1885) took a harshly critical view of administrative law, seeing it as somehow inimical to his vision of the rule of law (see especially, 'Rule of Law compared with Droit Administratif,' chap. 12).

9 Early exceptions to this dearth of published comment were: Arthur Lourie, 'Administrative Law in South Africa' (1927) 44 S.A.L.J. 10; S.B. Kitchin, 'Non-Judicial Tribunals' (1928) 45 S.A.L.J. 193; Ben Beinart, 'Administrative Law' (1948) 11 T.H.R.H.R. 204. The first systematic treatment of the subject

came in the form of M. Wiechers, *Administratiefreg* (Durban: Butterworths, 1973) in Afrikaans, followed by L. Baxter, *Administrative Law* (Cape Town: Juta, 1984) in English.

10 W.H.B. Dean, 'Our Administrative Law: A Dismal Science?' (1986) 2 S.A.J.H.R. 164.

11 Constitutional and statutory regulation of general administrative law did not occur until 1994.

12 This was one of the major areas in which state and individual came into conflict in the courts in the formative years of the Union of South Africa, after 1910. For an account of the appellate jurisprudence, see Hugh Corder, *Judges at Work* (Cape Town: Juta, 1984) at 169–88 [Corder, *Judges*].

13 [1912] A.D. 605.

14 Ibid. at 617–18, Laurence J.

15 Ibid.

16 *Shidiack v. Union Government*, [1912] A.D. 642 at 653.

17 For a detailed and outstanding account of this movement, see M. Chanock, *The Making of South African Legal Culture, 1902–1936: Fear, Favour and Prejudice* (Cambridge: Cambridge University Press, 2001).

18 For an account of the work of the Appellate Division in this area, see Corder, *Judges*, *supra* note 12 at chaps. 4–6.

19 *R. v. Padsha*, [1923] A.D. 281.

20 *Minister of Posts and Telegraphs v. Rasool*, [1934] A.D. 167.

21 *Sachs and Diamond v. Minister of Justice*, [1934] A.D. 11.

22 For a general account of the judicial record since 1950, see C.F. Forsyth, *In Danger for Their Talents: A Study of the Appellate Division of the Supreme Court of South Africa* (Cape Town: Juta, 1985). The pioneering and most extensive work on judicial attitudes to race and security is that of C.J.R. Dugard, *Human Rights and the South African Legal Order* (Princeton: Princeton University Press, 1978).

23 See *R. v. Abdurahman*, [1950] 3 S.Afr.L.R. 136 (A).

24 See *R. v. Lusu*, [1953] 2 S.Afr.L.R. 484 (A).

25 See *R. v. Ngwevela*, [1954] 1 S.Afr.L.R. 123 (A).

26 The 'constitutional crisis' caused by the repeated judicial declaration of invalidity of an act of the 'sovereign' Parliament is well known in Commonwealth legal circles. See generally, I. Loveland, *By Due Process of Law: Racial Discrimination and the Right to Vote in South Africa, 1855–1960* (Oxford: Hart, 1999). I daresay David Mullan had to study the constitutional implications of *Harris v. Minister of the Interior*, [1952] 2 S.Afr.L.R. 428 (AD) and the associated cases for his LLB degree in New Zealand in the mid-1960s.

27 *Collins v. Minister of the Interior*, [1957] 1 S.Afr.L.R. 552 (A.D.).

28 See e.g. *Minister of the Interior v. Lockhat*, [1961] 2 S.Afr.L.R. 587 (A); *Roussouw v. Sachs*, [1964] 2 S.Afr.L.R. 551 (A); *Loza v. Police Station Commander, Durbanville*, [1964] 2 S.Afr.L.R. 545 (A); *Schermbrucker v. Klindt*, [1965] 4 S.Afr.L.R. 606 (A); *South African Defence and Aid Fund v. Minister of Justice*, [1967] 1 S.Afr.L.R. 263 (A).

29 In its most submissive sense see David Dyzenhaus, 'The Politics of Deference: Judicial Review and Democracy' in Michael Taggart, ed., *The Province of Administrative Law* (Oxford: Hart, 1997) 279.

30 For a discussion of judicial appointments at this time, see Dugard, *supra* note 21 at 10–11.

31 See *In re Dube*, [1979] 3 S.Afr.L.R. 820 (N); *Komani N.O. v. Bantu Affairs Administration Board, Peninsula Area*, [1980] 4 S.Afr.L.R. 448 (A); *Oos-Randse Administrasieraad v. Rikhoto*, [1983] 3 S.Afr.L.R. 595 (A).

32 See *Mathebe v. Die Regering van die R.S.A.*, [1988] 3 S.Afr.L.R. 667 (A); *Lefuo v. State President of the R.S.A. and Government of QwaQwa*, [1990] 2 S.Afr.L.R. 679 (A).

33 *University of Cape Town v. Ministers of Education and Culture*, [1988] 3 S.Afr.L.R. 203 (C).

34 See the standard formula of the grounds of review set out in *JSE v. Witwatersrand Nigel Ltd*, [1988] 3 S.Afr.L.R. 132 (A) at 152, Corbett J.A.

35 *Administrator, Transvaal v. Traub*, [1989] 4 S.Afr.L.R. 731 (A).

36 The term is usually attributed to Lord Denning M.R. in *Schmidt v. Secretary of State for Home Affairs*, [1969] 2 Ch. 149, but the courts of England, Canada, and Australia only fully embraced the doctrine in the early 1980s.

37 *Republic of South Africa Constitution Act*, 1983, No. 110 of 1983, the so-called Tricameral Constitution, as Parliament had three houses, split along racial lines to accommodate whites, coloureds, and Indians. There were equivalent executive structures; the courts were not directly affected.

38 No. 74 of 1982. This 'modernized' legislation was one of the products of a government commission of inquiry, chaired by Judge of Appeal P.J. Rabie, who became chief justice soon afterwards, and was kept on in office controversially after reaching the age of retirement, at the height of the state of emergency.

39 No. 3 of 1953.

40 The years 1983 to 1990 were of course marked by widespread public revolt against all structures of government, which was unlawful in terms of the then legislative regime, and intermittent attacks by the guerrilla forces of the exiled organizations.

41 See e.g. *Minister of Law and Order v. Hurley*, [1985] 4 S.Afr.L.R. 709 (D);

Nkondo and Gumede v. Minister of Law and Order, [1986] 2 S.Afr.L.R. 756 (A); *M.A.W.U. v. Castell NO*, [1985] 2 S.Afr.L.R. 280 (D).

42 See e.g. *Bloem v. State President*, [1986] 4 S.Afr.L.R. 1064 (O); *Momoniat and Naidoo v. Minister of Law and Order*, [1986] 2 S.Afr.L.R. 264 (W); *Nqumba v. State President*, [1987] 1 S.Afr.L.R. 456 (E).

43 *Omar v. Minister of Law and Order*, [1987] 3 S.Afr.L.R. 859 (A) led the way, followed by *Minister of Law and Order v. Dempsey*, [1988] 3 S.Afr.L.R. 19 (A), and *Nqumba v. State President*, [1988] 4 S.Afr.L.R. 224 (A), among others.

44 See especially S. Ellmann, *In a Time of Trouble: Law and Liberty in South Africa's State of Emergency* (Oxford: Clarendon Press, 1992).

45 *In Staatspresident v. U.D.F.*, [1988] 4 S.Afr.L.R. 830 (A).

46 Vagueness was a well-established ground of review at common law, but the court held that it did not fall under the *ultra vires* doctrine, and so the ousting of the courts' jurisdiction in terms of s. 5B of the *Public Safety Act* of 1953 prevented it from exercising its authority to review.

47 For accounts of this process, see H. Corder, 'The Constitutionalisation of South African Administrative Law' (1997) 3 European Public Law 541, and C. Hoexter, *The New Constitutional and Administrative Law* (Cape Town: Juta, 2002), chap. 1.

48 *The Republic of South Africa Constitution Act, 1993*, No. 200 of 1993, s. 24 [*1993 Transitional Constitution*].

49 *Constitution of the Republic of South Africa 1996*, No. 108 of 1996, s. 33 [*1996 Constitution*].

50 See, chap. 2 of the Constitution. See also, the rights in s. 32 (access to information), s. 33 (just administrative action), s. 34 (access to court – an anti-ouster clause provision), and s. 35 (criminal process rights, of detained, accused and imprisoned persons). This is not a formal sub-group of rights. An important aspect is to note that all rights granted are subject to limitation according to a broad formula set out in s. 36, of which proportionality forms a key element.

51 For an account of its genesis, see L. du Plessis and H. Corder, *Understanding South Africa's Transitional Bill of Rights* (Cape Town: Juta, 1994) at 165–70.

52 The scope of the right to written reasons has been narrowed, for example; other aspects have been broadened, and the formulation considerably simplified.

53 *1996 Constitution*, *supra* note 49, s. 33.

54 *Promotion of Administrative Justice Act* (*PAJA*). No. 3 of 2000.

55 It entered into force on 30 November 2000.

56 *PAJA*, *supra* note 54, s. 3.

57 Ibid. s. 4.

58 Ibid. ss. 7, 9.
59 Ibid. ss. 5, 9.
60 Ibid. s. 8.
61 Ibid. s. 1(i).
62 Ibid. s. 6(2).
63 Ibid. s. 6(2)(f)(ii).
64 Ibid. s. 6(2)(h).
65 See *supra* note 45.
66 The test for proportionality is an integral part of the limitations analysis (s. 30) as adopted by the Constitutional Court from its first judgment *(S v. Makwanyane,* [1995] 3 S.Afr.L.R. 391 (S.Afr.Const.Ct.)) on the level of judicial review of legislative action. The Working Group of the Law Reform Commission, which proposed a draft act, included proportionality as a ground of review, but Parliament preferred the *Wednesbury*-unreasonableness formulation.
67 *PAJA, supra* note 54, s. 6(2)(i).
68 See the reference to 'accountability, openness and responsiveness' as founding values of the *1996 Constitution, supra* note 49, in s. 1(d), as well as the detailed guidelines and values for the provision of service to the public by the public administration in ibid., s. 195.
69 This element of balance or compromise was expressly set out in the 'postamble' to the *1993 Transitional Constitution, supra* note 47, and runs like a thread through the final constitution (see e.g. the manner of granting socio-economic rights to shelter, food, water, social and medical assistance in ss. 26 and 27) and the jurisprudence of the Constitutional Court thus far. See e.g. *A.Z.A.P.O. v. President of the Republic of South Africa,* [1996] 4 S.Afr.L.R. 671 (S.Afr.Const.Ct,) and *Government of the Republic of South Africa v. Grootboom,* [2001] 1 S.Afr.L.R. 46 (S.Afr.Const.Ct,).
70 The most detailed and recent study is to be found in J.R. de Ville, *Judicial Review of Administrative Action in South Africa* (Durban: Butterworths, 2003).
71 [1997] 6 B.Const.L.R. 708.
72 Granted now by the *1996 Constitution, supra* note 49, s. 84(2)(f).
73 A preliminary survey of the courts' reaction is to be found in D. Van Wyk, 'Administrative Justice in *Bernstein v. Bester* and *Nel v. Le Roux*' (1997) 13 S.A.J.H.R. 249.
74 For an account of the drafting aspect of the transitional constitution, see Du Plessis and Corder, *supra* note 51, at 191–200. The distrust with which the Appellate Division was regarded, chiefly on account of its record under the State of Emergency, was emphasized by the fact that the provincial divisions of the Supreme Court were in fact granted constitutional jurisdiction.

75 See the *1996 Constitution, supra* note 49, s. 168 (3).

76 [1998] 2 S.Afr.L.R. 1115 (S.Afr.S.C.).

77 As formulated in *Fedsure Life Assurance Ltd v. Greater Johannesburg Metropolitan Council,* [1999] 1 S.Afr.L.R. 374 at para. 96 (S.Afr.Const.Ct.).

78 Ibid. at para. 105. This case is significant for drawing the boundaries of 'administrative action,' the Constitutional Court holding that budgetary decisions of a municipal authority made after deliberation by an elected council were legislative and not administrative in nature, and so did not fall to be reviewed in terms of the right to administrative justice.

79 [2000] 1 S.Afr.L.R. 1 (S.Afr.Const.Ct.).

80 Ibid. at para. 135.

81 *Commissioner for Customs and Excise v. Container Logistics (Pty) Ltd; Commissioner for Customs and Excise v. Rennies Group t/a Renfreight,* [1999] 3 S.Afr.L.R. 771 (S.Afr.S.C.).

82 Ibid. at para. 20.

83 *Pharmaceutical Manufacturers Association of South Africa: In re Ex Parte President of the Republic of South Africa,* [2000] 2 S.Afr.L.R. 674 (S.Afr.Const.Ct.) [*Pharmaceutical Manufacturers*].

84 Ibid. at para. 44.

85 Ibid. at para. 33.

86 Ibid. at para. 45.

87 See the *1996 Constitution, supra* note 49, s. 8(2), as applied by the courts.

88 *Pharmaceutical Manufacturers, supra* note 83.

89 Ibid. at paras. 85–86, 90.

90 As has been described, in the absence of any entrenched rights and in the face of legislative and executive tyranny, applications for judicial review of administrative action were often the last resort within the law for those suffering under repression by the state.

91 The approach was known as the 'symptomatic unreasonableness' test. Even the unsatisfactory circularity of the '*Wednesbury* unreasonableness' of English law was too bold a step for the South African judiciary.

92 *1993 Transitional Constitution, supra* note 48, s. 24(d). There was a conscious decision not to constitutionalize 'reasonableness' at this stage: see du Plessis and Corder, *supra* note 51 at 169. Commentators, however, argued that the proper meaning of 'justifiability' was in fact 'reasonableness,' or at the very least a rational and coherent decision-making process. See E. Mureinik, 'A Bridge to Where? Introducing the Interim Bill of Rights' (1994) 10 S.A.J.H.R. 31 at 41.

93 *1996 Constitution, supra* note 49, s. 33(1).

94 For a recent comment on this, see H. Corder, 'Without deference, with respect' (2004) 121 S.A.L.J. 438.

95 In the constitutional arena, as regards judicial review of legislative action, the talk is of the 'counter-majoritarian difficulty' or the 'democratic deficit,' both of which have an indirect influence in the executive sphere.

96 One of the most influential authorities is the article by Dyzenhaus, *supra* note 29, which concentrates on the application of a deferential approach (as 'respect' not as 'submission') in Canadian law. In the United Kingdom, see J. Jowell, 'Judicial Deference: Servility, Civility or Institutional Capacity' [2003] P.L. 592.

97 See generally, J.W.F. Allison, *A Continental Distinction in the Common Law: A Historical and Comparative Perspective on English Public Law* (Oxford: Oxford University Press, 1994).

98 See also *Roman v. Williams N.O.*, [1998] 1 S.Afr.L.R. 270 (C), in which Van Deventer J. equated justifiability with proportionality, an approach that has not been followed.

99 *Carephone (Pty.) Ltd. v. Marcus N.O.*, [1998] 10 B.Const.L.R. 1326 (LAC).

100 Ibid. at paras. 31, 32, 35, 37 [emphasis in original].

101 Baxter, *supra* note 9 at 477–97, 522–29.

102 Section 6(2)(h).

103 [2003] 6 S.Afr.L.R. 407 (S.Afr.S.C.) [*Phambili*].

104 Ibid. at para. 47.

105 *Bato Star Fishing v. Minister of Environmental Affairs and Tourism*, [2004] 7 B.Const.L.R. 687 [*Bato Star*].

106 Ibid. at paras. 69, 110–115.

107 Ibid. at paras. 73–78.

108 Ibid. at paras. 107–108 and n. 88.

109 Ibid. at para. 76.

110 *PAJA*, *supra* note 54, s. 6(2)(h).

111 *Bato Star*, *supra* note 105 at para. 44, approving the approach of Lord Cooke of Thorndon in *R. v. Chief Constable of Sussex, ex parte International Trader's Ferry Ltd*, [1999] 1 All E.R. 129 at 157 (H.L.).

112 Ibid.

113 Ibid.

114 *Bato Star*, *supra* note 105 at para. 45.

115 See the discussion *supra* at notes 83–90 and accompanying text.

116 Other than to state, at para. 46, that it preferred the word 'respect' in this context, after quoting the views of Schutz J.A. a quo.

117 See *Logbro Properties C.C. v. Bedderson N.O.*, [2003] 2 S.Afr.L.R. 460 (S.Afr.S.C.) at para. 21, Cameron J.A. [*Logbro*]; *Phambili*, *supra* note 103 at para. 47, Schutz J.A.

118 See the discussion and sources referred to *supra* note 22.

119 See the discussion in Dyzenhaus, *supra* note 29; Mullan, *supra* note 5; and Grant Huscroft's contribution to this volume.

120 See e.g. Lord Lester, 'With Great Respect and Deference' in Richard Gordon, ed., *Judicial Review in the New Millennium* (London: Thomson/Sweet & Maxwell, 2003) chap. 1; Lord Walker 'Second Guessing Government: Judicial Deference and Human Rights' (lecture presented to the Oriel Law Society, Oriel College, University of Oxford, February 2005) and the several references to articles about deference in Britain.

121 See C. Hoexter, 'The Future of Judicial Review in South African Administrative Law' (2000) 117 S.A.L.J. 484.

122 See *supra* note 29; See also, Hoexter, ibid. at n.79.

123 Hoexter, ibid. at 484–99.

124 Ibid. at 500.

125 Ibid. at 501.

126 Ibid. at 501–2.

127 Ibid. at 502–13.

128 Ibid. at 513–19.

129 Ibid. at 519.

130 At appellate level, her views were quoted in *Logbro, supra* note 117 at para. 21, Cameron J.A.; *Phambili, supra* note 103 at para. 47, Schutz J.A.; *Bato Star, supra* note 105 at para. 46, O'Regan J.

131 *Bato Star*, ibid. at para. 48, O' Regan J.

132 Ibid. at para. 46. O'Regan J. cites Dyzenhaus, *supra* note 29 in support, and proceeds to quote from the speech of Lord Hoffmann in *R. (on the application of Pro Life Alliance) v. British Broadcasting Corporation*, [2003] 2 All E.R. 977 (H.L.) at paras. 75–76 in amplification of her views.

133 For a recent account, see K. Saller, *The Judicial Institution in Zimbabwe* (Cape Town: Siber Ink, 2004).

134 See e.g. *Jayiya v. Member of the Executive Council for Welfare, Eastern Cape*, [2004] 2 S.Afr.L.R. 611 (S.Afr.S.C.); *Ngxusa v. Permanent Secretary, Department of Welfare, Eastern Cape*, [2001] 2 S.Afr.L.R. 609 (E.); *Vumazonke and three others v. Member of the Executive Council for Social Development, Eastern Cape*, (25 November 2004) Eastern Cape Division 110/04, E. Cape Div., Plasket J.

135 See *supra* note 134.

The Importance of Being Contextual: Deference South of the Border

ALFRED C. AMAN, JR.

In a recent article, David Mullan notes the vigorous debate over judicial deference to agency decisions in Canada, the United States, and elsewhere, citing 'what appear to be irreconcilable differences in philosophy and approach among the protagonists whether they are judges, academics, agency or tribunal members, or practicing lawyers.'[1] Professor Mullan cautions against any simple and simplistic formula for resolving such differences. Indeed, as he observes, at the basis of these debates are issues for which 'there may be no absolutes as far as the nature and extent of judicial review is concerned and ... any particular set of principles may be highly contingent and context sensitive ... [I]t should be in no way surprising if the rubric and intensity of judicial review varies from era to era within particular jurisdictions.'[2] In short, judicial deference to agency decisions, especially agency interpretations of statutes, involves multiple and often complex relationships among courts and agencies, as well as the legislative and executive branches of government.

Professor Mullan's insights on the elusiveness of any single or unified principle of judicial review is especially apt when applied to *Chevron, U.S.A., Inc. v. Natural Resources Defense Council, Inc.*,[3] the leading case in the United States on judicial deference to agency interpretations of law. Like the leading Canadian case, *CUPE, Local 963 v. New Brunswick Liquor Corporation*,[4] which preceded *Chevron* by five years, *Chevron* represented a defining moment in judicial review of agency actions in the United States. Courts were no longer to decide for themselves if agencies properly interpreted ambiguous statutory terms. Unless Congress spoke directly to 'the precise question in issue,' courts would now defer to all 'reasonable' agency interpretations of ambiguous statutory terms.[5] The *CUPE* standard went even further, requiring courts to defer to administrative tribunals protected by a privative clause and acting within their jurisdiction, unless the agency interpretation was 'patently unreasonable.'[6]

Both standards sound simple and straightforward enough, but, in the United States at least, the application of *Chevron* has turned out to be fraught with difficulty and often controversial. *Chevron* has never provided a consistent touchstone for judicial deference decisions, but it did create a mood, one that implicitly argued in favour of congressional specificity, and failing that, explicitly granting much greater discretion to agencies interpreting ambiguous statutory terms. *Chevron* made judicial restraint and agency discretion over legal issues important tenets of U. S. administrative law, but it remains a source of intense debate in U.S. courts and in law journals, no matter how many times it is tweaked or applied in new ways.

Over the past twenty-five years or so, the deferential approach set forth in *CUPE* has also generated its share of controversy and confusion, though, as Professor Mullan notes, 'by and large, until recently, there has been little reason to believe that the Supreme Court would turn back on itself on the basic approach to the judicial review administrative action.'[7] Indeed, the subsequent evolution of *CUPE* was characterized by the expansion of the deference principles it espoused. Deference clearly has become an accepted tenet of Canadian administrative law, although today there appears also to be a resurgence of judicial review in cases in which one might have expected deference to apply.[8] Jurisdictional issues also seem to arise more frequently these days.[9] Nevertheless, as Professor Mullan concludes: 'the Court is still a long way from giving up on the basic philosophy of [deference] and reverting to the highly interventionist mode that characterized the relationship between the Court and the administrative process in the nearly 30 years between 1950 and 1979.'[10]

This essay will explore the development of doctrines of judicial deference to agency interpretations of law in the United States. The first part introduces *Chevron* deference and raises some basic questions: when will judges defer, and what is the theoretical basis of such deference? Specifically, what are they deferring to, how and why do they do it? As we shall see, *Chevron* was more about deference to the president and a particular political conception of the administrative process than it was about the technicalities of the decisions involved and the technical capacity of agency decision makers to make those decisions competently.

The second section focuses on judicial methodology, primarily discussing 'textualism' and the relationship of this approach to statutory interpretation to the legitimacy to be derived from deferring to executive power. It is argued that this kind of deference places great weight on the legitimacy to be derived by linking agency decisions to an elected official – namely, the president. A more contextual approach to agency decisions, however, shows how much may be at stake in such cases. This is particularly true since deference questions often arise today in the context of deregulation and policy changes designed to transform statutes by infusing them with economically-based goals and regulatory approaches. A close reading of the legislative history of many of the statutes involved would likely show that Congress never considered seriously nor necessarily intended such a transformation. As our discussion of *Chevron* will show, however, such cases often seem to be relatively easy ones for the application of deference. The agencies involved are not trying to expand their jurisdiction, but rather to limit it substantially. Nevertheless, the effects of such statutory interpretations can result in dramatic changes in policy without any significant congressional involvement in the process. In such contexts, deference to the executive branch[11] as a way of legitimizing such change risks transforming our regulatory system into a kind of parliamentary regime, which, of course, it is not, thereby undermining more democratic forms of change, such as statutory amendments or legislative repeals by Congress.

Deference in such contexts is even more problematic when it applies to agency policies made informally and, often, largely outside of public view. The final section turns to *U.S. v. Mead*,[12] a case that reintroduces some aspects of pre-*Chevron* approaches to judicial review. *Mead* is, perhaps, not so much a return to the past as it is a modern recognition of the complexities of context, particularly as agencies try to make policy in more informal and less transparent ways. The return of a more contextual approach to deference, at least in some situations, may not make decisions more predictable, but it may better ensure that courts discuss deference in more complex ways that take agencies and their law-making roles seriously.

Complexity often yields difficulties in predicting judicial outcomes in particular cases, but much of the complexity surrounding *Chevron* over the years arises not only from questions concerning what should be left to the discretion of a particular agency in a particular case, but also from judicial debates over the methodology to be employed when interpreting statutes – all statutes, not just those pertaining to administrative agencies. 'Textualism' is often invoked by the Supreme Court when interpreting statutes. This methodology, as we shall see, is deeply intertwined with another rationale for deference and that is, a strong desire to defer to executive power generally. Cases involving the application of *Chevron* deference often are battlegrounds for issues that go well beyond the respective institutional capabilities and limits of courts and administrative agencies.

This essay concludes that the future problems presented by the application of deference doctrines in the United States will involve more than predicting when courts will or will not defer to agencies. Rather, there may well be an over-extension of deference principles to cases involving executive power and constitutional rights. These issues are precisely the kinds of questions that courts should decide independently.

Deference: To What, How, and When

In *Crowell v. Benson*,[13] the U.S. Supreme Court long ago rejected the constitutional argument that article III of the Constitution prohibited Congress from vesting fact-finding authority in an administrative agency. In so doing, however, the Court distinguished questions of law, reserving these for independent judicial review. This ruling did not mean that courts would not defer to agency determinations of law. For the most part, they did so with regularity, especially in cases involving mixed questions of fact and law – that is, the application of statutory terms to facts found by the agency. Such deference was a judicial option, not a doctrinal necessity. The case law, however, was often ambiguous (even confused) in this regard, especially when questions of mixed fact and law were involved. Courts deferred to the outcomes in those cases with language that made it appear they were deferring to questions of law in the same way they deferred to agency findings of fact. They did this, in effect, by collapsing the law application stage of their analysis with the law formulation part of the process. In other words, some courts used deferential language with regard to questions of law, without making clear that they did so only because they independently agreed with the agency's underlying statement of the law involved.

Before examining *Chevron* in some detail, it is useful to set forth, briefly, the basics of the law of judicial review as it existed before *Chevron* was decided.

*Judicial Review, Pre-*Chevron

The leading pre-*Chevron* case on judicial review of questions of law, *National Labor Relations Board v. Hearst Publications, Inc.*[14] is a prime example of this approach. *Hearst* is often cited to support a limited judicial role in dealing with questions of law, particularly the application of statutory terms to the facts in a case, but it is no *Chevron.* The case dealt with the meaning of the statutory term 'employee.' Writing for the majority in that case, Justice Rutledge deferred to the agency in this way:[15]

> where the question is one of specific application of a broad statutory term in a proceeding in which the agency administering the statute must determine it initially, the reviewing court's function is limited. Like ... the Federal Communication Commission's determination that one company is under the 'control' of another ... the Board's determination that specified persons are 'employees' under this Act is to be accepted if it has 'warrant in the record' and a reasonable basis in law.

On closer examination, however, it is clear that the Court engaged in a much more thorough and independent analysis of the law than this oft-quoted language indicates.

Hearst arose from the refusal of four Los Angeles newspapers to bargain collectively with a union representing so-called newsboys who distributed their papers from newsstands on the streets. The newspapers argued that newsboys were not employees within the meaning of the *National Labor Relations Act* (*NLRA*). Though the union was properly certified, the newspapers refused to bargain with it. The National Labor Relations Board found that the newsboys were 'employees' under the act and ordered the newspapers to cease and desist in these violations, and to bargain with the union. The newspapers appealed. Though the Circuit Court of Appeals agreed with them, the Supreme Court reversed and affirmed the board's ruling.

The principal question for the Supreme Court was whether the newsboys were employees under the *NLRA*. Before deferring to the board's interpretation of this provision, however, the court carefully examined whether the board had, in fact, used the proper legal test in determining the scope of the statutory term 'employee.' The court first discussed, but rejected the argument that employees should be interpreted in accord with common law standards. The Court then considered whether state law should govern in this matter, and rejected that possibility as well. Instead, the Court concluded the issue in this case had to be 'answered primarily from the history, terms and purposes'[16] of the *NLRA* itself. In this case, 'it cannot be irrelevant that the particular workers in these cases are subject, as a matter of economic fact, to the evil the statute was designed to eradicate and that the remedies it affords are appropriate for preventing them or curing their harmful effects in the special situation.'[17] Having independently determined that the board's approach was in accord with its own view of the law, the Court deferred to the result reached by the board's application of the statute to the facts of this case. In short, the Court in *Hearst* engaged in a two-step analysis: Did the agency apply the proper test to the facts in this case? And, assuming the board used the proper factors in deciding what an employee was for purposes of the *NLRA*, was its application of that term reasonable? In step one, the Court engaged in *de novo* review. It deferred only when it independently determined the board was applying the statute properly.

Another important pre-*Chevron* case involved the legality of agency interpretive rules. In *Skidmore v. Swift & Co.*,[18] the Supreme Court reviewed an administrator's interpretation of the *Fair Labor Standards Act*. Seven firemen brought an action in Federal Court seeking compensation for their confinement to the fire hall three and a half to four nights a week. They had to be available only to answer any alarms that might arise. The men used their time as they saw fit, but they were required to stay in or close to the fire hall. The issue for the Court was whether their required presence constituted 'work' for purposes of the act.

The Court noted that this was not a case in which Congress utilized 'the services of an administrative agency to find facts and to determine in the first instance whether particular cases fell within or without the Act.'[19] Nevertheless, it was expected that the administrator, whose office was created under the act, would consider issues such as these and he set forth his views in an interpretive bulletin. Such documents did not have the force of law, nor were they developed in the context of rulemaking or adjudicatory adversarial proceedings. Yet, the Court noted that they were nonetheless 'made in pursuance of official duty, based upon more specialized experience and broader investigations and information than is likely to come to a judge in a particular case.'[20] The Court found the administrator's views rejecting petitioners' requests for overtime compensation persuasive in this case. Those views, expressed informally in an agency bulletin, were not binding generally, said the Court, but might be entitled to respect after a variety of factors were considered: 'The weight of such a judgment in a particular case will depend upon the thoroughness evident in its consideration, the validity of its reasoning, its consistency with earlier and later pronouncements, and all those factors which give it power to persuade, if lacking power to control.'[21]

This was, by and large, the broad outline of the law of judicial review when the *Chevron* case came up for decision. Prior to *Chevron*, courts did not intrude upon agency decision-making in most cases, and they were evidently willing to defer to demonstrated agency expertise. Yet, so far as what might be called pure questions of law – that is, the meaning of a statutory term as opposed to how it was applied to a particular set of facts – courts retained the right to decide the law. *Chevron* significantly altered this long standing principle.

Chevron v. NRDC

Chevron[22] began as a challenge to the repeal by the Environmental Protection Agency (EPA) of rules promulgated during the Carter administration pursuant to the mandates of the *Clean Air Act 1970*,[23] as amended in 1977.[24] These statutes directed the EPA to establish primary and secondary national standards of ambient air quality for various pollutants. Each state was to devise an implementation plan for each pollutant, setting forth its program for achieving the required air quality standards by a certain date.

In 1977 Congress amended the act to impose even more stringent requirements on states that had not yet reduced pollution to levels below the ambient standards in what were called nonattainment areas. These provisions required permits 'for the construction and operation of new or modified stationary sources'[25] of air pollution. A state could issue a permit for the construction of a new or modified major source in a nonattainment area only if the proposed source met these stringent requirements. The primary goal of these amendments was to reduce pollution in nonattainment areas. The legislative history suggests that cost was to be a factor in attempts to achieve this goal, but arguably not to the extent argued by the government in *Chevron*.[26]

Consistent with the apparent stringency of the 1977 amendments, the EPA during the Carter presidency viewed all individual pieces of plant equipment as 'stationary sources' of pollution within the meaning of the act. The relevant statutory provisions required all new sources of pollution, or modifications to major stationary sources, that increased the amount of pollution by more than one hundred tons per year to comply with the 'lowest achievable emission rate.' The Carter EPA applied this stringent standard to each piece of equipment in the plant that might potentially be replaced. In this way, the Carter EPA hoped that pollution in nonattainment areas would, in fact, begin to decrease.

In response to President Reagan's directive that agencies conduct a '[g]overnment-wide reexamination of regulatory burdens and complexities,' the Reagan EPA conducted an informal rule-making proceeding, which resulted in the repeal of the Carter EPA rules and the implementation of a so-called 'bubble' concept. Under the bubble approach, the EPA defined a major stationary source as the entire plant, rather than the individual facilities within the plant. It was thus possible to replace individual pieces of equipment within a plant without any pollution controls whatsoever, if the owner could show that the net increase in *total* pollution would not exceed one hundred tons per year. The entire plant was, in effect, encased in an imaginary bubble for the purpose of determining whether the requirements of the 1977 act should apply.

The net effect of the bubble concept was to lessen considerably the stringency of the Carter EPA rules. It allowed for the possibility that plants in nonattainment areas could essentially maintain the status quo when they replaced individual pieces of equipment rather than actually lower their overall level of pollution. The bubble concept thus helped replace the less cost-conscious regulatory approach to pollution control espoused by the Carter EPA and affirmed by the courts with a new regulatory approach designed to mitigate the costs borne by those creating the pollution. In so doing, it allowed the essentially consumer-oriented *Clean Air Act* to take on a distinct producer orientation.[27]

Achieving statutory goals in a more cost-efficient manner is almost always a valid goal, but the bubble approach arguably did more than lower the costs of achieving the act's regulatory goals. It was also likely to have a substantial impact on the curtailment of pollution in nonattainment areas. It enabled polluters to upgrade their equipment without necessarily lowering their total pollution rate. It was at least questionable whether Congress had authorized a regulatory approach that emphasized the costs of regulation while possibly maintaining the status quo in nonattainment areas. This was, however, the way the government argued the case in court.

In its brief to the Supreme Court, the EPA 'spoke' economics. It asked the court to '[s]uppose that it is economically desirable to modernize and expand the capacity of machine *A*, leading to an increase in its emissions to 700 units, and that at the same time emissions from machine *B* could be correspondingly reduced from 500 to 300 units.'[28] The EPA went on to argue that, under these circumstances, review prior to the granting of a construction permit would be pointless since the project would not adversely affect air quality. Thus, the EPA concluded:[29]

> [The bubble approach] ensures that emissions from new or modified sources *do not prejudice attainment;* it requires review of those projects that could interfere with achievement of national air quality standards. It also facilitates the statutory policies of industrial growth and modernization by eliminating the costs necessary to comply with new source review for projects that do not adversely affect air quality. And it gives a plant owner the flexibility to control emissions in the most efficient manner.

This is, essentially, an argument for accepting the environmental status quo at the least possible regulatory cost, but one that gives little weight to the fact that the 1977 act, as applied to nonattainment areas, was intended to achieve more than the status quo. The EPA's approach is seemingly at odds with the overall structure of the *Clean Air Act*, its legislative history, and at least one previous judicial interpretation of the act by the U.S. Court of Appeals for the District of Columbia Circuit.[30]

Arguably, and more importantly, using a market-oriented approach as the primary means of assuring environmental quality changed significantly the ends of the program mandated by Congress. This regulation did not easily lend itself to the use of the market as a means for achieving the *same* regulatory ends. The use of the market transformed the statute from a consumer-oriented statute to one with a distinct producer bias.

The Court in *Chevron* nevertheless took an approach to the appropriateness of the EPA's new definition of stationary sources that not only maximized agency discretion, but also avoided any real examination of the agency's dramatic change in philosophic approach. The *Chevron* Court was unwilling to take a hard look at the questions of law in this case, much less the questions of policy. It advocated, instead, a two-step approach to judicial review:[31]

> When a court reviews an agency's construction of the statute which it administers, it is confronted with two questions. First, always, is the question whether Congress has directly spoken to the precise question at issue. If the intent of Congress is clear, that is the end of the matter; for the court, as well as the agency, must give effect to the unambiguously expressed intent of Congress. If, however, the court determines Congress has not directly addressed the precise question at issue, the court does not simply impose its own construction on the statute, as would be necessary in the absence of an administrative interpretation. Rather, if the statute is silent or ambiguous with respect to the specific issue, the question for the court

is whether the agency's answer is based on a permissible construction of the statute.

To be acceptable, the agency's construction need not be 'the only one it permissibly could have adopted to uphold the construction, or even the reading the court would have reached if the question had arisen in a judicial proceeding.'[32] The *Chevron* approach thus maximizes agency discretion by defining narrowly the legal category in which courts are usually expected to intervene to 'the precise issue in question,' thereby enlarging considerably the residual discretionary functions of the application of law and the determination of policy, in which agencies are generally expected to excel. Underlying this deferential approach, however, was not necessarily a faith in agency expertise, but rather, a view of politics that placed great weight on the fact that agencies were controlled by the president and, thus, their discretionary judgments were the responsibility of the executive branch, which is accountable to the electorate. If Congress had not decided the precise issue in question, neither should a court, even though that issue had important legal and policy implications. Justice Stevens spoke in terms of presidential deference:[33]

> Judges are not experts in the field, and are not part of either political branch of the Government. Courts must, in some cases, reconcile competing political interests, but not on the basis of the judges' personal policy preferences. In contrast, an agency to which Congress has delegated policymaking responsibilities may, within the limits of that delegation, properly rely upon the incumbent administration's views of wise policy to inform its judgments. While agencies are not directly accountable to the people, the Chief Executive is, and it is entirely appropriate for this political branch of the Government to make such policy choices resolving the competing interests which Congress itself either inadvertently did not resolve, or intentionally left to be resolved by the agency charged with the administration of the statute in light of everyday realities.

The rationale used by the court in *Chevron* is similar in nature to that expressed by Rehnquist C.J. one year earlier in *Motor Vehicle Manufacturers Ass'n v. State Farm Mutual.*[34] That case dealt with the scope of judicial review appropriate not for questions of law, but questions of policy in a deregulatory context. The Reagan Department of Transportation sought to rescind a rule promulgated in the Carter administration that required automobile companies to, among other things, install air bags in their cars at a future date. None of the judges who reviewed the reasons given by the Department of Transportation for rescinding this rule (including the Court of Appeals and the Supreme Court), sided with the agency, but they differed as to how far a court might go in probing its reasoning.

Writing for four members of the Court, then Justice Rehnquist filed a separate opinion concurring in part and dissenting in part. He concurred because the agency gave no reason at all as to why they chose to eliminate air bags as an option for the automobile manufacturers, but for him and three others almost any reason would do. This was because, not unlike the majority in *Chevron*, the administrative process was conceived of as part of the executive branch and subject to the executive's discretionary power. The crucial paragraph in his opinion states:[35]

> The agency's changed view of the standard seems to be related to the election of a new president of a different political party. It is readily apparent that the responsible members of one administration may consider public resistance and uncertainties to be more than do their counterparts in a previous administration. A change in administration brought about by the people casting their votes is a perfectly reasonable basis for an executive agency's reappraisal of the costs and benefits of its programs and regulations. As long as the agency remains within the bounds established by Congress, it is entitled to assess administrative records and evaluate priorities in light of the philosophy of the administration.

The next section will analyse *Chevron* deference in light of this more politically-based rationale as well as other aspects of the deference doctrine that also have led to a good deal of inconsistency in its application over the years, so much so that recent decisions such as *U.S. v. Mead* [36] suggest a major gloss on *Chevron* deference, if not a *de facto* return to the *Hearst/Skidmore* era described above.[37] In particular, this section examines the role of textualism as a judicial methodology and its relationship to executive power in *Chevron* deference cases.

Textualism and Executive Power

Textualism

A textualist approach to interpretation of statutes is not necessarily devoid of context, but the context involved usually is limited to the face of the statute under consideration. As Judge Wald has written, '[t]extualism is a mode of statutory interpretation that relies on text and dictionaries to determine the meaning of statutory provisions and eschews reference to legislative history.'[38] As another commentator has noted, a judge using this interpretive methodology seeks to determine 'what an ordinary reader of a statute would have understood the words to mean at the time of enactment, not what the intentions of the enacting legislators were.'[39] As a result, legislative history is essentially eliminated as a tool of statutory construction, particularly when the court is engaged in step one of the *Chevron* analysis – determining whether Congress spoke to the precise question at issue.

The reasons for a textualist approach have been more fully expressed in various cases following *Chevron*, in which the Court has increasingly and openly engaged in a spirited methodological debate. In *Blanchard v. Bergeron*,[40] for example, though the Court dealt with a judicial rather than an agency interpretation of a statute, Justice Scalia forcefully articulated why he, at least, does not rely on legislative history in any context. In rejecting the Court's use of a Senate report that cited three federal district court cases favouring a particular statutory interpretation of an attorney's fee provision, he stated:[41]

> Congress is elected to enact statutes rather than point to cases, and its members have better uses for their time than poring over District Court opinions. That the court should defer to the citation of three District Court cases in a document issued by a single committee of a single house as the action of Congress displays the level of unreality that our unrestrained use of legislative history has attained. I am confident that only a small proportion of the Members of Congress read either one of the Committee Reports in question, even if (as is not always the case) the Reports happened to have been published before the vote ... As anyone familiar with modern-day drafting of congressional committee reports is well aware, the references to the cases were inserted, at best by a committee staff member on his or her own initiative, and at worst by a committee staff member at the suggestion of a lawyer-lobbyist; and the purpose of those references was not primarily to inform the Members of Congress what the bill meant ... but rather to influence judicial construction.

Given this view of legislative history, and the perception of the process as one characterized by diverse, self-interested, and often manipulative roles played by interest groups, as well as the fact that the *whole* Congress is unlikely to be aware of such interpretive subtleties,[42] any judicial quest for 'genuine' legislative intent is doomed to failure.[43] This is also true when a regulatory statute initially interpreted by an administrative agency is involved. For those who have this perception of the legislative process, an examination of congressional intent would only engage the Court in a review of the unprincipled give-and-take of the political process. If Congress was not precise in its intentions, the Court should defer to the agency, rather than enter the intensely political thicket of interpretation. Congress could, theoretically, correct this problem retrospectively and such a judicial approach to statutory interpretation may even encourage Congress to be more specific in future legislation.

These are significant arguments and they gain strength from their real-world understanding of the legislative process. But being realistic about the legislative process does not require an all-or-nothing judicial approach to legislative history and statutory interpretation. A sophisticated judicial analysis of a statute's history need not result in interest-group manipulation of a court, nor would it unduly expand the judicial role. Courts have the institutional competence to engage in such interpretation and, more important, they have the obligation to ensure that an administrative agency does not exercise any more power than Congress originally gave to it. Closing judicial eyes to the help that an examination of a statute's legislative history may provide only makes the fulfillment of that judicial role more difficult. Quite apart from attempts by interest groups to manipulate future statutory interpretations, an examination of a statute's legislative history can be very helpful. It can deepen considerably the court's understanding of the kind of regulation Congress may have intended, the type of market failure it sought to correct, and the regulatory values Congress sought to further with the statutory framework it created. It is particularly these value questions that tend not to be reflected on the face of the statute.

This is not to say that recourse to legislative history will always be illuminating. It can, however, reinforce a court's view of the proper interpretation of the statutory language in contention or raise serious doubts when a purely textual interpretation of a statute is juxtaposed with its legislative history. As Judge Wald has argued:[44]

> As a general matter, interpreting statutes is more difficult than one might think from reading judicial opinions. Once a decision is reached, we often mask much of the angst that is involved in getting there. Although judges' opinions often refer to 'plain statutory' language, the truth is that statutes

> are increasingly complex and technical, and a judge may not always be certain as to the meaning of the small print. As we conscientiously embark on our duty to ascertain what the words mean in the context of the statute's aims and purposes, we are almost inevitably drawn to the historical record of what the men and women who proposed and sponsored the legislation intended to enact. We feel better when their words confirm our reading of the text; we worry more when it contradicts the text. This does not mean, as the textualist Justices accuse, that we 'transform' every 'snippet of analysis' in congressional reports into 'the law of the land' or 'elevate to the level of statutory text a phrase taken from the legislative history ...' It does mean, however, that we think again when we face a contradiction between text and history, and we should.

The judicial willingness to 'think again' in the face of contradictions between text and history should extend to judicial review of agency interpretations of law as well.

Executive Power

Chevron relies heavily on deference to executive power in refraining from close judicial scrutiny of agency interpretations of law. This is based on several aspects of executive power – the legitimacy derived from the fact that the president is democratically elected every four years and, at least as to executive, as opposed to independent, agencies created by Congress, the president has direct responsibility over them, along with his overall responsibility under article II of the Constitution to 'take care that the laws are faithfully executed.'[45] These attributes and responsibilities of the executive branch are integrally tied up with the textualist approach that *Chevron* has advanced. They are a source of the doctrinal confusion that application of the case has caused, and represent issues that go well beyond the appropriate role for administrative agencies, and the relationship of courts to agencies. Taken as a whole, decisions that substitute inaction or economically-derived rules for previous approaches often shift power in ways that should involve the legislature directly and short of that, at least be subject to more than deferential judicial review.

A more contextual approach to statutory interpretation requires a judicial willingness to consider legislative history when reviewing the legality of agency action. It represents a mode of judicial interpretation that is more in accord with the underlying assumptions of a checks-

and-balances approach to the constitution, one that recognizes the importance of all three branches of government, not just executive power. A contextualist approach that includes an examination of legislative history assumes that there is and should be overlap between the oversight responsibilities of the courts and the executive branch because there may be some contexts, however rare, in which exclusive executive oversight might result in too much power being exercised by that branch of government. The executive has the duty to take care that the laws are faithfully executed, and it plays an important supervisory role when it comes to the federal bureaucracy. The courts, however, must make sure that the actions agencies take pursuant to executive directives fall within the powers that Congress gave to them. Such a judicial role is particularly necessary in deregulatory contexts.

Most agency questions of law involve affirmative regulatory actions that arguably exceed the authority of the agency that undertakes them. The primary question is one of power: did the agency have the power to take this step? In the New Deal context, prior to *Chevron,* these cases usually raised purely jurisdictional questions and came about due to agency attempts to extend their regulatory reach. In resolving these kinds of questions, courts, sometimes explicitly, but often implicitly, examined the relevant congressional history and statutory language and resolved all doubts in favour of agency power. Similarly, courts deferred to policy decisions, which were fully within agency discretion, but the context was always that of affirmative regulatory action. In a deregulatory context, *ultra vires* questions of this sort do not usually arise as such. If an agency has had the power to take certain affirmative actions, it may be assumed that it has the legal authority to pull back. The only real questions are *why* an agency would choose to exercise its power in this way. This requires an examination of what, in fact, the agency offers to put in place of the rules it seeks to withdraw.

As the *Chevron* case shows, some statutes require affirmative regulatory action to ensure that legislative goals will be attained. This is particularly the case when it comes to lowering pollution levels in nonattainment areas. Deregulation or the substitution of a market-based regulatory approach, however, may very well undercut the substantive goals of the statute involved. Using market means to achieve regulatory ends can transform those ends into something quite at odds with what Congress intended. It can, for example, result in a cost-conscious regulatory regime that encourages the maintenance of the environmental status quo, rather than its improvement. These are issues about which reasonable people may differ, and they are by no means easy issues to decide. A court should not automatically veto such agency change. But such change does raise *ultra vires* concerns, even in the context of a contraction, rather than an extension of regulatory power. It may seem that the legal power to do less at a lower cost would automatically be within the power of an agency that had previously tried to accomplish more at a higher cost, but the substitution of market means can result in a significant shift of statutory goals. Such questions of policy, law, or a mixture of the two require close judicial scrutiny because the very values Congress sought to promote may be at stake.

Even if we were to conclude that issues such as whether or not to resort to a bubble policy in pursuing the goals of the 1977 *Clean Air Act* were well within the EPA's powers, the deregulatory context in which they arise requires that a court reach that result after engaging in the same judicial soul searching applicable in most *ultra vires* cases. The agency is, in effect, reinterpreting its legal mandate. In a deregulatory context, this usually means that it intends to further market values that may or may not be part of the agency's enabling act or, more broadly, its regulatory constitution. The focus in such cases cannot simply be on the fact that policy issues are involved as if all policy issues are the same. The relationship of policy to statute differs, particularly in deregulatory contexts. Characterizing deregulatory decisions simply as an exercise of policy discretion blurs the usual pro-regulatory policy approaches of agencies with deregulatory and, quite possibly, anti-regulatory policy goals. Decisions such as these should be based on the substantive legislative bargains that are exemplified by the statute, its history, and the regulatory regime it creates. In such contexts, courts have an important oversight role to play.

Inconsistency and Jurisdictional Issues

There has long been concern that the apparently clear two-step approach in *Chevron* is not nearly as clear when it is applied. As argued above, this often has to do with the fact that the methodological approaches employed as well as the separation-of-powers assumptions being made go well beyond the doctrinal possibilities and uncertainties inherent in the language of *Chevron.* But the vagaries of the language used by the *Chevron* Court also give rise to less predictable outcomes. Courts, for example, often disagree over what is and what is not an ambiguous statutory term. As one judge has remarked, '[s]ome will find ambiguity even in a "No Smoking" sign.'[46] More important, in applying *Chevron*, courts are not at all in agreement on when and to what extent they should use legislative history to discern the meaning of an ambiguous statutory term.

Courts refer to 'the traditional tools of statutory construction,'[47] which in pre-*Chevron* days could and often did include the use of the overall context of the statute in question – its text, purpose, legislative history and substantive background considerations. Just what tools will be used or what constitutes the context of a statutory term is not always clear, but the further one gets from just the text of the statute, the further one gets from a relatively pure form of textualism. Even when the context invoked to explain a statutory term excludes legislative history, it can include other provisions of the statute in question, its overall structure and internal logic,[48] as well as other related congressional actions or inactions.[49]

In *Food and Drug Administration v. Brown & Williamson Tobacco Corp.*,[50] the Court reviewed the Food and Drug Administration's (FDA) regulations of tobacco under the Federal *Food, Drug and Cosmetic Act* (*FDCA*).[51] Its search for the meaning of the statutory terms 'drug' and 'drug delivery devices' was so broad as to utilize more traditional tools of statutory construction, including prior legislative actions and inactions if not legislative history, *per se*. Two factors, in particular, may have accounted for the departure from a relatively strict textualist approach used in some of the previous cases. First, this case represented an attempt by the FDA to expand its own jurisdiction, in a context in which it had resisted doing so for many years. Interpretive issues that can result in expanding an agency's jurisdiction can evoke a closer judicial look at congressional intent than what a plain meaning or textualist approach might suggest. More important, the policy issues involved in this case were so sensitive that the majority may very well have assumed that only Congress could address them and that it must do so directly. As Professor William Popkin has noted, 'the Court seems to conclude that the power to regulate cigarettes is too controversial to be achieved by an agency on the basis of uncertain legislative signals, at least where there are signs of periodic legislative review of the issue (that is, no legislative inertia).'[52]

Specifically, the FDA's regulations sought to reduce smoking by children and adolescents. Writing for the majority of the Court, Justice O'Connor agreed that the thousands of premature deaths caused each year by tobacco presented 'one of the most troubling public health problems facing our Nation';[53] however, the magnitude of the problem did not mean the agency had the power to deal with it. By a five to four vote, the Court invalidated FDA regulations prohibiting the sale of cigarettes to minors and concluded that Congress did not authorize the FDA to regulate tobacco.

At issue in this case was the meaning of the statutory terms 'drugs' and 'devices' in *FDCA*. The FDA took the position that nicotine was a drug and that cigarettes and smokeless tobacco were 'drug delivery devices,' thereby granting them the jurisdiction to regulate tobacco products. The Court invoked *Chevron* to guide its analysis of the agency's interpretation of the act. In so doing, the Court noted that in determining 'whether Congress has specifically addressed the question at issue, a reviewing court should not confine itself to examining a particular statutory provision in isolation.'[54] In concluding that FDA's interpretation of drug was not acceptable, the Court stated that it was necessary to look at the *FDCA* as a 'symmetrical and coherent regulatory scheme,'[55] noting that safety was the essential purpose of the act. To achieve this purpose and to be consistent with the overall regulatory scheme of the act, the Court concluded that if, indeed, nicotine was a drug covered by this act, the agency would have to have banned the use of tobacco and removed it from the market, not just regulate its use by minors.[56] Put in this light, it was clear that Congress never intended in this act to give the FDA such power. This was true, not only because of the regulatory structure of this act, but because in other legislative action, Congress specifically foreclosed the removal of tobacco products from the markets. Congress had enacted six separate pieces of legislation since 1965 addressing the problem of tobacco use and human health and, against this backdrop, never once did it even suggest the FDA had the power it claimed in this case. As the Court noted, '[t]aken together, these actions by Congress over the past 35 years preclude an interpretation of the *FDCA* that grants the FDA jurisdiction to regulate tobacco products.'[57] In effect, the Court held, when Congress passed the *FDCA* in 1938 it did not intend the FDA to exercise jurisdiction over tobacco.

This conclusion, however, would appear to contradict the plain language of the statute. In dissent, Justice Breyer argued that tobacco products fell within the statutory definition of drugs over which the FDA clearly had authority[58] and that the regulation of tobacco products was consistent with the broad purpose of the *FDCA* to protect public health. The majority, however, turned to an even broader congressional context by considering other legislative action as well as congressional silence.

Rather than defer to the agency, the majority concluded that it would be unlikely that Congress would implicitly delegate to the agency so important a policy decision as the use of tobacco. Indeed, the statute itself dealt only with products that 'were safe for [their] intended use.'[59] Congress would not have implicitly delegated regulatory authority over products such as tobacco that had no safe use. Even if the act itself was ambiguous, subsequent congressional acts showed that FDA jurisdiction over tobacco never was intended.[60]

Textualism in its purest forms may have reached its high point in the late 1990s. A variety of factors , including the controversial nature of the issues involved, the nature of the proceedings used to promulgate the agency's decision, and the institutional competence of the decision-makers became, once again, relevant factors for courts deciding whether or not to defer to agency determinations. This is particularly true in light of the Court's recent ruling in *U.S. v. Mead*.[61]

U.S. v. Mead: Back to the Future?

The Supreme Court's decision in *U.S. v. Mead*[62] returns at least a portion of the law of judicial review to what it was when *Hearst* and *Skidmore* reigned supreme. The question in *Mead* was whether a tariff classification ruling by the U.S. Customs Service was entitled to judicial deference under *Chevron*. Mead Corporation imported day planners which were classified in a way that made them free of duty. Customs, however, changed its position in a ruling letter classifying Mead's imported day planners in a way that made them subject to duty. The Court held that this ruling letter, in and of itself, was not entitled to *Chevron* deference because there was no indication on the part of Congress that it ever intended such a ruling to carry the force of law. Invoking *Skidmore v. Swift & Co.*,[63] the Court held the ruling was, nevertheless, eligible for judicial respect in accord with its persuasiveness, as *Skidmore* itself explained. The majority remanded the case to the court of appeals for a *Skidmore* assessment.

Prior to *Mead*, it was often argued that *Chevron* applied to any and all agency interpretations of ambiguous statutory terms, no matter what kinds of procedural formats were involved. *Skidmore* deference was, if not explicitly overruled, at least no longer relevant. *Mead* corrected this misapprehension: 'The authorization for classification rulings, and Custom's practice in making them, present a case far removed not only from notice and comment process, but from any other circumstances suggesting that Congress ever thought of classification rulings as deserving the deference claimed for them here.'[64] The majority went on to note that:[65]

> *Chevron* did nothing to eliminate *Skidmore's* holding that an agency's interpretation may merit some deference whatever its form, given the 'specialized experience and broader investigations and information' available to the agency ... and given the value of uniformity in its administrative and judicial understandings of what a national law requires.

The Court seemed to reserve *Chevron* deference for the review of proceedings that were the product of more formal agency processes: 'It is fair to assume generally that Congress contemplates administrative action with the effect of law when it provides for a relatively formal administrative procedure tending to foster the fairness and deliberation that should underlie a pronouncement of such force.'[66]

Justice Scalia vigorously dissented, predicting that 'we will be sorting out the consequences of the *Mead* doctrine, which has today replaced the *Chevron* doctrine, for years to come.'[67] His position was based, at least in part, on his desire to simplify judicial review in such cases. The majority, however, rejected what it called Justice Scalia's penchant for posing questions of deference as either/or choices. 'Justice Scalia's first priority over the years has been to limit and simplify. The Court's choice has been to tailor deference to variety. This acceptance of the range of statutory variation has led the Court to recognize more than one variety of indicators that Congress would expect *Chevron* deference.'[68] More important, the majority emphasized that what decided questions of deference for Justice Scalia was whether the agency action was 'authoritative.' The majority took a different approach: 'We think, in sum, that Justice Scalia's efforts to simplify ultimately run afoul of Congress's indications that different statutes present different reasons for considering respect for the exercise of administrative authority or deference to it.'[69]

There is no question that *Mead* adds to the complexity of deference determinations. What has and what does not have the force of law is not always easy to determine. But reopening the issue of which contexts demand deference and which do not is a good direction to be going in, even if the outcomes predicted in such cases may be less than clear. Deference should involve an analysis of all of the factors in any given case that suggest an agency decision would be better than a judicial decision. The more oriented this analysis is to these contextual factors, the more likely it is we shall have useful guidelines for future cases and an analysis that goes beyond relatively abstract methodological debates. A discourse focused on agency competence and behaviour in a particular case is preferable to abstract power debates based on theories of interpretation or a sense of executive power. The reasons for deference that are derived from such debates tend to be too general and formulaic; the real issues involving agency performance, the relationship of a court to an agency in a particular case, and the relative responsibilities of the respective branches of government in these situations are seldom considered openly.

Mead does not necessarily signal the demise of *Chevron* as Justice Scalia suggests it does in his dissent.[70] It deals primarily with agency processes that are informal and not as transparent and participatory as notice and comment rule-making. It can easily take five to seven years before rules promulgated pursuant to the rule-making procedures set forth in various agency statutes become final. This, however, raises another problem for the dissent: rule ossification. The agency processes themselves take time and rules that are controversial in any way are likely to be appealed to the federal courts as well as subjected to intense scrutiny by the Office of Management and Budget in the executive branch. On rare occasions, Congress itself might decide to veto certain rules pursuant to the *Congressional Review Act*. All of these reviews and the various criteria that are applied to proposed rules as well as the different fora in which they may be contested, slow the process down considerably. As a result there is increasing pressure on agencies bent on change to use informal processes – rulings, exceptions or other informal actions – to promulgate new policies more quickly.

For Justice Scalia, *Mead* will only increase ossification: 'Worst of all, the majority's approach will lead to ossification of large portions of our statutory law. Where *Chevron* applies, statutory ambiguities remain ambiguities subject to the agency's ongoing clarification ... *Skidmore* deference gives the agency's current position some vague and uncertain amount of respect, but it does not, like *Chevron*, leave the matter within the control of the Executive Branch for the future.'[71] Executive dominance in cases where the rulings involved are not just interstitial but fundamental should be subject to close judicial scrutiny. *Mead* does not prevent a court from doing so; it gives it the opportunity to be sure that the discretion the agency exercises is in accord with the statute and the agency's expertise. The problem in such cases is not the ossification of the agency rule-making process, but rather the profound impact certain kinds of informal regulatory change, often hidden from view, can have on democracy. Judicial deference in such circumstances must be carefully analysed.[72]

Conclusion

Like *CUPE, Chevron* deference is here to stay, though its uses are now more likely to be subject to contextual analyses. The factors involved in these analyses will always be subject to debate and there is no obvious set of principles available for all cases. There is no holy grail when it comes to determining how and when courts should or should not defer – no magic formula. Each case is different. In the end, the hard work of articulating the multiplicity of factors involved and their respective weights is what deference should be about and what courts should be able to do.

A great deal is at stake in the court's ability to do this. In considering deference to executive power in a post-September 11 world, for example, David Mullan notes the tendency of courts to defer to executive determinations, even when constitutional or Charter rights are involved. Indeed, he has argued that 'this approach to review is quite problematic and runs the chance of devaluing the application of the Charter as a vehicle providing protection against violations of the right to life, liberty, and security of the person,' for example, in cases involving torture. He goes on to state: 'More generally, it raises serious questions of the role of the courts in providing an antidote to executive excesses at times of heightened concerns about national security and the imminent threat of terrorism.'[73]

Similar issues await U.S. courts. For example, several cases currently in the lower courts in the United States[74] involve procedures drafted and applied by the Defense Department and applied to detainees and unlawful combatants currently held in Guantanamo. What degree of deference are those procedures due by a reviewing court, especially when constitutional issues are involved? To what extent will deference to the executive branch carry the day? However these cases are decided, they should not invoke a formulaic approach to the important issues involved. It is important, as David Mullan has argued, to develop a satisfactory set of principles for discerning the appropriate standard of review when constitutional rights and freedoms are involved.[75] In so doing, in these and other more typical agency cases, the hard work of judging can only highlight the importance of contextualism.

NOTES

1 David J. Mullan, 'The View from North America: A Canadian Perspective on Three Troubling Issues' (2005) 17 Can. J. Admin. L. & Prac. 167 at 168 [Mullan, 'View']. For discussions of deference doctrines in various common law jurisdictions, see Michael C. Tolley, 'Judicial Review of Agency Interpretation of Statutes: Deference Doctrines in Comparative Perspective' (2003) 31 Policy Studies Journal 421; Margaret Allars, 'Chevron in Australia: A Duplicitous Rejection?' (2002) 54 Admin. L.R. 569; Michael Taggart, 'The Contribution of Lord Cooke to Scope of Review Doctrine in Administrative Law: A Comparative Common Law Perspective' in Paul Rishworth, ed., *The Struggle for Simplicity in the Law: Essays for Lord Cooke of Thorndon* (Wellington, NZ: Butterworths, 1997) 189. Grant Huscroft discusses the Canadian conception of deference and Hugh Corder discusses deference in the South African context in their respective contributions to this volume.
2 Mullan, 'View,' *supra* note 1 at 169.
3 467 U.S. 837 (1984) [*Chevron*].
4 [1979] 2 S.C.R. 227 (S.C.C.) [*CUPE*]
5 *Chevron*, *supra* note 3 at 842–43.
6 *CUPE*, *supra* note 4 at 237.
7 Mullan, 'View,' *supra* note 1 at 171.
8 See, e.g., *Barrie Public Utilities v. Canadian Cable Television Assn.*, [2003] 1 S.C.R. 476 (S.C.C.).
9 See, e.g., *United Taxi Drivers' Fellowship of Southern Alberta v. Calgary (City)* (2004), 236 D.L.R. (4th) 385 (S.C.C.).
10 Mullan, 'View,' *supra* note 1 at 191.
11 Deference to executive discretionary decisions in Canada is discussed in Grant Huscroft's contributions to this volume.
12 533 U.S. 218 (2001) [*Mead*].
13 285 U.S. 22 (1932).
14 322 U.S. 111 (1944) [*Hearst*]. This subsection draws heavily on Alfred C. Aman, Jr. and William Mayton, *Administrative Law Treatise*, 2nd ed. (St Paul, MN: West Publishing, 2001) at paras. 13.7.1, 473–6 [Aman and Mayton, *Administrative Law*].
15 *Hearst*, ibid. at 131.
16 Ibid. at 124.
17 Ibid. at 127.
18 323 U.S. 134 (1944) [*Skidmore*].
19 Ibid. at 137.
20 Ibid. at 139.

21 Ibid. at 140.

22 *Chevron*, *supra* note 3. This subsection draws heavily on Alfred C. Aman, Jr., *Administrative Law in a Global Era* (Ithaca, NY: Cornell University Press, 1992) at 108–21 [Aman, *Global Era*].

23 Pub. L. No. 91–604, 84 Stat. 1676.

24 *Clean Air Act Amendments*, 42 U.S.C. ss. 7401–7642 (1982).

25 Ibid. s. 7502(b)(6).

26 As the Court noted in *Chevron*, 'the House Committee Report [to the 1977 Amendments] identified the economic interest as one of the "two main purposes" of this section of the bill' (*supra* note 3 at 851, citing H.R. Rep. No. 294, 95th Cong., 1st sess., 1977, 211). However, commentators and courts have argued that Congress intended cost to be a significant factor only if the economic viability of plants would be endangered. See T.J. Stukane, 'EPA's Bubble Concept After *Chevron v. NRDC*: Who Is to Guard the Guards Themselves?' (1985) 17 Nat. Res. Lawyer 647 at 663–64 [Stukane, 'EPA's Bubble Concept'], who describes the strictness of Congress's standards; R. Shep Melnick, *Regulation and the Courts: The Case of the Clean Air Act* (Washington, DC: Brookings Institute, 1983) at 96–103, who notes Congress's emphasis on the prevention of significant deterioration.

27 See S.D. Hays, 'The Politics of Environmental Administration' in Louis Galambos, ed., *The New American State* (Baltimore, MD: Johns Hopkins University Press, 1987) at 32–3.

28 See Stukane, 'EPA's Bubble Concept,' *supra* note 26 at 666 (quoting from the government's briefs of argument in *Chevron*).

29 Ibid. at 666–7 (emphasis in the original).

30 See *Alabama Power Co. v. Costle*, 636 F.2d 323 (D.C. Cir. 1979); *ASARCO, Inc. v. EPA*, 518 F.2d 319 (D.C. Cir. 1978). See also, J.L. Landau, '*Chevron, U.S.A. v. NRDC*: The Supreme Court Declines to Burst EPA's Bubble Concept' (1985) 15 Envtl L. 285 at 307–8.

31 *Chevron*, *supra* note 3 at 842–43.

32 Ibid. at 843 n.11.

33 Ibid. at 865–66.

34 463 U.S. 29 (1983).

35 Ibid. at 59.

36 *Mead*, *supra* note 12.

37 See *supra*.

38 Patricia Wald, 'Judicial Review in Mid-passage: The Uneasy Partnership Between Courts and Agencies Plays On' (1996) 32 Tulsa L. J. 221 at 241. This section draws heavily on Aman and Mayton, *Administrative Law, supra* at note 14 at paras. 13.7.4, 488–91 and Aman, *Global Era*, supra at note 22 at 108–21.

39 Thomas W. Merrill, 'Textualism and the Future of the Chevron Doctrine' [1994] Wash. U.L.Q. 351.
40 109 S. Ct. 939 (1989).
41 Ibid. at 941.
42 See, e.g., *Green v. Bock Laundry Mach. Co.*, 109 S. Ct. 1981, 1994 (1989) (Scalia J. concurring).
43 See, e.g., Antonin Scalia, 'Judicial Deference to Administrative Interpretations of Law' [1989] Duke L. J. 511 at 516.
44 See Patricia Wald, 'The Sizzling Sleeper: The Use of Legislative History in Construing Statutes in the 1988–89 Term of the United States Supreme Court' (1990) 39 Amer. Univ. L. Rev. 277 at 301.
45 *U.S. Const.* Art. II, s. 3.
46 See, e.g., *UAW v. General Dynamics Land Sys. Div.*, 815 F. 2d 1570 at 1575 (D.C. Cir. 1987).
47 See, e.g., *Chevron*, *supra* note 3 at n.9.
48 See, e.g., *Third Nat'l Bank v. Impac Ltd.*, 432 U.S. 312 at 322–3 (1977).
49 See, e.g., *Federal Housing Administration v. the Darlington, Inc.*, 358 U.S. 84 (1958).
50 529 U.S. 120 (2000) [*Brown & Williamson*].
51 21 U.S.C. ss. 301–95 (1994).
52 William Popkin, *Materials on Legislation: Political Language and the Political Process* (Mineola, NY: Foundation Press, 2000) 582–3.
53 *Brown & Williamson*, *supra* note 50 at 130.
54 Ibid. at 132.
55 Ibid. at 133.
56 Ibid. at 142.
57 Ibid. at 155.
58 Ibid. at 162.
59 Ibid. at 137.
60 Ibid. at 160–1.
61 *Mead*, *supra* note 12.
62 Ibid.
63 *Skidmore*, *supra* note 17.
64 *Mead*, *supra* note 12 at 231.
65 Ibid. at 234.
66 Ibid. at 230.
67 Ibid. at 239.
68 Ibid. at 236–7.
69 Ibid. at 238.
70 Ibid. at 246.
71 Ibid. at 247.

72 For an extended argument about various forms of democracy deficits brought on by globalization and the role administrative law can play to minimize these deficits, see Alfred C. Aman, Jr., *The Democracy Deficit: Taming Globalization through Law Reform* (New York: New York University Press, 2004).

73 Mullan, 'View,' *supra* note 1 at 205.

74 See, e.g., *Hicks v. Bush*, No. 02-CV-0299, *Al Odah v. Bush*, No. 02-CV-0828, *Habib v. Bush*, No. 02-CV-1130, *Kurnaz v. Bush*, No. 04-CV-1135, *O.K. v. Bush*, No. O4-CV-1136, *Begg v. Bush*, No. 04-CV-1137, *Khalid v. Bush*, No. 04-CV-1142, *El-Banna v. Bush*, No. 04-CV-1144, *Gherebi v. Bush*, No. 04-CV-1164, Boumediene v. Bush, No. 04-CV-1166, *Anam v. Bush*, No. 04-CV-1194, *Almurbati v. Bush*, No. 04-CV-1227, *Abdah v. Bush*, No. 04-CV-1254.

75 Mullan, 'View,' *supra* note 1 at 205.

Principle and Pragmatism: Administrative Agencies' Jurisdiction over Constitutional Issues

JOHN M. EVANS

I was delighted to be invited to contribute to this collection of essays to celebrate David Mullan's outstanding achievements to date as an administrative law scholar and educator, and I know that there will be many more after his formal 'retirement' from the groves of academe.[1] Equally important, in my view, has been his commitment to professional service in the broadest sense. For example, he has accepted more invitations to speak to members of administrative tribunals and judges than most of us have ever received,[2] and much of his writing has a strong pedagogical element from which we have all benefited.

I have known and admired David since 1978, when we first started collaborating on Evans, Janisch, Mullan and Risk, *Administrative Law: Cases, Text, and Materials*.[3] David contributed the last section, Remedies, to the prototype version in 1979 and to the first three editions.[4] Over the years, his influence spread throughout the book until, having outlasted those of us with shorter attention spans, he alone produced the fifth edition in 2003.[5]

The growth of David's contributions to the case book is reflected in the widening range of his writings on public law, much of which he distilled and refined in his outstanding text, *Administrative Law*.[6] His appointment as the Osler, Hoskin & Harcourt Professor of Constitutional and Administrative Law in the Faculty of Law, Queen's University, aptly recognized the broad scope of his interests in the institutional roles and relationships of courts and administrative agencies in our system of government, and the constitutional principles on which they are based.[7]

I thought it appropriate, therefore, to honour David by examining the jurisdiction of statutory decision-makers to decide constitutional issues arising from their administration of the public programs for which they are responsible, including challenges to the validity of their enabling legislation. The Supreme Court of Canada has brought to its treatment of this issue a blend of constitutional principle and pragmatism, and of the public interests in administrative efficacy and fairness to individuals, considerations which have very much been a *leitmotif* of David Mullan's work. I should also confess that my choice of topic may have been influenced by the fact that, as far as I am aware, David has written relatively little on the Court's most recent decisions on this topic and, for once, has thus left me something to say.[8]

The New Trilogy[9]: *Martin, Laseur,* and *Paul*

It is relatively unusual in administrative law for the Supreme Court of Canada to draw a line firmly beneath its previous decisions and announce that the law starts from here. Nonetheless, this is what it did in *Nova Scotia (Workers' Compensation Board) v. Martin* and its close companion, *Nova Scotia (Workers' Compensation Board) v. Laseur,*[10] and in *Paul v. British Columbia (Forest Appeals Commission).*[11] While the analysis in *Martin* builds in part on the foundations laid in the old trilogy,[12] the rationales and analytical framework adopted in *Martin* supersede the previous law, including the Court's much-criticized decision in *Cooper v. Canada (Canadian Human Rights Commission).*[13]

For present purposes, the facts of the new trilogy can be described simply. Mr. Martin and Ms. Laseur had been denied permanent impairment benefits for work-related injuries by virtue of amendments made in 1999 to Nova Scotia's workers' compensation legislation. These amendments excluded chronic pain claimants from the normal statutory benefits available under the scheme to workers with work-related injuries or illnesses.[14] Those claiming on the basis of chronic back pain were limited to a four-week 'functional restoration program,' and nothing thereafter.[15]

Mr. Martin and Ms. Laseur appealed from the Workers' Compensation Board (WCB) to the Appeals Tribunal, arguing that the statutory exclusion of chronic pain sufferers from regular benefits violated their right under subsection 15(1) of the *Charter* to equality under the law and to freedom from discrimination on the ground of disability. The tribunal held that it had jurisdiction to decide the *Charter* challenge to the validity of the legislative provisions barring those claiming on the basis of chronic pain from permanent impairment benefits. It also held that these statutory provisions violated subsection 15(1) and could not be justified under section 1. Accordingly, the tribunal decided the appellants' claims without regard to the provisions of the legislation that it had found to be in breach of the *Charter*, and hence were of no force or effect. The Nova Scotia Court of Appeal reversed the tribunal on both the jurisdictional and constitutional issues.[16]

In *Paul*, administrative officials had found Mr. Paul in breach of British Columbia's statutory forest practices code, which prohibited the unauthorized cutting of crown timber and harvesting of logs. He appealed to the Forest Appeals Commission, arguing that, as a registered Indian, he had an aboriginal right to cut timber and harvest logs on crown land. Accordingly, he said, since existing aboriginal rights are recognized in section 35 of the *Constitution Act, 1982*, the code must be interpreted so as to exempt activities undertaken pursuant to an aboriginal right. It was not alleged that the code itself was invalid. The commission made a preliminary ruling that it had jurisdiction to consider a defence based on an aboriginal right. This ruling was upheld on an application for judicial review, but set aside by the British Columbia Court of Appeal.[17]

In each of these three cases, the Supreme Court of Canada unanimously allowed the appeals and upheld the tribunals' jurisdiction to decide the constitutional questions in issue.[18] Gonthier J. wrote for the Court in *Martin* and Bastarache J. wrote in *Paul*. *Martin* is the leading case on this issue.

Gonthier J. identified the supremacy of the constitution over inconsistent laws, which is set out in section 52 of the *Constitution Act, 1982*,[19] as the constitutional basis for determining whether a legislature had conferred jurisdiction on a tribunal over constitutional issues arising from a matter before it. Consequently, since all institutions and officials of the state making legal decisions operate under the constitution, they must take it into account when interpreting and applying their enabling statute.[20]

In addition, many administrative decision-makers must be able to determine the validity of a statutory provision relevant for the determination of a dispute, and should not be required to give effect to laws that violate the constitution. Neither the *Charter*, nor any other component of the constitution, is some[21]

> holy grail which only judicial initiates of the superior courts may touch. The *Charter* belongs to the people. All law and law-makers that touch the people must conform to it. Tribunals and commissions charged with deciding legal issues are no exception. Many more citizens have their

> rights determined by these tribunals than by the courts. If the *Charter* is to be meaningful to ordinary people, then it must find its expression in the decisions of these tribunals.

Tribunals should thus disregard provisions in their enabling legislation to the extent of any inconsistency with the constitution. However, tribunal decisions on questions of constitutional law are entitled to no deference on judicial review, and are reviewable on a standard of correctness,[22] whatever standard may be applied to the administrative law aspects of their decisions. It seems from the Court's analysis in these cases that the standard of correctness also applies to a tribunal's determination of whether it has jurisdiction to consider and decide constitutional questions.

The Court reinforced constitutional principle with pragmatic considerations in order to justify its approach to administrative jurisdiction to resolve constitutional issues.[23] First, a party should not be forced to institute two legal proceedings in respect of a single matter: the constitutional issue before a superior court, and the administrative law issue before the tribunal. Second, a determination of the constitutional validity of an aspect of a statutory scheme requires a factual foundation that tribunals are often well placed to establish. Third, an assessment of a constitutional challenge also calls for an understanding of the statutory purposes and the implications for the functioning of the scheme of invalidating the impugned provision. The perspective on these issues of the specialist agency administering the scheme may provide valuable insights for a court when determining a constitutional challenge, even though the tribunal does not enjoy the same degree of independence from the executive as the courts.

Principle and pragmatism thus support the following general rule: 'Administrative tribunals which have jurisdiction - whether explicit or implied - to decide questions of law arising under a legislative provision are presumed to have concomitant jurisdiction to decide the constitutional validity of that provision.'[24] The Court stated further that the category of administrative decision-makers to which this rule applies is not limited to those performing adjudicative functions, although the fact that a tribunal's functions are adjudicative is an important indicator that it has jurisdiction to decide questions of law, including, presumptively, whether the statutory provision in dispute is constitutional.[25] However, the requirement that the tribunal must have the power to decide questions of law (or to make 'legal decisions')[26] limits the range of officials with jurisdiction to make constitutional determinations. First, let us consider two analytical steps.[27]

Step 1: Is Jurisdiction Presumptively Conferred on the Tribunal?

'The power to decide questions of law is the power to decide by applying only valid laws.'[28] Hence, a tribunal will be presumed to have jurisdiction to decide constitutional questions if it has jurisdiction to decide questions of law, a jurisdiction that is conferred by the legislature.[29] The first step in the analysis, therefore, is to decide if the legislature intended to confer, implicitly or explicitly, jurisdiction on the tribunal to decide questions of law.[30]

EXPLICIT JURISDICTION

A statutory provision empowering a tribunal to decide any question of fact or law arising from its administration of the legislation constitutes an *express* conferral of jurisdiction and triggers the presumption that the tribunal can determine any constitutional question necessary to resolve the administrative law issues before it.[31] In *Martin* the Court relied on two statutory provisions to conclude that the Appeals Tribunal had been explicitly granted jurisdiction to decide questions of law.

First, the *Workers' Compensation Act*[32] grants the WCB exclusive jurisdiction to determine all questions of law and fact arising under the relevant part of the act; on appeal from the board, the tribunal has power to affirm, vary or reverse the decision of the board's hearing officer.[33] Consequently, Gonthier J. reasoned, the tribunal must be able to decide any question within the jurisdiction of the board, including questions of law, a power that presumptively includes constitutional issues arising in the course of its determination of claims for workers' compensation.[34] Second, since subs. 256(1) of the *Workers' Compensation Act* provides for an appeal from the tribunal to the Nova Scotia Court of Appeal on any question of law, it must follow that the tribunal has the power to decide questions of law.

Hence, on the basis of these two provisions, the Court concluded that the legislature had *explicitly* conferred jurisdiction on the tribunal to decide questions of law and, therefore, that the first step in the analysis had been successfully negotiated.[35]

IMPLICIT JURISDICTION

If a tribunal's enabling legislation does not expressly confer on it jurisdiction to decide questions of law, the tribunal will still be presumed to have the power to decide constitutional questions if the legislature has *impliedly* granted it jurisdiction to decide questions of law. Whether such a power can be implied will, for the most part, be decided on the basis of the provisions of the enabling legislation when read as a whole. Four factors in particular should be considered in the search for legislative intent.

Functional necessity. The first factor is whether a power to decide questions of law is necessary to enable the tribunal to perform its mandate effectively. If it is, this is an important indication of a legislative intent to grant jurisdiction to the tribunal to decide questions of law: legislatures should be presumed to equip the agencies that they create with the legal tools needed to perform their statutory functions. This factor calls for an examination of the statute to determine the nature of those functions.

Because Gonthier J. found in *Martin* that the Workers' Compensation Appeals Tribunal had express jurisdiction to decide questions of law, it was not strictly necessary for him to apply the test for determining implied jurisdiction. Nonetheless, he did so, perhaps to illustrate the application of the factors to a set of facts.[36] Gonthier J. defined the tribunal's statutory mandate as resolving disputes over workers' compensation without resort to the courts.[37] The discharge of this mandate regularly requires the tribunal to interpret legislation other than its enabling statute, as well as to apply principles of the common law. Without jurisdiction to decide questions of law necessary to determine an appeal, the tribunal's ability to perform its statutory function would be severely impaired.

Similarly, in *Paul,* Bastarache J. concluded that the Forest Appeals Commission could not perform certain procedural statutory duties if it could decide only questions of fact.[38] In determining the scope of those duties he relied, in particular, on the rights of parties to make submissions to the commission on *law* and fact, and to appeal decisions of the commission to British Columbia's Supreme Court on questions of *law* or jurisdiction. He inferred from these provisions that the commission's functions include the determination of questions of law.

Nature and capacity of the decision-maker. The second factor is the nature of the decision-maker and its process. The adjudicative nature of a tribunal is an indication that it has an implied power to decide questions of law arising from its administration of the enabling legislation. Even if the tribunal is adjudicative, it is necessary to examine the legislation to determine whether it also has the practical capacity to decide questions of law. Indicators of a practical capacity to decide questions of law include: the independence of the tribunal from the relevant government department; its power to make rules of procedure; and its possession of legal powers to summon witnesses and to compel testimony. Whether a tribunal has the practical capacity to decide questions of law is to be determined primarily on the basis of its enabling statute.[39]

It was not disputed in *Martin* that the Appeals Tribunal was adjudicative in nature, that it was independent of the minister of labour, and that it had the requisite procedural powers. In particular, the tribunal was empowered both to extend the time in which it must render its decisions (presumably, to allow it more time to deliberate on more complex issues) and to provide the attorney general with an opportunity to intervene in proceedings raising a constitutional issue. Gonthier J. also noted that, while the legislation required only the chief appeal commissioner to be a lawyer, all tribunal members were in fact appointed from the bar.[40] However, Gonthier J. emphasized that a tribunal whose members were not statutorily required to hold legal qualifications could still be found to have an implied jurisdiction to decide questions of law on the basis of other aspects of the statutory scheme.[41] The application of the 'practical capacity' aspect of the test for determining implied jurisdiction to the facts of *Paul* was not considered.

The place of the decision-maker in the statutory scheme. The third factor in determining whether a tribunal has implicit jurisdiction to decide questions of law is the tribunal's place in the overall statutory scheme and, in particular, its interaction with other administrative decision-makers. The idea here seems to be that whether the legislature intended a tribunal to have jurisdiction to decide questions of law may be indicated by an examination of the scope of the jurisdiction conferred on other decision-makers in the same scheme, and the relationship between those decision-makers and the tribunal whose jurisdiction to decide questions of law is at issue.

In *Martin*, Gonthier J. did not spell out what he had in mind in connection with this factor, and did not apply it to the facts before him.[42] In *Paul*, however, the jurisdiction of other tribunals was relied upon as a basis for arguing that the commission had no implied power to decide questions of law. The argument was that, since the tribunals from which the commission entertained appeals had no power to decide questions of law, the commission could not have jurisdiction to reverse for error of law. Without deciding whether the premise of this argument was correct, Bastarache J. rejected it on the ground that, whatever the powers of a court may be when hearing an appeal from an administrative tribunal, there is no reason to suppose that, as a general rule, an administrative appellate body lacks the power to consider issues that the tribunal below could not.[43] On the other hand, Bastarache J. suggested that an express conferral of jurisdiction on an appellate administrative body to decide questions of law, but not on the tribunal below, militates against a finding that the tribunal *a quo* has an implied power to decide questions of law.[44]

Practical considerations. Finally, while other practical considerations favouring a tribunal's jurisdiction over constitutional challenges may be relevant to the contextual inquiry, their role would seem to be merely supporting in nature. The conclusions reached on the basis of an examination of the statutory scheme as a whole will normally be decisive.[45]

Thus, Gonthier J. held that, given the clear indications in the statute of the Appeals Tribunal's implicit jurisdiction to decide questions of law, the Nova Scotia Court of Appeal was wrong to consider the practical effect of clothing the tribunal with jurisdiction to determine constitutional issues arising under the relevant provisions of the act.[46] In particular, the tribunal's backlog of cases prior to the 1999 amendments of the legislation, which deprived claimants of full benefits on the basis of chronic pain, could not oust the implication of jurisdiction arising from the statutory scheme. Otherwise, whether a tribunal could decide constitutional questions could change from year to year, depending on the state of its backlog.[47] In any event, counsel for the Tribunal informed the Court, *Charter* challenges were not the cause of the backlog and would not significantly increase the tribunal's workload. On the other hand, enabling the tribunal to adjudicate *Charter* issues had important practical advantages to the administration of the scheme, including the creation by a specialist agency of a full record on which a court could review the tribunal's conclusion on a constitutional question, and the provision of relatively expeditious and inexpensive 'one-stop-shopping' for claimants wishing to raise both constitutional and administrative law issues to establish their entitlement to benefits.

Step 2: Is the Presumption of Jurisdiction Rebutted?

If a tribunal is found to have been granted, explicitly or implicitly, jurisdiction to decide questions of law, that jurisdiction presumptively includes constitutional questions arising from the tribunal's administration of the enabling statute. However, the presumption may be rebutted if, as Bastarache J. said in *Paul*, the legislature has 'expressly or by clear implication arising from the statutory scheme withdrawn from the Commission the power to determine related questions under s. 35.'[48] Practical considerations not arising from the statute itself will normally be insufficient to rebut the presumption that the tribunal's jurisdiction to decide questions of law includes questions of constitutional law.[49]

The Court did not examine this issue in the context of the facts of *Paul*, presumably because it was not argued that the presumption had been rebutted. In *Martin*, however, the Court considered the operation of the principle that the presumption that a tribunal's jurisdiction to decide questions of law includes constitutional issues may be rebutted. It was argued that the legislation denied the tribunal jurisdiction to decide *Charter* challenges because the chair of the board of directors had a statutory power to suspend an appeal to the tribunal and to direct it to the board of directors, when an appeal raised an issue of law or general policy that should be reviewed by the board of directors.[50] This provision rebutted the presumption, it was said, because it was inconceivable that the legislature intended the board of directors, an executive policy-making body, to decide *Charter* challenges to the legislation.

However, Gonthier J. rejected this argument on the ground that the legislation merely provided the board with an opportunity to craft a new policy to deal with an issue of general importance.[51] If the appeal were not abandoned, it would be heard and decided by the tribunal after the reference to the WCB's board of directors had been determined. Moreover, board policy is only binding on the tribunal to the extent that it is consistent with the act and regulations.

The Court did conclude that the duty of a hearing officer to refer to the chair of the board of directors appeals raising important or novel questions or issues of general significance, and the discretion of the chair to refer such appeals to the tribunal, relieved the WCB of the *obligation* to decide *Charter* issues thought to be more appropriately decided by the tribunal.[52] These provisions, in effect, impliedly excluded the general principle that an administrative tribunal with jurisdiction to decide related constitutional issues is under a duty to exercise that jurisdiction when it is invoked.[53] A statutory provision authorizing a tribunal to refer a question of law to a court similarly rebuts the mandatory nature of a tribunal's jurisdiction to decide constitutional questions.[54]

Finally, the Court considered in *Martin* whether the WCB's presumptive jurisdiction over related *Charter* issues had been rebutted. Not surprisingly, the Court held that the practical difficulties and additional burdens on the board's scarce resources that, in the board's view, would result if it had jurisdiction in regard to the *Charter*, did not rebut the presumption that arose from the express statutory conferral on the board of the power to decide questions of law.

The New Trilogy: A Preliminary Assessment

Tribunal members and their staff, lawyers, and judges will generally welcome the new trilogy for the relative clarity that it brings to the law. The Court has resolved some of the ambiguities in the old trilogy while salvaging some basic principles from it, and has recognized the flawed reasoning in its much-criticized decision in *Cooper*.[55]

Nonetheless, it will not always be easy to predict the outcome of the contextual analysis required to determine if a tribunal has implied jurisdiction to decide questions of law.[56] It would also be unrealistic to imagine that the Court's reasons can dispel all uncertainties, some of which I consider below.

Constitutional Imperatives

The Court repudiated definitively[57] the view first advanced by Lamer C.J. in concurring reasons in *Cooper*,[58] namely, that it is unconstitutional for a legislature to confer on administrative tribunals jurisdiction to decide constitutional questions, on the ground that this would violate the separation of powers principle since tribunals lack the courts' independence from the executive. Gonthier J. said that the separation of powers was adequately safeguarded by subjecting tribunal decisions on questions of constitutional law to review for correctness.[59] Indeed, he went further by leaving open the possibility that it might be unconstitutional for a legislature *not* to permit a statutory tribunal to determine constitutional questions arising under the legislation that it administers, when such a provision 'would place procedural barriers in the way of claimants seeking to assert their rights in a timely and effective manner, for instance by removing *Charter* jurisdiction from a tribunal without providing an effective alternative administrative route for *Charter* claims.'[60]

To my mind, it is quite remarkable that the Supreme Court of Canada would think it worth warning legislatures that they might not be able to leave to the inherent jurisdiction of the superior courts the determination of constitutional questions arising from the administration of a public program by a tribunal. Is it really that long ago that the Court was imposing serious limits on legislatures' ability to create administrative tribunals with jurisdiction to decide questions of law analogous to those within the jurisdiction of superior courts?[61]

In my respectful view, issues of institutional design involve choices, balances, and trade-offs that are nearly always best left to legislatures, which have a better informed overview than the courts of their administrative justice system and of the strengths, limitations, and needs of particular tribunals. It should be unthinkable that the courts would, for example, invalidate a statutory provision applying to a particular tribunal section 44 of British Columbia's *Administrative Tribunals Act,*[62] which states that a tribunal does not have jurisdiction over constitutional questions, a provision which applies to most of the province's tribunals.[63]

The Court seemed to have acknowledged its limited role in questions of institutional design in *Ocean Port Hotel Ltd. v. British Columbia (General Manager, Liquor Control and Licensing Branch),*[64] where it held that it is for legislatures to decide what degree of independence, if any, administrative tribunals should enjoy in the exercise of their statutory powers. The 'unwritten constitutional principle'[65] guaranteeing judicial independence is limited to courts, including provincial courts whose judges fall outside the protections provided to federally appointed superior court judges by sections 96–100 of the *Constitution Act, 1867*. It does not extend to members of administrative tribunals in the course of 'the exercise of a power that falls squarely within the executive power of the provincial government.'[66]

Ocean Port touches more directly on tribunals' jurisdiction over constitutional questions in that, writing for the Court, McLachlin C.J. emphasized that it was not argued that the tribunal's enabling statute violated the respondents' constitutional right to an independent tribunal under section 7 of the *Charter.*[67] This was presumably because counsel argued that the revocation of a liquor licence did not deprive the licensee of the right to liberty or security of the person. McLachlin C.J. thus seems to have left open the question of whether a tribunal with jurisdiction to deprive a person of the right to life, liberty, or security of the person (such as the Refugee Protection Division of the Immigration and Refugee Board) is required by the principles of fundamental justice to be independent.[68]

If independence is required for tribunals to which section 7 of the *Charter* (or para. 2(*e*) of the *Canadian Bill of Rights*[69]) applies, they may only be given jurisdiction to decide whether their enabling legislation infringes section 7 (on the ground, for example, that a provision is too vague) if they are sufficiently independent to satisfy the principles of fundamental justice. To this limited extent, a residue may remain of Lamer C.J.'s view that legislatures may not vest constitutional jurisdiction in tribunals because they are not independent.

Expanding Administrative Decision-makers' Jurisdiction over Constitutional Questions

The new trilogy seems to have broadened in three respects the circumstances in which a tribunal may be found to have jurisdiction to determine a question of constitutional law arising from an administrative proceeding otherwise properly before it.

First, prior to *Paul*, the Court only had to consider an administrative tribunal's jurisdiction over constitutional questions in the context of the *Charter*. In *Paul*, however, the question was whether the commission could consider a defence based on an aboriginal right protected by section 35 of the *Constitution Act, 1982*. Not surprisingly, the Court could find no principled or pragmatic basis for distinguishing in this context between *Charter* rights and constitutionally guaranteed aboriginal rights.[70] The same is presumably also true of constitutional questions concerning the division of powers.

Second, contrary to the teaching of *Cooper*, an administrative body may be found to have implied jurisdiction to decide questions of law, even when it is not performing adjudicative functions.[71] It is difficult to assess how significant an extension of the law this is likely to prove. I suspect that non-adjudicative decision-makers will rarely be found to have jurisdiction to decide questions of law. Few will have express jurisdiction to decide questions of law. Moreover, relatively few non-adjudicative decision-makers are likely to be found to have the implied jurisdiction to decide questions of law because, for example, of their lack of the practical capacity to make findings of fact and reach conclusions of law, or the nature of their interaction with adjudicative decision-makers in the statutory scheme.

Third, and most significant, the new trilogy says that a tribunal will be presumed to have jurisdiction to decide constitutional questions if it has the power to decide questions of law arising under the impugned statutory provision. The Court makes it clear that whether a tribunal can be presumed to have jurisdiction to decide *constitutional* questions must be inferred from whether the tribunal has explicit or implicit jurisdiction to decide *other* kinds of legal questions. Statements in the old trilogy suggesting that the inquiry is limited to whether the tribunal has explicit or implied jurisdiction over constitutional questions are wrong.[72]

So much is clear. Less clear, however, is how broad a tribunal's power to decide non-constitutional law questions must be before the presumption that it also has jurisdiction over constitutional questions is triggered. However, before addressing this question, I explore briefly what seems to me to be a lack of clarity about what constitutes an explicit, as opposed to an implicit, grant of jurisdiction.

Explicit or Implicit Jurisdiction

If the legislature has conferred explicit jurisdiction on a tribunal to decide questions of law, the tribunal will have jurisdiction to decide constitutional questions arising from the matter before it, unless the statute clearly withdraws it. A finding that jurisdiction has been conferred expressly makes it unnecessary to conduct the more broad-ranging contextual analysis required to determine whether the legislature has conferred that jurisdiction implicitly on a tribunal to decide questions of law.

Thus, for instance, if the tribunal has explicit jurisdiction, there is no need to decide whether a power to decide questions of law is necessary for the decision-maker to discharge its statutory mandate, or whether the decision-maker is performing adjudicative functions and has the kinds of composition, independence, and adjectival powers that give it the practical capacity to decide questions of law.[73] To characterize the conferral of jurisdiction as explicit not only reduces uncertainty of outcome and simplifies the task of lawyers and of the reviewing court, but also may be determinative of the outcome, where the tribunal would not be found to have implicit jurisdiction.

What constitutes a grant of explicit jurisdiction may thus be a matter of some practical import. One might have thought that a tribunal would only be found to have explicit jurisdiction to decide questions of law if its enabling legislation provided, in terms, that it has jurisdiction to decide questions of law. This is what the statutes considered in *Douglas College*[74] and *Cuddy Chicks*[75] provided. However, no such provision was contained in the *Workers' Compensation Act* considered in *Martin*. Rather, Gonthier J. inferred an express jurisdiction to decide questions of law from statutory provisions conferring the right of appeal to the tribunal from the WCB, which had express power to decide questions of law, and the right of appeal on questions of law to the court from the tribunal.

With all respect, I would have thought that, when the existence of a power to decide questions of law depends on drawing an inference of this kind from the powers conferred on other decision-makers in the administrative scheme, the jurisdiction of the tribunal is more appropriately regarded as implicit. The statutory provisions on which Gonthier J. relied in concluding that the tribunal had express jurisdiction might as easily have been considered as part of the implicit jurisdiction analysis, under the rubric, 'the interaction of the tribunal in question with other elements of the administrative system.'[76]

It is not altogether clear whether Bastarache J. regarded the enabling statute considered in *Paul* as containing an explicit or an implicit grant of jurisdiction. The statute did not expressly state that the commission had jurisdiction to decide questions of law. Bastarache J. started his analysis by referring to two statutory provisions which, in his view, made it 'clear that the statutory mandate given by the Code to the Commission requires the Commission to determine questions of law.'[77]

These provisions conferred on parties the right to make submissions to the commission on questions of law and to appeal from the commission to the court on questions of law. This reasoning might be seen as relevant to the first of the factors to be considered in determining whether a tribunal has implicit jurisdiction, namely, whether the power to decide questions of law is necessary to enable the tribunal to perform its statutory functions.

Bastarache J.'s consideration of whether the limited jurisdiction of the body from which the commission heard appeals precluded it from deciding questions of law also suggests that he regarded the commission's jurisdiction as implicit rather than explicit. However, he did not find it necessary to consider the nature and practical capacity of the commission – factors that are relevant to determining whether a tribunal has implicit jurisdiction to decide questions of law.

The statutory provisions found in *Paul* and *Martin* to support a finding that the legislatures had conferred jurisdiction on the tribunals to decide questions of law are sufficiently similar to suggest a difference of opinion between Gonthier and Bastarache JJ. about when jurisdiction is implicit and when it is explicit. To the extent that *Paul* proceeds on the basis of a narrower test for determining the commission's jurisdiction to decide questions of law to be implicit, it is, in my view, to be preferred to a broader test that can be satisfied on the basis of inferences drawn from provisions dealing with the powers of other decision-makers in the statutory scheme. The approach of Gonthier J. fits less well with the concept of 'explicit jurisdiction,' and is unduly vague as to how clear the inference must be in order to warrant a conclusion that the grant of jurisdiction is explicit.[78]

'Any Question of Law'

It is not easy to determine what kind of power to decide questions of law will give rise to the presumption that a tribunal has jurisdiction to decide questions of constitutional law that arise incidentally from an administrative proceeding. Gonthier J. said in *Martin* that, in determining whether the presumption is triggered, 'one must ask whether the empowering legislation implicitly or explicitly grants to the tribunal the jurisdiction to interpret or decide any question of law.'[79]

Under the old trilogy, a tribunal's jurisdiction over *Charter* questions could be inferred from a *general* power to decide questions of law. If this did not necessarily require a statutory power to decide *every* question of law necessary to resolve a dispute,[80] the power had to be sufficiently general to enable the tribunal to interpret and apply *some* statutes in addition to its enabling legislation.[81]

In *Cooper*, La Forest J. agreed that the administrative decision-maker in question in that case, the Canadian Human Rights Commission, had the power to interpret and apply the *Canadian Human Rights Act*,[82] its enabling statute:[83]

> Every administrative body, to one degree or another, must have the power to interpret and apply its own enabling statute. If this were not the case, it would be at the mercy of the parties before it and would never be the master of its own proceedings.

But, he continued, to conclude that a tribunal's power to interpret its own legislation is sufficient to confer jurisdiction to decide constitutional questions 'would be to accept that all administrative bodies and tribunals are competent to question the constitutional validity of their enabling statutes, a position this Court has consistently rejected.'[84]

However, when Gonthier J. speaks in *Martin* of the power to decide 'any' question of law arising under the statutory provision in question, he clearly does not mean that the tribunal must have the power to determine 'every' question of law before the presumption of jurisdiction to decide questions of constitutional law is triggered.[85] He rejects the utility of the distinction drawn in *Cooper* between a general, as opposed to a limited, power to decide questions of law. Rather, he said: 'It suffices that the legislator endow the tribunal with power to decide *questions of law arising under the challenged provision*, and that the constitutional question relate to that provision.'[86]

Martin is less clear, however, on an issue only practically likely to arise in the course of an examination of an enabling statute to determine if a tribunal has an *implied* jurisdiction to decide questions of law. Does a tribunal have jurisdiction to decide questions of law for the purpose of triggering the presumption that it can determine the constitutional validity of a provision in its statute if it is authorized to interpret only its enabling statute, including the impugned provision? If it does, then *Martin* would appear to have moved the law a lot closer to the position that La Forest J. said in *Cooper* 'this Court has consistently rejected,'[87] namely that all administrative tribunals have jurisdiction to decide constitutional challenges to the validity of their own legislation.

This is because the first factor to be considered in the search for implied jurisdiction to decide questions of law is whether such a power is necessary to enable the tribunal to discharge its statutory mandate. For, as La Forest J. pointed out in *Cooper*, without such jurisdiction, it would be next to impossible for a tribunal to exercise its power to make decisions on the basis of the provisions of its enabling statute. Without a power to interpret their enabling statute, how would statutory bodies or officials acting under statutory powers know when they are authorized to take administrative action and what action they may take? Administrative decision-makers can only implement the programs for which they are responsible through the exercise of the legal powers conferred by statute. Consequently, how can they carry out their statutory mandate if they have no power to interpret their enabling legislation?

Perhaps the best evidence that Gonthier J. meant that administrative decision-makers with power to interpret only their own statute would have presumptive jurisdiction over constitutional questions is his rejection of the utility of the distinction between 'general' and 'limited' questions of law: 'An administrative body either will or will not have the power to decide questions of law.'[88] The following passage seems to indicate that, for Gonthier J., the question is whether a tribunal has power to interpret the challenged provision in its enabling statute. If its legislation confers this jurisdiction, then, subject to the other criteria, the tribunal may determine the constitutionality of the provision:[89]

> [O]ne must ask whether the empowering legislation implicitly grants to the tribunal the jurisdiction to interpret or decide any question of law. If it does, then the tribunal will be presumed to have the concomitant jurisdiction to interpret or decide that question in light of the *Charter*, unless the legislator has removed that power from the tribunal. Thus, an administrative tribunal that has the power to decide questions of law arising under a particular legislative provision will be presumed to have the power to determine the constitutional validity of that provision. In other words, the power to decide a question of law is the power to decide by applying only valid laws.

On the other hand, Gonthier J. cited with approval the observation by La Forest J. in *Tétreault-Gadoury* that 'the power to interpret law is not one which the legislature has conferred lightly upon administrative tribunals.'[90] This suggests that a tribunal's power to interpret its enabling statute does not in itself confer jurisdiction 'to decide legal questions arising under the challenged provision,' to use the phrase regularly repeated in *Martin*, since most tribunals must be able to interpret their own statute if they are to be functional.

Even if most tribunals require a power to interpret their enabling legislation in order to perform their functions, the other criteria to be considered in the search for implicit jurisdiction are likely to narrow the range of constitutional decision-makers. As already noted, the criteria include: whether the tribunal's functions are adjudicative in nature; whether its enabling legislation has armed it with the practical capacity to decide legal questions; and the tribunal's interaction with other decision-makers in the administrative scheme.

Test-Driving the New Model

In an attempt to try out the new trilogy's test, I will consider its application to two cases where the Supreme Court of Canada held that an administrative agency had no implied jurisdiction to decide a *Charter* challenge to provisions in its enabling legislation, *Cooper* and *Tétreault-Gadoury*. Neither was said in *Martin* to have been wrongly decided. I shall then consider some cases decided after the new trilogy to see how lower courts are handling the new law.

HISTORY REVISITED: COOPER V. CANADA (CANADIAN HUMAN RIGHTS COMMISSION)[91]

Despite finding parts of the reasoning in *Cooper* to be erroneous, Gonthier J. said in *Martin* that the conclusion in *Cooper* that the Canadian Human Rights Commission had no power to apply the *Charter* was consistent with the governing principles as restated in *Martin*, 'given La Forest J.'s finding that the Commission had no authority, either explicit or implicit to decide questions of law arising under s. 15(*c*) of the *Canadian Human Rights Act*. It is thus unnecessary *at this time* to revisit the holding in that case.'[92]

However, as already noted, La Forest J. was of the view that the commission had no jurisdiction to decide questions arising under para. 15(*c*) because it did not have power to decide questions of law other than the interpretation of its enabling statute.[93] Hence, La Forest J.'s conclusion that the commission had no implicit jurisdiction to decide a question arising under para. 15(*c*) may appear suspect now that the new regime disregards the distinction between a limited and a more general power to decide questions of law. It is difficult, therefore, to accept without further analysis the assertion in *Martin* that *Cooper* was not inconsistent with the new learning, since the commission could not decide questions arising under para. 15(*c*). Indeed, Gonthier J. may have been hinting as much by declining to revisit the result in *Cooper* 'at this time.'[94]

Cooper arose from an airline pilot's complaint to the commission that he had been terminated by his employer because, on reaching sixty years of age, he was subject to the mandatory retirement provisions of the collective agreement governing the terms and conditions of his employment. Mr. Cooper alleged that this was discrimination on the ground of age and was thus contrary to the *Canadian Human Rights Act*.[95]

However, after an investigation of the complaint, the commission concluded that it did not warrant adjudication by the Canadian Human Rights Tribunal since Mr. Cooper's complaint fell within para. 15(*c*), which provided that, in certain circumstances, mandatory retirement does not constitute discrimination on the ground of age for the purpose of the act. The commission also rejected the complainant's *Charter* challenge to para. 15(*c*) on the basis of the decision in *McKinney v. University of Guelph,*[96] where the Supreme Court of Canada had held that an analogous provision in the Ontario *Human Rights Code*[97] did not violate the *Charter.*

In response to Mr. Cooper's application for judicial review, it was argued that the commission's dismissal of the complaint should be upheld, on the ground that the commission had no jurisdiction to consider whether para. 15(*c*) was contrary to subs. 15(1) of the *Charter* and hence of no force or effect. The Supreme Court of Canada agreed. Would the Court reach the same decision today on the basis of the new trilogy?

Since the commission does not have explicit jurisdiction to decide questions of law, the first question is whether it has implicit jurisdiction. In order to answer this question, the following inquiries are relevant under the new trilogy.

First, is a power to decide questions of law arising under the impugned provision of the act (namely, para. 15(*c*)) necessary to enable the commission to discharge its statutory mandate? The commission's functions include the investigation of complaints, the determination of whether or not they warrant being referred to the tribunal for adjudication and, when a complaint is referred, its prosecution before the tribunal. For present purposes, the commission's function of 'screening' complaints for adjudication by the tribunal is the most pertinent.

In order to dispose of Mr. Cooper's complaint, the commission would have to decide whether the mandatory retirement provision in the collective agreement governing the terms and conditions of his employment required him to retire because he had reached 'the normal age of retirement for employees working in positions similar to the position of that individual.' This may involve deciding questions of law – for example, the meaning of 'normal' and 'similar.'

Thus, if determining the applicability of para. 15(*c*) of the act is a question of law 'arising under the challenged provision,' the power to interpret it would seem necessary for the commission to perform its screening function. It is unclear to me what Gonthier J.'s view was on this issue. On the one hand, he accepted the finding of La Forest J. that the commission had no jurisdiction to decide questions of law, a finding that he made even though he conceded that the commission could interpret its own statute. On the other hand, however, Gonthier J. rejected the utility of the distinction drawn by La Forest J. between powers to decide general, as opposed to limited, questions of law.

Secondly, even if the 'functional necessity' factor supports the conclusion that Parliament had implicitly conferred jurisdiction on the commission to decide questions of law, the commission's functions are not adjudicative in the sense that it does not determine whether a respondent has breached the complainant's statutory rights. This is the function of the tribunal. The commission only decides whether to dismiss or refer the complaint by reference to several statutory criteria, including if, 'having regard to all the circumstances of the complaint, an inquiry into the complaint is' or is not 'warranted.'[98]

When the commission dismisses a complaint, its decision precludes the complainant from obtaining relief under the act; its decision is thus 'final' from the complainant's perspective. Hence, the commission is subject to the duty of procedural fairness when conducting its investigation of a complaint and determining whether an inquiry is warranted.[99] However, in the context of the human rights statutory scheme, this is probably not sufficient to render the commission's functions 'adjudicative' in nature.

As for the 'practical capacity' of the commission to decide questions of law, the relative independence of the commissioners[100] should be entered in the plus column, as should the fact that the commission is a sophisticated agency supported by a substantial staff.[101] However, since it lacks the other procedural indicia listed by Gonthier J., it is unlikely that the commission would be found to have the practical capacity to decide questions of law. In contrast, all members of the tribunal must be legally qualified,[102] and the tribunal is empowered to make procedural rules,[103] to administer oaths and receive evidence, and to decide procedural and evidentiary questions.[104]

Thirdly, in regard to the commission's interaction with other decision-makers, it is relevant to focus on the commission's relationship to the tribunal. The commission provides the sole means of access to the tribunal. If the commission dismisses a complaint, the complaint cannot be adjudicated by the tribunal[105] and the tribunal's jurisdiction to determine a person's rights under the *Canadian Human Rights Act* is exclusive. Breach of the act does not give rise to a cause of action in the courts.[106]

Consequently, if the commission's power to interpret para. 15(*c*) is insufficient to trigger the presumption that it can decide whether this paragraph is in breach of section 15 of the *Charter*, the tribunal will never be in a position to adjudicate the question. The same will be true of any other challenge made by a complainant on the ground that the act is constitutionally under-inclusive, in the sense that it does not prohibit the conduct of which he or she complains: consequently, such challenges must be commenced in the superior courts.[107] On the other hand, if the commission is unable to consider a defence to a complaint of discrimination based on an allegation by a respondent that the act is over-inclusive because it infringes a *Charter* right of the respondent, the commission may refer the complaint if satisfied that an inquiry is otherwise warranted. The respondent can raise before the tribunal a constitutional objection to the impugned provision as part of the defence to the complaint.[108]

The rationale for such an asymmetrical allocation of jurisdiction is not obvious. If Parliament has thought fit to confer jurisdiction on the tribunal to determine the validity of a provision in the *Canadian Human Rights Act* when the issue is raised by a respondent, why should the tribunal not also have this jurisdiction when complainants challenge a provision on the ground that it gives insufficient protection to their constitutional right to equality and freedom from discrimination? If the tribunal has this implied jurisdiction, then the commission must have the power to consider an allegation that the act is unconstitutionally under-inclusive. Otherwise, as La Forest J. pointed out, Parliament would be found to have given the tribunal a jurisdiction that it could never exercise because the commission could never refer such a question to it.

In short, the interaction of the commission and the tribunal in the statutory scheme may support the conclusion that the commission's power to consider questions of law goes beyond the interpretation of its enabling statute; it includes constitutional challenges to the act. When it appears to the commission that a complaint raises a constitutional question about the scope of the act that is sufficiently substantial to warrant an inquiry, the matter should go to the tribunal for adjudication.

It is not for me to opine here on whether, when all the factors are considered, the *Martin* analysis leads to the conclusion that the commission has implicit jurisdiction to decide questions of law. I would say only that I see nothing in the act to rebut the presumption that if the tribunal has power to decide questions of law under section 15(c),[109] it can also determine its constitutional validity.

TÉTREAULT-GADOURY V. CANADA (EMPLOYMENT AND IMMIGRATION COMMISSION)

Gonthier J. did not consider the decision in *Tétreault-Gadoury*[110] in light of the new analytical framework prescribed in *Martin*. Mme Tétreault-Gadoury's claim for employment insurance benefits was refused by the commission, solely because she had lost her job after turning sixty-five years of age.[111] She appealed this decision to a board of referees, the first level of external administrative appeal under the employment insurance scheme. She argued that the statutory disqualification of workers who lost their employment when they were over the age of sixty-five breached her *Charter* right to equality and freedom from discrimination on the ground of age and, since she otherwise qualified for benefits, subsection 31(1) could not provide a valid basis for refusing her application for benefits.

The board of referees dismissed the appeal without commenting on the constitutional argument. Instead of appealing to an umpire, the second level of external administrative appeal, the claimant applied to the Federal Court of Appeal for judicial review of the board's decision. The Court held that the board had jurisdiction over the *Charter* issue and that the statutory restriction on her entitlement to benefits violated Mme. Tétreault-Gadoury's rights under section 15 of the *Charter.*[112] The Supreme Court of Canada reversed, holding that the board had no jurisdiction to decide the constitutional challenge. Unlike the board of referees, the Court noted, the umpire had an express power to decide any question of fact or law necessary for the disposition of an appeal[113] and, therefore, no such general power could be imputed to the board by implication, even though the board had the 'practical capability to deal with *Charter* issues':[114] *expressio unius est exclusio alterius.*

Would a court today reach the same conclusion on the basis of the principles established by the new trilogy? Absent the conferral of an explicit jurisdiction on boards of referees to decide questions of law, the statutory scheme must be examined to determine whether Parliament implicitly conferred this jurisdiction.

It would seem that boards of referees could not perform their statutory function as appellate tribunals unless they could decide legal questions arising from their enabling legislation, including whether, when properly interpreted, section 31 disqualified Mme Tétreault-Gadoury from benefits. However, boards of referees are only required by statute to include in their written decision a statement of their findings of fact material to the decision[115]; they are not under a statutory duty to give reasons for their legal conclusions. It might be inferred from this that boards are not expected to decide questions of law. On the other hand, the omission of conclusions of law from a board's statutory duty to give reasons might be explained by umpires' limited power to scrutinize a board's decisions for errors of fact. If boards of referees did not have to set out the findings of fact on which they base their decisions, it would be very difficult for umpires to perform their statutory function by reviewing the record to determine if the appeal should be allowed on the ground that the board 'based its decision on an erroneous finding of fact that it made in a perverse or capricious manner or without regard for the material before it.'[116] Since umpires review the decisions of boards of referees on questions of 'pure' law on a standard of correctness,[117] the absence of reasons does not undermine their ability to determine if boards' decisions are erroneous in law.

In determining appeals from the commission, boards of referees are clearly performing adjudicative functions and have the practical capacity to decide questions of law.[118] If a power to interpret section 31 constitutes 'a power to decide questions of law arising under the challenged provision,'[119] then the factors considered above suggest that boards of referees have the power to decide questions of law for the purpose of triggering the presumption that they may decide constitutional challenges to their enabling legislation.

As for boards' interaction with other relevant decision-makers in the statutory scheme for the administration of employment insurance, the fact that an appeal lies to an umpire on the ground that the board erred in law in making its decision[120] may indicate that boards of referees also have the power to decide such questions.[121] On the other hand, the legal expertise of umpires, who must be serving or retired judges,[122] suggests that this is the level at which Parliament intended questions of law to be decided.

Also relevant here, of course, is the fact that, since umpires have an express power to decide any question of *law* or fact necessary for the disposition of an appeal,[123] and boards of referees do not, it might be thought that Parliament did not intend to confer the same power on boards by implication. This is the basis on which La Forest J. decided the case. However, the *expressio unius est exclusio alterius* maxim is no more than a presumption. The persuasiveness of the implied exclusion presumption depends on context. As Ruth Sullivan puts it, 'The force of the implication depends on the strength and legitimacy of the expectation of express reference. The better the reason for anticipating express reference to a thing, the more telling the silence of the legislature.'[124]

The presumption of implied exclusion was not used (or mentioned) in *Martin* as a reason for concluding that, because the WCB had an express power to decide questions of law and the Appeals Tribunal did not, Parliament cannot have intended to confer the power on the tribunal by implication. Indeed, Gonthier J. used the WCB's power to decide questions of law, and the right of the tribunal on appeal to confirm, vary or reverse the decision of a WCB officer, as proof that the tribunal had jurisdiction to decide questions of law. Boards of referees are not, of course, in the same relationship to umpires because they are the tribunals from which an appeal is made. However, Gonthier J. also regarded the existence of a right of appeal on questions of law from the tribunal to the Court of Appeal as an indication that the tribunal had the power to decide questions of law. Since the decision of a board of referees may be set aside by an umpire for error of law, might it not also be said that it can be inferred from this that the board had power to decide questions of law?[125]

My only point here is that *Martin* directs that the potency of the implied exclusion presumption must be put into context. Whether a tribunal has implicit jurisdiction to decide questions of law must be determined on the basis of a multi-factored, contextual analysis of the statutory scheme. If other considerations, including the right of appeal to an umpire on the ground of error of law, suggest that boards of referees have this jurisdiction, the presumption of implied exclusion may not necessarily suffice to compel the conclusion that they do not.

Some Recent Decisions

The Supreme Court of Canada's decisions in the new trilogy have been considered approximately twenty-five times in decisions by other courts to date. For the most part, *Martin* and *Paul* have been cited, without further analysis, to support the proposition that administrative tribunals have jurisdiction to determine a constitutional question arising in an administrative proceeding. The tribunals in question have had functions, procedures, and powers that locate them at the adjudicative end of the decision-making spectrum. I discuss below three cases that have considered, in a more substantive manner, the application of the relevant legal principles.

'QUESTIONS OF LAW ARISING UNDER THE CHALLENGED PROVISION'

As already noted, Gonthier J. repeatedly defines the first step of the analysis as requiring a determination of whether the administrative tribunal has explicit or implied jurisdiction 'to decide questions of law arising under the challenged provision.'[126] One possible meaning of this phrase is simply that, if a tribunal has jurisdiction to interpret the challenged provision and to determine whether it applies to a given set of facts, the tribunal can presumptively decide its constitutional validity.

In *Kroon v. Canada (Minister of Citizenship and Immigration),*[127] the issue was whether the Immigration Appeal Division (IAD) of the Immigration and Refugee Board had jurisdiction to determine a challenge under sections 7 and 12 of the *Charter* to the validity of section 64 of the *Immigration and Refugee Protection Act.*[128] As relevant to the facts of the case, section 64 provides that a foreign national, permanently resident in Canada, who has been found inadmissible on the ground of serious criminality, has no right of appeal to the IAD's 'equitable jurisdiction' to stay his deportation. Other permanent residents not falling under subsection 64(1) may appeal to the IAD against their removal from Canada. Mr. Kroon, a Dutch national with permanent resident status in Canada, was convicted of sexual assault on a child. Since he was sentenced to a term of imprisonment of more than two years, he was inadmissible on grounds of 'serious criminality' as defined by subsection 64(2), and had no right of appeal to the IAD.

The IAD has explicit jurisdiction to decide questions of law[129] and thus, under the new trilogy, a presumptive power to decide *Charter* challenges. Nonetheless, the Court held that the IAD's jurisdiction over questions of law did not extend to interpreting section 64.[130] Once the 'factual determination' was made at an admissibility hearing that Mr. Kroon was inadmissible on the ground of serious criminality, a finding which he had not challenged, the IAD had no jurisdiction to hear an appeal by Mr. Kroon and hence no power to decide any question under the challenged provision. His remedy was to institute a proceeding in the Federal Court for a declaration that section 64 was unconstitutional.[131]

Thus, *Kroon* decides that, even though an administrative tribunal has an apparently unlimited and explicit jurisdiction to decide questions of law, the presumption that this empowers the tribunal to decide constitutional questions is only triggered if the tribunal's power to decide questions of law extends to the interpretation of the challenged statutory provision itself. It may not be entirely clear whether a tribunal's power to decide questions of law limited to interpreting its enabling legislation, including the challenged provision, is *sufficient* to satisfy the first element of the implied jurisdiction test. According to *Kroon*, however, it is *necessary* that the tribunal's power to decide questions of law includes the interpretation of the challenged provision.[132]

The fact that the IAD did not have this power in respect of section 64 distinguishes *Kroon* from *Cuddy Chicks*, where the Court held that the Ontario Labour Relations Board had jurisdiction to determine the validity of a provision in the enabling statute excluding agricultural workers from the term 'employees,' thus precluding them from the right to unionize enjoyed by most other workers in the province. Presumably, the board might have had to interpret the statutory words 'employed in agriculture,' or to decide if they applied to the facts of a given case.

A 'PRACTICAL CAPACITY' CASE?

The question raised by *Singh v. Canada (Minister of Immigration and Citizenship)*[133] concerns the jurisdiction of an immigration officer to decide constitutional questions when making a pre-removal risk assessment (PRRA). These assessments are made to determine if the removal of persons from Canada to their country of nationality would expose them to a risk of torture, cruel and unusual punishment, or loss of life. However, a person is not 'at risk' for this purpose if the risk arises from the inability of the country to which the person is to be removed to provide adequate medical or health care.[134]

Ms. Singh told the PRRA officer that, if returned to India, she would likely die because she did not have the money needed to gain access to the kidney dialysis facilities in India that she required by virtue of her medical condition. She urged the officer to ignore subparagraph 97(1)(*b*)(iv) when conducting the risk assessment, on the ground that, to send her to certain death, violated her right under section 7 of the *Charter* not to be deprived of her right to life other than in accordance with the principles of fundamental justice. The officer rejected this plea, saying that she had no statutory authority to disregard provisions of the legislation that she was administering: 'PRRA officers are not considered a tribunal with the jurisdiction to consider *Charter* arguments.'[135]

On the interpretation of subparagraph 97(1)(*b*)(iv), the judge concluded that it applied to a situation where a person had no access to medical treatment because they could not afford it: health or medical care may not be 'adequate' if it is not available to a person who cannot pay for it. Thus, the question was whether the officer erred when she declined to determine the constitutional challenge to the validity of the provision. While acknowledging that the importance of the decisions made by PRRA officers to the individuals concerned was perhaps good reason why these officers should have been given jurisdiction over constitutional questions, the judge held on the basis of the tests in *Martin* as follows:[136]

> In the absence of an express grant, I cannot conclude that it was the intent of the legislator to confer upon PRRA officers an implied jurisdiction to

> decide constitutional questions of the kind urged upon the officer by the applicants. The pre-removal assessment process is not, in my opinion, an appropriate forum for the resolution of complex legal issues, including the interpretation and application of the *Charter*.

This analysis may be somewhat elliptical in the sense that it jumps directly to the question of whether Parliament intended PRRA officers to determine *Charter* challenges to their enabling statute, without plodding step-by-step through each of the contextual factors prescribed in *Martin* for deciding whether the officers have implicit jurisdiction over questions of law.[137] Nonetheless, the judge's bottom line seems clear: in *Martin* terms, PRRA officers lack the practical capacity to decide questions of law and, *a fortiori*, have no jurisdiction over constitutional questions. Administrative officials such as immigration officers lack both the independence and the procedural powers needed to build a record that could form the basis on which a court could review a determination of a constitutional question.[138]

PRIMACY OF THE ADMINISTRATIVE TRIBUNAL'S JURISDICTION

The issue in *R. v. Kátlodééche First Nation*[139] was whether a proceeding before the Canada Industrial Relations Board should be stayed on the ground that the board had no jurisdiction to determine a union's complaints of unfair labour practices against the governing body of a First Nation, since the *Canada Labour Code*[140] could not regulate the labour relations between the First Nation and its employees. For the *Code* to apply in these circumstances, it was said, would violate section 35 of the *Constitution Act, 1982*: the inherent aboriginal right to self-determination, including the right to self-governance, is an existing aboriginal or treaty right protected by that section.

The First Nation commenced an action in the Supreme Court of the Northwest Territories seeking declarations respecting the inapplicability of the *Code* to its labour relations with its employees, and an order staying proceedings before the board pending the determination of its action. The principal issue was whether the balance of convenience favoured granting the stay.[141] The First Nation argued that, even if the board had jurisdiction to determine the constitutional defence to the unfair labour practice complaints, it was principally an aboriginal rights issue, and thus not within the board's labour relations expertise, and therefore the Court should be regarded as the primary forum.

Vertes J. had no difficulty in concluding that the board satisfied the tests in *Martin* and *Paul* for determining whether a tribunal has jurisdiction to decide constitutional issues arising from a matter otherwise properly before it. In particular, the board has an express power under the *Code* to decide any question that may arise in a proceeding,[142] a power that must include questions of law. Further, Vertes J. added, 'there are no overwhelming practical considerations to rebut the presumption that it is capable of dealing with [the constitutional issue] in as comprehensive a manner as a court.'[143] Indeed, the capacity of labour boards to determine constitutional questions has been well established since *Cuddy Chicks*.

As for recognizing the primacy of the board's jurisdiction, subject to judicial review on a standard of correctness, Vertes J. emphasized the serious consequences of requiring the bifurcation of the issues. The union would not be able to obtain a determination of the unfair labour practice complaint until the Supreme Court had decided whether the *Code* applied to the governing body of the First Nation as an employer, and all rights of appeal had been exhausted. 'Just by raising an aboriginal rights issue, one cannot circumvent the tribunal's primary jurisdiction.'[144] The stay of the board's proceedings was refused.

Similar reasoning was recently adopted by the Supreme Court of Canada in *Okwuobi v. Quebec* (*Attorney General*),[145] where the Court held that persons wishing to challenge on constitutional grounds an administrative decision that their children had no right to minority language education could not bypass the appellate jurisdiction of the ATQ on questions pertaining to statutory provisions regarding language rights by going to the Quebec Superior Court for injunctive and declaratory relief.

The ATQ's statute empowers it to decide any question of fact or law necessary for the exercise of its jurisdiction,[146] thus triggering the *Martin* presumption that it has jurisdiction over questions of constitutional law. Further, unless otherwise provided, the tribunal's jurisdiction to decide questions of law is exclusive,[147] a clear legislative intent that the Court held all courts should normally respect.[148]

Although not able to grant a declaration of invalidity with respect to a statutory provision found to be unconstitutional, or to issue an injunction, the tribunal had broad remedial powers and could ignore a statutory provision that infringed a person's *Charter* right to minority language education. The Superior Court should only exercise its constitutionally entrenched power to issue injunctive relief, or to entertain a direct challenge to the validity of the language legislation, in unusual circumstances where this was necessary to fill a gap in the tribunal's remedial arsenal.[149]

CONSTITUTIONAL REMEDIES

On the strength of the supremacy provision in section 52 of the *Constitution Act, 1982*, *Martin* and *Paul* have expanded the range of administrative decision-makers with jurisdiction to determine the constitutional validity of their enabling legislation or of its application to particular facts. However, they have not broadened the more restricted circumstances in which tribunals have jurisdiction to grant a remedy under section 24 of the *Charter* for a violation of an individual's constitutional rights.[150] The respective spheres of operation of sections 52 and 24 have been described as follows:[151]

> If a law is inconsistent with the *Charter*, s. 52 of the *Constitution Act, 1982* provides that it is invalid to the extent of the inconsistency. On the other hand, if a government action is inconsistent with the *Charter*, s. 24 provides remedies for the inconsistency.

One consequence of the new trilogy may be that many more administrative decision-makers (especially those performing adjudicative functions and possessing procedural powers) will be found to have jurisdiction to determine the constitutionality of their enabling legislation than will be found to be 'courts of competent jurisdiction' with power to grant a remedy under section 24.[152] As a result, it may become important to determine the range of options available to a tribunal in order to vindicate the supremacy of the Constitution proclaimed by section 52, because it may not be a court of competent jurisdiction under section 24.

In addition to invalidating legislation that it finds to be unconstitutional, a court acting under section 52 may seek to align the statute with the Constitution by severing the invalid provisions of an otherwise valid statute, reading in words into a constitutionally under-inclusive statute, reading down a statute so as to limit its scope to the constitutionally acceptable, and suspending a declaration of invalidity, with or without granting a constitutional exemption for those who successfully instituted the action to have the legislation declared invalid.[153]

The extent to which an administrative tribunal with power to determine the constitutionality of a provision in its enabling statute may do anything but disregard a provision that it finds unconstitutional is not yet settled. However, it is not obvious to me why, in principle, tribunals should not have much the same powers as the courts to ensure the supremacy of the Constitution.[154]

On the other hand, unlike superior courts with inherent jurisdiction, administrative tribunals do not have, and cannot constitutionally be given, power to grant declarations of constitutional invalidity.[155] Hence, tribunals have no occasion to suspend a declaration of invalidity while the legislature considers how to fix the problem with the legislation identified by the tribunal or, perhaps, to grant constitutional exemptions.[156]

Conclusions

The comparative ease with which the Supreme Court of Canada has been prepared to permit administrative decision-makers to share with the courts responsibility for constitutional determination should be understood within the broader context of Canadian public law.

The Court has pioneered the idea in Commonwealth jurisdictions that administrative agencies have a valuable role to play in the elaboration of the legal framework within which they operate. Since the late 1970s, the Court has recognized the distinctive perspectives and specialist expertise of administrative agencies by providing them a considerable degree of latitude in the exercise of their decision-making powers, including in the interpretation of their constitutive instruments. Whether curial deference should be extended to a particular administrative decision and if so, how much, is determined on the basis of a multi-factored contextual analysis: developing, refining and, some would say, obfuscating, standard of review jurisprudence has been the principal preoccupation of Canadian administrative law over the last twenty years.

The development of a policy of judicial deference has been driven by a range of forces:[157] a willingness to impute to legislatures an intention to allocate decision-making responsibility in a manner that is best calculated to ensure effective public administration; a recognition that the meaning of statutory language is highly context-specific, ambiguous, and incomplete, and that a specialist agency's understanding of the program it is responsible for delivering is often more useful than traditional judicial interpretative skills in ensuring the effective interpretation of the law through which public programs are administered;[158] the judiciary's acceptance of the legitimacy of the aspirations and activities of the administrative state;[159] and the democratic impulse to make room for institutions that are often more accessible to the people than the courts for the resolution of disputes.

While courts do not defer to agencies on questions of constitutional law, an underlying rationale of both the old and the new trilogies is that administrative tribunals will often have something useful to contribute in the elaboration of constitutional norms in the context of particular regulatory schemes, as well as provide an effective forum for fact-finding. Standard of review and constitutional jurisdiction jurisprudence in Canada are justified by resort to both principle and pragmatism, and are grounded in contextual analysis, not abstract general rules.

Further, the *cri de coeur* adopted in *Martin* that the *Charter* belongs to the people, and is too important a part of the fabric of the Canadian system of governance to be left exclusively to the judges, fits well with a policy of judicial deference to administrative decision-making. This is particularly true in labour relations, where the parties agree on the process for resolving differences arising from collective agreements and on the choice of arbitrator, and where labour relations boards, which, among other things, police the collective bargaining process, include nominees of labour and management.

Nonetheless, judicial deference is not to be equated with judicial abdication. At much the same time that the Court was articulating its policy of deference to agencies' interpretation of their enabling legislation, it also established a constitutional basis for preventing legislatures from precluding all review of decisions by administrative decision-makers.[160] Similarly, while the Court has welcomed administrative tribunals into the circle of those able to pronounce on the validity of legislation, or of an order requested by a party, it has also insisted on retaining the courts' supervisory power to review for correctness the constitutional determinations of administrative agencies, and, when its exercise is needed, their original jurisdiction to enjoin unconstitutional conduct and to determine direct challenges to a statute's validity.

NOTES

I gratefully acknowledge the valuable research assistance of two of my law clerks, Kristi Ross and Andy Astritis. Thanks, too, to Lorne Sossin for his thoughtful comments. As usual, I am also indebted to my judicial assistant, Mireille Lalonde-Beaudoin, who has exceeded even her exacting standards in producing the final version of this text.

1 Being unsure whether 'despite' or 'as a result of' is the appropriate causal connector of the two halves of this proposition, I settled for the bland, but incontrovertible, temporal connection.

2 As co-chair of the Judicial Education Committee of the Federal Courts, I have been able to persuade David to speak on recent developments in administrative law at our annual education seminars. I can attest that his famed erudition, clarity, and sheer charisma as a legal educator have in no way been diminished by his absence from the law school classroom. His sessions are always rapturously received by my colleagues. It is no mean pedagogical feat for a teacher to be able to hold a bunch of judges spellbound for an hour by an exposition of the standard of review, and to have them demand that he be invited next year!

3 Over a period of some twenty-five years, tens of thousands of law students across English Canada, for better or worse, obtained their introduction to administrative law, and particularly to the law of judicial review of administrative action, from five editions of this book. See H. Wade MacLauchlan and Philip Bryden's contribution to this volume. Paul Emond, our impresario and publisher, should also be credited, or debited, for getting us together and overseeing the book's production and distribution through five editions.

4 1st ed. 1980; 2nd ed. 1984; 3rd ed. 1989.

5 David J. Mullan, *Administrative Law: Cases, Text and Materials* 5th ed. (Toronto: Emond Montgomery, 2003) [*Cases, Text, and Materials*]. With characteristic generosity, he acknowledged the use that he had made of a supplement that Hudson Janisch had prepared for his classes to bridge the eight-year gap between the appearance of the fourth and fifth editions. In addition to the Remedies chapters, David also contributed procedural fairness chapters to the 4th edition, which was published in 1995.

6 David J. Mullan, *Administrative Law* (Toronto: Irwin Law, 2001) [*Administrative Law*].

7 For a relatively recent statement of his position, which includes a firm, if somewhat unfashionable, belief among many Canadian academic public lawyers that courts have a legitimate part to play in democratic systems of governance, see David J. Mullan, 'The Role for Underlying Constitutional Principles in a Bill of Rights World' [2004] N.Z. Law Rev. 9.

8 I have read with benefit his discussion of the 'new trilogy' in a lengthy paper, entitled 'Administrative Law Update' which he developed from various presentations that he made in 2003 and 2004. In addition, our honorand's publications include extensive analyses of earlier forays by the Court on the topic: see, for example, *Administrative Law*, *supra* note 6 at 352–67; *Cases, Text, and Materials*, *supra* note 5 at 915–22.

9 Since I wrote this paper, the Court has rendered another decision on the topic, *Okwuobi v. Quebec (Attorney General)*, [2005] 1 S.C.R. 257 [*Okwuobi*],

which, thanks to the wonders of word processing, I have been able to integrate into the notes at a relatively late date in the production process.

10 [2003] 2 S.C.R. 504 [*Martin*]. While the dispositions in *Martin* and *Laseur* differed, the Court delivered a single set of reasons. As the differences between these two cases are not material to the issues of concern in this paper, I shall refer to the cases as one.

11 [2003] 2 S.C.R. 585 [*Paul*]. Although the reasons in *Martin* and *Paul* were released on the same day, 3 October 2003, *Martin* was heard on 9 December 2002, and *Paul* on 11 June 2003. The judgment in *Paul* allowing the appeal was given from the bench, presumably because, by that time, the Court was far enough along in its reasons in *Martin* to know the answer.

Martin contains the fuller treatment of tribunals' statutory jurisdiction to hear constitutional challenges. The only additional point in *Paul* on this question is that the reasoning in *Martin* is not limited to constitutional challenges based on the *Canadian Charter of Rights and Freedoms*. Most of the reasoning in *Paul* deals with another issue: does the doctrine of interjurisdictional immunity preclude a provincial legislature from vesting in a provincial administrative tribunal authority to decide constitutional issues of aboriginal rights when legislative competence with respect to Indians and lands reserved for the Indians is a federal head of power vested in Parliament by s. 91(24) of the *Constitution Act, 1867*? The Court said that it does not.

12 *Douglas/Kwantlen Faculty Assn. v. Douglas College*, [1990] 3 S.C.R. 570 [*Douglas College*]; *Cuddy Chicks Ltd. v. Ontario (Labour Relations Board)*, [1991] 2 S.C.R. 5 [*Cuddy Chicks*]; *Tétreault-Gadoury v. Canada (Employment and Immigration Commission)*, [1991] 2 S.C.R. 22 [*Tétreault-Gadoury*].

13 [1996] 3 S.C.R. 854 [*Cooper*]. The reasoning in the new trilogy is closer in spirit to the minority opinions expressed by Wilson and L'Heureux-Dubé JJ. in the old trilogy, and by McLachlin J. (as she then was) in dissent (together with L'Heureux-Dubé J.) in *Cooper*. La Forest J. was very much the architect of the 'old' jurisprudence on this issue, having written for the majority of the Court in each of the four cases.

14 *Workers' Compensation Act*, S.N.S. 1994–95, c. 10, s. 10B, as am. by S.N.S. 1999, c. 1, s. 1.

15 *Functional Restoration (Multi-Faceted Pain Services) Program Regulations*, N.S. Reg. 57/96.

16 *Martin v. Nova Scotia (Workers' Compensation Board)* (2000), 192 D.L.R. (4th) 611 (N.S.C.A.).

17 *Paul v. British Columbia (Forest Appeals Commission)* (2001), 201 D.L.R. (4th) 251 (B.C.C.A.), supplementary reasons (2001), 206 D.L.R. (4th) 320 (B.C.C.A.), allowing an appeal from (1999), 179 D.L.R. (4th) 351 (B.C.S.C.).

18 In *Okwuobi*, the Court also upheld the jurisdiction of the Administrative Tribunal of Québec (ATQ) to determine whether a provision of Quebec's *Charter of the French Language*, R.S.Q. c. C-11, complied with section 23 of the Canadian *Charter*.

19 Although the *British North America Act, 1867*, does not contain a supremacy clause, the Court's division of powers jurisprudence had always accepted that it was implicit in the nature of Canada's federal structure that legislation was invalid if it was beyond the powers of the legislature that had enacted it.

20 See, for example, *Little Sisters Book and Art Emporium v. Canada (Minister of Justice)*, [2000] 2 S.C.R. 1120 at para. 133 (broad statutory discretion must be exercised in accordance with the *Charter* because Parliament cannot authorize a violation of it).

21 *Cooper, supra* note 13 at para. 70, *per* McLachlin J. (as she then was) dissenting, and quoted with approval in *Martin* at para. 29. For the most part, *Martin* adopted the approach taken in *Cooper* by the now chief justice for determining whether the legislature has conferred *Charter* jurisdiction on a tribunal.

22 *Martin, supra* note 10 at para. 31. Gonthier J. appears thus to have framed quite narrowly the range of questions that are reviewable for correctness: questions of law involving the interpretation of the constitution. Did he thereby exclude from review for correctness findings of *fact* of constitutional significance, and even questions involving the *application* of the constitution to the facts as found? It would not be surprising if he intended to exclude findings of fact: see *Cases, Text, and Materials, supra* note 5 at 945–46.

It would be more surprising, however, if Gonthier J. meant that, as a general rule, courts should be deferential to tribunals' application of the constitution to given facts: I suspect that he did not. The jurisprudence is currently inchoate on the question of whether the standard of review normally applicable to a question of mixed fact and law should apply when the law in question is the constitution. Courts are yet to articulate the factors for determining when deference to a tribunal's application of the constitution to the facts is appropriate and when it is not.

23 See, however, Deborah K. Lovett, 'Administrative Tribunal Jurisdiction Over Constitutional Issues and the New *Administrative Tribunals Act*' (2005) 63 Advocate 177 [Lovett], who argues that the advantages of conferring constitutional jurisdiction on administrative tribunals are outweighed by such pragmatic considerations as the costs of further judicializing the administrative process and of imposing tasks that are removed from tribunals' core expertise.

24 *Martin, supra* note 10 at para. 3.
25 Ibid. at para. 47. This is one of the grounds on which the majority (which included Gonthier J.) in *Cooper, supra* note 13, is said in *Martin* to have erred.
26 Ibid. at para. 34.
27 Gonthier J. helpfully summarizes the analytical framework, ibid. at para. 48. As is its wont, the Court constructs some smaller steps to help us negotiate the bigger ones.
28 *Martin, supra* note 10 at para. 37.
29 On some constitutional aspects of the issue, see 386–88, below.
30 Gonthier J. refers in his reasons to a tribunal's 'explicit or implicit jurisdiction' to decide questions of law. I assume that this is not intended to refer to some difference in the jurisdiction itself, but simply to how the jurisdiction was conferred: that is, by express statutory language to this effect or by implication based on the statutory scheme when considered as a whole.
31 *Okwuobi, supra* note 9 at para. 31.
32 S.N.S. 1994–95, c. 10, s. 185(1).
33 Ss. 243 and 252(1).
34 *Martin, supra* note 10 at paras. 62–64.
35 Whether the grant of jurisdiction to decide questions of law was explicit or implicit was not considered in *Paul*, where Bastarache J. seems to have assumed that, if the commission had jurisdiction to decide questions of law, it had been conferred implicitly. On the distinction between an express and implicit conferral of jurisdiction, see 389–91, below.
36 Compare the suggestion that the Supreme Court should be prepared to assume a didactic role in showing lower courts how to conduct a functional and pragmatic analysis for determining the standard of review, see H. Wade McLauchlan, 'Transforming Administrative Law: The Didactic Role of the Supreme Court of Canada' (2001) 80 Can. Bar Rev. 281.
37 *Martin, supra* note 10 at para. 52
38 *Paul, supra* note 11 at para. 41.
39 This is in contrast to the 'practical considerations' that may play a small role in determining whether a tribunal has jurisdiction to decide constitutional questions: see 384, below.
40 *Martin, supra* note 10 at para. 53.
41 Ibid. at para. 54.
42 It was, however, argued in *Martin* that the power of the chair of the WCB to refer a question away from the tribunal to the WCB's board of directors, in order to give the board of directors an opportunity to formulate a policy, indicated that the tribunal lacked jurisdiction to decide questions of law. Gonthier J. treated this argument as an attempt to rebut the presumption

that the tribunal's power to decide questions of law included constitutional questions, and not as part of the contextual inquiry as to whether the tribunal had jurisdiction to decide questions of law: see *Martin*, ibid. at paras. 59–60.

43 *Paul, supra* note 11 at para. 43.

44 Ibid. at para. 44. He derived this example from the Court's decision in *Tétreault-Gadoury, supra* note 12: see 398, below.

45 On the limited role of 'practical considerations' in determining if the presumption that a tribunal's power to interpret a statutory provision includes deciding its validity, see *infra* note 50.

46 *Martin, supra* note 10 at para. 56.

47 On the other hand, a tribunal may appropriately take into account the existence of a backlog if it has discretion not to decide a question of law itself, but to refer it to a superior court: see further, 385, below.

48 *Paul, supra* note 11 at para. 45. In *Martin*, Gonthier J. was also of the view that the presumption could only be implicitly rebutted by a 'clear implication' to the contrary: *supra* note 11 at para. 61.

49 *Paul, supra* note 11 at para. 39: 'Practical considerations will generally not suffice to rebut the presumption that arises from authority to decide questions of law,' although they may be relevant where the statutory scheme makes 'more than one option available.'

50 See *Workers' Compensation Act, supra* note 14 at ss. 199(1) and (2), 200, and 248(1).

51 *Martin, supra* note 10 at paras. 59–60.

52 Ibid. at paras. 63–64.

53 La Forest J. stated in *Cuddy Chicks, supra* note 12 at 18, that a tribunal with jurisdiction to decide *Charter* issues cannot decline to exercise it. In an article written before the Supreme Court of Canada decided any of the cases comprising the old trilogy, I had suggested that tribunals should have discretion in determining when to exercise their jurisdiction over *Charter* challenges: J.M. Evans, 'Administrative Tribunals and *Charter* Challenges' (1988) 2 Can. J. Admin. L. & Prac. 13 at 38 [Evans, 'Administrative Tribunals']. I remained unrepentant after this idea was apparently scotched in *Cuddy Chicks*: Evans, 'Administrative Tribunals and *Charter* Challenges: Jurisdiction, Discretion and Relief' (1997) 10 Can. J. Admin. L. & Prac. 355 at 362–64.

54 Tribunals in British Columbia with jurisdiction over constitutional questions because the *Administrative Tribunals Act*, S.B.C. 2004, c. 45, ss. 43 and 44, apply to them, *may* or, at the request of the attorney general, must refer a constitutional question to the court by way of a case stated. Since section 43 has only been applied to the Labour Relations Board and the Securities

Commission, these are the only tribunals with express jurisdiction over all constitutional questions relevant to resolving the matter before them. In addition, section 45 has been applied to three administrative tribunals, the Employment Standards Tribunal, the Farm Industry Review Board, and the Human Rights Tribunal, so that they may consider non-*Charter* constitutional questions. See further Lovett, *supra* note 23 at 192–94.

55 In particular, Gonthier J. said in *Martin, supra* note 10 at para. 47 that, in determining whether a tribunal has jurisdiction to decide questions of law so as to give rise to the presumption that it can decide constitutional questions, the distinction between general and limited questions of law is unnecessary, and that implicit jurisdiction to decide questions of law is not confined to adjudicative decision-makers.

56 British Columbia has recently tackled the problem of uncertainty in its *Administrative Tribunals Act, supra* note 54, which contains consequential amendments to many enabling statutes in order, among other things, to specify which sections of the act apply to particular tribunals, including sections 43–45 which deal with tribunals' jurisdiction over constitutional questions. *On Balance: Guiding Principles for Administrative Justice Reform in British Columbia* (Victoria, BC: British Columbia Ministry of the Attorney General, 2002), a white paper prepared by the Administrative Justice Project for the Attorney General of British Columbia, concluded that few tribunals have the institutional capacity or expertise to decide *Charter* questions and recommended, therefore, that the list of tribunals with jurisdiction over constitutional questions should be short: see recommendations 30–34. However, legislatures' search for specificity and certainty may be frustrated by the strong generalizing tendency of the common law. Thus, because the Supreme Court of Canada has decided in the new trilogy that implicit jurisdiction to decide questions of law is not confined to adjudicative tribunals, it will be difficult for legislatures to be sure that they have identified all the statutory decision-makers that may have implied jurisdiction over constitutional questions.

57 *Martin, supra* note 10 at para. 47.

58 *Cooper, supra* note 13. A position similar to that of Lamer C.J. had been taken by Marceau J. in the Federal Court of Appeal prior to the trilogy: see for example, *Canada (Attorney General) v. Vincer,* [1988] 1 F.C. 714 at 725–7 (C.A.). Lamer C.J.'s concerns also surface in American jurisprudence: see Evans, 'Administrative Tribunals,' *supra* note 53 at 35; and, more recently, *Singh v. Reno*, 182 F. 3d 504 (7th Cir. 1999).

59 See further *supra* note 22. On the issue of when a superior court should exercise its *de novo* jurisdiction to determine a constitutional question over

which a tribunal has been given jurisdiction, see *Okwuobi, supra* note 9 at para. 38 and following, and the discussion at 404 below.

60 *Martin, supra* note 10 at para. 44.

61 A lot of the steam has been taken out of this issue by the Court's decision upholding tribunals' power to decide questions of law that were the same as or analogous to those within the exclusive jurisdiction of the superior courts if the power was conferred as part of a regulatory scheme: see Peter W. Hogg, *Constitutional Law of Canada*, 4th ed. (looseleaf) (Toronto: Thomson Carswell, 1997) chap. 7.3(e) [Hogg, *Constitutional Law*]. As a constitutional *quid pro quo*, legislatures cannot insulate administrative tribunals from judicial review on 'jurisdictional grounds': *Crevier v. Quebec (Attorney General)*, [1981] 1 S.C.R. 220 [*Crevier*].

62 *Supra* note 54.

63 Lovett, *supra* note 23 at 192–94.

64 [2001] 2 S.C.R. 781 [*Ocean Port*].

65 *Reference re Remuneration of Judges of the Provincial Court of Prince Edward Island*, [1997] 3 S.C.R. 3 at para. 83, per Lamer C.J.

66 *Ocean Port, supra* note 64 at para. 33. On the basis of this statement, it may be arguable that some administrative tribunals are so like courts in their functions, process, and powers that they should be regarded as exercising adjudicative, rather than executive powers.

67 Ibid. at para. 29.

68 Paragraph 2(e) of the *Canadian Bill of Rights* R.S.C. 1985, App. III, a quasi-constitutional instrument, contains a guarantee of a fair hearing in accordance with the principles of fundamental justice before most federal administrative tribunals. In *Bell Canada v. Canadian Telephone Employees Association*, [2003] 1 S.C.R. 884 at paras. 23–24, it was held that, because of the exclusively adjudicative nature of the functions of the Canadian Human Rights Tribunal and the importance of the interests that it determines, a high standard of independence is required in order to satisfy para. 2(e).

69 Ibid.

70 *Paul, supra* note 11 at paras. 36–37. But see Donald J.A. in the Court of Appeal, who thought that the determination of aboriginal rights was sufficiently more difficult than deciding *Charter* questions as to constitute a practical consideration militating against implying tribunal jurisdiction: *Paul v. British Columbia (Forest Appeals Tribunal)* (2000), 201 D.L.R. (4th) 251 (B.C. C.A.) at paras. 106–7. Interestingly, sections 43 and 45 of the British Columbia *Administrative Tribunals Act, supra* note 54, envisage that some tribunals may decide constitutional questions, while others may decide constitutional questions other than *Charter* questions.

71 *Martin, supra* note 10 at para. 47. At para. 54 Gonthier J. says that the adjudi-

cative character of the decision-maker would seem to be an important positive indicator that it has implied jurisdiction to decide questions of law. Contrast, however, para. 47, where he states that the Court in *Cooper* was wrong to regard it as 'a necessary (*or even preponderant*) factor in the search for implicit jurisdiction' [emphasis added].

72 Ibid. at para. 35.

73 However, as already noted, Gonthier J. performed the implicit jurisdiction exercise in *Martin*, even though he had found that the tribunal had express jurisdiction.

74 The *Labour Code*, R.S.B.C. 1979, c. 346, para. 98(g), considered in *Douglas College, supra* note 12, provided that an arbitration board had power to 'interpret and apply any Act intended to regulate the employment relationship of the persons bound by a collective agreement.'

75 The *Labour Relations Act*, R.S.O. 1980, c. 228, s. 106(1), considered in *Cuddy Chicks, supra* note 12, conferred on the board exclusive jurisdiction 'to determine all questions of fact or law that arise in any matter before it.'

76 *Martin, supra* note 10 at para. 48.

77 *Paul, supra* note 11 at para. 41.

78 The distinction between whether a statute applies to the crown expressly, or only by necessary implication, has been regarded in some cases as significant because interpretation statutes sometimes provide that legislation only binds the crown if it *expressly* so states: see Peter W. Hogg and Patrick J. Monahan, *Liability of the Crown*, 3rd ed. (Toronto: Carswell, 2000) at 283–87, where the authors suggest that the better reading of such interpretative provisions is that they include statutes that apply to the Crown by clear implication.

79 *Supra* note 10 at para. 36.

80 The power to determine 'all questions of law' was considered in *Cuddy Chicks, supra* note 12.

81 This was the position in *Douglas College, supra* note 12.

82 R.S.C. 1985, c. H-6.

83 *Cooper, supra* note 13 at para. 55.

84 Ibid.

85 The statute considered in *Okwuobi, supra* note 9, empowered the ATQ to decide 'any question of law necessary for the exercise of its jurisdiction.' In this context, 'any' clearly means 'every,' and was understood as such by the Court: see, e.g., para. 32.

86 *Martin, supra* note 10 at 37. Although the emphasis in this quotation is mine, Gonthier J. uses the italicized words no less than nine times in his reasons in *Martin*: see paras. 4, 35, 37, 39, 41, 48, 50, 58, 65. They do not appear in *Paul*. However, in *Tranchemontagne v. Ontario* (*Director, Disability Support Program*)

2006 S.C.C. 14 at para. 25, Bastarache J. states on the basis of *Martin*: 'Where a specific provision is being declared invalid, it is necessary to ensure that the tribunal is empowered to scrutinize it. Power to scrutinize other provisions is not sufficient, because the constitutional analysis is targeting one specific proivision.'

87 *Cooper, supra* note 13 at para. 55.

88 *Martin, supra* note 10 at para. 45. I would note that Gonthier J. does not reproduce the test under the old trilogy with complete accuracy. The distinction between 'general' and 'limited' related to the kinds of questions of law that a tribunal could decide, not to their jurisdiction. This is probably no more than a semantic quibble, and I have assumed that Gonthier J. did not intend to attach significance to his slight recasting of the distinction drawn by La Forest J.

89 Ibid. at para. 36.

90 Ibid. at para. 43, quoting *Tétreault-Gadoury, supra* note 12 at 33. La Forest J. made this comment in order to limit the scope of curial deference. Deference, he said, is due to a tribunal's interpretation of a provision in a statute within the area of its expertise. Hence, if the legislature authorized the tribunal to interpret another statute, a reviewing court could not consider whether the tribunal had interpreted it correctly. However, the mere fact that the legislature has authorized a tribunal to interpret a general public statute when necessary to resolve the dispute before it does not attract judicial deference to the tribunal's interpretation: *Egan v. McLeod*, [1975] 1 S.C.R. 517 at 519.

91 *Supra* note 13.

92 *Martin, supra* note 10 at para. 47 [emphasis added].

93 See, in particular *Cooper, supra* note 13 at para. 55, where La Forest J. found that, while the act indicated that the commission had power to interpret its enabling act, this was insufficient to confer jurisdiction over constitutional questions, because it did not also have jurisdiction 'to address general questions of law.'

94 Ibid.

95 *Supra* note 83.

96 [1990] 3 S.C.R. 229.

97 S.O. 1981, c. 53, para. 9(*a*).

98 See *Canadian Human Rights Act*, *supra* note 82, s. 44(3)(a)(i) and (b)(i). This is not to say, of course, that the questions addressed by the commission are altogether different from those that the tribunal has to decide. However, the commission only determines whether there is sufficient evidence to warrant an adjudication and whether, if the facts alleged by the complainant are true, she or he has made out a reasonably arguable case on the law.

99 *Radulesco v. Canada (Human Rights Commission)*, [1984] 2 S.C.R. 406. The duty would seem to have been applied subsequently to decisions by the commission that an inquiry by the tribunal is warranted: see *Cases, Text and Materials, supra* note 5 at 176.

100 See *Canadian Human Rights Act, supra* note 82, s. 26(3) and (4) (length of appointment to office and removal for cause or on address of Parliament).

101 For further details, see Canadian Human Rights Commission, *Annual Report* (Ottawa: Canadian Human Rights Commission, 1974).

102 *Canadian Human Rights Act, supra* note 82 at s. 48(3).

103 Ibid. at s. 48.9(2).

104 Ibid. at s. 50(3).

105 The commission's dismissal of a complaint may, of course, be the subject of an application for judicial review to the Federal Court.

106 See *Seneca College of Applied Arts and Technology v. Bhadauria*, [1981] 2 S.C.R. 181, an early case dealing with Ontario's human rights legislation.

107 As was the case, e.g., in *Vriend v. Alberta*, [1998] 1 S.C.R. 493, where the appellant sought a declaration in the Alberta Court of Queen's Bench that the provincial human rights statute infringed section 15 of the *Charter* because it omitted sexual orientation from the prohibited grounds of discrimination.

108 Despite the scepticism expressed by La Forest J. in *Cooper, supra* note 13 at para. 65, about the practical advantages to be gained from a tribunal's determining constitutional questions, I infer from paras. 63–66 of *Cooper* that he was of the view that, once the commission refers a complaint for inquiry, the tribunal had jurisdiction to decide constitutional questions, including challenges to the validity of a provision in the enabling statute.

The *Canadian Human Rights Act* was subsequently amended by S.C. 1998, c. 9, s. 27, by adding subs. 50(2) to give the tribunal power to decide all questions of fact and law necessary for determining a matter. This is an explicit jurisdiction over questions of law, giving rise to a presumptive power in the tribunal to determine constitutional challenges to its enabling statute.

109 That s. 50(2) now gives the tribunal explicit jurisdiction to decide questions of law might support an inference that, since this power was not also conferred on the commission, it does not have it implicitly.

110 *Supra* note 12.

111 See *Unemployment Insurance Act, 1971*, S.C. 1970–71–72, c. 48, s. 31(1), which at that time provided 'a period shall not be established for a claimant if at the time he makes an initial claim for benefit he is sixty-five years of age or over.'

112 [1989] 2 F.C. 245 (C.A.).

113 *Unemployment Insurance Act, 1971, supra* note 111, s. 117.

114 *Tétreault-Gadoury, supra* note 12 at 33–34.

115 *Employment Insurance Act*, S.C. 1996, c. 23, s. 114(3).

116 Ibid., s. 115(2)(*c*).

117 See, for example, *Budhai v. Canada (Attorney General)*, [2003] 2 F.C. 57 at para. 48 (C.A.)

118 On the procedure at a hearing before a board of referees, see now *Employment Insurance Regulations*, SOR/96-332, ss. 80–81. The independence from the commission of boards of referees is implicit in their tripartite composition: see s. 111(1) of the act.

119 *Martin, supra* notes 10 and 87.

120 *Employment Insurance Act, supra* note 115, s. 115(2)(*b*).

121 Compare *Martin, supra* note 10 at para. 49, where Gonthier J. regarded the rights of appeal on questions of law both to and from the tribunal as indications that the tribunal itself had power to decide questions of law.

122 On the appointment of umpires, see *Employment Insurance Act, supra* note 115, s.112(1)-(4).

123 Ibid., s. 117.

124 Ruth Sullivan, *Sullivan and Driedger on the Construction of Statutes*, 4th ed. (Markham, ON: Butterworths, 2002) at 187.

125 But see *Martin, supra* note 10 at para. 43, where Bastarache J. rejected the argument that an appellate administrative tribunal could not have wider powers than the tribunal *a quo*.

126 See *supra* note 86, where I list the nine paragraphs in *Martin* in which this phrase occurs.

127 (2004), 252 F.T.R. 257 [*Kroon*].

128 S.C. 2001, c. 27 [IRPA].

129 Ibid., s. 162(1).

130 *Kroon, supra* note 127 at paras. 32–33.

131 In fact, the applications judge went on to dismiss Mr. Kroon's constitutional arguments on their merits: *ibid.* at paras. 34–41.

132 See note 86.

133 [2004] 3 F.C.R. 323 (F.C.) [*Singh*].

134 IRPA, *supra* note 128, s. 97(1)(*b*)(iv).

135 *Singh, supra* note 133 at para. 8.

136 Ibid. at para. 30.

137 In *Martin, supra* note 10 at para. 35, Gonthier J. criticized a tendency in the previous cases to think that the relevant legislative intent was an intent that the tribunal could determine *Charter* questions.

138 Sadly, Ms. Singh died before the judge certified a question for appeal.

139 [2004] 8 W.W.R. 233 (N.W.T. S.C.) [*Kátlodééche*].

140 *Canada Labour Code*, R.S.C. 1985, c. L-2.

141 Courts exercise their discretion to grant stays by reference to the three criteria established in *RJR-MacDonald Inc. v. Canada (Attorney General)*, [1994] 1 S.C.R. 311: (1) the existence of a serious issue to be decided; (2) the possibility that, without a stay, the plaintiff would suffer irreparable harm; and (3) whether the balance of convenience favours the *status quo*.

142 *Canada Labour Code*, *supra* note 140, para. 16(*p*)

143 *Kátlodééche*, *supra* note 139 at para. 73.

144 Ibid. at para. 65.

145 *Supra*, note 9.

146 *An Act Respecting Administrative Justice*, R.S.Q. c. J-3, s.15.

147 Ibid., s. 14.

148 *Okwuobi*, *supra* note 9 at paras. 38–40

149 Ibid. at paras. 50–5.

150 Section 24 provides that a person who has been denied their *Charter* rights may apply to 'a court of competent jurisdiction to obtain such remedy as the court considers appropriate and just in the circumstances.' The leading cases on section 24 and administrative tribunals are *Weber v. Ontario Hydro*, [1995] 2 S.C.R. 929 at paras. 59–66 [*Weber*], and *Mooring v. Canada (National Parole Board)*, [1996] 1 S.C.R. 75. These cases establish that a remedy may only be given under section 24 if the decision-maker has jurisdiction over the subject matter, parties, and the remedy sought. Ultimately, whether a tribunal has jurisdiction to grant the remedy sought under section 24 is to be determined by asking if the tribunal's function and structure make it an appropriate body to grant the particular section 24 remedy requested: see *R. v. 974649 Ontario Inc.*, [2001] 3 S.C.R. 575 [*974649*]; *R. v. Hynes*, [2001] 3 S.C.R. 623.

151 *R. v. 974649 Ontario*, ibid. at para. 14 [emphasis in original]. A section 24 remedy will generally not be granted in a proceeding brought to impugn the validity of legislation: *Schachter v. Canada*, [1992] 2 S.C.R. 679 at 720.

152 Whether a tribunal can grant a remedy for breach of the *Charter* is said to depend on whether the tribunal has jurisdiction over the parties, the issue in dispute, and the remedy sought: *Weber*, *supra* note 150 at para. 63. A similar test was formulated by La Forest J. in *Cuddy Chicks*, *supra* note 12 at 14 for determining jurisdiction under section 52 as well, although it is unlikely that this continues to be the law after the new trilogy.

153 See generally, Hogg, *Constitutional Law*, *supra* note 61, chap. 37.

154 See Kent Roach, *Constitutional Remedies in Canada*, looseleaf (Aurora, ON: Canada Law Book Inc., 1994) at para. 6.660.

155 See, for example, *Okwuobi*, *supra* note 9 at para. 44.

156 See *Highline Produce Ltd. (c.o.b. Wellington Mushroom Farm)*, [2003] O.L.R.D. No. 4531 (O.L.R.B.).

157 One of the most thoughtful and articulate accounts of the intellectual origins of the 'pragmatic and functional revolution' can be found in the reasons for judgment of Wilson J. in *National Corn Growers Association v. Canada (Import Tribunal)*, [1990] 2 S.C.R. 1324 at 1331–46.

158 However, courts from time to time still harken to an earlier positivist view of the law by insisting that the interpretation of the enabling legislation is for the courts, and that the tribunal's expertise in the regulatory subject-matter is irrelevant to the determination of 'a purely legal question' about the meaning of a provision in the tribunal's statute which 'has no technical meaning': *Barrie Public Utilities v. Canadian Cable Television Association*, [2003] 1 S.C.R. 476 at paras. 14–16; and for a vigorous dissent from the narrow scope of expertise attributed by the majority to the tribunal, see the reasons of Bastarache J., ibid. at para. 88. Indeed, the most recent decision from the Court on this issue appears to suggest that, on an application to the Federal Courts for judicial review, correctness is always the standard of review for determining if a tribunal has made an error of law: see *Mugesera v. Canada (Minister of Citizenship and Immigration)*, [2005] 2 S.C.R. 100 at para. 37. See further, John M. Evans, 'Questions of Law and the Standard of Review' (2005) 18 C.J.A.L.P. 297.

159 The regulation of labour relations has been the bellwether of administrative law in Canada. Prior to the 1970s, courts regularly substituted their view of the interpretation of both collective agreements for those of arbitrators' chosen by the parties and labour relations statutes for those of the tripartite boards. Individualistic notions of freedom of contact and of the prerogatives of ownership found legal expression in the common law, including the interpretation of legislation, of which the judiciary was both creator and jealous keeper. Legislative attempts to protect these regimes from judicial review were ineffective. Appropriately, the courts laid the foundations of the contemporary law of judicial review in the context of labour relations: see Brian Langille, 'Developments in Labour Law: the 1981–82 Term' (1983) 5 Sup. Ct. L. Rev. 225 at 246–54.

160 See *Crevier*, *supra* note 61.

'Common Public Law in the Age of Legislation': David Mullan and the Unwritten Constitution

MARK D. WALTERS

> The original of the constitution ... is not to be found of record, but is beyond memory, and the law known only from practical proceeding and usage in Courts of Justice, as may appear by many laws made in the time of the Saxon Kings, of William the First, and Henry the First, yet extant in history, which are now received as common law.
>
> – *Thomas v. Sorrell* (1677), Vaugh. 330 per Vaughan C.J. at 358

> There is, as it were, back of the written Constitution, an *unwritten Constitution*, if I may use the expression, which guarantees and well protects all the absolute rights of the people. ... The[se] rights ... may not be preserved by express constitutional provisions, yet they exist in all their perfection, and no legislative enactment impairing them can be sustained.
>
> – *Hanson v. Vernon*, 27 Iowa 28 (S.C., 1869) per Beck J. at 73

In this chapter I will examine the account of public law developed in the work of David Mullan, with a view to identifying its underlying constitutional theory and, in particular, its position on the so-called 'unwritten constitution.' The struggle to reconcile concepts of written and unwritten law has a long history in the common law tradition. There is, at the level of theory, a deep connection between older assertions that the constitution is not 'of record' and later assertions that there is an '*unwritten Constitution*' behind or 'back of' the written constitution. This theoretical continuity should come as no surprise. The tension between written and unwritten law is really the tension between a conception of law as the conscious and creative product of political or sovereign will (usually recorded in writing), and a conception of law as reason revealed through the practices and customs of a special form of moral discourse (not contingent on writing). Each conception of law relates to valuable aspects of human flourishing – to the creative ability of people to make specific commitments to each other and to honour them over time, and to the inherent dignity of people that endures independently of the particular commitments they may or may not have made. There can be no final reconciliation of these two conceptions of law and the values they embrace; each generation of jurists must struggle to articulate a constitutional settlement between them, sensitive to the realities imposed by the legacy of the past but appropriate for the particular age.

David Mullan's account of public law is in one respect a critical explication of substantive legal doctrine, but in another respect it represents an extended discourse on the tension between written law and unwritten law. His scholarship in administrative and constitutional law stands as a monument to, using his words, 'the vitality of a common public law in the age of legislation.'[1] In the following analysis of Mullan's constitutional theory, I will argue that by 'common public law' Mullan means, in essence, the *unwritten constitution* and the special features of human flourishing that it embraces. I will suggest that Mullan offers a compelling account of the normative force of the unwritten constitution in this present 'age of legislation' – in an age, that is, of *written* declarations, conventions, statutes, codes, charters, and bills of rights. Mullan's public law is compelling, I think, because it resists theoretical dogmatism in favour of the balanced pragmatism characteristic of common law method at its best. In the end, he refuses to declare victory for either of the two competing conceptions of law; instead, his theory of public law is predicated on a vision of the common law as a form of equilibrium that balances law-as-sovereign-will and law-as-reason.

This is a critical time for debates about the unwritten constitution in the common law world. Extreme measures taken to address the fear of terrorism show how fragile our commitment to the rule of law may become. Judicial condemnations of these measures may be explained by exclusive reference to written human rights guarantees, but the judges themselves also speak of more fundamental and transcendent reasons for their conclusions – illustrating, I think, the importance of the assertion made by the Supreme Court of Canada in a different context that the rule of law is, in the end, an 'unwritten' constitutional value.[2] At the same time the idea of unwritten constitutional principles remains controversial. Reasonable lawyers respond differently to the idea – a point illustrated by the friendly debates between David Mullan and his co-instructor in the Advanced Constitutional Law seminar at Queen's, David Stratas, who, echoing Jeremy Bentham, calls unwritten constitutional principles 'imaginary.'[3] From other quarters, criticism of unwritten constitutionalism has been, as Professor Mullan observes, 'vehement, sometimes vituperative' in nature, and to defend the theory is to risk being branded as 'part of the conspiracy of judicial imperialism, antidemocratic, and just downright ignorant.'[4] This is, in short, a good time to reflect once again on the relationship between written and unwritten law – and in my view the measured scholarship of David Mullan, a valued colleague and mentor, provides an ideal context in which to do so.

The 'Remarkable Resurgence' of Unwritten Constitutionalism

In Canada, judicial recognition of unwritten constitutional principles as supreme law is a relatively recent development. Courts have long acknowledged that the Canadian Constitution is in part a 'common law constitution' based on principles 'inherited from the United Kingdom' – as confirmed by the acknowledgment in the preamble to the *Constitution Act, 1867* that the constitution is 'similar in principle' to the British constitution.[5] Although it was assumed that common law constitutional principles in Canada were, as in Britain, subject to parliamentary sovereignty, Justice Ivan Rand concluded famously in the 1950s that the preamble identified a 'political theory' that was elaborated by constitutional provisions establishing an 'institutional apparatus' of parliamentary democracy, and from this 'constitutional structure' certain political rights and freedoms – not at the time explicitly guaranteed – were 'by necessary implication' protected from legislative violation.[6] But it was not until the 1990s that the Supreme Court of Canada, citing Rand's theory, held that the 'Constitution of Canada' – the 'supreme law of Canada' – 'embraces unwritten, as well as written rules.'[7] From such unwritten principles as judicial independence, parliamentary privilege, federalism, democracy, the rule of law, constitutionalism, respect for minorities, and human rights,[8] specific rules and principles with 'powerful normative force' may be inferred by judges and imposed on state actors.[9] These unwritten principles do, however, retain a close relationship to the written text: unwritten principles are 'exterior'[10] to the written text but they exist '[b]ehind the written word' as the 'vital unstated assumptions upon which the text is based'; they 'emerge' from 'an understanding of the constitutional text itself, the historical context, and previous judicial interpretations of constitutional meaning.'[11] Some unwritten principles, like federalism, may be evidenced by provisions that secure 'political compromise[s]' that are not universal.[12] Other unwritten principles, like the rule of law, are said to be 'implicit in the very nature of a Constitution,' and so are regarded as universal norms inherent in the very idea of constitutional government.[13] The recent Canadian approach to the unwritten constitution therefore resembles in some ways the older American theory of an unwritten constitution 'back of' the written constitution, a set of 'implied reservations' that 'grow out of the essential nature of all free governments.'[14] It also resembles Australian cases that recognize political rights and freedoms as implied from the institutions of parliamentary government manifested in the 'text and structure' of the written constitution.[15] And, finally, it may be said to resemble arguments made in the United Kingdom that parliamentary sovereignty is controlled by the common law constitution, or that spirit of liberal legalism that is instantiated through the judicial interpretation of written laws in specific cases.[16] Indeed, these examples lend support to T.R.S. Allan's argument that all common law jurisdictions '*share* a common constitution' grounded in liberal conceptions of legitimate governance – a constitution that is ultimately more important than the different written constitutional provisions found in each jurisdiction.[17]

David Mullan championed unwritten constitutional rights long before they were rediscovered by the courts; indeed, he continued to celebrate Rand's 'confident assertion of implied constitutional values' even after the Supreme Court of Canada appeared in the 1970s to have rejected Rand's theory altogether.[18] Nevertheless, Mullan has expressed concerns about what he calls the 'remarkable resurgence' of implied or unwritten rights.[19] There is, he writes, something 'a little peculiar' about relying on the common law 'to reinvent itself' by reference to unwritten values after the adoption of written statutory or constitutional bills of rights that secure those values in a 'much more blunt and direct way.'[20] He is concerned, in particular, about the lack of structure the unwritten constitution imposes on woolly legal ideals; the effect that its re-emergence may have on the delicate balance of competing interests in the administrative state; the risk that it may draw judicial attention away from bills of rights and undermine the development of a vibrant new human rights jurisprudence; the confusion surrounding its place within the hierarchy of legal norms, in particular whether it *really* prevails over otherwise valid legislation; and, finally, the very use of the term 'unwritten' to describe the values it embraces.[21] Mullan is, however, what we might call a *constructive* critic of the unwritten constitution. True critics more sceptical of the idea will no doubt observe that Mullan's list of concerns fails to include the concern that they most commonly raise – namely, that the judicial assertion of unwritten constitutional principles unanchored in the positive law of either statute or constitutional text is an affront to the sovereign will of the legislature and a threat to democracy.[22]

In fact, many of Mullan's concerns about the unwritten constitution can be rephrased as concerns about the balance between judicial enforcement of transcendent constitutional values and judicial deference to legislative will and constitutional politics. For instance, his concern about the adjective 'unwritten' is that it might suggest that *any* common law constitutional principle qualifies as part of the supreme law, a result inconsistent with the still-fundamental principle of parliamentary sovereignty.[23] Although he accepts that the constitution is not just a set of 'text-based' rules, he concludes that the description of the non-text part as 'unwritten' may be exploited by critics who allege a 'conspiracy of judicial imperialism' in which un-elected judges make laws from thin air.[24] The reality, says Mullan, is that the so-called unwritten principles identified so far in Canada are very closely related to written constitutional texts: written and unwritten rules 'are not in reality sharply differentiated concepts but rather function on a spectrum.'[25] For reasons of principle, strategy and logic, then, Mullan concludes that the relevant principles should be described as 'underlying' rather than 'unwritten.' In short, Mullan *is* concerned about legislative sovereignty and democracy, but not in the same spirit as more sceptical critics of the unwritten constitution. Unlike those critics, Mullan appears far more interested in finding a principled explanation as to how sovereign legislative will and judicial ideas about transcendent values may be balanced than in seeking outright supremacy of the former over the latter.

Mullan's argument about the word 'unwritten' hints at a complex view about the relationship between written texts and transcendent norms. It also suggests that he might regard as mistaken an attempt to link his idea of 'common public law' to the *unwritten* constitution. In fact, labels are of secondary importance and one could easily substitute the terms 'common law,' 'underlying,' 'transcendent,' 'meta-' or 'antecedent' as descriptors for the relevant 'constitution' at issue.[26] My principal objective is to determine whether Mullan's work in public law suggests a theory of that constitution – whatever we call it – that may be useful to our understanding of how sovereign will and transcendent values interrelate. To this end, I will consider Mullan's views about common law and legislation generally and then his views about the constitutional foundations of administrative law before returning to his views about constitutional texts and the (so-called) unwritten constitution.

Balancing Legislative Will and Transcendent Values

The tension within the common law tradition between the conception of law-as-sovereign-will and the conception of law-as-reason is paralleled by debates in legal philosophy between legal positivism and what we might call legal rationalism.[27] This parallel is less obvious than it once was, for under the influence of H.L.A. Hart legal positivism has turned from sovereign command to official custom for an explanation of law's posited nature.[28] But many lawyers and judges remain sympathetic to the older positivist tradition associated with Bentham, a tradition that viewed law as (primarily) a matter of legislative will.[29] Bentham thought the common law was chaotic, irrational, and subjective, and argued for its replacement by legislation that, through exhaustive codification of progressive or utilitarian social reforms, would leave no room for judicial reference to substantive moral values. This form of normative legal positivism is therefore premised on the primacy of written legislative codes that, in the terminology developed by Joseph Raz, impose on judges 'exclusionary reasons' for their decisions – that is, 'second-order' reasons that exclude as irrelevant to judicial reasoning all 'first-order' or substantive reasons underlying legal rules.[30] David Dyzenhaus has argued recently that judges and lawyers who insist on looking to written legal texts and legislative intention and no further when explicating public or constitutional laws betray both Benthamite scepticism of the common law and Benthamite faith in written laws as codes – an attitude that is wrongheaded in common law jurisdictions that have not yet, and may never, undertake the scale of legislative codification of law that Bentham advocated.[31] It follows, Dyzenhaus argues, that judges in common law jurisdictions *must* be committed to some form of unwritten or common law constitutionalism; without written texts that purport to codify exhaustively all aspects of public law they simply have no choice.

In considering Mullan's approach to the relationship between common law and legislation it is first necessary to consider the unwelcome prospect that he is in fact a Benthamite in disguise – a serious charge in light of Dyzenhaus' argument. What is the evidence against him? First, Mullan clearly regards the state, and in particular its legislative branch, as the primary vehicle for attaining the common good. The theory of judicial deference towards administrative actors that he has advocated for over thirty years is ultimately premised on this view. Judicial review of administrative action should not, he argues, constitute a 'brake on legislative experimentation' or inhibit legislative 'methods of dealing with intransigent, social engineering problems.'[32] The common law should not frustrate the search for social justice by the welfare state. Second, Mullan has produced some withering attacks on the coherence of the common law – in particular the 'terminological nightmare' that by the late 1960s surrounded concepts such as 'jurisdiction,' 'judicial' and 'quasi-judicial' that were central to the common law system of public law remedies.[33] Indeed, Mullan advocated Bentham-like legislative reform that would have replaced the common law with comprehensive codes defining explicitly the occasions when and the grounds upon which judicial review of administrative action was available; he even ventured the suggestion – heretical to common-law constitutionalists in the Diceyan mould – that the job of review might be withdrawn from the common law courts altogether and given to a separate administrative tribunal modelled on the French Conseil d'état.[34] Finally, there is Mullan's response to the famous *Bhadauria* case.[35] In *Bhadauria* the Supreme Court of Canada held that the courts could not acknowledge a new tort action at common law based on discrimination in the workplace where the legislature had already enacted a statute on human rights that prohibited discrimination and created an elaborate administrative structure for the investigation, conciliation and adjudication of such claims.[36] Mullan agreed: although the human rights code in issue did not explicitly bar common law remedies, it was 'a complete code for the vindication of rights,' – a conclusion that follows, in his view, from the importance of 'judicial deference' to '[l]egislative choice' in the selection of methods for addressing complex social problems.[37]

Mullan's arguments do have a Benthamite tone. There seems to be little evidence here of the vitality of a common public law. Looking to Mullan's scholarship as a whole, however, it soon becomes clear that these selected examples reflect a commitment to democratic action and social justice but *not* a Benthamite legal philosophy. The legislative reforms in administrative law that Mullan advocated in his earlier work did not occur, and much of his subsequent scholarship has therefore focused on common law reform. In this respect, his work represents classic common law scholarship, integrating the search for just solutions with fidelity to existing lines of precedent and sensitivity to the institutional limits imposed on judicial decision-making. Mullan extols the virtues of common law method, in particular its ability to assimilate gradually into law, on a case-by-case basis, the lessons of practical or 'real life' experience – an ability, he says, that is not shared by legislation or judicial decision-making modelled on legislation.[38] To be sure, Mullan regards legislative codification as a shortcut to a framework of legal language that permits principled analyses of difficult problems, but he accepts that this framework of language can also be constructed by judges. The key to success in this endeavour, however, is judicial respect for the 'range of discourse' in the law that has 'evolved over a considerable period of time' through the cases – a respect, in other words, for the capacity of lawyers to use language in a 'subtle and ultimately useful manner' to structure argument and doctrine.[39] For Mullan, language is 'the tool with which lawyers and judges have to work' and 'refining and respecting language are the means by which effect is given to valid policy goals.'[40] It follows, according to Mullan, that judicial excursions into abstract theories of justice, fairness or natural law are inappropriate; substantive moral values find their life in the common law through the subtle process of practical reasoning by judges on a case-by-case basis.[41] It may be said, then, that common law for Mullan is not theoretical reason but practical reason – or, in Sir Edward Coke's terms, the 'artificial Reason' of judges.[42] Needless to say, no Benthamite could hold these views about the common law's rational potential.

But what of the common law's *vitality* in the public law sphere in this 'age of legislation'? How, in other words, do we explain Mullan's views on *Bhadauria*? His position on this case is, I think, somewhat more complex than the summary above suggests. Commitment to the common law constitution as a source of public law rights independent of legislative intention might suggest reasons of principle why human rights codes do not preclude common law remedies, but this same commitment might also suggest reasons of principle why they do. Indeed, Mullan identifies the principle of equal access to justice as one reason to defer to the legislature in this instance. He argues that insofar as the legislative human rights apparatus provides a public enforcement mechanism that relieves victims of discrimination from the burden of pursuing private legal actions, the principle of equal access to justice should be respected by common law courts rather than undermined through the creation of an unequal 'two-tier' system that gives rich victims the option of litigating their own claims at common law.[43] There are, in other words, principled reasons *above and beyond* simple submission to sovereign legislative will for judges to respect and promote the integrity of public institutions and social programmes established by the state for the common good – reasons that (we might say) could find a secure place within a theory of the unwritten or common law constitution.

We may conclude tentatively, then, that Mullan does not regard common law judges as bound to accept legislative rules as, to use Raz's term, second-order 'exclusionary reasons' for decisions. Instead, he seems to think that the judicial interpretation of legislation involves a direct and independent assessment by judges of the underlying first-order reasons for legislative rules, and that the scope they give to legislation and the corresponding scope given to related common law principles will ultimately depend on the degree of judicial deference that these reasons justify. Not only is Mullan's approach to common law and legislation very un-Benthamite in character, but his writings seem premised on a set of antecedent norms – an unwritten constitution – that explains when judicial deference to legislative sovereignty is warranted, and when it is not.

The Unwritten Law behind the Administrative State

Let me now turn to Mullan's approach to the constitutional foundations of administrative law to see if the tentative conclusions reached above are confirmed or denied. I will examine Mullan's writing on the judicial review of administrative action from three separate angles: the constitutional foundations of judicial review, the characterization of the grounds of judicial review, and the methods for determining the standard or intensity of judicial review.

The debate about the constitutional foundations of judicial review of administrative action is usually framed as a debate between, on the one hand, those who think that courts derive their ability to review the decisions of statutory authorities from the statutes that delegate decision-making powers, and, on the other hand, those who think that courts derive their authority to review such decisions from common law.[44] Advocates of the former position say that judicial review is explained by the *ultra vires* doctrine, the principle of upholding legislative intentions and parliamentary sovereignty by keeping statutory authorities within their statutory mandates. Advocates of the latter position say that judicial review is explained by common law doctrines relating to the rule of law that have normative force independent of legislative intention. This tension between law-as-sovereign-will and law-as-reason has a jurisprudential aspect, with legal positivists tending to support the former position and legal rationalists the latter.[45]

Once again, it is initially difficult to fit Mullan's work into this bipolar theoretical framework. Mullan explains the legal foundations of judicial review by weaving together arguments drawn from both sides of the divide. In his view, the fact that legislatures created the administrative state and conferred statutory decision-making powers on specialist tribunals without establishing a 'coherent system of appeals' and in full knowledge of the historical role played by superior courts at common law in supervising inferior tribunals confirms an implicit legislative intent that decisions of administrative tribunals should be subject to judicial review.[46] Indeed, he states that the principle of 'legislative supremacy' demands that statutory decision-makers be kept within their statutory powers, and that 'the common law of judicial review developed by the courts' secures this principle.[47] If we were to stop here, Mullan's argument would resemble what has become known as the modified *ultra vires* position, which seeks to reconcile judicial review with parliamentary sovereignty by insisting that it derives from legislative intent while at the same time acknowledging that the relevant intent must often be inferred from the interplay between legislative text and common law context.[48]

But Mullan does not stop here. He continues: 'Beyond questions of legislative intention, review for jurisdictional error can be justified on a more basic level yet. Notions of the Rule of Law and the position of the courts in constitutional history point to the desirability of providing a method by which statutory authorities can be confined within the limits of their statutory mandate.'[49] In other words, judicial review is justified, at least in part, by the 'role of an independent judiciary in the protection of basic constitutional and civil libertarian values.'[50] For Mullan, then, the foundations for judicial review are both written and unwritten and it is difficult to say that he gives ultimate priority to the written justification. He finds positivist and rationalist explanations for judicial review, but because he appears to give the rationalist explanation weight independent of the positivist explanation we may conclude that there must be, behind these explanations, some larger background (unwritten or common law) theory of the constitution that explains their normative force and relationship.

This reading of Mullan's position is illustrated by the fact that he offers different constitutional explanations for different types of judicial review. Judicial review of administrative officials appointed by the executive to carry out statutory functions may be explained, in part, by parliamentary sovereignty, but Mullan treats judicial review of the executive itself – ministers of the crown individually or collectively – differently. The greater deference traditionally shown by courts to ministerial or cabinet decisions is justified by orthodox constitutional theory: the government is distinct from Parliament but, by convention, members of the government are responsible, individually and collectively, to Parliament, and abuses of executive power are prevented or remedied through this democratic process of parliamentary accountability, not litigation.[51] This, at least, is the theory. The problem, says Mullan, is that 'the seemingly inexorable transfer of power from Parliament to the executive branch'[52] has reduced this theory to a 'myth' or 'fiction.'[53] In truth, the Westminster electoral model usually produces a 'democratic deficit' in which executives effectively control legislatures even when they do not have the backing of a popular majority.[54] In this context, judicial deference to the executive out of respect for the democratic mechanisms that check executive power is nonsensical. Mullan says that courts are, or ought to be, 'antidotes' for this problem because they may provide 'surrogate democratic processes' for the traditional forms of democratic control of executive power that have disintegrated.[55] Mullan accepts that, insofar as executives are forced by judicial review to pursue their policies through valid statutory forms, judicial review can be said to be helping Parliament to exercise its sovereignty: parliamentary sovereignty remains a justificatory principle for judicial review.[56] But he fears that parliamentary sovereignty has largely succumbed to an undemocratic form of executive sovereignty, and so he looks beyond it to a more abstract principle of democracy, manifested in surrogate form by the courts, as the true foundation of judicial review in this context. It is important, he argues, to acknowledge the right of individuals 'to have a role in the working out of constitutional arrangements in a forum' – that is, the courts – 'where they will not necessarily be overwhelmed by the force of government.'[57] Once again, his conclusions seem predicated on a set of unwritten normative assumptions, according to which legislative sovereignty is but one of several fundamental constitutional values that are balanced when explaining the constitutional foundations of judicial review.

It might be said that these debates about the unwritten constitutional foundations of judicial review were superseded in Canada once the courts identified a basis for judicial review in the written constitution.[58] But Mullan's response to Lord Cooke's argument, that judicial review of administrative actors for *all* errors of law on a standard of correctness should be regarded as part of the unwritten constitution of New Zealand, suggests otherwise. Mullan insists that Canada and New Zealand may not share 'the same pattern of unwritten and implied constitutional evolution' given 'political, historical and social' differences, and in Canada the evolution of the unwritten constitution leaves greater scope for legislative reform of the administrative state than Cooke's theory would allow in relation to New Zealand, despite the fact that judicial review enjoys written constitutional protection in Canada and does not in New Zealand.[59] In other words, the meaning of the written principle is informed by its unwritten context.

The second aspect of Mullan's work in administrative law to consider is his views on the *grounds* of judicial review. In Mullan's view, administrative law concerns itself with limits to administrative or governmental power arising from two distinct sources: the 'statutory regime' within which power is exercised, and the various 'common law restrictions' courts have been willing 'to graft onto those statutory regimes.'[60] 'For centuries,' Mullan writes, 'the common law courts have engrafted hearing requirements onto statutes that have made no specific provision for procedural protections.'[61] Courts describe these rights of natural justice or procedural fairness as 'common law' rights.[62] Mullan observes that courts often assume that the imposition of such rights can be linked to an implied legislative intention and thereby reconciled with parliamentary sovereignty.[63] However, he prefers the explanation given by John Willis in the 1930s and echoed by L'Heureux-Dubé J. in the 1990 *Knight* case[64] – that common law procedural rights are 'in the nature of unwritten constitutional guarantees' or a 'common law *Bill of Rights*' that apply whether or not the legislature intended them to apply.[65] '[P]retending' that courts infer these rights from legislative intent is, concludes Mullan, 'artificial.'[66] Still, he concedes that these transcendent procedural rights must be balanced against another 'fundamental value,' parliamentary sovereignty, and so must yield to alternative procedural measures found in statutes.[67]

As for the review of substantive discretionary decisions, Mullan's position could not be clearer: statutory discretion, he argues, is 'reined in' not only by the terms of empowering legislation but also 'sources external to the statute' like 'underlying constitutional norms'[68] or 'transcendent democratic, civil libertarian values.'[69] Indeed, the famous case of *Roncarelli v. Duplessis*,[70] in which the actions of a premier were measured against (in Mullan's words) the 'transcendent values of the Canadian polity,'[71] is celebrated by Mullan as 'one of the shining beacons in the entire history of the Supreme Court of Canada.'[72] The 'obviousness' of the limits on administrative or executive power imposed under the theory of *Roncarelli* comes not from the consideration of the text or purposes of the statute under which the power is exercised but, he argues, from 'a common law (or common sense) perspective of what would generally be impermissible under *any* Act.'[73] But Mullan's view in this area, as in others, is a balanced one. The statement by L'Heureux-Dubé J. in *Baker v. Canada*, that statutory discretion must be exercised 'in accordance with the boundaries imposed in the statute, the principles of the rule of law, the principles of administrative law, the fundamental values of Canadian society, and the principles of the Charter,'[74] is to be welcomed if it represents a confirmation of the basic principle of *Roncarelli*, but it is problematic in our 'pluralistic world' if 'fundamental values' are extended beyond rule of law ideals to embrace substantive moral values.[75]

The last aspect of Mullan's work on administrative law to consider is his treatment of the question of standards of review employed by courts when examining the decisions of administrative actors. Writing in 1999, Mullan stated that the transcendent value of Canadian judicial review law is now the principle of deference – not the rule of law or unwritten constitutional values or human rights, but *deference*.[76] By this Mullan means, of course, judicial deference to legislative decisions about the structure of the administrative state – a judicial respect, in other words, for the 'positive virtues of governmental policies and programmes.'[77] Is his position in this respect consistent with the vitality of a *common* public law or *unwritten* constitution? I think it is. Indeed, his position cannot be explained fully without invoking a robust conception of unwritten constitutionalism.

Nowhere is this conclusion illustrated more clearly than in Mullan's interpretation of the so-called pragmatic and functional test developed by Canadian courts to determine the standard of review in judicial review cases. The orthodox common law position was that superior courts reviewed errors of law made by inferior tribunals if they led to an excess of jurisdiction, or if those errors were made within jurisdiction but apparent on the face of the record. Legislative attempts to bar judicial review with ouster or privative clauses were read by courts as preventing the latter form of review but not the former. This conclusion made the distinction between jurisdictional and non-jurisdictional questions very important. The problem, in Mullan's view, was that by the late 1960s courts appeared to be edging towards the view that all errors of law were potentially 'jurisdictional' – which threatened the autonomy of specialist tribunals whose work was essential for the modern welfare state.[78] Some deference was owed by courts to administrative actors, but how much, and in relation to which questions?

A sensible solution began to emerge in Canada in the late 1970s when courts acknowledged that, if errors made within jurisdiction were protected by a privative clause, judicial review would not be on a standard of correctness, as it was in relation to jurisdictional questions, but on a standard of patent unreasonableness.[79] Still, the challenge of separating jurisdictional questions (for which correctness was the standard of review) from non-jurisdictional questions (for which deference was given and the standard of review was patent unreasonableness) remained. Since the late 1980s the courts have adopted the pragmatic and functional approach to meet this challenge, which essentially flips the analysis on its head.[80] Instead of determining which matters are jurisdictional and which are not as a method of defining the appropriate standard of review, courts simply focus on identifying the appropriate standard of review for each question (correctness, reasonableness, or patent unreasonableness), and this process defines the point at which an error is regarded as 'jurisdictional' and therefore reviewable.[81] In place of formalistic concepts such as jurisdiction, then, courts focus on several substantive factors, including the text of the relevant statute, especially the wording of any privative clauses; the purposes of the statute and the specific provision in issue; the expertise of the decision-maker as compared to that of the courts; and the nature of the question being reviewed (for example, whether it is a question of law or fact or mixed law and fact). In *Bibeault*, Beetz J. insisted that the value of the pragmatic and functional approach over formalistic analyses of jurisdiction is that it 'focuses the Court's inquiry directly on the intent of the legislator,' for the 'true problem of judicial review is to discover whether the legislator intended the tribunal's decision on th[e] matters [under review] to be binding.'[82]

Mullan praises the pragmatic and functional approach because it offers a substantive rationale for the principle of deference, but he offers a very different explanation for its constitutional basis. Whereas Beetz J. explains the approach solely in terms of legislative intention and parliamentary sovereignty, Mullan treats what he calls the 'parliamentary sovereignty justification'[83] for deference as separate from other justifications. In his view, the parliamentary sovereignty justification means that judges seek to identify and respect 'legislative will' and 'legislative choice' about the degree of autonomy administrative actors have from the judiciary.[84] Although he accepts that legislative intention is 'frequently underscored' by 'pragmatic considerations' relating mainly to the relative expertise of the decision-maker, he insists that these two sets of considerations are conceptually separate.[85] Moreover, he adds another set of considerations into the mix – namely, the 'constitutional role' of the courts in checking 'arbitrary and wrong-headed exercises of power' and in protecting 'individual rights and constitutional values.'[86] Mullan says that some of these constitutional values, like the rule of law, may point to less deference in certain instances[87]; others, like respect for regional and cultural differences within Canada, may point to more.[88] Mullan's argument, then, is that each of these three sets of factors – parliamentary intention, pragmatic factors relating to expertise, and transcendent constitutional values – must be given independent weight by judges when seeking the right balance of deference to extend to administrative actors. He considers that, over the last quarter-century in Canada, courts have reached an 'appropriate state of equilibrium' between these potentially competing considerations.[89] That this equilibrium is established through a form of judicial reasoning in which legislative intention is just one factor to be balanced with other constitutional values confirms the importance of the unwritten constitution to the theoretical structure of Mullan's account of public law.

Common Public Law and Bills of Rights

My argument thus far has been that David Mullan advances a conception of the common public law in which judicial articulation of an unwritten constitution establishes a constitutional structure within which judges balance a number of factors, including sovereign legislative will, pragmatic or utilitarian factors, and transcendent constitutional norms, and that this unwritten constitution can be seen to underlie his views on the constitutional foundations of judicial review, the grounds of judicial review, and the standards of judicial review. It is an *unwritten* constitution in which the importance of *written* law is acknowledged. One aspect of human flourishing that it embraces is the idea that people have the ability and need to create new forms of law to achieve the common good for each new age; deference to the written enactments establishing such law is therefore a fundamental tenet of the unwritten constitution. Another aspect of human flourishing that it embraces is the idea that certain important legal values transcend the particular regime of written law in place at any given time and form the normative backdrop for understanding rights and duties in public law, including the meaning of written laws. The question that I now want to address is how the unwritten constitution responds to efforts by a community to reduce supposedly unwritten or transcendent legal values, or some of them, to written form. How does the unwritten constitution respond to written bills of rights?

If my understanding of Mullan's common public law is right – if written law takes effect within a larger context of unwritten law – then under this theory a constitutional bill of rights like the *Canadian Charter of Rights and Freedoms*[90] or a statutory bill of rights like the *New Zealand Bill of Rights Act*[91] gains its legal force and meaning through judicial reasoning that balances the written instrument against all other parts of the unwritten constitution, including unwritten constitutional values such as the rule of law and human rights. This is not as controversial an idea as it sounds. The Supreme Court of Canada has, as seen, characterized unwritten principles as the unstated assumptions on which written constitutional texts are based. Mullan's work makes clear, however, that this underlying common public law accords significant deference to written constitutional laws.

There is, in other words, no starry-eyed reverence for transcendent constitutional norms in Mullan's theory. For Mullan, written constitutional texts – and the political acts of communities that lead to the adoption of written constitutional texts – matter. The constitutional entrenchment of a bill of rights signals emphatically the need for a 'heightened regard' by judges and other officials for the 'constitutional (as opposed to merely common law) interest[s]' protected.[92] Under Mullan's common public law there *is* a hierarchy of legal norms: common law and statutes are (generally) trumped by written constitutional provisions. So while Mullan accepts the conclusion in *Bhadauria* that a human rights statute might preclude the development of parallel *common law* remedies, he insists that such statutes cannot preclude the development of parallel *constitutional* remedies pursuant to a written bill of rights; an 'issue of constitutional law' like this deserves distinctive treatment.[93]

Because Mullan thinks that written constitutional texts make, or ought to make, real differences to the manner in which judicial reasoning shapes public law, he finds continued judicial reliance on unwritten constitutional values *after* the adoption of written bills of rights troubling. He observes that the enactment of written human rights guarantees has, at least in some areas, led to a 'revivified common law of judicial review' on human rights grounds, which has in turn made reliance on the relevant written instrument unnecessary.[94] In his view, however, direct reference to written human rights instruments may be preferable in such cases. Examining Mullan's reasons for this assertion – which, after all, does seem to contradict unwritten constitutionalism in its strong sense – is important to clarifying his view of the unwritten constitution.

The reason why judges ought to focus on written constitutional texts instead of unwritten contexts is, of course, the general obligation they have to respect the sovereign will of the legislature or the people whose actions led to the adoption of the relevant written constitution. If sovereign will is the ultimate source of law, then this justification for judicial deference to written constitutional texts is the only justification. We might say, then, that from this perspective written bills of rights are, in Raz's terms, second-order exclusionary reasons for judicial decisions – that is, they are authoritative in and of themselves without any need to refer to the first-order reasons, or substantive unwritten norms, that justified their adoption (though, of course, bills of rights, given their very nature, do direct judges to consider abstract moral or political rights in the course of textual interpretation).

Although Mullan does not address the status of written constitutions using Raz's terminology, my impression from the arguments that he makes about the relationship between written and unwritten constitutional law is that he does not regard written constitutional texts as second-order rules that exclude reference to first-order reasons. Instead, he seems to regard them as first-order reasons for decision to be balanced by judges against other first-order reasons for decision when determining difficult constitutional cases. This is simply another way of saying that he regards sovereign will as just one of several constitutional values to be weighed by judges when articulating a reasoned approach to public law. Of course, Mullan does insist that there are powerful reasons why, after this reasoning exercise, the balance will almost always favour judicial deference to written bills of rights. He explores two reasons, which we may classify as first-order reasons, why this is so.

First, he concludes that the success of any attempt by judges to construct a new framework for human rights based on abstract moral or political principles will be limited by the incremental nature of common law reasoning. Such a framework could emerge, but only gradually as existing legal language is refined. So, when a written code of rights is available to provide a shortcut to that end, the shortcut should be taken.[95] To regard the enactment of a written code as a sign to hasten or revivify the building of a common law structure of rights is, in Mullan's view, to divert judicial efforts from the more efficient and productive task of building a vibrant case law that might bring the written code of rights into full legal life. In short, a sound human rights jurisprudence is enhanced by judicial focus on textual interpretation where an appropriate written text exists.

Second, Mullan fears that if judges think about human rights within an unwritten or common law mindset – one that historically adopted a deferential stance toward executive and legislative power – the result will be the 'debasing of the coinage of rights and freedoms.'[96] The adoption of written guarantees can have a 'transformative impact' on our rights culture, an escape from limits inherent in 'the earlier world of the common law,' which will be missed unless judges direct their attention to the written texts.[97] So, here are two reasons *above and beyond* simple respect for and submission to sovereign will why Mullan thinks judges ought to articulate human rights through textual interpretation of written bills of rights rather than through common law or unwritten constitutional principles.

There are, in other words, sound unwritten constitutional reasons for giving written bills of rights a central place within judicial reasoning about public law. But it follows from this conclusion that there may also be sound unwritten constitutional reasons for de-emphasising or even disregarding written constitutional texts. Mullan suggests that where written constitutions leave gaps in legal protections that are not the result of conscious political design, resort to the unwritten constitution is justified. He acknowledges at least the possibility of two ways in which unwritten norms *may* limit written constitutional laws that have been effected through conscious political design: amendments to the written constitution, and use of the section 33 of the *Charter* (which permits legislatures to make laws notwithstanding certain *Charter* rights) in a manner that seriously violates fundamental unwritten norms *may* be impermissible.[98] Mullan is very cautious about these points, and does not state whether or not these arguments might be or ought to be accepted. Instead, he argues that advocates of unwritten constitutionalism must first do a better job explaining the theoretical foundations and the practical implications of the unwritten constitution before such arguments can be fully considered.[99] However, it is clear that the ill-defined aspects of unwritten constitutional principles – what precisely do they include and to what extent are they *really* justiciable in the face of contrary written laws? – concern Mullan, not because he fears their overuse by an anti-democratic judiciary but because, on the contrary, he fears that, without a coherent theory that provides concrete answers on these matters, their legitimacy will always be contested and their potential value for the sound articulation of public law compromised.

Before we rush to construct a grand theory explaining the unwritten constitution, however, we do well to keep in mind two cautionary points that Mullan makes. First, the search for a convincing practical and theoretical account of unwritten principles must, in a sense, be a work-in-progress. It is an enterprise that, says Mullan, must be shaped by the fluid nature of concepts like sovereignty and nation-state within the constitutional discourses of post-colonial societies like Canada, Australia, and New Zealand – a fluidity arising in part from the challenge made by aboriginal peoples to the mythologies that used to sustain national political and legal narratives in these jurisdictions.[100] Second, Mullan denies that any grand theory is really possible. On this point, once again, Mullan opts for rational pragmatism over theoretical dogmatism: 'So varied are the competing visions of what is the appropriate theory of constitutional law and interpretation and so deeply divided are the advocates of the various competing theories that there may ultimately be dangers to the constitutional order in recognizing the predominance of one theory over another.'[101] I take this to mean that the unwritten constitution, as a form of *common* public law, will only emerge through practical and measured reasoning over time, and that its strength may ultimately lie in its ability to resist theoretical extremes – to resist, in other words, any final victory for legal positivism or legal rationalism, any ultimate supremacy of either the conception of law-as-sovereign-will or the conception of law-as-reason.

Mullan's work stretches over interesting times. It offers sustained critical reflection about the nature of public law during a period of intense faith in the promise held out by the modern liberal-welfare state of securing the ends of social justice. But it also embraces a period during which intense scepticism has emerged about the prospects of the liberal-welfare state and its ability to deliver its promise of social justice. Finally, it embraces a present time of considerable unease about globalization and international security issues. In these turbulent times, state power often lurches in precarious and unaccountable ways, threatening the fragile constitutional, political, and social settlements of the past. For Mullan, the common law represents a stabilizing force – an 'equilibrium' – that seeks to uphold the promise of state power by correcting its excesses and its omissions.[102] If this practical vision of the common law underlies the unwritten constitution then it is, I think, a compelling moral foundation for constitutional theory in Canada and other common law jurisdictions. I, for one, am indebted to David Mullan for providing the insights that bring this theory to life.

NOTES

1 David Mullan, '*Wells v. Newfoundland*: Redefining the Status of Tribunal and Agency Members' (1999) 13 Can. J. Admin. L. & Prac. 117 at 136 [Mullan, 'Redefining the Status'].

2 On terrorism measures see *A (FC) and others (FC) v. Secretary of State for the Home Department*, [2005] 2 W.L.R. 87 (H.L); *Rasul et al. v. Bush, President of the United States et al.*, 542 U.S. 466 (2004). On the rule of law as unwritten see *Reference re The Secession of Quebec*, [1998] 2 S.C.R. 217 at paras. 32, 70–8 [*Quebec Secession Reference*].

3 In fact, Bentham said the common law, as system of general rules, is 'imaginary,' and he insisted that the expression 'unwritten law' is a 'paradoxical and unmeaning epithet': J. Bentham, *A Comment on the Commentaries: A Criticism of W. Blackstone's 'Commentaries on the Laws of England,'* C.W. Everett ed. (Oxford: Oxford University Press, 1928) at 125, 156.

4 David Mullan, 'The Role for Underlying Constitutional Principles in a Bill of Rights World' [2004] N.Z. Law Rev. 9 at 34 [Mullan, 'Role for Underlying Constitutional Principles'].

5 *Fraser v. Canada (Public Service Staff Relations Board)*, [1985] 2 S.C.R. 455 at 462–63.

6 *Saumer v. Quebec (City)*, [1953] 2 S.C.R. 299 and *Switzman v. Elbling*, [1957] S.C.R. 285 at 306.

7 *Quebec Secession Reference*, *supra* note 2 at paras. 32, 62. See also *Reference re Remuneration of Judges of the Provincial Court*, [1997] 3 S.C.R. 3 at paras. 83, 95, 100–3 [*Provincial Judges Reference*]. Section 52(1) of the *Constitution Act, 1982* defines 'The Constitution of Canada' as 'the supreme law of Canada.'

8 See *Provincial Judges Reference* ibid. (judicial independence); *New Brunswick Broadcasting Co. v. Nova Scotia (Speaker of the House of Assembly)*, [1993] 1 S.C.R. 319 (parliamentary privilege), *Quebec Secession Reference*, *supra* note 2 (federalism, democracy, the rule of law, constitutionalism, respect for minorities), and *R. v. Demers*, [2004] 2 S.C.R. 489 per LeBel J. at para. 83 (human rights).

9 *Quebec Secession Reference*, *supra* note 2 at para. 54.

10 *Provincial Judges Reference*, *supra* note 7 at para. 83.

11 *Quebec Secession Reference*, *supra* note 2 at paras. 49, 32.

12 Ibid. at para. 80.

13 Ibid. at para. 50.

14 *Hanson v. Vernon*, 27 Iowa 28 (S.C., 1869) at 73, and *Loan Association v. Topeka*, 87 U.S. 655 (1874) at 663. For an early defence of unwritten constitutionalism in the United States, see Christopher Tiedeman, *The Unwritten Constitution of the United States: A Philosophical Inquiry into the Fundamentals of American Constitutional Law* (New York: G.P. Putnam's Sons, 1890). In general, the theory was closely associated with the laissez-faire capitalist reading of the U.S. Constitution that was largely superseded by post-New Deal developments: see C.E. Jacobs, *Law Writers and the Courts: The Influence of Thomas M. Cooley, Christopher G. Tiedeman, and John F. Dillon upon American Constitutional Law* (Berkeley: University of California Press, 1954). For more recent discussions of unwritten constitutionalism in the U.S., see T.C. Grey, 'Do We Have an Unwritten Constitution?' (1975) 27 Stan. L. Rev. 703; Michael Moore, 'Do We Have an Unwritten Constitution?' (1989) 63 S. Cal. L. Rev. 107; Jed Rubenfeld, 'The New Unwritten Constitution' (2001) 51 Duke L.J. 289.

15 See e.g., *Lange v. Australian Broadcasting Corporation* (1997), 189 C.L.R. 520 (H.C.A.) at 566–7. See generally Jeremy Kirk, 'Constitutional Implications (I): Nature, Legitimacy, Classification' (2000) 24 Melb. U. L. Rev. 645.

16 See e.g., T.R.S. Allan, *Constitutional Justice: A Liberal Theory of the Rule of Law* (Oxford: Oxford University Press, 2001). For an overview, see Thomas Poole, 'Back to the Future? Unearthing the Theory of Common Law Constitutionalism' (2003) 23 O.J.L.S. 435. In the New Zealand context, see R. Cooke, 'Fundamentals' [1988] N.Z.L.J. 158.

17 Allan, *Constitutional Justice*, ibid. at 4–5.

18 David Mullan, 'Mr. Justice Rand: Defining the Limits of Court Control of the Administrative and Executive Process' (1979–80) 18 U.W.O. L. Rev. 65 at 76 [Mullan, 'Mr. Justice Rand']. Rand's implied bill of rights theory was seemingly rejected in *Canada (Attorney General) v. Dupond*, [1978] 2 S.C.R. 770.

19 David Mullan, *Administrative Law* (Toronto: Irwin Law, 2001) at 31.

20 David Mullan, 'A Comparison of the Impact of the New Zealand Bill of

Rights Act and the Canadian Charter of Rights and Freedoms on Judicial Review of Administrative Action' (2003) 1 N.Z.J.P.I.L. 115 at 147 [Mullan, 'Comparison of the New Zealand Bill of Rights and the Canadian Charter'].

21 These points are made in Mullan, 'Comparison of the New Zealand Bill of Rights and the Canadian Charter,' ibid.; Mullan, 'Role for Underlying Constitutional Principles,' *supra* note 4; Mullan, 'Underlying Constitutional Principles: The Legacy of Justice Rand' [forthcoming; Mullan, 'Legacy of Justice Rand']; and David Mullan, 'Deference from *Baker* to *Suresh* and Beyond – Interpreting the Conflicting Signals' in D. Dyzenhaus, ed., *The Unity of Public Law* (Oxford: Hart, 2004) 21 [Mullan, 'Deference from *Baker* to *Suresh*'].

22 See, e.g., Robin Elliot, 'References, Structural Argumentation and the Organizing Principles of Canada's Constitution' (2001) 80 Can. Bar Rev. 67 at 91–92, 95–97 (accepting LaForest J.'s assertion in his dissent in *Provincial Judges Reference*, *supra* note 7 at paras. 314–19, that unwritten constitutionalism 'subvert[s] the democratic foundation of judicial review').

23 Mullan, 'Legacy of Justice Rand,' *supra* note 21 at 16–18.

24 Ibid. at 16–21, and Mullan, 'Role for Underlying Constitutional Principles,' *supra* note 4 at 34.

25 Mullan, 'Legacy of Justice Rand,' *supra* note 21 at 22.

26 For a similar argument, see Luc Tremblay, 'General Legitimacy of Judicial Review and the Fundamental Basis of Constitutional Law' (2003) 23 O.J.L.S. 525 at 545; on antecedent norms generally, see Luc Tremblay, *The Rule of Law, Justice, and Interpretation* (Montreal & Kingston: McGill-Queen's University Press, 1997).

27 See, e.g., Mark Walters, 'Common Law, Reason, and Sovereign Will' (2003) 53 U.T.L.J. 65.

28 H.L.A. Hart, *The Concept of Law* (Oxford: Clarendon Press, 1961).

29 See generally G.J. Postema, *Bentham and the Common Law Tradition* (Oxford: Clarendon Press, 1986).

30 Joseph Raz, *Practical Reasoning and Norms* (Oxford: Oxford University Press, 1990).

31 David Dyzenhaus, 'The Constitution of Law,' Smuts Memorial Lectures, delivered at Cambridge University, 1–4 November 2004. Also David Dyzenhaus, 'The Genealogy of Legal Positivism' (2004) 24 O.J.L.S. 39 and David Dyzenhaus, 'The Politics of Deference: Judicial Review and Democracy' in M. Taggart, ed., *The Province of Administrative Law* (Oxford: Hart, 1997) at 280–81 [Dyzenhaus, 'Politics of Deference'].

32 David Mullan, 'The Uncertain Constitutional Position of Canada's Administrative Appeal Tribunals' (1982) 14 Ottawa L. Rev. 239 at 267 [Mullan, 'Uncertain Constitutional Position'].

33 David Mullan, 'The Federal Court Act: A Misguided Attempt at Administrative Law Reform?' (1973), 23 U.T.L.J. 14 at 15 [Mullan, 'Federal Court Act'].

34 Ibid. at 35–36, 43, 51–52. See also David Mullan, 'Reform of Judicial Review of Administrative Action – The Ontario Way' (1974) 12 Osgoode Hall L.J. 125 at 126, 130 [Mullan, 'Reform of Judicial Review']; David Mullan, 'One Plus Five Equals Six' [1971] N.Z.L.J. 512 at 513; and David Mullan, 'The Jurisdictional Fact Doctrine in the Supreme Court of Canada – A Mitigating Plea' (1972) 10 Osgoode Hall L.J. 440 at 446 [Mullan, 'Jurisdictional Fact Doctrine'].

35 *Seneca College of Applied Arts and Technology v. Bhadauria*, [1981] 2 S.C.R. 181 [*Bhadauria*].

36 David Mullan, 'Developments in Administrative Law: The 1980–81 Term' (1982), 3 Sup. Ct. L. Rev. 1 at 5–14 [Mullan, 'The 1980–81 Term'], discussing *Bhadauria*, ibid.

37 Ibid. at 8, 14, 64.

38 David Mullan, 'Fairness: The New Natural Justice?' (1975) 25 U.T.L.J. 281 at 298 [Mullan, 'New Natural Justice'].

39 David Mullan, 'Substantive Fairness Review: Heed the Amber Light!' (1988) 18 V.U.W.L.R. 293 at 307 [Mullan, 'Substantive Fairness Review'].

40 David Mullan, 'Natural Justice and Fairness – Substantive as well as Procedural Standards for the Review of Administrative Decision-Making?' (1982) 27 McGill L.J. 250 at 298 [Mullan, 'Natural Justice and Fairness'].

41 Ibid. at 266–85.

42 *Prohibitions del Roy* (1607), 12 Co. Rep. 63 at 65.

43 David Mullan, 'Tribunals and Courts – The Contemporary Terrain: Lessons from Human Rights Regimes' (1999) 24 Queen's L.J. 643 [Mullan, 'Tribunals and Courts'].

44 See e.g., essays in Christopher Forsyth, ed., *Judicial Review and the Constitution* (Oxford: Hart, 2000).

45 See e.g. David Dyzenhaus, 'Reuniting the Brain: The Democratic Basis of Judicial Review' (1998) 9 PL.R. 98.

46 Mullan, 'Jurisdictional Fact Doctrine,' *supra* note 34 at 444.

47 Ibid. at 445.

48 The argument is developed at length by Mark Elliott, *The Constitutional Foundations of Judicial Review* (Oxford: Hart, 2001).

49 Mullan, 'The Jurisdictional Fact Doctrine,' *supra* note 34 at 444–5.

50 Mullan, 'Reform of Judicial Review,' *supra* note 34 at 130. See also Mullan, *Administrative Law, supra* note 19 at 55–6.

51 David Mullan, 'Judicial Deference to Executive Decision-Making: Evolving

Concepts of Responsibility' (1993) 19 Queen's L.J. 137 at 157 [Mullan, 'Judicial Deference to Executive Decision-Making'].

52 Mullan, 'Role for Underlying Constitutional Principles,' *supra* note 4 at 35.

53 Mullan, 'Redefining the Status,' *supra* note 1 at 132 and Mullan, 'Judicial Deference to Executive Decision-Making,' *supra* note 51 at 157. Also Mullan, 'Mr. Justice Rand,' *supra* note 18 at 70.

54 David Mullan and Antonella Ceddia, 'The Impact on Public Law of Privatization, Deregulation, Outsourcing and Downsizing: A Canadian Perspective,' (2003) 10 Ind. J. Global Legal Stud. 199 at 244–45 ['Impact on Public Law of Privatization'].

55 Mullan, *Administrative Law, supra* note 19 at 136, and Mullan and Ceddia, 'Impact on Public Law of Privatization,' ibid. at 245. For other references to courts as surrogates for democratic checks, see David Mullan, 'Administrative Law at the Margins' in Michael Taggart, ed., *The Province of Administrative Law* (Oxford: Hart, 1997), 136 [Mullan, 'Administrative Law at the Margins'], and Mullan, 'Judicial Deference to Executive Decision-Making,' *supra* note 51 at 159.

56 Mullan, 'Mr. Justice Rand,' *supra* note 18 at 70, and David Mullan, 'Developments in Administrative Law: The 1982–83 Term' (1984) 6 Sup. Ct L. Rev. 1 at 28, 31 [Mullan, 'The 1982–83 Term'].

57 David Mullan, 'Standing After McNeil' (1976) 8 Ottawa L. Rev. 32 at 48 [Mullan, 'Standing After McNeil'].

58 *Crevier v. Quebec (Attorney General)*, [1981] 2 S.C.R. 220; *MacMillan Bloedel Ltd. v. Simpson*, [1995] 4 S.C.R. 725.

59 Mullan, 'Substantive Fairness Review,' *supra* note 39 at 302–3. The *New Zealand Bill of Rights Act 1990* (N.Z.), no. 109, which enjoys quasi-constitutional status, provides for a right to judicial review (s. 27). See P. Rishworth, G. Huscroft, S. Optican, and R. Mahoney, *The New Zealand Bill of Rights* (Melbourne: Oxford University Press, 2003), chap. 27.

60 Mullan, *Administrative Law, supra* note 19 at 9.

61 Ibid. at 156. Also Mullan, 'New Natural Justice,' *supra* note 38 at 310.

62 See, e.g., *Nicholson v. Haldimand-Norfolk Regional Board of Commissioners of Police*, [1979] 1 S.C.R. 311 at 319.

63 Mullan, *Administrative Law, supra* note 19 at 150, 156–57 and David Mullan, '*Board of Education of the Indian Head School Division No. 19 of Saskatchewan v. Knight*: The Emergence of a Free Standing Right to Procedural Fairness' (1990) 43 Admin. L. Rep. 230 [Mullan, 'Free Standing Right to Procedural Fairness'].

64 *Knight v. Indian Head School Division No. 19*, [1990] 1 S.C.R. 653 [*Knight*].

65 Mullan, *Administrative Law, supra* note 19 at 187, 150, and Mullan, 'Free

Standing Right to Procedural Fairness,' *supra* note 63, both sources citing John Willis, 'Administrative Law in Canada' (1939) 53 Harv. L. Rev. 251. See also *Knight*, at 668 ('There may be a general right to procedural fairness, autonomous of the operation of any statute.').

66 Mullan, *Administrative Law, supra* note 19 at 157, 187, and David Mullan, 'Developments in Administrative Law: The 1978–79 Term' (1980) 1 Sup. Ct L. Rev. 1 at 7–8 [Mullan, 'The 1978–79 Term'].

67 Mullan, *Administrative Law, supra* note 19 at 150. Also David Mullan, 'Procedural Codes: A Second Opinion' [1973] N.Z.L.J. 41; Mullan, 'New Natural Justice,' *supra* note 38 at 310.

68 Mullan, *Administrative Law, supra* note 19 at 10.

69 David Mullan, 'Judicial Deference to Administrative Decision-Making in the Age of the Charter' (1986) 50 Sask. L. Rev. 203 at 209 [Mullan, 'Deference in the Age of the Charter'].

70 [1959] S.C.R. 121 [*Roncarelli*].

71 Mullan, 'Judicial Deference to Executive Decision-Making,' *supra* note 51 at 164.

72 David Mullan, 'The Supreme Court of Canada and Tribunals – Deference to the Administrative Process: A Recent Phenomenon or a Return to Basics?' (2001) 80 Can. Bar Rev. 399 at 427 [Mullan, 'Supreme Court of Canada and Tribunals']. Elsewhere, Mullan describes the *Roncarelli* decision as 'venerable,' 'riveting,' 'seminal,' and 'our major administrative law decision': David Mullan, 'Judging the Judgment of Judges: *CUPE v. Ontario (Minister of Labour)* (2003) 10 C.L.E.L.J. 431 at 436 [Mullan, 'Judging the Judgment of Judges']; Mullan, *Administrative Law, supra* note 19 at 100, 102; Mullan, 'The 1982–83 Term,' *supra* note 56 at 31.

73 Mullan, 'Judging the Judgment of Judges,' *supra* note 72 at 450.

74 *Baker v. Canada (Minister of Citizenship and Immigration)*, [1999] 2 S.C.R. 817 at para. 56 [*Baker*].

75 Mullan, *Administrative Law, supra* note 19 at 114.

76 David Mullan, 'Recent Developments in Administrative Law – The Apparent Triumph of Deference!' (1998–9) 12 C.J.A.L.P. 191 at 192, 194 [Mullan, 'Apparent Triumph of Deference'].

77 Mullan, 'The Supreme Court of Canada and Tribunals,' *supra* note 72 at 403. Other statements supporting the principle of deference: Mullan, 'Deference in the Age of the Charter,' *supra* note 69 at 203–4, 223; Mullan, 'Apparent Triumph of Deference,' *supra* note 76; David Mullan, 'The Future of Canadian Administrative Law' (1991) 16 Queen's L.J. 77 at 77, 88 [Mullan, 'Future of Canadian Administrative Law']; David Mullan, 'Developments in Administrative Law: The 1983–84 Term' (1985) 7 Sup. Ct L. Rev. 1 at 46 [Mullan,

'The 1983–84 Term']; and Mullan, 'The 1978–79 Term,' *supra* note 66 at 28, 32, 75.

78 For Mullan's concerns in this respect about the logical implications of *Anisminic v. Foreign Compensation Commission*, [1969] 2 A.C. 147 (H.L.), see Mullan, 'The Federal Court Act,' *supra* note 33 at 38; Mullan, 'The 1978–79 Term,' *supra* note 66 at 28–32.

79 See *Canadian Union of Public Employees Local 963 v. New Brunswick Liquor Corp.*, [1979] 2 S.C.R. 227.

80 See *Union des employés de service, local 298 v. Bibeault*, [1988] 2 S.C.R. 1048 [*Bibeault*].

81 *Pushpanathan v. Canada (Minister of Citizenship and Immigration)*, [1998] 1 S.C.R. 982. The pragmatic and functional approach is discussed in Grant Huscroft's contribution to this volume.

82 *Bibeault*, *supra* note 80 at paras. 124, 126.

83 David Mullan, 'Judicial Deference to Executive Decision-Making,' *supra* note 51 at 151–2.

84 Ibid.

85 Ibid. On the separateness of these two considerations, see David Mullan, 'The Re-emergence of Jurisdictional Error' (1985) 14 Admin. L. Rep. 326; David Mullan, 'Future of Canadian Administrative Law,' *supra* note 77 at 78; and Mullan, 'Deference from *Baker* to *Suresh*,' *supra* note 21 at 52.

86 David Mullan, 'Establishing the Standard of Review: The Struggle for Complexity?' (2004) C.J.A.L.P. 59 at 93–94, 96 [Mullan, 'Establishing the Standard of Review'].

87 Ibid. Mullan cites *Baker*, *supra* note 74 at para. 65, which in turn cites with approval the idea of 'deference as respect' developed in Dyzenhaus, 'Politics of Deference' *supra* note 31 at 286.

88 Mullan, 'Substantive Fairness Review,' *supra* note 39 at 298–9.

89 Mullan, 'Establishing the Standard of Review,' *supra* note 86 at 96.

90 Part I of the *Constitution Act, 1982*, being Schedule B to the *Canada Act 1982* (U.K.), 1982, c. 11 [the *Charter*].

91 *New Zealand Bill of Rights Act 1990* (N.Z.), no. 109.

92 Mullan, 'Establishing the Standard of Review,' *supra* note 86 at 85. See also Mullan, 'Deference in the Age of the Charter,' *supra* note 69 at 218, and Mullan, 'Deference from *Baker* to *Suresh*,' *supra* note 21 at 55.

93 David Mullan, 'Tribunals and Courts – The Contemporary Terrain: Lessons from Human Rights Regimes' (1999) 24 Queen's L.J. 643 at para. 9.

94 Mullan, 'Comparison of the New Zealand Bill of Rights and the Canadian Charter,' *supra* note 20 at 118, 147.

95 See, e.g., Mullan, *Administrative Law*, *supra* note 19 at 114, and Mullan, 'Deference from *Baker* to *Suresh*,' *supra* note 21 at 30–1.
96 Mullan, 'Comparison of the New Zealand Bill of Rights and the Canadian Charter,' *supra* note 20 at 119.
97 Ibid. at 140.
98 Mullan, 'Role for Underlying Constitutional Principles,' *supra* note 4 at 15, note 19, and Mullan, 'Legacy of Justice Rand,' *supra* note 21 at 11, especially note 29.
99 Mullan, 'Role for Underlying Constitutional Principles,' *supra* note 4 at 32–38.
100 Ibid. at 32, 36–7.
101 Mullan, 'Legacy of Justice Rand,' *supra* note 21 at 50–1.
102 Mullan, 'Administrative Law at the Margins,' *supra* note 55 at 156.

David Mullan's Theory of the Rule of (Common) Law

DAVID DYZENHAUS

For more than thirty years, David Mullan has been charting the development of Canadian administrative law. He has done this not only by telling us where the administrative state has been, but also, like an ancient explorer venturing into unknown regions, he has provided perceptive charts of where the administrative state might productively go. Both kinds of charts have had immense influence, establishing him as Canada's foremost administrative lawyer since John Willis, and as one of the leading commentators on administrative law in the common law world. The influence of these charts is owed in part to a remarkable clarity when it comes to uncovering the tensions in and explaining the complexity of the administrative state. But it is also owed, in my view, to a sophisticated theory of the rule of law, one that had to be developed in order to give the charts both their descriptive precision and their prescriptive force.

The last claim is made despite the fact that, as far as I know, Mullan has always avoided abstract or theoretical statements of his position, preferring to stay quite close to the analysis of trends in practice.[1] But ever since I started reading his work, I have thought that such a theory was not just below the surface of his writing, waiting to be uncovered. Rather, it was in full view, if only one went to the trouble to gather its components in one place. What follows is my attempt at that task.

A Debate in the *University of Toronto Law Journal*[2]

In 1975 Mullan published a major essay on administrative law in the University of Toronto Law Journal titled 'Fairness: The New Natural Justice?'[3] When he wrote this article, it was generally accepted in Canada that the rules of natural justice applied to decisions that could be classified as judicial or quasi-judicial, whereas purely administrative decisions attracted no procedural protection. However, in England courts had begun to explore the idea that there was a general duty on public officials to act fairly. Other Commonwealth courts were following this path, and Canadian courts had begun to indicate their discomfort with the thought that a whole swathe of public decision-making attracted no procedural protection.

Mullan identified three reasons critics might think stood in the way of Canadian adoption of the doctrine of fairness: first, the parameters of the doctrine of fairness were 'extremely hazy'; second, the rules of natural justice are reasonably predictable but the new concept was so unpredictable that lawyers could no longer give safe advice; and third (and most serious), the new doctrine would lead to courts imposing inappropriate procedural requirements on officials, which would interfere with efficient decision-making.[4]

In response to the first criticism, Mullan pointed out that the doctrine was new and therefore of course hazy. He thus took the criticism to be of the 'common law way of law-making' and, because of his confidence in the common law's ability to render the doctrine useful on a case by case basis, he rejected this criticism.[5]

To the second criticism, he responded that natural justice was not as predictable as the criticism supposed. Not only was there the difficulty of classifying a decision as judicial or quasi-judicial, but once a decision was so classified a court still had to decide which of the rules of natural justice applied. In any case, it was high time to question the validity of the distinction between judicial and quasi-judicial decisions, on the one hand, and administrative decisions on the other. The difficulties in making the distinction tended to show that there was a spectrum of functions rather than a clear distinction, so Mullan suggested getting rid of the classification process altogether. He then posed a crucial question for Canadian administrative lawyers:[6]

> Why not deal with problems of fairness and natural justice simply on the basis that, the nearer one is to the type of function requiring straight law/fact determinations and resulting in serious consequences to individuals, the greater is the legitimacy of the demand for procedural protection but as one moves through the spectrum of decision-making functions to the broad, policy-oriented decisions exercised typically by a minister of the crown, the content of procedural fairness gradually disappears into noth-

> ingness, the emphasis being on a gradual disappearance not one punctuated by the unrealistic impression of clear cut divisions presented by the classification process?

Mullan claimed that the courts, unburdened by the classification process, could then ask the 'real questions' about appropriate procedural protections – that is, questions about what protections are appropriate in a particular context.[7] He saw that the idea of fairness might result in the addition of a classification process to the old one, citing as evidence Megarry J.'s dictum in *Bates v. Lord Hailsham of St. Marylbone*: 'Let me accept that in the sphere of the so-called quasi-judicial the rules of natural justice run, and that in the administrative or executive field there is a general duty of fairness.'[8] But Mullan suggested that the content of procedural fairness should diminish as one gets closer to the administrative end of the spectrum, without supposing that there are two separate standards.[9]

In response to the third criticism – that judges would apply procedures inappropriately – Mullan observed that, thus far, there was no real evidence of such a trend,[10] and noted that one bonus of the fairness approach was already in evidence: judges were willing to apply less than the full panoply of procedural requirements at the quasi-judicial end of the spectrum.[11] Thus, even at a time when administrative decisions were thought to be immune to procedural review, judges seemed to recognize that procedural requirements should be adapted or tailored to suit the needs of particular administrative settings.[12]

Mullan's article received two significant responses. The first was an endorsement by the majority of the Supreme Court in what is regarded as one of the most important judgments in Canadian administrative law, *Nicholson v. Haldimand-Norfolk Regional Board of Commissioners of Police*,[13] though the endorsement was qualified by the fact that the majority quoted with approval Megarry J.'s dictum which implied, as we have seen, that there were two different standards. The second was a 1978 article in the *University of Toronto Law Journal* by Martin Loughlin, the first publication by an academic who went on to become one of the United Kingdom's leading public lawyers.[14]

Loughlin did not regard the development of the idea of a duty to act fairly as evidence of a progressive trend in public law but rather as symptomatic of a crisis in the conception of the rule of law. In his view, administrative law had traditionally operated with a tripartite division of political power between the legislature responsible for enacting general laws, the administration, which was a transmission belt for implementing legislative directives, and the judiciary, which acted as the final arbiter of the law's interpretation and also ensured that the administration acted within the boundaries established by law. In addition, the concept of the rule of law included a principle of equality.[15] In the nineteenth century, judges tended to assert a supervisory jurisdiction over administrative bodies in accordance with this conception, while in the twentieth century, they realized that the administration was not a mere transmission belt, but was involved in developing the content of social-welfare legislation. Judges thus retreated somewhat from activist assertions of supervisory jurisdiction, a retreat marked by the classification of functions as administrative.

Loughlin sketched three strategies judges could adopt in order to cope with the breakdown in their conception of the rule of law, occasioned by the rise of the welfare state. They could be 'activist formalists' and simply impose natural justice on all administrative decisions, an imposition that would fundamentally distort the administrative process. They could be 'activist informalists,' which would require abandoning natural justice/adjudication as the one-size-fits-all model for procedures and developing in its place a flexible supervisory role. But that role, Loughlin argued, is inconsistent with the judge's role under the traditional conception, which sees judicial expertise as lying in adjudication. Activist informalism would require a court to go into controversial areas of policy 'which it is required to avoid' and also risked 'overjudicialization of administrative procedures.' Finally, there is the 'inactive formalist strategy,' the one adopted, which preserves the traditional model for quasi-judicial functions while leaving the administrative functions alone.[16] Here Loughlin seemed to agree with Mullan that the distinction between the two categories was unstable, and that in some cases the classification led to injustice.[17] So the question became whether Mullan's approach, which Loughlin took to be activist informalism, could do better.

On the basis of his analysis of English case law, Loughlin argued that activist informalism did not produce the flexible answers to real questions that Mullan had advocated. Rather, the courts found themselves unable to abandon formal classifications and they were clearly uncomfortable with, and bad at, weighing the interests at stake in determining the right level of procedural protection.[18] And Loughlin found evidence of the same problems in *Nicholson*.[19] The root of these difficulties, he claimed, was that activist informalism required judges to set themselves up as the 'supreme authority to determine which decisions will be made by what process.'[20] Further, they would have to engage in a kind of instrumental reasoning subversive of the rule-governed formalism that had provided courts with the basis for certainty. Mullan had suggested that a sufficient degree of consistency could be achieved through the development of principles pursuant, Loughlin conjectured, to a normative idea of the purpose of statutes. He surmised that Mullan's approach had something in common with Lon L. Fuller's, quoting the following passage from Fuller in support of the contention that a purposive approach does not necessarily destroy the notion of a rule:[21]

> The answer lies in the concept of *structure*. A statute or a rule of common law has, either explicitly, or by virtue of its relation with other rules, something that may be called a structural integrity. This is what we have in mind when we speak of the intent of the statute, though we know it is men who have intentions and not words on paper. Within the limits of that structure, fidelity to law not only permits but demands a creative role from the judge, but beyond that structure it does not permit him to go.

But such an idea, Loughlin asserted, rests on an 'imaginary consensus' that is supposed to make it possible for us to recognize fairness in practice.[22]

The upshot, on Loughlin's account, seemed to be that judges were faced with the fact that the formalism of their conception of the rule of law could no longer cope with the task of policing the administrative state. Judges had thus retreated from active to inactive formalism, but even that retreat could not preserve their conception. The alternative Mullan presented left judges as arbiters of instrumental rationality, a role to which judges were unsuited. They could try to stabilize things by appealing to a consensus about fairness but that consensus was a product of their imagination. Loughlin's diagnosis was thus, to say the least, pessimistic.

But before I proceed to evaluate his pessimism, it is important to have a clearer understanding of its basis. Fuller articulated his idea of the structural integrity of a statute in response to H.L.A. Hart's claim that the law, properly so-called, consists of rules with a determinate content. Their status as law is certified ultimately by a master rule that Hart, in later work, called the 'rule of recognition.'[23] Fuller's response was that this claim has to be seen as one made from within a particular tradition of thinking about law, the legal positivist tradition, which advances a particular conception of law because it understands the point of law as providing stability and order. But there are, Fuller argued, other ways of understanding law, including that of the common law tradition. The latter regards law not as a fully finished determinate product but as something that is continually in the process of being worked out in accordance with the sense of participants in legal practice of what comports best with what Fuller called the 'inner morality' of law, or in later work law's 'internal morality.'[24] While Mullan did not endorse Fuller's argument, his faith both in the principled resources of the law and his declared allegiance to the 'common law way of law-making' make it plausible to suppose that he would side with Fuller in this debate, adopting what I will refer to as the common law conception of the rule of law. But it is equally plausible to suppose that Loughlin endorses Hart's claim about law, and thus a positivist conception of the rule of law, at least to the following extent. Loughlin suggests that the rule of law is practicable if and only if law has a content such that the administration can be a transmission belt for it and judges can check what officials do to see whether it complies with law's content. If law fails to have such a content, judges will be cut adrift from their role.[25] Thus, the formal understanding of the rule of law is not just one conception among others. It is the only conception, at least the only conception in which judges have a central role as guardians.

It is also important to recall that the claim that law has a content does not specify what kind of law is at stake in a discussion of administrative law. It is ambiguous as between the kind of law that the administration was supposed to transmit (the substantive law of the statute that delegated authority to public officials) and the law of natural justice that judges had developed (the procedural law that described how officials were to make their decisions on substance). Mullan's article was concerned only with procedural law, while Loughlin's response dealt with both, though not altogether explicitly.

In light of the distinction between procedural and substantive law, Loughlin's argument can be reformulated as follows. In the nineteenth century, the formal conception of the rule of law was stable for two reasons. First, substantive law has a determinate content such that officials can transmit it and judges can check that they have done their job. Second, procedural law has a determinate content such that judges can check to see whether officials are complying with procedures. But when the first kind of law becomes indeterminate (because officials are given the task of creating its substance), judges are no longer comfortable with applying the content of procedural law to officials across the board. They thus confine the application of procedural law to the first kind of law only when that kind has a determinate content. But since the classification of substantive law into law with either determinate or indeterminate content is unstable and because injustices result from the classification, judges rethink their position and develop a category of indeterminate procedural law – fairness – that they will apply either across the board to substantive law or to substantive law when it is indeterminate. But this adds a second layer of indeterminacy – procedural indeterminacy – to the layer of indeterminate substantive law and perhaps to all of substantive law. Since the judicial role is predicated on law being determinate, judges can no longer successfully perform their role.

In the next section, we will see how Mullan's accounts of the development of Canadian administrative law, both substantive and procedural, support somewhat Loughlin's predictions about incoherence and provide evidence for some of Mullan's fears about resurgent formalism. However, to the extent that this is so, the evidence is of a crisis for Loughlin's conception of the rule of law rather than for the grander claim he made about the incoherence of the very idea of the rule of law.

Canadian Administrative Law since 1979

Substantive Review

In 1979, the same year the Supreme Court of Canada handed down *Nicholson*, it handed down an equally significant decision on substantive review, *CUPE Local 693 v. New Brunswick Liquor Corporation.*[26] Prior to this decision, judges had tended to review officials' interpretations of their enabling statute on a correctness standard, in line with the conception of the rule of law that says that judges are entitled to check to see whether officials have made a correct determination of the substantive content of their enabling statute. In order to protect officials from such intrusive review, legislatures would sometimes insert privative clauses into statutes – provisions that, with varying degrees of explicitness, told the judges not to review. On a literal interpretation, a privative clause precludes judges from any role in checking the legality of administrative decisions and thus seems to leave the officials with unlimited discretion – a law unto themselves. And this result seems to follow whether one adopts the positivist or the common law conception of the rule of law.

In order to avoid this apparently absurd result, judges adopted a formal distinction between two categories of error: errors about the jurisdictional limits on the official's authority, and error within those limits. A privative clause protected the latter but not the former, which were reviewable on a correctness standard. This distinction attempts to do the same kind of work as the distinction between quasi-judicial and administrative decisions by carving out a category where it makes functional sense for the administration to be free or almost free of judicial review while retaining a category where judicial control, traditionally or formally understood, is maintained. In addition, when it came to exercises of discretion (in contrast to interpretations of a statute), a formal distinction was drawn between a limited set of grounds of review (for example, bad faith) requiring a correctness standard, and the substantive decision that was in the discretion of the official.

As with the distinction between quasi-judicial and administrative decisions, problems attended both of the distinctions made in substantive review. First, the distinctions were unstable. This permitted, for example, judges who were so inclined to classify any official interpretation of law as jurisdictional in nature, thus permitting review on the correctness standard. In Loughlin's terms, such judges would be activist formalists since they were inclined to review all administrative decisions on the basis of their conformity with an allegedly determinate content of the law. Second, when judges took seriously the thought that there is a class of decisions that, as matter of form rather than principle, are immune to judicial review, the result was that those affected by those decisions were unprotected by the rule of law even when the decision affected some very important interest. When it came to review of discretion, it seemed that judges would review exercises of discretion when these were extremely unreasonable, so unreasonable that no rational person could make such a decision. But this standard of review was hardly likely to be met unless the official had acted in bad faith, or the equivalent, in which case the decision could be reviewed on that ground. So when it came to review of discretion, judges seemed to be, in Loughlin's terms, inactivist formalists, since a large swathe of administrative decisions attracted no, or virtually no review.

In *CUPE*, the Supreme Court warned judges of the dangers of being too ready to classify an official decision as jurisdictional in nature. In other words, the Court told judges to refrain from activist formalism. It also pointed out that the reason privative clauses had been inserted into statutes was to protect decisions that lay within the expertise of the officials charged with carrying out the mandate of their statute – decisions over matters that generalist judges were not qualified to judge. Thus judges should review such decisions, those at the core of official expertise, only if they were patently unreasonable – the standard that, as we have seen, was on occasion applied to discretionary decisions.

On one interpretation, *CUPE* seems an example of inactivist formalism: in the face of a privative clause, a formal signal from the legislature, judges should generally refrain from jurisdictional/correctness review and apply a standard that officials' decisions would meet unless they were patently unreasonable. In other words, there would be a small category of administrative decisions in which old-style correctness review was appropriate, hence in this respect the approach was formalist. But for the most part, administrative decisions would be largely immune from review, hence the judges would be inactive.

There were at least four problems with such an interpretation. First, while the privative clause was to be treated as a formal signal, *CUPE* provided no formal criteria for determining when an administrative decision fell into one category or the other. Second, it is hard to get a grip from *CUPE* on the content of the patent unreasonableness standard. It is a standard of review, so the decisions subject to it are not totally immune to evaluation. The question is whether the evaluation requires something in the decision that shows that the decision is absurd – that is, equivalent to bad faith – or whether something different is required. Third, in preserving the correctness standard for some undefined class of cases, the Court preserved the basis for formalism even as it tried to move away from a formalistic approach. Indeed, as we will see below, it is a puzzling and recurrent theme of the Canadian jurisprudence on jurisdiction (and it could be said in administrative law in general) that the Court seems unable to avoid preserving or reintroducing formalism in the very decisions in which it signals most strongly the need to move away from it.

Thus, the Supreme Court initially seemed to demonstrate the ongoing instability of the distinction between jurisdictional errors and the rest by succumbing to the temptation to classify errors as jurisdictional in order to apply a correctness standard. Conversely, and in reaction to these decisions, some judges warned not only against that tendency but also against the temptation when applying the patent unreasonableness standard to ask whether, if reasons were given for a decision, those reasons adequately supported the decision.[27] In this second regard, their concern was that any test that evaluated the fit between the substance of the decision and the reasons given for it would come dangerously close to correctness or merits review. In order to avoid this danger, they suggested, judges should review only on the basis that there was something manifestly or patently unreasonable about the decision.

The fourth problem is that *CUPE* was a more complex decision than the label of inactivist formalism can capture. The Court articulated a vision of the administrative state which suggested that it was necessary, legitimate, and that the officials who staff it are often much more expert than generalist judges when it comes to interpreting the law of their statutory mandate. Now, this vision of the administrative state could be interpreted as a kind of afterthought to the formal signal of a privative clause. In that case, the privative clause is all-important, since it indicates that judges should be wary of, or even refrain from, review, and thus judges may infer from legislative silence that review on a correctness standard is appropriate. Nothing turns on whether judges accept that vision or not. All that matters is whether they interpret the legislative signals correctly. But if the vision is taken seriously, as the reason for judges to adopt a different stance towards the administrative state, then the reason applies whether or not there is a privative clause.

Just as the fact that the legislature has indicated that an official must follow certain procedures or is fit to follow procedures (that is, is quasi-judicial) is not conclusive of the question what procedures are appropriate, whether or not the legislature has indicated that judges should be wary of substantive review is not conclusive of whether they should be wary. At least, in both procedural and substantive review, the formal expressions of legislative intent are not conclusive if one adopts Mullan's premise that what matters are the 'real questions.' One should not ask: 'Are the formal indicia for review present?' Rather, one should ask: 'What does fairness require in this context?' and 'Taking into account the context, what standard should judges apply in substantive review of this decision?'

But, as should be now clear, packed into the idea of the 'real' is that such questions cannot get full or real answers if the answers are based on form, if they are settled by what judges understand to be formal indicia of legislative intent. Rather, the questions are to be settled by the 'common law way of law-making.' In short, we have activist informalism across the board in both procedural and substantive review. Judges should actively inquire into the legality of administrative decisions but without any prejudice that legality is synonymous with consistency with formal criteria.

And so it came to pass, as the Supreme Court unpacked the idea of substantive review along activist informalist lines:

1 The approach to substantive review was termed the 'pragmatic and functional' approach to denote its attention to context and issues of relative institutional competence, and this approach was supposed to determine when judges should 'defer' to officials' interpretations of the law.[28]
2 The privative clause was no longer regarded as a necessary condition for deference – if an official deserved deference because of expertise, he or she should get it whether or not the legislature had indicated that this was the case.[29]
3 A spectrum of standards was developed for review, so that, depending on a set of factors including the importance of the interest affected by the decision, review could be on a correctness standard, patent unreasonableness, or 'reasonableness *simpliciter*.'[30]
4 Expertise was said to be a quality that had to be demonstrated – that is, it was not sufficient for a decision to be regarded as expert that it be made by someone who was presumably appointed because of his or her expertise. In other words, the official had to demonstrate that he or she had expertise in the quality of the decision.[31]
5 The idea of jurisdiction was said not to be a formal category that required correctness review but rather a label for those decisions which one concluded, using the pragmatic and functional approach, required correctness review.[32]
6 Exercises of discretion were said in *Baker* to be hardly different in kind from officials' interpretation of the law and thus were reviewable on the same pragmatic and functional approach.[33]
7 In *Baker* it was also suggested that there was a general duty on administrative officials to give reasons for their decisions, in part because without reasons expertise can neither be demonstrated nor evaluated.[34]

In retrospect, the duty to give reasons seems a precondition for the other developments listed above, since without it appropriate judicial scrutiny of administrative decisions seems futile, dependent often on an individual's luck in finding out details about the decision-making process to which he or she had no legal entitlement in the absence of an explicit statutory requirement. But the duty to give reasons is a duty within the category of procedural review and so *Baker* seems to demonstrate that even this classification – procedure and substance – has permeable boundaries. Moreover, as Mullan was the first to point out, *Baker* suggested that the rationale for the duty to give reasons was not only the utility of such a duty for effective review, but also that the dignity of the individuals whose interests were affected by officials' decisions required that there be such a duty.[35] And because of the symbiotic relationship between procedural and substantive review – without reasons there can be no effective review of substance – this value thus underwrites the whole of the judgment.

So *CUPE* seems to have laid the basis not for inactivist formalism but for something closer to activist informalism – 'closer to,' because at least at the level of rhetoric it seemed that activist informalism did not require, contrary to Loughlin, that judges set themselves up as the supreme authority to determine which decisions will be made by which process. That is, activist informalism did not necessarily amount to more intrusive review since the theme of deference that pervades the jurisprudence on substantive review, and which might come to pervade similarly the jurisprudence on procedural review, requires courts to defer to administrative decisions as long as the officials who make them offer adequate reasons.

However, in both procedural and substantive review there is strong evidence of persistent formalism, which might bear out Loughlin's argument that judges understand their role best under a formal conception of the rule of law. In procedural review, formalism resurfaced after *Nicholson* in the way that the courts developed new classifications according to which there is a class of administrative decisions immune from procedural review. Here the distinction was drawn between decisions that were more administrative and decisions that were more legislative in nature. In addition, the thought that there might be a qualitative distinction between the old quasi-judicial decisions, which attract natural justice, and the administrative decisions, which attract fairness, persisted.[36]

Similarly, in substantive review the idea that there is a category of decisions that inherently require correctness review will not go away: determinations of jurisdiction as well as interpretations of the Constitution, the common law, and statutes other than the official's enabling statute are thought to fall into this category. In addition, it seemed that the courts considered that no deference to an official's determination of the content of fairness was required. Moreover, the Supreme Court has continued to exhibit the puzzling theme of the Canadian jurisprudence on jurisdiction that it seems unable to avoid preserving or reintroducing formalism in the very decisions in which it signals most strongly the need to move away from it. Notably, the *Southam* decision (in which the reasonableness standard was introduced) was seen as one that potentially extended the logic of deference to administrative decisions that previously had not been thought to attract deference, those that were either unprotected by a privative clause or even made expressly subject to a statutory right of appeal. But in that same decision the Court held that if the provision in the enabling statute the official has to interpret is one that is quite general in nature – that is, the interpretation of it is not tied to the facts of the case but will affect future practice – on that ground alone courts should review on a correctness standard.[37] However, the interpretation of the provision of the statute that was at stake in *CUPE* was of this nature and the Court insisted in that case that it was at the core of the tribunal's jurisdiction and thus susceptible to review only on the patent unreasonableness standard. After *Southam*, it might thus appear that the Court in *CUPE* got things wrong, despite the presence of the privative clause.

It would then follow that the claim that the idea of jurisdiction should no longer be a formal tool of substantive review would be mere rhetoric. The courts would have simply replaced that idea with a bunch of discrete ideas (this is common law, constitutional law, a general proposition about a provision in the enabling statute, etc.), all formal markers for correctness review, that could put judicial review back in the pre-*CUPE* era.

Thus, in substantive review, it might well look as though judges cut adrift from their formal anchor find themselves caught between making ever more fine-grained determinations of what is best in the particular administrative context and simply asserting that a decision has to be reviewed on the correctness standard. The former strategy would be akin to the judgments of instrumental rationality about procedures which, we saw Loughlin argue, would take judges into territory they were ill-equipped to explore, and the latter might look like an appeal to a consensus that was wholly 'imaginary.' In the former respect, it seems notoriously difficult to distinguish reasonableness review, 'a somewhat probing evaluation of the reasons,'[38] from correctness review, so that it might seem that judges who engage in reasonableness review find themselves retaking the official's decision and striking it down if they would have reached a different decision in that context. Of course, part of the problem is that judges are not really 'in' that context. In addition, it is not at all clear that there is any real agreement as to what standard particular contexts require, so that while judges will appeal to what they take to be settled criteria in making that determination, it is not implausible to claim that the consensus to which they appeal is imaginary.

For similar reasons, Justice LeBel of the Supreme Court has, in a concurring judgment, penned an essay on substantive review that tracks carefully concerns Mullan had raised in an essay on deference as well as in a monograph on administrative law.[39] LeBel J. likened the Court's attempts to make sense of the three standards of review to 'watching a juggler juggle three transparent objects. Depending on the way the light falls, sometimes one thinks one can see the objects. Other times one cannot and, indeed, wonders whether there are really three distinct objects there at all.'[40] In his view, the Supreme Court could not remain unresponsive to the concerns of the legal community about predictability, workability and coherence of its jurisprudence on deference.[41] Following Mullan, LeBel J. noted that *CUPE* had invoked both a highly deferential standard and a 'historically interventionist one.'[42] Like Mullan, he expressed concern about possible slippage between the two standards, or between correctness and the relatively new standard of reasonableness.[43] Slippage occurred especially when courts sought to determine how they would have themselves decided the matter rather than, as LeBel J. advocated, asking whether the official's determination 'lacked a rational foundation.'[44]

Despite this concern, and a concern that correctness was too easily assumed to be automatically appropriate for certain categories of determinations,[45] LeBel J. thought that the main difficulty lay in distinguishing the patent unreasonableness standard from unreasonableness *simpliciter*. His concerns pertained to the immense difficulty in distinguishing between the two standards in any meaningful way. In the course of his careful discussion of the doctrinal issues, he offered the following powerful argument. It must be the case that a decision that is patently unreasonable is also unreasonable. But it must also be the case that a decision could be unreasonable but not patently unreasonable. Therefore, the patent unreasonableness standard by definition permits those subject to the law to have their fate determined by unreasonable interpretations of the law.[46] In other words, the distinction between standards presupposes that there is a class of unreasonable decisions that are immune from review because they fail to reach the pitch of patent unreasonableness.[47] Thus, as he saw it, the problems raised by the Court's jurisprudence had implications for the rule of law:[48]

> As a matter of statutory interpretation, courts should always be very hesitant to impute to the legislature any intent to let irrational administrative acts stand, absent the most unequivocal statement of such an intent ... As a matter of theory, the constitutional principle of the primacy of the rule of law, which is an ever-present background principle of interpretation in this context, reinforces the point: if a court concludes that the legislature intended that there be no recourse from an irrational decision, it seems highly likely that the court has misconstrued the intent of the legislature.

LeBel J.'s argument goes beyond Mullan's because he strongly indicates that the way forward is to get rid of the distinction between reasonableness *simpliciter* and patent unreasonableness, and simply to ask the real question whether the official's decision has a rational basis in the law. But he might then underestimate the extent to which the distinction between the correctness standard and the unreasonableness standard becomes problematic.

I have argued elsewhere that the answer might lie in getting rid of the correctness standard altogether.[49] There should be no category of decisions, including decisions that hinge on the interpretation of the Constitution, where the courts think that correctness is appropriate.[50] All that should matter is whether the official has offered an adequate justification for his or her decision. Indeed, my argument is merely an adaptation of Mullan's main claim in 1975. It accepts the idea that the content of procedural fairness should be determined on a spectrum by using a context-sensitive analysis, with the emphasis being on 'gradual disappearance not one punctuated by the unrealistic impression of clear cut divisions presented by the classification process.'[51] And it then transposes that same idea to the area of substantive review, so that the issue is more or less intense scrutiny of decisions, depending on the context. The only difference is, as I will make clearer in the next section, that I do not accept that the deference 'disappears into nothingness'[52] as one approaches the end of the spectrum where officials are most intensively scrutinized. And at this point it is worth noting that Mullan had often urged the courts to recognize that deference when it came to substantive review should logically be matched by deference when it came to procedural review,[53] and that *Baker* seemed to indicate, against the trend of Supreme Court jurisprudence, that the courts should consider deferring to the expertise of officials when it came to choice of appropriate procedures.[54]

LeBel J., as we have seen, is somewhat drawn to such an argument since he raised a question about whether it was appropriate that the correctness standard had to be invoked automatically if a decision fell into a particular category. But his reluctance to do more than raise the question shows the difficulty in the path of an activist informalist stance, where judges assume that all public officials must follow a principle of legality but they do not understand that principle in formal terms.

However, Mullan has recently signalled something of a retreat from activist informalism since he now seems to want to reinstate some clear-cut divisions in substantive review. Recall that Loughlin suggested that activist informalism would require judges to get into the instrumental rationality business, the business of second-guessing officials' determinations of the weight that should be given to considerations in a realm previously considered administrative and hence not amenable to review. Mullan now seems to accept that this is an implication of the move away from formalism, since he has argued that judges become illegitimately involved in correctness review if they reweigh the factors an official had to consider in order to come to a decision.[55] Thus he seems drawn to advocate a more conservative approach to review. And I will now show, through a discussion of the issue of weight in two Supreme Court decisions, that this conservative approach seems to be evidence of Loughlin's claim that judges and advocates of judicial review are ever subject to the grip of formalism.

Baker arose out of the argument by Mavis Baker, who had been living in Canada illegally for several years, that the minister of immigration should exercise her statutory discretion to stay Baker's deportation order on 'humanitarian and compassionate grounds.' The immigration officials charged with Baker's case decided against her despite the fact that she had Canadian-born children. The front-line official's case notes, which were disclosed to Baker even though there was no statutory duty to do so, provided strong evidence that prejudice drove the decision and that the fact that Baker had had children in Canada was for the official a factor that supported deporting her. The Court decided that a reasonableness standard governed such decisions, especially given the importance of the interest affected by them, and that a reasonable decision was one that gave appropriate weight to the interests of the children.

In the context of this case, it might seem that a court could comfortably invalidate the decision because the officials, far from giving appropriate weight to the children's interests, considered the existence of the children as a kind of aggravating factor in the light of their express concerns about the drain on Canada's resources that illegal overstayers like Baker in their view represented. But it could not be said that the officials had failed altogether to take children into account. So if all a court is entitled to do is to check whether a factor has been taken into account that had to be taken into account, it is not at all clear that in this respect there was anything wrong with the officials' decision. In other words, if all the officials had to do was tick the box – 'considered children's interests' – this should satisfy a court if the court is not permitted to reweigh. The fact that the officials drew adverse inferences from the fact that Baker had children might not be to the court's liking, but should not provide a basis for intervention.

There is something odd, even perverse, about this kind of reasoning. After all, noting the existence of children, whether or not one draws adverse inferences, is hardly equivalent to taking their interests into account. It is surely right that the very idea of taking children's interests into account when the deportation of their mother is at stake requires serious attention by the decision-maker to the question of what those interests are. It might thus seem that the officials could not offer the very same reasons that they in fact offered in *Baker* and survive review, even on an anemic standard.

Indeed, in *Baker* the Supreme Court found that the case notes disclosed such bias as to require invalidation of the decision on that ground alone. But that the Court went on to find that there was a duty to give reasons shows that it was anxious that a decision on the basis of bias alone would lead to officials taking care never to disclose their reasons. Moreover, a duty to give reasons was not sufficient to deal with the problem, as officials who were so minded could offer reasons that simply indicated that they had taken all the factors into account, while keeping their real reasons to themselves – that is, the tick-in-the-box approach. This is why the Court had also to find that the appropriate standard for review was the reasonableness standard. The officials had to demonstrate in light of the circumstances of the case, the interests at stake, and the relevant legal values that their decision was reasonable.

But while I concede that there is a difference between the standard tick-in-the-box approach and an approach that expressly takes account of factors but does so in a perverse fashion, I am not sure that this difference is visible to formalist judges. In this regard it is important to note that in the Federal Court, both at trial and in the Federal Court of Appeal, the judges found that the notes did not disclose bias and that the officials had taken the children's interests into account.[56] So I do not think one can be confident that an anemic, formalistic standard of review suffices even when officials are willing to display their real views.[57]

It thus seems inevitable to me that if the test for the court is whether there is a rational basis in law for the decision, a court cannot help but evaluate the basis in fact offered by the officials. Following LeBel J., one might argue that judges avoid crossing the line that demarcates legitimate review not by avoiding reweighing, but by not asking themselves whether they would have made the same decision as front-line decision-makers. In other words, their concern should be whether the officials did a decent job of justifying the decision they made, and not whether there was some alternative decision that the judges would have preferred.

However, as Mullan points out, those who regarded *Baker* as ushering 'in an era of much greater judicial intervention in discretionary decision-making' were concerned that the 'judgment invited either straight incorrectness review or unreasonableness review of the substance of discretionary exercises of power.'[58] In their view, the only way to avoid this result is to retreat to the patent unreasonableness standard. And, as Mullan makes clear, such a retreat must avoid talk of a requirement that officials must in some sense demonstrate a rational basis for their decision. Rather, the standard to be deployed is that their decision must not be utterly irrational, that is, one which amounts to a decision in bad faith.[59]

Out of this analysis, one can draw the following conclusions. First, for those who worry about judicial interventionism if reasonableness review of substance is permitted, the worry amounts to the claim that there is no real distinction between applying a correctness standard and applying a reasonableness standard. Second, in order to avoid the slippage from reasonableness to correctness, one should adopt the position that there are only two standards, correctness and patent unreasonableness. Third, in understanding patent unreasonableness, one should not ask whether there is a rational basis for the decision, as evidenced by the official's reasons, since this question invites reweighing (correctness review). In other words, one should reinstate *CUPE* on the inactivist formalist interpretation of that decision: judges should review on formal criteria only those few decisions that are properly susceptible to such review and for the rest – the vast majority – judges should avoid review unless there is something really, really wrong with the decision.

Mullan himself seems to accept these conclusions with one exception, as is made clear by his critique of the Supreme Court's decision in *Suresh v. Canada (Minister of Citizenship and Immigration)*.[60] Here, part of the issue the Court had to decide was the standard of review that should apply to the exercise of a ministerial discretion to declare a landed immigrant, or someone applying for that status, to be a 'danger to the security of Canada' and thus to be able to deport that person even though he would face a substantial risk of torture on return to his home country. It is important to note that the decision was handed down in the wake of September 11, 2001, and that the Court was explicitly mindful of what it perceived as the changed context, despite the fact that Suresh had no connection with any groups that were possibly connected to the attacks on the United States.

The Court considered the relevance of *Baker* and suggested that that decision did not authorize courts 'reviewing decisions on the discretionary end of the spectrum to engage in a new weighing process, but draws on an established line of cases concerning the failure of ministerial delegates to consider and weigh implied limitations and/or patently relevant factors.'[61] The Court distinguished the decision to declare someone a security risk and the decision whether he would face a substantial risk of torture following deportation on the basis that the former did not affect constitutional rights and so could be decided on straight administrative law principles, while the latter clearly did affect constitutional rights. However, it reasoned not only that the same patent unreasonableness standard applied to both decisions but also that the minister was entitled to deference on the same standard to a decision that someone should be deported despite the fact that he faced torture because national security considerations outweighed his interest in avoiding torture. This last conclusion is, as Mullan points out, hardly unequivocally supported by all the Court had to say on this topic.[62] But even if the Court did not mean what it seemed to say in this last respect, Mullan expresses grave concern that *Suresh* indicates that the courts should adopt a patent unreasonableness standard despite the fact that an individual's most important constitutional rights are at stake. He regards this position as an abdication of the Court's constitutional responsibilities. Following *Baker*, the standard in such cases has in his view to be at least reasonableness. However, Mullan says that he has no objection to the proposal that in other sorts of cases, reasonableness review should be understood more conservatively. For reasonableness does not allow in his view a 'complete re-evaluation of the overall decision on a reasonableness basis or a straight re-weighing by the reviewing court of all the various factors.'[63] His objection to *Suresh* is not that it advocates something like that conservative approach, but that it advocates that approach in the constitutional area.[64] Indeed, recently Mullan has offered this formulation of when it is appropriate for courts to defer: 'Deference is generally earned by statutory and prerogative bodies justifying outcomes by comprehensible reasons.'[65]

The standard of review suggested here is one that could be taken to imply that as long as one can understand the reasons offered by the decision-maker, one has a sufficient basis for deference. That Mullan used this formulation is significant as it indicates his sense of unease with any real test of the adequacy of reasons by judges outside of the area of *Charter*-protected interests. And in expressing this unease, he echoes those Supreme Court judges who worried about the pitfalls of such testing.[66] In short, it seems that Mullan's conservatism looks rather like a retreat to inactivist formalism – gung-ho, old-style correctness review where 'real' constitutional issues are at stake; otherwise and for the most part judges should back off review to the greatest extent possible.[67]

But if we go back to the Fullerian idea of structural integrity, which Loughlin thought could explain Mullan's approach in 1975 to the rule of law, the issue for the officials is not only the law of the statute under which they act. They must also show their fidelity to the more general commitments of their legal order, commitments to values that are considered fundamental because they express what we can think of as the moral mission of that order. In any liberal democratic legal order, one of these values is the dignity of the individual subject to the law. And, as Mullan was the first to point out, it is this value that underwrites both the procedural and the substantive parts of the Supreme Court's judgment in *Baker*.

But if the Court in *Baker* had adopted a more conservative, which I think can in this context be equated with a more formal, understanding of its role in reviewing official decisions, it would have made a mockery of its grander statements about the duty of public officials to uphold the rule of law.[68] If there is a duty on officials to give reasons, but those reasons are not subject to serious scrutiny, then the duty will be exercised in a *pro forma* way and those subject to the decisions will rightly feel that the claim to govern in accordance with the rule of law is simply a veneer over arbitrary decision-making. The situation will be no different from the one that prevailed when official exercises of discretion were said to be reviewable, but the grounds were very difficult to sustain in the absence of a duty to give reasons; nor will it be different from a situation where official interpretations of the law are reviewed on an utterly anemic standard.

So I want to suggest that Mullan's advocacy of a more conservative approach for the review of non-*Charter* matters runs the same risk that he warned against when he pointed out the pitfall of new classifications arising on the basis of Megarry J.'s dictum in *Bates v. Lord Hailsham*: 'Let me accept that in the sphere of the so-called quasi judicial the rules of natural justice run, and that in the administrative or executive field there is a general duty of fairness.'[69] Moreover, Mullan's view that *Charter*-based review should automatically attract a stricter standard than non-*Charter* review is in some tension with his claim in 1975 that lawyers need not fear the disappearance of the distinction between the quasi-judicial and the administrative. Recall that his reason was that experience had already shown that judges might rightly think that the mere fact that a decision would in the old days have been classified as quasi-judicial did not mean that it necessarily required the full panoply of natural justice. It should follow that the mere fact that a decision trenches on a *Charter*-protected interest does not in and of itself require more scrutiny than is required of decisions that trench on fundamental interests that are not directly or even indirectly protected by the *Charter*. That is, a decision that would have been classified as administrative might require the full panoply of natural justice and similarly a decision that trenches on a fundamental legal value not protected in the *Charter* might still require the strictest judicial scrutiny. What matters, as Mullan advocated, is to ask the 'real questions,' and the answers to these will require both an evaluation of how fundamental the individual interests are that are affected by the official decision and how appropriate the decision was in the particular context.

Mullan recognizes that his new conservatism is suspect from the perspective of certain versions of the rule of law that I and others have put forward. As he describes them, they deploy a conception of the rule of law 'as an underlying principle of Canadian constitutional law as a basis for placing normative constraints on the exercise of statutory power, constraints that transcend normal conceptions of parliamentary sovereignty and the positivist approach that it imposes on thinking about the limits of judicial review.'[70] In particular, he recognizes that such versions will resist the idea that there is a sharp distinction between review on the basis of entrenched constitutional rights and review on the basis of the values of the rule of law – the values of the common law constitution. As he says,[71]

> [I]t may be a fair reading of *Baker* to allow for more intense scrutiny of the exercise of broad discretions when their exercise involves underlying constitutional principles or considerations emanating from a substantive conception of the rule of law ... and the fundamental values of Canadian society. If so, the line between constitutional and administrative law review becomes even less pronounced. This sense of a continuum also emerges in the constitutional domain at least to the extent that there is legitimacy in at least some level of deference to the factual findings of decision-makers when constitutional rights are at stake.

But while Mullan suggests the above as a fair reading, he seems to be of two minds about whether to advocate it, inconsistent as it is with his conservatism about judicial review outside the constitutional area, where by 'constitutional' is meant the written text of a bill of rights. In the next section, I deal with his more abstract account of why such conservatism is important.

The Unwritten Constitution

In two recent lectures, the Ivan C. Rand lecture at the University of New Brunswick[72] and a lecture to the Faculty of Law at Auckland University,[73] Mullan discussed the role of unwritten constitutional principles in a world in which many legal orders have adopted bills of rights. While the lectures covered similar themes, there was something of a shift from the first to the second, reflected in the fact that while in the title of the first Mullan referred to 'unwritten' constitutional principles, in the second he preferred the label 'underlying.' His reasons for that shift are made clear in the Auckland lecture. Critics of the legitimacy of the project of what we can think of as common law constitutionalism – the project wherein judges articulate and rely upon unwritten constitutional values – use the term 'unwritten' pejoratively. They use it to point out what in their view is inappropriate judicial activism, 'part of the conspiracy of judicial imperialism, anti-democratic, and just downright ignorant.'[74] The term 'underlying,' in contrast, evokes a 'link between the text of the constitution and the claim being made, in that it invites inquiry as to the principles on which the text is based with a view to recognition of subsidiary or additional norms or rules of constitutional law that enhance the operation or effectiveness of the text.'[75]

By relying on this idea, Mullan hopes to avoid falling afoul of the deeply positivistic prejudice on which the criticism is based. According to that prejudice, Parliament is subject to constitutional law only when there is an entrenched constitutional text that sets out explicit legal controls on Parliament's otherwise supreme authority and explicitly delegates guardianship of those controls to judges. Mullan's hope is that the use of 'underlying' helps to answer these critics, because it anchors the values articulated by judges firmly in the text and requires that they accept the burden of showing how those values must be invoked in order to make sense of the text. The idea of underlying principles thus provides a useful middle ground on which to meet those who have the prejudice, since it concedes that constitutional controls on the legislature are appropriate only when there is an entrenched constitution. The difference between common law constitutionalists and the positivists is then perhaps only about the scope of those controls, and so the stage is productively set for an argument that the common law constitutional project 'can be located within a coherent and defensible version of a country's constitutional arrangements.'[76]

My disagreement with Mullan starts with his claim that one should concede to the positivists the middle ground that requires that text is the only legitimate basis for judicial review. For, as I will now argue, there is no middle ground to be conceded.

In the course of justifying his preference for 'underlying' over 'unwritten,' Mullan offers this side remark about the virtues of 'underlying': 'More radically, of course, ... [underlying] may also leave open the possibility of recognition of principles that have an existence independent of the explicit text of the constitution.'[77] Moreover, in the Rand lecture, he suggested that in those rare cases where a supreme court faces a constitutional crisis and text is of no help, judges must accept a responsibility to articulate an answer, even though by definition they are thus required to take their stand on unwritten constitutional principles. And at the end of the Auckland lecture, he declared his support for a position that states that the rule of law responds to 'moral imperatives.' 'Primary' among these, he says, is a 'conception of equality or mutual respect from which it is appropriate to move in striking down legislation that hits at core human rights values.'[78]

But one cannot confine unwritten constitutional values to the exceptional situations of constitutional crisis while reserving underlying principles for all other cases. Rather, as Mullan's support for a moral understanding of the rule of law suggests, the common law project starts with unwritten constitutional principles. Indeed, in his Rand lecture, Mullan says that when critics of the common law project speak of it as the 'promotion of "unwritten" principles,' they are not only 'misspeaking but also covering up the fact that 'written' and 'unwritten' are not in reality sharply differentiated concepts but rather function on a spectrum.'[79]

I prefer the metaphor of a continuum – of a progression of constitutional situations – to that of a spectrum, which connotes a set of diffused or decomposed situations. For my claim is that judicial review in public law is best understood as based on fundamental constitutional values on a continuum, ranging from the ordinary situations of common law judicial review to the more dramatic judicial interventions on the basis of an entrenched bill of rights, to the most dramatic examples when judges consider resort to unwritten constitutional principles to strike down legislation. None of these situations is more or less constitutional than any other.

Now it might be that examples of the last kind of situation are to be found more in hypotheticals than in experience, when judges or academics muse about situations in which Parliament does something so outlandish that judges would feel compelled to strike down the statute.[80] But significant here is Mullan's interpretation of the decision of the Australian High Court in *Australian Communist Party v. The Commonwealth*,[81] which struck down legislation banning the Communist party. Mullan suggests that at least the judgment of Dixon J. did not depend on the text of the division of powers in the Australian Constitution, nor on underlying principles of that text, but rather on the 'assumptions on which the Constitution was built' – for Dixon J., pre-eminently the assumption of the rule of law.[82]

Mullan is right to make this claim.[83] But certainly the judges in the majority, including Dixon J., tried for the most part as hard as they could to avoid the impression that they were relying on anything other than the text of the Constitution. They wanted to avoid relying not only on unwritten principles but also on underlying principles. Dixon J.'s dictum about the rule of law is the barest hint that they were doing something different.

But if it is the case that not only did they make the right decision but that, whatever they said, their decision depended on unwritten assumptions of which the Constitution was the expression rather than on the text of the Constitution, then, I am not sure that Mullan's middle ground exists. At least it does not exist, if we take the claim about assumptions to include not only the assumptions which the Constitution expresses, given the actual text, but also given the assumptions that any legal constitution necessarily expresses, whatever its text – for example, Dixon J.'s assumption that all officials and official bodies, including the legislature, are under a duty to preserve the rule of law.

The only difference text makes to the second kind of assumption, the principles of legal order,[84] is to the answer to the question about what a judge should do if the legislature chooses explicitly to override a constitutional principle. I do not want to suggest here that the existence of constitutional text is a precondition of a judge's authority to invalidate a statute. Rather, I want to suggest that one's view about whether or not text is a precondition is not as important as one's view about whether there are unwritten constitutional principles that a legal order necessarily aspires to realize.

For it is the question whether there are such unwritten principles that really distinguishes legal positivist from common law conceptions of the rule of law. To suppose that the important issue is the one about text and authority to invalidate is to fall into a positivist trap. The trap is the assumption that the test of whether there are such principles is whether a judge is entitled to invalidate a statute that clearly flouts one of the principles. But invalidity is a positivist obsession that should not distract those who adopt the common law conception of the rule of law.

Notice in this regard that a statute in Canada that invokes section 33 of the *Charter* to override a judicial determination of unconstitutionality is valid, but its validity does not detract from the status of that judgment. Similarly, the failure of the United Kingdom government or Parliament to respond positively to a judicial determination of incompatibility of a statute with the *Human Rights Act 1998* does not detract from the place given to human rights in the legal order; it simply shows that the government is unwilling to abide by its legal commitments. The statute remains valid but its incompatibility with human rights leaves an indelible question mark over it.[85] Finally, in a common law legal order where there is no written constitution, it might be the case that a statute will be upheld as valid even though it expressly gives officials the power to act unfairly and unreasonably in making decisions that affect important individual interests. Just as in the first two examples, in the last, the constitutional status of these principles is unaffected by the fact that judges might be unable to invalidate an overriding statute.

Six conclusions can be drawn from these examples. The first has already been indicated: the common law conception of the rule of law does not rest its claim about the existence of unwritten constitutional principles on the actual or alleged authority of judges to invalidate statutes that flout those principles. Rather, the principles are, to use Fuller's terminology, an internal morality of law to which legal order aspires. The judicial duty is to try to ensure that their decisions show the positive law, now drawing on Dworkin, in its best light, that is, its best moral light. But a particular law might be such that it can hardly or perhaps not at all meet these aspirations.

Second, the principles will inform judicial interpretation in a variety of situations, ranging from situations where the positive law is open to interpretation in their light, to situations where it is a strain to interpret the positive law in their light, to situations where it is impossible to interpret the positive law in their light. These situations are the points on the continuum I mentioned earlier, but they are all situations that raise constitutional issues. The ordinary situation of administrative law where a statute does not speak to the issue of fairness or even could be thought to indicate that fairness was not intended is no less constitutional in nature than the situation where a statute seems to violate a right protected in an entrenched bill of rights.

Third, the issue in these situations is not well described by the idea of ambiguity. It is a trope of positivist thought to claim that judges may resort to principles only when the positive law is ambiguous. Rather, one should see that there is an interpretive obligation on judges to achieve interpretations of the law that manifest the aspirations of legal order.[86]

Fourth, this interpretive obligation is not confined to judges. Given that these principles are aspirations of legal order, all public officials are required to attempt to live up to them. And given that judges do not have expertise about particular administrative contexts, it is the case that judges should be ready to defer to the interpretations of public officials within these contexts on condition that the officials provide both a reasoned and reasonable conclusion about how those principles are best manifested in their context. It is also the case that judges might not be best equipped to make more general claims about how such principles are to apply. Specialized legislative committees might, for example, be better suited to hammering out codes of administrative conduct.

Fifth, and following the last conclusion, it is incumbent on government and the legislature to put in place the constitutional resources necessary for the legal order to live up to its aspirations. One cannot deny that common law judges have been guilty of all sorts of bad behaviour when it came to the administrative state. But their mistakes have also stemmed from the fact that they had and still have to take on the task of guardians of the rule of law in situations where other legal institutions would be better suited, when these have either not been created or have not been given sufficient resources to do the job.[87]

The sixth and last conclusion is a theoretical one, which brings me back to Mullan's middle ground. It is, of course, the case that the written texts of the law – the positive law – are a crucial component of interpretation, whether it is judges or officials who are doing it. But the point of the positivist conception of law is to insist that real law is the determinate content of valid law, where determinate means determinable in accordance with tests that do not rely on moral considerations and arguments, including arguments about the principles of an internal morality of law. It is this conception of law that underpins, as we saw, the transmission belt account of the rule of law and it is the conception adopted by critics of judicial review. In their hands, it is deployed to claim that judges are entitled to exercise rule of law controls on officials when and only when these controls have been put in place by the legislature (or the written constitution) and it is clear what the legislature (or the constitutional framers) intended by those controls. They also claim that when the law, whether substantive or procedural, is indeterminate or ambiguous, the legislature has already indicated who may legitimately render the law determinate – the officials, not the judges. In short, for the critics of judicial review it does not matter whether the principles are said to be underlying or unwritten. In either case, judicial resort to them is illegitimate.

In my view, the way to answer such critics is not then by reliance on an alleged distinction between underlying and unwritten principles, but through pointing out the incoherence of their position. They will, with rare exceptions, subscribe to something like the aspirational view of the rule of law, although at the same time they wish either to keep judges on the margins or to exclude them altogether.[88] At root, what they distrust is the common law way of developing an account of the rule of law, precisely the 'common law way of law-making' in which Mullan put his confidence in 1975.

But even more important to such an answer is the elaboration of a positive account of judicial review. And, following my remarks in the last section, I do not think that such an account can be successful if it is conservative, in the way we have seen Mullan suggest it should be. For, as I have suggested, and as Mullan seems clearly to recognize, such conservatism carries the risk of resurgent formalism. It would be far better to see that the best interpretation of the Supreme Court's later jurisprudence is that the shift in focus from decision to reasons for decision, and the development of the third standard of review, reasonableness *simpliciter,* shears the correctness standard off the continuum of standards of review. In other words, even the most probing evaluation is to some extent deferential, since judges operate with a presumption that the reasons offered by the tribunal for its decision could justify a decision, which is not necessarily the decision that the court would have reached had it operated in a 'vacuum.'[89] And filling the vacuum is not desirable because of some natural abhorrence, but because what fills it is the expert understanding of the tribunal about how the law is to be interpreted in its specialized context. If that is right, then there is no correctness review, only more or less intense scrutiny of reasons, whether tribunals are engaged in interpreting the law of their enabling statute, or of another statute, or the common law, or the provisions of a written constitution, including, if there is one, a bill of rights.

I suggest that this approach is more consistent with Mullan's theory of the rule of (common) law than the conservative approach he has recently articulated. As he clearly saw in 1975, and has hammered home on many occasions since, it is not easy to escape the grip of formalism. In this respect, he and Loughlin agree. In order to escape that grip, one has to show not only how the area of administrative action that had been thought not to attract review is reviewable, though on principled, not formalistic grounds. One also has to show that principled rather than formalistic grounds apply to the area that had been thought to be unproblematically susceptible to review. Further, one must be wary of new candidates that are claimed to require formalistic review. The point is that formalistic grounds cannot live comfortably in the same conceptual space as principles. In a way, this was Loughlin's insight when he coined the category of activist informalism. The idea, as we have seen, was that Mullan had correctly seen that judges were trying to establish a general regime of legality for the administrative state, which required that they escape the distorting grip of formalism. But as we have also seen, Loughlin did not think that judges could escape this grip because their only resource was law, formally understood.

I should note that Loughlin did not, in later work, use the categories of activist and inactivist formalism or activist informalism. Rather, he used another tripartite division: conservative normativism, liberal normativism, and functionalism.[90] However, roughly speaking, conservative normativism is the same set of attitudes that characterize inactivist formalism – formal review for what was traditionally reviewable, with a question mark over the rest – while liberal normativism seems to be a new version of activist formalism – gung-ho, judicial review of everything. Activist informalism has, however, no equivalent in this later work, though functionalism is, I think, supposed to be the non-normativist (or realistic) response to the same pressures on formalism that lead to activist informalism.

Loughlin clearly prefers functionalism. However, he regards his functionalist predecessors, especially John Griffith, as too positivistic and formalistic[91] and in general unable to account for the normative character of law. He thus seems to yearn for some combination of realism/functionalism with an understanding of the normative nature of law. I have argued elsewhere that this yearning leads to deep tensions in Loughlin's work precisely because he wishes at all costs to avoid falling into the liberal camp, which understands the normativity of law as having to do with fundamental values such as the dignity of the individual.[92] This is not the place to rehearse those arguments. Rather, I wish to point out that all of Mullan's work in administrative law has sought to marry a normative account of law with a realistic or functionalist account of the different competencies of the institutions of legal order. Moreover, while Mullan has taken care not to allow his political commitments to intrude into his research, there is no doubt that, in his view, the dignity of the individual and associated liberal values are inherent in the rule of (common) law project. His example shows the depth of the challenge that public lawyers face as they attempt to elaborate an account of the rule of law appropriate to the complexities of the administrative state. As important, though, is that Mullan teaches us the necessity of the attempt to rise to that challenge through the elaboration of a principled account of the rule of law.

It might, however, be said that this chapter is far from articulating anything as grand as a theory of the rule of law. It might also be said that to the extent that I have articulated some elements of a theory, it might look as though at least some of them have been foisted by me on Mullan, rather than being Mullan's own.

My first response is simply that my own account of the rule of law has been worked up over seventeen years of trying to make sense of Canadian administrative law – a journey that began in 1989 when I sat in on David Mullan's administrative law class at Queen's and whose every step has been guided by the charts I described at the beginning of this chapter.

My second more complex response is that the virtues of the 'common law way of law-making' are not that easily theorized.[93] Its best academic exponents appreciate its pragmatism, manifested in its ability to adapt its sense of what is appropriate to the needs of practice; its particularism, manifested in its development of principles on a case-by-case basis; its commitment to evolution, manifested in an openness to changes in the understanding of the content of legality; and also its aspirational nature, captured most famously in the metaphor of law working itself pure. But the combination of these virtues means that its exponents cannot move to too a high a level of abstraction from what the practitioners are doing, for any grand statements of principle or attempts to impose a rigidly coherent structure on the common law risk undermining its virtues.

It might also be the case, though I have not addressed this issue here, that the common law way requires a constant to-and-fro between attempts to loosen the grip of rules and formal categories by articulating principles and attempts to stabilize and make principles predictable by formalizing them, which is to say capturing them in rules and categories. As part and parcel of this requirement, one would expect to see a pattern of advances and retreats as the practitioners experiment with new ideas in the pragmatic spirit of their tradition. And if this last claim is right, then Mullan's theory of the rule of (common) law might well be far superior to the one I could be accused of foisting on him.

NOTES

I thank the editors for excellent comments on drafts of this chapter.

I first encountered David Mullan when I taught at Queen's University in the late 1980s. My chapter records my intellectual debt to him. In this note, I wish to record a more personal debt. I arrived in Canada as what is now called the 'trailing spouse' – the academic who trails behind the academic spouse whom the university really wants. The Queen's Law Faculty was at that time a fractious place and there was understandably little interest shown initially in someone who was likely there on contract for only a short period and who in any case had a perpetual hangdog air as he would have preferred to be in his home country – South Africa. Dave went out of his way to welcome me, to try to make me feel at home, and to encourage me to think differently about my place in Canada. I am far from being the only recipient of the generosity of an unusually humane and decent man, but I would like to acknowledge here how much it meant to me.

1 The closest he has come to providing a theory of the rule of law is his introductory chapter to David J. Mullan, *Administrative Law: Cases, Text, and Materials*, 5th ed. (Toronto: Emond Montgomery, 2003), formerly edited by J.M. Evans, H.N. Janisch, R.C.B. Risk, and Mullan [Mullan, 'Cases, Text, and Materials']. H. Wade MacLauchlan and Philip Bryden discuss the impact of this book in their contribution to this volume.

2 This debate has recently been revisited in an article to which I am much indebted: Geneviève Cartier, 'Procedural Fairness in Legislative Functions: The End of Judicial Abstinence?' (2003) 53 U.T.L.J. 217.

3 D.J. Mullan, 'Fairness: The New Natural Justice?' (1975) 25 U.T.L.J. 281 [Mullan, 'Fairness'].

4 Ibid. at 297.

5 Ibid. at 298.

6 Ibid. at 300.

7 Ibid. at 300–2.

8 [1972] 1 W.L.R. 1373 at 1378 (Ch. D.) [*Bates*].

9 Mullan, 'Fairness,' *supra* note 3 at 303.

10 Ibid. at 310–14.

11 Of course, that procedural protection might be watered down at the quasi-judicial, adjudicative end of the spectrum could be seen as a cause for concern and thus a reason for preserving the distinction. (See D.H. Clark, 'Natural Justice: Substance and Shadow' [1975] P.L. 27, who concludes at 63: 'While natural justice casts a lengthening shadow, the shade serves only to conceal the decline in its substance.') As suggested in the text, Mullan seemed to think the potential for this to happen could be productive, if the context warranted less than the full panoply of procedural protection. At other times, as is also suggested in the text, he seemed to think that in fact one would get progressively less protection as one journeyed closer to the administrative end of the spectrum. As I will show later, the same tension crops up in his 'conservatism' about review when the interests affected by the administrative decision are not protected by an entrenched bill of rights.

12 Mullan, 'Fairness,' *supra* note 3.

13 [1979] 1 S.C.R. 311 [*Nicholson*].

14 Martin Loughlin, 'Procedural Fairness: A Study of the Crisis in Administrative Law Theory' (1978) 28 U.T.L.J. 215 [Loughlin, 'Procedural Fairness'].

15 Ibid. at 216.

16 Ibid. at 220–1.

17 Ibid. at 222.

18 Ibid. at 230. Loughlin identified a third problem: a tendency to let the existence of a procedural code determine the issue of the fairness of the procedure.

19 Ibid. at 230–6.

20 Ibid. at 237.

21 Ibid. at 237, quoting from Lon L. Fuller, 'Positivism and fidelity to law – a reply to Professor Hart' (1958) 71 Harvard L. R. 630 at 670.

22 Loughlin, 'Procedural Fairness,' *supra* note 14 at 238.

23 H.L.A. Hart, 'Positivism and the Separation of Law and Morals' reprinted in H.L.A. Hart, *Essays in Jurisprudence and Philosophy* (Oxford: Clarendon Press, 1983) at 49. For the idea of the rule of recognition, see H.L.A. Hart, *The Concept of Law* (Oxford: Clarendon Press, 1961).

24 Lon L. Fuller, *The Morality of Law* (New Haven, CT: Yale University Press, rev. ed. 1969).

25 In later work, Loughlin expressly distances himself from the legal positivist understanding of law. See, e.g., Martin Loughlin, *Public Law and Political Theory* (Oxford: Clarendon Press, 1992) at 19–23 [Loughlin, *Public Law and Political Theory*]. He also does not in this later work use again the categories of activist and inactivist formalism or activist informalism. Rather, he uses another tripartite division – conservative normativism, liberal normativism, and functionalism. I will discuss this shift at the end of this chapter.

26 [1979] 2 S.C.R. 227 [*CUPE*].

27 See, e.g., *National Corn Growers Association v. Canada (Import Tribunal)*, [1990] 2 S.C.R. 1324, per Wilson J. and *Dayco (Canada) v. CAW-Canada*, [1993] 2 S.C.R. 230, per Cory J.

28 *U.E.S. Local 298 v. Bibeault*, [1988] 2 S.C.R. 1048 at 1088. It is telling that this approach was named in a decision that was soon criticized for using the correctness standard inappropriately.

29 *Pezim v. British Columbia (Superintendent of Brokers)*, [1994] 2 S.C.R. 557, and *Canada (Director of Investigation and Research) v. Southam Inc.*, [1997] 1 S.C.R. 748 [*Southam*].

30 *Southam, supra* note 29, read together with *Baker v. Canada (Minister of Citizenship and Immigration)*, [1999] 2 SCR 817 [*Baker*].

31 *Southam, supra* note 29 at para. 62.

32 *Pushpanathan v. Canada (Minister of Citizenship and Immigration)*, [1998] 1 S.C.R. 982 at para. 28.

33 *Baker, supra* note 30 at para. 54.

34 Ibid. at para. 43.

35 David Mullan, '*Baker v. Canada (Minister of Citizenship and Immigration)*: A Defining Moment in Canadian Administrative Law' (1999) 7 Reid's Administrative Law 145.

36 Mullan has addressed these problems on several occasions. See e.g., David Mullan, 'Natural Justice: The Challenges of *Nicholson*, Deference Theory

and the *Charter*' in Neil R. Finkelstein and Brian MacLeod Rogers, eds., *Recent Developments in Administrative Law* (Toronto: Carswell, 1987).

37 Again, authority for this proposition is a decision that also provides the basis for extending deference: *Southam, supra* note 29 at paras. 36–7.

38 Ibid. at para. 56.

39 *Toronto (City) v. CUPE, Local 79*, [2003] 3 S.C.R. 77 [*Toronto (City)*], following David J. Mullan, 'Recent Developments in Standard of Review' in Canadian Bar Association of (Ontario), *Taking the Tribunal to Court: A Practical Guide for Administrative Law Practitioners* (2000) [Mullan, 'Recent Developments'], and David J. Mullan, *Administrative Law* (Toronto: Irwin Law, 2001) chap. 3, 'Jurisdiction' [Mullan, 'Administrative Law'].

40 *Toronto (City)*, ibid. at para. 63, quoting Barry J. in *Miller v. Workers' Compensation Commission (Nfld.)* (1997), 154 Nfld. & P.E.I.R. 52 (Nfld. S.C. (T.D.)) at para. 27.

41 Ibid. at para. 64.

42 Mullan, *Cases, Text, and Materials, supra* note 1 at 69–70; *Toronto (City), supra* note 39 at para. 88.

43 *Toronto (City), supra* note 39 at para. 96.

44 Ibid. at para. 97.

45 Ibid. at para. 67.

46 Ibid. at paras. 100–27.

47 Ibid. at paras. 132–3.

48 Ibid. at para. 133 [emphasis in original].

49 One bonus would be that one would get rid of the oddity of having incorrect but reasonable decisions considered valid. The change here might be viewed as merely terminological but language is expressive of ideology and a change in terms often signals and even promotes real shifts in stance.

50 David Dyzenhaus, 'Constituting the Rule of Law: Fundamental Values in Administrative Law' (2002) 27 Queen's L.J. 445.

51 Mullan, 'Fairness,' *supra* note 3 at 300.

52 As Mullan indicated might happen with the content of fairness. See text accompanying note 7.

53 Mullan, 'Fairness,' *supra* note 3.

54 *Baker, supra* note 30 at para. 27.

55 David Mullan, 'Deference from *Baker* to *Suresh* and Beyond: Interpreting the Conflicting Signals' in David Dyzenhaus, ed., *The Unity of Public Law* (Oxford: Hart, 2004) at 21 [Mullan, 'Deference'].

56 The judges did not, however, concede that there was a duty to take the children's interests into account. But they did not see fit to quote the case notes,

a striking omission to say the least. See (1995), 101 F.T.R. 110 and [1997] 2 F.C. 127 (F.C.A.).

57 Hence I disagree with Michael Taggart, who argues that *Baker* could be dealt with as a straightforward case of statutory interpretation. Taggart says that 'to an administrative lawyer from the southern hemisphere, *Baker* looks like a straightforward statutory interpretation case.' That is, the phrase 'humanitarian and compassionate considerations' required the applicant's family situation to be considered so that the children's interests were a mandatory relevant consideration. Taggart does recognize that courts are reluctant to review the weight given to such a consideration but says that courts in both Australia and New Zealand say that if an 'obviously important factor is given very little weight ... the judges may infer unreasonableness.' See M. Taggart, 'The Tub of Public Law' in Dyzenhaus, *The Unity of Public Law*, *supra* note 55 at 462–63. But there is a step in the claim that judges may infer unreasonableness that makes the issue more than one of straightforward statutory interpretation. Before one can infer unreasonableness, one has to infer that a reasonableness standard is appropriate and that inference cannot be read off the statute. That anemic standards of review allow unreasonable results to survive as valid legal decisions is a cost that has to be accepted if one wants to avoid the risks of reasonableness review of the substance of administrative decisions. For a complex analysis of the issue of weight, see David Herling, 'Weight in Discretionary Decision-Making' (1999) 19 O.J.L.S. 583. At 589, Herling recognizes that the claim that a factor is a mandatory relevant one does not by itself get one to the conclusion that judges are entitled to evaluate whether officials gave the factor sufficient weight. In order to get to that conclusion, one needs the help of common law techniques plus, he suggests, one has to deem the legislature to have knowledge of these techniques.

58 Mullan, 'Deference,' *supra* note 55 at 27, referring to J.L.H. Sprague, 'Another View of *Baker*' (1999) 7 Reid's Administrative Law 163.

59 Mullan, 'Deference,' *supra* note 55 at 28.

60 [2002] 1 S.C.R. 3 [*Suresh*].

61 Ibid. at para. 37.

62 Mullan, 'Deference,' *supra* note 55 at 41–5.

63 Ibid. at 55.

64 Ibid. at 59.

65 David J. Mullan, 'Establishing the Standard of Review: The Struggle for Complexity?' (2004) 17 Can. J. Admin. L. & Prac. 59 at 94.

66 He also echoes the left critics of judicial review in Canada. See, e.g., John Willis, 'To the Editor' (1951) 29 Can. Bar. Rev. 584: judges 'are not now – and

never should be – allowed to set aside [administrative] action on the ground of unreasonableness; their sole concern must be with *intra vires* or *ultra vires*.' For further development of this line of thought see Harry Arthurs, 'Rethinking Administrative Law: A Slightly Dicey Business' (1979) 17 Osgoode Hall L.J. 1 at 32.

67 To some extent his position could already be seen in his essay on the *Charter* and administrative law, where he argued that administrative decisions affecting *Charter*-protected interests must receive more judicial protection than interests that are not so protected: David Mullan, 'The Impact of the *Charter* on Administrative Law: The Meaning of Fundamental Justice' in *Public Interest v. Private Rights: Striking the Balance in Administrative Law* (Winnipeg: Law Society of Manitoba, 1991) at 27.

68 *Baker, supra* note 30 at para. 56.

69 See text accompanying note 9.

70 Mullan, 'Deference,' *supra* note 55 at 54.

71 Ibid. at 59.

72 David Mullan, 'Unwritten Constitutional Principles – The Legacy of Justice Rand' (forthcoming) [Mullan, 'Unwritten Constitutional Principles'].

73 David Mullan 'The Role for Underlying Constitutional Principles in a Bill of Rights World' [2004] N.Z. Law Rev. 9 [Mullan, 'Underlying Constitutional Principles'].

74 Ibid. at 34.

75 Ibid. at note 2.

76 Ibid.

77 Ibid.

78 Ibid. at 37, with the expression of support at 38.

79 Mullan, 'Unwritten Constitutional Principles,' *supra* note 72.

80 Ibid. at 37–38.

81 (1951) 83 C.L.R. 1.

82 Mullan, 'Underlying Constitutional Principles,' *supra* note 73 at 27–8, quoting at 28 Dixon J.'s famous dictum at 193 of the judgment.

83 See David Dyzenhaus, 'Constituting the Enemy: A Response to Carl Schmitt' in Andras Sajo, ed., *Militant Democracy* (Utrecht: Eleven International Publishing, 2004) at 15.

84 Constitutional text, of course, makes a substantive difference both by articulating principles that would not otherwise be thought to be fundamental and by giving specifications of and structure to principles that would be thought to be fundamental even in the absence of text.

85 Notice that both section 33 of the *Charter* and the *Human Rights Act* use language that assumes that the judges have the last word when it comes to the

interpretation of the rights. Critics of judicial review sometimes argue that this language rigs things unfairly, as it tells us that the legislature does not have interpretative authority since the courts' correct interpretation has either to be overridden or ignored. See, e.g, Jeffrey Goldsworthy, 'Judicial Review, Legislative Override, and Democracy' in Tom Campbell, Jeffrey Goldsworthy, and Adrienne Stone, eds., *Protecting Human Rights: Instruments and Institutions* (Oxford: Oxford University Press, 2003) at 263. When these arguments are put on democratic grounds they are incoherent as long as it is the case as the text is democratically adopted. Further, these critics fail to see that the legislature is given interpretative authority as long as the courts will invalidate a statute or declare it incompatible with human rights only if the statute cannot survive a reasonableness or proportionality test. These critics see the issue as all or nothing – either the judges have exclusive authority or the legislature does. This all-or-nothing view is endemic in the positivist tradition, leading to a view of legal order as a battle between what Murray Hunt has aptly called 'competing supremacies.' See Murray Hunt, 'Sovereignty's Blight: Why Contemporary Public Law Needs the Concept of "Due Deference",' in Nicholas Bamforth and Peter Leyland, eds., *Public Law in a Multi-Layered Constitution* (Oxford: Hart, 2003) at 337. For similar reasons, the critics suppose that the constitution has to be understood as the written constitution interpreted in a way that is true to some narrow textualist approach (perhaps combined with a doctrine of original intent) if it is not to collapse into the judges' views of the constitution. Thus, they have to resist any claim that there are unwritten constitutional principles.

86 See Murray Hunt, *Using Human Rights Law in English Courts* (Oxford: Hart, 1997).

87 See David Mullan, 'Willis v. McRuer: A Long Overdue Replay with the Possibility of a Penalty Shoot Out' (2005) 55 U.T.L.J. 535. Proponents of the left critique of judicial review often patronizingly accuse those who wish to make sense of judicial review of not having a grip on reality, or worse, wishing to mystify or even deceive. But they rarely deal with the reality of the paucity of resources available to ensure the rule of law, nor deliver any detailed account of alternatives.

88 This point is very effectively and politely made by Mullan in his review of *Without the Law: Administrative Justice and Legal Pluralism in Nineteenth-Century England* (1987) 12 Queen's L.J. 106.

89 As La Forest J. put it in the first decision in a trilogy of cases where the Supreme Court of Canada decided that a tribunal could entertain a *Charter*-based challenge to a provision in its statute – *Douglas/Kwantlen Faculty Assn. v. Douglas College*, [1990] 3 S.C.R. 570 at 605. For my detailed discussion of

these issues, see 'Constituting the Rule of Law: Fundamental Values in Administrative Law' (2002) 27 Queen's L.J. 445.

90 Loughlin, *Public Law and Political Theory, supra* note 25.

91 See, e.g., ibid. at 197–201.

92 David Dyzenhaus, 'The Left and the Question of Law' (2004) 17 Can. J.L. & Jur. 7.

93 See A.W.B. Simpson, 'The Common Law and Theory' in A.W.B. Simpson, *Legal Theory and Legal History: Essays on the Common Law* (London: Hambledon Press, 1987) at 359.

The Writings of David Mullan

Books

Administrative Law in 1 *Canadian Encyclopedic Digest*, 2nd ed. (Toronto: Carswell, 1973) chap. 3 (171 pp); also published separately as a stand alone monograph *Administrative Law* (Toronto: Carswell, 1974); supplements prepared 1974 and 1976 (60 pp); 2nd ed., 1980 (275 pp); 3rd ed., 1996 (610 pp); 1997 supplement (102 pp); 1998 cumulative supplement (168 pp)

Administrative Law (Toronto: Irwin Law, 2001) (583 pp) (a volume in the Essentials of Canadian Law Series)

(with Allan Manson), eds., *Commissions of Inquiry: Praise or Reappraise?* (Toronto: Irwin Law, 2003) (547 pp)

Published Casebooks

'Parol Evidence and Rectification' in C. Boyle and D.R. Percy, eds., *Contracts: Cases and Commentaries*, 1st ed. (Toronto: Carswell, 1978) 451–94; 2nd ed., 1981, 595–639; 3rd ed., 1985, 605–50; 4th ed., 1989, 589–635 (plus 'The Requirement of Writing,' 243–74); 5th ed., 1994, 287–319 and 623–70; 6th ed., 1999, 'Remedies,' 809–952; 7th ed., 2004, 'Remedies,' 821–970

Administrative Law: Cases, Text and Materials, a casebook prepared in collaboration with J.M. Evans, H.N. Janisch, and R.C.B. Risk, published in temporary lithographed form by Emond-Montgomery Press, August 1979 (1248 pp); published 1st ed., 1980 (1085 pp); lithographed supplement, 1982 (117 pp); 2nd ed., 1984 (994 pp); lithographed supplement, 1986 (271 pp); 3rd ed., 1988 (1194 pp); 4th ed., 1995 (with J.M. Evans and H.N. Janisch) (1519 pp); 5th ed., 2003 (sole author) (1438 pp)

Remedies: Cases and Materials, a casebook prepared in collaboration with J.

Berryman, J. Cassels, T. Cromwell, S. Sadinsky, R.J. Sharpe and S.M. Waddams, 1st ed. (Toronto: Emond Montgomery Publications, 1988) (1071 pp); 2nd ed., 1992 (1107 pp); 3rd ed., 1996 (1284 pp); 4th ed., 2001 (1403 pp)

Chapters in Books and Published Conference Proceedings

'Ombudsman at Work' in *New Zealand's Heritage* (Wellington: Paul Hamlyn Ltd, 1973) vol. 7, 2728–32

'What Use Can and Should be Made of a Declaratory Remedy in Modern Administrative Law?' in H.N. Janisch, ed., *Administrative Law Remedies* (Halifax: Faculty of Law, Dalhousie University, 1974) 44–56

'Fairness: The New Natural Justice?' in H.N. Janisch, ed., *Current Issues in Administrative Law* (Halifax: Faculty of Law, Dalhousie University, 1975) 1–14

'The Modern Law of Tenure' in H.N. Janisch, ed., *The University and the Law* (Halifax: Faculty of Law, Dalhousie University, 1975) 102–15

'The Scope and Principles of Statutory Appeals from Administrative Action in Nova Scotia' in H.N. Janisch, ed., *Government Regulation and the Law* (Halifax: Faculty of Law, Dalhousie University, 1976) 81–107

'Attainment of Objectives and Jurisdiction' in H.N. Janisch, ed., *Telecommunications Regulation at the Crossroads* (Halifax: Faculty of Law, Dalhousie University, 1976) 149–64

(with B.G. Hansen) 'Private Corporations in Canada: Principles of Recovery for the Tortious Disablement of Shareholder/Employees' in L. Klar, ed., *Studies in Canadian Tort Law* (Toronto: Butterworths, 1977) 215–72

'The Common Law of Contract: A New Equity?' in M.T. Hertz, ed., *Is the Common Law Dead?* (Halifax: Faculty of Law, Dalhousie University, 1977) 38–55

'Human Rights and Administrative Fairness' in R.St. J. Macdonald and J.P. Humphrey, eds., *The Practice of Freedom: Canadian Essays on Human Rights and Fundamental Freedoms* (Toronto: Butterworths, 1979) 111–37

'Access to Information and Rule-Making' in J. McCamus, ed., *Freedom of Information: Canadian Perspectives* (Toronto: Butterworths, 1981) 54–73

'Procedural Fairness: Nicholson and the Tasks Ahead' in *Proceedings of the Administrative Law Conference: Held at the Faculty of Law, University of British Columbia, 18–19 October 1979* (Vancouver: U.B.C. Law Review, 1981) 219–36

'Comment' [on D.M.M. Goldie, 'The Federal Court'] in *Proceedings of the Administrative Law Conference: Held at the Faculty of Law, University of British Columbia, 18–19 October 1979* (Vancouver: U.B.C. Law Review, 1981) 38–42

'Comment' [on D.J. Jordan, 'Tortious Liability of Public Officials: A Proposal for Evolution'] in *Proceedings of the Administrative Law Conference: Held at the*

Faculty of Law, University of British Columbia, 18–19 October 1979 (Vancouver: U.B.C. Law Review, 1981) 181–85

'Unfairness in Administrative Processes - The Impact of *Nicholson* and the *Charter of Rights*' in *Isaac Pitblado Lectures on Advocacy: Rights and Remedies - New Developments* (Winnipeg: Law Society of Manitoba, 1983) 68–99

'Standing: The Relevance of the Constitutional Cases to Administrative Law' in *Isaac Pitblado Lectures on Advocacy: Rights and Remedies - New Developments* (Winnipeg: Law Society of Manitoba, 1983) 172–76

'The Developing Law of Procedural and Substantive Fairness' in E.S. Case, P.Z.R. Finkle, and A.R. Lucas, eds., *Fairness in Environmental and Social Impact Assessment Processes* (Calgary: Canadian Institute of Resource Law, Faculty of Law, University of Calgary, 1983) 15–28

'Review of Subordinate Legislation on the Merits' in *Second Commonwealth Conference on Delegated Legislation*, Volume 2, *Documents of the Conference* (Ottawa: 1983) 229–37, and Volume 3, *Transcript of Proceedings* (Ottawa: 1983) 118–35

'Administrative Tribunals: Their Evolution in Canada from 1945 to 1984' (A study paper for the Royal Commission on the Economic Union and Development Prospects for Canada) in I. Bernier and A. Lajoie, eds., *Regulations, Crown Corporations and Administrative Tribunals* (Toronto: University of Toronto Press, 1985) 155–202

'The Law of Canada' in J. Bell and A.W. Bradley, eds., *Governmental Liability: A Comparative Study* (London: United Kingdom National Committee of Comparative Law, Comparative Law Series, vol. 13, 1983) 59–83

'Natural Justice – The Challenges of *Nicholson*, Deference Theory and the *Charter*' in N.R. Finkelstein and B.M. Rogers, eds., *Administrative Law – Recent Developments and Emerging Issues* (Toronto: Carswell, 1987) 1–52, and in *Développements récents en droit administratif* (Montreal: Les Éditions Yvon Blais, 1987) 1–57

'The Impact of the *Charter* on Administrative Procedure: The Meaning of Fundamental Justice' in *The 1990 Isaac Pitblado Lectures: Public Interest v. Private Rights: Striking the Balance in Administrative Law* (Winnipeg: Law Society of Manitoba, 1991) 29–81

'The Contribution of the Federal Court to Judicial Review' in *The Federal Court of Canada – An Evaluation* (Ottawa: Federal Court of Canada, 1991) 27–42, and in *Le Bulletin* (Journal of Quebec Administrative Law Society) (October 1991) 1 and 3–5

'Anton Piller Orders: Life at the Extremity of the Courts' Powers' in J.B. Berryman, ed., *Remedies: Issues and Perspectives* (Toronto: Carswell, 1991) 189–217

'Where Do Tribunals Fit into the System of Administration and Adjudication?

A Canadian Perspective' in R. Creyke, ed., *Administrative Tribunals: Taking Stock* (Canberra: Centre for International and Public Law, Australian National University, 1992) 1–20

'Common and Divergent Elements of Practices of the Various Tribunals: An Overview of Present and Possible Future Developments' in *Special Lectures of the Law Society of Upper Canada 1992: Administrative Law: Principles, Practice and Pluralism* (Toronto: Carswell, 1992) 461–80

'The Ombudsman of Ontario: Some Issues of Authority' in C. Samson and J. McBride, eds., *Solutions de rechange au règlement des conflits / Alternative Dispute Resolution* (Sainte-Foy: Les Presses de l'Université Laval, 1993) 341–60

'Administrative Law at the Margins' in M. Taggart, ed., *The Province of Administrative Law* (Oxford: Hart Publishing, 1997) 134–59

'Legitimate Expectation in Canadian Public Law' in *Contemporary Law, 1998* (Cowansville, QC: Les Éditions Yvon Blais, 1999) 519–40

'Tribunals and Courts: The Contemporary Terrain – Lessons from Human Rights Regimes' in G-A. Smith and H. Dumont, eds., *Justice to Order: Adjustment to Changing Demands and Co-Ordination Issues in the Justice System in Canada* (Montreal: Les Éditions Thémis, 1999) 119–34

'The Role of the Judiciary in the Review of Administrative Policy Decisions: Issues of Legality' in M-J. Mossman and G. Otis, eds., *The Judiciary as Third Branch of Government: Manifestations and Challenges to Legitimacy* (Montreal: Les Éditions Thémis, 2000) 313–76

'Appeals from Ontario Securities Commission Determinations – The Standard of Review' in A.I. Anand and W.F. Flanagan, eds., *Selected Topics in Corporate Litigation* (Toronto: Carswell, 2001) 287–98

(with Allan Manson) 'Introduction' in A. Manson and D. Mullan, eds., *Commissions of Inquiry: Praise or Reappraise?* (Toronto: Irwin Law, 2003) 1–10

(with Allan Manson) 'Lessons from Walkerton' in A. Manson and D. Mullan, eds., *Commissions of Inquiry: Praise or Reappraise?* (Toronto: Irwin Law, 2003) 499–516

'Deference from *Baker* to *Suresh* and Beyond: Interpreting the Conflicting Signals' in D. Dyzenhaus, ed., *The Unity of Public Law* (Oxford: Hart Publishing, 2004) 21–61

'The *Charter* and Administrative Law' in *The 2002 Isaac Pitblado Lectures on The Charter: Twenty Years and Beyond* (Winnipeg: Law Society of Manitoba, 2004) chap. 10, 1–32

'Bifurcation of the Ontario Securities Commission's Functions: The Competing Concerns' in A.I. Anand and W.F. Flanagan, eds., *Conflicts of Interest in Capital Market Structures* (Toronto: Carswell, 2003) 147–49

Articles, Reports, and Commentary

'Was Justice Really Seen to Be Done?' (1969) 3 N.Z.U.L. Rev. 440–42
(with G.D.S. Taylor) 'Recent Developments in New Zealand Administrative Law' (1969) 32(1) New Zealand Journal of Public Administration 60–84
'Some Developments in Administrative Law (1970)' (1971) 33(2) New Zealand Journal of Public Administration 76–96
'Not In the Public Interest: Crown Privilege Defined' (1971) 19 Chitty's L.J. 289–95
'Administrative Law - Universities - Judicial Review of Administrative Action – Natural Justice' (1971) 49 Can. Bar Rev. 624–32
'One Plus Five Equals Six' [1971] N.Z.L.J. 512–14
'The Pursuit of Truth - At What Cost?' (1972) 5 N.Z.U.L. Rev. 164–9
(with J.D. Whyte) 'Who Must Obey the Laws?' (1972) 79 Queen's Quarterly 97–9
'Legal Education for Professional Practice: Ontario and New Zealand Experiences' (1972) New Zealand Law Society Newsletter (No. 31, August 1972) 11–14
'The Jurisdictional Fact Doctrine in the Supreme Court of Canada: A Mitigating Plea' (1972) 10 Osgoode Hall L.J. 440–9
'Developments in New Zealand Administrative Law (1971-72)' (1973) 35(2) New Zealand Journal of Public Administration 1–28
(with R. Beaman) 'The Constitutional Implications of the Regulation of Telecommunications' (1973) 2 Queen's L.J. 67–92
'Procedural Codes: A Second Opinion' [1973] N.Z.L.J. 41–2
'Abuse of Discretion: Jurisdictional Error?' (1973) 5 N.Z.U.L. Rev. 280–4
'The Federal Court Act: A Misguided Attempt at Administrative Law Reform?' (1973) 23 U.T.L.J. 14–53
'Reform of Judicial Review of Administrative Action: The Ontario Way' (1974) 12 Osgoode Hall L.J. 125–78
'Code of Civil Procedure: The $32 Statute' (1974) 2(6) Caveat 2–4
'Confusion Perpetuated: *The Judicial Review Procedure Act* Before the Divisional Court' (1974) 22 Chitty's L.J. 297–302
'The Declaratory Judgment: Its Place as an Administrative Law Remedy in Nova Scotia' (1975) 2 Dal. L.J. 91–120
'Judicial Review of Administrative Action' [1975] N.Z.L.J. 154–66
'Fairness: The New Natural Justice?' (1975) 25 U.T.L.J. 281–316; reprinted in D.J. Galligan, ed., *Administrative Law* (New York: New York University Press, 1992) 471–506
'Reform of Administrative Law Remedies – Method or Madness?' (1975) 6 Federal Law Review 340–66

'Standing After McNeil' (1976) 8 Ottawa L.R. 32–49
'Recent Developments in Nova Scotian Administrative Law' (1975–76) 2 Dal. L.J. 870–915
'Judicial Restraints on Administrative Action: Effective or Illusory?' (1976) 17 C. de D. 913–26
Annotation to *Nugent v. Board of Rosetown School Unit No. 43* (1977) 2 Canadian Cases on the Law of Torts 325 (3 pp)
'Recent Developments in Nova Scotian Administrative Law' (1977–78) 4 Dal. L.J. 467–558
'*Martineau and Butters v. Matsqui Institution Inmate Disciplinary Board*: Its Potential Impact on the Jurisdiction of the Trial Division of the Federal Court' (1978) 24 McGill L.J. 92–111
Annotation to *Mensink v. Dueck* (1979) 9 Canadian Cases on the Law of Torts 149 (4 pp)
'Developments in Administrative Law: The 1978-79 Term' (1980) 1 Sup. Ct. L. Rev. 1–76
'Mr. Justice Rand: Defining the Limits of Court Control of the Administrative and Executive Process' (1979-80) 18 U.W.O.L. Rev. 65–114
'Developments in Administrative Law: The 1979-80 Term' (1981) 2 Sup. Ct. L. Rev. 1–47
'Natural Justice and Fairness: Substantive as well as Procedural Standards for the Review of Administrative Decision-Making?' (1982) 27 McGill L.J. 250–98
'Developments in Administrative Law: The 1980-81 Term' (1982) 3 Sup. Ct. L. Rev. 1–64
'The Uncertain Constitutional Position of Canada's Administrative Appeal Tribunals' (1982) 14 Ottawa L.R. 239–69
'The Legal Nature of Professorial Status at Queen's' (1982) 9(5) Qufacts 5–8
Annotation to *Everett v. King* (1982) 20 Canadian Cases on the Law of Torts 1 (4 pp)
(with Innis M. Christie) 'Canadian Academic Tenure and Employment: An Uncertain Future?' (1982–3) 7 Dal. L.J. 72–121
'Developments in Administrative Law: The 1981-82 Term' (1983) 5 Sup. Ct. L. Rev. 1–76
'Alternatives to Judicial Review of Administrative Action - The Commonwealth of Australia's Administrative Appeals Tribunal' (1983) 43 R. du B. 569–94; reprinted in Canadian Institute for the Administration of Justice, *Judicial Review of Administrative Rulings* (Cowansville, QC: Les Éditions Yvon Blais Inc, 1983) 441–66
'Fairness and Natural Justice' (1983) 4 Canadian Regulatory Reporter 5-19–5-24

Annotation to *Seaspan International Ltd. v. Office and Technical Employees' Union* (1983) 1 Administrative Law Reports 98 & (1984) 2 Administrative Law Reports 218 (2 pp)

'The Review of Delegated Legislation on its Merits' (1983-84) 6(4) Canadian Parliamentary Review 5–7

'Developments in Administrative Law: The 1982-83 Term' (1984) 6 Sup. Ct. L. Rev. 1–48

(with Andrew J. Roman) '*Minister of Justice v. Borowski*: The Extent of the Citizen's Right to Litigate the Lawfulness of Government Action' (1984) 4 Windsor Y.B. Access Just. 303–51

Annotation to *Saanich Inlet Preservation Society v. Cowichan Valley Regional District* (1984) 2 Administrative Law Reports 12 (1 p)

Annotation to *B.C. Coal Ltd. v. Wrend* (1984) 3 Administrative Law Reports 82 (3 pp)

Annotation to *Williams v. Kaplan* (1984) 3 Administrative Law Reports 113 (2 pp)

Annotation to *Carey v. R.* (1984) 3 Administrative Law Reports 158 (3 pp)

Annotation to *Attorney General of Quebec v. Grondin* (1984) 3 Administrative Law Reports 267 (2 pp)

Case Comment: *Energy Probe v. Atomic Energy Control Board of Canada* (1984) 5 Administrative Law Reports 191 (8 pp)

Annotation to *Bibeault v. McCaffrey* (1984) 6 Administrative Law Reports 239 (3 pp)

'The Re-emergence of Jurisdictional Error' (1985) 14 Administrative Law Reports 326–37

'Developments in Administrative Law: The 1983-84 Term' (1985) 7 Sup. Ct. L. Rev. 1–61

'"Fairness" in the Employment of University Faculty' (1986) 11 Queen's L.J. 264–92

'Judicial Deference to Administrative Decision-Making in the Age of the *Charter*' (1986) 50 Sask. L. Rev. 203–23

(with Andrew J. Roman) Annotation to *Consolidated-Bathurst Packaging Ltd. v. International Woodworkers of America* (1986) 16 Administrative Law Reports 37 (3 pp)

Annotation to *Thomas v. Mount Saint Vincent University* (1986) 19 Administrative Law Reports 146 (6 pp)

'*Consolidated-Bathurst* and the Dominion Stores Pension Fund Case: Different Approaches or Reconcilable Differences?' (1987) 21 Administrative Law Reports 215–19

'The Supreme Court of Canada and Jurisdictional Error: Compromising *New Brunswick Liquor*?' (1987) 1 Can. J. Admin. L. & Prac. 71–101

'The Reach of Section 7 of the *Charter*' (1987) 24 Administrative Law Reports 203–5

'The Universities and the Principles and Remedies of Public Law' (1987) 25 Administrative Law Reports 212–18

'The Supreme Court of Canada and Government: Openness and Accountability Versus Efficiency and Effectiveness' (1987) 27 Administrative Law Reports 29–45

'Substantive Fairness Review: Heed the Amber Light!' (1988) 18 V.U.W.L.R. 293–310

'The Administrative State: Theory or Pragmatism?' (1990) 40 U.T.L.J. 362–68

'*Board of Education of the Indian Head School Division No. 19 of Saskatchewan v. Knight*: The Emergence of a Free Standing Right to Procedural Fairness' (1990) 43 Administrative Law Reports 230–7

'Confining the Reach of Legitimate Expectations' (1990) 44 Administrative Law Reports 245–51

'"But Some Animals Are More Equal Than Others" – Even Under the *Charter*' (1991) 44 Administrative Law Reports 276–87

'Of Chaff Midst the Corn' (1991) 45 Administrative Law Reports 264–72

'The Future of Canadian Administrative Law' (1991) 16 Queen's L.J. 77–94

'The Procedural Obligations of Tribunals and Agencies That Do Not Hold Hearings' (1991) 47 Administrative Law Reports 130–48

'A Blast From the Past: A Surreptitious Resurgence of *Metropolitan Life*?' (1992) 5 Administrative Law Reports (2d) 97–108

'*Canada Assistance Plan*: Denying Legitimate Expectation a Fair Start?' (1992) 7 Administrative Law Reports (2d) 269–92

'Jurisdictional Error Yet Again: The Imprecise Limits of the Jurisdiction-Limiting *Canada (Attorney General) v. P.S.A.C.*' (1993) 11 Administrative Law Reports (2d) 117–23

'Bradco: Refined Reiterations of the Rubric of Review' (1993) 12 Administrative Law Reports (2d) 219–29

Annotation to *Furey v. Conception Bay Centre Roman Catholic School Board* (1993) 17 Administrative Law Reports (2d) 46 (3 pp)

'Judicial Deference to Executive Decision-Making: Evolving Concepts of Responsibility' (1993) 19 Queen's L.J. 137–78

'Policing the *Consolidated-Bathurst* Limits: Of Whistleblowers and Other Assorted Characters' (1993) 10 Administrative Law Reports (2d) 241–66

'The Role of Lawyers to Professional Disciplinary Bodies' (1994) 13(3) Advocates' Soc. J. 10–24

'Damages for Violation of Constitutional Rights: A False Spring?' (1995) 6 N.J.C.L. 105–27

'Quebec Unilateral Secession Reference: "A Ruling that Will Stand the Test of Time"' (1998) 9 Public Law Review 231–6

'Recent Developments in Administrative Law: The Apparent Triumph of Deference!' (1999) 12 Can. J. Admin. L. & Prac. 192–212

'Tribunals and Courts: The Contemporary Terrain: Lessons from Human Rights Regimes' (1999) 24 Queen's L.J. 643–65

'Deference Deferred: The Immigration and Refugee Board' (1999) 7 Reid's Administrative Law 97–103

'*Baker v. Canada (Minister of Citizenship & Immigration)*: A Defining Moment in Canadian Administrative Law' (1999) 7 Reid's Administrative Law 145–62

'*Wells v. Newfoundland:* Redefining the Status of Tribunal and Agency Members' (1999) 13 Can. J. Admin. L. & Prac. 117–46

'Revisiting the Standard of Review for Municipal Decisions: When is a Pile of Soil an "Erection"?' (2000) 13 Can. J. Admin. L. & Prac. 319–30

'The Supreme Court of Canada and Tribunals – Deference to the Administrative Process: A Recent Phenomenon or a Return to Basics?' (2001) 80 Can. B. Rev. 399–432

(with Deirdre Harrington) 'The *Charter* and Administrative Decision-Making: The Dampening Effects of *Blencoe*' (2002) 27 Queen's L.J. 879–912

'*Ocean Port Hotel* and Statutory Compromises of Tribunal Independence' (2002) 9 C.L.E.L.J. 189–209

(with Antonella Ceddia) 'The Impact on Public Law of Privatization, Deregulation, Outsourcing, and Downsizing: A Canadian Perspective' (2003) 10 Ind. J. Global Legal Stud. 199–246

'A Comparison of the Impact of the New Zealand Bill of Rights Act and the Canadian Charter of Rights and Freedoms on Judicial Review of Administrative Action' (2003) 1 New Zealand Journal of Public and International Law 115–55

'Judging the Judgment of Judges: *CUPE v. Ontario (Minister of Labour)*' (2003) 10 C.L.E.L.J. 431–55

'*Voice Construction*: One Swallow Does Not a Summer Make?' (2004) 11 C.L.E.L.J. 113–138

'Establishing and Applying the Standard of Review: The Struggle for Complexity?' (2004) 17 Can. J. Admin. L. & Prac. 59–97

'The View from North America: A Canadian Perspective on Three Troubling Issues' (2004) 17 Can. J. Admin. L. & Prac. 167–205

'The Role of Underlying Constitutional Principles in a Bill of Rights World' [2004] N.Z. Law Rev. 9–38

(with Martha Boyle) 'Raising and Dealing with Issues of Bias and Disclosure' (2005) 18 Can. J. Admin. L. & Prac. 37–59

'An Old Codger and the Frontiers of the New Technology,' Canadian Association of Law Teachers Bulletin, April 2005, 9–11

'Willis v. McRuer: A Long-Overdue Replay with the Possibility of a Penalty Shoot-Out' (2005) 55 U.T.L.J. 535–74

'Tribunals Imitating Courts – Foolish Flattery or Sound Policy?' (2005) Dal. L.J. 1–25

Published Study Papers

Frustrated Contracts Law (Study Paper for Nova Scotia Law Reform Advisory Commission)(Halifax: Queen's Printer, 1976) (69 pp)

The Federal Court Act: Administrative Law Jurisdiction (Background Paper for the Law Reform Commission of Canada) (Ottawa: Supply and Services Canada, 1977) (117 pp)

Rule-Making Hearings: A General Statute for Ontario? (Study Paper for the Ontario Commission on Freedom of Information and Individual Privacy) (Toronto: Queen's Printer, 1979) (232 pp)

Unpublished Study Papers

Study Paper for Canadian Bar Association Commission on Federal Court of Canada, 'History and Constitutional Basis of the Federal Court of Canada' (1978) (44 pp)

Study Paper for Manitoba Law Reform Commission, 'Reform of Administrative Law Remedies' (1979) (128 pp)

Study Paper for Ontario Law Reform Commission's Contract Law Amendment Project, 'Unconscionability' (1981) (155 pp)

Study Paper for Canada Employment and Immigration Commission, 'Immigration Officers and the Duty of Procedural Fairness' (1987) (27 pp)

(with the Hon. Coulter A. Osborne Q.C. and Bryan Finlay Q.C.) 'Report of the Fairness Committee to the Ontario Securities Commission' (2004) (104 pp)

Book Reviews

Review of J.A. Farmer, *Tribunals and Government* (1975) 21 McGill L.J. 315–19

Review of D.P. Jones and A.S. de Villars, *Principles of Administrative Law* (1986) 31 McGill L.J. 555–60

Review of H.W. Arthurs, *'Without the Law': Administrative Justice and Legal Pluralism in Nineteenth-Century England* (1987) 12 Queen's L.J. 106–17

Review of D.J. Galligan, *Discretionary Powers: A Study of Official Discretion* (1988) 38 U.T.L.J. 420–24

Review of Peter Hogg, *Liability of the Crown*, 2nd ed. (1991) 10 Windsor Y.B. Access Just. 263–71

Review of Stephen Legomsky, *Specialized Justice* (1991) 10 C.J.Q. 183–87

Review of Lorne Sossin, *Boundaries of Judicial Review: The Law of Justiciability in Canada* (2000) 38 Osgoode Hall L.J. 221–27

Review of Susan Kneebone, *Tort Liability of Statutory Authorities* (2000) 26 Monash U.L. Rev. 397–404

Review of Jack Williams, *Cricket and Race* (2002) 19 Sociology of Sport Journal 437–40